ERRATA

Persons and Places
Critical Edition
1986

The following are corrections for errors in the captions under illustrations in the text.

24.   Charles Augustus Strong
25.   Robert Dickson Smith, Jr.
          (later Robert Dickson Weston-Smith)
26.   Julian Codman
27.   Warwick Potter

The list of illustrations on page [ix] correctly identifies each illustration.

The Works of George Santayana

Volume I

George Santayana in the 1930's.
By permission of George Santayana
Papers, Rare Book and Manuscript
Library, Columbia University.

Persons and Places

Fragments of Autobiography

George Santayana

edited by
William G. Holzberger and Herman J. Saatkamp, Jr.
with an Introduction by Richard C. Lyon

Critical Edition

The MIT Press, Cambridge, Massachusetts, and London, England

The preparation of this volume was made possible in part by a grant from the Program for Editions of the National Endowment for the Humanities, an independent Federal agency.

Additional funding was provided by Corliss Lamont.

COMMITTEE ON
SCHOLARLY EDITIONS

AN APPROVED EDITION

MODERN LANGUAGE
ASSOCIATION OF AMERICA

Portions of Chapters I, II, III, VII, VIII, IX, X, XII, and XIII of *Persons and Places: The Background of My Life* were first published in 1943 and 1944 in *Atlantic Monthly*. *Persons and Places: The Background of My Life* was first published in 1944 by Scribner's in New York and by Constable in London. *The Middle Span* (*Persons and Places,* vol. 2) was first published in 1947 by Scribner's in New York and by Constable in London. *My Host the World* (*Persons and Places,* vol. 3) was first published in 1953 by Scribner's in New York and by Cresset Press in London. A one-volume edition containing *Persons and Places: The Background of My Life, The Middle Span* and *My Host the World* was published in 1963 by Scribner's.

© 1986 Massachusetts Institute of Technology

Manufactured in the United States of America

Library of Congress Cataloging-in-Publication Data

Persons and places.

  Santayana edition project.
  Bibliography: v. 1, p.
  Includes index.
  1. Santayana, George, 1863–1952. 2. Philosophers—
United States—Biography. I. Holzberger, William G.
II. Saatkamp, Herman J.
B945.S24A3   1986   191 [B]   86-10492
ISBN 0-262-19238-1 (v. 1)

Contents

III

Editorial Appendix

Illustrations

Acknowledgments

The editors are grateful to many persons and institutions for their important contributions to and generous assistance in the preparation of this volume. Members of the Society for the Advancement of American Philosophy were instrumental in starting the project. In particular, John Lachs proposed a critical edition of *The Works of George Santayana*, and Morris Grossman initiated the establishment of an editorial board. Throughout the project Mrs. Margot Cory, Santayana's literary executrix, graciously assisted the editors in a considerate and cooperative manner. Helen Agüiere, Margot Backas, Richard Ekman, George Farr, Kathy Fuller, and Dorothy Wartenberg of the Research Division of the National Endowment for the Humanities provided information and guidance. Principal financial support was supplied by the National Endowment for the Humanities. Dr. Corliss Lamont also gave sustained financial support. Additional funds were given by David Bidwell, Arthur Eldredge, Nathaniel R. and Kathy Sturgis, Robert S. Sturgis, and David Wapinsky.

The central location for the Santayana Edition from 1977 to 1985 was the University of Tampa. The following persons at Tampa gave the Edition assistance and support: Provost Michael J. Mendelsohn; Provost Edwin Wilde; Dr. Mark Lono, Vice President for Public Affairs; Professor Clayton Long, Area Coordinator for Computer Science; Professor Eustasio Fernández, Area Coordinator for Modern Languages; Professor Robert L. Harder, Philosophy Area; and Louise Erk, Accountant. Lydia Acosta, Director of Merl Kelce Library, and librarians Marlon Pethe, Jeff Sowden, and Mary E. Fleury have been especially helpful.

In 1985, Texas A&M University became the headquarters for the Santayana Edition. The following persons at Texas A&M have also assisted and supported the Edition: Dr. Daniel Fallon, Dean of the College of Liberal Arts; Dr. Arnold D. Vedlitz, Associate Dean; George D. Parker III, Assistant Provost; Charles M. Stoup, Senior Academic Business Administrator; Jo Ann Treat, Steve Garrett, and Nancy Merrill, Texas A&M Research Foundation; Katherine J. Jackson, Librarian,

Sterling C. Evans Library; Dr. Michael Quick, Manager of New Technology; John Kane, Micro Support Center; Marsha Newton, Texas A&M University Development Foundation; Professor John McDermott, Department of Philosophy and Humanities; and Professor Luis F. Costa, Head of the Modern Languages Department. We are indebted to Samuel Hose for his translations of Spanish.

Bucknell University serves as a supplementary location for the Santayana Edition. Bucknell administrators who have supported the Edition and faculty who have contributed their special knowledge to preparation of the first volume are Dr. Frances D. Fergusson, Vice President for Academic Affairs; Dr. Wendell I. Smith, Vice President for Planning and Administration; Dr. Larry D. Shinn, Dean of the College of Arts and Sciences; Professor Mills F. Edgerton, Jr., Director of Spanish; Professor George F. Folkers, Director of German; and Professor James M. Heath, Chairman of the Classics Department. Ann M. de Klerk, Director of Library Services, and George M. Jenks, Collection Development Librarian, Ellen Clarke Bertrand Library, have been especially helpful.

This volume could not have been completed without the dedicated efforts of the Santayana Edition staff. Special thanks are given to principal editorial assistants Shirley Cueto and John W. Jones at the University of Tampa, Donna Hanna-Calvert at Texas A&M University, and Annegret Holzberger at Bucknell University. We extend gratitude and appreciation to our research assistants: Sallie Beavers, Tracy Bowman, James M. Capollini, Dan Comminsky, Lisa Comstock, James Evans, Deborah Fegan, Patricia French, Kimberly Kailing, Pat Kimbrell, Constance Kingsley, Lisa Kline, Austria M. Lavigne, Nina Leonard, Sandra Malafronte, Michele Mann, Nina Mollica, Linda Nagle, Cyndi Neal, Kathleen O'Neill, Alice Perrin, Sharon McBriar Sercombe, Nancy M. Wilfong, Dawn Winkelman, and Diana Yeager at the University of Tampa; Robin Baker, Kris Frost, and Brenda Sims at Texas A&M University; Afsaneh Bahar, Hugh Bailey, Kathy Bittner, Elizabeth Smith Brown, Beth Davis, Lori Fraind, Tracy Cohen Greenfield, Karen Hoffnagle, Caroline Keller, Frances Liu, Laurie Russell, Cherri Lee Smith, Roberta Visaggio, Jeanne Wiggers, and Wendy Van Wyck at Bucknell University.

We wish to acknowledge the invaluable assistance of the professional staffs of the many libraries and archives where we have worked in preparing this volume, and particularly, Katherine Dibble and Norma Mosby, Boston Public Library; Kenneth Lohf, Bernard Crystal, and

Rudolph Ellenbogen, Butler Library, Columbia University; William H. Bond and Marte Shaw, Houghton Library, Joanna Robinson, Widener Library, and Harley Holden, William Whalen, and Robin McIlheny, Harvard Archives, Harvard University; Kenneth Blackwell, Bertrand Russell Archives, Mills Memorial Library, McMaster University; John Stinson, The New York Public Library; Jean F. Preston, Princeton University Library; Daniel C. Williamson, Temple University Library; Decherd Turner, Ellen Dunlap, and Kathy Henderson, Harry Ransom Humanities Research Center, University of Texas; Michael Plunkett, University of Virginia Library; Susan Bellingham, The Library, University of Waterloo; and the librarians of the Bodleian Library, Oxford University, and King's College Library, Cambridge University.

The following have graciously permitted us to print excerpts from letters and from other unpublished materials:

Rare Book and Manuscript Library, Columbia University
Mrs. Margot Cory
Houghton Library, Harvard University
Princeton University Library
Charles Scribner's Sons, Publishers
Robert S. Sturgis
Rare Book and Manuscript Collection, Temple University Libraries
Harry Ransom Humanities Research Center, The University of Texas at Austin
Special Collections, The Library, University of Waterloo

Special thanks to Jo Ann Boydston for her support and advice concerning textual scholarship, to Hugh J. Dawson for his help in preparing the *Notes to the Text*, to Richard C. Lyon for his assistance with the *Notes to the Text* and the genealogies of Santayana's Spanish and American families, and to Charles Scribner, Jr., Chairman of Charles Scribner's Sons, Publishers, for his considerable assistance and cooperation. Other individuals to whom the editors are indebted for assistance in the preparation of this volume include Professors James E. Abbott, John Anton, Willard Arnett, Jerome Ashmore, Richard Bernstein, Justus Buchler, David R. Chesnutt, Arthur Danto, Jude Dougherty, Hoyt Edge, Morris Grossman, Speed Hill, Angus Kerr-Lawson, Paul Kuntz, John Lachs, Irwin C. Lieb, Eugene Long, John O. McCormick, Douglas MacDonald, Stephen Meats, John Michelsen, Joel Porte, Hilary Putnam, Andrew J. Reck, Richard Rorty, the late Herbert W. Schneider, Beth

Singer, Irving Singer, Ignas Skrupskelis, John E. Smith, T. L. S. Sprigge, Richard Sylvester, and Henny Wenkart; also Mildene Bradley, Helen Osborne, Miriam Palmerola, and Betty Stanton of MIT Press; Elizabeth Muhlenfeld, inspector for The Center for Scholarly Editions; Benjamin K. Glazebrook of Constable Publishers; G. Thomas Tanselle of the Guggenheim Foundation; J. Donald Freeze, S.J., Provost of Georgetown University; Javier Jiménez-Ugarte, Consul General of Spain at Houston; Jesús MªSanchidrián Gallego, director of *Piedra Caballera*; Mario Galán Sáez, Alcalde of Avila; Robert S. Sturgis and the late Eduardo Sastre Martín, members of Santayana's family; the Mother General of *Clinica della piccola Compagnia di Maria*, Rome; Anthony Rota of Bertram Rota Ltd., Booksellers; Spanish poet, Jorge Guillén; Rome art dealer, Richard Schneider; and Dino Rigacci of Villa le Balze.

This list is inevitably incomplete, and to all those persons whose names are not included here but who helped realize this edition of Santayana's autobiography the editors extend deep thanks.

INTRODUCTION
Richard C. Lyon

I. The Subject of *Persons and Places*

Reviewing in 1944 the first volume of George Santayana's auto-biography, *Persons and Places*, Edmund Wilson noted that it belongs to a class which includes very few examples. "Few first-rate writers," he observed, "have done stories of their lives which are among their major productions." Wilson could find precedents only in Yeats's memoirs and *The Education of Henry Adams*—although a year later, in his review of the second volume, he would find another parallel in Proust's *Remembrance of Things Past*. Like those books of reflective reminiscence, Santayana's autobiography supplies a store of thought, feeling, and observation "that the author had not got out in his other works: not merely the facts of his career but a searching and subtle study of the meaning for him of his experience."[1]

Santayana's turn in his late years to the writing of personal history was not sudden or surprising. He had already, in 1936, given fictional form to many of his recollections in *The Last Puritan*—"A Memoir in the Form of a Novel." And his philosophic principles seemed almost to require that sooner or later he should make articulate the form and meaning of his own story. He had always insisted that understanding must be, can only be historical understanding. His five-volume *Life of Reason* (1905–06), the work which secured his place as a major force in the philosophy of the new century, had been a survey of the miscellaneous career of western man—of the forms of his religions,

1. Edmund Wilson, "Santayana: A Boyhood Between Spain and Boston," *New Yorker* magazine, January 8, 1944, pp. 56–58.

societies, arts, and sciences—designed to mark within that history, and so recover for present memory, some of the pitfalls and quandaries and above all the achieved harmonies discoverable in the past. (In our time politicians and historians have tirelessly seized on Santayana's words of warning to those who will not remember the past: they are condemned to repeat it.) But a long memory, he thought, is necessary not only to those who would judge the present or devise a future for man free of calamitous surprises. It is necessary to anyone who would discover his own deepest nature. For Santayana self-definition required—not introspection and confession, our modern ways to salvation—but retrospection, an attentive regard for the recurrences, rhythms, and patterns of one's own life history, a watchful observing of one's affinities and aversions over time.

In the writing of *Persons and Places*, as during his life, Santayana looked steadily both ways: toward the circumstances of his personal career and toward the recorded experience of western man. The facts of his life—so little known and so often the subject of rumor and gossip before the book's appearance—are amply here: the story of his early childhood in Spain and his repeated returns, of his thirty years at Harvard, first as a student, then as a luminary of its Golden Day, and of his later years as a solitary and a wanderer in Europe. Yet his unusual private history depends for its meanings on man's history. As we follow his narrative, we come to see that the precision with which he is able to locate himself in time and define his vocation has as its necessary condition a wide-ranging historical imagination. From the past he draws the terms and categories and alternative ways of thinking and feeling about the world which make possible his naming of his deepest affinities. These fusings of private and human history and the playing of one against the other, the easy leaps from present to past, from the personal to the general and the cosmic are the motions of a mind which could define itself in no other way.

His apprenticeship to the past made of Santayana a relentless critic of the present; he was often at odds with his time and place, and often rebuked the modern world in the name of habits of mind which he thought had been too long forgotten. Above all he found in ancient Greece and Rome the clarity and scope which his own nature demanded. He once said that of all periods in history he would have felt most at home in the age between Alexander and Caesar, and he was pleased by the title bestowed on him by a friend, "the antique sage." Yet he spoke also for the Catholic mind. An unbeliever, he suggested the moral and poetic force which Christianity might yet have for an age of unbelievers. And he sometimes thought of himself as the last of the Victorians, speaking as had Arnold and Ruskin and Pater for the recovery of the past not for its own sake but as it may serve present sensibility and the full range of the spirit's needs—as also it may serve to remind us of better times when religions and philosophies and works of art were the vital expressions of an ongoing general life. From his student days until his death in Rome in 1952, he felt himself to be a man born out of season.

In recent years we have become aware, encountering Santayana's voluminous marginal entries in the books of his library, of the unrelenting responsive energy he brought to his reading, and how extensive it was. Among the philosophers whose thought most influenced his own one might name Plato and Aristotle, Democritus and Lucretius, Aquinas, Leibniz, Spinoza, Hume, Hegel, Schopenhauer. I cite these names in particular for the reason that various critics at various times have suggested that Santayana's own philosophy may be found entire in one or more of them. But if in our time his genius is coming to be recognized anew, it is a recognition of his power to assimilate and appropriate for his own reflection the work of these and many other thinkers—not only philosophers but historians, critics, poets, and dramatists. Their views are deployed within the field of his own disposing intelligence, indefatigable in its quest for order, coherence, and a final unity in its comprehension of the world. That is another way of saying that the intelligence at work here is radically original. So also is the *temper* of his mind.

It is not easy to characterize Santayana's genius—his mind's atmosphere, the essential quality of his response to the world. One critic has remarked on what a quiet mind he had, and surely that is right. Santayana would teach us to sit still; he once thought of his life in America as a "protest of quietness" against our clamorous irrationality. Someone has observed that Santayana writes as if human history were over and all thinking done. Certainly this is one of his characteristic notes. The mood of retrospection (as in his occasional use of the past tense in reflecting on the contemporary scene) sometimes gives to his writing the tone of the memorialist. Santayana himself has spoken of his feeling of "detachability" from the present, from the persons, places, and ideas among which he moved. A dispassionate quality, a cool impersonality marks his judgments—a quality which should not be confused with a want of fellow feeling, although that is a charge brought by more than one accuser. Satiric wit, amused irony, candid appraisals which are not always kind appear often in his reflections, but "the tears of things" and pity for mankind impel his words more often than laughter. Tragedy cuts deeper, he thought, than comedy.

We may say of Santayana's detachment that it often carries the accent of the nineteenth century's alienated man. He took up very early a place at the margins of society, and along with many another nineteenth-century social critic, artist, and philosopher chided the world of utilitarian democracy, a world become prosaic and acquisitive and very sure that Providence was on its side. (Of all words in the modern lexicon, Santayana said, the word "progress" was for him the most odious.) The tone of this watchful outsider's voice can range from gentle amusement to ironic mockery to preacherly denunciation.

From the nineteenth century we may borrow another and very different vocabulary to suggest the particular temper of Santayana's mind. Lionel Trilling came closest, perhaps, to naming his quality when he invoked the English Romantics' image of the mountain peak to explain the kind of exhilaration induced in him by his reading of Santayana's letters.[2] It was the Romantics, he observes, who celebrated the mind's power to escape the distractions of the daily round and the oppressions of convention by rising above them. On a mountain top, and only there, one could escape the prison-house of the world and see things below in their vivid particularity, and see them justly, in their true relations. This "unsanctioned altitude"—unsanctioned by the prepotent modern censors who find looking down undemocratic— Trilling evokes in order to suggest "the kind of mental sensation" Santayana imparts.

The metaphor is telling. Reading Santayana we have the sense that he holds the quotidian world clearly in view, yet sees it steadily in its ephemerality and littleness. Perspectives open on perspectives which open on yet other perspectives beyond, and "we feel, in this illumined large, / The veritable small. . . ." Wallace Stevens also, in his poem of tribute to Santayana, required a spatial metaphor.[3] Through the eyes of the old philosopher and citizen of Rome we follow "the majestic movement / Of men growing small in the distances of space":

2. Lionel Trilling, "That Smile of Parmenides Made Me Think," in *A Gathering of Fugitives* (Boston, 1956), p. 153.
3. Wallace Stevens, "To an Old Philosopher in Rome," *The Collected Poems of Wallace Stevens* (New York, 1965), p. 508.

It is as if in a human dignity
Two parallels become one, a perspective, of which
Men are part both in the inch and in the mile.

In *Persons and Places* Santayana himself employs a spatial, a geographic metaphor to explain his life and mind. Although it does not emerge explicitly until the third volume, the metaphor of travel and the traveler serves in multiple ways to join his life's history to his philosophy. It tellingly conveys the intent and spirit of his journeying mind; it supplies a range of meanings which illuminate his theories of "essence" and "spirit"; and it points to the literal fact of his travelings, underscoring the unusual circumstances of his life as an ocean-shuttling native of Spain and professor at Harvard. In the summary figure of the book's conclusion, Santayana appears to himself in retrospect to have been a wandering stranger here, a transient in the inn of a busy innkeeper called the world. The risks of cliché in the metaphor are obvious, but it had for Santayana a precise force, and a wide range of implications. As his chosen *persona* it lies very near the center of his autobiography.

To the image of the Olympian or of the outsider the metaphor of the traveler adds the idea of the active explorer, intent on discovering the ways man has found to live.

The precision and variety of alien things fascinate the traveller. He is aware that however much he may have seen, more and greater things remain to be explored, at least ideally; and he need never cease travelling, if he has a critical mind.[4]

Stevens called Santayana "the inquisitor of structures," a name suggesting the inquiring, appraising surveyor, visiting one after another of the moral and intellectual and architectural habitations which the imagination of western man has devised for itself as accommodations to the elements. A steady vitality of response to the new remained with Santayana until his death at the age of eighty-eight. So curious was he even in his later years to learn how and where the modern spirit lived that he sometimes wearied of all backward glancing. In a letter to his American editor in 1936 the seventy-two-year-old philosopher, balking at a proposal that he write new prefaces to his old

4. *Persons and Places*, p. 448.

books, protested that he was "tired of myself, of my old self, and . . . want to see fresh aspects of things, and of things as remote as possible from the old 'problems.' "[5]

But we would be mistaken if we understood Santayana to be a Romantic in quest of novel sensations, unexperienced emotions, or revolutionary conceptions. Few observers of our modern life have been so caustic as he in criticizing those who seek experience for its own sake and prize the new for its newness. Everywhere—and not least in his autobiography—Santayana insists that settled affections, defined tastes, and an intellectual *point d'appui* must accompany the traveler if further experience is not to be all vacuous stares, fondlings of emotion, and inconsequent cerebrations.

Nor was his traveling a hopeful quest for utopia:

> Your sanguine man who sets forth enthusiastically for El Dorado nurses a secret passion for the happy home. For that reason he is restless in his accidental lodgings and risks everything in the hope of discovering other lodgings where he would enjoy for ever an unclouded happiness. The born traveller, on the contrary, is not pining for a better cage.[6]

Why this scepticism concerning the dreamer's visions of a happy home, a better society? How shall we reconcile it with the Santayana who declared himself a lover of the ideal, of all those visions of perfection (as he wrote to William James) which we may catch only for a moment but which inspire our days and justify our existence? Santayana is, after all, the poet-philosopher who urged us to cultivate the endless forms of the imagination, and among them images of social felicity as rich as we can make them. He testifies in *Persons and Places* to his own lively visions of ancient Greece and modern England, and they were touchstones for his judgments of societies and human possibility. But that, he explains here, was the young Santayana. He later rejected those visions—not as suggestive ideals but as readings of reality. He grew to see them as projections of a dreaming mind too disposed to substitute its own ideals for historical fact, and parts for wholes. And in the passage before us it is the political realist and Burkean conservative in Santayana who notes the utopian's tendency to confuse dream and reality, as if heaven just might lie around earth's next

5. Santayana to John Hall Wheelock, April 2, 1936, unpublished letter.
6. *Persons and Places*, p. 447.

bend. Political activists are not his target here, although he mistrusted reformers. His doubts go out to the seekers of instant salvation, whose extravagant hope breeds a chronic disaffection with present circumstance, and so prevents them from making their peace with things.

If Santayana's travels of the intellect cannot be likened to the Romantic's courting of the new or the seeker's quest for the one right place, what impelled his lifelong searching of man's works? In 1930, in an essay titled "A Brief History of My Opinions," he observed that his traveling ancestors and the stories of the colonial Philippines which he heard them tell were a constant stimulus to his boy's imagination:

> From childhood I have lived in the imaginative presence of interminable ocean spaces, coconut islands, blameless Malays, and immense continents swarming with Chinamen, polished and industrious, obscene and philosophical. It was habitual with me to think of scenes and customs pleasanter than those about me. My own travels have never carried me far from the frontiers of Christendom or of respectability, and chiefly back and forth across the North Atlantic—thirty-eight fussy voyages; but in mind I have always seen these things on an ironical background enormously empty, or breaking out in spots, like Polynesia, into nests of innocent particoloured humanity.[7]

In *Persons and Places* Santayana repeats and elaborates this observation but adds two further explanations of his passion for travel. One incentive, he writes, was aesthetic, his love of the picturesque and the ludicrous in man's polyglot costumes, manners, buildings, theories. And "a kindred but less innocent motive was satirical," the ironic pleasure of marking everywhere men's delusions in mistaking the surface of experience (appearances) for its ground (matter) and in thinking themselves and their works important to the cosmos.[8] The laughter of the gods, looking down on man's career, marking his "dramatic poses and pert egoisms," was always in Santayana's ears.

Behind or within these various explanations of his love of travel we can identify, I think, a single informing intuition: Santayana's profound, recurring sense of the contingency of existence—his sense of how

7. Santayana, "A Brief History of My Opinions," in George P. Adams and William Montague, editors, *Contemporary American Philosophy* (New York, 1930), p. 240.
8. *Persons and Places*, p. 448.

arbitrary is the fatality which imposes on the watching, enduring self this precise irrevocable world and not another. This awareness repeatedly governs the language of his explanations, as in his talk of "the ironical background enormously empty" against which he always saw the shows of the world, or his sense of all events and conventions as magical patterns in a kaleidoscope, delightful to the eye but deeply unintelligible with respect to their source. Santayana's surveys of human arts and philosophies are finely sympathetic to each in turn—yet he seems to ask us to see at last what each is not, to look before and after and around it so we might understand its merely local place on the wide map of history he spreads before us. And the limits of the terrain opened to us are by no means the limits of man's history; seen at a sufficient distance all our works appear as transitory episodes in a universal flux, tropes which nature has so far realized, and for no reason we may call sufficient. That the world should have taken these forms rather than others is, in this light, a perfect marvel of exclusion. For it is in the nature of mind to outrun in its conceiving what merely happens to exist or to have once existed. Its native vocation lies in ranging beyond the facts, beyond even the facts of the history of the human imagination, into the infinite region of possibles which Santayana called the realm of essence. "If ever [the born traveller] got to heaven," he writes in these pages, "on the next day he would discover its boundaries, and on the third day he would make a little raid beyond them. Imagination is potentially infinite."[9]

The mind active in this way may be called the imagination, but in his systematic philosophy Santayana more precisely named it "spirit." By spirit he did not understand a mysterious or dynamic power at work in the world or in the self, but simply the scanning light of attention in man, the witness of all that passes before him. Spirit when it wakes is a child of wonder, amused, puzzled, perhaps dismayed that it should find itself in this body amid these particular scenes.

> The free spirit in us knows that whatsoever may be offered
> to it is but a reversible accident, and though we are com-
> pelled to be absorbed ignominiously in such accidents, yet

9. *Ibid.*, p. 447.

the interesting side of those accidents for the intellect is
only their character and their reversibility.[10]

To see the world under the aspect of its contingency is to recognize
simultaneously the absurd limits of the existing world and the illimitable
range of intellect—quickened in its perception of the present precisely
because it sees the present against a background of the absent. Spirit,
addressed to all being, is most truly itself as a traveler, participating
vicariously in the lives of other persons and places. It is self-tran-
scendent. The self is left behind in the spirit's repeated acts of imaginative projection.

If we say that the spirit, moving freely in the realm of essences,
enjoys an absolute dominion, we must do so with Santayana's keen
sense for the limits of metaphor. From its own vantage the traveling
spirit is indeed intrinsically free—yet only on its own ontological plane.
The philosophic idealist who suggests that mind makes its world as
it goes is in Santayana's eyes the egoist *in excelsis*. For when we look
toward the material forces (however science names them) which sustain
the world and humankind, we must say of the spirit that it is helpless,
a passive witness and not itself a force. Spirit is the spirit of some
body. It is born of a particular animal psyche. It is the vagrant offspring
of an individual organism limited and specific in its powers, formed
and checked by its environment. For these reasons the spirit and the
psyche often have a troubled life together. As "a rank outsider, a child
rebellious to the household, an Ishmael ranging alone,"[11] the spirit
wishes to be altogether free of the ignominious limitations of its home
orbit, and may be disheartened or grow defiant when pinned down
by its domestic commitments. Mother Psyche, for her part, will remind
her child of his origins and very particular inheritance, and of the real
possibilities open to him in a world narrowly circumscribed. She will
exact his loyalty to home traditions, warning her Ishmael that his
aspiration to sympathy with all things may lead to aimless drifting
and dissolution.

The spirit aims at self-transcendence, the psyche at self-definition.
Spirit looks to the ideal; the psyche must look to the world, anxiously

10. *Ibid.*, p. 447–448.
11. Santayana, *Platonism and the Spiritual Life* (New York, 1927), p. 69.

hoping to match circumstance to its needs. Spirit is all imagination; the psyche asks what may rationally be believed. Among all the subjects of Santayana's philosophic reflection in *Persons and Places*, the rival claims of spirit and psyche and their fateful interplay are nearest the center of his concern. And they are so because they lie near the center of his life's history. Santayana refused to disallow in himself either the aspiration of the spirit or the stern lessons of the psyche. He would somehow accommodate them both. In its largest outline, *Persons and Places* tells the story of that difficult accommodation in his own life.

We may mark four events—critical turns of fortune or moments of personal decision—which played a part in forming Santayana's vocation as "the inveterate stranger." When he was five, his mother deserted him (he does not hesitate to use the word), leaving him with his father in his boyhood home, Avila, Spain, while she settled in Boston with her children of a previous marriage. Three years later he was transplanted from Avila to Boston where (back now with his mother but no longer with his father, who returned to Spain) Santayana was consigned to kindergarten at the age of nine. In his mid-thirties his growing sense of separation from all the persons and places he loved required a radical settlement of his accounts with despair, the "metanoia," as he calls it here, which led him to a renunciation of self. When he was forty-eight he resigned his Harvard professorship and left America for good to take up the life of a wandering observer. An orphan and an involuntary exile from Spain, an ascetic and a voluntary exile from America. In the simple recital of these names and events we may find suggestion enough of the complex inheritance and difficult choices of a *déraciné*, one who was freed (and wished to be free) from home commitments, yet who tirelessly sought his native place, a country of the mind to which he might give his full allegiance. And in these events we may discover, I think, something of the origins of Santayana's conceptions of the spirit and the psyche. In important ways his own spirit and psyche were the protagonists of his personal drama.

Consider, for example, the shock of dislocation which the young Spanish boy must have felt on finding himself transplanted to Boston. The open sky and moors and ancient stone walls of Avila were suddenly, unaccountably supplanted by the high narrow houses of Beacon Street and back views of wooden sheds and wooden fences. Nothing in the boy's experience resembled what now met his eye. The cold blear landscape must have seemed an apparition, a stage set perhaps, summoned by magic to displace his familiar Spain. In the midst of so much that was strange, finding himself a stranger even in his own household, his philosophy may have been born. For his sense of the world as an inscrutable accident, imposingly present yet present for no reason, lies (I have suggested) near the center of his philosophy. How should he not feel that Boston was a "reversible accident"?

In its place Santayana could from his earliest days substitute the scenes of his Avila childhood—or the images of coconut islands summoned by his parents' tales of the tropics. The young boy avidly cultivated the images of all that was not-Boston: he was an unhappy stranger at first. If he made plans "of vast palaces and imaginary islands, where I should one day be monarch, like Sancho Panza,"[12] if he began to read omnivorously, these were clearly means of consolation. Boston might be made to recede even further in the presence of Alexander's Persia, Quixote's Spain, the *Arabian Nights*, or Byron's Italy. These were the refuges of a solitary, Santayana's worlds within. And yet as he began to move with ease and success at the Latin School and then Harvard College, he saw no reason to abandon his dramatic visions, the bright images of other places and other persons, as if only the here and now could honorably dominate a man's mind and engage his energies. His Castilian's sense of life as dream emerges clearly in Santayana's early sonnets; the young solipsist wishes to "forget that I am I," wishes to shake off the incubus of self in order that his imagination might range wholly free.

"[T]hose ideal universes in my head . . . had nothing to do with the wretched poverty-stricken real world in which I was condemned to live. That the real was rotten and only the imaginary at all interesting seemed to me axiomatic. That was too sweeping; yet allowing for the rash generalisations of youth, it is still what I think. My philosophy has never changed."[13] Early and late Santayana would insist on the prerogatives of spirit: to be homeless is its inevitable condition, to travel forever is its innate vocation, to be free is its aim and justification. Doubtless in the 1880's this preference for the imagination meant no more than a love of daydreams in the midst of business, yet in the '90's the philosopher, wishing to understand that preference, began

12. *Persons and Places*, p. 154.
13. *Ibid.*, p. 167.

his systematic exploration of that old conundrum about the reality of the ideal and the ideality of the real.

As a counterweight and corrective to his ideas of spirit and essence, he began to develop his conception of what he would call "the realm of matter," and (under the influence of Aristotle) of the psyche, the physical principle of an organism's equilibrium and development, the self in its biological ground, made manifest in its observable patterns of growth and response. This leap from talk of the spirit and its dominion (the language of philosophic idealism) to talk of the psyche and its organization (the language of physical science) has dismayed more than one reader, but Santayana would have us see them simply as two sharply distinguished levels of life in a human body, the psyche subtending and informing the conscious life of spirit. For while pure spirit may itself be heedless of its origins, reflection will lead us to see that its fortunes are governed by a predisposed self in commerce with its specific environment.

Even as the young transcendentalist at play among his worlds without end, for whom Boston was merely a curious local apparition, Santayana was always too much the realist to court seriously the idea that the cosmos was in him and not he in the belly of the cosmos. We may even find in his early disaffection with the world a single source for his conceptions of both spirit and psyche, for precisely to the degree that he wished to escape from the world he acknowledged its irremediable presence. Importunate circumstance—Cambridge, America, his mother and teachers, an absent father, the demands of study and teaching—not only filled insistently the foreground of his awareness, they exacted commitments and required responses, the responses of an active choosing agent. He perceived that in fact the self cannot be inactive, for it responds steadily and spontaneously—with aversion and desire, envy and delight, love and hate—to all that comes before it. Clearly, to pick his way through the world a man must discern his deepest nature, the recurring chords and rhythms of his psyche, and simultaneously he must study the habits of an ancient intractable world outside, the world in which his fortune must be spun out, an accident within an accident.

Clarity in these directions provided a sharp corrective to the young Santayana's dramatic indulgences. To have lived wholly in the spirit, the autobiographer observes, would have been to live in "suspended animation and the sense of infinite potentiality unrealised," wedded to the "crystal vision, umbilical contemplations." He was driven early to the recognition that "I might prefer ideally an imaginary Atlantis to any earthly island; but how puerile and helpless to languish after it and not at once to make the best of the real world?"[14] Making the best of the real world was not, however, easy. The society in which he found himself was pledged to optimism, hustle, and duty. So far from providing supports to sustain him, it contradicted everywhere his aspiration to quietness, it denied the worth of the past, denied the worth of almost all the things he loved. The hawkers and boosters, he thought, had seized even the academy. Americans may have paused sometimes in their service to progress long enough for a lesson in applied Culture, but all was a service to this world. "There was nothing subterranean acknowledged in it," he wrote, "no ultimate catastrophe, no jungle, no desert, and no laughter of the Gods." Instead there was "the furious impulse to make money, to make machines, to make war."[15]

To define his difference became a moral imperative. It was a task made all the more difficult by a number of converging circumstances about which he tells us in his autobiography. In his early thirties events delivered him to a dark night of the soul: the deaths of his father and a beloved young friend, the unfortunate marriage of his half-sister Susana ("the strongest affection in my life"), the sense he had of youth and friendship as past and of his future life as "solitary, obscure, trivial, and wasted."[16] These were the things that induced his metanoia, a renunciation that brought Santayana a new accession of power—or of peace. To this decisive resolution of conflict he devotes a chapter of his autobiography. Pride, desire, self-aggrandizement, the will to possess—these particular (and normal) outworkings of the psyche he now explicitly denied in himself. His psyche, he insists, was not thereby atrophied; rather, the range of its reactions was enlarged—but its reactions would now issue in pure contemplation, and out of his self-denial came self-possession. His calling, he now knew, would be that of a solitary and traveling spirit, without claims for its self. Through his metanoia he had, after all, found a place for Atlantis in the real world.

14. *Ibid.*, p. 170.
15. Santayana, "The Idler and His Works," in *The Idler and His Works and Other Essays* (New York, 1957), p. 8.
16. *Persons and Places*, p. 424.

Yet the world continued to press hard on his spirit: Harvard, Boston, the U.S.A. were no less insistent and no less offensive. They posed a problem which would require another sort of solution.

Almost from the day of his first appointment as an instructor at Harvard Santayana planned for his retirement. Plain living and careful saving (despite his yearly summers in Europe) became almost a point of pride, and by 1912 a bequest from his mother together with his savings enabled him to resign his professorship. In January of that year, twenty-three years after he had begun to teach philosophy, he sailed for Europe and would never return to America. It was a deeply wished-for escape. Santayana's steady aversion to American worldliness and jingoistic self-righteousness had always made him (certainly in the eyes of President Eliot) a possibly dangerous subversive in the halls of Cambridge academic enterprise—an enterprise whose ultimate sanction and real mission (however unconscious) was, he felt, the preparing of willing young servants for the industrial state. Nor was he ever at ease in the role of professor. The task of instructing, if possible uplifting those congregations of the Harvard young—not on Sundays but daily, by calendar and clock—often proved onerous; the preceptor often felt himself a beast of burden. In company with all dreamful poets or scholar gypsies waiting intently for sparks from heaven, Santayana could not happily turn on and turn off the spout of professorial exegesis and opinion at the dictate of the classroom bell. In a chapter originally designed to be the conclusion of *Persons and Places* (and posthumously published as "The Idler and His Works"), he observes that even his early writing was done under the compulsion of institutional expectations. Both the impetus to write and the themes of his first books—with the emphatic exception of his poems, which "belonged to me, expressed me, and were addressed essentially to nobody else"— derived from his public role, the requirements of Department and College, and the language and preoccupations of current philosophic disputation. "The academic subjects were suggested or imposed by circumstances, and I appear there in the costume and under the mask of an assumed character. The acting is sincere enough, but the part is conventional."[17]

To these comments on Santayana's Harvard years two observations should be appended. If he felt himself an actor in the wrong play or an alien stranded on barbarian shores, he did not sulk. To the demands

17. "The Idler and His Works," p. 5.

of his teaching he apparently brought great energy and conscience. Not from Santayana himself but from his students we have learned of his lasting influence on many of them, and we have heard a hundred stories of his generosity and touching kindness to students and colleagues. Santayana as the aloof, dandified, aesthetical snob of the Harvard Yard is a mythical figure, imagined by those who did not know him. And we may observe that he did in fact achieve a reconcilement of sorts during his years of teaching, a temporary peace with opposing circumstance. For a time, for so long as necessary yet intermittently, he let the boundaries of Cambridge and Boston be the boundaries of his world. The prisoner acquiesced in his confinement; the caged philosopher forgot the freer air of Europe. This self-induced forgetfulness, a kind of blunting of his full critical awareness, made of Santayana's last fifteen years at Harvard a period, he said, of somnambulism. These years would become a blur in his later memory. On one occasion he reflected that his truce with America must have been the result of the "instinct of courtesy." "When I am here in the midst of the dull round," he wrote to Susana, "a sort of instinct of courtesy makes me take it for granted, and I become almost unconscious of how much I hate it all." That recognition came a few weeks before his last departure from America; in the same letter he now felt free to confess that "I am very sick of America and of professors and professoresses, and . . . I am pining for a sunny, quiet, remote, friendly, intellectual, obscure existence, with large horizons and no empty noise in the foreground."[18]

Once in England, Santayana was free to become the wandering observer he had wished to be at least since his graduate-student days in Germany. In the year which followed he would be in London, the English Cambridge, Avila, Madrid, Paris, Rome, and Florence—places which became over the next forty years fixed points of his ambit. But it was not simply the freedom to live and travel in Europe which Santayana now possessed; his escape from the exactions of professional life gave him the freedom essential to the vocation of the artist-philosopher. His writings begin to manifest after 1912 an expansiveness, an audacity, a *joie* which had not appeared before in his public phi-

18. Santayana to Susana Sturgis de Sastre, December 7, 1911, in *The Letters of George Santayana*, ed. Daniel Cory (New York, 1955), p. 110.

losophy. In *Egotism in German Philosophy* (1916), *Character and Opinion in the United States* (1920), *Soliloquies in England* (1922), *Dialogues in Limbo* (1926), and *Platonism and the Spiritual Life* (1927) his imagination ranges over new themes and writers and places; metaphors multiply and acquire new resonances; the tensions of his inner dialectic find outlet now in the contending voices of dramatized dialogue. His soliloquies, dialogues, and retrospective judgments of America and the German philosophers were so many ways to accommodate at last the complexity of his own experience and mind, to give expression to emotions and insights buried or neglected by the professorial somnambulist. For all his years and wisdom Santayana was still, in his own eyes, a young philosopher trying to be born.

II. The Genesis of *Persons and Places*

By striking nearer the nerve of his innate philosophy in this period, Santayana opened a new and lively commerce with his past. The radical intuitions of his youth which had found spontaneous expression in his poems re-emerge in this period, more boldly articulated than before, and tempered or qualified only in the sense that they join a multitude of other views which challenge the exclusive authority and final adequacy of the young man's insights. And these acts of self-recovery brought with them attendant recollections of his personal past. Santayana speaks in *Persons and Places* of his recognition, after arriving in England and discovering that his old London rooms on Jermyn Street would no longer be available, that "the prospect backward had begun decidedly to gain on the prospect forward." He was approaching fifty. Yet it was not to be until several years later, with the end of the distraction and distress he felt during the years of World War I, that the stored impressions of his past life came to the forefront of his thinking. In 1920, after settling in Rome for the first of what would be his thirty winters there, he wrote to Mrs. Frederick Winslow in Boston of a recent turn in his reflections. He had been thinking, he said, of his days at the Boston Latin School and of his years at Harvard as an undergraduate. "It is wonderful how much I live in things long past." And he spoke of his "mystical" sense that all of his history would one day lie before him in its indelible truth: "My dear Mrs. Winslow, there is a time coming, or a day beyond all time when everything will return to us without being dug up; or to put my mysticism differently, when we shall cease to be irrationally concentrated and absorbed in the passing moment, and shall spread ourselves out, justly and veraciously, over the whole of our lives. I am old enough to be almost doing that already."[19]

We may conjecture that it was at this time that Santayana began to reminisce in writing. At any rate we find him in May 1924 reporting to his great-nephew, George Sturgis, "I am writing something which I call 'Persons and Places' in which I mean to give some account, historically accurate but selective, of some scenes and characters that have remained in my memory." He does not conceive it as an autobiography, he tells Sturgis; it is rather "a chronology of my life," "an authoritative document" which might serve as a corrective to mendacious biographers.[20] And yet two months later, at Cortina d'Ampezzo in the Italian Dolomites (where, he reports, he often feels on his long walks "a wonderful elation") he announces to Sturgis, "I have begun to write an Autobiography."[21]

Santayana continued to work on *Persons and Places* for another year; then, from the summer of 1925 until 1932, all reference to it drops from his correspondence. The writing of another book had usurped the place of the autobiography in his attention: *The Last Puritan*. He had contemplated writing a novel—although he had conceived it as a novel exclusively about college life—in the early 1890's. Now, so many years later and (one conjectures) as a direct result of the quickening of memory attendant on his autobiographical writing, the story of young Oliver Alden, his fictional hero, had begun to acquire form. Fiction now took precedence over fact, yet without abatement of Santayana's retrospective mood. Whether at work on the novel or the autobiography he could continue to draw from his now vivid past.

Santayana did not complete his novel until 1934, but in the meantime two circumstances impelled him back to the autobiographical notebooks in which he had begun in 1924 and '25 to record his impressions of

19. Santayana to Mrs. Frederick Winslow, May 3, 1920, unpublished letter.
20. Santayana to George Sturgis, May 13, 1924, unpublished letter.
21. Santayana to George Sturgis, July 29, 1924, in *The Letters of George Santayana*, p. 216.

persons and places. In the winter of 1932 the Boston Latin School *Register* asked him, as its first editor, for a contribution to its 50th anniversary issue. "I couldn't very well refuse," he wrote to his young secretary, Daniel Cory, "and have got interested in the thing for its own sake, going far beyond what is required for the occasion." Also that winter his old classmate Boylston Beal had settled in Rome, and their talks as they strolled the Borghese gardens doubtless carried them back to the Harvard Yard and the Berlin of the 1880's. Reporting these things to Cory, Santayana observed, "I am getting very reminiscent."[22] It is not surprising to find that at the end of that month, January 1932, he has resumed writing *Persons and Places* and is "writing with gusto."[23]

But sustained attention to his autobiography was to be more short-lived in this period than in 1924–25. Invitations to speak on Spinoza at the Hague and on Locke before the Royal Society of Literature deflected his interest once more. When he returned to Rome in the fall of 1934 after giving these, his last public lectures, he resumed the writing and revision of his novel, afterwards turning to the task of completing the final two volumes of his masterwork, *The Realms of Being.* Not till 1940 did he go back to that "pile of MS which I call 'Persons and Places.'" Early that year he began a regular morning regimen of reminiscences—an occupation he found delightful, for he had lived to complete his *magnum opus*, and he was able at last to turn from the exactions of theory to what he laughingly called his "complete, rambling, endless, philosophical and satirical stream of recollections."

Santayana completed Volume I in an astonishing spurt, writing two hundred pages of manuscript during "a very industrious holiday" at Fiuggi in the summer of 1941. On October 12th he dispatched the manuscript to Scribner's in New York. But World War II now intruded into the quiet routine of the old philosopher: he was to learn five days later that manuscripts and printed matter were no longer accepted in the Italian posts; his manuscript of Volume I was returned by the Rome post office. With the entry of the United States into the war two months later, all his lines of communication with America would be broken—all but one. Scribner's in New York, aware that a valuable

22. Santayana to Daniel Cory, January 5, 1932, in Daniel Cory, *Santayana: The Later Years* (New York, 1963), p. 90.
23. Santayana to George Sturgis, January 28, 1932, unpublished letter.

literary property was now out of reach, ingeniously contrived with the help of the Irish poet Padraic Colum and officials of the Vatican and the American Embassy in Madrid to have the manuscript sent in the Vatican diplomatic pouch to Spain, from whence the American Ambassador directed it to the United States. This quiet stratagem was carried out in the summer and fall of 1942. A little over a year later, in January 1944, Volume I of *Persons and Places* was published in its American edition.

Unsurprised and unperturbed by the war, Santayana, now settled in the convent-clinic of the Little Company of Mary (an English order) in Rome, went on re-living his life, continuing every day to set down his recollections. He completed his autobiography almost at the same time that communications with the United States were re-opened in the summer of 1944. The following December, after revising Volume II, he sent the manuscript by military post to New York through the courtesy of an American soldier, one of the many who now sought him out in the Via Santo Stefano Rotondo. It was published by Scribner's in the spring of 1945.

Santayana wished the publication of the third volume of his autobiography to be postponed until after his death, in order to avoid any possible embarrassment of persons still living who were discussed in its pages, or of their children. Although he permitted its first and last chapters to be published in *The Atlantic Monthly* in its issues of December 1948 and January 1949, *My Host the World* did not appear until 1953, a year after his death.

III. The Organization of *Persons and Places*

I have noted that the importance to man of a long memory is an insistent theme in Santayana's writings. The poet especially, he argued, is committed to carrying into the present a long and various experience of the world. The artist with the highest aspiration, the *altissimo poeta* of Santayana's *Three Philosophical Poets* (1910), seeks "to hold and suspend [the past] in a thought," to concentrate in one moment of intense reflection, in a single dramatic perspective, the impressions and suggestions of a lifetime. He must then make articulate his vision so that "others may be able to decipher it, and to be stirred by it as by a wind of suggestion sweeping the whole forest of their memories."[24] Like the three poets of his study, Lucretius, Dante, and Goethe, the artist Santayana speaks of is a maker of fictions: his personal history is the source but not the subject of his imaginative constructions. "Correlative objects," Santayana had argued several years earlier—characters, images, a plot—must be found to embody the artist's impassioned conceptions.[25]

But the philosopher also, like the poet, must bring to a focus the multitudinous past, "concentrating and liberating the confused promptings left in [him] by a long experience." And the philosopher, too, seeks to transmute personal history into the terms of an impersonal art, converting the particular into the universal, the merely subjective into the objective. A major thesis of *Three Philosophical Poets* is that both poet and philosopher aspire to join their lives to their words about life. For all their differences, both aim at those articulations of life which subsume and give coherence to associative values of the most diverse kinds—an image, a narrative, a conception responsive to a voluminous experience which we are able to appropriate and make ours. Such marryings of the mind and the world require the difficult fusing of word and spirit, language and emotion, theory and observation—and, as a prior condition of them all, a fusing of past and present.

I have suggested that Santayana's escape from Harvard marked a new beginning in his own pursuit of these aims. He would commit himself after 1912 to accommodating his deepest experience within a frame of language, a genuinely expressive and systematic philosophy which would be the adequate mirror of his mind and the world it contemplated. He began to infuse "more and more of myself into the apprehension of the world and its opinions, until in *Realms of Being* the picture of them becomes itself a confession and an image of the mind that composed it."[26] *Realms of Being* (1927–40) realizes consummately Santayana's ambition in all its depth and scope. Its terms, categories, and figurations are controlled by a mind committed to

24. Santayana, *Three Philosophical Poets* (Cambridge, Mass., 1910), p. 20.
25. Santayana, "The Elements and Function of Poetry," in *Interpretations of Poetry and Religion* (New York, 1900), p. 277. Santayana's pupil at Harvard, T. S. Eliot, silently appropriated this conception, terming it the "objective correlative."
26. "The Idler and His Works," p. 6.

seeing things whole and conceiving them integrally—without sacrifice of the actual complexity of experience and without trimming the world to the measure of hidden preconceptions. The extraordinary coherence and final unity of this four-volume work is at once formal (it responds to both logical and literary criteria of entailment and mutual implication among its terms), personal (it is the work of a unified sensibility which joins here the intellectual and affectional sides of its nature), and representational (in and through his orderings Santayana reveals the world to us, makes it available to our conceiving in new and unsuspected ways—and as a whole). We are able to see his *Realms* now as one of the last of a vanishing species, a comprehensive philosophy raised on the bedrock of examined first principles, in and through which a mind achieved its self-definition.

Persons and Places did not have its source in ambitions so large, nor has it the kind of organic unity so striking in *Realms of Being*. When, in his sixties, Santayana began to make personal history itself the subject of his writing, he thought of his reminiscences as a series of sketches, of scenes from the past and individual portraits of people who had, for whatever reason, left indelible impressions in his memory. Santayana did not think of himself as the subject of *Persons and Places*. From the first notebook jottings of the early 1920's down almost to the time of the first volume's publication, he thought of the book as a sequence of "disjointed recollections," "satire and gossip"—but "no confessions." He wished to discount the merely personal, to see his subjects as in themselves they were, and not always or not only as they may have influenced his own life and mind. In the spring of 1939 he characterized his book as "notes and reminiscences. . . , partly about myself and my family, but chiefly about friends and old haunts." "These fragments," he observed in another letter of the same period, "will hardly compose an autobiography."[27]

It is to this initiating conception that *Persons and Places* owes its form as a collection or gathering. It is not a work whose every image and episode subserves a central vision, as Joyce or Proust deployed the materials of personal history. Nor is it a chronological narrative designed to demonstrate the autobiographer's advance on chaos and dark night. Although the chapter on his metanoia and the concluding pages of the chapter on "The Church of the Immaculate Conception" are telling accounts of crucial turns in his development, the book as a whole does

27. Santayana to Otto Kyllmann, April 4, 1939, unpublished letter.

not find a focus in rites of passage or the evolution of a mind. Moreover its episodes, though everywhere they are made to yield their meanings, do not issue in a single dramatic perspective or summary insight. To grasp the full implications of many comments here we need to go to several of his other books. Nor is Santayana's narrative designed to be the portrait of an age—although he once referred to it wryly as "a humdrum chronicle of *faits divers* for some future antiquary to dig up to illustrate the low state of society in my time."[28] These incisive portraits of the persons and places he has known convey a wealth of information about his times, but they are not designed to summarize an epoch, illustrate a governing historical thesis, or append a moral to the times.

To notice these things is not to say, however, that *Persons and Places* lacks organizing conceptions. The intelligence at work in the midst of these memories conspicuously drives toward connection, form, unity, an architectonic impulse clearly apparent in the short runs—in the single paragraph or chapter or portrait which draws its life from a governing insight or impression. His chapter on "Avila," for example, is a self-contained essay, integrating a miscellany of observations in a sustained meditation on the power of tradition. His sketches of cathedrals incorporate a multitude of observed details yet locate these works in history and suggest their human meanings. His portraits of people always reach, by means of his characteristic interfusing of sympathy and wit, toward discovery of the center of his subject's personal and social being.

Some of the book's themes and images, however, join chapter to chapter. I have suggested two ways in which one may think about the book as a whole: through its recurring metaphor of the traveler, and as the story of Santayana's difficult extrication of his spirit from the meshes of circumstance in which he found himself. Both of these motifs are implicit in a geographic design which, on one occasion, Santayana pointed to as having ordered his materials. Writing in 1945 to his Scribner's editor, John Hall Wheelock, he observed that his double heritage, his residence in and allegiance to Europe and America, had determined the division of his autobiography into three parts.[29]

28. Santayana to (Mrs.) Asta Fleming Whiteside, December 8, 1944, in *The Letters of George Santayana*, p. 353.
29. Santayana to John Hall Wheelock, February 23, 1945, unpublished letter.

The first volume, *Persons and Places* (the title which Santayana wished to be used for an eventual one-volume edition of the complete work) tells of his coming to the United States, and of his life in this country up to the time of his leaving for graduate study in Germany. (For that purpose he must tell us of his family background and early history in Spain, and since he wished to complete his portraits at one sitting, he draws from his subject's full life-history and from all the impressions which he himself had gathered in his own lifetime. Thus, for example, in a single early chapter we learn of his father's family origins, his subsequent history, and his death: a biography-in-little.) The second volume Santayana thought might be titled "On Both Sides of the Atlantic," for it speaks of the Harvard professor and the summer traveler in Europe, a twenty-four year period of divided residence and divided commitments. The third volume, *My Host the World*, is "all on one side": it tells of his European years following his resignation from Harvard. If, he wrote to Wheelock, the last volume includes accounts of his metanoia in 1893 and of his year at King's College, Cambridge, in 1896–97, that is because these events were crucial for his decision to leave America. They were anticipations of "my eastward migration, material and moral." They pointed him toward Europe.

This is the *mise-en-scène* of the inner and outer drama told here: America, America/Europe, Europe. It is, more specifically, the story of a trans-Atlantic mind plying its way between Avila, Spain on the one side, and on the other Harvard and Boston, U.S.A. Santayana renounced neither. How should he? They had formed him, provided the inevitable terms of his awareness, been the fated contexts in which he must come to clearness. "My real nucleus was this combination, not easily unified."[30] Despite his many aversions to Harvard he recognized the favoring wind it provided for the would-be voyager: its intellectual vitality and sincerity, its wealth of books, its friendliness gave him "a maximum of air, of space, of suggestion." So also did Avila, but despite his deep love of the "austere inspiration of these mountains, these battlemented city walls and these dark churches" he found the place "too old, shrunken, barren and high and dry to impose its limitations on a travelling mind." As a son he acknowledged

30. *Persons and Places*, p. 449.

the beneficent influence of both foster parents, yet recognized and would not be constrained by their provinciality. "The extreme contrast between the two centres and the two influences became itself a blessing: it rendered flagrant the limitations and the contingency of both."[31]

Santayana's fidelity to his sources—whatever their differences and contrarieties, and however much he felt inwardly divided between Europe and America—brought his mature recognition that the civilization of Christendom was his native place. "[M]y heritage was that of Greece, of Rome ancient and modern, and of the literature and philosophy of Europe. Christian history and art contained all my spiritual traditions, my intellectual and moral language."[32] When he began in the 1920's to spend his winters in Rome it was not with the idea of settling there permanently, but it is not surprising that in time— as the circle of his travels diminished, and, with the coming of war, he was confined altogether to Rome—Santayana should feel that the eternal city had been his "fated centre of gravity and equilibrium."[33] There, he said, he came to feel nearer his own past and the past and future of his world than in any other place. Into Rome had come and out of Rome had gone most of the winds of doctrine and faith whose history and worth he had spent a lifetime studying. *Omnium urbis et orbis ecclesiarum, mater et caput*, the Lateran inscription says, and Santayana made it his salute also: "mother and head of my moral world."

He felt at home there; it was not home. To settle at last in Rome was not to come back at last to the Church, a penitent and believer. Though a Christian civilization had been the carrier of the traditions and language which had engaged him—beliefs, practices, writings pre-Christian and pagan, Catholic, Protestant, and secular—he could not in the end identify himself wholly with any one of them. On the contrary, as the moral crossroads of his world, Rome was a constant stimulus to new forays into the past and new discoveries of human possibility. At the end of his chapter on "Travels" Santayana observes that he could preserve in Rome better than anywhere else "my essential character of stranger and traveller, with the philosophic freedom that this implies."[34] To the end he demanded for himself the "privilege of ubiquity," the indefeasible right of the imagination to go on visiting

31. *Ibid.*, p. 98.
32. *Ibid.*, p. 449.
33. *Ibid.*, p. 467.
34. *Ibid.*, p. 467.

all ages and countries, participating in all minds and selves, while refusing a commitment of the whole heart or the whole mind to any.

In refusing to accept as his own the doctrines and faiths of true believers of every stamp, had Santayana failed, after all, to find his place, a belief of his own, a self? No: within his "realms" he had found his true *locus standi*. Within this structure of his own making built over many years he had realized his mind and world. The luminous register of his settled convictions (as it had been also an indispensable means to their discovery), it provided a center and sure vantage in all his travelings. More than that: it encouraged and justified them. For he had come to see how unnecessary, constricting, and tyrannous *belief* can be. Believe we must—in the external world, for example, or in other minds—but he thought most men oversubscribed in their articles of belief, pledged to the support of gratuitous doctrines born of assertiveness or the need of dogmatic certitude or of sheer imaginative exuberance. By rescinding our unnecessary commitments of mind, we open ourselves to the new and the alien, and look justly, because undogmatically, at the world's diversity. We might say of Santayana's mature philosophy that in it he had found a home and come to rest, or with equal justice we might speak of it as his fighting faith. Both observations, however, deflect attention from that most striking characteristic of his philosophy—its openness to rival perspectives, diverse intuitions, alternative ways of feeling. Among philosophic habitations with claims to completeness, Santayana's is unique in the size and number of its windows.

This is the philosophy which would find its further, most personal expression in *Persons and Places*. By the time Santayana came to set down these scenes from his past, he did not need to make up his mind and character as he went along. His mind was formed, his tastes sure, his character definite. As we go with him on this recollective ramble it is this—the self-knowledge and self-possession of the guide—which makes the trip a series of illuminations, and no sightseer's tour. He is not concerned to show us what he knows. He has no thesis to brandish. Santayana would simply have us see what he sees—mark the lines of a building or a character, recover an event, note a landscape in their essential qualities. Because this realist's intent is served as it

must be served by "an artist recomposing what he sees" (what Santayana thought every traveler ideally should be), his recollections have
form and meaning. Hence, like the artist-traveler, the reader too "can
carry away the picture and add it to a transmissible fund of wisdom,
not as further miscellaneous experience but as a corrected view of
the truth."[35]

Though the "antique sage" of this autobiography is a man of im-
movable principles, they are principles which justify and require a
quick and moving imagination. The terrain of his ramble is not only
astonishingly diverse; we are invited to see it in lights to which we
are not accustomed. The young Santayana who in his early books set
out to say in English "as many un-English things as possible" continues
to speak here as a European who would remember, and who would
have us remember, many a forgotten way of thinking and feeling
about the world. We may feel steadily rebuked in our provinciality,
but we can hardly grudge him the lesson.

35. *Ibid.*, p. 449.

I

Fragments of Autobiography

I

My Place, Time, and Ancestry

A document in my possession testifies that in the parish church of San Marcos in Madrid, on the first of January, 1864, a male child, born on the sixteenth of the previous December, at nine o'clock in the evening, at No. 69 Calle Ancha de San Bernardo, was solemnly christened; being the legitimate son of Don Agustín Ruiz de Santayana, native of Zamora, and of Doña Josefina Borrás, native of Glasgow; his paternal grandparents being Don Nicolás, native of Badumès, in the province of Santander, and Doña María Antonia Reboiro, native of Zamora; and his maternal grandparents being Don José, native of Reus, Catalonia, and Doña Teresa Carbonell, native of Barcelona. The names given him were Jorge Agustín Nicolás, his godparents being Don Nicolás Ruiz de Santayana, and Doña Susana Sturgis; "whom I admonished", writes Don Joaquín Carrasco, who signs the certificate with his legal *rúbrica* or flourish, "of their spiritual relationship and duties."*

*Don Paulino Corrales Diaz, Presbítero, Licenciado en Sagrada Teología y Cura Proprio de la Parroquia de San Marcos de esta Corte, y en su nombre D. Prudencio M. Gil y Arguso, encargado accidentalmente del Despacho.

Certifico: Que en el libro décimo de Bautismos que se guarda en este archivo al folio setenta y cinco se halla inscripta la siguiente partida, que copiada literalmente dice así:

En San Marcos de Madrid a primero de Enero de mil ochocientos sesenta y cuatro, yo Don Joaquin Carrasco, Teniente Mayor de Cura de la misma bauticé solemnemente en ella a un niño que nació el diez y seis de Diciembre del año último, a las nueve de la noche, en la Calle Ancha de San Bernardo, Nº 69, c^{to} 2º, hijo legítimo de D^{n} Agustín Ruiz de Santayana, natural de Zamora, y de Dª Josefina Borrás, natural de Glasgow (Escocia); abuelos Paternos, D^{n} Nicolás, natural de Badumes (Santander) y Dª Maria Antonia Reboiro, natural de Zamora, Maternos, D^{n} José, natural de Reus (Tarragona) y Dª Teresa Carbonell, natural de Barcelona: Se le puso por nombre Jorge, Agustín, Nicolás, y fueron Padrinos D^{n} Nicolás Ruiz de Santayana y Dª Susana Sturgis, a quienes advertí el parentesco espiritual y obligaciones, y lo firmé Joaquin Carrasco = Rubricado.

A shrewd fortune-teller would have spotted at once, in this densely Spanish document, the two English names, Glasgow and Sturgis. Where did they come from, what did they forebode? Might not seeds of my whole future lie buried there? And if the diviner had had preternatural powers, he might even have sniffed something important in those last, apparently so effete and perfunctory words, that Doña Susana Sturgis, who was my mother's daughter by a former marriage and then twelve years of age, had been forewarned of her spiritual relationship and duties: not that she should forbear marrying my godfather, my uncle Nicolás, who was a major in the Spanish army, with a wife and child, and forty-five years old; that was canonical red-tape nothing to the purpose; but that she was called by Providence to be really my spiritual mother and to catechise my young mind. It was she that initiated me into theology, architecture and polite society.

With parents evidently Catalans of the Catalonians, how did my mother come to be born in Glasgow, and how did she ever marry a Bostonian named Sturgis? These facts, taken separately, were accidents of travel, or rather of exile and of colonial life; but accidents are accidents only to ignorance; in reality all physical events flow out of one another by a continuous intertwined derivation; and those odd foreign names, Sturgis and Glasgow. They were in fact secretly allied and their presence here had a common source in my grandfather's character and circumstances and in the general thaw, so to speak, of that age: incongruous wreckage of a great inundation.

Not that I would nail the flag of fatalism to the mast at the beginning of this retrospective voyage. What we call the laws of nature are hasty generalisations; and even if some of them actually prevailed without

---

Concuerda con su original. (San Marcos de Madrid a tres de Septiembre de mil novecientos diez y nueve)

Prudencio M. Gil Arguso

(rubricado)

sello
de S. Marcos

V$\underline{^o}$ B$\underline{^o}$

Sello de la Vicaría
General, Madrid-Alcalá

El Provisor interino
D$\underline{^n}$ Bernardo Barbajero

(rubricado)

exception or alloy, the fact that these laws and not others (or none) were found to be dominant would itself be groundless; so that nothing could be at bottom more arbitrary than what always happens, or more fatal than what happens but once or by absolute chance. Yet in the turbid stream of nature there are clear stretches, and traceable currents; and it is interesting to follow the beginnings and the developments of a run here and a whirlpool there, and to watch the silent glassy volume of water slip faster and faster towards the edge of some precipice. Now my little cockle-shell and the cockle-shells of the rest of my family, and of the whole middle and upper class (except the unsinkable politicians) were being borne along more or less merrily on the surface-currents of a treacherous social revolution; and the things that happened to us, and the things we did, with their pleasant and their hopeless sides, all belong to that general moral migration.

My grandfather, José Borrás y Bufurull, belonged to a well-established family of Reus, of the sort that possess a house in the town and a farm in the country. In this as in other ways many old towns near the Mediterranean preserve the character of ancient cities or *civitates*, and Reus in particular is a place of great dignity in the eyes of its inhabitants, who are reputed to speak habitually of "Reus, Paris, and London". But José was a younger son, and the law of entail or *mayorazgo* still prevailed at that time in Catalonia, so that the house and land and an almost Roman authority as head of the family fell to his eldest brother. Yet dignity to the classic mind does not involve great wealth or much *Lebensraum*, and younger sons, even in Reus, had to seek their fortunes away from home. They might indeed expect hospitality or a little aid from their families in time of stress, but were well aware that in the ancestral estate and community there was no place or occupation for more than one household at a time. There was the Church always tempting them, if it tempted them; there were the other professions, and there was the New World, or at least Cuba and the Philippines. One of my grandfather's brothers had actually combined these opportunities, become a monk, and later been established as a parish priest in Montevideo or in Buenos Aires.* The

---

*A history of the Borrás family of Reus has been published, but it contains hardly any information about my grandfather and none about my mother. In some respects the traditions recorded there diverge from those that my mother handed down; they may be more accurate, as my mother had no great interest or respect for the past. The exact facts in any case are not important, and I report the impressions that I have gathered.

ultimate resource, among all my Spanish acquaintance and relations, was some post under the government; and my grandfather might very well have sought his fortunes no further afield than Barcelona, or at most Madrid; but he went much further. Economic considerations were probably not uppermost in his mind; if they were, his career must have disheartened him. Those were unsettled and unsettling times, the repercussions of the French Revolution had not spent themselves, and emancipation of mind was sure to follow, if it had not preceded, being cast loose upon the world. In any case we know that my grandfather, far from becoming a monk like his brother, became a Deist, an ardent disciple of Rousseau, and I suspect a Free-mason; and when a French army entered Spain, in 1823, to restore the shaken authority of Ferdinand VII and the absolute monarchy, José Borrás was compelled, or thought it advisable, to leave the country. The story goes that he fled first to Las Palmas, in the Balearic Islands, where he saw and wooed Teresa Carbonell, a stout blonde with very blue eyes (my mother's eyes were also blue and large); and that after a romantic marriage he persuaded her to follow him in his wanderings. In my certificate of baptism, however, Teresa Carbonell is set down as a native of Barcelona, which is not strictly incompatible with her living later at Las Palmas, or her family belonging there; but she and her whole history are wrapped in some obscurity, and suggest various problems that I have no means of solving.

One of these problems is why my grandfather should have chosen Glasgow for a place of refuge, and what he did there. Mahon, in the neighbouring Minorca, had long been in British occupation, and occasions may have presented themselves to sail from there to Scotland, or perhaps to Lancashire; and he seems to have remained in these parts for some years, probably giving Spanish lessons and in any case learning English. This exile in poverty and obscurity, in so remote, cheerless, and industrial a scene, may not have been altogether unwelcome to him. Catalans are industrially and economically minded; novelty and distance allure them; and who knows how many utopias and ideologies, and what reflections on the missed opportunities of human government and art may not have kept his brain and his heart warm in that chilly climate. All I can say is that his thirst for exploration or his longing for a simpler and more ideal society carried him eventually across the Atlantic, to rural, republican, distinguished, Jeffersonian Virginia. Here, if anywhere, mankind had turned over a new leaf, and in a clean new world, free from all absurd traditions and tyrant mortgages, was beginning to lead a pure life of reason and virtue. With slavery? Perhaps that was only a temporary necessity, a kindly apprenticeship to instil into the simple negro a love of labour and of civilised arts; and as the protection of industries might be justified provisionally, until they could become well-rooted, so domestic servitude might be justified provisionally, until the slaves were ripe for freedom. Be that as it may, José Borrás either came well recommended or ingratiated himself easily into the democracy of Winchester, Virginia, becoming (as a florid testimonial averred) one of its most honoured and beloved citizens; so much so that as the years revolved, and a change of government in the liberal direction had occurred in Spain, his Winchester friends induced Andrew Jackson, then President of the United States, to appoint him American consul at Barcelona. Thus his cordial attachments in exile enabled him eventually to return home, not only safely but gloriously, and with some prospect of bread and butter.*

*The President of the United States of America
to all who shall see these presents, greeting.

No ye, that reposing special trust and confidence in the abilities and the integrity of Joseph Borras of Spain, I have nominated and by and with the advice and consent of the Senate do appoint him consul of the United States of America for the Port of Barcelona, in Spain, and for such other parts as shall be nearer thereto than the residence of any other consul or vice-consul of the United States within the same allegiance,—and do authorize and empower him to have and to hold the said office and to exercise and enjoy all the rights, preeminences, privileges, and authorities to the same of right appertaining, during the pleasure of the President of the United States for the time being; HE demanding and receiving no fees or perquisites of office whatever, which shall not be expressly established by some law of the United States. And I do hereby enjoin all captains, masters, and commanders of ships and other vessels, armed or un-armed, sailing under the flag of the United States as well as all others of their citizens, to acknowledge and consider him the said Joseph Borras accordingly. And I do hereby pray and request Her Majesty, the Queen of Spain, Her governors and officers to permit the said Joseph Borras fully and peaceably to enjoy and exercise the said office without giving or suffering to be given un to him any molestation or trouble, but on the contrary to afford him all proper countenance and assistance; I offering to do the same for all those who shall in like manner be recommended to me by Her said Majesty.

In testimoney whereof I have caused these letters to be made patent, and the seal of the United States be hereunto affixed.

Given under my hand at the City of Washington, the third day of March in the

An element of mystery or mystification hangs about this home-coming. The date of my mother's birth, according to her official papers, was 1828, but there is reason to believe that in reality it was 1826. When she was brought to Spain in 1835 the shocking fact appeared that she had never been christened. Was there no Catholic priest in Glasgow in those days, and none in Winchester, Virginia? Had no travelling ecclesiastic been met with in all those wanderings? No doubt her father's enlightened principles made him regard all religious practices, morally and philosophically, as indifferent, while socially it was advisable that everyone should be affiliated to the religious customs prevalent in his country. But what was to be my mother's country? If it were to be Scotland or Virginia, she ought to be christened and brought up a Protestant; if it were to be Spain, it was imperative that she should be a Catholic. The matter therefore had to be suspended until the question of final residence was settled; although it may seem singular that my grandmother should have wholly acquiesced in this view and allowed her daughter to grow up, as they say in Spain, a Moor. Now, however, the matter had to be patched up as expeditiously and quietly as possible. Friends and relations, even clerical advisers, are very accommodating in Spain and very ingenious. The age of seven, the canonical age of reason, when one begins to sin of one's own accord, was the right age for confirmation; young Josefina was small for her age; let her official age be reduced to seven years, let a private christening, to supply the place of the missing documents, be smuggled in before the confirmation, and then the child would be launched quite legally and becomingly in her religious career, with confession and communion to follow immediately. This wealth of sacraments, raining down on her unprepared and extraordinarily self-reliant little soul, seems not to have left much hunger for further means of grace; my mother always spoke of such things as of troublesome and empty social requirements; and even ordinary social requirements, like visiting, rather annoyed her, as if they interfered with her liberty and interrupted her peace. On the whole, however, her ten years or more of girlhood in Barcelona seem to have been

---

year of our Lord one thousand eight hundred and thirty-five, and of the Independence of the United States of America the fifty-ninth.

(Signed)   Andrew Jackson

By the President

(SEAL)   John Forsyth, Secretary of State.

gay and happy—the only frankly happy period of her life. Without being robust, her health was perfect, her needlework exquisite, her temper equable and calm; she loved and was loved by her girl-friends; she read romantic verses and select novels; above all, she danced. That was the greatest pleasure in life for her: not for the sake of her partners, those were surely only round dances, and the partners didn't count; what counted was the joy of motion, the sense of treading lightly, in perfect time, a sylph in spotless muslin, enriched with a ribbon or a flower, playing discreetly with her fan, and sailing through the air with feet that seemed scarcely to touch the ground. Even in her old age my mother never walked, she stepped. And she would say, in her quaint, perhaps Virginian, English: "Will you step in?" She was not beautiful, and prematurely regarded herself as an old woman, and put on a white lace cap; but she had good points and made a favourable ideal impression, even if she did not positively attract. I can imagine her in her young days, agile of foot and hand, silent and enigmatic behind her large sunken blue eyes, thin lips, and brown corkscrew curls, three on a side, setting off her white complexion. If men did not often make love to her, especially not the men who care specifically for women, she amply took her revenge. Her real attachments, apart from her devotion to her father, were to her women friends, not to crowds of them, but to two or three and for life. To men as men, even to her two husbands, she seems to have been cold, critical and sad, as if conscious of yielding to some inevitable but disappointing fatality.

I will translate a letter written to her by my father, dated Jan. 28, 1888, when I was in my second year at the University of Berlin, and it began to seem clear that I should drift into an academic life in America.

"My dear Josefina; I have had much pleasure in taking note of your kind letter and of the verses which, while thinking of me, you wrote twenty-five years ago. A volume would be requisite for me to recount the memories I have of our relations during now little less than half a century. When we were married I felt as if it were written that I should be united with you, yielding to the force of destiny, although I saw plainly the difficulties that then surrounded such a union, apart from those that would not fail to arise later. Strange marriage, this of ours! So you say, and so it is in fact. I love you very much, and you too have cared for me, yet we do not live together. But it is necessary to keep in mind the circumstances peculiar to our case. I have always believed that the place in which it would be natural for you to live was Boston, in consequence of your first marriage which determined the course of your whole life. My position has offered and now offers no inducement, none, to balance the propriety or necessity of that arrangement. On my side, I could not then or later leave my own country for good, in order to live in Boston, when in view of my age and impediments it was impossible for me to learn to speak English well and to mix in that society. Here I have been a help to my family, and there I should only have been an encumbrance.

"I should have wished that Jorge should not have been separated from me, but I found myself compelled to take him in person and leave him in your charge and in that of his brother and sisters. Unhappy compulsion! Yet it was much better for him to be with you than with me, and I prefer his good to my pleasure."

How much in this was clearness of vision, how much was modesty, how much was love of quietness and independence? It is not a question for me to decide, but there was certainly something of all those motives. Education such as I received in Boston was steadier and my associations more regular and calmer than they would have been in Spain; but there was a terrible moral disinheritance involved, an emotional and intellectual chill, a pettiness and practicality of outlook and ambition, which I should not have encountered amid the complex passions and intrigues of a Spanish environment. From the point of view of learning, my education at the Boston Latin School and at Harvard College was not solid or thorough; it would not have been solid or thorough in Spain; yet what scraps of learning or ideas I might have gathered there would have been vital, the wind of politics and of poetry would have swelled them, and allied them with notions of honour. But then I should have become a different man; so that my father's decision was all for my good, if I was to be the person that I am now.

II

My Father

Origin of the name Santayana.

•

The towns Santillana and Espinosa.

The name Santayana is derived by phonetic corruption from that of a small town in the Cantabrian hills, not far from the sea and from Santander. This name was originally Santa Juliana, doubtless that of some shrine or hermitage; but in Latin, as in Italian, *J* is only a double *i* or *y* the consonant, and the consonant *y* in Spanish is often confused with the stronger sound of *ll*, or the Italian *gl*; so that Santa Juliana could variously yield in the vernacular to Santa Iliana, Santallana, Santayana, and Santillana. This last is the present name of that village; and on the other side of Santander, towards the south east, lies the village of Espinosa; so that my witty friend and translator, Don Antonio Marichalar, Marqués de Montesa (from whom I borrow the above etymology), half in banter and half in compliment finds in those seaside mountains, opposite one another, the native soil of Spinoza and of myself. But if I cannot be mentioned without a smile in the same breath with Spinoza for greatness of intellect, he cannot be compared with me for Spanish blood. He was a Jew; his ancestors could have found their way to Espinosa only as they did later to Amsterdam, or he himself to The Hague, or I to America; whereas, if the reader will look back to the first page of this narrative, he will see that my grandfather was born in the province of Santander, though not at Santillana, and that his wife and my father were born at Zamora, in Leon, my grandmother having the distinctly Portuguese or Galician surname of Reboiro: so that my ancestry on my father's side points distinctly to northwestern Spain, and Celtiberian blood; while my mother's origins were as unmistakably Catalonian and Balearic; rooted, that is, in those northeastern shores that look towards Provence and towards Italy and have linked Spain for many ages with the whole Mediterranean world. Through Christianity and through commerce culture if not blood certainly flowed into that half of my ancestry from the ancestry and true home of Spinoza; and there is more affinity between our minds in pure cosmic speculation than in any local or ancestral ties: for in spite of my profound attachment to his system of nature, I miss in his moral sentiment precisely that Castilian disdain and independence, that pagan lust and love of beauty, which might have been drawn from my race. In his ideal of happiness he was too Jewish and too Dutch for my taste: consented to be led to pasture in fat meadows beside the still waters. Quietness and personal frugality I love, but only in the shadow of historic greatness and monumental grandeur of the will. The grandeur of the universe is physical only, cruel, and stained with every form of baseness. The spirit within me says with the Indians and with the Romans: *Maggior mi sento.*

Vicissitudes of the family name. The name Santayana is tolerably well known in Spain. My father had a book of the eighteenth century written by one of the family on the subject of international trade, advocating the Spartan policy of isolation and autarchy. My father didn't call it Spartan, but monkish; and it was based perhaps more on fear of heresy than on love of political independence; but the author was not an ecclesiastic, but a man of affairs. My two forlorn unmarried aunts, older than my father, used to tell me that our family was noble and allied to the house of a Marqués de Santayana then existing in Madrid; but they had no means of tracing the relationship, nor did my father give the least attention to questions of this kind; so that I know nothing of my ancestry beyond his own time. Moreover our family name is really Ruiz, a very common one; and perhaps the addition of *de Santayana* was as accidental in our family as the addition of *de Espinosa* must have been in a family of Amsterdam Jews. Dropping Ruiz and retaining only Santayana was my father's doing, and caused him some trouble in legalising his abbreviated signature in formal documents. He loved simplicity, and thought plain Agustín Santayana as pompous a name as his modest position could carry. I sympathise with the motive; but why not drop the Santayana and keep the Ruiz, which was the true patronymic? Legally I still possess both; and the question has no further importance, since with me our branch of the family becomes extinct.

Gil Blas de Santillana. If I were looking for ancestors there is only one known to fame to whom I might attempt to attach myself, and he is Gil Blas, whose blood I should rather like imagining I had in my veins. I feel a natural sympathy with unprejudiced minds, or if you like with rogues. The picaresque world is the real world; and if lying and thievery and trickery are contemptible, it is because the game is not worth the candle, not because the method is unworthy of the prize. If you despise the world, and cheat it only to laugh at it, as the Spanish rascals seem to do, at least in fiction, the sin is already half forgiven. When the rogue tires of the game or is ruined by it, he may unfeignedly turn his free spirit towards higher things, or at least, like the good thief in Calvary, may recognise their existence. Those who lack the impudence and nimbleness of the rascal, cannot help admiring his knowledge of things, and his quick eye; and the very meanness and triviality of his arts will keep him from thinking, as sinners do on a larger scale, that they are altogether heroes. Gil Blas doesn't become a saint—his biographer is a Frenchman—but becomes a good bourgeois, rich and happily married. It is a sort of redemption, though the Spanish spirit in him demanded another sort. The worthy solution would be found not in prosperity (too nearly what the unregenerate Gil Blas was pursuing) but rather in devotion, religious in its quality, even if not in its object: the solution that the poet Zorilla, a friend of my father's in their youth, puts into the mouth of the reformed Don Juan, reformed, that is, by love.

> ¿No es verdad, ángel de amor,
> que en esta apartada orilla
> la luna mas clara brilla
> y se respira mejor?

> Angel love, is it not true
> that on this sequestered shore
> the moon shines as ne'er before
> and to breathe is something new?

The true Spanish democracy.   Gil Blas represents also the sort of spiritual democracy that is characteristically Spanish, Christian, or Oriental, utterly contrary to the venemous hatred and envy, lined with ambition, of the democratic demagogue. An unprejudiced man will be ready and happy to live in any class of society; he will find there occasions enough for merriment, pleasure, and kindness. Only snobs are troubled by inequality, or by exclusion from something accidental, as all particular stations are. Why should I think it unjust that I am not an applauded singer (which it was in me to be) nor a field-marshal nor a puppet king? I am rather sorry for them, I mean, for the spirit in them, certainly not freer than in me. Success and failure in the world are equally distracting, equally devastating. The pure gain in any career is sprinkled over it like dew; it does not depend on the species of plant that receives it, save that the plant must exist and must spread its living texture to the elements. That is a great privilege, and a great danger. I would not multiply or inflate myself of my own accord. Even the punctilious honour of the Spanish gentleman is only an eloquent vanity, disdaining many advantages for the sake of a pose. Why assume so much dignity, if you have it not? And if you have it, what need have you of parading it? The base and sordid side of life must be confessed and endured humbly; the confession and the endurance will raise you enough above it.

My father's nurture.   This Spanish dignity in humility was most marked in my father. He lived when necessary and almost by preference like the poor, without the least comfort, variety, or entertainment. He was bred in poverty, not in the standard poverty, so to speak, of the hereditary working classes, but in the cramped genteel poverty of those who find themselves poorer than they were, or than they have to seem. He was one of twelve children, imposing the strictest economy in the household of a minor official, with insecure tenure of office, such as his father was. For supper they had each a small bowl of garlic soup—something that my father loved in his old age, and that I also liked, especially if I might break a raw egg into it, as those twelve children were certainly never allowed to do. You fry some garlic in a pan with some olive oil; when crisp you remove the larger pieces of garlic, add hot water, according to the size of the family, with thin little slices of bread, no matter how dry, *ad libitum*, and a little salt; and that is your supper. Or perhaps, with a further piece of bread, you might receive a slice of cheese, cut so thin that the children would hold it up to the light, to admire its transparency, and to wink at one another through the frequent round holes.

That oil and water will not mix is disproved not only by this excellent garlic soup but also by a salad, *gazpacho*, that somewhat corresponded to it in the South. Bread, tomatoes and cucumbers, with oil and vinegar, and some slivers of raw onion, if you were not too refined, composed its substance, all floating in an abundance of water; so that if hunger was partly mocked, thirst at least was satisfied, and this is the more urgent need in a warm climate.

The national diet.   If supper at my grandfather's was only bread and water, with condiments, breakfast probably included a tiny cup of thick chocolate into which you might dip your bread, before you drank your water; for a glass of water after chocolate was *de rigueur* in all classes in old Spain. The difference between simplicity and luxury was only this: that the luxurious had an *azucarillo*, a large oblong piece of frosted sugar blown into a light spongy texture, and flavoured with lemon, to be dissolved in the glass of water. At midday the daily food of all Spaniards was the *puchero* or *cocido*, as the dish is really called which foreigners know as the *pot-pourri* or *olla podrida*. This contains principally yellow chick-peas, with a little bacon, some potatoes or other vegetables and normally also small pieces of beef and sausage, all boiled in one pot at a very slow fire; the liquid of the same makes the substantial broth that is served first.

My father was educated at Valladolid, I don't know first under what schoolmaster, but eventually at the university there, where he studied law; and he at least learned Latin well enough to take pleasure in translating all the tragedies of Seneca into Castilian blank verse: a pure work of love, since he could expect no advancement, perhaps rather the opposite, from such an exhibition of capricious industry. Nor was that his only taste; he also studied painting, and quite professionally, although he made no great progress in it. His feeling for the arts and sciences was extraordinarily different from that which prevailed in the 1880's in English-speaking circles. As to painting all in England was a matter of culture, of the pathos of distance, of sentimental religiosity, pre-Raphaelitism, and supercilious pose. Even the learned and the gifted that I saw in Oxford were saturated with affectations. My friend Lionel Johnson was typical: although thirty years later, during the war, I had other distinguished friends in Oxford, Robert Bridges and Father Waggett, who were not in the least affected. But my father could not understand the English mind, greatly as he admired and respected the practical lordliness of Britain. Speaking once of Newman, he said he wondered why Newman broke with the Anglican establishment. Was it so as to wear a trailing red silk gown? I had some difficulty in making him admit that Newman could have been sincere; perhaps it was possible if, as I said, Newman had never doubted the supernatural authority of the Church. But of inner unrest or faith suddenly born out of despair my father had absolutely no notion. Could he ever have read the Confessions of his patron saint, Saint Augustine? Was that not a natural sequel to the tragedies of Seneca?

My father's way of painting. As to painting, my father's ideas were absolutely those of the craftsman, the artisan following his trade conscientiously with no thought or respect for the profane crowd of rich people who might be babbling about art in their ignorance. This jealous professionalism did not exclude speculation and criticism; but they were the speculation and criticism of the specialist, scientific and materialistic. He viewed the arts in the manner of Leonardo, whom probably he had never read. In talking about the pictures in the Prado, which I had seen for the first time, he approved of an observation I made about *El Pasmo de Sicilia*, that all the figures were brick-coloured except that of Christ, which was whitish—a contrast that seemed artificial. He said I had been looking at the picture to some purpose. But he was disappointed when he questioned me about the Goyas, because I said nothing about the manner of painting, and only thought of the subjects, the ladies' fashions, and the sensuality of the eighteenth-century notion of happiness, coarser in Goya than in Watteau.

His methods were no less workmanlike than his thoughts. His easel, his colours, ground by himself with a glass pestle and carefully mixed with the oil, his palette, and his brushes were objects of wonder to my childish heart. I was too young to catch the contagion and try to imitate him; but afterwards, when drawing became a pastime for me (as it still is) I wondered sometimes if my father's example and lessons would have helped me to make the progress in draughtsmanship which I have never made. And I doubt that they would have helped me. Because composition and ideal charm which are everything to me in all the arts seemed to be nothing to my father. I might have acquired a little more manual skill, and corrected a few bad mannerisms; but I should soon have broken away and turned to courses that he could not approve. Yet I think that he himself suffered in his painting, as in his life, from the absence of any ideal inspiration. He was arrested by the sheer mechanics of the art, as I was arrested by ignorance of them; and he remained an amateur all his life in his professionalism, because after measuring his drawing, and catching the likeness (since his paintings were all portraits) and laying on his first strata of colour, he would become uncertain and discouraged, without a clear vision of what might render his picture living, distinctive, harmonious, and in a word *beautiful*.

Refuses to When I once asked him, apropos of his liberal politics,
have ideals. the hollowness of which I already began to feel, what ideal of society he would approve, he said he had no *ideal*. "I don't know what I want, but I know what I don't want." We laughed, and the matter ended there, since discussion with him was rendered difficult

by his extreme deafness; and few things seem worth saying when one has to reduce them first to a few words, and to make and impose an express effort in order to communicate them. But in my reflections afterwards it has often occurred to me that this position, knowing what you don't like but not knowing what you like, may be sincere enough emotionally, but not intellectually. Rejection is a form of self-assertion. You have only to look back upon yourself as a person who hates this or that to discover what it is that you secretly love. Hatred and love are imposed on the spirit by the psyche, and though the spirit may have no image of the end pursued, but only of jolts and obstacles on the way, there could be no jolts or obstacles if the life of the psyche had not a specific direction, a specific good demanded, which when disclosed to the spirit will become an ideal. Not to know what one wants is simple absence of self-knowledge. It is abdication— my father was inclined to abdicate—and the insistence on *not* wanting this, or *not* wanting that, becomes an unamiable exhibition of the seamy side of your nature, the fair face of which you have turned downwards. Now my father hated shams, among which he placed religion, and hated complicated purposes or ambitions, with all the havoc they make; from which expressed dislikes it would be easy to infer that he loved the garden of Epicurus, with simple natural pleasures, quietness, and a bitter-sweet understanding of everything. This garden of Epicurus, though my father would have denied it, was really a vegetable garden, a convent garden; and it seemed strange to me that a man who had been so much at sea, and seen so many remote countries, should take such a narrow and stifled view of human nature. He was tolerant and kindly towards the minor vices and the physical ills of mankind; he was tightly and ferociously closed against all higher follies. But is it not an initial folly, to exclude all happy possibilities and condemn oneself to limp through life on one leg? If it be legitimate to live physically, why isn't it legitimate to live morally? I am afraid that my father, unlike my mother, was not brave.

Modesty and scepticism. In some directions, however, my father was docile and conservative. He had a great respect for authority in science or letters, and would quote Quintilian in support of his own preference for limited views: *Ad cognoscendum genus humanum sufficit una domus:** For exploring human nature one household is large enough.* Yet

---

*Probably a confused memory, mine or my father's, of Juvenal, *Satire XIII*, 159–60:

Humani generis mores tibi nosse volenti
Sufficit una domus.

when authority made for boldness of thought or for ambitious aims, he mocked it. In the region of Avila, which is some 4,000 feet above the sea level, the heath is strewn with many boulders, large and small, often fantastically piled one over another; and one day when we noticed a particularly capricious heap of them, I said what a pity it was that we hadn't a geologist at hand to tell us about the origin of this odd formation. "What would be the use of that?" said my father. "He would tell us his theory, but he wasn't there to see the fact." Hobbes had said the same thing: "No discourse whatsoever can end in absolute knowledge of fact"; and I have made the *authority of things*, as against the presumption of words or ideas, a principle of my philosophy. Yet we materialists cannot consistently reject the evidence of analogy between one thing and another, since materialism itself is an interpretation of appearance by certain analogies running through things, and helping us to trace their derivation. There are glaciers in movement today in other mountainous regions the effects of which on the rocks they carry with them may be observed, as also the effect of running streams and beating waves in rounding and smoothing pebbles: so that those boulders on the skirts of the Castilian mountains may be plausibly explained by analogy. But my father feared to be cheated; and whenever he suggested anything a bit paradoxical, he would hasten to disown any personal responsibility for it. "I haven't invented that myself", he would say; "I have read it in a printed book, *en letras de molde*, in black and white." There seemed to be a curious mixture in his mind of the primitive man's awe for any scripture, with the sceptic's distrust of every theory and every report. And yet this very distrust tempted him to odd hypotheses at times to explain the motives behind what people said or imagined. If a visiting lady told us something interesting, which in my relative innocence I supposed might be true, it would startle me to hear my father say, as soon as she had turned her back: "I wonder *why* she said that."

Indecision and discouragement.   Respect for authorities is fatal when the doctors disagree and the pupil is not self-confident enough to give direction to his freedom. My father's style in painting, for instance, inclined to clear shadows, pure outlines, and fidelity to the model, with little thought of picturesque backgrounds or decorative patterns. Had he had greater decision and dared to follow the ideal that he denied he possessed; had he simplified his surfaces boldly and emphasised characteristic features and attitudes without exaggerating them, he would have painted like Manet. But perhaps when he was at work on a canvas that promised well, he would visit the Prado, and some lurid figures by Ribera would catch his eye, or the magic lights in darkness of Rembrandt, and he would come home and spoil his picture by incongruously deepening the shadows. Stronger imaginations than his have been distracted and defeated by rival contagions; he at least was conscious of his defeat, and finished very few of his portraits; and he deputed even these to be finished when in reality they were scarcely begun.

His success as an official. He stopped half way also in the law, which was his chosen profession, but for different reasons. Here he had not the blessed independence of the painter, consulting only his own inspiration. He had to think of tradition, of clients, of magistrates, of personal and political influences and intrigues; and his natural diffidence and dislike of rigmarole stood in his way. His family had no influential connections, and when still a very young man he accepted a post in the government service in the Philippine Islands. In this career, save for the effect of a tropical climate on his health, he did very well. Modesty combined with intelligence are prized in subordinates; and I had myself an opportunity, without any supernatural privilege of watching my father with his superiors in Manila before I was born, to see how he had behaved. My father's last post had been that of financial secretary to the "Captain General" or Governor General of the Philippines, who at that time had been General Pavía, Marqués de Novaliches. Now at the time of the revolution that dethroned Queen Isabella II, this general, then in Spain again, had been the only one to remain faithful to his sovereign, and actually to oppose Prim and Serrano in a battle at Alcolea, in which he was wounded and easily defeated. Now in 1871, when my father and I were living alone in Avila, my mother and sisters having gone to America, Novaliches and his lady came to live in Avila, in the palace that was later the Military Academy; and in their solitude and provincial retirement they seemed to relish the society of my father, with whom they had so many old memories in common. They had a carriage — the only one then in Avila — in which they took a daily drive along one *carretera* or another, or perhaps to the green hermitage of Sonsolès at the foot of the mountains opposite: a favourite walk of ours also. Sometimes they would send word, asking my father to accompany them; and as he and I were then the whole family, it was inevitable that I should go too.

Driving with the Marqués and Marquesa de Novaliches. Conversation on those occasions was naturally above my head, as I was seven years old; and after the first day I was promoted to a seat on the box beside the coachman, where I could watch the horses and the front wheels in motion to my heart's content. The landscape of that region has character, but no charming features such as a child might notice; indeed it is striking how entirely children and common people fail to see anything purely pictorial. Women and babies seem to them lovely, and animals attract their attention, as being human bodies curiously gone wrong or curiously over-endowed with odd organs or strength or agility; but the fact escapes them that light and shade or outlines in themselves are something. It was unusually mature of me, in ripe years, to re-discover *essences*—the only things people ever see and the last they notice. From that coachman's box my young mind saw nothing but the aesthetics of mechanism; yet my unconscious psyche kept a better watch, and I can now evoke images of impressions that meant nothing to me then, but that had subtler significance. Now I can see how deferentially my father sat on the front seat of that carriage, listening to the General's thick voice: for he had been wounded in the jaw and tongue, so that he had an impediment in his speech and wore a black beard—of the sort I don't like—to conceal the scar. Every now and then he made a one-sided grimace that I still recall, as well as the serene silent figure of the Marquesa at his side, dressed in black, passive and amiable, but observant, and when she spoke saying something always kind and never silly. She had the air, so common in Spanish ladies, of having suffered, being resigned, and being surprised at nothing.

My father's politics. My father couldn't have particularly relished the General's talk, which must have turned upon the politics of the hour, the intrigues of his rivals and his own wrongs; but my father had heard such talk all his life, and was not impatient. He liked to know and to read the opinions most opposed to his own. He actually preferred *El Siglo Futuro*, the Carlist and clerical newspaper, to the liberal sheets. I daresay it was written in purer Castilian, but that was not his chief reason for reading it: he wished to understand, he said, why Spain made so little progress. "Progress" of course meant material development and assimilation to England and France. I think that intellectually my father had no other political criterion; yet emotionally he remained a patriot, or at least, without considering what virtues were proper and possible for Spain, he suffered at the thought that his country should be inferior in anything; and he once surprised me, in talking about Gibraltar, by saying that if he could he would put a vast quantity of dynamite under the Rock and blow it up with all the English on it. I had had a different feeling when I first caught sight of St. George's Cross flapping defiantly in the strong wind at Europa Point. What a symbol, I thought, of commercial greatness, far-reaching adventure, and universal security! As a Spaniard I might wince at that usurpation, but as a man I thought it a small sacrifice for Spain to make to the general good order of mankind. That was in 1887; fifty years later, history had taken another turn and the oceanic lordship of Britain had become an anachronism. I write this in 1940 when I don't know whether Gibraltar is to remain British or not: but if it does, it will be a temporary matter. Britannia no longer has the exclusive resources or the aristocratic temper that made it dramatically fitting for her to rule the waves.

Vain projects for a career in Spain. We soon left for America, and Novaliches and his lady also left Avila on the return of the Bourbons, and resumed a place in the great world: not a leading place any longer, but a sort of grandfatherly place in the background of affairs. Once, some fifteen years later, when I was to pass through Madrid, my father gave me a letter of re-introduction to the old General. I was then (1887) in that appealing phase of youth when one's heart and intelligence are keenly active, but unpledged; and if Novaliches or the Marquesa should take a fancy to me, might they not still have enough influence to secure a place for me in the army, or at court, or in some government service, where my knowledge of foreign languages might be useful? English, my strong point, was as yet little studied in Spain, and even my German might have seemed an accomplishment; unfortunately it was my Spanish that limped, although that defect would soon have been remedied had I remained in Spain. These illusions floated, I know, in my father's mind, and they tempted me also imaginatively; but practically, had it ever come to a choice, I should have dismissed them. They would have led me into a slippery and insecure path, full of commitments, personal obligations, and false promises, very different from the homely plank walk across the snow that was open to me in America. I have never been adventurous; I need to be quiet in order to be free. I took my letter to the General's house, but he was out of town; and this little accident, which we might have foreseen, as it was mid-summer, sufficed to discourage us. We took it instinctively for an omen, symbolising the insurmountable difficulties in the way of our hopes. We had no money. We had no friends. My mother not only would not have helped, but would have cut off the allowance of $500 that she was giving me—exactly what she received from "Uncle Russell"—and would have regarded my action as an ungrateful rebellion against her and a desertion of my duty. The desertion, though excusable, was really hers, because nothing would have been more natural and proper than for her to return to Spain, being a Spanish subject, especially a few years later when for her daughters it then would have been a most welcome change. Only her son Robert, then thoroughly Americanised and planning marriage, would have been separated from her, not my father or my sisters or me. But her will was adamant, once it had taken shape; and without her aid—apart from the unpleasantness and responsibility of the quarrel—I could not have weathered the storms and the prolonged calms of such a voyage in Spanish waters. How her passionate will found expression in words may be seen in a letter, unusually rhetorical for her, that I will translate literally: it deals with this very point of a possible military career for me in Spain, although the essential question—sticking to her or sticking to my father and my country—is not mentioned.

No date (about 1880)

"I am glad that our son has no inclination to be a soldier. No career displeases me more, and if I were a man it would repel me less to be a hangman than a soldier, because the one is obliged to put to death only criminals sentenced by the law, but the other kills honest men who like himself bathe in innocent blood at the bidding of some superior. Barbarous customs that I hope will disappear when there are no Kings and no desire for conquest and when man has the world for his country and all his fellow-beings for brothers. You will say that I am dreaming. It may be so. Adieu."

Divergent liberalism of my parents.   In repeating the part of this letter about the hangman and the soldier, my father once observed, "I wonder in what novel your mother had read that." Perhaps it had been in a novel; but I suspect that the words may have come from her father's lips, or out of the book of maxims drawn from all sages, from Confucius to Benjamin Franklin, that my grandfather had collected and published, breathing the spirit of Locke, Rousseau, and *Nathan der Weise*. My father was as strong a liberal as my mother; but he had studied Roman law and looked upon government as an indispensable instrument for securing peace and prosperity. Arcadia and the state of nature were among the ideals that he refused to have. He had lived among the Malays in the Philippines, the most blameless of primitive peoples, and he spoke kindly of them; but the only Malays he respected were those that had become Mohammedan and warlike—pirates, if you like—and had kept their independence. He was modest enough not to hate superiors, as my mother did; he admired them.

Not an Anglomaniac.   When I ask myself what it was that he admired, say in the English or in the Romans, and what he respected them for, I think it was not that he had any inner sympathy with their spirit. The English I know he didn't understand; their whole poetic, sporting, frank, gentle side was unknown to him. He thought them only stiff, determined, competent, and formidable. They were all captains of frigates pacing the quarter-deck. And they were all rich, oppressively rich; because in his respect and admiration for the English there was an undercurrent of contempt—as towards people who are too well dressed. If you wish to be thought a gentleman among the English, he would say, you must shave and change your linen every morning, and never eat with your knife. The only time I remember him to have been annoyed with me was, during my first visit to him in 1883, when we had made an excursion to the Escurial, going third class at night from Avila, because in the morning, before we had breakfast, I wanted to wash my face and hands. "*¡Cuantos requisitos!*" he exclaimed, How many requirements!

Nor an old Roman.   As to the Romans, I am uncertain of his feelings. He often quoted them as great authorities, especially the line of Lucretius about *Tantum religio potuit suadere malorum.* But it was the thought, the political wisdom, in them that he cared for. He took their Greek refinements, as the true Romans took them, for mere accessories and matters of fashion. When I once wrote out for him (he had few books) the well-known little ode to Pyrrha in the first book of Horace, he was arrested at the word *uvida*, and remarked on the interweaving of the concordance between adjectives and nouns. Of the poetry, of the Epicurean *blasé* sentiment, he said nothing. If I had written out the first ode of the fourth book, through which so much pierces that is disquieting, what would he have said? He might have shrugged his shoulders at pagan corruption: societies are like human bodies, they all rot in the end, unless you burn them up in time. But he was no soldier, not merely no soldier temperamentally in that personally he shrank from conflicts rather than provoked them, but no soldier morally or religiously, in that he saw nothing worth fighting for. Of course, you fought for your life, if attacked: that was a mechanical reaction of the organism. But he could have felt no sympathy with the martial regimen and martial patriotism of an ancient city. There was something sporting about it, a club of big boys, only hereditary, sanctified, made eloquent and mysterious by religion. The Spaniard is an individualist; he can be devout mystically, because that is his own devotion to his own deity; but socially, externally he distrusts everything and everybody, even his priests and his kings; and he would have distrusted the *Numina* of Romulus and Remus.

He takes to manual work.   In his old age my father's eyes became so weak that it was almost impossible for him to read or write. Painting he had long since abandoned; and in order to while away the time he took to carpentering and to framing and polishing steel clothes-horses, of which there was soon one in every room in the house. I think he was happier in these rude occupations than he had been when more occupied with politics and ideas. He felt better, and his mind could choose its own themes, rather than the unpleasant events of the moment. Nature is far kindlier than opinion. When one faculty perishes, the others inherit a modicum of energy, or at least forget gladly, now that they are free, that formerly they were subordinate. Anything suffices, if nothing more is demanded; and mankind, let us hope, will dwindle and die more contented than it ever was when it waxed and struggled. I at least have found that old age is the time for happiness, even for enjoying in retrospect the years of youth that were so distracted in their day; and I seem to detect a certain sardonic defiance, a sort of pride, in the whining old beggars that look so wretched as they stretch out a trembling hand for a penny. They are not dead yet; they can hold together in spite of everything; and they are not deceived about *you*, you well-dressed young person. Your new shoes pinch you, and you are secretly racked by hopeless desires.

John Smith his house.   The house in which my father spent his last years, and which afterwards fell to me and was the only property I ever had in Spain, was built by an Englishman named John Smith, who had come to Avila as a railway foreman or contractor when the main line from the French frontier to Madrid was constructed. He had settled in Avila and established the hotel—*la fonda del inglés*—opposite the cathedral, to which all foreigners stopping in Avila were compelled to go. I must have seen him, but have no clear memory of him; only of the stories told about his outrageous Spanish, and of his long friendly relations with my father. They were once in England together; it must have been in 1867 when my father took Robert to London; or in 1873 on his way back to Spain from Boston; anyhow Smith conducted him to Grantham, his native town, and regaled him with an oxtail soup that, in my father's estimation, was "fit to resurrect the dead". The relish of it I am sure confirmed him in his rooted admiration for England. The fundamentals are fundamental and in England they were solid. Who, on such oxtail soup, would not conquer the world? It seems that on some occasion—perhaps at that convivial moment—my father had lent Smith a considerable sum of money; which Smith naturally never found it quite convenient to pay back; on the other hand a little more ready cash, especially if you are establishing a hotel or moving out altogether from one country to another, is eminently useful; so that it was agreed that my father should buy Smith's house, who would thus cancel his debt and get a little ready money in addition.

This house, one of the first in the town as you come from the Station, was opposite the Church and convent of Santa Ana, where above a stone cross and a modest row of trees, the rocky soil rises a little above the road and forms a sort of terrace or little square. It was a working-man's dwelling, what in England is called a cottage, but commodious; there was ample room for my father and aunt, for me and Susana, and eventually for my other old aunt and my cousin Elvira. In the first place it was a whole house, not divided into apartments; and it possessed a walled space, called a garden, in the rear, with a low wing on one side, which with its kitchen formed a complete dwelling by itself. This "garden" contained an apricot tree and some bushes, and one accidentally picturesque feature, which perhaps I was alone in noticing. The back wall, of uncut stones and mortar, coincided with a private aqueduct belonging to another convent in the neigh-bourhood, called popularly *Las Gordillas*; and between the top of our wall and a broad arch of this aqueduct, there remained a semicircular space, exactly like those filled by Raphael's frescoes in the *Stanze* at the Vatican; only that instead of the *School of Athens* or the *Dispute of the Sacrament*, nature here had painted a picture of the *Valle de Amblés*, to which Avila owes its existence, with the purple sierra beyond: a picture everywhere visible to the pedestrian round about Avila, yet here concentrated and framed in by its stone setting into a perfect and striking composition.

Life in Avila in the 1880's. The ground before this little house was neither town nor country: virgin earth with rock emerging in places and preserving its irregular surface; but stone paths had been laid across it roughly, in the directions that people were likely to take, and served as stepping-stones in case of mud or pools of water; for there was no drainage. We had a well, with an iron pump, in the house, so that only the water for cooking and drinking needed to be fetched from the public fountains. Sometimes, in summer, when the purest water was desired, a donkey, with four large jars in the pockets of a wicker saddle, brought it from some reputed spring in the country. This primitiveness was rather pleasant and on the whole salubrious; we lived nearer to mother earth; nor was it exclusively Spanish. At Harvard, I used to bring up my coal and water daily from the cellar of Hollis Hall, or water in summer from the college pump opposite.

The servants' pleasures. Going to the fountain (as it was called) was a chief occupation for servants in Avila, whether girls or men, and also a chief amusement, as were the innumerable errands they were sent on; it gave them a breath of air, a little freedom from the mistress's eye, and a lovely occasion for gossip and for love-making. Without going to the fountain and without errands (since all messages were sent by word of mouth, never by written notes) the life of domestic servants would have been prison-labour. As it was they knew everybody, heard everything, and saw wonderful things.

Plain lodgings. John Smith had built his house in the style of the country, but on a plan more regular and symmetrical than usual. A passage paved in stone like the paths outside, and on the same level, led from the front door to the garden; and on each side were square sitting-rooms with alcoves: every sitting-room in Spain having such a whitewashed sleeping cubicle attached to it. I always occupied the room immediately to the left of the entrance; while my father had the back room upstairs (the other being the kitchen) because it was the only sunny room in the house. There had been an open verandah running outside this room, through the whole width of the house; but my father turned it into a glazed gallery, himself making and fitting all the woodwork necessary. This, with my father's room behind it, was the pleasantest place in the house, and we habitually sat there, and made it the dining-room. There was little furniture of any sort; a table and a few chairs could be easily moved anywhere: only the bookcases and a *chaise-longue* remained always in my room, which had been meant for the study; while the room over it, possessing a sofa, two arm-chairs with oval backs, and an oval mirror, suggested the ladies' parlour. Susana occupied it whenever she came to Avila, and on other occasions my cousin Elvira.

In the midst All this formed a meagre, old-fashioned, almost in-
of death we different stage-setting to my father's life: the real drama
are in life. was his health. He was a wiry and (for a Spaniard) a tall man, and lived to the age of seventy-nine; and long walks and long sea voyages in comfortless old sailing-vessels were nothing to him. Yet he was a hypochondriac, always watching his symptoms, and fearing that death was at hand. Whether this was congenital or the effect of insidious ailments proper to tropical climates, I do not know: but the sense of impediment, of insecurity, was constant in him. It defeated any clear pleasure in any project, and mixed a certain bitterness with such real pleasures as he enjoyed. They were snatched, as it were, from the fire, with a curious uneasiness, as if they were forbidden and likely to be punished. And this when theoretically he was absolutely rationalistic, materialistic, and free from moral or physical superstition. Perhaps, if a man's bowels are treacherous, he cannot trust anything else. Dysentery removes all the confidence that the will has in itself: the alien, the irresistibly dissolving force is too much within you. Moreover my father had other obvious discouragements to face: poverty, deafness, semi-blindness; yet these, if his digestion had been good and strong, I don't think would have cowed him. He had plenty of Castilian indifference to circumstances and to externals, plenty of independence and capacity to live content with little and quite alone. But the firmness of the inner man must not be undermined by a sour stomach: that, at least, seems to have been my father's experience. Yet intelligence and brave philosophy were mixed strangely with this discouragement. On one of the many occasions when he thought, or dreaded, that he might be on his death-bed, he felt a sudden desire for some boiled chicken, without in the least giving up his asseveration that he was dying; and as his deafness prevented him from properly modulating his voice, he cried out with a shout that resounded through the whole house: *¡La unción y la gallina!* "Extreme Unction and a chicken!" Extreme Unction only, be it observed. That is the last sacrament, to be received passively, without saying a word. It would put him to no inconvenience. To have asked for confession

and communion would have implied much talking; he was too far gone for that. Extreme Unction would do perfectly to avoid all unpleasantness regarding his funeral and burial in holy ground. Nobody would need to be distressed about his soul. And meantime, since these were his last moments, and the consequences of any imprudence would make no difference, why not boldly indulge himself one last time, and have some boiled chicken? That, I am confident, was his thought. And he had the chicken. The last sacrament, this time, was not required.

III

My Mother

A romantic
interlude. I have already recorded my mother's parentage with what little I have gathered about her childhood; and in the sequel there will be occasions to mention many other events in which she was concerned. Yet the crucial turn in her life, her migration to Manila, and her first marriage, remain to be pictured; I say pictured, because the bare facts are nothing unless we see them in a dramatic perspective, and feel the effect they had on her character and the effect that her strong character had on them. Between her father's return to Barcelona, to act as American Consul there, and the time, thirty years later, when my own observations begin, I must interpolate a little historical romance: because my mother's history during those years, her sentiments, and even her second marriage were intensely romantic. Romantic in a stoical key, when the heroine is conscious of her virtue, her solitude, and her duty.

Those dancing years of girlhood, with their intense girl-friendships, their endless whisperings and confidences and discussion of toilets and tiffs and other people's love-affairs, with their practice at the piano, their singing-lessons, and their lessons in the languages—for my mother could read and half-understand French, although she never spoke it— would have had a natural end in being courted and married; especially in Spain, where young people easily become *novios*, or acknowledged sweethearts, without any formal engagement to be married. To go to the papa and make an express demand for the young lady's hand, and to obtain leave to visit the family daily, would be an ulterior step, on which the wedding would follow presently; but to have *relaciones* or to be *novios* is a free and indefinite courtship, permitting no liberties, and involving no blame, should the courtship be broken off by either party. It might be described in Anglosaxon terms as a trial engagement. Now this normal development seems not to have occurred in my mother's case; I never heard the least hint that she had ever had a *novio* either in Barcelona or in Manila. In her the first flower of youth did not bring its natural fruit; it was cut short by the pruning-hook.

Removal to the Philippines. Whether my grandfather's appointment as consul in Barcelona lapsed with the change of Presidents in the United States, or whether those strictly legal fees to be received by him were disappointing, or whether other difficulties arose, I do not know; but he was still a Spanish subject, and after a change of government in the liberal direction had occurred both in France and in Spain, his friends were able to obtain for him what promised to be a lucrative post in the Philippine Islands. This was further geographically than Virginia, but politically and socially much nearer home; and perhaps the oceanic distance and the idyllic state of nature of the natives in those unspoiled latitudes tempted his imagination, as much as the easy life and future pension tempted his advancing years. At any rate, he decided to go; and it was obvious that his daughter, who was devoted to him and was the apple of his eye, must accompany him. Distant lands were not unknown to her, nor coloured people. Her first memories were about a "Grandmother Locke" in whose house they had lived in Virginia, and the darky children that ran half-naked about it. The sea had no terrors for her; perhaps she positively preferred the excitement of a real danger, with the sense of her own courage in facing it, to the fading trifles that had entertained her until now. The problem was her mother, who seems to have been less willing to leave her friends and country for the second time. They were really her friends and country, something that was not true in her daughter's case nor, in a moral sense, even in her husband's; because with his opinions a certain irritation at all things Spanish was hardly to be avoided. It is easy to acknowledge the backwardness or poverty of one's country, and to be happy there, when one thinks those things relative and unimportant, and the contrary advantages treacherous and vain. The Arab is not ashamed of his desert, where he is alone with Allah; but the pupil of the French Revolution, dreaming of multitudes all possessing a multitude of things, and of the same material things, cannot rest in a few old customs and a few simple goods. He has a bee in his bonnet; or rather his head is a veritable bee-hive, and the only question for him is in which direction to fly. My grandfather, though perhaps a little weary, was determined to launch forth again in pursuit of fortune; but my grandmother wouldn't go. She was very fat; she was not young; perhaps she felt that she had not much longer to live; perhaps she had a premonition that this adventurous project might go wrong, and that her husband and daughter might come back to her before they expected. If so, she would have been half right, as are the best premonitions. She died soon; her husband never returned; and new dawns opened before her daughter in which she counted for nothing.

An old-fashioned voyage. The voyage from Cadiz to Manila, round the Cape of Good Hope, lasted six months, included the inevitable worst storm the Captain had ever encountered, with death yawning before the passengers in every hollow between the black waves; and it included also the corresponding invention of something to do in good weather. My mother then made the first of her bosom friendships, with a young lady I believe of Danish or Dutch extraction but Spanish breeding named Adelaida Keroll; she learned to play chess; and her father gave her lessons in English, to brush up her Virginian baby-talk, which must have been rather forgotten during her ten years in Barcelona.

The confusion of tongues. And what language, I may ask incidentally, would she have habitually heard or spoken in Barcelona between 1835 and 1845? Castilian, no doubt, officially and in good society; but surely Catalonian with the servants and in the streets; and was not Catalonian also the language that her parents spoke when alone together? Perhaps not. That was not yet an age when disaffected people were nationalists; they were humanitarian and cosmopolite; they were purists in politics and morals, theoretical Brutuses and Catos, inspired by universal ideals and categorical imperatives of pure reason. In any case, I have only heard a very few words of Catalonian, bits of proverbs or old songs, from my mother's lips. Yet she may have spoken it fluently at one time. She was not given to reminiscence or to fondness for past things. Had we not lived in America later, I might never have heard her say a word in English, which had been one of her first languages; even in America she never spoke it easily or if she could help it. Her Spanish, however, was far from perfect; and perhaps a certain confusion and insecurity in her language contributed to render her so prevailingly silent. The things she was likely to hear or able easily to express were of little interest to her; and it annoyed her to be troubled about them.

My mother's philosophy. In the 1880's, when we lived in Roxbury (a decayed old suburb of Boston) a rich widow who lingered in a large house round the corner, and had intellectual pretensions, came to call and to invite my mother to join the Plato Club—all the very nicest ladies of the place—which met at her house once a fortnight in winter. My mother thanked her, and excused herself. The president and host of the Roxbury Plato Club would not take no for an answer. Might not my mother *develop* an interest in Plato? Would she not be interested in *meeting* all those superior ladies? In what then *was* she interested? What did she *do*? To this my mother, driven back to her fundamental Philippine habits, replied without smiling: "In winter I try to keep warm, and in summer I try to keep cool." Diogenes could not have sent the President of the Plato Club more curtly about her business.

I am convinced that this contempt of the world, this indifference and pride, had a double root in my mother. Partly it was native independence, like that of the wild bird that refuses to be tamed; but partly also it was a second mind, a post-rational morality, induced in her by the one great sorrow and disappointment in her life, of which I shall speak presently. She put on a resigned despair, a profound indifference like widow's weeds or like a nun's veil and mantle, to mark herself off as a stricken soul, for whom the world had lost its savour. The sentiment was sincere enough and rendered easy to adopt by that native wildness and indolence of the bird-soul in her, which it seemed to justify rationally; yet her change of heart could not be complete. It was romantic, not religious. She kept intact her respect for the world in certain directions, and even a kind of negative snobbery. She could not forgive the shabby side of things for being shabby, or the weak side of people for being weak; while she sternly abdicated all ambition in herself to cultivate the brilliant side, or to hope for it in her children; and this renunciation was bitter, not liberating, because she still craved and needed that which she knew she had missed.

Nature pure, society corrupt. Was it only English that her father taught her during those six months out of sight of land? What better occasion for instilling true wisdom into a virgin mind, so ready to receive it? Just at the crisis, too, when frivolous amusements were being abandoned together with all familiar faces and ways, and a violently different climate, frequent earthquakes, torrential rains, a new race of human beings, and a simpler, more primitive order of society were to be encountered. I like to believe that during some of those starlight nights or lazy afternoons under an awning in the slow swell of a tropical sea, my mother must have imbibed those maxims of virtue and philosophy to which she always appealed: commonplace maxims of "the enlightenment", but taken by her, as by her father, for eternal truths. Pope's *Essay on Man* contains them all in crisp epigrams; and it was in this oracular form that my mother conceived them, as if self-evident and recommended by their luminous simplicity to every virtuous mind. All else was unnecessary in religion or morality. Nor was there any need of harping on these principles or of preaching them. Hold them, appeal to them in a crisis, and they would silently guide you in all your actions and judgments.

Refinement essential to virtue, but virtue sufficient for refinement.   I never accepted these maxims in my own conscience, but I knew perfectly what they were, without being expressly taught them, as I was taught the catechism. They were implied in every one of my mother's few words and terrible glances. And she was almost right in thinking that, without much express admonition or direction from her, they would suffice to guide us safely in all circumstances; because they were not really confined to being "virtuous". We knew that it was equally obligatory to be "refined". To be a *persona fina* was to be all right; refinement, to her mind, excluded any real vices. Her notion of what was right, like the Greek notion, did not divide the good from the beautiful. And this had a curious reverse effect on the education of her children. We were expected to be refined, but that did not mean that we were to have any advantages or accomplishments. It was quite sufficient to be virtuous. Of course we were to be educated: enlightenment and virtue (again a Greek notion) were closely allied. It was not religion that made people safely good, it was reason. If she had not felt so poor, no doubt we should have been sent to the best schools or had the best private tutors, according to prevailing fashions. But the object, in her mind, would still have been to make us personally more virtuous and enlightened; it would not have been to widen our interests or our pleasures and to open the way for us to important actions or interesting friendships. Nor, in the case of the girls, would the reprehensible object have been that they should find distinguished rich husbands, or any husbands. They could be virtuous at home, where they belonged; and if they were virtuous, they ought to be happy. The result of this was that two of her children had little education and led narrow dull lives; while the other two, Susana and I, had to make our friends and pick our way through the world by our native wits, without adequate means or preparation, and without any sympathy on her side, quite the reverse. Our new interests—religion, for instance—separated us from her and from the things she trusted. We were not virtuous.

Disappointment and disaster.   Whether or not the seeds of this stern philosophy were sown in my mother's mind during those six months at sea, the end of the voyage put that philosophy to a severe test. Not all vessels took so long, even going round the Cape of Good Hope; and there was also the overland route by Alexandria, and camel-back to Suez. Despatches from Spain, sent after my grandfather's departure, had reached Manila before him; and he learned to his dismay that in Madrid there had been a change of ministers, and that the post promised to him had been given to somebody else. Yet as justice does not exclude mercy in God, so injustice does not always exclude it in men. The Captain General of the Philippines enjoyed some of the prerogatives of a viceroy, since distance from superiors always leaves some room for initiative in subordinates; and another post was found for my unfortunate grandfather, an absurdly modest one, yet sufficient to keep body and soul together. He was sent as governor to a small island—I think it was Batang—where there were only natives, even the village priest being an Indian. Terrible disappointment, do you say? But was not this the very ideal realised? What a pity that Rousseau himself, so much more eloquent than poor José Borrás, could not have been sent instead to that perfect island, to learn the true nature of virtue and happiness!

Matter has the last word in morals.   I am not sure that Rousseau or my grandfather need have been disappointed with the moral condition of Batang; perhaps it was just what they would have desired. Or if there were any unnatural chains binding those blameless children of nature, the chief gaoler and tyrant in this case was happily the philosopher himself, who might devote his energies and his precepts to relaxing those bonds and might win the supreme reward of making himself superfluous. No: the real obstacle was not moral; perhaps the real obstacle never is moral. If it were, the surrender of some needless prejudice, a slight readjustment of some idle demand, might immediately solve it. Are those blameless children of nature, for instance, promiscuous in their loves? Instead of crying, How shocking! the moralist has only to familiarise himself with their view, sanctioned by the experience of ages, in order to recognise that promiscuity may be virtuous no less than a fidelity imposed by oaths and fertile in jealousy and discord. But here the physician and the historian may intervene, and explain the origin of exogamy, monogamy, and the cult of virginity. Perhaps, as a matter of fact, promiscuous tribes are weaker, more idiotic, easier to exterminate than those that take it into their heads, no doubt superstitiously, to observe all sorts of sexual taboos. Perhaps it was the ferociously patriarchal family that made the strength of the Jews and of the Romans. The force as well as the obstacle in nature is always physical. So it was with my unlucky grandfather, and so it would have been with Rousseau, had he ever found himself safe and sovereign in his ideal society. The state of nature presupposes a tropical climate. A tropical climate is fatal to the white race. The white race must live in the temperate zone, it must invent arts and governments, it must be warlike and industrious, or it cannot survive. This fatality of course is not absolute or immediate; white men may live in the tropics, protecting themselves by a special regimen, and returning home occasionally to recover their tone; but if they leave children in those torrid regions, the children will die out or be assimilated, in aspect and temperament, and probably also in blood, to the natives.

Now when my grandfather found himself relegated to Batang, he was not a young man; he was a battered and disappointed official, a man of sedentary habits, studious, visionary, and probably careless about his health. It was noticeable in Spain and Italy, until very recent times, how little most people seemed to sleep, how much they smoked, how they never bathed or took exercise, how yellow was their complexion, how haggard their eyes. I don't know that my grandfather carried this neglect of the body and abuse of its powers further than other people did; probably he was more continent and abstemious than the average. He was an enthusiastic moralist and idealist, and it is only fair to suppose that his life corresponded with his principles. But now, in the decline of life, he was suddenly transferred to a tropical climate entirely new to him, without advice or such resources, medical or other, as even a tropical colony would have afforded in its capital city; and he succumbed. His wife also had meantime died in Barcelona; and my mother was left an orphan, without property or friends, alone at the age of twenty in a remote island peopled only by Indians.

Virtue in act. It was at this crisis that she first gave proof of her remarkable courage and strength of character. With what ready money she could scrape together, and with her jewels for security, she bought or hired a small sailing-vessel, engaged a native skipper and supercargo, and began to send hemp for sale in Manila. If she was without friends in a social sense, the people round her were friendly. Two of her servants, her man cook and her maid, offered to remain with her without wages; and her skipper and agent proved faithful; so much so that in a short time a small fund was gathered, and she began to feel secure and independent in her singular position. She adopted the native dress: doubtless felt herself the lady-shepherdess as well as the romantic orphan. And she was not without friendly acquaintances and friends of her father's in Manila who were concerned at her misfortunes and invited her to come and live with them. In time, offers of protection came even from greater distances. Her uncle the monk, then in charge of a parish in Montevideo, wrote asking her to join him, and be his housekeeper. Although I have heard nothing, I cannot help thinking that her other uncle or cousins in Reus, and her mother's relations, would also have offered to take her in—such orphan cousins or wards are found in many a bourgeois Spanish family—if she had seemed to desire it. But she did not desire it; and I don't know how long her life according to nature, to virtue, and to Rousseau might have continued, but for an accident that I almost blush to record, because it seems invented. Yet it was real, and is referred to in my father's letter of 1888, already quoted.

Jupiter thunders on the left. That solitude, at once tragic and protective, was one day disturbed by a fresh arrival. Batang had remained without a governor; but at last a new governor, a young man, was sent from Manila. Now two white persons, a young man and a young lady without a chaperon, alone together in a tropical island formed an idyllic but dangerous picture; and it became necessary for that young lady in order to avoid scandal to return to a corrupt civilisation. Thus the life of pure virtue, as I might show if I were Hegel, by its inner ironical dialectic transformed itself into conventional life; and fate laughed at the antithesis that prudence and decorum opposed to its decrees; because, though my mother proudly turned her back on that young intruder, and went to live with friends in Manila, he nevertheless was destined, many years later, to become her second husband and my father.

Return to Manila to live with the family of Iparraguirre. The friends with whom she took refuge were a Creole family in Manila, for I think the head of it was not a government official but a merchant or landowner long established independently in the country. His name was Iparraguirre, a Basque name rich in resounding r's, and carrying my fancy, I don't know by what association, to the antipodal sea-faring peoples of Carthage and of Japan. The Basque element is an original but essential element in the Spanish race; it is sound, it is needed; but divorced from Castile it would lose itself like those other ancient peoples with strange languages that are driven to the uttermost coasts of all continents, to hibernate there without distinction or glory: Laplanders, North American Indians, Highlanders, Welshmen, Bretons, and one might be tempted to add, Irishmen, Basques, and Norwegians. Here a distinction seems to be requisite; for the Norwegians may seem to be, geographically, a primitive people driven to the uttermost verge of the habitable earth, yet biologically they are a fountain-head and source of population, rather than a forlorn remnant. They multiply and migrate; and though they are not great conquerors (for their home strength and perhaps their moral development is not firm enough for that) they become a valuable ingredient in other countries and peoples. This is or may be the case with the Scotch also, and with the Irish; and I like to think that it is true of the Basques. I have known South Americans of distinction who bore the names of Irazusta and Irarrázabal; as if something Magian or Carthaginian could resound at the limits of the new world. However, if the Basques are to propagate their virtues it must not be in the tropics; and in the family of Iparraguirre there was only one child, Victorina, who became my mother's second intimate and life-long friend; so much so that afterwards, in Madrid, where Doña Victorina had gone with her husband, Don Toribio de la Escalera, who had been an officer in the Spanish army, the two families lived together for a time; and we have always regarded Mercedes, Doña Victorina's only child, as one of our family.

Doña Victorina. As I remember Doña Victorina she was a diminutive wizened old woman, so round-shouldered and sunken in front as to seem a hunchback; but it was not her spine that was bent but her shoulder-blades that were curved forward, making her little convex back rounded and hard like that of some black insect. My mother too had the right shoulder-blade somewhat bent forward and protruding a little behind, which she said was the effect of continually stretching the arm round the frame of her embroidery; but if that were the cause, Doña Victorina must have embroidered with both hands at once. Nevertheless this little dark lady made a pleasant impression; she was lively, witty, affectionate, interested in everything and everybody, and her bright eye and suggestion of a smile—never laughter—made you feel that she wished you well but had no illusions about you. I can understand that her vivacity in repose—for like my mother she never moved about or did anything—should have made her a perfect companion for my mother, a link with the gay world, as Susana was later, that never pulled you or attempted to drag you into it. Doña Victorina was entertaining, she knew everybody and had known everybody, whereas my mother, if left to herself, was silent and sad.

It was Doña Victorina that received me when I first came into this world, and wrapped me in a soft brown shawl that she and Mercedes have often shown me, and which Mercedes still keeps at the foot of her bed, to be pulled up at night, in case of need, as an extra coverlet. They must be good shawls and good friends that have lasted in daily use for eighty years.

Doña Victorina was pious, and this, it might seem, would have proved an obstacle to such an intimate friendship with my mother; yet it did not. There are many kinds of piety. I imagine that Doña Victorina's was of the ancient, unquestioning, customary kind, remote from all argument or propaganda; emotional and sincerely felt, but only as the crises of life are felt emotionally, deaths, births, weddings, fêtes, and travels. So you went to mass or to a novena, to confession and communion, punctually and with the appropriate sentiment, in the appropriate dress (always black); and you returned to your other employments and thoughts with the same serenity and simplicity. It all was one woof; the appointed dutiful, watchful, shrewd, and passionate life of woman. My mother skipped the piety: it was not in her private tradition; but piety in others did not offend her, and the mere absence of it in her did not offend anyone.

A rational marriage. For the orphan living with the Iparraguirres dancing could hardly have been again the chief of social pleasures. It was too warm for much dancing in Manila; but people drove out in the late afternoon and went round and round the promenade, to look at one another and take the air. When the Angelus bell rang, all the carriages stopped, the men took off their hats, the ladies, if they liked, whispered an *Ave Maria*, and the horses made water. But there were some houses where people gathered for a *tertulia*, a daily *salon* or reception; and I suppose there were occasional official balls. Anyhow young people could make eyes at each other and marriages could be arranged. My mother always spoke contemptuously of love-making and match-making: yet she herself was twice married, and not by any simple concatenation of circumstances but in spite of serious obstacles. Passion may inspire determination in a Romeo and Juliet; in my mother I think determination rather took passion's place. She decided what was best, and then defied all difficulties in doing it. Now it was certainly not best, or even possible, to remain for ever a guest of the Iparraguirres. Victorina any day might be married, and what would the orphaned Josefina do then? Go to Montevideo to keep house for her uncle, the parish priest? Wouldn't it be wiser and more natural herself to marry? Certainly not any one of those Creole youths or Spanish officials who in the first place did not particularly court her, and in the second place were not virtuous. However, there was one wholly exceptional young man in Manila, tall, blond, aquiline, blue-eyed like herself, an American, a Protestant, and unmistakably virtuous. And that young man, probably as little passionate as herself, and as little trustful of the Spanish young women as she was of the Spanish young men, could not but be visited by kindred thoughts. Was not this grave, silent, proud orphan wholly unlike the other young girls? Was she not blue-eyed like himself? Did she not speak English? Had she not lived in Virginia, which if not as reassuring as Boston, still was in the United States? And as he found on inquiry, if she was not a Protestant, at least she was no bigoted Catholic, but a stern, philosophical, virtuous soul. Was she not courage personified, and had she not suddenly found herself alone and penniless and, like Benjamin Franklin, made her own way in the world? Was she not a worthy, a safe, a suitable, even an exceptionally noble and heroic person to marry? And was it not safer, more suitable, and more virtuous for a merchant in the Far East to be married to a foreigner than not to be married at all?

Ecclesiastical obstacles cleared by the British Navy. Such convergent reflections found ways of expressing themselves, and the logical conclusion was easily drawn. A virtuous marriage meant safety and peace for him in his old bonds, and it meant safety and peace for her, who had no dread of novelty, in new bonds rationally chosen. By all means, they would be married; but there was an obstacle. No legal marriage was then possible in Manila except in the Church; and the Church there had not the privilege of granting dispensation for a marriage to a non-Catholic. Everybody, including the Archbishop, was sympathetic and free from prejudice; but a petition would have to be sent to Rome for a special license. This would involve long delay, perhaps a year, and of course some expense; and much worse, I am sure, from my mother's point of view, it would involve a conspicuous act of submission to ecclesiastical authority, such as her pride and her liberal principle would never submit to. Yet it would have been useless to take extreme measures, and to declare that she was a non-Catholic herself; there was no non-Catholic marriage possible within Spanish jurisdiction. I am not sure whether her free principles would have gone so far as to justify her in eloping, and going to live with George Sturgis unmarried. Perhaps not; whether such a course would have seemed to her nobly virtuous, or not virtuous at all, but disreputable, I cannot say. She was capable of taking either view. It was he, perhaps, who might have blushed at such an idea; not only a foreign but an illegitimate union to be reported to Boston! However, a brief voyage to China, not more than ten days, might have sufficed to make that union legitimate, and to remove all reproach or legal impediment from any possible children. But accident offered a simpler means of effecting this purpose. There happened at that time, April, 1849, to be a British man-of-war at anchor in Manila Bay. The deck of that ship was British territory, and of course there was a Chaplain, who being a jolly tar, would not object to marrying a Unitarian to a Papist. Indeed, although the thing was not then fashionable, he might have contended that theologically he was a Catholic, that he stood in the truly apostolic succession, and was blessing a truly Catholic marriage. In any case, the ceremony and the certificate of marriage under British law were legal; and we may imagine the wedding party, the bride and bridegroom, all the Iparraguirres, all the members of the House of Russell and Sturgis, and the nearer friends of both setting out in the ship's cutter, manned by its double row of sailors, and flying the white ensign, borne to the frigate, and cautiously but joyfully climbing the ladder up the great ship's side. And perhaps, if the Captain was jovial, as he doubtless was, there may have been a glass of wine, with a little speech, after the ceremony.

The young husband's mentality. This important event—important even for me, since it set the background for my whole life—occurred on the 22nd of April, 1849, chosen by George Sturgis for being the thirty-second anniversary of his birth. This choice of his birthday for his wedding is characteristic; as was also his sanguine assertion, only half facetious, that his son Victor, because born in the Tremont House in Boston, would be some day President of the United States. Such fancies are in the tone of the Sturgis mind, inclined to pleasantry that is too trivial to be so heartily enjoyed; and these jester's jests are apt to have some sad echo. That future President of the

United States did not live to be two years old, and his confident father had preceded him to the grave.

Loss of the first-born child. When this double bereavement fell on my mother, eight years after her marriage, she was already deadened to sorrow and resigned to living on resolutely in a world that no longer could please her or could wound her deeply. Ten months after the wedding she had given birth to a beautiful boy, blue-eyed like his parents, fair, and destined to have yellow hair though at first quite bald; and his nature at once showed itself no less engaging than his appearance; for when only fifteen months later he found he had a little sister, who sometimes couldn't help calling their mother's attention to herself, he, far from being jealous, was most tolerant and kind, and would even give the baby his toys, although she was too small to appreciate them. The contrast between the two babies was marked, and had a lasting influence in our family. Susana, the second child, was in the first place only a girl; and although my mother had all due respect and affection for her own sex, and as I have said, was more attached to her women friends, to one or two of them, than even to her two husbands, yet she had no artificial illusions about womankind, their rights, or their virtues. They were, in most things, inferior to men; she would have preferred to be a man. So that the fact that Susana was only a girl while Pepín was a boy instituted the first point of inferiority in her. Then curiously, she didn't have blue eyes, like her parents, but only hazel eyes and a great lot of brown hair; as if nature had wished to mark the fact that she was not at all angelic, like her brother, but belonged to a lower, much lower, moral species. And as she grew up, she showed no signs of unselfishness, but on the contrary a lively desire to have her own way, and to take the lead in everything. Our mother actually had to defend the too self-sacrificing Pepín, and later the too self-sacrificing Josefina, from Susana's prepotency. Because the curious part of it was, that not only poor little Josefina later, but even Pepín, seemed *to like* doing as Susana wished, and *to imitate* her; which was a dangerous tendency that would have to be suppressed. However, not much suppression of Susana was necessary in those years; the great occasion presented itself only many years later, in regard to me; for Josefina was so tepid and had so few resources and so little initiative, that in regard to her it was almost a blessing that Susana should be there to take the lead.

Until the age of two Pepín had seemed to be in perfect health, even if rather gentle and oldish for a baby; but at that age signs of fading away began to appear, and became slowly more pronounced. No remedies, no care, no change of residence could arrest them, and seven months later the perfect child died.

There is an oval miniature of Pepín in a low-neck green frock, like a lady's; he appears wide awake, pale, with very thin fair hair. This miniature was set in a circle of pearls and worn in the old days by my mother as a brooch, to pin a lace shawl over her bosom.

Was it only the climate? Was the death of this child due only to the effects of a tropical climate? I am not in a position to judge; but none of his brothers and sisters had a strong constitution. Even Susana, who seemed to be the most vigorous, was not rightly put together; and Robert, who seemed normal and commonplace, had a latent contradiction in his nature. I may return to this subject later. If I am right in suspecting that, eugenically my mother and her first husband were not well matched, and that there was something hybrid in all their children, that latent weakness would only have reinforced the often fatal effect of a tropical climate on children of European race. That little Victor should have succumbed also is not to be wondered at: born in Boston, he was subjected to a long sea voyage to Manila, to a season of that climate, and then to an agitated long journey by sea and land to London, where he decided that he had seen enough of this world, and escaped from it at the age of one year and seven months. Perhaps, on the other hand, these voyages and this speedy removal to a temperate if trying climate,—"bracing", Bostonians call it—may have saved the other three children from a gradual decline or relaxation of fibre, if not from an early death.

My mother's despair. The loss of her first born did not affect my mother as it would any mother, especially a Spanish mother. There were no violent fits of lamentation, no floods of tears, no exaggerated cult of the grave or relics of the departed. Especially in a woman who has or is expecting other children, as was the case here, such wild sorrow has its period: the present and the future soon begin to gain healthily upon the past. But with my mother this event was crucial. It made a radical revolution in her heart. It established there a reign of silent despair, permanent, devastating, ruffled perhaps by fresh events on the surface, but always dark and heavy beneath, like the depths of the sea. Her husband, with his sanguine disposition and American optimism, couldn't understand it. He wrote worried letters home, expressing his fears for her life or her reason. He didn't see the strength in this coldness. Her health was not affected. She continued to bear children at frequent intervals—five in seven years. She did not neglect her appearance, her embroidery, her friends, or her flowers. She spoke little, but she never had been loquacious; and when, in a brief interval between babies, he proposed a voyage to Boston, to present her and the children to his family, she readily agreed. This marriage for him had been extremely happy. He described his domestic bliss in glowing terms in his letters. Was it not a happy marriage for her also? Of course it was. Why then this deadly calm, this strange indifference? Why these silent steps, grave bows, and few words, such as people exchange at a funeral?

Many Spanish women live in this way the life of a Mater Dolorosa, and are devout for that reason to Our Lady of the Seven Sorrows, with seven swords fixed in her heart. They give a religious or pictorial turn to their despair; but at bottom they have the same experience that my mother congealed into a stoical philosophy. She knew that her father's positivism and humanism and thirst for progress had a black lining; and she had the courage to wear his mantle with the black side out. Let the world see the truth of its own madness. She at least would not pretend not to see it.

However, let me not exaggerate. This second life, this mystic unmasking of the commonplace and the obvious, was not explicit in my mother. She didn't know what her real philosophy was: her verbal philosophy remained the most trite and superficial positivism. Her depth was entirely psychic, passionately dispassionate, intensely determined and cold; but her intelligence had no depth. It was borrowed, and borrowed not from the best sources, but from the intellectual fashions of her father's time. Therefore, in her outward life and actions, she showed a persistent attachment to persons and to principles that really meant very little to her. This paradox must be accepted and understood if we are to explain the two apparently contrary bonds with which now, in this first voyage to Boston, she outwardly bound herself. One was her attachment to the whole Sturgis family, much more hearty than her attachment to her husband personally, of whom she never spoke with enthusiasm or even with deference. The other was the unwilling but somehow inescapable bond with my father.

Jupiter thunders on the left for the second time. For by a second curious chance, or perhaps by an unconscious or even conscious attraction, my father was one of the passengers in the same clipper ship, *Fearless*, that took her and her husband with their three little children, Susana, Josefina, and Roberto, in the record time of ninety days from Manila to Boston. He was on his way to Spain on leave, for the sake of his health; and by taking this roundabout course not only had a chance of visiting New England, New York and even Niagara Falls, but of getting a glimpse of England also, and yet reaching Spain no later than those who had set sail for it directly at the time of his departure from Manila. For from New York to Liverpool there was already a line of steamers.

My father's first and second thoughts about New England. There is an unusually enthusiastic letter of my father's describing the lovely scene in some genteel suburb of Boston—very likely the very Roxbury that seemed so shabby thirty years later, when we lived there. It was a Sunday morning, and under the arching trees between their neatly painted separate and comfortable wooden dwellings, the happy citizens and their well-dressed wives and children walked with a quiet dignity arm in arm to church. It seemed the perfection of human existence, at last realised on earth. Whether if my father had understood the spoken language and had followed those model citizens into their meeting-house, he would have been as much edified by their mentality as he was by their aspect, I do not know; but his impressions on his second visit to the United States were rather different. From 1856 to 1872, from a rural suburb to a half-built quarter of the town, from summer to winter, from the "flowering of New England" to its industrialisation, from the prime of his own life to its decline, many things no doubt had changed to lower the key of his judgment. But I was surprised, knowing his earlier impressions, by something he said when, towards the end of his life, I showed him some comic verses I had just scrawled comparing America with England, in which I satirised the American man, but paid a gallant compliment to the ladies. And he said, "No. The women there are just as second-rate as the men." Did he—he was so apprehensive—take that passing compliment of mine too seriously and think that I might be in love and meditating marriage with an American? Or had his earlier view itself been coloured by amorous sentiments awakened during that recent voyage in an American ship by an interesting young mother, seen and conversed with for ninety days on deck and at table? Perhaps it is rash to identify in any case the moral colour of a memory with the moral colour originally proper to the fact remembered. Sunday morning in Roxbury, by a lucky chance, may once have seemed ideal, and that impression, while warm, may have been recorded in a letter;

and some decades later the memory of that same scene, qualified by later discoveries, may have looked mediocre or even ridiculous, like the clothes that were the fashion thirty years ago. Even if Roxbury and the Puritan Sunday had proved elevating to behold by the stranger, they might mean boredom in a slum to the native unable to escape from them. Which of these judgments shall we retain? My philosophy would retain both, each proper to the ideal essence then present to the spirit; but it would discount both, and smile at both, as absolute assertions about that poor material ever changing congeries of accidents which was Roxbury in fact, or those unrecoverable manifold feelings which truly echoed and re-echoed through the emptiness of a New England Sunday.

Boston in 1856.   What Boston first thought of my mother or she of Boston I can only infer from their relations in later years; these relations were always friendly and theoretically cordial but never close. Indeed, when she first arrived in Boston she was expecting another child. It was born there, in the hotel that stood in Tremont Street directly north of the grave-yard adjoining the Park Street Church. I remember this *Tremont House* clearly. It had rounded red-brick bay windows like bastions, and the glass in some of the square window-panes had turned violet, a sign of venerable age. In 1856 it may have passed for a fashionable place, being near the rural Common yet not far from State Street and the centre of business. The principal churches were scattered round it—the Park Street Church, the Old South, King's Chapel, and St. Paul's—while round the corner the eye was caught by the State House with its classic dome, model for all Capitols in the New World. And almost opposite was the theatre, called the Museum, because before entering it your cultured mind was refreshed by the sight of a choice collection of plaster antiques, including the Apollo Belvedere, as well as by cases of stuffed birds and mammals that surrounded the grand entrance hall. Here even Emerson and Margaret Fuller are said to have gone to see not merely a play but a ballet, carrying a bag of peanuts for the entr'actes; and when the leading dancer had made her last pirouette and her last sweeping curtsy, Emerson is said to have exclaimed, "This is art!" To which Margaret Fuller replied with added rapture, "Ah, Mr. Emerson, this is religion!"

Such was certainly the aura of Boston in the 1850's; but there were gentle lights really burning in some of those houses, with no exaggeration of their range or brilliance: Ticknors, Parkmans, Longfellows, and Lowells with their variously modest and mature minds. I came

too late to gather much of that quiet spirit of colonial culture, that
felt itself to be secondary and a bit remote from its sources, and yet
was proud of this very remoteness, which gave it the privilege of being
universal and just. In my time this spirit lingered only in Professor
Norton, but saddened by the sense of being a survival. I also knew
Lowell, in his last phase; I once shook hands with Longfellow, at a
garden party in 1881; and I often saw Dr. Holmes, who was our
neighbour in Beacon Street; but Emerson I never saw; while William
James and Judge Holmes and "Jack" Chapman, etc., belonged
to a younger generation, more scatter-brained and dispersed, and
revolutionary, without any real dominion, however distant and water-
colourish, over the universal scene. They tried to paint in oils, impres-
sionistically, with masculine dashes of colour; but everything was
confused, amateurish, out-of-focus, and violently useless.

My mother approves of it on moral grounds.   All this was nothing to my mother, who was too proud
to pretend to care for what didn't concern her. That
which she saw and prized in Boston was only what the
Sturgises represented: wealth, kindness, honesty, and a
general air of being competent and at home in the world. They belonged to the aristocracy of commerce, the only one my mother
respected and identified with the aristocracy of virtue. The titular
nobility of Spain and other European countries, which she knew only
by hearsay, was only the aristocracy of undeserved privilege and luxurious vice. It was detestable; it was also out of reach; and she felt
doubly virtuous, being cut off from it physically as well as morally.
In Boston her friends were at the top, where they deserved to be;
and although her friendship with them was little more than nominal,
she was content to be counted among them; and this feeling made
her heroic resolution to break away from all her associations and go
to live in America very much easier than it might have seemed. Cli-
matically, socially, intellectually she was moving into a strange world,
but morally she felt she was moving into her true sphere. It was the
sphere of her principles and her imagination. She soon found that in
practice she could play no part in it; but that did not change her
theoretical conviction that it was the *right* place to live in. There the
mighty had fallen from their seat, and the righteous had been filled
with good things.

Death of George Sturgis.   A superstitious person might have been alarmed at
the omens and accompaniments of this first visit to Bos-
ton; for old Nathaniel, her father-in-law, whom they

presumably went to see, died soon after their arrival, and George Sturgis, her husband, died soon after their return to Manila not only prematurely and unexpectedly, for he was scarcely forty, but in the midst of a disastrous commercial venture, which left the widow with inadequate means. But my mother had not a vestige of superstition; and her courage and coolness, her quick and intrepid action, on this occasion contrasted oddly with the utter apathy and despair that had overcome her on the death of Pepín. The pathetic but not uncommon loss of an infant had paralised her; the loss of a young husband, the prospect of a complicated journey half round the world, alone with four little children, and the prospect of life in a strange society and a strange climate in reduced circumstances, seemed to revive her energies and to make her more alert and self-possessed than ever.

The widow's firmness. Yet this had occurred once before, on the death of her father, when she had no experience and no resources, which this time was not the case: for now she was not penniless; her brother-in-law Robert gave her a present of ten thousand dollars to help her over the crisis, and she had recently made the acquaintance of the whole Sturgis family in Boston, where a share, one-eleventh, of her father-in-law's estate remained for her support. She would have to give up her easy colonial life, with numerous servants and old friends, and with nothing exacted of her except the usual civilities and the usual charities. Yet she was not in the least perturbed. I almost think that she was relieved, liberated, happy to abandon burdensome superfluities and reduce her life to the essentials; and as to the demands that her new environment would make on her perhaps she did not foresee them, and in any case she had ample strength to resist them. The admiration she aroused at this time was well deserved but not very intelligent. People supposed her to be bearing up under a terrible sorrow and cutting herself off from the dearest ties, in order to do her duty by her children; but the fact was that the most tragic events now could not move her deeply, and the most radical outward changes could disturb her inner life and daily habits very little. She had undergone a veritable conversion, a sweeping surrender of the Old Adam, of all earthly demands or attachments; she retained her judgments and her standards, but without hope. I am confident of this, because at about the same age I underwent the same transformation, less obviously, because in my case there were no outer events to occasion it, except the sheer passage of time, the end of youth and friendship, the sense of being harnessed for life like a beast of burden. It did not upset me, as the revolution in her circumstances did not upset my mother; but it separated the inner self from the outer, and rendered external things comparatively indifferent. I recorded this conversion in my Platonising sonnets; my mother expressed it silently in the subsequent fifty years of her life.

Grand removal to Boston.   If clearness about things produces a fundamental despair, a fundamental despair in turn produces a remarkable clearness or even playfulness about ordinary matters. That tragic journey of the young widow with her four little orphans to the antipodes was planned and carried out in rather a lordly way. She would not go again in that nasty little clipper ship *Fearless*, or the like of her, where the passengers were cooped up for three months like the poultry under the benches on deck; she would go grandly, overland, and when possible by steam packet. She believed in progress. On her way, she would visit her eldest and richest brother-in-law in London. And she would travel with two maids and quantities of luggage. When travel was still difficult, it was still pompous. She carried not only all her personal belongings, shawls, laces, fans, fancy costumes, and family heirlooms, but chess-men and chess-boards, Chinese lacquer tables, and models of native Philippine houses in glass cases, with their glass trees, fruits, animals, and human figures. She even took with her, to look after the baby, a little Chinese slave, *Juana la china*, whom she had bought and had had christened and of course liberated. She believed in progress, and she was making one.

The visit to her brother-in-law Russell in London no doubt left its mark in her mind. It set the standard of propriety and elegance for her in the way of living in Northern and Anglosaxon countries. It combined, with the tropical charms of Manila, to make Spain, for instance, seem to her most inferior. Possibly it set the standard too high; because after that heroic effort to settle down in Boston she does not seem to have taken root there; and three years later, at the outbreak of the American Civil War, she left Boston again for Spain. It was not to be more than a temporary visit; her Boston house was merely let, and she meant soon to return to it. Yet she was away for eight years. During those three years in Boston, 1858–1861, she had an English governess for the children, a Miss Drew, whose correct British locutions, such as "make haste" instead of "hurry up", I sometimes detected in my sisters, when they spoke English; she had a French maid for herself, in addition to Juana, the Chinese girl; in spite of her hatred of priests and indifference to religion, she took a pew in the Catholic pro-Cathedral in Castle Street—an almost disreputable quarter for true Bostonians to be seen in; and she seems to have made only one personal friend, an old maiden lady who was a neighbour and sometimes sat with her over their fancy-work. In fine, I gather that from the first my mother lived in Boston as she did in my time, entrenched in her arm-chair in her corner between the window and the fire, with a novel or a piece of embroidery to occupy her mind, expecting no visits, receiving them formally and almost silently if they came, going out for a stroll in good weather to take the sun and air, watching our movements and the servants authoritatively but as it were from a distance, and seldom interfering, and in all things preserving her dignity and also her leisure. Perhaps she resented the tendency, meant for kindness, to assimilate and absorb her, and she emphasised her separateness in self-defence, as I had to do afterwards in personal and intellectual matters. Boston was a nice place with very nice people in it; but it was an excellent point of vantage from which to start out, if you belonged there, rather than a desirable point to arrive at if you were born elsewhere. It was a moral and intellectual nursery, always busy applying first principles to trifles.

Life with old friends in Madrid. Was my mother cloyed with too much Boston, was she really troubled by anti-slavery agitation and war, or was she merely attracted by the idea of seeing her friend Victorina again, who had followed her husband to Madrid? I confess that none of these reasons seem to me sufficient to explain, in so calm a person, such a disturbing and unnecessary journey. However, the journey took place; and in 1862 my mother and her three children were living in Madrid with Don Toribio, Doña Victorina and the little Mercedes, then five or six years old. I remember this joint household very well, as it was re-established some years later, when I had come into the world. In Spain Santa Claus is nobly and religiously replaced by the Three Kings or Wise Men of the East that brought presents to the Infant Jesus; and in the absence of chimneys (except in the kitchen) children hang out their stockings or place their shoes in the balcony with which every window not on the ground floor is provided. It was *el día de reyes* and we had not forgotten to put out our shoes on the night before; the good Kings had taken the hint and left something for each of us; but what was our glee that Don Toribio who had foolishly put out his big shoe also, found nothing in it but a raw potatoe!

Jupiter thunders on the left for the third time.

In Madrid there was naturally a circle of retired or transferred officials and military men who had served in the Philippines, and who liked to renew old acquaintance and recall common experiences. Among these retired officials, at that moment, was my father. Don Toribio and Doña Victorina of course knew "Santayana", as they always called him. Without being a society man, he was liked for his wit and for his well-informed conversation. He spoke little—he was very prudent—but he spoke well. It was inevitable that he and my mother should meet again. If I were writing a novel and not a history I should be tempted to invent here a whole series of incidents and conversations that might have occurred during those ninety days in the clipper ship *Fearless* six years before, and to indicate how the scattered little impulses then awakened, now, when all checks to free expression were removed, could gather head, combine their currents, and become an irrepressible force. But I have no evidence as to what really may have brought these two most rational persons, under no illusion about each other or their mutual position and commitments, to think of such an irrational marriage. It was so ill-advised a union that only passion would seem to justify it; yet passion was not the cause. I say so with assurance because there is not only the fact of their ages, nearly forty and nearly fifty respectively, but there are my mother's verses, kept in secret and sent to my father twenty-five years later, when it was likely that the two would never meet again; and there are also certain expressions of my father's about love and marriage, which it would not be proper for me to repeat, but which show that my mother, a widow who had had five children, could not have been the object for him of an irresistible love. It was an irresistible *daemonic* force, a drift of circumstances and propensities, as in one more throw at dice, or one more picture to paint. Things on the whole *drove* them to that action; but both he and she performed it unwillingly and with full prescience of the difficulties in store. My mother's verses are melancholy and sentimental, containing nothing specific, but the tone is that of renunciation. It is *impossible*, she feels, to entertain the idea that nevertheless has presented itself and has seemed tempting. The lines seem to have been written when her mind was still undecided, as if to encourage herself to resist, and to give up the project. It still remains obscure what the irrational force was that nevertheless carried the day.

IV

The Sturgises

For my purposes the Sturgis family begins with the children of Nathaniel Russell Sturgis of Mount Vernon Street, Boston, who died in 1856. These children were twelve in number, like those of my paternal grandfather in Valladolid, but some died in childhood and five others had disappeared before I was taken to America; although their children often come into my story, and cast more or less reflected light on their departed parents. It is only by reflected light that I am able to picture the old gentleman, on a rainy Sunday afternoon, sitting far apart with his newspaper, while Susan Parkman his wife read the Bible aloud to the children; but the reflected ray comes from a sure source, from Sarah, the eighth of those children, afterwards Mrs. Francis George Shaw, mother of the Robert Gould Shaw, colonel of a negro regiment raised in Massachusetts, whose monument stands at the edge of the Common opposite the State House in Boston. She was aunt to my brother and sisters, and by a pleasant arrangement that at once was established, I too called her "Aunt Sarah", and repeatedly stayed at her house in Staten Island or in New York. The family were Unitarian, but apparently with varying degrees of radicalness and fervour; and it was with a twinkling eye and great gusto that "Aunt Sarah", who was a woman of spirit and warm convictions, told me the story. Her mother, she said, was reading about Jonah and the Whale; and her father, whose people came from Cape Cod and who knew what's what about whaling, put down his paper—what political gazette or commercial bulletin could he have been perusing in 1825?—and said solemnly: "Susan, do you expect the children to believe that nonsense?" "I thought," "Aunt Sarah" confided to me, "I thought, George, that my father was a wicked man."

If the father was wicked, at least the eldest son, whom we called "Uncle Russell", was virtue personified—I don't mean moral virtue only, but *virtù* of every description. Unfortunately it is again only by reflected light that I ever saw him, although several of his children or grandchildren were among my best friends, and he was prominent among the lares and penates worshipped in our own household. For both my father and my mother seemed to think him the perfection of manhood, as exalted as he was kind, a centre of dazzling wealth and exquisite benefactions. His career had begun in the East, in Manila and China; but somehow from there he passed to England, and eventually became a partner, at one time I think senior partner, of Baring Brothers in London. He was twice married and had two distinct families, two sons and a daughter married to Bostonians and honestly though gently American, and three other sons and a daughter brought up and settled in England, and although their mother was an American, perfectly English. I knew, more or less intimately all these seven establishments, in two of them, one in England and one in America, I was a frequent guest; and as this relation lasted for half a life-time, I had the melancholy pleasure of watching them in their early glory and in their gradual obscuration, dispersion, and decline. This theme will recur often; it has become a *leit-motif* in my view of life; and the first great, slow, tremendous variation upon it was made by the splendid Russell Sturgis himself. Of his great days I have seen many traces; all his children's households were at first prosperous, fresh, luxurious, recognisable copies of the parental grandeur; but the reflection paled, as the sun itself descended. Perhaps Russell Sturgis remained too long at his post, or perhaps other greater circumstances altered the fortunes of Baring Brothers; but everybody knows that after being for years, with the Rothschilds, the greatest banking-house in the world, it got into difficulties, was rescued by the goodwill of the government, but sank into comparative obscurity. When I was first in London, in 1887, my mother had instructed me to pay my respects in her name to our great "Uncle Russell"; and after I had been there a week or two, learned the ropes, got suitable clothes, and found myself alone and at leisure, I called one afternoon, at the right hour, at the mansion in Carlton House Terrace where the old gentleman still lived. The air of the great house, even externally, was rather cold and abandoned, but after I had rung the bell twice, a dignified old butler opened the door a little. When I asked for Mr. Sturgis and offered my card, the man explained civilly, in a sort of sick-room whisper, that Mr. Sturgis didn't see anyone, that he was not very well, but that I might see Mr. Henry Sturgis. When I said I would see Mr. Henry Sturgis, the butler seemed surprised. Mr. Henry Sturgis didn't live there; and he gave me an address in Marylebone where I might call upon him.

That was the nearest I ever got to "Uncle Russell"; but I learned from discreet hints dropped by his son Henry, when I saw him some days later, that it was not simple old age or simple illness that kept his father in seclusion. The distinguished head of all the Sturgises, who had united great abilities to the good looks, affability, sound sense, and kindness common to the whole tribe, no longer possessed those abilities. He in whom the not too brilliant intellect of the family had been focussed and concentrated, had lost it. It would be no pleasure now, his son had said, for him to see me nor for me to see him. That was the melancholy report I had to send to my mother.

I am sorry, in opening this family-picture gallery, to turn in this way my first and most imposing portrait to the wall; but they are all to be works of my own brush, not done by the fashionable painters or photographers of those old days, and no living image of Russell Sturgis is in my possession. But I can give him a name, in lieu of a portrait, and will call him and his generation the Great Merchants: a type that in America has since been replaced by that of great business men or millionaires, building up their fortunes at home; whereas it was part of the romance and tragedy of those Great Merchants that they amassed their fortunes abroad, in a poetic blue-water phase of commercial development that passed away with them, and made their careers and virtues impossible for their children.

Nathaniel's second son, Henry, repeated the success of his brother Russell on a smaller scale, and ended with a more decided reverse, which however he died in time scarcely to witness. He had not been long dead when I first reached Boston in 1872, and his stately house, which I passed daily on the way to school, was pointed out to me with a certain funereal reverence. He was also far less fortunate than Russell in his children: most of them died before him; the ominous word *dissipated* was whispered, or positively hissed, by the ladies when they felt obliged to mention some of them. Only two survived, Fred, who was a doctor in New York and whom we seldom saw, and Nena, who on the contrary seemed more like one of us than any other of the Sturgises. Not that we saw her often, for she was an expatriate, having just enough money to live in decent pensions in Europe, like so many English and American spinsters: but that only increased our points of contact, which were initially numerous. Besides being a Sturgis she was, like my brother and sisters, an East Indian; lively, erratic, and as her name, Nena, suggests, with something pseudo-Spanish or Creole about her. Her mother had been born of British parents in

India, and I believe had lived there most of her life; at any rate, she was exotic, and Nena too seemed exotic in Boston, like ourselves. She even pretended to know a little Spanish picked up from her father. He like his brothers had been at one time or another connected with the house of Russell & Sturgis in Manila, of which an uncle of theirs had been a co-founder; and they had taken kindly to the place and its lazy opulence, as had my mother also. Their easy Spanish exempted her from having to dig up her little old-fashioned English phrases, as she had to do in conversation with the other Sturgises. Nena was Spanish at least in having *disposición*, the inclination to assume accomplishments without much training; she composed and sang and even published some "Songs of the Pyrenees", in a language which certainly was neither Spanish nor French. Eventually, at a mature age, she married a cultivated Englishman named Middlemore who wrote for the *Saturday Review*. They both loved Italy, ultimately became Catholics, and died romantically within a few days of each other. I staid with them for a week-end in 1887, in a pleasant house they had taken in the English country; that was shortly before their conversion and death, for they put off pledging themselves about the other world until they were about to enter it, and discover whether they were right or wrong. From my room I heard them discussing in the passage whether I was so much of a Catholic as to require fish on Fridays. "No," said the intuitive Nena, "he is a *philosophe*." Philosophical in-difference she assumed in me also in another direction, when she had her legs massaged in the drawing-room in my presence—and this in the nineteenth century. She was forty-three and I was twenty-three, ages that might make such a liberty innocent, or else very dangerous. In fine, she was *corriente* and *despreocupada* (it seems as if only Spanish epithets could fit her); I mean that she had no nonsense about her, was a man's woman, and a good sort. With one degree more of beauty and several degrees more of wealth she might have cut a charming figure in society.

A curious thing was that with this sympathy between us and Nena and with my mother's admiration for the Sturgis character and ethics, Nena's detested step-mother, the *bête noire* and stage villain of the whole Sturgis comedy, should have been a special friend of ours. "Aunt Lizzie", as we called this formidable lady, was a tall strong woman of fifty or more, with black hair and bushy eyebrows that met over her nose and a bass voice; in which it was impressive to hear her tell how her brother, an unemployed clergyman, with whom she had had a law-suit, had attempted to poison her, all for the sake of the wretched pittance that remained to her. She had also attempted to break her admirable husband's will, but to no purpose; her reduced circumstances obliged her to live about in boarding-houses or with poor relations, no doubt souring her high temper and making her a dangerous enemy. She was a native of Worcester, Mass. and not a safe self-restrained Bostonian. She seemed mysterious and sordid like some gaunt ghostly figure from Hawthorne's desolate New England. My mother alone was able to retain her favour; so much so that our house was filled, if not beautified, by remnants of the pictures and furniture from "Uncle Henry's" dismantled house in Beacon Street. This loan was welcome to my mother who, without having any knowledge or taste in matters of fine art, was accustomed to a certain air of luxury in her surroundings; and it saved "Aunt Lizzie" the cost of storage. For it would have been against her principles to *sell* anything: everything that once was legally hers she held for ever with a grasp of iron. She even hinted, or actually proposed, coming to live with us, of course as a paying-guest; but this was too much. My mother above all things loved liberty, self-government, and silence; things not to be preserved where "Aunt Lizzie" was enthroned. It would have been an offence to the other Sturgises, and a constraint to ourselves. We should have had to speak English at table, as if we were not at home. We should also have had to double up, at least my sisters would have had to share the same room; and our domestic economy, however modest otherwise, always provided that each of us should possess his or her private room as a castle. It might be small, like my narrow one-windowed den at the top of the house, but it should be sacred. I doubt whether this practice is altogether wholesome in youth. Animals are born and bred in litters. Solitude grows blessed and peaceful only in old age.

This habit of privacy turned our house, quite unintendedly, into a little monastery. In a monastery there is strict community in externals, in hours, food, manners, and mode of dress, while in theory and sometimes in fact each member remains inwardly a hermit, and silent in his thoughts and affections. The system suited me perfectly, since nature had framed me for a recluse and only the contrary force of circumstances kept me for many years from complete retirement; but that system perhaps had an unfortunate influence on my brother and sisters, who would have been happier and more truly themselves if they had been carried along, body and soul, by an irresistible social medium. They instinctively sought such a medium, perhaps thought they had found it, but were never really unified or inwardly content. They had not the requisite inner clearness and force, such as my mother and I had, to thrive on a deliberate moral independence and a profound solitude.

I think I half understand why my mother was faithful to that objectionable virago, our "Aunt Lizzie". My mother was faithful to everything she once accepted—faithful, that is, within limits, as she was even to my father. This was part of her fidelity to herself. She might seldom or never see her oldest and best friends; she didn't need them; but she always remembered and cherished them as they had first figured in her life, as they ought to prove, if they in their turn would only remain faithful to what she had believed them to be. Now she had deliberately and for ever accepted all the Sturgises: not so much because they were her husband's family as because, being his family, they made her husband himself much more acceptable than he would have been individually: for individually the virtuous George Sturgis was rather negative. The simplicity of the Sturgis mind was decidedly marked in him; whereas in Henry, and of course in Russell, if it was present at all, it had assumed the noble characters of integrity, decision, and benevolence. Now "Aunt Lizzie" was Henry's widow; she belonged to the great generation; she had been once accepted, and she should never be disowned. How should the Sturgises be offended, when it was for their sake that she was treated decently? My mother never cooled towards any of them because they hated "Aunt Lizzie", and why should she cool towards "Aunt Lizzie" because she hated *them*? Besides, there was perhaps a certain bond between the sisters-in-law in their common poverty and isolation. For my mother, though she never had any lawsuits or quarrels and was no doubt esteemed by all her first husband's people, was inevitably neglected by them. They came to see her, if at all, once or twice a year, for a visit of ten minutes. It was not their fault. She had nothing to tell them, they had to make talk: how many children their children already had; how sad that so-and-so had died; what a pity that so-and-so had failed, and had been obliged to move to a smaller house; but how bravely and cheerfully everybody put up with everything. And so, goodbye, they must be off; and they were so glad to find her looking so well. With "Aunt Lizzie" conversation had more substance. There was a common background; and to hear long accounts of the misdeeds of one's relations and of one's own trials was something to which my mother must have been accustomed in Spain and in Manila: it was the staple of feminine confabulations; and, given my mother's perfect passivity, it was like hearing a novel read aloud; and my mother read many novels. They helped to pass away the time, and required no answer. Anyhow, friends the two sisters-in-law remained to the end. In her will, the Dragon left all those terrible yet space-filling mid-Victorian pictures and sofas and stuffed little arm-chairs and Chinese dovetailing tea-tables to my mother, to live with until death.

Rarest of our Sturgis visitors but most picturesque was "Uncle Samuel", third son of old Nathaniel, of Mt. Vernon Street, and of Susan Parkman, his wife. Perhaps he called only once, perhaps twice; the dear gentleman was not often let out from Somerville, where he resided in private apartments at the Insane Asylum.* Sound commonsense people, roseate optimists, as the Sturgises were, they were too Bostonian not to have at least one mad member, even in the Great Merchant generation; and "Uncle Samuel's" was an appropriately mild case. He seemed, in these lucid intervals when he was allowed to go visiting, most amiable, dignified, and even happy. Indeed, why should he not have been secretly a philosopher, saner than any of us, like Hamlet laughing at all the world and pretending to be mad in order to be free to laugh at it unmolested? But no: such complexities, as I have already hinted, were far from the Sturgis mind. It was straightforward, believed in what it saw, and in what sounded right. It had just enough rope to go once round the intelligible world; to go round it twice, like a philosopher, was beyond them. Had "Uncle Samuel" attempted such duplicity, I am sure he would have been much madder than he was. It was rather simplicity that perhaps he had carried a little too far; so far, that the moral comfort of not apprehending too much had passed into the practical inconvenience of apprehending too little. At any rate, he visibly took excellent care of his person, if not of his affairs. He was a tall, handsome, courtly old gentleman, beautifully dressed in the style of his first youth. The change in men's fashions had not been radical enough to render his figure ridiculous; I remember only one singular detail. His long-tailed coat, cut like what is now worn for full dress in the evening, was double breasted and buttoned in front; and a thin line of white waistcoat peeped out beneath it. Beau Brummel might have approved, but comment must have been caused in Beacon Street. In his conversation

*Later removed to Danvers.

there was nothing especially queer. We smiled on one another; explained our state of health, remarked upon the beautiful weather, so summer-like for the season, till finally, smiling even more pleasantly, he rose, extended his hand to us all in the right order, said he was pleased to have found my mother looking so well, which compliment she of course returned, amid our approving murmurs. She thanked him for his visit; my sisters and I accompanied him to the front door, and stood there while he went down the steps, and as he turned into the street beyond the little grass-plot, he once more elaborately took off his very tall top hat, and sent us a parting smile.

My mother certainly had reason to be flattered by the courtesy of such a visit. If her mad but punctilious brother-in-law had extended his unaccustomed walk to one of the last houses in the Mill Dam, to pay his respects to the foreign and remarried widow of a younger brother whom he had hardly known, save as a young boy, was not this a proof of the esteem in which the Sturgis family had held her from the beginning? That esteem had surmounted a very just initial prejudice against foreign marriages; and the surprise of finding the Spanish stranger so firm and courageous, and consistent in her actions, and in her independence, had survived in this shattered mind, as it might not have survived if overlaid by years of commonplace acquaintance.

Decay, in ways less tragic but more unlovely, ate at other points into some branches of this vast family tree, in spite of its general green and flourishing appearance. It was the impecunious boughs, as lacking sap, that first showed this tendency to wither. One of Nathaniel's daughters, for instance, had married the Reverend John Parkman, her cousin, and had had three children, who in their turn, with the greatest difficulty, produced a single bud between them for the third generation. I never knew the parents nor the son Theodore, who had fallen in the Civil War, and scarcely remember the daughter Bertha, who also died young and unmarried. But Alice, the other daughter, was one of our family friends, and unforgettable. She too was condemned to remain unmarried for years, a circumstance entirely contrary to her express wishes, and even to her moral principles. I don't know whether her father's theology, like her sister's name Bertha, was German, but Alice had a romantic German flavour to her mind. She read books on education, and had precise ideas on the vocation of motherhood and on the propriety of large families. She would tell us about it, shaking her curls, and stretching out her feet, the toes turned in and touching, in a voluntary little fit of the giggles. She planned to have at least eight children, four boys and four girls; but a husband had not turned up. The war had depleted the ranks of elder solid reasonable suitors; and after the financial panic of 1873, and the Boston fire, and the prolonged hard times, young lovers, however amorous their hearts might be in secret, couldn't pop the question for lack of means. Ultimately, however, Alice discovered a derelict of the Civil War, a *mutilé*, now a pronounced pacifist, still suffering from a nasty wound that had left one of his arms weak and much shorter than the other; he could still shake hands with it (for unluckily it was his right arm) but so limply and unwillingly that you were afraid it was causing him acute pain. Everything seemed to cause him acute pain, or at least serious misgivings, even his engagement to Alice. His aspect, in one way, belied his principles and his limpness, for he wore a fan-tail black beard, like a ferocious Parsee, from the centre of which shone his bright red cheeks and beady black eyes. He told us, in depressed accents, that soldiering was something horrible that left a man utterly ruined physically and without hope of advancement in any decent business; yet he was willing to contemplate matrimony if the lady could bring some contribution to the heavy expenses of a home. Unfortunately his name was Smith, but he was willing to change it—the name of Parkman was in greater danger of becoming extinct—and certainly it seemed to us, though of course he couldn't touch on such a delicate subject, that with Alice's programme for a nestful of babies, it would be carrying coals to Newcastle to have them all Smiths. On second thought, however, in view of her age (thirty-four) and of her husband's difficulties, she reconsidered her demands as a mother, and would not insist on any precise number of children. "William and I", she explained to us afterwards, "have decided to let nature take her course." Wasted, alas, was all that German learning and idealism about eugenics and the scientific amelioration of the race. But nature was not vindictive. They had one child.

Much more fruit grew on the branch of the Sturgises that sprang from Elizabeth, fourth child of old Nathaniel. This bough was refreshed by much golden sap; some of the lady's descendents became or married people of note in the great world; and besides the connection through the Sturgises I had a private wire to them through my friend Beal, who married into that family. Elizabeth's marriage at first would not have suggested much scope for her progeny. Her husband was a sort of gentleman-farmer whom we called old Mr. Grew, a rustic not only in appearance and humour, but also by virtue of actually cultivating a large estate in the country, including a high hill, with his ancestral farmhouse standing on the very top of it. On some occasion we spent a holiday there, either as guests of the family or simply as invited to occupy the house in the absence of the owners: a discreet form of hospitality sometimes practised by our truly kind rich relations. We had no country house, nor money to make excursions and live in hotels; and no place could be more airy than the top of Hyde Park Hill (for so it was called); and doing our own housekeeping there for a week or two would be less constraining, and even less expensive, than being invited to stay in a large establishment. For old Mr. Grew, though rustic, was rich, and his son Henry—who was our special friend and protector—was even more so. Henry Grew had made a private fortune in China, being one of the oldest of the second generation, and the only one to imitate his uncles the Great Merchants; this circumstance no doubt helped to interest him in my mother; and his wife liked my sister Susana. Our relations with the Henry Grews, if not intimate, were therefore always cordial. Yet all was not well with the Grew family. There was a skeleton in the closet. Everybody re-membered but nobody ever mentioned the existence of Henry's sister Lizzie. It was she, in that whole generation of Sturgises, that was paying the toll of madness: not placidly, in an almost pleasant abstraction, like her uncle Samuel, but horribly, hopelessly, wildly, through a long series of years. Her fate haunted the mind of all her relations in the midst of their prosperity, and it might have served to recall their thoughts to ultimate realities; but I think their effort was to hush, to suppress that unpalatable lesson, and to go on living as if it were not true. They had passionately rejected the horrible Christian doctrines of hell and of infant damnation; and here was a young girl, one of themselves, a howling maniac. Everything, they wished to think, was for the best; but how make out that Lizzie's unmerited torments were for the best, prolonged for twenty years and ending only with her death? Surely the argumentative Sturgises—for they were argumen-tative though not critical—must have felt this contradiction to their remaining religious pretenses, surging like a ground swell beneath the smooth surface of their lives. The suspicion rendered them secretly uncomfortable and distressed. The Furies exist; and though there is no need of harping on their existence when they are in hiding, we ought nevertheless sometimes to bring them on the stage, as the Greeks did; not in order to poison natural gladness, but in order to enjoy that gladness more humbly, as a passing gift and not as a right or a possession. Life is strong enough to get on without lies. Once our bow made to the primeval powers, we can accept good fortune when it comes as a feast of uncovenanted music. And this feast is no accident, as our torments often are. If fate were not radically kind we should not have existed to complain that it is incidentally so cruel.

Against the drain of this secret tragedy the moral budget of the Grews had many assets to its credit, some of them brilliant. The two brothers Henry and Ned were prosperous, but with a curious difference, characteristic of old Boston. Ned was much younger, handsomer, and one would have thought in every way destined to play a larger part in the world. Yet somehow he remained socially in the shadow. His wife came from some family that nobody knew, and they moved somehow on the outskirts of Boston society—at least such was the impression that gossip made on our ears. I believe they even lived in the wrong street, or on the wrong side of their street; for in Boston moral colour was not confined to actions or sentiments, but saturated things and places. Perfection resided on the eminence of Beacon Hill, but only within limits, and it might extend, more and more cautiously into the flat filled-in land to the west, along the sunny side of Beacon Street and Commonwealth Avenue. The shady side of Beacon was permitted to a well-established family like the Coolidges, but for most people it was dangerous, and proper only for doctors, dentists, or strangers; while the shady side of Commonwealth Avenue and of course Newbury Street was out of bounds. In Marlborough Street the sunny and shady sides were almost indifferent; both were blameless, but modest. I think it was in Marlborough Street, and on the *sunny side*, that the Ned Grews lived; perhaps they had lived somewhere else before: anyhow a sort of negative magnetic field seemed to surround them, for which I know no reason. In the next generation, however, this spell was broken. Boston had grown larger; it had grown less important; the currents of the age circulated more freely through it, and the centre of the whirlpool, even intellectually, was no longer there, but in New York. Later still, during the war of 1914–1918, even Washington became a social and moral focus: and this change, radical for Boston, may be seen mirrored in the Grew family. Henry's son resisted the dreadful revolution, drew in his horns, went native, reverted to his grandfather the farmer and actually went to live on the top of Hyde Park Hill, although the town at the foot of it had already become an industrial suburb. Meantime Ned's son had somehow burst the local barriers, gone into the government service and become the American ambassador to Japan.

The age of the great merchants was past, even that of the great capitalists began to be threatened. Perhaps the world is blindly and painfully returning to a normal economy. The contempt for public office, for army, navy, and government services that prevailed among the great merchants and in the liberal era could not long be maintained. Either the merchants must become the governing class, as in England, or they must cease to form the upper class, as they unmistakably did in New England in the nineteenth century. A normal upper class is composed of the lords of the land, who govern and defend it.

Henry Grew's was a typical instance of the Sturgis simplicity of mind: he was affectionate, sensible, careful, busy, and a little fussy. His views and his hopes were what everybody expected them to be. Yet simplicity of mind is a most inadequate phrase to describe this Sturgis quality. A fact, particularly a moral fact, cannot be covered by any one word; each term is like a radius drawn to the intended centre, but drawn from a particular point of the circumference; and there are numberless other points from which the same centre could be reached with equal precision. These reflections are suggested to me by the difference between Henry Grew, who was simple, and his wife, who was not. Yet his wife—Jane Wigglesworth, whom we called "Cousin Jennie"—was no less affectionate, sensible, careful, and busy than her husband, and also a little fussy. Why was she not also simple? Her thoughts no doubt were clearer than his, more theoretical and finer; but she too was a Unitarian, and I have often heard that religion praised by those who profess it for its *simplicity*. The simplest of things is nothing; and the charm of religious nothingness was probably what drew people originally to that form of worship; you could feel religious without any intellectual consequences. This also attracted other people to ritualism: but "Cousin Jennie" could not evade religion so easily. Unitarian or not, she would always have been spiritually intense; she would have lived in a higher world as well as in this one; and that excludes simplicity; it complicates, it inverts, it reverses conventional perspectives. Her Unitarian opinions could not abolish her Puritan emotions. She disbelieved in hell with the same fervour with which her ancestor Michael Wigglesworth had gloated on it. Hell for him and the absence of hell for her vindicated the same religious intuition: the holiness and justice of God. Yet both couldn't help worrying. Worry was ineradicable in "Cousin Jennie". There were so many dangers on every side; it was so *dreadful* that people should be so blind and should so degrade themselves and one another. This is probably why she liked my sister Susana, who was a fervent Catholic, but merry, and trusted her with the children. It was a comfort that religious intensity should produce peace; and it was a bond that religious intensity should exist. Such peace is not simple but secondary, wise, spiritual, or what the Church calls supernatural. That is, it flows not, as with the optimistic Unitarians who have shed all Puritanism, from expecting things to be all right, but from living fundamentally in another sphere, from which the wrongness of things seems a ground for liberation from their ascendency. If you renounce inwardly your natural lust for pleasure or reputation or for life itself, the loss or the insecurity of those things ceases to touch you deeply: but if those things come to you, you enjoy them heartily for the time being, not expecting them to last.

One difficulty that Jennie Grew found distressing was the training of her children in manners. They must learn good manners, yet they must not be forbidden to do anything unless it is morally wrong. Now, is it morally wrong to make a noise in blowing your nose? Or is it morally wrong not to wipe your nose when you *ought* to wipe it? If only hurting others be morally wrong, must this hurt be physical? Or would a slight disgust caused at seeing children with their noses running be such an infringement of the happiness of others as to make a running nose a *moral* delinquency? Now so much casuistry and hesitation and self-consciousness do not produce truly good manners even in the older people who ought to be models; whereas truly good manners in them would produce good manners in their children by imitation. This seems not to have occurred to the Grews; and perhaps it would hardly be true in America, because young people there mix in every sort of society, and they come home to teach their parents rather than to learn from them.

It is curious how much liberty is restricted by the idea that everybody ought to be free and independent. The field of elective morals then extends over everything, and the notion that you *ought to choose* your manners and your opinions prevents them from ever being spontaneous and really expressing your mind. Only people in whom manners and judgments are ingrained can laugh at convention, and can turn a somersault when occasion demands without turning a hair. The Sturgises, Nena for instance, had this aristocratic gift. They had sureness in liberty, perhaps because not being very imaginative they liked to do harmless entertaining things rather than anything perverse. For Bostonians they worried very little, disapproved very little, and were not pontifical. The milk of freedom in them didn't turn sour.

There is a little love-story connected with the Henry Grews which I will tell as I heard it from the lips of the lady-gossips in the early 1890's, when it was new; but how far it is true (except for the happy issue) I have no means of knowing. If I asked the persons concerned, some of whom are still living, they would probably think me impertinent, and refuse to tell me the true facts. Let it then pass for fiction, and not be published until everyone is dead who figures in it. I have already spoken of Henry Grew's son who "went native" and returned to his grandfather's farm. Very different was the path chosen by his eldest sister, Jessie. Everybody remarked how like she was, when a young girl, to a Dresden figurine, delicacy personified, in form, motion, and colour. Nobody was ever whiter or pinker or blonder, nobody sweeter or more graceful. When her brother was in College, he sometimes brought a friend of his to the house, a big, dark and (if one must say it) rather gross-looking young man, with decided manners, and well-informed categorical views expressed with the opposite of bashfulness. His name was Jack Morgan. Jack and Jessie, by all the rules of St. Valentine, had to fall in love; and so they did, but not for St. Valentine's day only. They said they wished to be married. Old Mr. Morgan, the original great banker with the huge red nose, said this was premature, they were too young, the flirtation must be broken off and Jack must go to London, to the branch of the Morgan bank there, and forget his dainty provincial sweetheart in the gay capital. He went; but it was less easy for her at home, to endure the separation. The white in her cheek grew whiter, the pink paler; she began to cough a little; and with the dreadful shadow of her mad aunt darkening his mind, her affectionate anxious father became alarmed. Things not improving with time, but growing slowly worse, he finally took the step of writing to Mr. Morgan, relating the facts. Might not Jack be authorised to return, at least for a visit, so that they might discover whether his absence was really the cause of the girl's pining away. It might not be that. It might be only delicate health—heredity. Mr. Morgan agreed heartily; he had no objection to the match; he had only wished to test the reality of the young people's attachment; and their youth would cease to be an objection if their attachment were so strong, since an early marriage, where there was true love, was a great insurance for a young man's steadiness and for his success in the world. So all ended happily; and the Sturgis family in the third generation became allied to as important a banking-house as that in which in the first generation it had played a personal part.

How I came to be named after "Papa George".   I leave what more I may have to tell about these elder branches of the Sturgis tree until I come to the part some of them played in my own life; as I leave also the fruits that ripened on the ninth branch, which was that of "Papa George", as I might call my mother's first husband, father of my brother and sisters, who was, as it were, my step-father by anticipation and after whom I was named. This rather odd fact was due to the original innocent sentiment of my sister Susana, who as the reader may remember was my godmother, and in that capacity had a nominal right to give me a name. She could just remember her father, having been six years old when he died, and it was she, apparently, who suggested that I should be called Jorge, a rather unusual but not unknown name in Spain. That my father should have smiled and made no objection, I can understand, in view of his modesty and ironical turn of mind. He thought his predecessor a good soul, but a simpleton; and somehow his expectation about me seems to have been that I should be a simpleton too, perhaps in order not to count on too much and then be disappointed. He liked to aim low, not trusting his star, and perhaps calling me Jorge in memory of "Papa George" was a subtle sign of such resignation. When I first returned to Spain in 1883, and we went out together for our first walk—my father and I were great pedestrians—he pointed out to me the first donkeys we came across, and said: "*¿Reconoces los compañeros de tu infancia?* Do you recognise the companions of your infancy?*" I recognised them. But it was not I that ever played with donkeys. It was my brother Robert, Robert *Sturgis*, who had once had a donkey for a pet in his childhood. I reminded my father of this, and we laughed about it.

A more puzzling point would be to ask why my mother saw no objection to calling me Jorge, after her first husband. Might not my father resent it? No doubt he said he didn't in the least; but wasn't there some indelicacy on her own part? She was passive, very passive unless her path was crossed; and her path in the matter of children had been crossed once for all by the death of her first born. I too might have been named José, after her own father, or *Pepín*, her pet-name for that lamented child. But no, that would have been sacrilege. I think in my early childhood she sometimes felt a certain analogy between her lost darling and me, who was her first-born by her second marriage, after five years of widowhood; but the illusion was soon dispelled. I was too inferior; and to institute any such comparison would have damned me at once. Why then establish this strange link with the past by calling me Jorge? Anyhow, Susana had her way— she often did—and there was something prophetic about this mingling of Sturgis traditions with my little person. Jorge, translated back into George, has become a part of my *nom de plume*.

Amy White with the red hand. I should hardly mention the tenth child of old Nathaniel at all, or her branch of the family tree, not a luxuriant one and unknown to me save for one sprout; but this one had a peculiarity that impressed my young mind. Her name was Amy White; a spare, active, intelligent spinster, a little older than my sisters, and like any other friendly spinster, save for a horrid secret about her: she had a red hand. She always wore a glove, of course (this was Boston), and I never was permitted to see the offending member; but my sisters had once seen it, when they were children, and Amy, to prove that she could be naughty if she liked, had pulled off her glove and driven away all the little girls playing in Boylston Place by brandishing her crimson hand in their faces. Of course, it was not other people's blood that had stained it, but only her own; it was an enormous birth-mark; but the suggestion of gore remained, and a vague affinity with *The Scarlet Letter*. Poor Amy White had no other distinction; and though she lived to old age, we soon lost sight of her. Obscurity—we were obscure too—hid us from one another. If she had been rich, this matter of the red hand might have kept her an old maid, partly out of pride on her part, partly out of a slight disinclination in shallow wooers; but it would not have isolated her or led her to hide in some corner. There were many rich old maids in Boston; some of them remained single precisely because they were rich, and had no need of marriage to give them all the comforts and luxuries of a home; and they were little hunted for their money. A poor young man, vaguely amorous (for mad love was improbable) would rather turn to a helpful poor young woman who would be attached to him, than to a luxurious rich one, with her fine friends and family ethics, who would keep him in leash like a poodle. Had Amy been rich, I say, she might have remained single with a good grace. She could have become soft and gracious; she could have been surrounded by books, friends, and flowers; she could have busied herself with charities or with some favourite learned speciality, like

Miss Grace Norton with Montaigne. The red hand wouldn't have mattered then; the glove, properly varied and always clean, would even have seemed a mark of distinction, like the ribbon of an order. Red-handed and poor, however, she couldn't be an attractive figure or a happy woman. She was not perceptibly soured; yet a chill wind of difficulty, of misfortune, of solitude played about her, and the world seemed to grow empty wherever she went.

James Sturgis 1822–1888.

•

Lower status of professional men and officials.

James, eleventh and penultimate child of old Nathaniel, like all his brothers, except silly Samuel, was a man of business and though he belonged to the generation of the Great Merchants, he was not one of them. If ever he went a-fishing for to catch a whale, it was, like Simple Simon, in home waters; yet he was often wrecked, having no judgment, and remained as sanguine as ever and unsinkable. He would have done better in a government office, if any self-respecting Bostonian in those days had ever thought of a government career. Not only the civil service was taboo, but also the army and navy (except, of course, during the Civil War, and temporarily); and it is significant that none of the Sturgises of that generation were professional men, lawyers, doctors, or clergymen. One of Russell's sons, John, of the American branch became an architect under the sign of Ruskin and perpetrated the pseudo-Italian terra cotta and brick Museum of Fine Art in Copley Square never completed, and soon afterwards pulled down. A grandson of Russell's, Clipston, later adopted the same profession, as well as High Church Anglican sentiments; and two of his younger brothers were at one time or another masters at the Groton School; but all this was under strong English influence and in another phase of New England culture. Of Russell's English sons, one was occasionally a Gladstonian Member of Parliament, and the other two occasionally wrote novels; but they all were unmistakable gentlemen of leisure. The glamour of the Great Merchants was gone, in spite of their father's glory: the glory of a sunset, perhaps, and to be admired without being imitated. But in Boston, in the middle of the nineteenth century, no one who was ambitious, energetic, or even rich thought of anything but making a fortune; the glamour was all in that direction. The Adamses were not, and always said they were not, Bostonians; and the orators, clergymen, and historians of the day, as well as the poets, though respected and admired, never dominated the community: they were ornaments and perhaps dangers. The great affair, the aristocratic path to success and power, was business.

"Uncle James", whose head was full of projects, confidently took that path, and though he sometimes slipped and "failed", he never failed finally. He would start afresh and begin to make money; there was always some speculation that could help him to do that, and renew in him the sense of prosperity. He was not a mere Micawber; he really prospered at times. For safety, he had a nice home-keeping unfashionable wife with a small fortune of her own which evidently he was prevented from managing; and whenever he was bankrupt, they moved to a smaller house in some side street, and lived on the wife's income until business looked up again, when the family would come out once more into the social sunshine.

My prejudice against him.

•

The snare of cordiality.

I bore "Uncle James" a grudge. In the first place I didn't like him: and the world is rather sharply divided for me into the people I like and the people I don't like. Philosophy and charity counsel me to correct this caprice, and I don't theoretically build on it; but it persists in my inner feeling, and it is not wholly arbitrary. I dislike the people I dislike for some reason; they offend some natural ideal within me. For I do not either like or dislike people interestedly but absolutely disinterestedly, artistically, erotically; and this their harmony or disharmony with my psychic impulse, has its human importance. After all I am a man; what I like and dislike probably is, fundamentally, what any honest reflective person would like or dislike. "Uncle James" never offended me personally or did me any intentional harm; he would have been kind to me, like all the Sturgises, if there had been occasion; nevertheless I didn't like him. He had a full round beard, and I cannot like that. A long white, or grey, or even yellow beard, especially if clean, forked, or blown into strands is suitable for Michaelangelo's Moses or Charon in his bark, or even for God the Father: but a round short full beard like Saint Peter's is vulgar. That key-note was taken up in "Uncle James" by his commonplace talk, his hurry, his bustling, unperceptive manners. How inferior to "Uncle Samuel", who was so elegantly mad! But no wonder; James was some fifteen years younger, the world had grown commoner, and he had passed his life making and losing money. Only success, great success, can ennoble that; a success that debouches into something that is not money-getting. Moreover, "Uncle James" was cordial. That is the well-meant American substitute for being amiable; but it won't do. It is being amiable on principle and about nothing in particular; whereas true amiability presupposes discernment, tact, a sense for what other people really feel and want. To be cordial is like roughing a man's head, to jolly him up, or kissing a child that doesn't ask to be kissed. You are relieved when it's over.

The snare of   However, all this may be silly prejudice on my part.
speculation.   My real grievance touches something more positive. "Uncle James" was the only Sturgis of the first generation surviving in Boston during the 1870's and 1880's. It was to him that my mother inevitably turned for advice in money-matters. In domestic economy she was firmness personified, never miscalculated her resources or left a debt unpaid (as I never did); but about investments and general business she knew absolutely nothing. "Uncle James", on the contrary, thought he knew everything. Just before the panic of 1873 he was sure of a boom: real estate, especially in the Back Bay and on the water-side of Beacon Street, was rising and rising in value. Now the house in which my mother lived, and which James himself, very likely, had chosen for her in 1868, when she first went to live in Boston, was in the depths of Boylston Place. That spot, genteelly retired in the '60's, had become unsuitable for two young girls about to enter society; several of the houses had become boarding-houses, or something even worse. On the other hand, business was flooding Boylston Street, just at the head of Boylston Place, and could not fail to run down that little slope and flood Boylston Place also. Let my mother move from Boylston Place but not sell her house, No. 17, because what with the business flowing down (in his imagination) from the busy street above, and the boarding and other houses requiring just such central but retired spots to flourish in, that property would prove a bonanza: the rent could be increased with every new lease. It would be perfectly safe, therefore, to put a slight mortgage on that house, and with the ready money so secured—say $10,000—buy cheap for $25,000 a very nice new little house on the water-side of Beacon Street, just the place socially for the girls, even if it was one of the last houses on the Mill Dam, surrounded by empty, half-flooded lots, and swept all winter by icy winds. Of course this $25,000 house couldn't be bought for only $10,000; it would be necessary to put a little mortgage, say $15,000, on this house also. But that was only a momentary affair; when the value of the house had risen, it could be sold, and the mortgage on both houses payed off, leaving enough to buy a new and better house elsewhere. The girls would both be happily married then and something different, perhaps in Longwood, would then suit my mother best for her old age.

Boylston Place. Why didn't my mother consult "Uncle Robert" (of whom more presently) or Henry Grew before agreeing to this transaction? How could she, so prudent in her own affairs, not shudder at the thought of that double mortgage? Apparently, she was simply deceived; or perhaps she, too, was allured by the idea of greater elegance, or (more likely) by the sense of the *necessity* or *duty* of living where she ought to live for her children's welfare. Why else should she have come to Boston or to America at all? And wouldn't it be unthinkable that she should have left Spain, where with her income she could live very well, in the style of the country, and where Susana already had had several suitors, in order to live in a disreputable back alley in Boston? I call it disreputable dramatically, as my mother would have called it if she had understood; but it was simply Bohemian. Vercelli's Italian restaurant was there in my time, and the Tavern Club, the only club I ever belonged to in Boston; and I frequented both, until they became stuffy and tiresome, and I preferred the Napoli in the North End, which was more genuinely Italian. However, "Uncle James" was right in thinking that it was now a place where "nobody lived"; and this was a reason for selling the Boylston Place house, though not for mortgaging it, and much less for buying another that absorbed half my mother's capital and was an ugly comfortless narrow mean slice of a house, built for speculation.

The Boston fire. In the year 1872 there was a great fire in Boston. I well remember the night in which my brother Robert — who was then clerk in "Uncle James's" office and had the keys to it — was called up in the small hours by "Uncle James" himself; they must rush in a cab to get all the papers out of the safe; the fire was gaining ground in the business quarter, the post-office was in flames, State Street threatened; just look out of the window and see the glare. Robert, who was then nineteen years old, awoke with difficulty, took some time to understand, but then got ready in the twinkling of an eye, because like all American youths he loved nothing better than "going to a fire". When he was gone, I too got out of bed — we slept in the same bed then — and looked out of the window. I could see a suffused light in the night sky, but no real beautiful flames; and I went back to bed philosophically. How much "Uncle James" lost by the fire, I don't know. India Building in State Street, in which my mother had a share and which now, if the Boylston Street house was unlet, became the sole source of her income, luckily was not burned; but the ravage was impressive, and Robert took me to look at it, full of the contagious excitement and even pride felt by the Bostonians at having had such a big fire. People wouldn't speak of the London fire any more; they would say the Boston fire. Unluckily for Boston, Chicago had had an even bigger fire; and more unluckily, in my opinion, Boston had no Wren to rebuild the town. That was the era of an abominable architectural medley of styles imitated from picture-books by professional speculators and amateur artists: the scourge of Ruskinism.

A financial crisis. It never rains but it pours, and that same year 1872 was marked by one of those periodical crises that now are well-known and expected, but that then seemed an inexplicable cataclysm, contrary to the certainty of perpetual progress and prosperity proper to the nineteenth century and to America. It was a financial deluge. Everybody suddenly felt poor: business unexpectedly shrank; Uncle Jameses failed in every family. Hard times came, especially (with those two mortgages, and the deflation, increasing their relative amount, undertaken by the government) to my mother and to us. The Beacon Street house could not be sold or let until nine years later, and the Boylston Place house, though usually well let, was even longer on our hands. It was not sold until Robert, having ceased to work in other people's offices, took to administering property, which he did admirably, getting us all out of our penury into gradually increasing comfort, as his son has continued to do by the wisdom of his investments. But the predicament at first was so serious for us that "Uncle James" (himself no doubt ruined) evidently felt ashamed of having got my mother into such difficulties, and wrote to his brother Russell in London. Russell at once responded to the appeal, and promised my mother an allowance of £100 a year, which he inserted in his will, so that she enjoyed it until her death in 1912: a real benefit to us all and particularly to me. For I, not being a Sturgis, had no natural share in her money, which came from her first husband. But her first husband himself had had the temperament of his brother James, at least as regards business, and had in his last years, made rash investments of his savings, founding I don't know what rope-factory or other foolishness in Manila; so that on his death, there was hardly enough money for my mother with her young children—they were four then—to carry out the approved plan of taking them to Boston and establishing herself there. It was the youngest of the brothers, Robert, then at the height of his fortunes in China (although but thirty-four years of age) that came to the rescue, making her a present—as a rich bachelor could—of ten thousand dollars. That sum, my mother always regarded as her own, not her first husband's or her children's; and later it came nominally to devolve upon me, as I may have occasion to relate in its place.

To this "Uncle Robert", the third of the Great Merchant brothers, and twelfth child of their generation, I will come presently; but first I must exhibit three minor portraits: miniatures of "Uncle James's" three children. They are not unpleasing pictures but like the small ones that hang in the side rooms in museums, often having the spirit of their epoch more clearly indicated than in the greater canvasses.

Two old bachelors out of place. As none of the great generation were professional men or government officials or political figures, so none were bachelors or old maids—except merry Samuel, who I daresay would have married a dozen times had he been at liberty. This was patriarchal, and characteristic of a prosperous, ambitious, enterprising race. But now we come to a novel fact: "Uncle James" had two very presentable sons, Charley and Frank, apparently in good health and of good habits; yet they both remained single until their deaths at the age of sixty-four and sixty-nine respectively. Why so? I can suggest only one cause: poverty. Not pauperism, of course; they were always well-fed, well-dressed, and well-lodged; and I suppose they (with their sister) divided their mother's little fortune between them in the end, and had just enough to live on in modest bachelor apartments and some secondary club. But they were poor for their class and for their friends. They couldn't establish a household of the sort they would have liked. Yet that was not all. They apparently had nothing to do. Whether perhaps Frank, who certainly went to College, also studied law, I don't know; but I never heard that he practised it; and as to Charley, his elder brother (who had a round beard like his father) he never was known to do anything but potter about in the New England back country and shoot birds. There was a distinct class of these gentlemen tramps, young men no longer young who wouldn't settle down, who disliked polite society and the genteel conventions, but hadn't enough intelligence or enough conceit to think themselves transcendentalists or poets, in the style of Thoreau or of Walt Whitman. That is what they would have wished to be, but they were too well-bred, too citified. Why didn't they go to live in Europe? Frank, especially, had a suggestion about him of being a possible artist or wit: why didn't he paint or write or do something? It was the failure of nerve, the sense of spent momentum, of being sons of Great Merchants, but without either need or opportunity for enterprise, and without money enough to be important men about town. Superfluous persons who felt themselves superfluous: dry branches on the green family tree.

A woman in hers. Nothing withered, however, about their sister Susie, one of the five Susie Sturgises of that epoch, all handsome women, but none more agreeably handsome than this one, called Susie MacBurney and Susie Williams successively after her two husbands. When I knew her best she was a woman between fifty and sixty, stout, placid, intelligent, without an affectation, or a prejudice, adding a grain of malice to the Sturgis affability, without meaning or doing the least unkindness. I felt that she had something of the Spanish feeling, so Catholic or so Moorish, that nothing in this world is of terrible importance. Everything happens, and we had better take it all as easily or as resignedly as possible. But this without a shadow of religion; none of the Sturgises (except the Susie Sturgis that was my sister) had any inward religion; and the outer religion they had sometimes was either nominal or absurd. Morally, therefore, she may not have been complete; but physically and socially she was completeness itself, and friendliness and understanding. She was not awed by Boston. Her first marriage was disapproved, her husband being an outsider and unreliable; but she weathered whatever domestic storms may have ensued, and didn't mind. Her second husband was like her father, a man with a chequered business career; but he too survived all storms, and seemed the healthier and happier for them. They appeared to be well enough off. In her motherliness there was something queenly, she moved well, she spoke well, and her freedom from prejudice never descended to vulgarity or loss of dignity. Her mother's modest solid nature had excluded in her the worst of her father's foibles, while the Sturgis warmth and amiability had been added to make her a charming woman.

"Uncle Robert" and "Aunt Susie". I have mentioned the gift that "Uncle Robert" made to my mother when she was left a widow in Manila with four young children and insufficient means. His fortune had been made so quickly that he soon left China and returned home, to marry. His wife was just the woman a bachelor of thirty-five coming home from China would choose, a feminine, tall, pretty woman, to whom money, good food and fine clothes would signify happiness. Her name was Susie, and she became the eldest, "Aunt Susie", of the Susie Sturgises. Susan is a dreadful name, but is Susie an improvement on it? I like to call my sister Susana, as we called her at home and as everybody of course did in Spain, where she married and spent the last forty years of her life; but everybody called her Susie—Spanish Susie, for distinction—in Boston, and I had to call her so among them, and even when I wrote to her in English; but we habitually spoke Spanish together, unless the subject was so un-Spanish as to require the Boston vernacular. "Aunt Susie", then, was rather a showy and shallow woman; affectionate, and in particular attached to Susana: but her husband matched her only as contraries may be said to match, or to make matches. She was fat, he was thin; she was blonde, he was dark with transparent side-whiskers; she was physical, he was (for a Sturgis) intellectual. You would have taken him for an English gentleman: he probably lived among them in China, and caught their quiet, experienced, imperturbable ways. After Canton (where I think he had lived) Boston was too cold a climate for him; his lungs were weak; and he went to live in Philadelphia.

The Philadelphia Sturgises. It was to Philadelphia, to his uncle Robert's, that my brother Robert (named after that uncle) was directed, when he was sent to America, in 1867, to be thoroughly Americanised. He arrived, and was temporarily adopted by his uncle Robert's family. This ought to have been a close bond; and towards the girls, especially Rita, he always retained an admiring attachment; but I am afraid it was not reciprocated. Robert had neither the gifts, the tact, nor the money that would have allowed him to take the place that a slightly older and half-foreign cousin with any ability could so easily have taken in such a family: he was simply a well-meaning poor relation to whom one musn't be unkind. Moreover the three sons of "Uncle Robert" were not boys to look up to my brother— far otherwise—or that he could understand: for he never understood men or could get on with men: only with women, and with those who were not too exacting. Now "Uncle Robert's" four girls were, in different ways, exacting, and justly exacting. Rita, the eldest, though the least beautiful, made a good impression, by her intelligence and high feeling. She was like her aunt Sarah, public-spirited and morally intense, without any religious fanaticism. She married in Philadelphia, I believe happily, but I never saw her or her children after the first years. Lily, the second girl, was pretty and very tall; not, I suspect, looking beyond the sphere of rich local society for her interests or standards. The same might be said of the third sister, the Susie Sturgis that shone among the good-looking Susie Sturgises for a true beauty: not classic, a little like her mother, inclining too much to sensual charm, but really the ideal of a woman appealing to the senses, without, of course, quite knowing, when she was a young girl, the secret of her power. She learned it afterwards, however. She married a rich young man about town who had courted her for years, whom she liked, but who drank; after eighteen years of wedded life she divorced him, and married twice again, as she said, for money; yet in the end had only just enough to live on. Here is one more instance of the decline of the idle plutocracy: they peter out.

Last flashes of old acquaintance. Out of a clear sky these three sisters, whom I hadn't seen or heard of for forty years, wrote to me apropos of *The Last Puritan*, not by way of protest (it is the commoner people in America who protested) but simply by way of reminiscence and friendliness, or as in Lily's case, to get my autograph. Susie's letter was the most interesting; she told me what I have just repeated about her marriages, and offered me two comic statuettes that had belonged to her father, caricatures of Gladstone and Disraeli; which I thanked her for but begged her not to send, as I had nowhere to put them, and lived with a hand-bag for all my earthly possessions—a slight exaggeration: at present (1942) I possess five valises, and nine cases of books and papers stored where I shall never get at them until after this war. I asked Susie to send me her photograph instead: but I reflected afterwards, when she didn't send it, that my request had been stupid: because I meant, of course, an old photograph of what she was at seventeen, but couldn't frankly say so: and she wasn't going to send me one of what she may be now, at seventy-one.

The youngest of the sisters remains to be mentioned, who didn't write, but said to a friend that she would have done so, except that she heard her three sisters had, and thought that was enough; but I am sorry because she, Maisie, the youngest of all that second generation of Sturgises, was one of the nicest, a favourite of my sister Susana, a suggested lady-love for myself, almost a lady-love of Warwick Potter's, and married to Warwick's bosom friend, Edgar Scott. With these antecedents, apart from being a quasi-cousin, she would have had special lights for judging *The Last Puritan*. She was far nearer to me in mind than any of her immediate family; in her there was something unworldly, something more subtly refined; and she actually sent her son Warwick to see me in Rome when he was doing the grand tour. I was touched by this attention and this double revival of the friendly past; but the young man seemed to me washed out and commonplace;

they all seem to me washed out and commonplace, in comparison to their parents, as they were in the 1890's. That was not only a time when my own eyes and sympathies were fresh, but when the plutocracy was itself self-confident and bouyant; not only the plutocracy, but the cultivated inner circle within it or gravitating round it, to which I may be said to have belonged. Poetry and art, religion also, were our real interests; sport, fashionable society, and travel, good wines and good books were our pleasures, and we were not haunted yet by the spectre of decline, of war, of poverty, of a universal bureaucracy, and of a vulgar intelligentsia.

V

My Sister Susana

Her importance in my life. I knew the Sturgis clan in two ways, first at home, since my half-brother and half-sisters were characteristic Sturgises in their different directions, and then as friends freely chosen for personal reasons, where our nominal relationship merely furnished an occasion for discovering some real affinity. Of my personal friends among the Sturgises I will speak as they turn up: for these were all social friendships with fixed periods and circumstances, not friendships of the spirit. But the Sturgis influence flooding me at home was primordial and I might almost say pre-natal. It imposed on me my Christian name, and it gave me my second mother or godmother, who, by virtue of her remarkable Sturgis warmth and initiative was I think the greatest power, and certainly the strongest affection, in my life. This bond, added to the fact that she was my sister, makes any attempt to describe her embarrassing for me and perhaps unbecoming. Yet she must be described, else this narrative would miss its object. I intend my recollections to be only fragmentary, but only by excluding things that are of no importance, or all too human and well-known to everyone in his own person; not at all fragmentary in the sense of leaving out the bull's eye from my target. Let me then tell the story of Susana's life and thereby allow her, as far as possible, to describe herself.

Her vivacity. I have mentioned how, even in early childhood, when she had an older brother, she took the lead; and this became a matter of course when she was the eldest and also far more lively, wide awake, and competent than her brother and sister. In their lessons and in their games she ruled the roost. In Boylston Place, when she was from six to nine years of age, she was the captain of all the children that played in the street; and if this practice seems not very genteel, we must remember that in Boston, local society was both select and democratic, given an acceptable quarter of the town; and that as Boylston Place ran down hill, it afforded in winter an irresistible chance for "coasting", that is, for tobogganing with single or even with double or longer sleds. There were big boys in the neighbourhood who naturally assumed the duty of steering; but Susana remained the arbiter of what should be done, and how. For a little Spanish girl, fresh from tropical Manila, to command in this winter sport shows her easy adaptability, her gift of inspiring confidence, and the willingness with which people spontaneously caught her enthusiasms.

Her enthusiasm for Queen Isabella the Second.   Her enthusiasms sometimes were rather extraordinary. It was not only others that caught them from her, she herself caught them like a disease and was greatly their victim; because they were all far from expressing her whole nature, or even its fundamental needs. Her religion was the chief instance of this; but the trait appeared earlier. In the summer of 1863, when I had announced my intention to come into this world but had not yet made my appearance, the family lodged at La Granja, the small imitation of Versailles not far from the Escurial, where Queen Isabella and her Court spent the season; and the public were not excluded from the park where the Queen took her daily drive. Naturally when she passed, people took off their hats or curtsied, and sometimes a group might even raise a discreet cheer. Now for some inexplicable reason, Susana was captivated by this little ceremony: she would not for the world miss seeing the Queen drive by, and she would be the first to run forward, wave her handkerchief, and cry: *¡Viva la Reina!* As this happened repeatedly, the Queen noticed it, and inquired: *¿Quien es esta niña, que se ha enamorado de mí?* "Who is this child that has fallen in love with me?" Isabella was not unaccustomed to have people, not children, protest that they loved her; but one of Susana's Sturgis characteristics was that she showed her feelings in her face, often without knowing it; and the *élan* of her movements and the light in her eye were unmistakable evidences of her emotions. She *was* in love with the Queen. How and why was a mystery. Isabella was a stout and not beautiful woman with a bad complexion; but she was frank, amiable, hearty, and easy-going (like the Sturgises) and there was the glamour of her station, her coach, her guards, and her gracious smiles. Then there was a family in Don Toribio's circle who held some position at court: *Doña Primitiva*, widow of a General Orà who had been executed for some *pronunciamiento* or conspiracy, and her daughter *Milagros*, a young woman of bold spirit who smoked cigars and was said to go about at night dressed as a man, so as to see "life". These ladies naturally retailed much Court gossip, which Susana may have listened to, and they, being in favour with the Queen, would naturally tend to describe her generous and regal qualities rather than those that might have seemed too primitively human. At any rate, Susana's enthusiasm continued, until one day the Queen stopped her carriage, beckoned to Susana, asked her her name, and after a few amiable words, said goodbye with some vague reference to the future.

Abortive contacts with the Court. Nothing more occurred, I believe, at La Granja; but later in Madrid it was arranged that Doña Primitiva should take Susana to the Palace to be formally received by the Queen. It would have been indispensable, in ordinary circumstances, that my mother should have accompanied her daughter and been received also; but my mother's state of health served as an excuse. For my mother never under any circumstances would have gone to kiss a Queen's hand, and such a Queen too, so little virtuous or stoical; and the odd thing is that she should have allowed Susana to go; but it was like my mother to let things take their course, provided she was not personally involved in the proceedings. She hated royalties as she hated priests, but it did not ruffle her, it rather entertained her, that her friends and even her daughter should be interested in such follies, and should have so much to tell about them. After all, it was more vivid than a printed novel, especially as Susana was a good mimic and would act out for us at home all that she might have seen and heard abroad.

This policy of *laissez-faire* had unpleasant consequences in this case, as in many others; for some years later, when we had moved to Avila, a virtual invitation came through the Marqués de Novaliches for Susana to become a lady-in-waiting to the Infanta Isabel, who was of the same age; and my mother was so enraged that she refused to see Novaliches at all, pretended to be ill, and left it to my poor father to explain and to make excuses: that for the moment Susana's mother was ill, that she was about to start with her daughters for the United States, and that the project of Susana's figuring at Court was incompatible with the plans of the family and with their modest resources. Susana I presume knew nothing of this proposal until long afterwards; and I never heard her express any regret that it was not accepted. But my father, who had dutiful feelings towards Novaliches, was placed in an awkward position; and my mother herself was embittered and made uncomfortable. This incident, as well as the attentions of several young men courting Susana, no doubt hastened my mother's resolve to escape to Boston, and fostered a certain distrust and resentment that was latent in her towards Susana from the first. Susana, she felt, was not loyal to her; she preferred other people and other principles. Unluckily escaping to Boston did not correct this disloyalty. From the clutches of dissolute courts and undesirable lovers Susana fell into those of the Jesuits and of religious enthusiasm.

Danger of being duped by a warm imagination. She had always warmed toward religious doctrines and practices, as she had warmed toward anything interesting and vivid, such as children's games, social pleasures, or a reigning Queen in her brilliant equipage. She was abundantly alive, and all these were spontaneous ways of giving shape to life and of enjoying it intensely. This enjoyment, in her case as in mine, always had in it a touch of comedy or even of mockery. In regard to Queen Isabella this touch of satire became conscious in time or even dominant, and while Susana never lost her sympathy with that queen and with all royalties, she saw and admitted their weaknesses and laughed at her own pleasure in those vanities. Thus she rendered her pleasure double and rendered it pure. But in respect to religion she fought against all dramatic insight or transcendental laughter. She felt the laughter coming round the corner, and she attempted to run away from it, to condemn it in herself as a diabolical temptation. It was a sad business to have to be absolutely solemn, convinced, and fanatical, against her nature and to the ruin of her possible happiness.

Society in Avila. From the age of fifteen to eighteen, when we lived in Avila, Susana had rather a limited field in which to display her adaptability, but she seems to have dominated it easily, and to have been happy in it. There was a small, modest, and grave provincial society, Avila being the quietest and most unspoiled of provincial capitals. *Tertulias* gathered together the local worthies and officials, and the town contained half a dozen presentable young men. There was a Casino, with a café on the ground floor, and upstairs a billiard-room and a dancing hall, with a small stage to it. Here an inner circle, called *El Chenique* sometimes performed amateur plays. These plays and occasional dances seem to have been the principal amusement for the young people. Susana took a leading part in them; yet I should hardly have become aware of it by her own report, because she seemed to have forgotten those early years, but our sister Josefina remembered them vividly, could recall all the people's names, and could recite the greater portion of the plays they acted, which were in verse. Josefina, who was two years younger than Susana, and most timid and dull, took little or no part in those gaieties; but she was always present at them, as she couldn't be left alone at home, and her silent mind, having nothing else to occupy it, retained every detail of her sister's doings and sayings. She and I in after years could thus reconstruct whole farces, *La Casa de Campo* and *Las Hijas de Elena* in which Susana, who had completely forgotten them, had played the heroine. Yet the impressions of those years, though overlaid, were not destroyed. When life in America had proved a failure for her, in society, at home, and in the convent where she had been a novice, Susana returned instinctively to Avila, renewed old acquaintance with one or two quiet devout ladies of the place, lived in my father's poor man's house, and eventually married one of those presentable young men (now a widower with six children) whom she had danced with in *El Chenique.*

Second immersion into Boston life. America affected Susana exactly as it affected me. The people, principally the admirably kind and civilised Bostonians who became our friends, excited our interest, attached our affection, and won our complete confidence. We laughed with them and not at them, and we thought and judged as they did on current and social matters; but beneath and in the end there was a chasm. It was only with friends of the heart, chosen friends, friends who at bottom had the same religion or philosophy with ourselves, that this chasm could be bridged; and for Susana, in this direction, it was requisite that her friends should be Catholics. Now, when she found herself again in Boston at the age of eighteen, none of the Sturgises or of their friends were Catholics; but at first that seemed not to matter, and she plunged heartily into that society, as it was in her nature to do. Yet her view of the Sturgis family and of Boston in general, as she unfolded it to us merrily at home, though friendly and kindly, was frankly comic; and none of her cousins, female or male, became intimate friends of hers or admirers. It took time—this was Boston—for the admirers and intimate friends to appear. There was a great obstacle to be surmounted: our comparative poverty. Susana couldn't dress or travel as the rest did; she couldn't invite anybody to the house. There were two sets of people, however, with whom this obstacle didn't count: the very rich and self-satisfied, who might even be attracted by an interesting young friend to help and to protect;

and the semi-foreign Catholic families that were discovered to exist even in polite Boston. To these two classes Susana's true and lasting friendships were confined.

Intimacy with Miss Sara Lowell. Of the highly placed, patronising, and somewhat older friends, the most important was Miss Sara Lowell. (It was essential to leave out the *h* in Sarah, or rather to transfer it to the first syllable and to call the lady *Sahra*.) Her traditions and standards were of the highest, and as the youngest and favourite child of a rich father, alone with him at home, she was mistress of establishments both in town and country. With Susana she could discuss all her other friends freely, as to a fresh, uninformed, and sympathetic audience. The two would sleep in the same bed, so as to have perfect privacy and endless time for confabulation. And somehow the religious question, that must have arisen in passing always conscientious and ultimate judgments on everything and everybody, seems never to have disturbed this unclouded intimacy. Miss Lowell was of course a Unitarian, and an ornament of King's Chapel; but she was a woman of the world; and I suspect that she smiled to herself a little about the proprieties, thought them expedient but not indispensable or eternal; and a few amiable pagan myths repeated or devotions practised by a younger and less well educated companion far from displeasing her, may have seemed to her engaging. They indicated the need of something beyond reason; a need that all reasonable people must end by feeling. Miss Lowell in the end felt this need in her own life; and when everybody had understood that she meant to remain single, being perfectly happy in her virgin state and finding nobody worthy of her hand, she suddenly announced her engagement to a widower as rich as herself. This widower had two sons, no longer little children; and the story reached me (the reader may imagine by what channel) that one day one of the boys by chance caught sight of his step-mother before the long glass in her dressing-room, and exclaimed—those being the days of exuberant bosoms and bustles—"But mama, you are all ups and downs!" And when the lady, who was short and plump, said he was unkind, he protested: "I am not unkind, I like it." From this domestic scene I gather that the accomplished Sara, being a sensible woman, valued the ups and downs in her person, as well as the ups, and never the downs, in her fortune.

Catholic families in Boston: the Homers.
The foreign Catholic families that became Susana's closest friends in Boston were two in number, the Homers and the Iasigis. The language in both families was French, although English inevitably tended to intrude more and more into their conversation, as it did in our own house, until in the end, for instance, I always spoke English with my brother Robert, and sometimes with Susana, although never with my mother or with my sister Josefina. This was particularly true of the Homers, because the head of that family was a pure American, so that at table—apart from whisperings among the ladies—the official language was English. Susana and I often had luncheon or early dinner at the Homers on Sundays, and as a boy I knew that household very well. There were four daughters, the eldest a little younger than Susana, and the youngest a little younger than I, but no boys; and as Mr. Homer always disappeared when we rose from table, the atmosphere of the house was thoroughly feminine, Catholic, and foreign.

In *The Last Puritan* the Boscovitz family is drawn in part after the Homers. Mrs. Homer was a native of Gibraltar where her father and later her brother held the practically hereditary post of American consul; but her mother came from Marseilles and she herself had been educated in a French convent. She had been married off to "Homer", as she always called him, in the French fashion, because he was well-off, and had been carried away to Boston helplessly, where she lived like a lap-dog in a cushioned basket, with her brood of daughters, her little belongings, and her devotions to occupy her mind. She was a great comfort to Susana, a link with the genuine human, Mediterranean, non-hypocritical world; and Susana in turn must have been an enlivening influence in that too domestic circle. The girls had various fates, none of them happy. The eldest died while still young; the second vegetated, alone and impoverished, I don't know where; the third, who had refused to marry my brother Robert, accepted one of the Iasigis instead, a thoroughly corrupt and falsely jolly *viveur*, who was sentenced to fourteen years in prison for embezzling a trust; and his poor wife, somewhat coarsened but brave, received him back after that punishment and went to live with him in retirement, on her own slender fortune, in a spirit of Christian duty and sacrifice.

A false religious vocation.
There was at least this ray of spiritual heroism and light in that moral tragedy: but what shall I say of the fourth daughter and her history? At the time of her first communion she developed an intense mystical devotion so absorbing

as to cut her off, at heart, from everything else, and so lasting that she was thought to have an unmistakable vocation to a religious life. She thought so herself, and became not only a novice, but a professed nun at the same Carmelite convent in Baltimore where Susana had made an abortive attempt to find her moral quietus. What ensued is a secret, which Susana either did not know or was pledged not to reveal; but a psychologist may perhaps guess it. The nuns secured what is extremely rare, a full dispensation for the youngest Miss Homer from her solemn vows; and at about the age of thirty she left the convent, and went to travel about alone. Her mother's relations and perhaps Susana's example led her to go to Spain; and I have Mercedes' account of the appearance and behaviour of the emancipated Carmelite nun. She was fashionably dressed, scented, and painted; her conversation was free and unorthodox; she exchanged glances and even notes with strangers at the theatre or in the streets. Poor Mercedes was on the point of breaking off relations, when the gay traveller left Madrid for Barcelona, where she had cousins, and where she married one of them and perhaps settled down.

Contrast with Susana's difficulties in a convent. This was a painful story for Susana, because it seemed a caricature or diabolical revelation of her own career, in what might have been its unconscious motives and difficulties; but I do not think the two cases similar at bottom. In the caricature the moving force was erotic, and the discovery that it was erotic and only erotic throughout explains everything: the girlish devotion, the vows, the scandal in the convent, and the dispensation obtained in Rome; but with Susana the social instinct, the general inclination to sympathy, gaiety, and fun far outbalanced anything erotic: the Sturgises have much genial warmth, but little or no passion. In the convent it was not Susana that shocked the nuns, or was enlightened about any unavowed elements in her supposed vocation. She was merely restless, uncomfortable, and bored; she found she could not dismiss the world from her heart; and she left the convent sadly, disappointed at her failure, which she liked to attribute to not being young enough and strong enough to begin a new and austerer life. And her religious faith and tone of mind were not in the least altered by this discovery. On the contrary, she hoped to preserve the Carmelite spirit, in so far as it was expressible in a life in the world.

The Iasigis. In blood the Iasigis were far more exotic than the Homers, since the father was a Turk and the mother nominally a Greek, but in language, religion, aspect, and breeding entirely French. Her mother at least must have been a Frenchwoman somehow married in Smyrna, from which the family came. There was a sharp division in it between the six males and the six females. Mr. Iasigi was visible only at meals, which were gargantuan; a short fat thick-lipped Levantine of the most unprepossessing and disquieting kind. You felt that he could think of nothing but sensuality and money; but I daresay he had hidden virtues. His sons, in different degrees, all took after him; the eldest and most decent ended by making a good marriage in Boston, as if he meant to foreswear all foreignness and become an ordinary respectable citizen; but fate overtook him. Business or pleasure had carried him on a trip to Havana, and on the return his steamer was wrecked and he was found drowned in his locked cabin. Of the second son, who married one of the Homers, I have already said enough; and the other three had the good sense to transfer themselves as soon as practicable to Europe, doubtless to Paris, to enjoy life after their own hearts.

The ladies, on the contrary, all kept within conventional bounds, and for the most part became pious old maids or pious mothers; only one came later within my range. She had married a young Bostonian whose inclinations were perhaps those of her own brothers; but he had been satisfied with dipping into Bohemian life in France and Germany, learning to speak those languages with a deceptive fluency, and studying a little music. He could then return to Boston as an art critic, and as a friend (since he was not rich enough to be a patron) of all artists, musicians, and actors. He and his good-natured agreeable wife held open house on Sunday evenings (when theatres and concert-halls were closed); there was beer with pretzels, and all artistic or Europeanised Boston, from Mrs. Gardner down, frequented those easy receptions. I remember speaking there with the prima donnas Sembrich and Emma Eames and with Madame Paderewska. I asked the latter about the fidelity of the men in Poland to the Church; and she said that they all *had* to remain good Catholics, because a soul lost to the Church meant a soul lost to Poland. This Eastern way of identifying religion with nationality gave me a useful hint for the interpretation of both.

In Boston but not of it.   These things befell after Susana's time in Boston. For her the Iasigis and the Homers were friendly households, nests of marriageable girls, where she could break away from the restraints of polite hypocrisy and could take comfort in feeling that her religion was no anomaly but perfectly natural, traditional, and a matter of course. It was the Bostonians who were eccentric and self-banished from the great human caravan. I found the same comfort in ancient literature and philosophy, which carried me beyond the Church and beneath its foundations. It is all a *Santa Maria sopra Minerva*. But towards Boston and Protestantism Susana and I had exactly the same feelings.

Susana's handicaps in fashionable or intellectual circles. I recognise now that the ripest and most settled circles in Boston were difficult for us to move in because of our poverty and lack of early friendships in that society. It was a little like the aristocracy in England, shy and secluded from strangers, but immensely simple and gentle when once you were inside. It was very difficult, for instance, for Susana to go to "parties". She had hardly any suitable clothes; she had to incur each time a relatively large expense in hired carriages, gloves and hairdresser; and she was not as accomplished or as well-informed about Boston history and people as were the leading families. Then, as she grew older, she had none of those political or artistic enthusiasms that might bring the older young ladies together. And as to the men—and one went to "parties" to be seen by the men—I suspect that Susana found them dull. She was accustomed to be made love to, and they didn't make love; not unless they deliberately intended to propose marriage. But very few, hardly any of them, intended to do that for the present. Society thus became a skirmish at very long range in a very wide field, with little danger of wounds, and no danger at all of death. Was it worth while?

Feeble admirers. I am not sure that in all those years in Beacon Street, when she was between twenty and thirty, she received a single express offer of marriage. She had admirers; but none of them such as she could seriously encourage. The best of them, a young architect terribly marked by the small-pox, was poor; and though matters went far enough for her to read Ruskin's *Stones of Venice* (which I profited by, and built my love of architecture upon) poverty on both sides made further progress impossible: and there would have been another difficulty to overcome, namely, the difference in religion. Religion was gaining on her with the fading of youth. Without having had, I believe, any serious disappointment in love, for she did not love men, she only loved their attentions, spinsterhood certainly was leaving her heart unemployed, and even her women friends were growing less communicative, less intimate, more preoccupied with their other affairs.

Family quarrels about religion. There was only religion to fill the void; and this had a disastrous effect in our own household. Josefina had always followed Susana, up to a certain point, in this as in other things, but mechanically and without any spark of emotion. There was no danger in that quarter. But I was a boy, becoming adolescent, and naturally inclined to live in the imagination. That I should catch Susana's interest in architecture, and spend my afternoons drawing plans of palaces and fronts of cathedrals, was all to the good: it occupied my young mind harmlessly; but that I should love images and church functions and the mysteries of theology was dangerous and morbid; and who was to blame for it but Susana? A conflict against Susana and against Catholicism thereupon filled our household, divided it, and ended by a separation of all parties, morally and even materially, and the separate entrenchment of each combatant in his own camp.

That Susana, being my godmother, deliberately took me in hand from the first day of my arrival in Boston, and in teaching me English and Mother Goose taught me also my prayers in English and my advanced catechism—for I already knew the elements of Christian Doctrine and Sacred History—is certain; but I think there was a complete blindness on my mother's part in supposing that any deep or permanent attachment to religious faith on my part could be achieved by Susana: and that for the reason that Susana was herself without it. I understood what she taught me very much better than she did, and I had a much greater affinity than she to a religious life; she tried it and couldn't bear it; I could have borne it gladly, if I had wished to try it.

Difference between her and me on this subject. There was another difference. She thought religion a matter of fact, like the geography of the Fiji Islands and the ways of the natives there; and as those ways were reported to be so grand and so captivating she was anxious to be convinced that the reports were true and that she might ultimately go and live in those Islands. Now I was aware, at first instinctively and soon quite clearly on historical and psychological grounds, that religion and all philosophy of that kind was *invented*. It was all conceived and worked out inwardly, imaginatively, for moral reasons; I could have invented or helped to invent it myself, if I had gone in for it; and I could have accepted it and enlarged it by my own insights if like all original religious souls I had fancied myself inspired. Such invention need not be dishonest, if it is taken for a revelation. But you can't go for the proof or confirmation of it to the Fiji Islands, or to any other part of the existing universe; you must place it, and live by it, on quite another plane. In a word, I was a spontaneous modernist in theology and philosophy: but not being pledged, either socially or superstitiously, to any sect or tradition, I was spared the torments of those poor Catholic priests or those limping Anglicans who think they can be at once modernists and believers. They can be only amateurs, at best connoisseurs, in religion. The rest for them will be only a belated masquerade.

Thus I, who was the nominal prize at stake, came out of this family quarrel without feeling a blow, and my mother, if a little hardened and embittered, was not much changed by it. But for Susana it was tragic; though perhaps not worse, perhaps more satisfactory on the whole, than it would have been to vegetate and wither, an impecunious old maid, in self-satisfied Boston.

The crisis came on slowly, and was never sharply terminated. It did not leave a scar but an ailment; and it kept passing, to the end of Susana's long life, through various phases.

Rapproche-ment **with the Philadel-phia Sturgises.**   In 1876 "Uncle Robert", head of the Philadelphia Sturgises, died; and the widow invited Susana to spend a few weeks with her, to cheer her up and keep her company. This was a somewhat unexpected proof of liking from a quarter that had never seemed sympathetic; for while "Uncle Robert" showed a traditional good-will towards us, including me, for he gave me my first nice book, a well illustrated copy of *Robinson Crusoe*, "Aunt Susie" seemed too much preoccupied with her clothes, her babies, and her gaieties to take more than a perfunctory notice of her husband's poor relations. But Susana had the gift of inspiring confidence; she was a Sturgis; she was young, available, and a person in need of being befriended. This visit to Philadelphia resulted in a lasting affection on Susana's part not so much towards her aunt as to the youngest of the children, Maisie, with whom for years afterwards, from Spain, she carried on a desultory correspondence. And the visit had another consequence that helped, as it were, to colour a little more pleasantly, the sunset of Susana's day in Boston. "Aunt Susie" sent her two trunks full of her almost new dresses, rather gay dresses, useless for a widow in mourning; and these dresses in lingering adaptations and transformations, helped to furnish Susana's wardrobe for several years. I remember them well to this day. The best was the salmon-coloured dress, as we called it, although at night it seemed only a brilliant yellow; it was elaborate with a looped overskirt, yellow satin bow-knots and scalloped edges, and a wealth all over it of little lace flounces. There were other gowns, less ornate and good for daily use, that outlasted the fashions; and there were some that never were worn at all, because Susana's interest in society had begun to flag, and she had at best but little pleasure in dress. She wished to look well, of course; but the how and the why of it escaped her. Neither she nor Josefina were good at needlework. Had they resisted their mother's lessons and example, or had nothing been done to initiate them into these arts? I think both causes coöperated; and it was a pity in many ways.

The great climacteric. The first five years that we lived in Roxbury, which included my undergraduate days at Harvard, were the darkest in Susana's life. She was between thirty and thirty-five years of age; her Boston sewing-circle, her Boston parties, were things of the past; there was sullen disunion and hostility at home; and there were no new interests. She read and re-read the works of Santa Teresa; she conceived plans of offering up her life in sacrifice for the salvation (which seemed unlikely) of the rest of her family; and she considered whether she might not have a vocation to tread in Santa Teresa's footsteps. Her confessor was Father Fulton, head of the Jesuit College attached to the church of the Immaculate Conception, where we usually went to high mass on Sundays—Susana and I only, because Josefina, thoroughly frightened by our mother's intense hostility to the Church, had given up going. Father Fulton, who belonged I believe to a Maryland Catholic family, had a rather philosophical mind; a little sleepy, like his half-closed eyes, not perhaps quite healthy, as his sallow complexion and heavy cheeks were not quite healthy. He admired the metaphysics of Coleridge; and perhaps understood it better than he did the feminine heart. There is a curious cruelty mixed sometimes with American shrewdness and humour. The sharp mind finds things queer, crooked, perverse; it puns about them; and it doesn't see why they shouldn't be expected and commanded to be quite other than they are; but all this without much hope of mending them, and a sardonic grin. My old teacher Royce had something of this perverse idealism, and I suspect there was something of it in Father Fulton. Didn't he see that Susana's imaginary vocation was false? He probably saw no reason why, *a priori*, it should not have been true; and he didn't positively dissuade her from testing it. When the test was applied, he advised her not to persist; but this experiment had involved untold conflicts, doubts, vacillations, and disappointments, which might have been avoided by a little more wisdom.

Her unfitness for the monastic life. I was living at Harvard and it was only for week-ends that I went to Roxbury. I remember one day, coming home with Susana from church, I said I thought I was better fitted than she for the cloister; and she replied, "You have *one* of the things required. You are *detached*." This was her way of expressing the fact that she lacked this necessary element. She lacked it so completely that she was most unhappy in going to the convent by her own free will, and quite happy (according to my mother) in coming out of it (against her will, according to her own account) by the advice or injunction of her superiors. I accompanied her to Baltimore; there was no simplicity, no ease, in her way of entering the convent or of being received there. She was too old, thirty-four, and too full of old memories and attachments to be happy in a round of mystical devotions; she was tired, and became sleepless. She insisted in her letters, and in her talk to the end of her life, that she loved our mother very much. These protestations seemed to me very strange; apart from the old childish bond that goes with blood and early associations, she *couldn't* love our mother very much: only enough to suffer, as I did not, from her hostility to everything we most cared about. Perhaps this morbid love (for there was something cowed or cowardly about it) was hypnotic and allied to forgotten experiences; perhaps it was only a verbal cloak for Susana's love of people in general, and her craving to be loved. In any case, it was a symptom of her radical unfitness for an ascetic regimen.

She tries it and gives it up. She had been for three months in the convent as what they called a Postulant, dressed in her own clothes but following the routine of the community, and had grown much attached to the Mother Superior and to the Mistress of Novices, when she became a novice herself, having her hair cut, and wearing the nuns' habit with a white veil in lieu of the black one. Talking with my cousin Elvira and me some years later in Avila, she said that this attachment, especially to the Mistress of Novices (who acted I suppose as a sort of female confessor or spiritual director) was the strongest she had ever felt in her life; and this assertion, making due allowance for dramatic exaggeration, seems to me interesting. It shows that she had never been much in love with any of her admirers, nor with her future husband, who was then courting her once more; and that her love for our mother had never been spontaneous, but a sort of unwilling and resentful love, a sense of subjection to an irrational influence. I saw a letter or two written afterwards by this nun to Susana; they were commonplace pious motherly letters; but motherly affection was new to Susana, and especially a motherly affection extending to spiritual troubles and needs, and bringing spiritual consolation. If when a girl she could fall in love at sight with a commonplace Queen, for being motherly and amiable, it is intelligible that as an unhappy woman she should have fallen in love with a gentle nun, for being wise and motherly. It is a wonderful thing to come upon intelligence and a guiding hand in the realm of spirit.

In spite of these affectionate ties and precisely because of this intelligent guidance, before six months of novitiate were over it was agreed that Susana should leave the convent. Then our mother did a very kind thing such as her usual manner would not have led us to expect: she with Josefina left Robert alone in the house with one servant (I was at College) and went to spend the winter in a boarding-house in Baltimore, so that Susana should not have to return home directly, and might have the relief of a wholly new scene and new faces.

She returns to Spain. When they came back to Boston I was on the point of leaving for Avila and for an indefinite student-life in Germany. I could not observe Susana's conduct or moods; but I believe she lived almost in seclusion, saw none of her old friends, and during the next winter decided to return to Spain, at least for some years, where she could live with Doña Victorina and with my father alternately. This was practicable, because when Robert reached his majority, the trust my mother had established on the occasion of her second marriage terminated, and her Sturgis children came into their money. It was a most modest sum, at that time only a few hundred dollars a year: but this was enough to get on with in Spain, living with old friends, and contributing a little to the household expenses.

Our finances improve. I went to meet her in September 1887 at Gibraltar, and returned with her to Avila; and in the winter she joined Doña Victorina and Mercedes in Madrid. But she still had, as it were, one foot in the stirrup. Could she live on in this way, as paying guest at other people's houses, for ever? Would she return to dreary

Roxbury? Could she persuade our mother to move back to Spain and reunite the family? Only one circumstance was favourable. Robert had taken charge of the family property and was doing very well in his investments. Without venturing on what is called speculation, he bought and sold safe investments with excellent judgment. The Beacon Street house had long been sold, the house in Boylston Place and India Building were sold at good prices, and the family income increased steadily, until it became ten times what it had been in the beginning. Had Susana foreseen this development, which would have enabled her to set up a comfortable establishment of her own in Spain, she might have been content to do so. She had friends enough, and would have made many more; and the current affairs of the world, political and social, would have kept her mind occupied and her wits sharp.

She marries an old admirer and spends the rest of her life in Avila. But how could this favourable turn of fortune be foreseen? She was simply a little better off, but still had only a slender income; and she was alone. Unfortunately, not being a Sturgis, I had no share in the family trust, and had to earn my living; otherwise Susana and I at that time, about 1890, could have joined forces and lived very happily together, by preference in Avila. There are nice old houses there, one of which we could have restored and turned into a dignified and peaceful residence; and both summer and winter there, in one's own house with a few modern conveniences, are pleasant and healthy. But the gods otherwise decreed: and Susana decided to marry her old admirer Celedonio Sastre, in spite of his crusty old provincial habits and his six children. Her married life forms another chapter, which I need not write separately. Glimpses enough of it will come in the course of my own visits; for Avila never ceased to be a place of frequent pilgrimage for me so long as Susana was alive.

Circumstances had thwarted or misled her impulses. Old age—she lived to be seventy-seven, as Josefina did also—changed her character very little; perhaps time did not change her at all, but only brought out more clearly—worldly respect and timidity being gone—her frank and sensible humanity. It had been veiled by untoward circumstances and sophisticated intellectually. Poverty and religion had long constrained and misled her. I do not mean for a moment that it was incongruous for her to be a believing Catholic. It was not only congruous with her temperament, but essential to her breeding and background and to the place she filled in the world.

Why else should her good American relations have turned to her and hugged her in their troubles? Catholicism is the most human of religions, if taken humanly: it is paganism spiritually transformed and made metaphysical. It corresponds most adequately to the various exigencies of moral life, with just the needed dose of wisdom, sublimity, and illusion. Only it should be accepted humanly, traditionally, as part of an unquestioned order, a totalitarian moral heritage, like one's language and family life, leaving religious controversy to the synods and metaphysical speculation to the schools. The synods and the schools make enormous assumptions, and perhaps reason on them correctly: that is a question of art and technique with which the layman had better not meddle; but as to the need or importance of those assumptions each man and each society decides afresh, and instinctively, because the controversies that agitate the public are inevitably superficial, making contrary and hasty assumptions of their own, without knowing it.

Materialistic misunderstanding of spiritual things. Susana's misfortune was that her instinctive and ardent sympathy with Catholic and Spanish conventions was crossed by controversy and strained speculatively, when she had no capacity for speculation; so that instead of finding peace and a secret symbolic life in religion, she turned religion into a problem and a torment. She became fanatical against her natural good sense, and was worried about the salvation of her friends and relations as if that were not in God's hands, and as if the salvation of souls were a physical event, like the saving or drowning of passengers in a shipwreck. That was exactly how the early Christians conceived it, so that her zeal was strictly orthodox; but this only shows how orthodoxy must be taken with a grain of salt, to keep it sweet and prevent it from turning into madness. The pity was that both in religion and in family life circumstances should have suppressed and embittered the native warmth of her nature, her need of being impassioned. She needed to be carried away, to be ravished; and since the days of being ravished by irresistible bold men were gone, she dreamt of being ravished, like Santa Teresa, by sacrifice and prayer. But Susana was not made either for prayer or for sacrifice, but decidedly, like the other Sturgises, for that natural joyous enthusiasm and kindness which are their own reward. Before sacrifice and prayer can be self-rewarding a revolution has to be worked in the soul; and though Susana knew of this, she never experienced it in her own person. It would have required her to key her nature up to a note that it was incapable of sustaining.

Profound coincidence of body and mind.   I have said nothing of Susana's appearance and physique, yet what is more important in life than our bodies or in the world than what we look like? And not only for a woman. The crusty old Hobbes observes that good looks are a power even in a man, since they predispose women and strangers in his favour. But women and strangers are not all fools, and there is something unprejudiced and disinterested in a first impression that runs deeper than any laboured or conventional judgment. Body, character, and mind are formed together by that single hereditary organising power which the ancients called the psyche or soul; so that however much the mind or the body may be distorted by accidental influences, at bottom they must always correspond; and the innocent eye often catches this profound identity. We are arrested by a beautiful body because the sight of it quickens in ourselves the same vital principle that fashioned that body. And so too any deformity or distortion offends us in beings akin to ourselves, and ways of life contrary to ours seem to us monstrous even to look upon, like the wallowing hippopotamus opening a vast mouth half as large as himself. Chaos is fertile in monsters destroyed as soon as they appear, but definite species establish and perpetuate themselves unchanged where the seasons revolve steadily and the very enemies of life are so constant that means of defence may be prepared against them. In the human family it is an open question how far in-breeding will perfect or debilitate a type, and how far half-breeds may form new and healthy races.

Susana's appearance.   I like to muse on this theory apropos of my brother and sisters and of the American melting-pot in general. My mother's first marriage seems not to have been eugenically a perfect match. Of five children two died in infancy and of the other three only Susana could be compared to her ancestors in vital fibre; and yet in her an odd constitutional disharmony was visible to the eye. She had elements of pure beauty, but neither her face nor her figure was well composed. Most arresting were her large clear eyes, between hazel and green, and *à fleur de tête*, with delicately penciled almost invisible eyebrows much higher up; and this effect of aristocratic innocence was reinforced by the high smooth forehead; so that when she was a young girl she could have posed in a *tableau vivant* for *La Belle Jardinière*. Yet those beautiful eyes were rather too close together, and that calm forehead was too narrow; the oval of the face, in time, became decidedly pear-shaped; and if the little mouth went perfectly with the eyes, the nose that intervened was too long and pointed, and too flat under the forehead. Altogether this countenance, when animated, arrested and held people's attention. In a Victorian epoch when ladies were not made up, it was conspicuous for a youthful white and ruddy complexion and a great liveliness, because those Madonna-like eyes surprised you by their subtle changes in expression, their involuntary unaffected confession of eagerness, intelligence, or fun. In conversation everything was fused into a vivid personality, but in repose you couldn't help wishing that so many good points had been combined differently.

It was especially in her figure that the disharmony was obvious. Above the waist Susana was slender, as if designed by the same hand as her eyebrows; but if the upper half of her figure imitated Raphael, the lower half most successfully imitated Rubens. She had very small hands and feet, quite Spanish, with short fingers proper for a dumpy woman; yet she was tall, American in her movements, and entirely without our mother's deftness and grace. She and her sister would never dance: they were conscious of doing it so badly that they refused to do it. As Susana grew older her weight became too great for her small feet, walking tired her and soon grew painful. For a time after her marriage she had a small victoria in which she could drive, but in the end she ceased to go out, even to church, and set up a chapel at home, where a Dominican from the great monastery of Santo Tomás, in the valley beneath her windows, might come to say Mass on Sundays and feast-days, and give her Communion.

Her true self. The imperfections I could not help seeing in Susana and the points—very few—on which we did not sympathise, were a source of unhappiness to me, for she occupied a niche in my pantheon where I could never place any other creature. I remember how seriously my father upset me one day, after Susana had returned to Spain and had lived with him for a season, when he said: "Ah, *Susanita*, whom we thought the world of, so exceptional, so sprightly, so perfect, now she has become a woman like any other woman." There was truth, I couldn't deny it, in this judgment, but there was no charity. Susana was still herself, we are all always ourselves at bottom, however disfigured by the incrustations of life. She had been defeated by unhappy circumstances, forced out of her native element, denied the *Lebensraum* necessary to her nature; and charity will always judge a soul not by what it has succeeded in fashioning externally, not by the body or the words or the works that are the wreckage of its voyage, but by the elements of light and love that this soul infused into that inevitable tragedy.

VI

*Avila**

Accidental connection with Avila. Avila became by chance the headquarters of my family in Spain; we had no hereditary bond with that ancient and noble town. The first of us to go there was my uncle Santiago, sent no doubt by his official superiors, as a sort of punishment, to the worst of government posts. I fear he was rather a merry and lazy fellow, given to drink, and not useful in the office; yet his chiefs had the virtues as well as the vices of nepotism; and if advancement went automatically to their relations and to persons recommended by the big-wigs, still room was made for the ne'er-do-wells also in the smallest and dullest of provincial capitals. My father lighted on Avila because his brother was there; and the place recommended itself on acquaintance for being in the Old Castile of his youth, healthy, tranquil, and cheap. My mother too was willing to go and live there when, in 1866, she agreed to postpone her return to America. At least the town was accessible, being on the main line between Madrid and Paris, habitable in summer as well as in winter, and safely remote from the Court, from fashion, and from corrupt society. After three years she was finally able to escape with her daughters; yet unsuspected associations remained in their young minds with unsuspected virtues in that place, so that both eventually returned to live and to die there; and there they both are buried.

Excellent *Aussichtsthurm.* As for me, I was scarcely three years old when we moved to Avila, and I was nearly seventy when it ceased to be the centre of my deepest legal and affectionate ties. That these ties, albeit the deepest, should have left me so remarkably free was a happy circumstance for my philosophy. It taught me to possess without being possessed, yet it gave me a most firm and distinctive station. For the freest spirit must have some birthplace, some *locus*

---

*Pronounced *Ah'vilah*, from the Latin *Abŭla*, from which the official Spanish adjective, *abulense.*

some *locus standi* from which to view the world and some innate passion
by which to judge it. Spirit must always be the spirit of some body.
Now the chance that made me an exiled Spaniard and linked me in
particular to Avila (rather, let us say, than to Reus) was singularly
fortunate. The austere inspiration of these mountains, these battlemented city walls and these dark churches could not have been more
chivalrous or grander; yet the place was too old, shrunken, barren,
and high and dry to impose its limitations on a travelling mind; it
was a mountain-top and not a prison. Standing there, the spirit was
situated, challenged, instructed; it was not controlled.

So too   The same thing, by another happy chance, might be
Boston and   said of my other principal point of attachment, namely,
Harvard.   Boston and Harvard College. The extreme contrast between the two centres and the two influences became itself a blessing:
it rendered flagrant the limitations and the contingency of both. Granted
that I was to awake in Spain in the nineteenth century, I could have
found myself in no place less degraded than Avila; and granted that
I was to be educated in America and to earn my bread there, I could
have fallen on no place friendlier than Harvard. In each of these places
there was a maximum of air, of space, of suggestion; in each there
was a minimum of deceptiveness and of the power to enslave. The
dignity of Avila was too obsolete, too inopportune, to do more than
stimulate an imagination already awakened, and lend reality to history;
while at Harvard a wealth of books and much generous intellectual
sincerity went with such spiritual penury and moral confusion as to
offer nothing but a lottery ticket or a chance at the grab-bag to the
orphan mind. You had to bring a firm soul to this World's-Fair; you
had to escape from this merry-go-round, if you would make sense of
anything or come to know your own mind.

The typical   In quality Avila is essentially an *oppidum*, a walled city,
oppidum.   a cathedral town, all grandeur and granite; yet it is so
small as to seem in the country. Step out of one of the lofty gates
and you are at once amid wheat-fields or on rocky and windy moors.
At this altitude primitive bald nature has coexisted for ages with the
tightest and most fortified civilisation, ecclesiastical and military. Here
no one need hanker after *rus in urbe*; he has the opposite, which is
almost an equivalent. He has what we might call *urbs ruri*, or rather
oppidum in agris. *Urbs ruri* would be a good name for some great English
country-house with its park, and its subject farms and villages; for in
the mansion there would be all the social amenities and sophistication

of London, and yet, looking about, the eye would see nothing but emerald lawns and blue horizons, while at the gates the thinly-peopled country would lie open to all lordly sports, from hunting and shooting down to driving, walking and golf. Avila, on the contrary, is an instance of *oppidum in agris*; not a private seat to which the great retire for pleasure and quietness, but a defensible eminence, perhaps with an ancient place of pilgrimage in it, where the country people have collected and walled in their granaries, leaving an open space in the midst for their meetings and fairs. Here in time the surrounding landlords will build themselves town houses, and perhaps come habitually to live, without surrendering their farms or neglecting their farming interests. They will form the ruling class, the *patres conscripti*, of the little republic, the typical ancient town, with its local religion and its gradually developing political eloquence.

Imperialist influences and dominations. Very likely the original pre-Roman *Abula* was a town of this kind; but that native simplicity has not survived the passage of migrations and conquests, armed with alien imperial force, or with the force of immensely contagious militant religions. After the Romans and the Visigoths, the Moors swept over this region, but have left no such traces of their arts as may be seen at the not very distant Toledo. The great walls, the glorious crown of Avila, might have looked much as they do now in the Moorish epoch, for they are such as prevailed during the whole Byzantine millennium, from the fourth to the fourteenth century; but in their present form they belong to Christian times. There is a sweep and unity in their plan that indicate royal government and national resources; this had become a stronghold of kings against rival kings. And with this two new features, foreign to the ancient city, impressed themselves on Avila, and still, in their decay, lend it its dominant character: the seats of the nobility and those of the clergy. In my day several great families still had houses in Avila, to which some of them sometimes returned, Oñate, Superunda, Santa Marta, Parcent; but aristocratic families from different provinces and kingdoms had long intermarried, so that each great title might go with estates scattered all over Spain; and estates in the province of Avila, or palaces in the town, were not likely to be those of most importance to the family or favourite places for them of residence. Many great houses were therefore neglected, or turned into public offices or private apartments. Better preserved, even if somewhat shrunken and depopulated, were the convents and churches. The former Jesuit College, built into the walls and replacing the upper part of them over the *Rastro*, had become the bishop's palace; and many monasteries and convents, rather hidden behind blank walls, occupied large mysterious spaces in the town or choice positions in the suburbs. Avila was a distinctly clerical town, with Santa Teresa for its native patron and chief glory.

Market-days.   Yet the fundamental realities are still in evidence. The town walls, for all their massiveness, do not shut out the country from the eye. At every turn, through one of the city gates, or over some bastion, the broad valley remains visible, with its checkerboard of ploughed fields and the straggling poplars lining the strait roads, or clustered along the shallow pools by the river; and at night, in the not too distant mountains, the shepherds' fires twinkle like nether stars. Or if the townspeople are too busy and near-sighted to remember the country, the country every Friday morning invades the town, and fills the market place with rustics and rustic wares. At dawn they ride in from their villages in groups, on their trembling little donkeys, the man or woman perched on the hind quarters, behind the four-pocketed wicker saddle-bags brimming with scarlet tomatoes, bright green and red peppers, lettuce, and yellow chick-peas or clod-coloured potatoes. In my time the peasant costumes, though tending to disappear, were still prevalent: the men in broad black hats, short jackets, bright sashes and leather greeves, attached like armour over their knee-breeches and blue stockings; and the women bell-like in their wealth of brilliant flannel petticoats, worn one over another, and the topmost on occasion pulled up to serve as a shawl, and protect the many-coloured kerchiefs covering their heads and shoulders. Nor was garden produce all that these self-sufficing peasants brought to market: there were also home-made garments in plenty, such as *alpargatas*, or canvas shoes with rope soles, and country crockery, *botijos* and *cántaros*, shining in their newness, and no less smooth and rotund than the gorgeous melons and watermelons of mid-summer.

No danger that such a town should think itself self-supporting like a capitalist, or existing by divine right to rule and instruct the world. The country has created the city, built it up at the cross-roads between one threshing-ground and another, where the bridge crossed the river, and the riding-paths met leading beyond the valley to the neighbouring market-towns. From the country each city still draws its wealth and sustenance, as well as the fresh hands required for its multiplying trades, the servants for its great houses, and the young soldiers to be enlisted, by force or by bribes, in its feuds and conquests.

The feast of
Corpus
Christi. Markets and fairs were dwarfed at Avila, however, by the religious feasts, doubtless much decayed in my day, yet still imposing. I remember the procession of Corpus Christi, wonderful in my childish eyes. And this not at all on account of the *gigantones*, grotesque card-board and cambric giants that formed the comic part of the show. These were monstrous primitive caricatures such as the raw mind loves, originally no doubt often obscene, and were still allowed to precede or to follow the religious pageant, like an Aristophanic farce after three tragedies. No: farce and even obscenity fall flat in early childhood; it is lovely marvels that entrance. Yet it was hardly the theological mystery that impressed me, the Eucharist as a means of grace: that too requires experience to comprehend it, and a second mind. The lovely mystery glittered on its own spectacular plane, the wonder was intrinsic to it, like that of the stars. To have explained would have cheapened it. At the age of six or seven I could feel the happy excitement of this feast, without words to express it or ideas to justify it; but had words and ideas been at my command, they would have been like those that come to the French writer Alain on such an occasion. The occasion creates emotion, and the emotion creates intuitions to focus it and to lend it form. Was not this the festival of the summer solstice? Did not the summer sun and the June roses fill it with light and fragrance? Was not everybody happy and gaily dressed? Did not tapestries and damasks hang from the balconies, or where these were lacking, at least some gay coverlet or shawl or table cloth? Did not gold thread and tinsel shine everywhere from vestments and banners? Were not the sun's rays doubly reflected from the golden monstrance that seemed to imitate them? And as the Host approached, borne high in a silver shrine amid lights and flowers, did not doves, let loose from some window, soar and circle in the upper air, while handfuls of rose-leaves fluttered down like snowflakes on the procession? And the Host itself, the mystic centre of all this joy, what was it but the bread of life, white wheaten bread sublimated into the pure principle of eternal happiness? For although hidden from the eye, the red wine that can turn to blood was not absent from the heart, and every holiday influence seemed fused together into this sacrament of union.

Pagan and
Christian
symbolism. All this might be conceived to be the latent burden of my childish wonder, if the eventual poet who gave form to it had no further experience and no contrary inspiration: it is all that Alain cares to note, whose philosophy is rich in casual intuitions, but without foundations or results. What a sensitive child might feel, and a pagan satirist might recognise in this pageant might indeed not go beyond the echo of some cult of the sun and the harvest, of golden Apollo and golden Ceres, not without some reminiscences of Bacchus. We might even go a step further and see here only a prelude to the *Pervigilium Veneris* with its unforgettable refrain: *Cras amet qui nunquam amavit, quique amavit cras amet.* But that would be to take a false turn in the reading of history, a turn that, at the cross-roads, history did not take. To reach Corpus Christi moral evolution had to move in the opposite direction. These little boys and little girls dressed in white, fresh from their first communion, are not simply preparing to make love, and tomorrow to sing *Little Roger Coming Home from the Fair*. Very likely some of them will do so, but it will not be in continuation of this ceremony: they will do it rebelliously, sullenly, or sneakingly, perfectly aware of their change of front. This feast commemorates the institution of the Eucharist on the eve of the Passion. It was moved from Maundy Thursday only because too much overshadowed there by Calvary still to come; whereas now, after Pentecost, it could be celebrated joyfully, and be felt to be an initiation into a happy but transfigured life; a sacrament of love, indeed, but of a love made selfless by renunciation and sacrifice. The sun, the banners, the rose-leaves, the young children are not out of place in this feast; they rhyme with the new joy and innocence to be achieved; the purity of nature harmonising perfectly, while it lasts, with a chastened purity of spirit.

Those to whom such things seem nonsense must be puzzled at the vogue that the cult of the Sacrament has acquired in the present conceited but distracted age: it seems incongruous with dominant industrialism and with opinion controlled by the daily press. Perhaps it is a safety-valve, a self-defensive movement of the human psyche, threatened with absolute servitude, like that of the working ants.

The feast of **La Santa.** The rich, the polite, the well-informed about everything, would perhaps see more in the other feast that I chiefly remember at Avila: an autumn feast, the apotheosis of a reforming and literary woman. Santa Teresa was a native of Avila, and remains the patron saint and chief celebrity of the town. She is not buried there, her heart alone is kept as a relic in the chapel built over the room in which she was born; and her beautiful image, an image almost identified with her now by local sentiment, stands or rather kneels over the same altar. It is a wooden image, movable and fit to be carried in procession: only the attitude and the face and hands manifest the artist; the rest is dressed in the Carmelite habit, modified by a gorgeous mantle, a golden nimbus, and many jewels. Yet the sculptor and the saint triumph over these accessories, and we see the enraptured nun, pale and heroic, lifted from the earth by the power of faith and love. Yet Santa Teresa was eminently sane; she was considerate of circumstances, of particular cases, of human weakness and the humours of fate; she was distinctly modern. She can appeal to the pragmatist in the believer: a dangerous tendency, it seems to me, that carries religion into politics and, almost inevitably, coarsens religion itself into a sort of celestial politics and diplomacy. One world is enough, to my feeling, and I should wish religion to digest and transmute this life into ultimate spiritual terms rather than commit us to fresh risks, ambitions, and love-affairs in a life to come. But my impulsive half-American sister was an ardent disciple of Santa Teresa; and something unsatisfactory in Susana's piety perhaps prejudices my judgment in respect to the perfection of her model. Religion in Susana seemed to remain always strained, and did not sweeten her old age. Did she perhaps doubt the truth of her faith, and did she assert it so persistently precisely because, at heart, she doubted it? Santa Teresa had no such secret unrest; but perhaps she would not have escaped it had she breathed for twenty years an American atmosphere. Fixity of tradition, of custom, of language is perhaps a prerequisite to complete harmony in life and mind. Variety in these matters is a lesson to the philosopher and drives him into the cold arms of reason; but it confuses the poet and the saint, and embitters society.

Religious courtesies and rivalries. In Avila, in these processions of Santa Teresa, there were charming survivals of popular naiveté, worthy of the middle ages. The Saint was too great, the crowds too large, for everything to go on in her own church: ten days before the feast she was borne to the Cathedral, where the image of the Virgin Mary was brought out from her chapel to welcome the pilgrim; and the two statues, one to the right the other to the left of the high altar, presided over the ensuing novena. When this was finished, another procession was formed to carry the Saint back to her own home; but such was her ascendency in heaven as well as on earth, that the Virgin Mary herself could not forbear to accompany her parting guest at least half way on the journey. At the appointed place, an open square where the eye could extend for some distance, the procession halted. Santa Teresa, who preceded (ecclesiastical etiquette requiring that the greatest shall come last) then turned completely round, and made three deep obeisances to the Queen of Heaven, who amid the delighted whispers and gratified vanity of the crowd actually made an obeisance in return, and then majestically moved away towards the Cathedral; whereupon the Saint resumed her homeward progress. So much for popular piety: but the pious also have their little human dissensions. At another hour there was another procession, by a rival confraternity, carrying a different newly bought image of Saint Teresa, in the style of Saint Sulpice. And why? Because the regular Confraternity of Santa Teresa, whose property the old venerable image was, was said to be in the hands of rich men and ecclesiastics; and the artisans had seceded and formed a different confraternity of their own, with a modern pink and white image, plain painted stucco without silks or jewels, that they liked better.

First sight of Avila from the north. To confirmed pedestrians like my father and me the friendly if rugged visage of Avila appeared more in its environs than within its walls. Each time that, coming from Paris in the 1880's and 1890's, after my second night in the train, the dawn warned me that I must be approaching my destination, it was always with a beating heart that I looked for the names of the last stations, Arévalo, then Mingorría; after which, at any moment, I might expect to see on the right, sloping down gently towards the bed of the invisible river, the perfect walls of Avila, every bastion shining clear in the level rays of the sun, with the cathedral tower, in the midst rising only a little above the line of battlements, and no less imperturbably solid and grave. The stone in that level sunlight took on a golden tint, beautiful and almost joyful against the blackish rocks and arid slopes of the descending hills, only relieved here and there by fringes of poplars or dark green oaks. The landscape near Avila (that, I suppose, of an extinct glacier) is too austere to be beautiful, too dry and barren; yet it reveals eloquently the stony skeleton of the earth; not a dead skeleton like the mountains of the moon but like the mountains of Greece, vivified at least by the atmosphere, and still rich in fountains and in hidden fields. After all, Castile is not so high and dry as Arabia, which also has its green spots; the whole Spanish table-land slopes gently westward and southwestward towards Portugal and the Atlantic, whence come its rains and where its rivers debouch without impediment. Avila sits on the very tip of a tongue of high land stretching in this direction; and its peculiar picturesqueness depends on the circumstance that, although situated among the northern foothills of the Castilian sierras it does not look northward but southward toward those very mountains, from a parallel minor spur. Being more often cold than warm, it has turned its face and opened its windows to the sun. From the promenade of the Rastro or from my brother-in-law's house on the crest of the same southern slope, the eye consequently dominates the pleasanter and more humane aspect of the country. At one's feet lie the roofs of a picturesque suburb, not without its church and belfry; in the fields beyond rises the great monastery of Santo Tomás; you see the long straight roads, sometimes lined with trees, that cross the broad valley, and you may even catch a glimpse of the river, although in summer it is little more than a string of pools, with a little water trickling from one to another, or hiding amongst heaps of stones and stretches of sand. Beyond all this, to close the vista, rise the sharp peaks of the Sierra de Avila, and the more distant and massive Sierra de Gredos, both alike purple to the eye, and as it were liquified by excess of light.

The hermitage of Sonsolès. In this direction there was an interesting goal for a long walk in cool weather; and a walk is pleasanter when it is directed to some specific spot, where one may stop, look about, and rest a little before turning satisfied homeward. This was the Hermitage of Our Lady of Sonsolès, a large stone chapel with a farmhouse attached, built on an eminence at the foot of the sierras, with a grove of trees before it, a fountain, and some stone benches. In my father's day we seldom visited it, because my visits then fell in mid-summer, and the walk across the whole valley was long and dusty in the sun; but later, when I could stay with my sister in the autumn, I could walk there alone, or sometimes accompanied by my brother-in-law who however rode his mule, while I and his son Rafael (my usual companion) went on foot.

My brother-in-law's devotion to the *numen loci*. Celedonio, middle-aged and heavy, didn't come on my account, although he pretended to do so. He came on a religious pilgrimage. My fondness for this excursion served only as a hint to his secret conscience, that perhaps he had neglected Our Lady of Sonsolès too long. On these occasions it was therefore in order to enter the Chapel, and to kneel for a while in prayer, or as if praying, before the miraculous image. My brother-in-law's piety was of a primitive, prudential, and chthonic kind, not at all theological. He with his whole family marched dutifully together to confession and communion once a year at the

Easter season, according to the precept of the Church, and he went to mass on Sundays, unless something prevented; but he would have nothing to do with modern devotions, or the people who, as he said, *se comían a Dios*, gobbled up God, every day. Religion to his mind was and ought to be a formality, like calling on the authorities, respecting the written law, and keeping up the ancient dignity of church and state. One mustn't offend the powers that be: and these powers, according to his agricultural sense of cause and effect, were mysterious and multi-form. Our Lady of Sonsolès was one of them. He carried in his waistcoat-pocket a small silver reproduction of her image, and as Sonsolès was visible from the windows of his dining-room, before sitting down at table, he invariably went to the window, as if to examine the look of the weather, pulled the little image out of his pocket, lifted (as if to scratch his head) the cap he always wore in the house, muttered a word or two in the direction of Sonsolès, and kissed the tiny amulet before slipping it back into its hiding-place. This was his private grace before meat, good for his whole household, well-known to everybody, but never spoken of.

Two miracles and a problem. On occasion, however, Celedonio would tell us about the miracles worked by this particular *numen*. One was commemorated by the votive model of a seventeenth century ship that we might all see hanging from the rafters of the Chapel at Sonsolès, and depicted in the large painting on one of the walls. Someone, in a storm at sea, had invoked the aid of Our Lady under this advocation, and had been saved from shipwreck. Had I been quite at ease in Celedonio's company (as I never was) I might have asked him whether he thought that, if this mariner had invoked, say, Our Lady of the Pillar instead of Our Lady of Sonsolès he would have been less likely to escape. And if he had hesitated, I then could have aired my own strictly orthodox theology and said that the intercession of the Virgin Mary would of course be equally efficacious under whatever name she was invoked; but that the prayer, in each person, might be more spontaneous and trustful, and therefore worthier of being heard, if it were associated with the favours and the cultus familiar to him at home. Celedonio would have (or should have) congratulated me on this explanation; but he would certainly have thought me a dangerous person if I had asked whether, if that mariner had invoked not the Virgin Mary but Castor and Pollux, he might have been no less earnest and no less worthy of his reward. Whatever name we may invoke, is not prayer always essentially addressed to whatsoever real power we may depend upon to liberate us from the troubles that pursue us? Superstition may variously deceive the fancy; it never changes the allegiance of the heart, which I suppose is all that matters from a spiritual point of view.

Celedonio's allegiance, at least in his old age, was solidly prudential, and such as befitted a farmer, a lawyer, an administrator, and a *pater familias*. Perhaps in his youth he had had dreams: he had been in love with Susana, a love apparently never quite extinguished: for he had hung opposite his desk, where he could see it whenever he looked up from his papers, or stopped to light a cigarette, an oil painting of Susana, at the age of fifteen, holding me in her arms, done in those early days by my father, after a photograph; and there were certain romantic vistas in his mind concerning Spanish history, and in particular concerning this shrine of Sonsolès. He vouched personally for a modern miracle proving its sanctity. A certain person, whom at first he named, but who later became vague and might ultimately have been identified by tradition with himself, was one day riding across the valley when he was overtaken by a violent thunderstorm, and imprudently took shelter under a solitary oak by the wayside. The oak was struck and riven by lightning; the horse was killed, and the rider's clothes burned; yet the man had raised his eyes towards Our Lady of Sonsolès, had invoked her protection, and had miraculously escaped.

Natural religion at home. Without counting on miraculous favours, I too felt a genuine sanctity, a pagan sanctity, hanging about Sonsolès. Nothing forbidding, nothing ominous, but a sort of invisible sympathy of all things with man, when he takes his place gladly among them. The sanctuary was old, simple, solid, nobly placed on the hillside, with an enclosed grove before it, and a stone fountain, from which the water flowed in paved channels among the trees, keeping the grass green in the shady places. Chapel, farmhouse, and barns were contiguous along one side of the enclosure, all equally familiar possessions, ancestral, and tended with equal prudence and care. Poultry, a dog and a cat, even a stray pig or two formed a happy family, not useless near a temple, any more than the donkeys and sheep in the background; for this was a place of pilgrimage, travellers must be refreshed, and there was even a rude space serving as a bull-ring at the yearly feast when a fair was held, with great concourse from the neighbouring villages. From these coarse pleasures and hub-bub in the hot sunlight, and from these troubles of the poor, it was all the more grateful to slip for a moment into the darkness of the cool oratory, and visit the Virgin in her placid unearthly splendour. The universe, our own souls, then revealed to us another dimension, beside those of our labours and sorrows.

The chapel was a perfect little temple, dark and windowless save for some opening in the roof. No modern ceiling or plastered walls or wooden flooring, but only rough stone everywhere and bare rafters; yet the shrine was ornate, and the image of Our Lady of Sonsolès, rather less than life-size, stood magnificently dressed and crowned, her white and gold mantle and rich veil being piously worked and renewed on occasion by Celedonio's daughter and other young ladies of Avila. "Sonsolès" means, or may mean, *they are suns*; and the place has a coat of arms or at least an emblem, rudely sculptured here and there on the stone, representing three faces of Sol, encircled by rays, like so many monstrances; for such symbols have transferable applications, and what depicts visible radiance may also indicate the diffusion of divine grace.

Still waters run deep. At heart Avila itself only repeats on a grander scale this same religious and human theme; only that the rustic setting has disappeared, and repentant paganism has become more Byzantine, more mediaeval, enclosed and overshadowed as it is by such high military and monastic bulwarks. The place in my time was in part ruinous and neglected, reduced to 6,000 inhabitants from the 30,000 it is said to have had in its day; for almost half the area within the walls, that slopes down to the river from what might be called the upper town was deserted within its circle of battlements and towers, and occupied only by heaps of rubbish, and a few nondescript huts and stone enclosures, where occasional stray pigs and poultry might be encountered. Even in the upper part many old mansions and chapels were closed, sometimes only the great door, with a wrought-iron balcony over it attesting their ancient dignity. Yet dignity was not absent from the good people that remained, leading a simple, serious, monotonous provincial life, narrowed by poverty and overhung more obviously than busier places seem to be by the shadow of illness, sorrow, and death. Almost all the women appeared to be in mourning, and the older men also. There was nothing forced or affected in this: people were simply resigned to the realities of mother nature and of human nature; and in its simplicity their existence was deeply civilised, not by modern conveniences but by moral tradition. "It is the custom", they would explain half apologetically, half proudly to the stranger when any little ceremony or courtesy was mentioned peculiar to the place. If things were not the custom, what reason could there be for doing them? What reason could there be for living, if it were not the custom to live, to suffer, and to die? Frankly, Avila was sad; but for me it was a great relief to hear that things were the custom, and not that they were right, or necessary, or that I ought to do them.

How much respect did these grave, disillusioned, limited people of Avila have for their conventions, and in particular for their religion? Not much, I think, at bottom; but nothing else was practically within their range; and if something else had been possible for them, would it have been better? The more intelligent of them would have doubted this, and resigned themselves to their daily round. What they had and what they thought was at least "the custom"; they could live and express themselves on those assumptions. Their inner man, in bowing to usage, could preserve its dignity. In breaking away, as the demagogues and cheap intellectuals wished them to do, they would have fallen into mental confusion and moral anarchy. Their lives would have been no better, and their judgments much worse. They could never, at the time when I knew them, have come to feel at home in a society where nothing was any longer "the custom", either in opinion or in conduct. Everything in Avila, the walls, the streets, the churches, the language, still bore witness to a faded but abiding civilisation; and it was not impossible for me to heighten and vivify the picture, as I projected it into the past, and turn it into a proud, distinct, and uncompromising power, such as a corrupt world would have to respect and to fear.

The ravages of reform. Every tourist with a guide-book may learn that in Avila the Cathedral, San Vicente, Santo Tomás, and the Chapel of Monsén Rubí are notable monuments in which the whole troubled history of Gothic architecture might be studied, if there were not elsewhere so many purer examples of each of those phases. Architecture, especially Gothic, was a passion of my youth, when I searched and analysed everything of the kind that I spied anywhere, and a pinnacle, or the tracery of a window arrested my eye as if it had promised to be Helen in all her glory. But that illusion is gone, and Avila is not a place to encourage it. On the contrary, it is a place where I have felt the profounder power of unintended harmonies, of accidents, not happy in themselves, that merge into a background for happiness—I mean of happiness for a philosopher who can live happy in the intellect, amid the lovely promise and quick ruin of all other happiness. Lovely promise and quick ruin are seen nowhere better than in Gothic architecture, all exuberance, freedom, and instability, "vaulting ambition" in stone, original sin thinking it could glorify repentance. Oriental luxury invaded classic art in Byzantium; and the purely aesthetic and geometrical glory of this art appears better when the Christian occasion for it does not exist, as among the Moslems. It could then supply a myriad lovely settings for poetry, for love, and for unbridled imagination, all without imposing a moral on the arabesques of creation. And to religion it could leave the empty and silent dome, where the solitary mind might settle its account with the universe. Our Gothic on the contrary became insatiably lavish in ornament and in all sorts of distracting curiosities; and I like it best when the hand of time or of chastisement, has intervened in that orgy, which tended to become tiresome, and has introduced a new style, a different taste, an imperious broom, sweeping away half those golden cobwebs. Sometimes the incongruous addition is more beautiful than the background on which it intrudes; and many a Gothic church would lose its charm if you removed the renaissance tombs or the baroque porches. After all, it was only by the force of its own restlessness that Gothic was superseded.

Spoliation of the Cathedral.   The irony of progress was illustrated in my time even in the Cathedral of Avila. There were formerly magnificent red damask hangings round the chancel and choir. They covered the wall beneath the triforium and the upper half of the arches into the aisles, the lower half being screened by the no less magnificent wrought-iron and brass railings. They made the whole inner space warm to the eye and nobly secluded to the heart. The sanctuary then seemed something like a throne room and audience chamber for the Most High. It was regal without loss of sublimity or mystical suggestion, since the vault still soared far above this earthly luxury, and vast sombre spaces remained open in the direction of the nave and of either transept. Nor was the public cut off, as in eastern churches, from viewing the ceremonies. Room was left for them between the sanctuary and choir; for the Spanish practice of placing the choir west of the transepts allows the laity to flood the very centre of the scene of worship. It is the favourite station for the officially devout, benches being sometimes provided there; while the unpretending Christian can still see and hear everything from the aisles, without being observed among the observers. These intimacies and charms of divine worship are missed by the superior critics who deplore such intrusion of the choir into the nave. That the tunnel of a long nave is thereby blocked seems to them an aesthetic sacrilege; but to me it seems a devotional advantage, and even a poetic one; because a partial veiling of beauty often enhances it, and the screens that enclose the choir, without interrupting the continuity of the clerestory and the vault, diversify the scene beneath, and supply appropriate places for monuments and altars. Therefore to a more Catholic age those red damask hangings seemed an appropriate ornament for a church, and they lent to the Cathedral of Avila, which is rather cold and severe, a special humanity and splendour. Nevertheless, some years ago, the Chapter sold the whole to an American, doubtless a Jewish dealer, for twenty thousand dollars. They said that the damask was rotting, that they needed the money for structural repairs in the fabric of the Cathedral itself, and that without the damask the architecture of the church would appear to more advantage.

Inner disaffection. These excuses seem to me as lamentable morally as the loss of the hangings is aesthetically. No doubt those hangings needed overhauling; but if the silk was rotting, would any shrewd Chicago millionaire or his careful wife want them in their bright new home? No doubt the government architects that direct repairs in national monuments did not always act as the Chapter would have wished, if they acted at all; and no doubt twenty thousand dollars, to be spent as they directed, was an unprecedented temptation to the bishop and canons. But if any of them said that to remove so great an ornament to the cultus would better reveal the beauties of the edifice, he must have been a sad Catholic and a false lover of the arts. Churches are built for prayer, not to exhibit the history of architecture; and it was a sound instinct in Christian times to assume that all richness and beauty might be laid at the foot of the Cross. Nothing that man naturally loves need go unconsecrated, if only it be sacrificed in part and in part redeemed. Moreover, it is not true that the damask hid anything worth looking at. The Cathedral of Avila is noble, but no part except the apse is particularly original or interesting. The student could examine every detail sufficiently before, while to the poet the bare stone walls—for there is much flat empty surface here without any riot of sculptured niches, windows, or galleries— seem now exposed to too much light, common, comfortless, bleak and discouraging. The vandalism that has devastated the interior of almost all churches elsewhere had now begun to attack them even in Spain. They were becoming sepulchres for the religion that built them.

Meditations   This church, faded and neglected but still glorious, was
at high mass.   the last in which I have been able to hear mass with
inward satisfaction. For one thing, there was no sermon in the morning.
To separate the mass from the sermon shows a genuine respect for
both. The liturgy and the eventual discourse are alike assumed to be
worth attending to, each for its own sake. Then at the high mass here
the rite was performed honestly, simply, in less than an hour, as a
traditional ceremony, without any affectation of personal devotion or
unction. It was the ancient Church still living, not the modern witling
trying to invent some combination of mystery and flattery to attract
the half-educated public. The little acolytes scampered about as if at
play, swung their heavy silver censers with gusto, and let the chains
rattle and the great puffs of smoke escape at each high turn of the
pendulum, as if pleasure and duty had never been better matched.
The music was rough, gusty, and not very classical, but at least brief;
and like all the rest it was not offered to the public for admiration
but performed simply to conform, as well as might be or was usual,
to the prescriptions of the liturgy. Here was ancient priestly religion,
as acceptable to the truly intelligent as their native language or their
accidental governments, not because miraculously right or perfect but
because ingrained in all their traditions, part of the soil and substance
of their only possible life, to be transmitted with the inevitable variations
to the next generation, if this generation is not to be wholly disinherited
and barbarous.

I did not feel at all disinherited, although never a partaker in those
rites. I respect them, I like them, and I refuse to use them for any
baser purpose. They celebrate inevitable human passions and joyful
hopes; and I shed no tears if those hopes and passions in myself have
had their day. Why envy illusions? Insight is not only calmer, but
more sympathetic and charitable; because each passion or hope when
alive sees hateful enemies in every other passion and hope, whereas
insight sees in each the good to which it aspires. In pure religion and
in art all these rival goods may be celebrated without contradiction
or disloyalty; for after all it is only the profane that expect art and
religion to serve their private passions. Those who have passed the
pons asinorum in the inner life know that the function of art and religion
is precisely to transfigure those private passions so that, far from being
served, they may all serve religion and art.

It was not, however, for the high mass on Sundays that I most often
visited the Cathedral, or lingered there with the most pleasure. Any

day at any hour, to make a short cut from street to street or to escape from the sun at the hot hours, I could traverse the dark cool aisles, or sit for a while in the transept, measuring the vaults with the eye, examining the rather nondescript stained glass, or the agreeable if somewhat obscure paintings in the great gilded reredos, or the two charming pulpits, or the sculptures in some old altar or tomb. Enough scent of wax and of incense clung to the walls to preserve the atmosphere of the cultus, and the focus of it, where some old man or old woman might be seen kneeling in prayer, was usually some modern shrine; this was still a living church, not a museum or a ruin. That circumstance, like Avila itself, pleased and consoled me. Everything profound, everything beautiful had not yet vanished from the world.

.

VII

Early Memories

Of early childhood I have some stray images, detached and un-datable, called up occasionally for no reason, after the fashion of dreams. Indeed, sometimes I suspect that they may be fragments of old dreams, and not genuine recollections; but in that case, where did the old dreams come from? For autobiography it might be no less pertinent, and even more telling, to report them if they were dreams than if they were true memories, because they would show how my young mind grew, what objects impressed it, and on what themes it played its first variations.

A vain   These images are all visual. I remember the *sota de*
infant.   *copas* or knave of cups in the Spanish cards, with which I was playing on the floor, when I got entangled in my little frock, which had a pattern of white and blue checks; and I can see the corner of the room, our *antesala*, where I was crawling, and the nurse that helped me up. I also remember sitting in my mother's lap, rather sleepy, and playing with a clasp that could run up and down the two strands of her long gold chain, made of flexible scales; she wore a large lace collar, and had on a silk gown which she called *el vestido de los siete colores*, because the black background was sprinkled with minute six-petalled flowers, each petal of a different colour, white, green, yellow, brown, red, and blue. Clothes and colours evidently had a great fascination for me: the emphasis may have been partly borrowed and verbal, because I heard the women constantly talking *chiffons*; but the interest was congenial. I have always been attentive to clothes, and careful about my own; and in those days of innocence, it was by no means indifferent to me whether with my white summer dress I wore the plain everyday blue sash, which I despised, or the glossy and fresh silk tartan, that made me feel more like myself. Yet I retain a memory, that must have been much earlier, of quite another kind. One evening, before putting me to bed, my mother carried me to the window, sitting on her arm, and pulled back the *visillo*, or lace curtain

that hung close to the glass. Above the tower of the Oñate house opposite, one bright steady star was shining. My mother pointed it out to me, and said : *"Detrás de ese lucero está Pepín"*; Pepín, her lamented first-born, was behind that star. At the time this announcement neither surprised nor impressed me; but something about my mother's tone and manner must have fixed her words mechanically in my memory. She seldom spoke unnecessarily, and was never emotional; but here was some profound association with her past that, for a moment, had spread its aura about me.

My brother Robert in Avila.   Another set of memories can be dated as not later than my third year, because they introduce my brother Robert, who left Avila when I was three and he was twelve. We occupied the same little room behind our mother's and next to the school-room; and I remember our pillow-fights, or rather games, because Robert had a tender heart and was nice to his baby-brother. He was forbidden to purloin any part of my food, but might stick out his tongue in the hope, not always disappointed, that with my fork I might delicately place a morsel upon it. It was a feat of equilibrium on my part, as well as of magnanimity, and I remember it for both reasons. Also the crisp potatoe omelette, fried in oil, that I had for supper, and that I still pine for and seldom obtain; and the napkin, white on the black and red table-cover, on which the feast was spread. The first toy I can remember was also in Robert's time at Avila, for it was given me by his Alsatian tutor, Herr Schmidt: a velvety grey mouse that could be wound up to run across the floor. And finally I can remember distinctly the occasion of Robert's departure. We all went to the station to see him off; for my father was taking him as far as London, from where his cousin Russell Sturgis (the Evangelical major with the side-whiskers and the shapely calves) was to convey him to America to be put to school. But it is not any emotion connected with leave-taking for an indefinite absence that remains in my mind: only the image of young Robert's back, walking before me at a particular corner where we had to go in single file. He wore a long grey coat with a braided mantelette or short cape covering the shoulders; above which I can still see his grey cap and the tightly curling brown hair escaping and bulging out under it. Whether I was actually walking too or was being carried does not appear from the picture. The self in these clear and fixed intuitions remains wholly transcendental and out of sight. It is doing its duty too well to be aware that it is doing it.

His German tutor. That Robert should have had an Alsatian tutor in Avila (who also taught the girls) may seem odd. It was one of those unstable and unsatisfactory compromises that were involved in the circumstances of my parents' marriage. For a time they lived in Madrid, in the flat where I was born: but Madrid has a bad climate, with great heat in summer and cold winds in winter; it made a second residence necessary for the hot months, and was expensive and, for my mother, socially distasteful. Moreover, she had to go back to Boston; my father knew it, but kept finding reasons for putting the thing off. Finally, very characteristically, my mother took the law into her own hands, secretly made all the arrangements and one afternoon escaped with all of us, save my father, in the express train for Paris. There my father's remonstrances reached her. They were so eloquent, or backed by such threats of action (since he had a right at least to retain *me*) that we all finally returned. It had been agreed that we should live in Avila. But what education could Robert or the girls receive there? None! Therefore a private tutor was imperative, and somehow a young Alsatian was found who seemed to possess all the requirements. French and German were native languages to him, he spoke a little English, and would soon learn Spanish. His demands were modest and his character apparently excellent. So Herr Schmidt was installed as a boarder with a poor widow who lived on the ground floor, and there were daily lessons in the sunny little room at the back of the house which became the schoolroom. I don't know what idealistic cobwebs the German Minerva might have spun there had not her labours been interrupted; but presently a German Cupid had flown in over the flower-pots in the open window, and tangled those learned threads. For although this was before the Franco-Prussian War, young Schmidt showed all the sentimentality and push of a pure German; he believed in discipline and thoroughness, and the duty of founding all instruction on German geography, in the native language; so that between the difficult and most clearly articulated names of *Harzgebirge* and *Riesengebirge* he would whisper in Susana's ear: "*Je vous aime avec rage.*" She was hardly sixteen, and he had to be sent away, which no doubt he thought a great injustice; for he wrote a long letter explaining his worthiness to be Susana's husband, and his willingness to go to America and establish himself there — on nothing a year.

A new
drama begins
with the same
stage-
setting.

It was this collapse of superior international education at home that had made it urgent to send at least Robert at once to school in America, and that separated me from my elder brother for the next five years. Two more years elapsed before my mother and sisters also departed. I remember nothing of that interval; but after they went my uncle Santiago, with his wife María Josefa and his daughter Antoñita, came to live with us, and a new and distinct chapter begins in my experience. The scene, the persons, the events are still present to me most vividly. I didn't feel deeply or understand what was going on, but somehow the force of it impressed my young mind, and established there a sort of criterion or standard of reality. That crowded, strained, disunited, and tragic family life remains for me the type of what life really is: something confused, hideous, and useless. I do not hate it or rebel against it, as people do who think they have been wronged. It caused me no suffering; I was a child carried along as in a baby-carriage through the crowd of strangers; I was neither much bothered nor seriously neglected; and my eyes and ears became accustomed to the unvarnished truth of the world, neither selected for my instruction nor hidden from me for my benefit.

My aunt
María Josefa.

My aunt María Josefa was frankly a woman of the people. She was most at home in her kitchen, in a large blue apron that covered most of her skirt; and I shall never forget the genuine fresh taste of the fried peppers and eggs, and the great soft cake or *torta* that came from her hands. She was a native of Jaén, with a strong but pleasant Andalusian accent and exaggerated rhetoric. Her every word was a diminutive or an augmentative, and her every passion flowed out in endless unrestrained litanies of sorrow or endearment. She could hardly read or write, and her simplicity or humility was so great that she would casually observe that her daughter Antoñita had been a *siete mesina* or seven-months child; from which anyone could gather the reason for her marriage. For my uncle this marriage had been unintended and undesirable; he was much too young and she was much too common; but having got the poor girl into trouble he nobly made the *amende honorable*; and terrible as the sacrifice would have been if he had had much ability or ambition, as things were it rendered poverty perhaps easier to bear. Poverty was not the only misfortune they had to put up with: but when the worst was over, I found my aunt living in Granada with a brother who was a tanner. This was in the summer of 1893, when I had reached Spain via

Gibraltar. My mother and I were in the habit of sending María Josefa a small allowance, so that she was well received and respected in her brother's household. The tannery occupied the court of an old, possibly a Moorish, house; the skins hung drying from the gallery; and my aunt's brother, in order to do the honours of the city (as if I had not been there before, or had no guide-book) took me to see the University, which indeed it would not have occurred to me to visit. In the library there was a large globe; and in order to make talk, which rather ran dry between us, I said I would show him the voyage I had just made from America. I was doing so when he asked, "But which is Spain? — What, that little spot? I thought it was this", and he pointed to Africa. It occurred to me that some great wits before him had seen no difference between Africa and Spain; but I didn't go into the intricacies of that opinion. As to my aunt, of course she was then old, fat, and broken, but calm and strangely silent. She had protested enough, and this was the fifth act of her tragedy, all storms subdued and equalised in resignation. Yet one more trial awaited her. Her brother died before her, and she had to retire to her native village near Jaén, from which soon no more answers reached us to our letters.

Her daughter's love-affairs. Not the person, *tía María Josefa*, in whose hands my mother could have wished to leave me at the age of five! But my mother's mind was made up and inflexible; it was made up abstractly, in scorn of particulars and of consequences. She had put off her departure only too long, and now she *must* go. Besides, strange as it may seem, she was well disposed towards my father's relations, as they were not towards her. She seldom spoke of them, but when she did it was amiably, even sympathetically. She seems to have trusted María Josefa, as one might a devoted old nurse; and this trust was deserved, because in relation to me María Josefa behaved perfectly. Moreover there was Antoñita, who but for her love-affairs and marriage would have looked after me more playfully than her mother. Antoñita was a nice girl, a friend of Susana's, pretty and with a latent depth of feeling which made people think her not insignificant, in spite of her simplicity and lack of education. My mother had liked her, and helped her to get prettier clothes. But she was ripening into womanhood and preoccupied with love. I remember her first *novio*, or acknowledged lover, the youngest of the Paz brothers, who were among the leading bourgeois families of Avila; and I think there was more between him and Antoñita than the local conventions allowed to *novios*. He came to the house, which is contrary to the rules:

novios should meet only in public places, in sight of their elders, or talk together at the window, the girl sitting inside the *reja*, or in the balcony, and the young man standing in the street. This was called *pelando la pava*, plucking the turkey, or conjugating the verb *amo*, I love. There was a great attick over a part of the house, accessible from my father's room or studio, where he painted; and from one of the big beams of the roof hung a trapeze, arranged, I suppose, for my benefit. Into that attick the lovers would wander alone, whether to admire my performance, or not suspecting that I might be swinging there, I didn't know. That something was brewing became evident on another occasion. We were sitting one evening or late afternoon in the *café del Inglés* (for the lamps were lighted) when suddenly my aunt got up, evidently very angry, bundled Antonia and me out of a side door; and once in the adjoining *portal* or *porte cochère*, began violently beating Antonia with fists and claws, with such a flood of imprecations as only my aunt was capable of. All I could gather was that the poor girl had been *looking* at somebody: no doubt, as I now conjecture, at young Paz, at another table, making love to another girl. Anyhow, my aunt had worked herself up to such a rage that, being subject to fits, she fell full length with a loud bang on the stone floor. She fell exactly as *prima donnas* and murdered heroes fall on the stage; and apparently as harmlessly, for I heard no more of the whole affair. Relations with Paz were evidently broken off; there were no more trips to the attick, where I did my swinging undisturbed; and presently a very different *novio*, this time meaning business, appeared on the scene.

Rafael Vegas.   What brought him to Avila I do not know; probably some great lawsuit, for he was a lawyer, and ostensibly an important person, *bellâtre*, with well-oiled curly black locks and silken side-whiskers and the beginnings of a paunch, on which a conspicuous gold chain with dangling seals marked the equator. He was a widower with two little girls, but still young, not over forty; for people spoke of his brilliant prospects rather than of his brilliant past, and he had a still beautiful mother whom my father and I once visited in Madrid. She received us in her boudoir, or rather in the alcove attached to it, for she was still in bed, but elaborately prepared to receive callers. There were great lace flounces to her sheets, over a red damask coverlet, and she wore a lovely fresh peignoir and little cap, from which two great black braids hung down over her two shoulders, ending in coquettish knots of blue ribbon. What she and my father were talking about I didn't understand, but I felt I had never been in such a luxurious nest before, so much carpeted, so much curtained, so softly upholstered, and so full of religious and other bric-a-brac.

With such a mother, Rafael Vegas must have begun life convinced that he was a distinguished and fashionable person, and that his clients, when he had them, should pay him handsome fees. Nor could he have helped being a ladykiller, having not only the requisite presence and airs, but the requisite temperament; for he was no vulgar libertine, but a genuine lover of the fair sex, who demanded to conquer and to possess his conquests exclusively. He might have liked a harem, but he despised a brothel. His success with the ladies, young and old, was immense and in one sense deserved, since his admiration for them was sincere. That he was truly subject to the tender passion was proved by his courting and marrying two of my pretty and penniless cousins, beginning with Antoñita. Nothing but love could have prompted him in these cases; but to them it seemed a dazzling match, that meant initiation into a higher social sphere, as well as into all the mysteries of untried passion.

A wedding in the dark. The wedding took place secretly in the small hours of the night, because a rowdy custom subjected widowers, on their new bridal night, to a *cencerrada*, or derisive serenade of cowbells, if the date and place of those mysteries could be discovered. Everything was therefore kept as dark as possible; only the immediate family was summoned, and they at the last moment, and only a cup of chocolate offered afterwards to the sleepy company before the newly married pair vanished to some unknown hiding-place. I was of course present, and impressed by the strangeness of going out at night into a dark street and a dark empty church, with a knot of people whispering and hastening, with much trepidation, as if on some criminal errand. We were in our ordinary clothes, the bride in black, with a lace mantilla. It was all over in a moment. I was bundled to bed again, and might have thought it a dream, but for the talk afterwards about everything. Rafael's emphatic personal dignity would have suffered sadly had he not escaped the *cencerrada*; and he managed it cleverly, by not going on any wedding trip (he may also have been short of money) but establishing himself at once in our house, with his two daughters, in the best front rooms left vacant by my mother and sisters, who were in America. For a day or two, however, bride and bridegroom occupied my bedroom, because it looked out on a tangle of little courts and walled gardens, quite shut off from any street. On the first morning I followed the housemaid there—after all it was my room—when she took in their breakfast to the happy pair. The two cups of chocolate were on a particularly fresh and well-filled tray, with *azucarillos*; there was a bright brass bed, wholly unknown to me, and a gorgeous red damask coverlet, and great lace flounces to the sheets, like those, or the very same, that on that other occasion, in Madrid, I saw setting off the charms of Rafael's black-browed mother. Rafael and Antoñita lay smiling and rosy on quite separate pillows; they said good morning to the servant and me with unusual good humour, and people all day indulged in witticisms and veiled expressions which I didn't quite understand.

Rafael and his daughters come to live with us. I now had playmates in the house, two well-dressed little girls about my own age; but we didn't like one another. It was made clear in every direction that our house and our standard of living were not such as the Vegases expected, and they bore us a grudge for causing them to be lodged and fed so badly. Yet our double or triple *ménage* was kept up for a year or more until an event supervened that brought disaster to my uncle's family and eventually sent my father and me to America.

Antoñita was soon quite obviously in what was called an interesting condition. The place that children come from was no mystery to me, although I was only seven or eight years old. I was already a calm materialist; not that in another direction I was less knowing in theology; and if anyone had made the mistake of telling me that babies came in bandboxes from Paris, I am sure I should have scornfully replied that God, and not milliners had made me; and that as God was everywhere, it was just as easy for him to make babies in Madrid or even in Avila as in Paris. Yet Antoñita's baby, that God was undoubtedly making in Avila, was very long in coming to light. She continued more and more strangely to enlarge, until her haggard and unseemly condition, and murmurs and consultations in the family, began to suggest that something was wrong. Perhaps the date for the expected event had been miscalculated; or perhaps some complication prevented nature from bringing it about. At last one evening there was much agitation in the house, with strangers coming in, and long consultations; and I began to hear from Antoñita's room (which was my mother's room back to back with mine, but with no communication) piercing cries and weeping invocations of all the heavenly powers. This presumably lasted all night, since it was still going on when I woke up in the morning; and then there were more consultations with strange doctors and exhibition of surgical instruments. At one moment I remember my aunt bursting into the passage, with a bundle of blood-stained linen in her hands and floods of joyful tears, crying: "She is saved, she is saved!" Yet later we children were taken to our neighbour's on the second floor, where we didn't know the people; and on the way out I saw, in a small wooden box that might have held soap or candles, a dead child lying naked, pale yellowish green. Most beautiful, I thought him, and as large and perfectly formed as the child Jesus in the pictures; except that where the navel ought to be he had a little mound like an acorn, with a long string hanging out of it.

A reason why mankind is so ugly and so unhappy. The image of that child, as if made of green alabaster, has remained clear all my life, not as a ghastly object that ought to have been hidden from me, but as the most beautiful of statues, something too beautiful to be alive. And it has suggested to me a theory, doubtless fanciful, yet which I can't think wholly insignificant, concerning the formation of living things. They are all formed in the dark, automatically, protected from interference by what is called experience: experience which indeed would be impossible if there were not first a definite creature to receive it and to react upon it in ways consonant with its inherited nature. This nature has asserted itself in a seed, in an egg, in a womb, where the world couldn't disturb its perfect evolution. Flowers and butterflies come perfect to the light, and many animals are never more beautiful, pure, and courageous than when they first confront the world. But man, and other unhappy mammals, are born helpless and half-shapeless, like unbaked dough; they have not yet become what they meant to be. The receptacle that held them could not feed them long enough, or allow them to attain their full size and strength. They must therefore be cast out into the glare and the cold, to be defeated by a thousand accidents, derailed, distorted, taught and trained to be enemies to themselves, and to prevent themselves from ever existing. No doubt they manage to survive for a time, halt, blind, and misshapen; and sometimes these suppressions or mutilations of what they meant to be adapt them to special environments and give them technical knowledge of many a thing that, if they had been free, they might never have noticed, or observed only poetically, in a careless and lordly way. But every living creature remains miserable and vicious, so long as in serving other things it has to suppress itself: and if that alien world must needs be served, the only happy solution, and one that nature often finds, would be for the unfit species to perish outright—there is nothing ignoble in perishing—and for a different species to appear whose freedom and happiness would lie in contact with those particular circumstances and mastery over them. I say to myself, therefore, that Antoñita's child was so exceptionally beautiful, and would doubtless have been exceptionally brave and intelligent, because he had profited longer than is usual by the opportunity to grow undisturbed, as all children grow in their sleep; but this advantage, allowed to butterflies and flowers, and to some wild animals, is forbidden to mankind, and he paid for it by his life and by that of his mother.

Death of Antoñita and its consequences. For she had not really been saved; only a false hope made my aunt think so for a moment; and on Antoñita's death, it would have seemed natural that Rafael and his two little girls should have left us and gone to live elsewhere in their own more luxurious way. But not at all. Primitive human nature in my aunt María Josefa yielded absolutely to every passion in turn, put up with every trial, but survived and clung no less passionately to whatever was left. Her grief on this occasion was violent, but violent only by fits, as when each new visitor came to condole with her, and she had to repeat the whole story, with appropriate floods of tears, sobs, and lamentations. She even said at times that now she knew there was no God, because, with all her prayers and vows, no God could have allowed her poor innocent daughter to suffer so horribly to no purpose. Her heart thus unburdened, however, she couldn't but take comfort in that splendid man, her son-in-law, and devote herself to his service and care for his little girls. Rafael therefore not only remained in our house, but became all-important in it, as if my father had not existed. Nor could I be looked after exclusively, when after all I had my own mother to love me, even if a thousand leagues away, and there were those two darlings to rescue from the shock of having lost their second mama as well as their first one. Moreover my uncle Santiago, though he said little, was beginning to go daft. Not on account of his daughter's death. He used to say, when people expressed their sympathy, that his real loss had come when she was married. I don't think this observation in itself a sign of dementia; but it indicated a general despair and passivity that went with his taking refuge in drink, and finally in idiocy. For idiocy may begin by being partly acted, like Hamlet's madness, in order to mock the facts, until the mockery becomes an automatism, and the facts are lost altogether. Years afterwards, when he was at his worst, he would walk ceaselessly round and round the house, half singing half moaning, always repeating the same sounds, and crushing a piece of paper in his hand. He had recovered the animal capacity—such an insult to the world!—of still doing his old trick, no matter what might be going on. The marvel is how many individuals and how many governments are able to survive on this system. Perhaps the universe is nothing but an equilibrium of idiocies.

Our household breaks up.   My father was mildness itself on ordinary occasions, but sometimes could be aroused to reveal his hidden and unusually clear mind, when all his command of terse language and his contempt for the world would flow out in a surprising and devastating manner. I was not present, but I gathered from stray comments overheard afterwards, that he had had an explanation of this sort with Rafael and María Josefa. At any rate, they suddenly left us. My father and I remained in what seemed that vast house, alone with one little maid servant. Such an arrangement could not be permanent and doubtless was not meant to be so; and presently we too said farewell to that house for ever and to Avila, as far as I was concerned, for eleven years.

First and important lessons.   During the three years that I was separated from my mother I went more or less to school. It was a large darkish room on the ground floor in the public building directly opposite our house; but the entrance was not in our street, and I had to go round the Oñate tower into the lane at the back, where the school door was. We children stood in *corros* or circles round the teacher—I think sometimes only an older lad—and recited the lesson after him. I don't remember any individual questions or answers, nor any reading or writing, yet we did learn somehow to read and write. I had two books: the *cartilla*, with the alphabet and the different syllables, with easy words following; and the catechism, perhaps in a later year. This was itself divided into two parts, one Sacred History, with pictures in it, of which I remember only Moses striking the rock from which water gushed; and Christian Doctrine, of which I remember a great deal, virtually everything, because it was evidently an excellent catechism, so that after learning it I have been able all my life to distinguish at the first hearing the *sapor haereticus* of any dangerous doctrine. Especially present to me is the very philosophic dogma that God is everywhere, by his essence, by his presence and by his power:

of which, however, the first clause has always remained obscure to me; for if God is everywhere by his essence, it would seem to follow that everything is essentially divine—a vulgar pantheism; so that the meaning must be something very recondite and highly qualified, which escapes me. But the other two clauses are luminous, and have taught me from the first to conceive omnificent power and eternal truth: inescapable conceptions in any case, quite apart from any doctrines of historical Judaism or Christianity. I have reasserted them, in my mature philosophy, in my notions of the realm of matter and the realm of truth: notions which I am happy to have imbibed in childhood by rote in the language of antiquity, and not to have set them up for myself in the Babel of modern speculation. They belong to human sanity, to human orthodoxy; I wish to cling to that, no matter from what source its expression may come, or encumbered with what myths. The myths dissolve; the presuppositions of intelligence remain and are necessarily confirmed by experience, since intelligence awoke precisely when sensibility began to grow relevant to external things.

VIII

I am Transported to America

At sea for the first time.   My first voyage—if I hadn't been deadly seasick— might have initiated me into the life of primitive mariners, for we sailed the high seas in an open boat. It was a little freight steamer plying from Bilbao to Cardiff, hardly more than a tug; and though it had a small bridge and a deck house aft, it was open to the sky forward, and visibly freighted with reddish earth, which I believe was iron ore. The Bay of Biscay in such a craft confirmed its bad reputation; but on the third day there was sunshine and smooth sparkling water, and I recovered instantly. A quick and complete recovery is characteristic of my ill turns in general, and particularly of seasickness, which purges the system of its poisons. If I could have secured this advantage without the horrid prolonged trials that produced it, I might have gladly become a sailor. I love moving water, I love ships, I love the sharp definition, the concentrated humanity, the sublime solitude of life at sea. The dangers of it only make present to us the peril inherent in all existence, which the stupid ignorant untravelled land-worm never discovers; and the art of it, so mathematical, so exact, so rewarding to intelligence, appeals to courage and clears the mind of superstition, while filling it with humility and true religion. Our world is a cockleshell in the midst of overwhelming forces and everlasting realities; but those forces are calculable and those realities helpful, if we can manage to understand and to obey them.

A child's impressions of England.   We were in the Bristol Channel, in sight of the Welsh coast: smooth grassy hillsides, grey-green in the slight mist and dotted with little white houses. But there was something far more interesting for me to watch; several boats with white sails, probably small yachts, bending and tacking in the almost imperceptible breeze. A British note: a first hint to me of that brave, free, sporting side of the youthful Anglosaxon character which I was later to love so much. For if in most things it is contrast that makes me admire and trust the unspotted young Englishman, in one respect it is affinity; I too love the earth and hate the world. God made the first, and man, with his needs and his jealousies, has made the second.

On landing, an ungainly ridiculous side of this world, and especially of Britain, became suddenly present. We had plumped on a Sunday into a British non-conformist industrial town. Ugliness and desolation could not be more constitutional. Perhaps we lodged in a too modest quarter, too near the port; but nothing was in sight save rows of mean little brick houses all alike, a long straight street, wet with the rain, and not a soul stirring. However, the rain ultimately ceased, and on going out for a stroll we came upon a forbidding castle wall, closely skirted by what evidently was the old High Street of the place; and we learned that this was the seat of the Marquis of Bute, the great landlord of that region. Another British note: the living survival of mediaeval features, material and moral, in the midst of modern England.

**The *Samaria*   The next day we travelled to Liverpool, where I re-
of 1872.**   member nothing but the docks, with long inclined ways, paved with cobble-stones, leading down between great warehouses to the water's edge. There we crept into a small rowboat, that was to convey us to our ship. Several large vessels were riding at anchor in the stream: my father pointed to the ugliest and most dwarfish of them and said that this would be ours. No help for it now, I reflected: but at once my eye was attracted by a line of little flags running from stem to stern, over the top of the two masts. What did that mean? My father explained that dressing the ship in that fashion, although a British vessel, was a compliment courteously paid to the United States, because most of the passengers were Americans, who on that day were celebrating the anniversary of their Declaration of Independence. This incident has fixed the date of my first sailing to America unerringly in my mind: it was the Fourth of July, 1872.

The Cunard steamship *Samaria* of that date was a vessel of 3,000 tons, with a squat red smokestack between two stumpy masts, and a bowsprit like a sailing-ship. Sails were indeed often set, in order, it was said, to steady her, but probably also to help her along; for never vessel was more distinctly an old tub. She stood high, black, and short above the water, looking rusty and almost derelict; however, she bore us safely, if not steadily, to Boston in twelve days. I was again terribly seasick most of the time; and my father, if not exactly seasick, being an old sailor, suffered from severe and prolonged indigestion, which he said upset and discouraged him altogether, and spoilt his whole visit to the United States. I, at least, had intervals when I was well, and hungry. A nice young woman, Irish she said, took pity on me and tried to entertain me; but we couldn't talk. I didn't know a word of English or she of Spanish; and my father, who read English perfectly, could neither pronounce it nor understand it when spoken; so that with English-speaking people he was reduced to uttering single words, if they could be recognised as he sounded them, or to writing them on a piece of paper. His deafness added to the difficulty, and made it impossible for him to surmount it. Nevertheless my young Irish friend and I got on well enough without a common language: the goodwill in what we might say was always intelligible. I afterwards often saw her family, for they occupied the pew immediately in front of the one in which my sisters and I sat at the Church of the Immaculate Conception; but our acquaintance never went beyond an occasional bow and discreet smile. My particular friend, the young lady, for some reason was never there. I have a dreamy recollection of hearing that she was the invisible contralto that sang with so charming and rich a voice in the choir; I am not sure of it, but in any case I liked to think so.

The Cunard Wharf at East Boston, Robert, and his blue ribbon.

The day of our arrival was very warm, with the damp suffocating heat of the New England summer; there was naturally some confusion in landing, and everything seemed odd and unaccountable. It was a sordid scene. I saw no stone quays, such as I associated with ports, at Bilbao, at Portugalete, and lately on a grand scale at Liverpool. No docks; only a wooden pier raised precariously on slimy piles, with the stained sea-water running under it; and on it a vast wooden shed, like a barn, filled with merchandise and strewn with rubbish. America was not yet rich, it was only growing rich; people worked feverishly for quick returns, and let the future build for the future. But there came my brother Robert. I shouldn't have recognised him, nor he me, after those five years: a pale pimpled youth not yet eighteen, of middle height, with a narrow chest and sloping shoulders; and a straw hat with a bright blue ribbon: yet the tightly curling brown hair, quite dry and brittle (we both grew prematurely bald) was unmistakably Robert's: besides, he spoke Spanish, and very soon I was quite at home with him. But I had never seen a man in a straw sailor-hat before, and the blue ribbon didn't please me. Of course I had no idea that blue ribbons might have a meaning: 'varsity blues, royal blue, the Garter, or the record in Atlantic passages or choice champagnes: there was no question of any of those things in Robert's case. His ribbon was an accident, a caprice of the hat-maker's, seconded by thoughtless taste in the buyer. I say thoughtless, not to say crude: because I nurse a sort of moral sense about colours, and in artificial objects a plain unmitigated blue seems to me vulgar. Robert had pale blue eyes, innocent and sometimes a little watery. To pale blue my colour-sense makes no objection, nor to dark blue; these have separate moral qualities, proper in their place; and the lightest blue eyes always possess a mysterious centre and several shades in the iris. I could have positively liked the blueness of Robert's eyes, and even that of his ribbon, if it had matched them.

Buggies. Once on terra firma, or rather on the rough planks of the Cunard Wharf, in what resembled the baggage room of a large station, I looked about for the carriages and horses. Carriages—anything with wheels—had been my favourite toys. Mine had been little ones, that I could pull round and round the dining-room table on a string; but more exciting, in Madrid, had been the real carriages, so smart and shining, with their gay red or yellow wheels, their high-stepping horses, their solemn coachman and groom, and the smiling ladies inside. But what did I see here? I daresay there were vehicles of various sorts; but just in front of me, what first caught and held my attention, was something like a large baby-carriage suspended high in air on four enormous skeleton wheels: Robert called it a buggy. The front wheels were almost as large as the back wheels, with the rims almost touching. Those front wheels were too high to slip under the body of the carriage; in turning, the near tire was apt to scrape against the side with an ominous and unpleasant sound, so that it was impossible for a buggy to face about sharply; this littlest of carriages could make only a great sweep, and was in danger of upsetting at every corner.

Symbols of the Yankee Spirit. Here by chance my eye, at the first moment of my setting foot in the new world, was caught by symbols of Yankee ingenuity and Yankee haste which I couldn't in the least understand but which instinctively pleased and displeased me. I was fascinated by the play of those skeleton wheels, crossing one another like whirling fans in the air, and I was disgusted by such a dirty ramshackle pier for a great steamship line. I think now that the two things expressed the same mentality. That pier served its immediate purpose, for there we were landing safely at it; it hadn't required any great outlay of capital; and what did it matter if it was ugly and couldn't last long? It might last long enough to pay, and enable the company to build a better one. As for the buggy, its extreme lightness economised force and made speed possible over sandy and ill-kept roads. The modest farmer could go about his errands in it, and the horsey man could race in it with his fast long-tailed pair. Never mind if in the end it turned out to be like some experimental and too ambitious species of insect, that develops an extraordinary organ securing an immediate advantage but leading into fatal dangers. Abstract ingenuity is a self-rewarding sport. The taste for it marks the independence of a shrewd mind not burdened by any too unyielding tradition, except precisely this tradition of experimental liberty, making money and losing it, making things to be thrown away, and being happy rather than ashamed of having always to begin afresh.

Commercial means of conveyance. Robert somehow guided us and despatched our things to Beacon Street; it was a complicated process and a complicated journey, a ferry and two horse-cars, beside three short walks; but it was economical, ten cents each for the trip, and twenty-five cents to send the trunk by express: whereas a "hack" (a hired landau) would have cost five dollars. The method of sending luggage by express seemed to us obscure and disquieting. How could we trust all our worldly goods to a stranger, paying him besides in advance, and meekly accept in exchange a coarse brass medal perforated with a number? There was a twin medal perforated with the same number, which the expressman kept; and Robert said he would attach this to our trunk, having taken a note of the address to which that number should be despatched; and the trunk was sure to arrive safely and speedily. Although my own scepticism was not yet fully developed, neither my father nor I were by nature inclined to faith in the unintelligible: however, being born travellers, we were ready in a new country to bow to a new logic and a new ethics; and we trusted Robert and the mysterious order of nature.

Theory of trust and credit. Our faith proved entirely justified: and though my father perhaps never felt at home in this system of trust and credit, fearing the confidence tricks of omnipresent rascals, I soon learned to swim happily with my eyes closed on this stream of business convention, which indeed at this moment is supplying me with a comfortable income coming, as far as my direct action or perception goes, from nowhere. But I have meditated on this point, and think I see the principle of it. Life, physical life, would be impossible without bold and risky presumptions about the future and without the opportune course of nature, coming to meet and to reward those presumptions. Millions of seeds, thousands of hopes, are frustrated; but there is enough adaptability in living beings, and enough constancy in things, for some arts to prosper, and to establish elaborate correspondences, long threads of co-operative tradition, between specific ways of living and the circumstances of such life. This, which happens obscurely in the depths of animal psyches, happens on the surface in human arts. When these arts have been long established with little remembered change, people think it a matter of course that things should proceed in that way, and are shocked if any accident, as they call it, produces what they call an anomaly; and they never perceive that they are daily building on faith over a sleeping volcano. Now a commercial society at first knows very well the risks it is running: ships sent out never return; stores are burned or pillaged; coin must ring true before it is accepted; and treasure must be kept hidden at home and guarded night and day with fear and trembling. But this state of things is so wasteful that merchants can afford to pay highly for a government that can give them security: and governments supported by trade will then police the country and the seas in the interests of trade, subordinating all other interests. But faith, trust, credit, security are the life-blood of trade: when strictly protected by courts and prisons, they will reduce the expense of business enormously, and enable the merchant not only to grow rich and remain rich, but to supply the public with endless commodities at reasonable prices. And this is why, on landing in Boston in 1872, my father and I were able safely to commit our trunk to the expressman (police, courts, and prison would have got him instantly if he had stolen it) and could be conveyed from East Boston to Beacon Street at the expense of fifty-five cents instead of five dollars. But we had not the lordly pleasure of driving in our private carriage, or the excitement of carrying swords and pistols, in case bandits should waylay us.

My family reunited. Events looked forward to with trepidation, when at length they occur, often fall flat. I was going to see my mother and sisters again after three years! Husband and wife were to be reunited! Well, when Robert said, "This is our house", and we walked up a little flight of stone steps to a half-open door in a row of doors, belonging to a narrow high house exactly like the house next to it, nobody seemed to inhabit that house or any of the others.

It was the dead season, July 16th, and the whole street was deserted. However, before we got to the last step, a second door further in was opened; we were expected; there were faces peering out; Susana and Josefina in white dresses, and, much smaller, my mother wearing a cap and looking very grave. We kissed each other all round, and Susana cried. (We had forgotten to kiss Robert at the Wharf.) Why did Susana cry? Was it mere excitement, nerves? Or was she already— she was twenty-one—secretly regretting Spain and her *beaux jours?* They took us into the dining-room to show us the "beautiful view" from the back of the house—a great expanse of water, with a low line of nondescript sheds and wooden houses marking the opposite bank. It was Bostonian to show us the view first; but we noticed that this dining-room was hung with many oil paintings, little Dutch or classic Italian landscapes, still life, and over the mantelpiece an old portrait: some Elizabethan worthy in a ruff and puffed sleeves, with a large ring on his fat fore-finger. My father naturally had begun by examining these pictures, all copies, of course; and we learned that the Elizabethan gentleman was supposed to be Lord Burleigh, but that "Uncle Henry", whose pictures these had been, had bought it because he thought the personage looked like a Sturgis and might have been one of his ancestors. My father must have been amused at this, it was so typical of the Sturgises; but he never spoke of it. As for me, what interested me was to find the large sofa so soft when I sat on it. One might ride on the springs as if on horseback.

It was inevitably Susana who took me in tow and who began to teach me English. I learned some verses by rote, about a bird's nest, out of a brightly coloured and highly moral book for young children. They ended, as I pronounced them, as follows:

> You mahsthnoth in play-ee
> Esteal the bords away-ee
> And grieve their mahther's breasth.

I am impervious to moralising. The moral of this was wasted on me—I was not a young child—and if I had had an impulse to steal any bird's nest or bird's eggs, or even to climb any tree, it would not have been these nursery rhymes that could have dissuaded me. But I had no such impulse, and no such opportunity, which made this moralising, like all moralising, ring hollow in my ears. The lady who said many years later that she envied me for not having a conscience, didn't altogether misread me.* Like my mother I have firmness of character; and I don't understand how a rational being can be wrong in being or doing what he fundamentally wishes to be or to do. He may make a mistake about it, or about the circumstances; or he may be imperfectly integrated, and tossed between contrary desires, not knowing his own nature or what he really wants. Experience and philosophy have taught me that perfect integrity is an ideal never fully realised, that nature is fluid and inwardly chaotic in the last resort, even in the most heroic soul; and I am ashamed and truly repentant if ever I find that I have been dazed and false to myself either in my conduct or in my opinions. In this sense I am not without a conscience; but I accept nobody's precepts traversing my moral freedom.

I learn to speak good English. As to my pronunciation, it improved rapidly and unawares. I then had a good ear and a flexible tongue, and the fact that English was a foreign language to me positively helped me to learn it well and to speak it, for instance, much better than Susana or Robert, or most of the boys in my successive schools. For among our friends and my teachers there were some who spoke excellent English, traditionally or by careful chastening of the Yankee vernacular; and I could easily distinguish the better of my models from the worse. We were expressly taught pronunciation and declamation; and declamatory American speech, in the 1870's, though blatant and sometimes infected with the Calvinistic drawl, still was at bottom noble and pure. The irregularity of English sounds and their subtlety was an interesting challenge: far from irritating, it attracted me, and made me sensitive to its finer shades; so that even before I had heard an English voice or lived in England, my English was good. In 1887, Russell** once asked me to join him at his grandmother's, Lady Stanley of Alderley, a great and venerable personage; and after we had exchanged a few phrases, Lady Stanley said, "But how well you speak English!" That is a back-handed compliment that one ordinarily prefers not to hear, since it implies that one evidently speaks like a foreigner: but in this case, as I was considered a Spaniard, it was not rude; and I explained that I had been educated in Boston. "But you haven't an American accent", the lady insisted. I reminded

*This incident is related, with variations, in the *Prologue* to *The Last Puritan*.
**The name *Russell* in these pages, unless otherwise indicated, designates John Francis Stanley, second Earl Russell. His brother Bertrand, who was also my friend, I venture to call "Bertie".

her of the culture of Boston, and protested that all my English was American, as I had been but three days in London. "No," she admitted, "you haven't a *London* accent. You speak like Queen Victoria." Let this stand as early testimony to my English speech: I spoke like Queen Victoria.*

---

*At my nicest, perhaps, but not always. And didn't Queen Victoria have a German accent?

IX

No. 302, Beacon Street

Our family prison for nine years. The house to which Robert had guided us, though the most commonplace of houses and meanly built for speculation, is perhaps worth describing. We passed the next nine years in it—all the later years of my boyhood; and its character and the life we led there are indelible not only in my memory but no doubt in my character and sentiment. I was unhappy there. At school nothing was imposed on me that I could complain of; there were no grinding tasks and no punishments; but until the last two or three years, when I formed close friendships and awoke to literature, it was all dead routine, and insufficient. A great void remained, which nothing at home could fill. The family was deeply disunited, and each member unhappy for a different reason. One of the boys at school, Davis, who had once come to lunch with us, said afterwards that we seemed to live as if in a boarding-house. This was not true at bottom, or at first, because on our Spanish side we formed a true family; but life in America gradually dispersed our interests and our affections. I found my own centre later, at Harvard; and then the bond with my mother's house, when Susana had returned to Spain and Robert was married, became pleasant and peaceful. Once or twice I spent a whole summer there, reading in the Public Library near by, and preparing my lectures. But that was no longer in Beacon Street; the scene was more retired, more modest, more suitable. There was no longer the pressure of poverty or of tiresome dissensions. It was the placid retreat of an old age without joy, but without claims.

The Back Bay in the 1870's. Our house was at that time one of the last on the water-side of Beacon Street, and there was still many a vacant lot east of it, where on passing in sharp wintry weather it was prudent to turn up one's coat collar against the icy blast from the river; as also, for the matter of that, at every cross-street. On the opposite side there were straggling groups of houses running further west along the Mill Dam, under which, at some points, the tide flowed in and out from the Back Bay, the shallow lagoon that originally extended to Boston Neck, turning the town almost into an island. The water in 1872 still came up to Dartmouth Street and to what is now Copley Square. Among the provisional features of this quarter were the frequent empty lots, ten or fifteen feet below the level of the street. These lots were usually enclosed in rough open fences, often broken down at the corners, from which a short cut could be made diagonally to the next street; and by this we schoolboys were quick to profit, for a free run on rough ground amid weeds and heaps of rubbish. The architecture of these half-built streets was conventional and commercial: no house of more than four storeys, no apartment-houses, no fanciful architectural styles, only two or three churches, closed except at the hour for services on Sundays. To go to Mass we had to walk over the Dartmouth Street railway bridge and some distance beyond, into the South End. I liked the spire at the corner of Newbury and Berkeley Street, and often walked that way in order to watch it. It looked to my eye, fed on copperplate views of English Cathedrals, a bit of genuine Gothic: but the brick Italian Gothic introduced by Ruskin, as well as Richardson's personal memories of Provence, left me quite cold, in spite of *The Stones of Venice*. They were indeed absurdly out of place, bastard, and theatrical.

Workings of a "producer's economy". Ours was one of two houses exactly alike; yet as they were only two, we could distinguish ours without looking at the number displayed in large figures on the semicircular glass panel over the front door: for ours was the house to the left, not the one to the right. The pair were a product of that "producer's economy", then beginning to prevail in America, which first creates articles and then attempts to create a demand for them; an economy that has flooded the country with breakfast foods, shaving soaps, poets, and professors of philosophy. Our twin houses had been designed to attract the buyer, who might sell his bargain again at a profit if he didn't find it satisfactory; and this was precisely the ground on which my mother was persuaded to buy her house, not expecting a financial crisis and a sudden but prolonged disinclination on the part of the consumer to buy anything that he didn't need. The advantages in our house were in the first place social or snobbish, that it was in Beacon Street and on the better or fashionable waterside of that street; which also rendered every room initially attractive, since it had either the sun if in the front or the view if in the rear. This view of a vast expanse of water reflecting the sky was unmistakably impressive, especially when the summer sunset lit up the scene, and darkness added to distance made the shabby bank opposite inoffensive. Gorgeous these sunsets often were; more gorgeous, good Bostonians believed, than sunsets anywhere else in the world; and my limited experience does not belie them. The illumination often had a kaleidoscopic quality, with fiery reds and yellows; but at other hours and seasons the aerial effects of the Charles River Basin were not remarkable. Moreover, the grand attraction of the water view was marred by two counter-effects discovered eventually by enthusiastic purchasers. One was the immediate foreground, modified but not removed afterwards, when the embankment was added. Under your nose was a mean backyard, unpaved, with clothes or at least clothes-lines stretched across it; and mean plank fences divided it from other backyards of the same description, with an occasional shed or stable to vary the prospect. Under your nose too,—and this was the second counter-effect—rose now and then the stench from mudflats and sewage that the sluggish current of the Charles and the sluggish tides that penetrated to the Basin did not avail to drain properly. However, this was chiefly noticeable in summer, when Beacon Street people were expected to be out of town; they made no loud complaints; and the democracy in general was not yet aroused to the importance of town planning for its own sake. The age was still enamoured of *laissez-faire*; and its advantages were indeed undeniable. For the government it meant a minimum of work, and for the public it meant a minimum of government.

Our white elephant offered attractions also for the investor; the town was rapidly spreading in that direction, land-values were sure to go up, and the house would become every year more central and more desirable. Finally, it was a small house, with only two rooms on each of the principal floors: comfortable and cosy, therefore, for a rich spinster or for an ambitious young married couple; especially as with its reception-room and large dining-room on the ground floor, and its front and back parlours upstairs, it lent itself to entertaining on a moderate scale. That it had only two decent bedrooms, one bathroom, and no backstairs, wouldn't matter with a very small family. **Our domestic arrangements** But we happened to be a family of five, demanding five separate rooms. Entertaining of any description was out of the question for us, apart from the expense, since our mother didn't pay visits or go anywhere, or wish for any society; and at that moment she possessed neither the objects nor the money necessary to furnish decently those superfluous reception rooms. She therefore turned the front parlour into a bedroom for herself, while my sisters occupied the two good rooms on the second floor, and Robert, the cook, the housemaid and I had the four small cubicles in the mansard or French roof. At least, this was the ultimate and normal arrangement; but when my father and I arrived, the family prejudice against doubling up had to be overcome for the time being. Not, however, in the case of my father and mother; for she resigned the front parlour to him and moved to one of the rooms above, the two girls being crowded into the other, while I was tucked, as a waif new to the New World, not only into Robert's room but into his bed, which happened incongruously to be a large double one. My mother had taken on her furniture from previous tenants or from "Aunt Lizzie"; and the double beds, not being wanted, had a tendency to pass out of sight into the upper regions; one falling in this way to Robert's lot. But this cohabitation with my elder brother didn't last long; it was contrary to my mother's instincts and habits; and soon a small bed was provided for me and I was moved into the adjoining little room, as into my own castle.

A non-Freudian initiation into sexual matters   The few months that I slept with Robert were not useless in my education. In those days nobody agitated the question as to how children should be informed about the secrets of life; it was left to life to divulge them. Now Robert, at eighteen, was the most innocent of beings, and mentally he remained so, even after he was a husband and father. He had had no sexual adventures or associations except of the most trivial sort; and if ribaldry ever amused him, it had little malice in it, and never rose above the clownish level; as his taste in literature also was of the crudest, and stopped at Mark Twain's *Jumping Frog* and Macaulay's *Lays of Ancient Rome*, learned at school in lieu of a classical education. Yet he was in the full flood of adolescence; his very innocence rendered him indiscreet; and I heard from him and observed in him what are the trials of young manhood, long before they could trouble me in my own person. This vicarious experience was like the vicarious experience I had had in Avila concerning the birth of children, the love-affairs, the quarrels, the torture, and the tragedies that encircle it. I was not much moved at the time or consciously interested; I was too young; but I was informed and prepared; so that the minor vices and even the anomalies of sexual life had nothing to surprise me, when I came upon them later in books or in the broad world. It was not at all as if I had been taken aside very gravely by a parent or teacher, and given a lesson in human physiology, as if in the biology of insects. That might have instructed me verbally, and left me as ignorant of the world, as my teacher might very likely have been. Nor had I been left to discover the facts by chance, perhaps in sinister surroundings and with sad results. The normal world itself had instructed me; I had seen its operation in the life. There could therefore be, initially and towards all mankind, sympathy in my knowledge and knowledge in my sympathies.

Sad architecture.   The strip of land that our house occupied was nineteen feet wide, and not far from ten times as long, since it stretched from the edge of the public road over the "side-walk", broad and paved with brick, which it was the tenant's duty to keep swept and reasonably free from snow; over the grass plot in front of the house; and behind the house over a long backyard, and the alley outside, to the water's edge. The brick façade was meagre and graceless; my architectural fancy often conceived how easily those twin houses might have been rendered symmetrical, homelike, and even pleasing, in the Dutch manner, if the two doors had been placed together in the middle, and if the steps, the little upper platform, and the steps on either side leading down to the basement had been combined into one picturesque design. The sash or guillotine windows too might at least have retained the square panes of the colonial period, instead of the hideous plate glass that was thought an "improvement". But the builder was no artist; he made one drawing for one cheap house, and for economy built two of them, his capital or his courage not permitting him to build a dozen.

The family centre.

•

Literary entertainments.   To this unsuitable residence our habits adapted themselves as well as might be. The small room beside the front door became our family sitting-room. It was sunny and cosy; on cold evenings, when the furnace proved insufficient, it could be at once warmed and ventilated by lighting the fire; and by day it afforded us the feminine Spanish entertainment of looking out of the window and watching, a little below our own level, the stray passers-by. It was here that I sat, close by the window, doing my fancy drawing and reading, which occupied me much more than my school lessons. We had one study-hour out of the five at the school in the morning, and that sufficed for most of my preparation; but I took my Latin book, and one or two others home, where I could read them aloud to myself, of course in my bedroom, and gather a rhetorical impression, with little profit to my scholarship. The back wall of that little sitting-room was covered by a large bookcase with glass doors, which contained the eighth edition of the *Encyclopaedia Britannica*, Lane's *Arabian Nights*, and a lot of old books that nobody opened. But we had a few Spanish books, and could get others from the Boston Public Library. In this way, I read Oliver Optic's stories for boys, doting on the sea-faring and the oceanic geography; also Abbot's *Lives*, of which I remember *Alexander the Great* and *Mary Queen of Scots*. We also had Motley's and Prescott's pseudo-Spanish histories: but I knew enough to spew them out of my mouth at the first tasting. The sectarian politics and moralising of most historians made history an impossible study for me for many years: not ancient history, of course, nor Plutarch's *Lives*, which we had at school to read out of at sight, and not Gibbon, when I came to read him; because although Gibbon's bias is obvious, it is entertaining, and by the time I came to him I was willing to laugh at absurdities whether in church or state or in philosophic opinion, without feeling that ultimate truth was in the least affected by such accidents or by the derision of worldly wits.

During the first years Susana and Robert would read aloud to us in the evening, at first in Spanish: *Don Quixote* in its entirety (save the *lunares*)* and *Un Servilón y un Liberalito* by the pious lady-novelist "Fernán Caballero". Then, because our interesting Spanish books were exhausted, or because Robert, especially, found English easier, they shifted to Shakespeare, and read *Julius Caesar* and *Romeo and Juliet*, of which I remember liking the first and thinking the second inexpressibly silly. There the practice died out. We had no more reading aloud, but Susana and I often read the same books separately. When I became fond of poetry, I tried to interest her in it, but failed. She liked nothing I showed her except Byron's *Don Juan*, because, she said, it was as good as prose.

Our choice of engravings. The walls of this little sitting-room were hung exclusively with engravings, most of which had adorned "Uncle Henry's" house. There were official large portraits of Napoleon the Third and the Empress Eugénie in their regalia, theatrically posed and very pompous; also an affecting scene in an English

*Facetious name for the Tales interspersed: literally *moles*.

churchyard, full of yew and weeping willow, and showing a brave little boy and a sweet little girl, sitting and holding hands on the edge of a newly made grave, strewn with wild flowers; while above their heads, a large white angel in muslin, the spirit of their departed mother, spread her hands and her great wings over them in protection and blessing. To take away the taste of this, like a savoury after a milk pudding, there hung near it a framed collection of *Poor Richard's Proverbs*, with quaint little eighteenth century illustrations for each maxim. I learned most of them by heart, but can remember only

> *Early to bed and early to rise*
> *Makes a man healthy and wealthy and wise*

and *Three removes are as bad as a fire*. I wished Franklin had said something crushingly true and materialistic about the Angel Mother and about Napoleon the Third's corsets and waxed moustache; but I was willing to nurse illusions about the Empress Eugénie. She had been the queen of fashion in her day, she was Spanish, and she might be said to look a little like Susana idealised.

Perspectives open in architecture and philosophy. The article in our *Encyclopaedia* on architecture, which I studied persistently, was an excellent corrective to Ruskin, to Ferguson's *History of Architecture*, and to the taste of my time. The illustrations were all plans, elevations, and sections; and the only styles treated were the classic and the "Italian". There were no perspective views. I was thus introduced to the art professionally; and the structural interest became as great for me as the picturesque. Yet as I was never to build anything except in fancy, and even if I had become an architect could never have built great English country seats like those depicted in my text, I turned all those technicalities to imaginative uses. Here were the magnificent houses in which the English nobility lived; I had only to supply the landscape, the costumes, and the characters—and vivid representations of all these were accessible to me,—in order to complete the picture, and bring it to life. English high life, before I had seen anything of it—and I have never seen much, except at Oxford and Cambridge—at once established itself in my regard side by side with ancient and with Catholic life as one of the high lights of history. The notion of belittling any one of them—or of belittling any other civilisation, because less known to me—never crossed my mind; and as one style of architecture does not prevent the others from being equally beautiful and proper in their time and place, so the whole mental and moral civilisation that flourished with that style must be accepted as right and honourable in its day. This principle is applicable to religions and philosophies, in so far as they too are local and temporary; but in so far as the universe and human nature are constant, it is evident that a single system of science will serve to describe them, although the images and language will constantly differ in which that system is expressed. In the last resort, all mutations must help to fill out a single history of things, that doubtless never will be finished or written. There is no vacillation in the truth about vacillations; and in this sense philosophic insight, if humble and sane, is as perennial as its object.

In regard, however, to rival forms of art or civilisation, I was directed from the beginning towards impartiality, which does not imply omnivorousness or confusion. All beauties are to be honoured, but only one embraced.

X

The Latin School

Philosophic parenthesis and apology. When I search my memory for events and feelings belonging to my earlier boyhood in America, from the age of eight to sixteen, I find for the most part a blank. There are only stray images, like those of early childhood, with no sense of any consecutive interest, any affections or sorrows. And yet I know that my feelings in those years were intense, that I was solitary and unhappy, out of humour with everything that surrounded me, and attached only to a persistent dream-life, fed on books of fiction, on architecture, and on religion. I was not precocious; I may have had more ability than the average boy, but it was lavished on boyish thoughts; and a certain backwardness, or unwilling acceptance of reality, characterises my whole life and philosophy, not indeed as a maxim but as a sentiment.

Why have I forgotten all those years? The causes are no doubt physical, but the effects may be expressed in literary terms. The past cannot be re-enacted except in the language and with the contrasts imposed by the present. The feelings of children, in particular, although intense, are not ordinarily long-lived or deeply rooted. We cry desperately or we silently hate for not being allowed to do this or to have that; but these objects are trifles. If we remembered those occasions they would seem to us indifferent; we should be ashamed to confess those feelings, or we should laugh at them with superior airs: as if the things that now preoccupy us, if we outgrew them, could seem to us more momentous. Thus vast portions of the past—almost all our dreams, almost all our particular thoughts and conversations— become unrecoverable. Our accepted, organised, practically compulsory habits shut them out. But these habits themselves will change more or less with time and with circumstances. Even what we still think we remember will be remembered differently; so that a man's memory may almost become the art of continually varying and misrepresenting his past, according to his interests in the present. This, when it is not intentional or dishonest, involves no deception. Things truly wear those aspects to one another. A point of view and a special lighting are not distortions. They are conditions of vision, and spirit can see nothing not focussed in some living eye.

Something like this was in Goethe's mind when he entitled his essay on his life *Fiction and Truth* or *Poetry and Truth*; not that any facts were to be reported inaccurately or invented, but that his mature imagination, in which those facts were pictured, could not but veil them in an atmosphere of serenity, dignity, and justice utterly foreign to his original romantic experience. I am no Goethe; the atmosphere of my aging mind is not Olympian, and in retrospect it cannot help lending to my insignificant contacts with the world some flavours that Goethe's wisdom had washed out, though they were not absent from his younger days: I mean salt, pepper, and pity for mankind.

One year at a Kindergarten.   Of Miss Welchman's Kindergarten in Chestnut Street, my first school in Boston, I remember only that we had cards with holes pricked in them, and coloured worsted: that we were invited to pass through the holes, making designs to suit our own fancy. I suppose this was calculated to develop artistic originality, not to convince us how trivial that originality is, and how helpless it is without traditional models. I remember also that I used to walk home with another boy, not so old as I, but also much older than the other children; that there were banks of snow on both sides of the path; and that one day—this must have been in spring for there was a bush with red flowers in his grass-plot—he said something very strange as he left me, and ran up the steps into his house. I reported what he had said to Susana, who pronounced it *pantheism*: perhaps it was that those red flowers were opening because God was awaking in them. This shows how far my English had got in that Kindergarten and how we lisped metaphysics there.

Another year at the Brimmer School.   The Brimmer School, where I went during the next winter, 1873–1874, was the public grammar school of our city district, although more than a mile from our house, in the depths of the South End. I had to walk the whole level length of Beacon Street, cross the Common, and go some distance down hill in Tremont Street to Common Street, where the school was situated, looking like a police-station. It was a poor boys' free school, the roughest I was ever in, where the rattan played an important part, although usually behind the scenes, and where there was an atmosphere of rowdiness and ill-will, requiring all sorts of minor punishments, such as standing in the corner or being detained after school. I don't know what lessons we had, except that there were oral spelling-matches, in which naturally I didn't shine. A word spelt aloud (as some Americans like to do facetiously, instead of pronouncing it) still puzzles me and leaves me dumb. Nevertheless, partly because I was older and bigger than most of the boys, I soon became "monitor", and had my little desk beside the teacher's, a woman, facing the whole class. This distinction was invidious, and there were attempts at chasing me or hooting at me when we got out of school. Only once did it come to blows; and inexpert as I was at fisticuffs, or rather wrestling, I was taller, and managed to hold my own, and make my nasty little enemy sneak away sullenly. And I was not friendless. There was another boy from the West End, Bob Upham by name, with whom I usually crossed the Common; this was the danger-zone, since in the streets there were policemen who understood these things and would stop hostilities. On that occasion Bob Upham behaved according to the strictest rules of honour, standing by me sympathetically, but without interfering, and he afterwards said that the other boy had "very nearly got me". But I hadn't been at all hurt, and never have had another opportunity to try my hand at the manly art, in which no doubt I should have been a miserable failure.

I begin at the Latin School at the Eighth Class, then the foot of the ladder. By a happy chance it was possible to transfer me the next year to a much better school, the historic Latin School where from the earliest times to the then most recent all well-educated Bostonians had been prepared for college. The School Committee in the City government had that year decided to try an experiment, and establish a preparatory course of two years, to precede the six traditional classes. The experiment was not long continued, but I profited by it, and passed eight full years in the Latin School, thus being more of a Latin School old boy than almost anybody else. We were not lodged during those preliminary years in the regular Schoolhouse, but at first in Harrison Avenue, and later in Mason Street. Both these places, as well as the Schoolhouse in Bedford Street, were in a central quarter of the town. I still had to cross the Common, but now to West Street, whence it was but a step to all those schoolhouses.

Somnambulistic periods in life. More than once in my life I have crossed a desert in all that regards myself, my thoughts, or my happiness; so that when I look back over those years, I see objects,

I see public events, I see *persons and places*, but I don't see myself. My inner life, as I recall it, seems to be concentrated in a few oases, in a few halting-places, *Green Inns*, or sanctuaries, where the busy traveller stopped to rest, to think, and to be himself. I say the *busy* traveller, because those long stretches of spiritual emptiness were filled with daily actions and feelings, later in my case often with giving lectures and writing books: yet all was done under some mechanical stimulus, the college bell, the desk, the pen, or the chapter planned: old thoughts and old words flowing out duly from the reservoir, until the college bell rang again, and the water was turned off. Of myself in those years I have no recollection; it is as if I hadn't existed, or only as a mechanical sensorium and active apparatus, doing its work under my name. Somnambulistic periods, let me call them; and such a period now seems to begin and to last for two-thirds of my Latin School days.

Frozen ears.   Certain detached images, with the crude spectral col-
ouring of a child's picture-book, remain from this first somnambulist season. At the school in Harrison Avenue I can see the yellow wainscotting of the school-room, and the yellow desks; and especially I can see the converging leaden sides of the sink, where on one winter morning the teacher—now a man—sent me to thaw out my ears, frozen stiff on the way to school. I was to bathe them in cold water; there was sharp pain and subsequently enormous blisters; but the accident never recurred, although I resolutely refused all scarves, pads, or ridiculous cloth rosettes, such as the women recommended to protect those asinine organs. I found that a little pressure, applied at the right moment, at once brought the warm blood coursing back, and prevented trouble. Cold, rain, and wind, unless there were dust, never spoilt my pleasure in the open air when I was young; on the contrary, I liked them.

Our first   I remember also my first Headmaster at the Latin
Headmaster   School, Mr. Gardner by name: a tall gaunt figure in some
and his
Parisian   sort of flowing long coat—of course not a gown—with
pronunciation   a diminutive head, like the nob of a mannikin. The in-
of French.   significant occiput was enlarged, however, as if by a halo,
by a great crop of dusty brown hair. Was it a wig? That suspicion seemed to my mocking young mind curiously comic and exciting. What if it were a wig and should fall off? What if we hung a hook on an invisible wire over the door, to catch it as he sailed out?

One day on his rounds of inspection the Headmaster found us having our French lesson. A headmaster has to pretend to know everything, and the pretense soon becomes a conviction. Mr. Gardner at once took over the duty of teaching us his super-French. "The French word *bonne*", he said, "is pronounced in Paris—I have been in Paris myself— exactly like the English word *bun*." Now, I had heard a good deal of French out of school. There had been the French *bonne* Justine, the Alsatian tutor who loved *avec rage*, and the Catholic families in Boston who chatted in French together. And hadn't I inherited from my sisters *La Jeune Abeille du Parnasse Français* and couldn't I say by heart:

> *Et ma plus belle couronne*
> > *De lilas*
> *Sera à toi, ma bonne,*
> *Si tu me dis où Dieu n'est pas?*

If *bonne* sounds exactly like *bun*, would Mr. Gardner maintain that *couronne*, save for the first letter, sounds exactly like *you run?* I was sure that it was as ridiculous to call a *bonne* a bun as to call a bun a *bonne*. But apparently headmasters were like that; and I kept my phonetic science to myself with the immense satisfaction of feeling that I knew better than my teacher.

Mr. Capen.   I may add that at that time our French master was not a Frenchman, but a Yankee farmer named Mr. Capen, whom we called Old Cudjo, and who had a physiological method of acquiring a Parisian accent without needing to accompany the Headmaster to Paris. He would open his mouth wide, like the hippopotamus at the Zoo, and would insert a pencil, to point out exactly what parts of the tongue, lips, palate, or larynx we should contract or relax in order to emit the pure French sounds of *u, an, en, in, un,* and *on.* Nobody laughed. I think the boys were rather impressed for the moment by the depth of Mr. Capen's science, and the hopelessness of profiting by it. He was not a man to be trifled with. He had a most thunderous way of playing what he called *Voluntaries* on the piano; and rumour had it that he had stolen a march, under a heavy handicap of years, on his own son, by marrying the girl his son was engaged to.

The Bedford Street Schoolhouse.   Scraps of rude, quaint, grotesque humanity; bits of that Dickensian bohemia still surviving in my day in certain old-fashioned places, of which I shall have occasion to speak again. But the image that for me sets the key to them all, appeared when we moved to the Bedford Street Schoolhouse. It seemed a vast, rattling old shell of a building, bare, shabby, and forlorn to the point of squalor; not exactly dirty, but worn, shaky, and stained deeply in every part by time, weather, and merciless usage. The dingy red brick—and everything in that world was dingy red brick—had none of that plastic irregularity, those soft pink lights and mossy patina that make some old brick walls so beautiful; here all the surfaces remained stark and unyielding, thin and sharp, like impoverished old maids. This house was too modern to be as solid as the Hollis and Stoughton Halls that I afterwards lived in at Harvard; it had been built in a hurry, and not to last long. The windows were much larger, but blank and sombre; their cold glassy expanse with its slender divisions looked comfortless and insecure. When up three or four worn granite steps you entered the door, the interior seemed musty and ill-lighted, but spacious, even mysterious. Each room had four great windows, but the street and the courts at the side and rear were narrow, and overshadowed by warehouses or office-buildings. No blackboard was black; all were indelibly clouded with ingrained layers of old chalk; the more you rubbed it out, the more you rubbed it in. Every desk was stained with generations of inkspots, cut deeply with initials and scratched drawings. What idle thoughts had been wandering for years through all those empty heads in all those tedious school hours! In the best schools, almost all school-time is wasted. Now and then something is learned that sticks fast; for the rest, the boys are merely given time to grow and are kept from too much mischief.

A ramshackle wooden staircase wound up through the heart of the building to the fourth storey, where the Hall was; and down those steep and dangerous curves the avalanche of nailed-hoofed boys would come thundering, forty or eighty or two hundred together. However short their legs might be, it was simpler and safer, if not altogether inevitable, to rush down spontaneously with the herd rather than hold back and be pushed or fall out or be trampled upon or deserted.

The school-teacher's fate. And the teachers, though it is not possible for me now to distinguish them all in memory, were surely not out of keeping with their surroundings: disappointed, shabby-genteel, picturesque old Yankees, with a little bitter humour breaking through their constitutional fatigue. I daresay that for them as for me, and for all the boys who were at all sensitive, the school was a familiar symbol of fatality. They hadn't chosen it, they hadn't wanted it, they didn't particularly like it; they knew of no reason why it should be the sort of school it was; but there it stood, there they somehow found themselves entangled; and there was nothing else practicable but to go on there, doing what was expected and imposed upon them. You may say that for the teachers at least, in that age of individual initiative and open careers, a thousand alternatives were, or had been, possible; and you may say that they could not have been altogether insensible of their high vocation and the high vocation of their country, to create gradually and securely a better world, a world free from superstition, from needless hatreds, from unjust inequalities, and from devastating misery. Yes: but all that was negative; it consisted of things to be got rid of and avoided, and in America the more obvious of them had actually been escaped. Officially, especially now that slavery had been abolished, everything was all right. Everybody was free. Everybody was at work. Almost everybody could be well educated. Almost everybody was married. Therefore almost everybody was, or ought to be, perfectly happy. But were the teachers at the Latin School, perhaps the best of American schools, happy? Or were the boys? Ah, perhaps we should not ask whether they were happy, for they were not rich, but whether they were not enthusiastically conscious of a great work, an endless glorious struggle and perpetual victory, set before them in the world. And I reply, not for myself, since I don't count, being an alien, but in their name, that they decidedly were conscious of no such thing. They had heard of it; but in their daily lives they were conscious only of hard facts, meagreness, routine, petty commitments, and ideals too distant and vague to be worth mentioning.

Mr. Fiske and my difficulties in Greek. Those teachers were stray individuals; they had not yet been standardised by educational departments and pedagogy. Some were like village schoolmasters or drudges; elderly men, like Mr. Capen, with crotchets, but good teachers, knowing their particular book and knowing how to keep order, and neither lax nor cruel. Others, especially Mr. Fiske, afterwards headmaster, and Mr. Groce were younger, with a more modern education. They might have been college professors; they loved their subjects, Greek and English, and allowed them to colour their minds out of school hours. In a word, they were *cultivated* men. I was an unprofitable though not unappreciative pupil to Mr. Fiske, because I didn't learn my Greek properly. That was not his fault. If I could have had him for a private tutor I should have become a good Grecian: it would have added immensely to my life and my philosophy. But I was only one of forty; I was expected to study dryly, mechanically, without the side-lights and the stimulus of non-verbal interests attached to the words. In Latin, I could supply these side-lights and non-verbal interests out of my own store. Latin was the language of the Church, it was old Spanish. The roots were all my roots. But Greek roots were more often foreign and at first unmeaning: they had to be learned by hammering, to which my indolence was not inclined. And there was another difficulty. My apprehension of words is auricular; I must *hear* what I read. I knew, with small variations, what was the sound of Latin. I had heard it all my life; slovenly and corrupt as the Spanish pronunciation of it may be, at least it is something traditional. But what of Greek pronunciation? How should Homer sound? How should Sophocles? How should Xenophon or Plato? The artificial German Greek that we were taught—without even a proper *o*—was impossible. I tried many years later, when I was in Greece, to learn a little of the modern language, in hopes that it might react on my sense for the ancient texts and make me feel at home in them; but the time was too short, my opportunities limited, and I was too old to be quick in such a matter.

How shall we pronounce it?   Even as it was, however, I learned a little Greek at school after my fashion, and one day surprised Mr. Fiske by reciting a long speech out of *Oedipus Tyrannos* for my ordinary declamation. He couldn't believe his ears, and afterwards privately congratulated me on my pronunciation of the *o*'s. But that didn't make me master of the Greek vocabulary or the Greek inflections. I didn't *study* enough. I learned and remember well what I could learn from Mr. Fiske without studying. He was an exceedingly nervous shy man; evidently suffered at having to address anyone, or having to find words in which to express his feelings. His whole body would become tense, he would stand almost on tiptoe, with two or three fingers in the side pocket of his trousers, and the other two or three moving outside, as if looking for the next word. These extreme mannerisms occasioned no ridicule: the boys all saw that there was a clear mind and a good will behind them; and Mr. Fiske was universally liked and admired. This, although his language was as contorted as his gestures. He always seemed to be translating literally and laboriously from the Greek or the German. When he wished to fix in our minds the meaning of a Greek word he would say, for instance: "χαράδρα, a ravine, from which our word *character*, the deeply graven result of long-continued habit." Or "καταρρέω, to flow down, whence our word *catarrh*, copious down-flowings from the upper regions of the head." We didn't laugh, and we remembered.

Mr. Groce and English poetry.   Very different was dapper Mr. Groce, our teacher of English composition and literature, a little plump man, with a keen, dry, cheerful, yet irritable disposition, a sparkling bird-like eye, and a little black moustache and diminutive chin-beard. I suspect that he was too intelligent to put up patiently with all the conventions. Had he not been a public-school teacher, dependent on the democratic hypocrisies of a government committee, he might have said unconventional things. This inner rebellion kept him from being sentimental, moralistic, or religious in respect to poetry; yet he *understood* perfectly the penumbra of emotion that good and bad poetry alike may drag after them in an untrained mind. He knew how to rescue the structural and rational beauties of a poem from that bog of private feeling. To me this was a timely lesson, for it was precisely sadness and religiosity and grandiloquence that first attracted me in poetry; and perhaps I owe to Mr. Groce the beginnings of a capacity to distinguish the musical and expressive charm of poetry from its moral appeal. At any rate, at sixteen, I composed my first longish poem, in Spenser's measure, after *Childe Harold* and *Adonais*, full of pessimistic, languid, Byronic sentiments, describing the various kinds of superiority that Night has over Day. It got the prize.

The novelty of being praised and its small use.   That year I won several other prizes, and began to be a personage in my own estimation, because other people, in my little world, began to take notice of me. At home I had never been petted or praised, and my conceit, which was rather disdain for other things than claims for myself, had had only itself to feed upon. Being noticed had a good effect on me, in awakening my sympathy in return without, however, either establishing or much modifying my good opinion of myself. Neither praise nor blame has ever done so. On the contrary, if people praise me I almost always feel that they praise me for the wrong things, for things which they impute to me out of their preconceptions, and which are not in me; and the blame often, though not always, has the same source. Yet blame is apt to be more keen-scented than praise; praise is often silly; but blame, though it may be baseless objectively, probably indicates a true perception of divergence from the critic's standards; so that relatively to the critic, it is seldom mistaken.

Criticism, favourable or unfavourable, I think has done me very little good. For one thing, it has been almost always belated, and founded on something that privately I had already sloughed off, as being an accidental and borrowed element. For instance, by far the most admired of my sonnets is sonnet three of the first series, about Columbus and the Other World, written when I was twenty, in the midst of my religious indecision, but framed in and published ten years later, when the decision had been made and found satisfying. So in my earlier prose, Americans like whatever in form or substance savours of America, and English people turn away in disgust from those very qualities, quite happy on the contrary at any expression of my admiration for themselves, however qualified and playful this admiration may be at bottom. Sentiment is neither dogma nor precept, and I express what I feel without pledging myself to feel it always. Frank as I may be, I doubt if any of my old friends has understood my character; and no philosophical critic seems to have found the key to my very perspicuous philosophy.

Vanity of the importance that youth gives to itself. To my inner man, therefore, the favours and buffets of society have been like those of the weather: most pleasant and most unpleasant, but insignificant: mere irritants to vanity. I am constitutionally vain, vain like a young woman; not that I particularly overestimate my powers or my works. I don't think myself a great poet or a great philosopher. Of course I accept all my opinions; that is a joke that fate plays upon us; but I am acutely conscious of this fatal predicament, which knocks absolutism out of one's pretensions and renders comparisons and preferences all partial and arbitrary. I am acutely conscious also of my great defects, bodily, passional, intellectual, and moral. I am in almost everything the opposite of what I should have wished to be; and my puerile vanity lies precisely in feeling these misfortunes keenly, and being most unphilosophically troubled at the figure I cut and the slips I make. Less now, perhaps, than when I was young; because now I can disregard more sincerely the accident that these good or bad characteristics are attributable to *me* rather than to another creature; and now I can allow them the weight, for good or for evil, that justly belongs to them in the world; and this weight is slight.

Declamation. I have mentioned declamation: that was another stimulus to vanity. Inwardly it was one more dramatic indulgence, one more occasion for fantastically playing a part, and dreaming awake, as I did in making plans of vast palaces and imaginary islands, where I should one day be monarch, like Sancho Panza; and this slides into the sphere of my youthful religiosity, of which more presently. But, socially considered, declamation was an effort *de se faire valoir*, to make oneself count, to gain a momentary and fictitious ascendency over others. Momentary and fictitious, because our declamation was pure oratory. It had nothing of that political timeliness which characterises young people's debates in England. With us, the subject matter was legendary, the language learned by rote, stilted and inflated, the thought platitudinous. Apart from the training in mere *elocution* (as indeed it was called) it was practice in feigning, in working up a verbal enthusiasm for any cause, and seeming to prophesy any event. Very useful, no doubt, for future lawyers, politicians, or clergymen; training for that reversible sophistry and propaganda that intoxicates the demagogue and misleads the people.

I begin to play a conventional part. That prize-day in June, 1880, in the old Boston Music Hall, marked my emergence into public notice. It abolished, or seemed to abolish, my shyness and love of solitude. I could now face any public and speak before it; and this assurance never forsook me afterwards, except when sometimes, in my unwritten lectures or speeches, I found myself out of my element, had nothing to say, or was weary of saying it. In reality I was always out of my element in teaching and in society, and was saying something forced. The dramatic practice of accepting a brief, or developing an argument helped me for a time. I could be sincere and spontaneous in the logic of my theme, even if the ultimate issue were unreal or problematical; and in reviewing the history of philosophy this critical honesty is enough, and supplies the information and the dialectical training that are officially required. Nevertheless this was not preaching a gospel. It did not come from the heart. It left the pupil unguided and morally empty, and in the end the teacher felt himself a drudge. My shyness came back in what Hegelians would call a higher form: I was no longer timid or without resource, but rebellious against being roped in and made to play some vulgar trick in a circus. My love of solitude reasserted itself, not that I feared the world, but that I claimed my liberty and my *Lebensraum* beyond it. In solitude it is possible to love mankind; in the world, for one who knows the world, there can be nothing but secret or open war. For those who love war the world is an excellent field, but I am a born cleric or poet. I must see both sides and take neither, in order, ideally, to embrace both, to sing both, and love the different forms that the good and the beautiful wear to different creatures. This comprehensiveness in sympathy by no means implies that good and evil are indistinguishable or dubious. Nature sets definite standards for every living being; the good and the beautiful could not exist otherwise; and the failure or lapse of natural perfection in each is an irreparable evil. But it is, in every case, a ground of sorrow to the spirit, not of rage; for such failure or lapse is fated and involuntary. This sorrow in my case, however, has always been mitigated by the gift of laughter; that helped me both to perceive those defects and to put up with them.

Kinship of laughter and tears.   Between the laughing and the weeping philosopher there is no opposition: *the same facts* that make one laugh make one weep. No whole-hearted man, no sane art, can be limited to either mood. In me this combination seems to be readier and more pervasive than in most people. I laugh a great deal, laugh too much, my friends tell me; and those who don't understand me think that this merriment contradicts my disillusioned philosophy. *They*, apparently, would never laugh if they admitted that life is a dream, that men are animated automata, and that the forms of the good and beautiful are as various and as evanescent as the natural harmonies that produce them. They think they would collapse or turn to stone or despair and commit suicide. But probably they would do no such thing: they would adapt themselves to the reality, and laugh. They might even feel a new zest in living, join in some bold adventure, become heroes, and think it glorious to die with a smile for the love of something beautiful. They do not perceive that this is exactly what national leaders and religious martyrs have always done, except that their warm imagination has probably deceived them about the material effects of what they were doing.

Lampooning the teachers.   My lachrymose prize-poem about the beauties of darkness was not my only effusion. The habit of scribbling mocking epigrams has accompanied me through life and invaded the margins of my most serious authors. Mockery is the first puerile form of wit, playing with surfaces without sympathy; I abounded in it. During the winter of 1880–1881 our class, then the second class, formed a society to meet once a week in the evening and have a debate. We hired a bare room in Tremont Street, opposite the Common, with a few benches or chairs in it; someone would propose a resolution or advance an opinion, and the discussion would follow. When my turn came, I read a little satire on all our teachers, in verse, saying very much what I have said about them above; only that my account was more complete, included them all, and treated them less kindly. It had a great success, and the boys wanted to have it printed. Printed it was, but not as it originally stood. "Holy Moses", for instance, which was the nick-name current for our Headmaster, Moses Merrill, was changed to the less irreverent and more exact phrase: "lordly Moses", and many other things were modified. Then the whole was enveloped in a tirade, of a sentimental sort, about the Bedford Street Schoolhouse, which was about to be abandoned for a new building in the South End. A lot of copies were printed, perhaps two or three hundred; and on the day of our Farewell public Declamation in the Hall, the Headmaster somehow got wind of its existence, and said, "We hear that one of the boys has written a poem about leaving this old Schoolhouse: will he get up and read it." I had a copy in my pocket: I got up, and read the longish sentimental part, and then sat down again, leaving out the personalities. For the moment, all was well; but other boys and some outsiders got copies; and the disrespectful gibes at the teachers became public under their noses.

I am forgiven and treated with favour. It was a day or two before Christmas, and the School was not to meet again for ten days or more: however, after consulting with the family at home, I went to see the Headmaster at his own house, and explained how everything had happened. He wasn't severe; I had been really very complimentary to him, and had come spontaneously to apologise. But he said I had better write to the various teachers, explaining that I had only intended the thing as a private joke, without any thought that it would become public; and that I must particularly apologise to Mr. Chadwick, whom I had spoken of unkindly, and who felt the blow. When School met again, Mr. Merrill made us a long speech; but nothing more happened. And official sentiment towards me was not unfavourably affected. This appeared at the opening of the next term. My class had to elect the Lieutenant Colonel of the Boston School Regiment, the Colonel that year coming from the English High School; and by a majority of one vote they elected Dick Smith, and then me unanimously for Major of our Battalion. But the Headmaster reversed the order, and appointed me Lieutenant Colonel and Dick Smith Major, without giving reasons, at which legal but arbitrary exhibition of favouritism on the Headmaster's part, Dick Smith's father took him out of the School; and I became both Lieutenant Colonel and Major, both offices being almost sinecures.

First false semblance of immersion in the world. These incidents established me during my last year as in a sense the leading boy in my School, far as I was from being at the head of my class; yet in my irregular way I was not bad at my studies, and got six honourable mentions in my Harvard entrance examinations. This capacity of mine to pass examinations and to win prizes was doubtless what had caused Mr. Merrill to prefer me to Dick Smith for the head of the School Battalion; because Dick Smith was a clean manly boy and a gentleman, but not an intellectual luminary. This sporadic brilliancy of mine seemed to render me a better representative of the School as a whole. A surprising and only momentary phenomenon. In reality I remained there, as I remained later at Harvard for twenty-five years, a stranger at heart; and all the false appearances to the contrary would not have misled anybody (as they did not mislead President Eliot and the intelligent public at Harvard) if athletics had been important at that time in the School; but although there was, I believe, a base-ball team it was an obscure unofficial affair; else my complete uselessness, either as performer or as manager in such sports, would have at once set me down for a stray individual of no importance to the life of the place. Not that I had then, or ever, any *ideal* hostility to sport or to polite society or even to politics or trade. As customs, as institutions, as historical dramas, these things interest and please me immensely and excite my imagination to sympathy with this form of them or antipathy to that other form. But I can truly live only in the reaction of the mind upon them, in religion, poetry, history, and friendship. If I take a practical part, it is only by putting on a domino for the carnival. I am capable of that impulse, I can feel the fun and the intoxication of it; but the louder the rout the greater the frivolity; and the more complete the relief of stripping off the motley, washing away the paint, and returning to solitude, to silence, and to sincerity.

XI

The Church of the Immaculate Conception

The more I change the more I am the same person. When I began, in this small way, to play a part in the world and to be absorbed in it, was I awaking from my childish day-dreams—my imaginary architecture and geography and my imaginary religion—and entering into real life? Or was I being seduced and distracted from my natural vocation, and caught in the vortex of a foolish dance where I could neither shine as a reveller nor find satisfaction as a mind?

Now when at an advanced age I look back upon my whole career, I think I can reply to this question. At bottom there was no real change, no awakening and no apostasy. There was only a change in the subject matter on which my fancy worked. I had new materials for my dreams, and other terms in which to express my secret aspiration. Instead of being an ineffectual poet I became, at intervals, a mediocre player; in both directions I was simply the artist. There was ultimately no material issue, in either case: it all inevitably ended in nothing. But in both cases there was a passing music of ideas, a dramatic vision, a theme for dialectical insight and laughter; and to decipher that theme, that vision, and that music was my only possible life.

This is a book of memoirs, not of philosophical argument, and I have no wish to brow-beat the reader into accepting my theory of myself or of anything else. Let me return at once to my narrative and let him judge the facts for himself.

Early Mass at the German Catholic church. In the Boston of my boyhood there were two churches served by the Jesuits. The more modest one was a parish church for the German-speaking population, in which the Jesuits were missionaries under the direct authority of the Archbishop. Here I used to go sometimes to an early Mass on Sundays, always alone. Mass was said in the basement, low, dark, flat-roofed, and perfectly bare, except for the altar, and the Stations of the Cross hung round the walls. But it was filled with a devout decent crowd, chiefly men; and they sang in unison several German hymns, simply, gladly, and unaffectedly, yet rather musically, as if they were singing glees. I thought that here must be the origin of the Protestant practice of psalm-singing: they had knocked off most of the Mass, but kept the popular German accompaniment of a general chorus, as in the Greek tragedies. Yet what a difference between these Catholic effusions, which were not substitutes for the ritual but a private and spontaneous participation in it, and the perfunctory, inaudible pretense at keeping up with the paid quartet that was really performing; where the music was not good enough to be listened to for a concert, and the words too crude and obsoletely doctrinal to express anybody's feelings—at least not in those Unitarian churches which, at that time, I was being taken to against my will. It was in order to find myself for a moment in a religious atmosphere that I got up before dawn on those winter mornings, and took that double walk at a great pace, perhaps over snow, in any case through deserted streets in biting weather. But I liked the communal spirit of those people, devout and unspoiled; I liked their singing, without myself understanding the words; and though the priest turned round after the Gospel and said something in German, it was not a sermon, only a few announcements or admonitions for the coming week; and the strange language lifted me out of time and place, into the universal fold of all pilgrim spirits. I also liked the long double walk, with its slight tang of hardship, I who never had real hardships to bear; and breakfast afterwards seemed better than usual. Walking has always been my sole form of exercise; and then I never went out merely to walk, but only to get to and from school; and here was the same kind of errand, only more voluntary, done with a more concentrated mind.

If later I was taken to some Unitarian church, it didn't matter. It seemed a little ridiculous, all those good people in their Sunday clothes, so demure, so conscious of one another, not needing in the least to pray or to be prayed for, nor inclined to sing, but liking to flock together once a week, as people in Spain flock to the *paseo*, and glad to hear a sermon like the leading article in some superior newspaper calculated to confirm the conviction already in them that their bourgeois virtues were quite sufficient and that perhaps in time poor backward races and nations might be led to acquire them.

Architecture and music at *The Immaculate Conception*.   The other church served by the Jesuits was entirely their own, being attached to their Boston College, and built and managed according to their taste and traditions. It was not a parish, but attracted unattached or inquiring people from any quarter. Jesuit policy did not forbid certain attractions not found in poorer churches. The edifice was not—as often happened in those days—a Protestant meeting-house turned into a church; nor did it attempt to rival the picturesqueness of an ivy clad village church in a bosky churchyard. It was frankly urban and rectangular, like a hall or temple without columns, and without tower or belfry. The custom of the country demanded that the interior should be filled with pews, so that there could be no freedom of movement and no true vistas; yet the double row of high Ionic columns was imposing, and there were square vaults over the aisles, and a tunnel vault in the nave, without a clerestory. The whole was plaster or stucco, in my time painted white; nevertheless the ground-glass windows subdued the light, and turned the whole, for the benevolent eye, into an inoffensive harmony in greys. There was florid music: organist and choir attempted the most pretentious masses, Bach, Mozart, Schubert, Verdi, and on occasions threw in Rossini's *Stabat Mater* and Gounod's *Ave Maria*. On the great feasts we even had an orchestra in addition. I liked this rococo music, and I still remember and sing it to myself with pleasure. It *transports*; the means may be at times inferior, but the end is attained. The end is to escape to another world, to live freely for a while in a medium made by us and fit for us to live in. Not all that is artificial is good, because the artifice may escape control and become stupid or even vicious; and much that is natural is good, because we are vitalised by it; but only the artificial can be good expressly.

The preaching.   The adjoining College naturally required a good many teachers, so that a number of priests were available for preaching in the church, some of them, however, not quite masters of the English language. One pale Italian in particular was admirable on difficult points in the religious life, as for instance on the words: *My God, my God, why hast thou abandoned me?* The spiritual aspiration to abandon oneself here corrected the Jesuit tendency to view salvation as a matter of legal give and take between God and man. We couldn't be saved, I know, if we didn't exist, and in that sense we must cooperate in our salvation; but the point is to be saved from ourselves morally while physically retaining our personal being and limitations. Tradition, since Plato, calls this method *mortification*; and the secret of it sometimes pierces through the machinery of religious ethics. More frequent and noted preachers, however, were the two successive heads of the College, Father Fulton and Father O'Connor. The latter was a young and very oratorical Irishman, eloquently proclaiming Catholic Truth against all heresies. It is not difficult for a man with a ready tongue and a good memory to pluck moral and theological arguments from the patristic garden. St. Augustine alone will furnish flowers for a thousand good sermons. And this practice of repeating ancient authorities cannot be taxed with laziness. More diligence and more conscience are shown in ransacking the Fathers than in ventilating one's casual notions; and Catholic preachers at least are expected to preach the gospel, and not some message new to the age. But the gospel arouses different feelings and meets with different opposition in successive times; and a mind sensitive to these influences can therefore preach it more usefully than if he merely echoed the words of the gospel itself. Father Fulton, of whom I have said something as confessor to my sister, was not eloquent; he was not warm; but he could explore the dialectics not only of doctrine but of sentiment; and it was in unravelling the complexities of our divided allegiance that I found him an instructive guide.

Architectural reveries in church.   There was a feature in the interior of this church that, in my empty head, led to much architectural theorising. The sanctuary, which was square, had an ordinary double vault lower than that of the nave; so that we were for ever faced by two round arches of the same span, one two or three yards over the other. The space between them was awkward, and the architect had done nothing to disguise or relieve it. I knew very well that in basilicas the apse is often much lower than the nave; but there the semicircular apse was not a sanctuary meant to house the altar, but only the head of the choir, round which the clergy had their stalls, with the bishop's or superior's throne in the middle; while the altar stood out in front, under an architectural canopy, and was approached by the priest from his end, looking eastward over the altar, and over the people beyond it; for in the original Christian basilicas in Rome the entrance is at the east end. Moreover, the arch of that apse is not surmounted by another arch, since the nave has a wooden roof, either showing the rafters or closed with a flat ceiling. In either case the arch has a rectangular setting, like a triumphal arch, and the triangles in the corners are adorned with mosaics or frescoes, to which they are admirably adapted. But in chapels or later churches, where the altar is set against a wall, or as in the cathedrals stands at the extreme *chevet* or east end of the choir, the vault is never lower over the chancel or choir than over the nave: on the contrary, it might well be higher— as for instance it is at Le Mans and at Carcassonne—with excellent effect and significance; while at St. Peter's the altar with its immense *baldacchino* stands under the vault of Michaelangelo's dome, five hundred feet high.

Baroque doing its duty. Our local architect, then, whatever his models or reasons, was guilty of a solecism in designing those two equal closely superposed arches, and that chancel vault lower than his nave; but I was ready to forgive him in view of the favourable atmosphere that his interior, as a whole, offered me for meditation. The reredos contained three paintings, and the side altars in the aisles two more, all warm in colour and acceptable in design— very likely copies of late Italian masters; their white plaster setting, with grouped columns, was graceful and pleasantly touched with gold in the mouldings and ornaments; and above was a sensational baroque curved pediment, broken in two, with two ecstatic saints kneeling perilously, but divinely confident, on the inclined upper surface of the two separated fragments. It was symmetrical, it was decorative, it was full of motion and enthusiasm. It warned me that there are more things going on in heaven and earth, and in oneself, than are dreamt of in our philosophy.

Religious art at its worst. When you looked, however, a little higher up, you saw things depicted as going on in heaven which, whatever may go on there, should not be so depicted on earth. Art, like mind, has its own categories and grammar for symbolising realities beyond it, and makes nonsense if it violates them. Our language cannot control its objects, yet could not even indicate them if it destroyed itself. What you saw above that reredos, filling the whole space under the vault, was a painting, a fresco, I suppose, of the Assumption. The figure of the Virgin Mary was at the very top, as in Titian's *Assumption*, fore-shortened, and clothed in the same dark red and dark blue; a heavy, materialistic, unworthy conception of the subject. Out of place here, too, since this church was not dedicated to the Assumption but to the Immaculate Conception. The Assumption is an alleged event; it is conceived to have occurred on earth, at a particular place and time; so that a treatment like Titian's, with the foreshortening, and with the drama of wonder and surprise in the crowd of witnesses, is not unjustified; and there the artist had a super-abundant technique to exhibit in painting a great variety of gesticulating figures, a landscape, and an Italian sky. The Immaculate Conception, on the contrary, is a theological idea,* the notion of a human soul created perfect and spotless, with a body subject, like a flower, to the direct, unconscious, unimpeded magic of that soul. Why, then, not have filled this space with the accepted representation of the Immaculate Conception, after the manner of Murillo? An ethereal, girlish, angelic Madonna, clothed with the sun (the image is based on a passage in the Apocalypse), with the moon at her feet and the stars encircling her head, would have filled the centre of the composition. Her garments would have been, in texture and colour, like the sky and the light clouds; she would have floated as the sun in midheaven, and everything would have been tinted and softened by the radiance of a pervasive yet hidden light that she seemed to shed. In that heaven, any number of seraphs and cherubs that the artist could paint or could draw might have flown or soared as in their native element.

Cherubs? Seraphs? No: half a dozen large young women in modest evening gowns (except that their feet were bare), one pure yellow, one sea-green, another terra-cotta, all with correspondingly large wings, like the Angel Mother in our engraving at home, yearned aesthetically upward: and the central ones seemed anxious to hold up the Madonna, as if she were not levitating of her own accord. I don't know what models, if any, this composition may have followed, but it didn't please me. I was glad when on feast days a canopy with red and white hangings was set up to hide it, and to turn the altar, with all its lights and flowers, into a sort of throne. Regal and priestly grandeur, even

---

*The non-theological reader must not be misled into thinking that the "Immaculate Conception" refers to the *Incarnation of Christ* without an earthly father, or to what Anglicans improperly call the "Virgin Birth". There is indeed a Catholic doctrine of the *perpetual* virginity of Mary, the *birth* of Christ being no less miraculous than his incarnation; a doctrine that my first Spanish catechism beautifully expressed by saying that the child Jesus passed from his mother's bosom into her arms as a ray of sunlight passes through a pane of glass, without breaking or staining it. This might properly be called the "Virgin Birth", and is entirely distinct from the doctrine of the Incarnation contained in the creed, and a later refinement upon it. The doctrine of the "Immaculate Conception", on the other hand, asserts that *the soul of the Virgin Mary herself* (though she was begotten and born like other people, except that her parents were unusually old) *did not inherit original sin from Adam*, being exempted by prevenient grace, in view of the redemption to be worked by her Son. As an inscription on her monument in the Piazza di Spagna in Rome has it, *Sanctificavit tabernaculum suum Altissimus*, the Most High had sanctified his tabernacle.

dimly suggested, has always impressed me. In Egypt, in those colossal temples and profound sanctuaries, I envied the priests that once officiated there, faithful to immemorial traditions, and learned in mysterious conventions. It was somnambulism, but in a noble setting, healthful, protective, capable of perpetuating itself for generations, and of rendering human life humanly better rather than worse.

The sex of angels. If ever I complained to my sister of those female angels and wondered how learned Jesuits could countenance such a lapse, she would say that angels were sexless, so that if artists might represent them as young men or boys or infants, why not, on occasion, as women? Theologically, this was correct; angels are sexless, since they have no bodies, and according to St. Thomas, are each the only member of its species; so that in them any complications connected with reproduction are excluded *a priori.** But theology—especially in regard to angels!—is something secondary: vision, inspiration, tradition, and literature come first. A Christian painter is not called upon to invent some form in which pure spirits might appear, nor is he likely to have seen them himself. What concerns him is not what they may be in heaven, but what they look like when visiting the earth. Now imagination has its specific hereditary idioms, just as the senses have; and if the artist be a Christian working for a Christian people he will be spontaneously borne along by the same tradition that has inspired the doctrines and visions of his Church; otherwise he would falsify the poetic character and tone of the themes that he illustrates. This will not deprive him of originality; he can be stylistic, hieratic, or picturesque, according to his taste or training; but he will cease to be a religious artist if he contradicts the revelation he has inherited.

Angels in Scripture. Now in what form have angels appeared? The angels that came to Abraham's tent, and the one that wrestled with Jacob, were certainly men; and in the Old Testament it often seems that angels were strangers or travellers that gave some warning or left a mysterious impression, and only afterwards were recognised to have been "angels of the Lord", or vehicles for a divine oracle. The angel that appeared to Mary is understood to have been the archangel Gabriel, certainly no less masculine, if less military, than his companion Michael; so much so that his figure, like that of St. Joseph, was avoided in early Christian art, until the idiom of the faith

---

*I refer to Catholic theology. In the *Jewish Book of the Jubilees,* assigned to about 100 B.C., we are informed that the angels in heaven are circumcised.

had become native to the popular imagination, and it could be left free without danger of becoming equivocal. Then those innumerable charming Annunciations could be designed, where Gabriel is a royal page, as deferential as he is smiling and beautifully attired, gracefully bending the knee, gracefully delivering his embarrassing but important message, and ready gracefully to retire, perfectly pleased with himself and with his performance.* Or if direct and strangely crude evidence on the sex of angels were required it might be found in Genesis, where the angels sent to warn Lot cause a most embarrassing commotion in Sodom. Graver ambassadors are the two "young men" in white raiment seen sitting by the empty tomb on Easter morning, who speak mystically of not looking for the living among the dead. It is as if the soldiers on guard had turned, in the Evangelist's fancy, into young priests. They come to bring tidings of martyrdom and of a transfigured life. Sex is not absent here, as it is not absent in the monk or mystic; it is expressly mentioned; yet it appears only in the firmness with which it is suppressed.

My idealisms never my genuine beliefs.   Such was the mechanism or logic or poetry of mere ideas that occupied my mind when a boy: not expressed, of course, as I now express it, but intensely felt by me to determine the only right or beautiful order possible for the universe. Existence could not be right or beautiful under other conditions. But was existence beautiful or right? Quite the opposite; according to my youthful heart, existence was profoundly ugly and wrong. The beautiful remained imaginary. My daily life had nothing to do with it. Reality meant a dull routine of getting up in the morning, walking to school, sitting there for five hours, walking home, eating not very palatable food, and going to bed again. I was bored. I hadn't enough to do or enough to learn. At school there was nothing but lessons; and lessons in a large class, with indulgent teachers and slack standards of accuracy, meant perpetual idleness. I could have learned twice as much in half the time, had a better pace been set for me and more matter. In the absence of matter, I dreamt on a hungry

*Cf. Saint Bernard in Dante:

> . . . "Baldezza e leggiadria
> quant' esser puote in angelo e in alma,
> tutta è in lui; e sì volem che sia. . . ."
> Par. xxxii, 109–111.

stomach. But those ideal universes in my head did not produce any firm convictions or actual duties. They had nothing to do with the wretched poverty-stricken real world in which I was condemned to live. That the real was rotten and only the imaginary at all interesting seemed to me axiomatic. That was too sweeping; yet allowing for the rash generalisations of youth, it is still what I think. My philosophy has never changed. It is by no means an artificial academic hypothesis; it doesn't appeal at all to the professors; it is a system of presuppositions and categories discovered already alive and at work within me, willy-nilly, like existence itself, and virtually present not only in the boy but in the embryo.

Impertinence of moralistic philosophies   I say "within me", because there I have finally deciphered it by analysis; but it was not peculiar to me. It was common then in certain circles and was called pessimism. Pessimism is an accidental moralistic name for it; because the philosophy in question is a system of cosmology, a view of nature and history; moral preferences or judgments are not central in it. Whether a particular man is pessimistic because he dislikes the truth, or likes the truth and feels optimistic, makes but a slight difference in that total truth; and such a feeling, turned into a sentence pronounced on the universe, seems, either way, rather impertinent. We speak of the fair, says a Spanish proverb, as we fare in it; and our personal fortunes may justly colour our philosophy only if they are typical and repeat the fortunes of all living beings. I am not ashamed of my childish pessimism; it was honest; and it showed my courage in not letting my preferences cloud my perceptions nor my perceptions abash my preferences. The clash between them was painful but not unnatural, and was destined to grow less painful with time, and this without any loss either of realism or of honour.

In spite, then, of my religious and other day-dreams, I was at bottom a young realist; I knew I was dreaming, and so was awake. A sure proof of this was that I was never *anxious* about what those dreams would have involved if they had been true. I never had the least touch of superstition. To follow the logic of dogma and keep the feasts, if not the fasts, of the Church was a part of the game; and the whole allegorical pseudo-historical pageant passed through my mind un-challenged, because I felt intimately the dramatic logic that had inspired it. But no logic can upset facts; and it never occurred to me to shudder at the doctrine of eternal damnation, as the innocent Unitarians did, or to be overawed by it, as were the innocent Calvinists. Hell is set down in the bond, like Shylock's pound of flesh: the play requires it. Of course damnation must be eternal, because every loss and every pain is irremediable. The consolation or peace said to wipe evil away, cannot wipe it out: you may forget it, but if you say you have annulled it, you are lying. Nothing that has ever occurred can be annulled. That is what eternal damnation means, or might be said to mean by a thinking being. But if you suppose that in an Inferno like Dante's you may soon be jumping about naked in a fiery furnace, you are dreaming. You are confusing poetry with fact. Never had I the least fear of a material hell or desire for a material heaven. The images were so violent, so childish, as to be comic.

Sentimentality and cynicism about religion. The force of images is equivocal, reversible, hard to recover in memory. Two of my earliest effusions in verse were entitled *To the Moon* and *To the Host*. The images were similar, and the sentiment in both cases was similar. The Host, I said, was "clear in faith's divine moonlight". It was "my only friend", much as the moon, to Endymion, might be the only goddess. And I sighed that my faith was "too like despair". The last word, what I really aspired to, was "peace". For this purpose the machinery of the sacraments was not needed. I had no wish to go to confession and communion, else I should have done so. My faith was indeed so like despair that it wasn't faith at all; it was fondness, liking, what in Spanish is called *afición*; I indulged in it, but only north-north west, and keeping my freedom. I heartily agreed with the Church about the world, yet I was ready to agree with the world about the Church; and I breathed more easily the atmosphere of religion than that of business, precisely because religion, like poetry, was more ideal, more freely imaginary, and in a material sense falser.

Those verses were written when I was fifteen or sixteen, and before my prize-poem; seven years later, when I had studied philosophy and travelled, the same position is described, more cynically, in the Byronic manner. The lines are entitled *At the Church Door*; I will quote one stanza from memory:

> Ah, if salvation were a trick of reason,
> How easily would all the world be saved!
>   But roses bloom not in the winter season
> Nor hope of heaven in a heart enslaved.
>   To break the bond with earth were easy treason
> If it were God alone the bosom craved;

> But we have chosen thrift and chosen rest
> And with our wings' plucked feathers built our nest.*

Here the drama had become frankly subjective: the turn it would take depended on the weather. Ideal flights, reason, heaven, and union with God did not compose another world or carry us there; they were methods, directions, or goals of thought, habits that the human spirit developed under favourable conditions, when it was free. But for the most part, and especially then (in the 1880's), the mind was wretchedly servile, vulgarised, and absorbed in instrumentalities. And the worst of it was that we had lost courage and forsworn our vocation. We were not like a good dog that, if compelled to cross a river, hurries to the other bank, and shakes the water vigorously from his skin as soon as he gets there; we wallowed in our muddy bath like pigs in a sty, pretended that we positively enjoyed it, and paid our philosophers in obsequiousness if not in money for telling us that at least we were doing our duty.

My intellectual materialism firmly established with little change in my religious affections. From the boy dreaming awake in the church of the Immaculate Conception, to the travelling student seeing the world in Germany, England, and Spain there had been no great change in sentiment. I was still "at the church door". Yet in belief, in the clarification of my philosophy, I had taken an important step. I no longer wavered between alternate views of the world, to be put on or taken off like alternate plays at the theatre. I now saw that there was only one possible play, the actual history of nature and of mankind, although there might well be ghosts among the characters and soliloquies among the speeches. Religions, *all* religions, and idealistic philosophies, *all* idealistic philosophies, were the soliloquies and the ghosts. They might be eloquent and profound. Like Hamlet's soliloquy they might be excellent reflective criticisms of the play as a whole. Nevertheless they were only parts of it, and their value as criticisms lay entirely in their fidelity to the facts, and to the sentiments which those facts aroused in the critic.

---

*A friend of mine who was a bird-fancier (I mean who liked shooting) observed that here I had hit on a true simile without knowing it; some birds did pluck their feathers in nest-building, but from their breasts, not from their wings. I believe I corrected my manuscript accordingly, spoiling the sense: because what I meant was that we sacrificed our capacity for flight, under pressure of blind commitments or in mere apathy.

Two insights yet to come: that the forms of the good are divergent, and that each is definite and final. Two other important steps remained to be taken before my philosophy was wholly clarified and complete: I shall speak of them when it comes to my successive books. Yet it may be well to mention those two points here, in order that the skein of my meditations at the Immaculate Conception may be seen unravelled. One step was to overcome moral and ideal provinciality, and to see that every form of life had its own perfection, which it was stupid and cruel to condemn for differing from some other form, by chance one's own. The other step, rising above the moral dissolution that might invade a man who cultivated an indiscriminate sympathy with every form of life, made it clear that sympathy and justice themselves are only relative virtues, good only in their place, for those lives or forms of life that thereby reach their perfection: so that integrity or self-definition is and remains first and fundamental in morals: and the right of alien natures to pursue their proper aims can never abolish our right to pursue ours.

Scepticism intervenes. Why, before taking these final steps, had I stood so long "at the church door", with regret at never having really lived inside? I might prefer ideally an imaginary Atlantis to any earthly island; but how puerile and helpless to languish after it and not at once to make the best of the real world? I think there was a congenital transcendentalism in me, long before I heard of transcendental philosophy or understood it. I had a spontaneous feeling that life is a dream. The scene might entirely disappear at any moment, or be entirely transformed. There could be no *a priori*, strictly no even empirical presumption against anything whatsoever. The volume and solidity of one apparition, of one imposed world, could never insure its perpetuity, much less prevent the reality or perpetuity of a thousand other worlds.

Transcendentalism formally true and materially empty. Now this, I am still convinced, is an invincible intuition: and for that reason I respect the Indian way of developing it philosophically, but do not respect the German way; because the Germans try to limit the possibilities of being and of illusion, to their home dialect, by a wretched persistence in Hebrew egotism and conceit; whereas the Indians give the mists of illusion liberty to drift, and cultivate only the pure light and peace of the spirit. At the same time, this invincible intuition, in its absoluteness and purity, leaves the mind empty and rescinds all faith. If it were the principle of life (which it is not) it would

condemn us to suspended animation and the sense of infinite potentiality unrealised: to crystal vision, umbilical contemplations, and my
childish verses *To the Moon* and *To the Host*. The light of spirit is indeed
pure and unprejudiced, open, like the young eye, to whatsoever there
may be. But this light is kindled by something else and it must fall
on something else, if it is to reveal anything. It is kindled in an animal
psyche, in a living perishable heart; and it falls on the world in which
that heart and that psyche have been formed, and is deeply dyed in
their particular passions. If, then, we are to see or to believe in anything,
it must be at the bidding of natural accidents, by what I call animal
faith; and the alternatives open to pure spirit are not open to rational
belief. Rational belief must have other guides than sheer imagination
exploring infinite possibilities. Those guides can be, logically, nothing
but accidents; but they have a compulsory presence and evoke an
inescapable adhesion, confidence, and trust; which trust is fortified by
experiment and found trustworthy.

My instinctive transcendentalism or solipsism was, as I think, quite
right analytically; but I was confused in playing with it as a criterion
or judge of beliefs. Beliefs have an earthly origin and can be sanctioned
only by earthly events.

XII

First Friends

It was also at the age of sixteen that I began to notice the characters and quality of the other boys, and to find my ideal affinities. I say ideal affinities, because I had always had instinctive or canine friends: boys or girls—for there were several girls—with whom I played or prattled, or danced at the dancing-school. There, at about the age of ten, I had a sort of *amourette*: absolutely groundless and silent, but absolutely determined. I remember the child perfectly. She had a dark complexion and curly black hair, and stood very straight, but gracefully. She was the first example to me of that admirable virtue cultivated by French actresses: eloquent stillness. I don't think she ever said a word, and I very few: but we always took each other out to dance, and were partners for the cotillion. Her name was Alice White, and I have never seen or heard of her afterwards. It was the friendship of two genteel kittens, who played gravely with the same ball, and eschewed the rest of the litter.

A less enigmatic companionship of my boyhood was with Charlie Davis. He was a soft blond youth, a little older and taller than I, but mentally younger: our great pleasure was to laugh about everything, like silly girls. But in our daily walks from school we must have gabbled on many subjects, because after some years—he left school young to go into an office—he became a Catholic, and asked me to be his sponsor at his Christening. I was; and I remember later his desire to enter a religious order, to which his previous incidental entanglements with the fair sex proved a fatal obstacle. Must all novices be virgins? Probably only in that (Paulist) order, and in America. Our friendship died out: but he continued all his life to write occasionally to my sister Susana, partly on religious subjects and partly in a tone of amiable banter and comic pessimism. Let us hope, if I didn't save my own soul, that I saved the soul of Charlie Davis.

He was by no means my first friend. The first was Gorham Hubbard, at Miss Welchman's Kindergarten: the next was Bob Upham, at the

Brimmer School: and in him I first tasted two of the sweets of friendship, which have regaled me since in many a "nice fellow": guidance or good judgment in practical matters—which it is always a pleasure for me to follow if I can trust the author: and the quality of simple gentleman, a clean upstanding independence and sureness in everything personal and moral. My favourite young gentlemen haven't always turned out well: they have often gone to the dogs; but that was on account of a virtue which lent them such a chivalrous aristocratic charm: namely, independence, indifference to public opinion, and courage in running risks. I had also had several fancy-friends—little more than dream-images of a foolish sentimental sort: but the reality of their persons mattered little; they were simply knobs on which to hang my own reveries. But now, in my second class year, the manly note sounds for the first time. A common intelligence, a common readiness—*spes animi credula mutui*—allies two young men in the presence of a common world.

My first real friend was Bentley Warren. We two with Dick Smith (who afterward took his mother's name, Weston) formed what we called the Triumvirate. Warren was the link between the other two of us, who hadn't very much in common, except perhaps a better breeding than most of the boys at the Latin School. This school, being public, (i.e. free), was naturally frequented by the ambitious poor— Irish boys wishing to be priests, lawyers, or doctors, Jews wishing to be professors, and native Americans, like Warren and Smith, whose families were in reduced circumstances. It was my mother's straitened means that caused her to send me there, instead of to some private school; and I should perhaps have seemed an entirely different person, and had an entirely different life, if this genteel poverty, and this education in a public day school, among the children of humble parents, had not fortified in me the spirit of detachment and isolation. Not that the most luxurious American surroundings—such as I afterward had some contact with—would ever have made an American of me. America in those days made an exile and a foreigner of every native, who had at all a temperament like mine.

Warren's father, who had recently died, had been a Democratic congressman, elected in an off year of public dissatisfaction in a suburb of Boston, usually Republican: but two years of life in Washington, together with inherited dissentient opinions, had given his son a freer intelligence and a more varied experience than little Bostonians were apt to have. I often went to Mrs. Warren's on holidays to tea; and

Warren sometimes came to lunch at our house. His Democratic views—
if he had them—were not rabid; his most intimate friends were Harry
and Jim Garfield, sons of the future President of the United States;
and he left school at the end of our second class year in order to
enter Williams College with the Garfields, a year before the rest of
us were expected to be ready for the university. Dick Smith, too, on
account of a tiff which his father had with the Headmaster, left school
early during our last year; so that as far as friendship was concerned—
so new to me but so important—the end of my school life would have
been desolate, but for a mere chance. Not that my relations with
Warren were broken off: we wrote each other long letters; and four
years later, in 1885, I went to Williamstown for the festivities at his
graduation. I think it was my first journey undertaken merely for
pleasure, and at my own expense. Ward Thoron had invited me to
his grandfather's at Lenox, and I combined the two visits. I have been
to Williams and to Lenox again: to read a lecture in the one (on
Shelley) and to "Ja" Burden's wedding in the other. There had been
intervals of twenty or twenty-five years: Harry Garfield was president
of the College; we spoke of Bentley Warren and of the old days, but
with how different a sentiment! For me those things had passed into
the empyrean, into an eternal calm where their littleness or their
greatness was nothing and their quality, their essence, everything: for
him they were merely early, unimportant phases of the business which
occupied him now, and not to be regarded on their own account.
When I mentioned Bentley Warren, Garfield said: "Oh, yes. He is
one of the Trustees of our College." From this I gathered two things:
that Warren had been "successful" and was now rich; and that for
Garfield this fact was what counted in Warren rather than their early
friendship. I expressed surprise that in their Faculty Room they had
no portrait of his father—an old member of the College and a President
of the United States; and he said it was not for him to suggest that.
Why not? Because it might seem egotistical? But why didn't his Trustees
or whoever governed behind him—for Presidents of colleges are secondary powers—take a gentle hint, or spontaneously attend to something so obviously proper? I suppose they were always thinking of
the future. A portrait in the Faculty Room would hardly have been
an advertisement; it would only have been an act of homage. Let the
past paint its own pictures.

My school friends were gone; but just beyond school bounds a new
friend appeared, Edward Bayley. I was Lieutenant-Colonel of the Boston

School Regiment, the Colonel that year being from the English High School which, back to back with the Latin School, was housed in the other half of the same new building. On some matter of vital importance to our forces it became necessary for me to consult my superior officer. We met by appointment, and found that the high questions of epaulettes or of buttons were soon disposed of; but that first interview made us fast friends. We happened to live in the same quarter of the town, the Back Bay, about a mile from our schools, and we at once established the custom of waiting, he for me or I for him, at the corner, so as to walk home together. Yet this did not last many months, because that winter my mother moved to Roxbury, having at last got rid of the dreadful burden of our Beacon Street house; so that I saw my new friend only occasionally, or by express appointment. But that made no difference. The bond was established, silently of course, but safely. Even the fact that he was not going to College, but directly into some place of business, so that as it actually came about, we never saw each other, after that year, and hardly a letter passed between us, made no difference in our friendship, though it entirely separated our lives. Strange enchantment! Even today, the thought of that youthful comradeship, without incidents, without background, and without a sequel, warms the cockles of my heart like a glass of old port.

There is a sort of indifference to time, as there is a sort of silence, which goes with veritable sympathy. It springs from clear possession of that which is, from sureness about it. Those who are jealous, jealous of time, of rivals, of accidents, care for something vague that escapes them now, and that would always escape them; they are haunted souls, hunting for they know not what. Not so those who know what they love, rest in it, asking for nothing more. If circumstances had led Bayley and me to go through life together, we should have stuck to each other against any incidental danger or enemy; there would have been something to tell about our comradeship; but there would have been nothing new in our friendship. Clearness and depth in the heart, as in the intellect, transpose everything into the eternal.

Is that all? What did he do? What did he say? What did he stand for? I confess that after sixty years I have to invent a theory to account for this fact. I have to compare that sudden, isolated, brief attachment with other friendships of mine that had something of its quality, but were circumstantially more describable. We were eighteen years old, and there was nothing in us except ourselves. Now in himself, apart from circumstances, Bayley was like Warwick Potter, only stronger.

In Warwick the same type of character, weaker although at the time of our intimacy he was much older, was made describable by his social background and breeding. He had been brought up in the most select and superior way in which it was then possible to be brought up in America. Not through mere wealth or fashion; because his widowed mother was neither very rich nor very well connected: he and his brothers would point out with glee that their mother's relations were a little common. But their father had been a general in the Civil War, and their uncle was the Anglican Bishop of New York: pontiff, that is, to the cream of rich and fashionable America. Moreover, Warwick and his brothers had been among the very first pupils of Mr. Peabody, on founding the Groton School; so that they received the fresh imprint of all those high and amiable intentions, and all that personal paternal care and spiritual guidance which it was Mr. Peabody's ideal to supply. School had been a second home to Warwick, and a real home. For, more than his brothers, he was sensitive to this type of distinctively English, homelike, refined sentiment, by which religion was merged in romantic and artistic memories, as well as in political pride, and in the sheer love of nature and freedom; only the sporting and military side of this education had not yet been much developed. This was to come later, with a certain standardised mentality and political ambition. In the early 1890's the rich dreamt of culture rather than of leadership. Warwick, who was young for his age, was particularly open to new impressions, plastic, immensely amused, a little passive and feminine. It was hard to say what he would have turned into if he had lived. As yet the dominant trait in him, as in Bayley, was clear goodness, the absence of all contaminations, such as the very young are sometimes proud of. He was sure, in great things as in little, to prefer the better to the worse; he delighted in pleasant ways and people, and he was religious. Love of historic Christianity opened to him a wonderful world existing before and beyond America. He felt at home in England and in the Church. He was civilised.

Now, how did it happen that Bayley who had nothing of that breeding and education, nevertheless possessed the same or a deeper intelligence of spiritual things? Why did a strictly Puritan and inward religion in him, far from producing narrowness or fanaticism, produce charity and hospitality of mind? Not that he was in the least what was called liberal, that is, indifferent and vaguely contemptuous towards all definite doctrines or practices, and without any discipline of his own. On the contrary, he was absolutely loyal to his own tradition, and master of it; he was made, finished, imposing in the precision of his affections. He had perfect integrity (where Warwick had only blamelessness), yet he had sweetness too, affection for what he excluded from his own sphere, justice to what he renounced, happiness in the joys of others that were not joys to him, so that his very limitations were turned into admirable virtues. Here was this manly boy, taller and stronger than I, firmly and contentedly rooted in his New England Presbyterianism, yet accepting, respecting and even envying *me* for being everything that he was not and did not expect to be. There was no shadow of the pathos of distance in this; it was honest religious comprehension that there are many vintages in the Lord's vineyard, and many different things that are beautiful and good. Where did Bayley learn this?

In his spiritual heritage there were doubtless certain naturalistic maxims that may have struck him in sermons or in casual reading. There was Milton, with his Latinity and his Italian sonnets; and there was the young Emerson, a sort of Puritan Goethe, the Emerson of *Nature*, before he had slipped into transcendentalism and moralism and complacency in mediocrity, in order to flatter his countrymen and indirectly to flatter himself. I may be reading ideals of my own into that very young man, in whom nothing of the sort may ever have come to light; but potentially I cannot help thinking that in him there was something more that those great men never possessed: I mean devotion, I mean humility and renunciation. A dumb inglorious Milton who was not a prig, an Emerson with warm blood, who was not proud or oracular or cosmographical, and never thought himself the centre of the universe. Young Bayley was my first, perhaps my fundamental, model for *The Last Puritan*.

It was doubtless the discovery that we were both—but differently—religious, that made us so quickly sure of each other. Never was trust more instinctive, more complete, or more silent. It has lasted in silence for sixty years. Not long ago I asked a Boston friend who turned up at Cortina about these very first friends of mine, Warren and Bayley. Did he know them? Were they still living? What had become of them? And I was not surprised to hear the warmest eulogy of both, although my informant was a Lyman of the Lymans and a Lowell of the Lowells, while Warren and Bayley were not descendants of the Boston Brahmins. And I said to myself, "Oh, my prophetic soul!" My earliest friendships were not illusions.

XIII

The Harvard Yard

Joys of the poor student. If fortune has been unkind to me in respect to my times—except that for the intellectual epicure the 1890's were enjoyable—in respect to places fortune has been most friendly, setting me down not in any one centre, where things supposed to be important or exciting were happening, but in various quiet places from which cross-vistas opened into the world. Of these places the most familiar to me, after Avila, was the Harvard Yard. I lived there for eleven years, first as an undergraduate, later as instructor and proctor. No place, no rooms, no mode of living could have been more suitable for a poor student and a free student, such as I was and as I wished to be. My first room, on the ground floor in the north-east corner of Hollis, was one of the cheapest to be had in Cambridge: the rent was forty-four dollars a year. I had put it first for that reason in my list of rooms desired, and I got my first choice. It was so cheap because it had no bedroom, no water, and no heating; also the ground floor seems to have been thought less desirable, perhaps because the cellar below might increase the cold or the dampness. I don't think I was ever cold there in a way to disturb me or affect my health. I kept the hard-coal fire banked and burning all night, except from Saturday to Monday, when I slept at my mother's in Roxbury. An undergraduate's room in any case is not a good place for study, unless it be at night, under pressure of some special task. At other times, there are constant interruptions, or temptations to interrupt oneself: recitations, lectures, meals, walks, meetings, and sports. I soon found the Library the best place to work in. It was not crowded; a particular alcove where there were philosophical books at hand, and foreign periodicals, soon became my regular place for reading. I could take my own books and note-books there if necessary; but for the most part I browsed; and although my memory is not specific, and I hardly know what I read, except that I never missed *La Revue des Deux Mondes*, I don't think my time was wasted. A great deal stuck to me, without my knowing its source, and my mind became accustomed to large horizons and to cultivated judgments.

My modest budget.   As to my lodging, I had to make up my sofa-bed at night before getting into it; in the morning I left the bedding to air, and the "goody", whose services were included in the rent, put it away when she came to dust or to sweep. I also had to fetch my coal and water from the cellar, or the water in summer from the College pump that stood directly in front of my door. This was economy on my part, as I might have paid the janitor to do it for me; perhaps also to black my boots, which I always did myself, as I had done it at home. But my life was a miracle of economy. I had an allowance from my mother of $750 a year to cover all expenses. Tuition absorbed $150; rent $44; board at Memorial Hall, with a reduction for absence during the week-end, about $200; which left less than one dollar a day for clothes, books, fares, subscriptions, amusements, and pocket-money. Sometimes, but very rarely, I received a money-prize or a money-present; I had no protection or encouragement from rich relations or persons of influence. The Sturgises were no longer affluent, and as yet they hardly knew of my existence. Later, when their natural generosity could (and did) express itself, it did so in other ways, because I was already independent and needed no help. Yet on my less than one dollar a day I managed to dress decently, to belong to minor societies like the Institute, the Pudding, and the O.K. where the fees were moderate, to buy all necessary books, and even, in my Junior year, to stay at rich people's houses, and to travel. Robert had given me his old evening clothes, which fitted me well enough: otherwise the rich people's houses could not have been visited.

I miss the accomplishments of a gentleman.   Doing my "chores" was something I rather liked, as I still brush and pack my own clothes for pleasure, and shave myself, and walk everywhere rather than drive, circumstances permitting. A little manual work or physical exercise changes the stops agreeably, lengthens the focus and range of vision, reverts to the realm of matter which is the true matrix of mind, and generally brings judgment and feeling back into harmony with nature. I have never had a man-servant, and later when I lived in hotels I seldom called on the servants for any personal service not in their common routine. This trait is a heritage from the humble condition of my father's family and my mother's reduced circumstances during my boyhood. I had not an aristocratic breeding; not only was I not served, but I was taught no aristocratic accomplishments, not even riding or driving or shooting or dancing. What is a gentleman? A gentleman is a man with a valet: originally he also had a sword, but in my time that was obsolete except for officers in full uniform; a bank-account could take its place. But having many servants, though it makes a man a master, does not make him a gentleman. He is not one because his wife may keep servant-girls in the house; he is one only if he has a body-servant of his own. This defines the Spanish gentleman as well as the English gentleman, yet differently. The relation in Spain is or was more confidential, more general, more moral: the man served his master in all his affairs. In England, it is more a matter of laying out all his master's things. However, I confess that the mere fop is not a complete gentleman, however dependent he may be on his valet. To be a complete gentleman he should also have a horse, and should ride it gallantly. Don Quixote, too, had a horse, as well as a servant.

J.B. Fletcher and the original sin of professors. Life in the Yard for me, during my second period of residence there, 1890–1896, had a different quality. I hadn't a horse or a valet, but could count on enough pocket-money, a varied circle of friends, clubs and ladies' society in Boston and Cambridge, and the foreglow and afterglow of holidays spent in Europe. The first year, when I had only one foot in the stirrup and was not yet in the saddle as a Harvard teacher, I lived in Thayer; graceless quarters and the insecure stammering beginnings of a lecturer. The only thing I remember is the acquaintance I then made with my next-door neighbour, Fletcher, who was afterwards a professor of Comparative Literature and made a translation of the *Divina Commedia*. He was also a football player; and I remember one day when I was violently sick at my stomach—my digestion in those days being imperfect—he thought to help me by holding my head (a common illusion among helpful people) and his grasp was like a ring of iron. He was a very good fellow, with a richer nature than most philologists, and firm morals. We had long talks and discovered common tastes in literature and the arts; but he didn't remain at Harvard, and I lost sight of him. Even if he had been at hand, we should hardly have seen each other often: there were things in us fundamentally inaccessible to one another. Besides, though I became a professor myself, I never had a real friend who was a professor. Is it jealousy, as among women, and a secret unwillingness to be wholly pleased?

Or is it the consciousness that a professor or a woman has to be partly a sham; whence a mixture of contempt and pity for such a poor victim of necessity? In Fletcher, and in the nobler professors, the shamming is not an effect of the profession, but rather, as in inspired clergymen, the profession is an effect of an innate passion for shamming. Nobody feels that passion more than I have felt it in poetry and in religion; but I never felt it in academic society or academic philosophy, and I gave up being a professor as soon as I could.

My rooms in Stoughton.   The next year I again had my pick of rooms in the Yard, securing No. 7 Stoughton, in the south-east corner of the first floor, where I stayed for six winters. Here there was a bedroom, and my coal and water were brought up for me by the janitor; on the other hand I often made my own breakfast—tea, boiled eggs, and biscuits—and always my tea in the afternoon, for I had now lived in England and learned the comforts of a bachelor in lodgings. Only—what would not have happened in England—I washed my own dishes and ordered my tea, eggs, milk and sugar from the grocer's: domestic cares that pleased me, and that preserved my nice china— a present from Howard Cushing—during all those years. There was a round bathtub under my cot, and my sister's crucifix on the wall above it: only cold water, but the contents of the kettle boiling on the hearth served to take off the chill. I had also acquired a taste for fresh air, and my window was always a little open.

Modernness of the morning bath.   One day a new goody left the bathtub full of slops, explaining that she hadn't known what to do with it; it was the only bathtub in her entry. I had myself taken only recently to a daily sponge-bath. When I was an undergraduate, few ever took a bath in Cambridge; those who lodged in private houses might share one bathroom between them, and those who went to the Gymnasium might have a shower-bath after exercise; but your pure "grind" never bathed, and I only when I went home for the week-end. In Little's Block I believe there was a bathroom on each floor; but Beck was the only luxurious dormitory where each room had its private bathroom. Habits, however, were rapidly changing. Violent exercise and fiercely contested sports were in the ascendent among the athletes; this involved baths, but not luxury. Yet luxury was in the ascendent too; and the polite ideal of one man one bathroom, and hot water always hot, was beginning to disguise luxury under the decent names of privacy and health.

Baths
meretricious.
•
Baths
austere.
My father used to say that the English had introduced baths into Christendom from India; but I suspect that it was luxury and the *femmes galantes* of the eighteenth century that did it. What could be more un-English than a languid female in a turban, not unattended, and not without a semi-transparent clinging garment, like that of a statue, getting in or out of a marble bath like an ancient sarcophagus, itself draped and lined with linen sheets? These were the refinements of luxury and mature coquetry. And the Christian background appears in the gown worn in the bath, according to the monastic precept of never being wholly naked. No such scruple exists in England, or among athletes. The tone there is masculine and hardy, with a preference for cold water and the open air. Robert Bridges, the most complete of Englishmen, at the age of eighty, used to take his cold bath every morning in the lounge-hall of his house, before a roaring wood fire. Here was Sparta rather than India transported to the chilly North.

And baths
superstitious.
In Spain, in those days, there were no baths in houses. My sister procured an immense zinc tub, in the middle of which, when it was full, a special stove had to be introduced to heat the water, which a special donkey laden with four earthen jars had to fetch from the fountain; the thing didn't work, and I doubt that she took more than one or two baths. For me she got a manageable little hip-bath which I found quite sufficient. Yet baths, medical baths, were not unknown even in mediaeval Avila. They were prescribed for certain ailments. You went to the establishment as to a pilgrimage; the water was that of a particular spring, mineral or miraculous, gushing forth at that spot; and you took always an odd number of baths, probably nineteen or twenty-one (never twenty!) according to some Pythagorean superstition of ancient medicine. When they were well the good people of Avila no more thought of bathing than of drinking tea; yet I never came there on any decent person who offended the nose. Complexions certainly were seldom fresh or ruddy; but it is working-people's clothes that smell; only the feet, head, and hands gather dust and grime. The protected parts of the skin shed their excretions and become clean of themselves, if only the clothes are well washed and aired.

The old and
the new
Harvard.
Hollis and Stoughton were twin red-brick buildings of the eighteenth century, solid, simple, symmetrical and not unpleasing. No effort had been made by the builders towards picturesqueness or novelty; they knew what decent lodgings

for scholars were, and that there was true economy in building them well. The rectangular wooden window-frames divided into many squares, flush with the walls, and painted white, served for a modest and even gay decoration. There was a classic cornice, and the windows immediately under it were square instead of oblong and suggested metopes, while the slope of the roof also was that of a temple, though without pediments at the end. On the whole, it was the architecture of sturdy poverty, looking through thrift in the direction of wealth. It well matched the learning of early New England, traditionally staunch and narrow, yet also thrifty and tending to positivism; a learning destined as it widened to be undermined and to become, like the architecture, flimsy and rich. It had been founded on accurate Latin and a spell-bound constant reading of the Bible: but in the Harvard of my day we had heard a little of everything, and nobody really knew his Latin or knew his Bible. You might say that the professor of Hebrew did know his Bible, and the professors of Latin their Latin. No doubt, in the sense that they could write technical articles on the little points in controversy at the moment among philologists; but neither Latin nor the Bible flowed through them and made their spiritual lives; they were not vehicles for anything great. They were grains in a quicksand, agents and patients in an anonymous moral migration that had not yet written its classics.

The interior.   In both these old buildings I occupied corner rooms, ample, low, originally lighted by four windows, with window-seats in the thickness of the wall, which a cushion could make comfortable for reading. Between the side-windows the deep chimney-stack projected far into the room, and no doubt at first showed its rough or glazed bricks, as the low ceiling probably showed its great beams. But an "improvement" had spoiled the dignity of these chambers. The rage for "closets" invaded America, why I am not antiquary enough to know. Was it that wardrobes and chests, with or without drawers, had become too heavy and cumbrous for an unsettled population? Or was it that a feminine demand for a seemly "bed-sitting-room" had insisted on a place of hiding for one's belongings? Anyhow, in 19 Hollis both the side-windows had been hidden by oblique partitions, going from the edges of the chimney stack to the front and back walls, and enclosing the desired closets, not large enough for a bed, but capable of containing a washstand, trunks, and garments hanging on pegs. Luckily in 7 Stoughton this operation had mutilated only one angle, and left me one pleasant side-window open to the south, and affording a glimpse of Holden Chapel and the vista then open over the grass towards Cambridge Common.

The outlook.   Yet it was the outlook to the east, from both rooms, that was most characteristic. The old elms in the Yard were then in all their glory, and in summer formed a grove of green giants, with arching and drooping branches, that swung like garlands in the breeze. This type of elm, though graceful and lofty, has a frail air, like tall young women in consumption. The foliage is nowhere thick, too many thin ribs and sinews are visible; and this transparency was unfortunate in the Harvard Yard, where the full charm depended on not seeing the background. In winter the place was ungainly and forlorn, and not only to the eye. The uneven undrained ground would be flooded with rain and half-melted dirty snow one day, and another day strewn with foul ashes over the icy pavements. This was a theme for unending grumbling and old jokes; but we were young, and presumably possessed snow-boots called "arctics" or thick fishermen's boots warranted water-tight. Anyhow we survived; and as bad going for pedestrians is made inevitable during winter and spring by the New England climate, the Yard was not much worse in this respect than the surrounding places.

The gain and the loss in "modern improvements".   Holworthy in my day was still nominally the "Seniors' Paradise", but not in reality: in reality those who could afford it lived in private houses, in Little's Block, or in Beck. Holworthy preserved, as it has sometimes recovered, only the charm of tradition. The two bedrooms to each study favoured the pleasant custom of chumming; but as yet Holworthy had no baths, not even shower-baths, and no central heating. Modern improvements seem to me in almost everything to be a blessing. Electricity, vacuum cleaning, and ladies' kitchens render life simpler and more decent; but central heating, in banishing fireplaces, except as an occasional luxury or affectation, has helped to destroy the charm of home. I don't mean merely the ancient and rustic sanctity of the hearth; I mean also the home-comforts of the modern bachelor. An obligatory fire was a useful and blessed thing. In northern climates it made the poetry of indoor life. Round it you sat, into it you looked, by it you read, in it you made a holocaust of impertinent letters and rejected poems. On the hob your kettle simmered, and the little leaping flames cheered your heart and ventilated your den. Your fire absolved you from half your dependence on restaurants, cafés, and servants;

it also had the moralising function of giving you a duty in life from
which any distraction brought instant punishment, and taught you the
feminine virtues of nurse, cook, and Vestal virgin. Sometimes, I confess,
these cares became annoying; the fire kept you company, but like all
company it sometimes interrupted better things. At its best, a wood
fire is the most glorious; but unless the logs are of baronial dimensions,
it dies down too quickly, the reader or the writer is never at peace;
while a hard-coal fire (which also sometimes goes out) sleeps like a
prisoner behind its iron bars, without the liveliness of varied flames.
The ideal fuel is soft coal, such as I had in England and also in America
when I chose; like true beauty in woman, it combines brilliancy with
lastingness. I congratulate myself that in the Harvard Yard I was never
heated invisibly and willy-nilly by public prescription, but always by
my own cheerful fire, that made solitude genial and brought many a
genial friend who loved cheerfulness to sit by it with me, not rejecting
in addition a drink and a little poetry; no tedious epic, but perhaps
one of Shakespeare's sonnets or an ode of Keats, something fit to
inspire conversation and not to replace it.

**Bohemia
and the
Harvard
Lampoon.**   The quality of the Harvard Yard, both in its architecture
and its manners, was then distinctly bohemian: not of
the Parisian description, since no *petite amie* or *grande
amie* was in evidence, but of the red-brick, lodging, tavern
and stable-yard bohemia of Dickens and Thackeray; yet being in a
college, the arts and the intellect were not absent from it altogether.
I had not been many days a Freshman when I had a glimpse of this.
A note was slipped by hand through my door, inviting me to go that
evening to a room in Holworthy, where two Seniors interested in
things Spanish would be glad to see me and to talk about them. I
went. The two young men were commonplace and easy-going. They
didn't actually speak Spanish but had an idea that they loved gypsies
and Moors, the *Alhambra* of Washington Irving and the *Carmen* of
Mérimée. There was a mysterious curtain cutting off a corner of their
room; and the talk soon drifted from Spain to painting Venuses from
the model. Was that done here, I wondered, and was the model about
to emerge from behind that curtain? That would surely have been
contrary to College discipline; did these bold Seniors not care about
that, or was I the greenest of Freshmen and were they trying to impose
upon me? I saw little or nothing of them after that evening; probably
I was less Spanish or less bohemian than they expected. But by chance
they gave me a useful hint. If I myself drew a little, why didn't I draw

something for the *Lampoon*; and one of them suggested a subject: a mother with two or three daughters mistaking "Holyoke House" for a hotel and arriving with luggage and asking for rooms there. I made the drawing and sent it to the appropriate address; and soon I received a visit from the "President" of the *Lampoon* Board, who said they accepted my drawing but wished to keep it for the Class Day number— nine months hence—and meantime wouldn't I send them something else. Naturally, I did so; and was thereupon elected a member of the *Lampoon* Board.

I become one of an inner circle. This was a decisive event in my Harvard life. Two other Freshmen, Felton and Sanborn, had also been elected; and they asked me to come and sit at their table in Memorial Hall. Felton's chum, Baldwin, was also there, and some other friends; so that I immediately found myself in a little circle of more or less lively wits and seeing them every day at meals, apart from any personal sympathies. In time, the inner circle narrowed down to four, the three I have mentioned and myself. We kept up our comradeship at table for four years; and Sanborn and I became personal friends on intellectual grounds.

Sad history of Tom Sanborn. In those days Freshmen at Harvard were still at school. Courses were prescribed, and we sat in alphabetical order, to be marked present or absent. Sanborn and I were therefore likely to sit next to each other: not always, because those who had passed in French had to take German, and *vice versa*, and in some subjects the two hundred and fifty Freshmen were divided into more or less advanced classes. But I remember especially in Natural History 4, where Professor Shaler set forth "all the geology necessary to a gentleman", sitting next to Sanborn. We had separate chairs but one running desk in front of us, so that we could easily overlook one another's notebooks; and we amused ourselves in matching triolets, not always on that "concatenation of phenomena" which Shaler was impressing upon us.

Sanborn was a poet of lyric and modest flights but genuine feeling, not naturally in harmony with the over-intellectualised transcendentalism of Concord, Massachusetts, where his father was a conspicuous member of the Emersonian circle. There was more of Chaucer in him than of Emerson or Wordsworth: even Shakespeare—except in the songs—he found too heavy and rhetorical. These exclusions were involuntary; he was not in the least conceited about them, but on the contrary felt that he was a misfit, shy, ungainly in appearance, and at a disadvantage in the give and take of conversation or action. These maladjustments, a few years later, led to a tragic end. His father had found him a place in the office of *The Springfield Republican*. That town offered little to keep up his spirits. He fell into the company of loose women, as at College he had sometimes succumbed to drink—not often, yet disgracefully. I think I understand the secret of these failings, gross as they seem for a man of such delicate sensibility. He was unhappy, he was poor, he was helpless. The sparkle of a glass, the glitter of a smile, the magic of a touch could suddenly transport him out of this world, with all its stubborn hindrances and dreary conventions, into the *Auberge Verte*, the green paradise, of his dreams. Yet this escape from reality was necessarily short-lived, and the awakening bitter and remorseful. The strain was too much for Sanborn. His discouragement became melancholia and began to breed hallucinations. He knew only too much about madness, as everybody did in old New England, and he feared it. He cut his throat in his bath with a razor, and we buried him in Concord, in sight of the optimistic Emerson's grave, after a parlour funeral, with the corṣe visible, at which his father read a few not very pertinent passages from the Upanishads and the Psalms.

Felton and Baldwin.   The other *Lampoon* men were more normal and better adapted to their social medium. Felton and Baldwin were not New Englanders, rather Southern, without crotchets and with unaffected old-fashioned literary tastes, leaning towards the sentimental and the nobly moral; leanings likely to grow more pronounced in later years, under the sacred influences of home and of political eloquence. They loved Thackeray; and Felton would read aloud *"Wait till you come to forty-year."* Their room, No. 1 Thayer, was the reality under the literary fiction of a *Lampoon* "Sanctum". We gathered there to compose our parts of the fortnightly edition; chiefly drawings, although sometimes the column of puns entitled *"By the Way"* was concocted by us cooperatively, in the midst of a thousand interruptions. I never wrote for the *Lampoon*; even the text for my sketches was usually supplied for me by the others, who knew the idioms required. My English was too literary, too lady-like, too correct for such a purpose; and I never acquired, or liked, the American art of perpetual joking. What we printed was a severe selection from what we uttered: it had to be local, new or fresh, and at least apparently decent. Speech in this circle, if not always decent, never became lewd. There was an atmosphere of respect for holy things, of respect for distant or future lady-loves, and also of self-respect. We were not very intimate friends. The *Lampoon*, the Yard, the College had brought us together; and when we scattered the comradeship ceased. I scarcely knew what became of Felton or Baldwin. In recent years I unexpectedly received a letter from Baldwin, not reawakening old interests or old friendship, but full of conventional cordiality and platform sentiments. I should have preferred silence: because the young Baldwin had been an engaging person, who inspired trust and affection, and I recall the circle in which we moved with the warmest pleasure.

Ernest Thayer.   The man who gave the tone to the *Lampoon* at that time was Ernest Thayer, not one of our group. He seemed a man apart, and his wit was not so much jocular as Mercutio-like, curious and whimsical, as if he saw the broken edges of things that appear whole. There was some obscurity in his play with words, and a feeling (which I shared) that the absurd side of things is pathetic. Probably nothing in his later performance may bear out what I have just said of him; because American life was then becoming unfavourable to idiosyncrasies of any sort, and the current smoothed and rounded all the odd pebbles.

William Randolph Hearst.   In our last year or two, the *Lampoon* possessed a business manager whose name is everywhere known, and who is identified, perhaps more than anyone else, with that inexorable standardising current, namely William R. Hearst. He was little esteemed in the College. The fact that his father was a millionaire and a Senator from California gave him an independence that displeased the undergraduate mind, and his long cigars were bad form in the Yard. Yet his budding powers as a newspaper owner and manager made him invaluable to the *Lampoon* in its financial difficulties. He not only knew how to secure advertisements, but he presented us with a material *Sanctum*, carpeted, warmed by a stove, and supplied with wooden arm-chairs and long tables at which all the illustrated comic papers in the world were displayed as exchanges for our little local and puerile *Lampy*. How easily a little cool impudence can deceive mankind! Yet the enterprise of our business manager, in this affair, was of little use to us. Two or three times two or three of us may have gone into that new *Sanctum* (for we were also supplied with keys) and looked at those startling comic papers, most of them unintelligible and grossly coloured; especially the *Vie Parisienne* and the other French sheets, so different in prevalent theme from our decent and childlike fun. I myself actually read some of the longer stories in the *Vie Parisienne*: there was a certain overtone there of satire and subtle humour, sometimes even of pathos, as in Guy de Maupassant and Théophile Gautier; and the conventionalised illustrations showed a giraffe-like ideal of feminine beauty, very unlike the dumpy realities, as if a taste for elegance were struggling against mere sensuality. Yet the thing was horribly monotonous, and had been done better in *La Maison Tellier* and *Mademoiselle de Maupin*. We turned a cold shoulder on Hearst's munificence, and continued to meet and to bring forth our laboured witticisms, not without laughter, in Felton and Baldwin's room.

Theatricals.   To the Harvard Yard in spirit, though not topographically, may be assigned my other contacts with college life during those first four years. Athletics did not figure among them. I never took any exercise except walking, and I seldom went, as yet, even to watch the games, which in the case of football was then done as in England, standing at the side lines, the crowd being kept back only by a chalk mark or a rope. This "Harvard indifference" was not due to intense study on my part, or to misanthropy. I played the leading lady in the Institute Theatricals of 1884, and two years later, though I no longer looked at all deceptive in feminine clothes, I was one of the ballet in the Hasty Pudding play. These amusements, with rehearsals and a noisy trip to New York as a theatrical company, involved a good deal of intimacy for the moment, and I remember the names and faces of some of my companions, and some of the tunes we sang, chiefly from *Martha*; but for the most part scenes and persons are completely erased. I have a very short memory, except for such things as I absorb and recast in my own mind; so that I am a good observer and critic, but a bad historian: let the reader of this book take warning.

Crosby Whitman.   One figure, however, still stands clear before me out of that medley: Crosby Whitman, our musician and director, in whom, as in many a person, I felt a true potential friendship behind a slight acquaintance. Besides the love of music and of Miss Mary Anderson, he had a kind of cosmopolitan competence or normality that I seem to have noticed in the best people of the American West. They moved swimmingly in the midst of all the current conventions and noises, but they seemed to make light of them, as your good Bostonian never could. They were not "taken in" by the tastes, opinions, and pleasures that they played with as in a carnival. Crosby Whitman was a man of the world.

The O.K. and my after-dinner poems. More intellectual, at least nominally, were the literary groups or societies of which for me the O.K. and the *Harvard Monthly*, when that was founded, were the most important. The members of these two were largely the same, and included *Lampoon* men as well; but the O.K., which later gave excellent dinners, had the advantage of running over into the class of merely intelligent or even athletic leaders of the College. In a commercial civilisation, these were likely to be much *better beings* than the professional scholars or intellectuals, *better beings* even than the future lawyers, though these might have more historical and rhetorical attainments. I liked to feel a spark of sympathy pass from those sound simple active heirs of the dominant class to my secret philosophy; and sometimes the spark did pass, and in both directions. It was at the O.K. dinners, in the 1890's, that I read my *Athletic Ode* and *Six Wise Fools*. Helped by the champagne, these trifles caught fire. The play of ordinary wit and sentiment, with a light touch and a masculine note, appeals to a side of the heart not reached by the standard poets; it moves from convention to sincerity, where the standard poets move from sincerity to convention.

The *Harvard Monthly* and Alanson Bigelow Houghton. The *Harvard Monthly* was founded by A. B. Houghton, afterwards American ambassador at Berlin and London. His literary quality was in marked contrast with Sanborn's, as was also his character and fate. Houghton was as rich as Sanborn was poor; he was ambitious and bitter, nominally preoccupied with socialism and pessimism, not, I think, in a clear speculative spirit, but rather as scandals and dangers that the leaders of liberalism and plutocracy must somehow overcome. His conscience and critical faculty were not at peace about the way in which his father made money; it was chiefly in a glass factory; and the son would ask himself how many glass-blowers died each year from blowing into those furnaces. In the good old times they would have died of famine, the plague, drink, war, or the gallows—not perhaps gentler ways of keeping down the population below the means of subsistence. But that was not the question. The question was, Is material civilisation worth while? Is the dull anonymous unhappiness that it steadily diffuses more tolerable than the sudden and horrible scourges that fall upon primitive peoples? Or should the question of happiness be ignored altogether, as German philosophy ignores it, and should the criterion be placed in more and more complex formal achievements? In the end Houghton would seem to have adopted the latter alternative, if we may judge by his brilliant career; but in his student days, at Harvard and in Germany, the problem of human suffering dominated his judgments. In verse he was scornful and revolutionary, with a good deal of verbal facility and technical ingenuity, after the manner of Swinburne. His versification was not slovenly, even when it was empty or trite. This was remarkable in America, and marked a certain documentary precision and authority in his mind, that doubtless contributed to his subsequent official distinction.

His philosophy of life   I knew Houghton very well; we discussed all manner of subjects. In 1898 he unexpectedly made me a visit in Brattle Street. He glanced about my quarters disapprovingly, sucked his enormous cigar, and said magisterially that it was a sad mistake to try to swim against the stream. I have never been aware of swimming against any stream: I have merely stood on the bank or paddled about in the quiet back-waters. From there I may have observed that the torrent was carrying down more or less wreckage. My philosophy throws no challenge to those who rush down the very middle of the rapids and rejoice in their speed. However, the monition addressed to me by the wise Houghton revealed the dilemma in which he had found himself, and his own decision never to swim against the current. I wonder if he was ultimately satisfied with his career. Perhaps his success fell short of his hopes, and perhaps his conscience about the way the world is run was never quite at rest. Yet he was actively abetting the dominant procedure, no doubt wishing to improve it in detail, but in any case determined to keep it going full blast. Was it faith in a divine direction of things and the course of history being the Last Judgment? Or was it the force of vested interests and formed habits drowning the still small voice of the spirit?

The collegiate ideal superseded.   After this glance into the great world taken from the Harvard Yard, I will add nothing more about that place. It has lost its character and its importance. When President Lowell was planning his "Houses" to be built by the river, he very kindly urged me to remain and take part in the experiment. I could have lived very like a Don at Oxford or Cambridge. But it was too late. My heart might have been in the thing twenty years earlier, and perhaps then the transformation of Harvard into a university of colleges might have been socially more successful. But by 1912 the non-collegiate additions had become too numerous and too important for such a re-organisation. The community too had outgrown the instinct for a secluded life. Colleges were fundamentally conventual and religious; on which foundation specific precious traditions, social and sporting, might develop, together with an exact but familiar and humanistic learning. Now looser, wider, more miscellaneous interests had invaded every mind. — But I am not writing a history of Harvard University. I know very little about it. I knew only the Harvard Yard.

XIV

First Return to Spain

The chief event of my Freshman year occurred towards the end of it. I received—what was unprecedented—a note from home, asking me to be in my room on the following evening, because my mother and sisters were coming to lay before me an important proposal. I guessed at once what it would be, although no hint had been dropped on the subject. I was to go to Spain that summer to see my father.

I am sent to see my father. My mother evidently felt profoundly the recent relief to her finances, and wished to be generous. Sending me to college, even on my modest allowance, had already consumed perhaps a fourth of her income; yet she still had money to spare, and desired to do more. She had done nothing for my father during these ten years; in a certain sense she had done nothing for *me*; for giving me food and lodging and a hundred dollars a year for clothes, books, and pocket money, was something she owed to herself. She could not have allowed a child of hers to beg or to go in rags; and even in sending me to college she was carrying out a plan of her own, and trying to make me into what she wished me to be, rather than into what my father or I secretly desired. But now in letting me go to see him, she was doing us an unselfish kindness, relenting as it were and letting us, for a moment, have our own way. Neither my father nor I had made any such suggestion; but it was impossible that he shouldn't wish to see his son grown up; and everybody knew at home how I longed to travel, to see again with my own eyes old towns, cathedrals, castles, and palaces, and also the classic landscape of Europe: because in America, at least in the parts I knew, nature as well as society seemed to lack contrast and definition, as if everything were half-formed and groping after its essence.

My body and my mind disagree about the sea. Late in June I started accordingly on my first journey alone, and sailed from New York in the steamship *Werra* for Antwerp. Robert had looked up the various routes possible, and it had been decided that I should go and return by the Belgian or Red Star line. The ship was decent, as standards stood in those days, but second rate, perhaps of 5,000 tons; and as usual I was dreadfully seasick; so much so that the doctor and the stewardess took pity on me, some ladies became interested (I was nineteen years old) and a bed was rigged up for me on deck, where as they said I should enjoy the sunshine and the air. The fresh air was indeed a relief but the glare an added nuisance; and the coming and going of people, and their talk, only intensified the general instability of everything. I was too ill for the moment to be ashamed of myself; but when I once got back to my cabin, although I wasn't alone even there, the feeling of shame came over me. They say dying animals go into hiding; and I could understand that instinct. There are phases of distress when help is neither possible nor desired. It is simpler, easier, more honest to be seasick alone, and to die alone. The trouble then seems something fated, not to be questioned, like life itself; and nature is built to face it and to see it out. Much as I suffered at sea, I was always ready to go to sea again: such a trial leaves the will unaffected, as nightmares do: you start afresh as you were, perhaps more merrily and with a deeper courage. The thing will pass, the ghosts will vanish. There is no reason for changing your purpose.

Mrs. X of Cincinnati. When I appeared on deck again, looking and feeling perfectly well, shaved and in fresh linen, I was congratulated. One particular lady of uncertain age, who now explained that she was Mrs. X of Cincinnati, Ohio, had to be thanked for the kindness she had shown, or at least intended, on the day of that disgusting exhibition which I was heartily sorry to have made of myself. A young man should be hardier, and I had been sicker than any girl. Mrs. X had brought me a raw egg in brandy, and insisted I should swallow it, which I had done with dire results: brandy on such occasions is a brutal remedy that my throat, not to say my stomach, abhors. Now, it was eleven o'clock in smooth sunny weather, there was no question of brandy, but only of a cup of broth and a biscuit, which we had together. I must come, she said, to sit in *their* chairs, and take a vacant place there was at *their* table. *They*, she explained, were her son (she had been married very young) and her niece, not *daughter*, who was sixteen. I had to say that of course a young girl of sixteen couldn't be her daughter. Even the boy seemed surprising. Yes, she said, he was very tall for his age; but she didn't tell me how old he was, because nice people mustn't lie.

A girl of sixteen might have seemed the natural affinity for a boy of nineteen: but not at all. The niece was to be regarded as a mere child, and my special friend was to be Mrs. X herself. She certainly was more entertaining, deeply interested in all the higher subjects, very refined, and very religious. She spoke of "plumes", and embroidered the words *Holy, Holy, Holy* in gold upon altar-cloths. They were going all the way up the Rhine, it was such a beautiful trip, so romantic and so full of historic associations. Didn't it tempt me? It tempted me; but frankly I had no extra money for trips, and must go straight to Avila to see my father. It was too bad, she said, that I had no extra money; but it was nice that I should be going straight to see my old father, after such a long absence. Her husband too was old, too old to enjoy travelling, but he was happy in thinking how many interesting experiences the family were having, and it was wiser and pleasanter for him to remain at home, he so loved his dog and his garden and his beautiful books, all the English standard authors bound uniformly and making such a splendid decoration for his sunlit library wall. I must come some day to Cincinnati and see their delightful home. I should love it. And by the first of September they expected to be in Paris: perhaps I might be there at the same time, on my way back from Spain. We must try to arrange it.

A glimpse of Antwerp.   We parted at Antwerp on these terms, having exchanged addresses, and promised to keep each other informed of our movements. I had just time to see the marketplace with the Cathedral spire, like a group of inverted icicles rising above it; and inside, besides the general splendour of a great living place of worship, I admired the two magnificent, if theatrical, pictures by Rubens at the head of the two aisles, especially the *Descent from the Cross*. Yet this is too classic, too Michaelangelesque for Flanders; I could have wished to carry away some humbler and more intimate memories: but the gorgeousness of Rubens blotted out the rest.

Predicaments of a green traveller.   In Paris I saw nothing, merely driving from one station to the other; but at the Gare d'Orléans I found myself in the sort of difficulty that inexperience will fall into. I had provided myself with just the amount of French money that I had calculated would be sufficient, leaving a decent margin for emergencies; and at the ticket-office, I asked, as planned, for a second-class ticket to Avila. I could have a ticket to Avila the man said, but only first class for the express: the ordinary trains, with second and third class, would take more than two whole days for the journey. I counted my money. I could take a first-class ticket and have fifteen francs left. Would that be enough for meals and tips on the journey? I would risk it. It was only thirty-six hours, two nights and one day; at a pinch, I could have a sandwich instead of a dinner. It wouldn't kill me.

During the next ten years I repeated this journey many times; the expense was about the same if I went first class without stopping, or second class with two or three stops on the way: a method that avoided long nights in the train, and enabled me, by varying my voyage and landing at Cherbourg or England, or even Gibraltar, to see the principal sights in all France and Spain, without making trips expressly for that purpose. My architectural passion was thus richly satisfied: it was only Italy that remained to be explored and lived in when I became relatively independent.

Arrival in Avila.   My fifteen francs, however, were only just enough to pay my way on that first occasion; and I found at Irún that I had only a few coppers in my pocket and couldn't telegraph to my father, as had been agreed, that I was arriving at 5.30 the next morning. It was broad daylight, being early in July, and I recognised the walls and the Cathedral tower, touched by the rising sun, before we reached the station. But there was nobody to receive me, and no vehicle. Not even anybody to carry my valise. I left it with the guard, and started alone on foot, immensely happy, and remembering perfectly that station road and the place among the first houses to the left, opposite the church and convent of Santa Ana, where Don Juan the Englishman's house stood, which was now my father's. There it was, the middle one of three humble two-storey buildings, not properly lined up, and painted in varying weatherworn yellows or greys, with red tiled roofs. I pounded the middle door with the knocker. No answer. Finally a neighbour, from a window over the bakery in the house to the left, put out her dishevelled head and said, "Knock hard. They are all deaf in that house." I knocked harder; until the window over my door was opened also, and another head, evidently the housemaid's, peered out, and looked at me with an air of inquiry. — "*Don Agustín* lives here, doesn't he? I am his son." — She smiled, wished me a good arrival, and said they were expecting me, but not that morning. *El señor* was still in bed, *La señora* (his sister María Ignacia) was in the garden. And presently the door was opened for me. At the end of the stone-paved passage running through the house, I could see the so-called garden, and my aged aunt standing there, stooping a little, with a watering-pot in her hand. The maid tactfully ran ahead and announced me loudly, and after embracing my aunt, whom I had never seen before, I had some difficulty in making her hear and understand why I hadn't telegraphed. Then I was led up to my father's room, where the same embraces and the same explanations, under the same difficulties, were duly repeated. But it was all right now; and rather characteristic of a young son from half round the world to arrive home with just twopence in his pocket.

Impressions of my father. My father looked much as I remembered him. When middle-aged he had seemed to me simply old; now that he was really old, he seemed no older, only deafer; a disadvantage for me—besides the fact that my powers of expression in Spanish were limited, for I had read, and even now have read, hardly any Spanish books. But deafness was almost an advantage for him in conversation. It gave him a free field, and I soon discovered how entertaining and witty his talk could be. His views were distinctly *views*, partial, definite, and humorous. They were not at all the fruit of scientific thinking. He was rather like an ancient sage, a satirist and proverb-maker; his wit lay in putting things in a nutshell—into which naturally they couldn't go in their entirety. When he talked about persons and events these miniatures were excellent; they caught the traits relevant to his purpose. It was only when given out as general truths that his summings up became sophistical and monotonous.

Difference between Latin and Anglosaxon liberalism. To be monotonous, sophistical, and utterly intolerant is the characteristic of the liberalism that he seemed to have adopted as final and absolute: I belong to the next turn of the tide. The fifty years between our ages thus made a perfect contrariety in our fundamental principles; but they made him all the more valuable for me, so to speak, as a classic, as a point of reference in thought; because the same principles, as they are found in English-speaking people, are not held so radically or intelligently but enveloped in various national, religious, commercial, or sentimental interests that confuse the issue. In him the narrowing and desiccating force of this philosophy, helped no doubt by old age, became conspicuous; and I wondered how so penetrating a mind in regard to particular facts and persons, could be satisfied with such jejune second-hand theories. Anti-clericalism was the dominant crotchet: hatred of religion had acquired all the dogmatism and intolerance of religion with none of its advantages. For it was noticeable in my father how comfortless (except for the assumption that things were improving and apparently were to go on improving for ever) I say how comfortless his philosophy was; whereas in the Anglosaxon world, it is all veiled and emotionalised by a sort of music, like the empty trite words by the swelling harmonies of an anthem.

Both worship prosperity, but the one is poor and the other rich. This difference is capital. It makes the whole moral lesson and speculative interest of my many visits to my father, of which this was the first. And I think now I can distinguish wherein that difference lies. Liberalism, Protestantism, Judaism, positivism all have the same ultimate aim and standard. It is prosperity, or as Lutheran theologians put it, union with God at our level, not at God's level. The thing all these schools detest is the ideal of union with God at God's level, proper to asceticism, mysticism, Platonism, and pure intelligence, which insist on seeing things under the form of truth and of eternity. You must be content, they say, to see things under the form of time, of appearance, and of feeling. Very well: yet the question returns why my father's view, which doctrinally was the same as the Anglosaxon, was morally and emotionally so different. And to this question I reply, that prosperity may be the ideal of the poor, or it may be the ideal of the rich; and it may be accompanied by domestic, national, and religious joys, or by domestic, national, and religious bitterness. My father's was the bitter poor man's liberalism; the liberalism of the dominant Anglosaxon is that of the joyful rich man. This colours differently their common ideal of prosperity; but prosperity remains the ultimate ideal of both. For this reason Latins who are rich, either in possessions or sympathies, can hardly be liberals. They love the beautiful.

Our different views of Anglosaxon life. This point touches the heart of my intellectual relations with my father, and also my judgment, very different from his, on English and American civilisation. Both the side of it that he admired, and the side of it that I admire and love, were foreshadowed in Bacon's *New Atlantis*. Bacon was the prophet of the rich man's Utopia; he had the liberal's worship of prosperity, and the pragmatic esteem for science and dominion over matter as means to that end; and when my father saw the partial realisation of that prophecy in England and America, he was filled with respect and envy for it, and chagrin that his own country was so backward in those profitable inventions and methods. But Bacon's ideal had another side, the successful rich man's delight in nobility and splendour; he was a courtier, and still nursed the classic ideal of a hierarchy of the arts, with a magnificent pageant of virtues and dignities, like the celestial choirs come down to earth. His New Atlantis was not to be merely prosperous, but solemnly ordered, glorious, and beautiful. Now just as in Bacon's mind this Roman or Byzantine vesture clothed a pragmatic skeleton, so in England and even in the United States, the cult of splendour and aristocratic ways of living and feeling endured and in some circles entirely hid the commercial and industrial mechanism beneath it. There was an intense poetic, sporting, and religious life. Of this my father knew nothing, or shrugged his shoulders at it, as at vanities that may be forgiven in a society that, in more serious matters, is thoroughly sound and utilitarian. Now it was precisely this free, friendly, laughing side of Anglosaxon civilisation that I liked and cultivated: it could not have existed, I know, without the material prosperity that supports it; at least it could not have existed in these special forms. Yet friendship, laughter, and freedom were not invented in the nineteenth century; and the modern forms of them are good only for re-enacting those ancient glories.

Don Pelayo.   It was not at long range only, like Lucretius, that my father could observe the evils occasioned by religion. His only friend in Avila, who at once courteously came to salute me, was a clerical, and a sad wreck. Whether his ruin was due directly to clericalism might be doubted; it was due rather to cards; but indirectly cards might be due to indolence and boredom, these to lack of national prosperity, and this in turn notoriously to clericalism. So that Don Pelayo, for that was his name, was a victim of the system that he so perversely advocated. Here was a perpetual thorn in my father's side; and yet the prick was a stimulant. It enlivened him and kept his exasperation always pleasantly fresh and green.

Don Pelayo expressed himself well, even grandly. His Castilian, like my father's, was of the purest, only that he loved rhetoric, as my father did not. His rounded periods were often Ciceronian. His model among the living, however, was only Cánovas del Castillo, prime minister whenever the conservatives were in power, whom he called "*el monstruo de la edad presente*", the monster, meaning the marvel, of the present age. Cánovas was neither a monster nor a marvel, but a plausible intriguing politician who made the best of a bad job. Perhaps he was less pernicious than his rival, the liberal Sagasta. He allowed Spain to draw her natural breath and to change spontaneously; he did not attempt to destroy her life and character, and to turn her into a capitalist plutocracy with an industrial proletariat, things equally contrary to her nature; because the Spanish people is a poetic people and Spanish greatness is a chivalrous greatness.

Sagasta and liberal government in Spain.   Sagasta, on the contrary, and the forces he represented, were corrupt to the core. I remember what my brother-in-law, a wiser head than Don Pelayo, said about Sagasta in 1898, after the battle of Santiago. The better Spanish cruisers had been sent to Cuba without their heavy guns. Where were those guns? In the pocket of the minister of marine. "How", I asked, "can Sagasta not be ashamed of himself, and how can he remain in office?" "He would have died of shame," my brother-in-law said dryly, "if he were capable of the feeling."* Such was Spanish government under a foreign parliamentary regime.

Castilian grandeur in misery.   Don Pelayo had studied at the University of Salamanca, but learning was not his strong point. Even the astronomy of Ptolemy was unknown to him. One evening we were walking in the Paseo de San Roque (a rough terrace by a convent wall, with an open view) and admiring the stars, particularly numerous and brilliant in the rarified atmosphere of Avila. "They say", Don Pelayo meditated, "that the earth is suspended in the void without any support. That is impossible. If it had no support, it would fall to the ground." Unfortunately his practice was no wiser than his theory. In his youth he had divided a small patrimony with his two sisters, but had soon dissipated his share, and gone to live with them at their expense. Finding nothing else to do, he continued to play cards in small taverns with only copper coins for stakes. As he was very near-sighted and his companions unscrupulous, he would find, even if he won, that he had only false pennies in his pocket. He would bring them up one by one in the light to his better eye, and exclaim sadly: "But all these coins are ignoble!" He felt himself Job-like; there was verbal majesty in his misery. My father used to say, that in spite of his grandiloquence, Don Pelayo would sell all his religious and political

---

*The original was more terse: "*Se hubiera muerto de vergüenza, si la tuviera.*"

principles for one peseta. I think he might have sold them, because
he needed the peseta; but he would have cheated the devil in doing
so, because his ideal allegiance to them would have remained
unchanged.

I was told that in winter, when my father took his walk soon after
his mid-day dinner, Don Pelayo would sometimes arrive just before
dinner was served. "No, thank you," he would say, "I have dined
already; but if I may I will have the pleasure of sitting at table with
you, while you eat." A place would be made for him; a heaping plate
of chick peas and the other ingredients of the *puchero* would be placed
before him, and he would resign himself to taste it. "*Empalmo*", he
would say: "I make a connection, I catch the branch train." It was
true that the poor man had already dined—the day before yesterday.

Saragossa   My stay in Avila that year, 1883, was not long. I made
and the   a tour to Catalonia, in order to visit relations, and by
Virgin of   the way I saw a good many impressive things. I have
the Pillar.   already mentioned that my father and I made an excursion to the Escurial; later I went alone to Madrid and to the Prado,
to Saragossa, to Tarragona, to Barcelona, and finally to Lyons and
Paris. It was a varied feast for my hungry eyes. Most of those places
have become familiar to me in later years, but of Saragossa, which I
have hardly revisited, my memories belong to that early time, and
are vivid. There was *La Seo*, the cathedral, Gothic in style but preserving
the square plan of the mosque that it replaced: seven lofty aisles, with
rows of chapels in addition, and with the rich choir and sanctuary
making an enclosed island in the middle. To me, who love shrines
and individual devotions and freedom of movement in sacred places,
this arrangement seemed ideal. A Jewish friend whom I once took to
see the Pantheon in Rome pronounced it the first *religious* place he
had found there; and I can understand that feeling. It belongs to what
Spengler calls *Magian* religion and art; it reappears in the mosque of
Omar—a Christian church—and in many other mosques. At Saragossa
it is combined, as at St. Sophia, with the Christian theme of salvation,
in all its complexities, historical, personal, and eschatological. There
are a thousand mediations, unknown to the pure Moslem; but they
do not destroy the sublimity or the inwardness of a total surrender
of man to God. In Saragossa there is also *La Lonja*, a picturesque hall
with twisted columns, the mediaeval merchants' Exchange. We are
in the Mediterranean world; might be at Pisa or Palermo, or even at
Damascus. Finally there is *La Virgen del Pilar*; but here the architecture

is vast, dreary, modern, and when I saw it hideously painted. The only interest, the only beauty, is devotional and centred in the glittering shrine of the Pillar itself.* *El Pilar* is the sanctuary of Spanish patriotism and chivalry: it is the point, as Delphi was to the Greeks, of their conscious contact with fate and with eternity. It is therefore truly sacred. That the legend should be childish or the statue ordinary makes no difference: what matters is the range of human need and aspiration that has been focussed here. I therefore went to the back of the shrine, where the jasper pillar is accessible to the public through an oval opening in the wall; and I kissed the hollowed place that had been worn down by the kisses of generations. Not that I expected any wish of mine to be furthered by such a ceremony: I was only offering up all my wishes, to be sacrificed or fulfilled as the issue might determine. In any case, I was quickening in myself the sense of their precarious fortunes and eternal claims. I kissed at once the beauty of the beautiful and the rod that smote me and drove me from its presence.

My father's cousin, a Canon of Tarragona, whom I called *tío Nicolás*.

The goal of my journey, however, was Tarragona: for there a cousin and contemporary of my father's, Don Nicolás Zabalgoitia, was a Canon in the Cathedral. Spanish custom calls a parent's cousin an uncle; courtesy therefore compels me to speak of the Canon as *tío Nicolás*; but he is not to be confused with my real uncle Nicolás Santayana, my father's brother, a major and my godfather, from whom I took my third Christian name. The Canon, however, was not my only relation in Tarragona. My father's eldest sister, my aunt Mariquita, lived with him and had kept house for him all their lives; and with them, at that time, lodged my father's youngest brother, Manuel, with his wife and two children. More than half my entire Spanish connection lived under that roof: so that my father, who was always loyal to his family bonds, thought I ought to accept the invitation of my *tío Nicolás*, and make the acquaintance of that whole household.

A shadow in his life.

Towards *tío Nicolás* my father had an old affection, as for a brother; yet like all my father's affections, it was mixed with bitterness. In their youth Nicolás had been put in a mon-

*Voir Notre-Dame, au fond du sombre corridor,
  Luire en sa châsse ardente avec sa chape d'or
  Et puis m'en retourner.

Victor Hugo, Hernani

astery and had become a monk: yet scarcely had he taken his vows, when all the monasteries in Spain (except a few devoted to supplying missionaries for the Colonies) were suppressed by the government, and the monks dispersed. In time, a place was found for the waif as parish priest in some village, where he had to keep house and needed a housekeeper. Now my grandmother, as I have already indicated, was punctilious and vehement in her piety, poor, and burdened with a family of twelve children, for whom places had to be found in the world. Unfortunately the two eldest were daughters, not inclined apparently to become nuns; yet their mother doubtless thought that life in a clerical atmosphere would be better for their temporal and eternal welfare than would some modest commonplace marriage. Now that the young priest, their cousin, needed a housekeeper, would not the eldest sister, Mariquita, be suitable for that office? Surely a great confidence was manifested here in divine grace, to put a young man and a young woman, practically strangers to each other, under one narrow roof, where they were compelled by their cousinship to live on equal terms, not as master and servant, for day after day all summer and night after night all winter. A triumph of chastity over propinquity would surely have been admirable in such circumstances, but the contrary was more probable. Could not my experienced grandmother or her confessor foresee it? A child, called a niece, before long was seen playing in that village parsonage; and although for some reason no more children appeared, the constraint and forced mendacity in such a household, added to its poverty, were not pleasant to consider.

My father's affectionate tone and loyal conduct towards his family never varied, whatever at any moment might be his feelings. He sometimes quarrelled with them, and spoke of them sharply to other persons; but the quarrels were soon made up, and he reverted to his fundamental tolerance and even deference towards all mankind. It was characteristic of him to combine a kind of enthusiasm and extreme courtesy of manner with a total absence of illusions about the person so favoured. It was so, I suspect, that he had courted my mother, as it were against his will. Fate had allied him to her as it had to his blood relations. In itself the conduct of my *tío Nicolás* had nothing to surprise anybody. Everybody would say of him what Mephistopheles said of Gretchen: He was not the first. That was what his ecclesiastical superiors must have said of him. The thing was unfortunate but had to be overlooked; and it didn't interfere with his continuance in the priesthood or his ultimately becoming a canon.

Later complications. Yet irregularities breed irregularities, and the worst, from my father's point of view, was yet to come. He had managed to secure, for his youngest brother Manuel, a small post in the Philippine Islands. It opened a career for the young man and could ultimately secure him a pension. Spain was not then a capitalist country. Nobody had "money". There were some great landlords, and some modest ones, like my brother-in-law; there were lawyers and doctors; and the rest of the middle class, including the engineers, professors, military men, and ecclesiastics, held their positions under the government, and expected pensions, not only for their widows and minor children, but for their unmarried daughters for life. A post under the government, especially in the colonies which had a separate and less political administration, was a virtual settlement: it gave a relative sense of security. What, then, was my father's chagrin, when his brother Manuel was leaving for Manila with the prospect of a decent career, to find his cousin Nicolás and his sister Mariquita had married off their "niece" to the young Manuel, who had sailed on his first voyage already burdened with a wife! It was an outrageous marriage. The girl was not only a cousin but also a niece of her husband's; and he, who as a young bachelor might have made his way in Manila in any society, was condemned to wallow (*acochinado*, my father said) in a tropical pigsty, poor, unknown, and without ambition. It was he, retired on a miserable pension, with his wife Hermenegilda and his two surviving children, Manuela and Juan, that I found living at Tarragona with my *tío Nicolás* and my aunt Mariquita.

An unattractive family, unpleasantly complicated, crowded in a modest ill-furnished flat: yet at once I had occasion to see the human necessity of that loyalty to one's blood, apart from one's inclinations, which my father practised, and to put it in practice in my turn. For I brought no blessing to that family. On the contrary, I involuntarily imposed upon them endless trouble and responsibility, which they faced bravely; and they placed me under a permanent obligation to acknowledge and to assist them.

I fall ill on arriving. It had been a hot journey to Tarragona: especially at the station in Lérida, where I had to wait several hours between trains, the heat had been oppressive. When I reached Tarragona, I easily singled out my *tío Nicolás* by his clerical robes; a stout, sound, white-haired old gentleman, dignified and affable; and with him my uncle Manuel, passive, modest, limp, and insignificant. At the house, my two aunts and two cousins were duly embraced. I was feeling a little dazed, not at all well. They had prepared an elaborate supper. I could eat nothing; excused myself on the ground of fatigue and of the great heat. But finally my head began to turn. I was unmistakably very ill, and had to be put to bed. They told me afterwards that I had been delirious, talked sometimes in English, sometimes in Spanish, but about imaginary things, and that the doctor had spoken of a high gastric fever. But after a day or two an irruption appeared. They said they were relieved. I was better. It was "only small-pox", and a mild case.

It was "only the small-pox".   It was nasty and for a time troublesome; but when the blisters dried up and the crusts fell off, I had rather a pleasant convalescence. They had told me not to scratch my face, as that would make the marks permanent; but I have no marks whatever on my body, where I was free to scratch, and a few, not very obvious, precisely on my nose. My father had come to Tarragona on hearing the news, and my mother had telegraphed asking for a bulletin by cable; and this could be brief and favourable, as by that time I was well, though the red spots remained visible for some months.

Sights in Tarragona.   The Cathedral was directly opposite, and my father and I used to walk in the cloisters: we are both given to pacing a room, like a beast in a cage; but a continuous cloister has all the advantages of an enclosed smooth space with those of fresh air in addition. It was a nice cloister, with the dark grey castle-like cathedral overshadowing it, and one immense slanting palmtree spreading its crown victoriously over all human obstructions in the direction of the sun. We were by the shores of the Mediterranean, and a short walk would take us to the ancient citadel, overhanging the nutshell port. It was my first glimpse of that sacred sea; but the foreground at that moment was more vividly in my mind than the distances, geographical and historical; only some years later, when I went by sea from Malaga to Gibraltar did the full sense of ploughing those Homeric waters come over me, of which I expressed something in the Ode written on that occasion. Here the accent fell on ancient Tarraco, with its Roman castle still standing, and its so Spanish mixture of Carthaginian and Celtic suggestions. This had been the capital of all northeastern Spain—how much more noble and Spanish than modern Barcelona!—and the archiepiscopal see still retained vestiges of its ancient pre-eminence. Its canons wore red silk cassocks, like cardinals, with purple stockings; and *tío Nicolás*, who had been a handsome man, looked very grand in his vestments.

The Canon's conversation and character. He had a jovial temperament and carried his heavy burden, both of flesh and of responsibility, with a good grace. And he was no fool. When I heard him and my father talking together, though at least in my presence their conversation was discreet and general, I couldn't help making comparisons and wondering which of them had the sounder and riper mind. My father was far better informed and freer to express himself; yet *tío Nicolás* seemed to be at home in a rich humanistic world of men, of affairs, of convention and of religion on which my father had turned his back with a strange hatred. I can sympathise with the preference for obscurity and solitude. I prefer them for myself also; but that does not condemn the world in its own eyes, or in those of justice, or remove the glory and inner interest of its adventures. I felt that *tío Nicolás* liked all that was likable, without being deceived by it: and this seemed a kindlier and wiser sentiment than constitutional derision of everything that one might have discarded in one's own life. I could see why he had been made a canon. Without eminence for either learning or virtue, he had a certain native elegance in speech and manners. His latinity, if not impeccable, was familiar and pleasant, and he felt the full afflatus of theological poetry and wisdom, however qualified his faith might be. Once when I complimented him on his robust health, he shook his head with a smile, and said "*Senectus isa morbus*; do you understand that?" I certainly understood *senectus* and *morbus*; but what was *isa*? Sounded like Greek for "equal"; was it Latin? Yes, he said; it meant "itself". —Oh, *ipsa*! "Old age is itself a disease." — Yes, that was it; but they pronounced it *isa*. And we talked sometimes of chants and church music. I knew only what I had heard at the church of the Immaculate Conception; but I used to sing parts of the mass and of Rossini's *Stabat Mater* about the house: something quite natural in that sort of family, where the housemaid sings while she makes the beds. Spanish chants have no solemnity: they are as precipitate and perfunctory as the recital of the Rosary; which doesn't preclude a general devout posture of mind in the process. It might even seem more religious only to *indicate* the burden of a prayer, rather than to mouth the words in order to impress other people. Worship should be addressed to God, not to an audience. Be that as it may, *tío Nicolás* was far from sanctimonious; he liked sometimes to be a bit naughty. At three o'clock he was obliged, in spite of the heat, to cross the street to the Cathedral, to be present at Vespers; for if a canon was absent, he was fined one peseta. Referring to this regulation, and smoothing his robe, he would recite as he went heavily down the stairs:

Cantemos del Señor las alabanzas
para llenar nuestras panzas

"Let us sing the praises of the Lord, in order that we may fill our bellies." Pleasantry? Cynicism? I think a mixture of both. After all the sentiment is not very different from the key-note of Hebrew piety;* and the Psalter needs to be taken liturgically, and very symbolically, if it is still to serve for spiritual expression. I don't wonder that the old canons should have found Vespers rather sleepy and useless, the music not having been raised, as in Anglican services, into an independent vehicle of sentiment, or stimulus for it.

My theory of his secret sentiments. What did *tío Nicolás* really think of his profession? I doubt that he knew himself, or much cared to ask. He was at home in the conventions, could not break away from them without ruining himself and his family, and had no inner desire to break away. It is not as if he had been a philosopher with a clear contrary system of beliefs. He was a man of the world without any contrary system. Your genuine and profound sceptic sees no reason to quarrel with any ruling orthodoxy. It is as plausible as any other capable of prevailing in the world. If you do not think so, it is simply because that orthodoxy is not familiar to you, or not congenial. In a different age, or with a different endowment, you would have rested peacefully in it like the rest of mankind. And from the point of view of happiness, decency, art, and imagination, you might have been better off. Such, I suspect, would have been the philosophy of *tío Nicolás*, if he had framed one for himself: but he was content to quote the approved answers to all puzzling questions, and to let the Church and the Fathers bear the responsibility. It was not our fault that we were born. Is it our fault that we believe what we believe? To be incurious and at peace in such matters might even be a mark of profound faith, if the intention were to conform to the divine order of things in courage and silence, without knowing what precisely this order may be.

---

*Cf. Psalm 33(34): 9,10.
  Gustate et videte quam bonus sit Dominus: beatus vir qui configit ad eum.
  Timete Dominum, sancti ejus, quia non est inopia timentibus eum.

Poverty and cynicism in his family. The worst symptoms of infidelity that I saw in that family were in the women. Not unintelligibly. It was they who had suffered most from poverty, since there had always been enough to eat, but not enough to appear in the world as women like to appear. And it was they who had suffered most from the latent disgrace of their position, and the dread of gossip and insults. They owed society a grudge for making their life difficult. They had not sinned against nature, but the world had sinned against them by its cruel tyranny and injustice. They were therefore rebels, impotent rebels, against all the powers that be, celestial and earthly. My aunt Mariquita was smiling and silent; she smiled feebly, passively, equivocally at everything, even at death and illness, and hardly said anything. When *tío Nicolás* died and she came to live with us in Avila, she would lock herself up in her room, where she didn't allow even the servant to penetrate; and when she came out for meals, she would hardly eat, insisting on mixing vinegar with everything. These were crotchets of extreme old age; but what her secret thoughts must have been appeared in her "niece" Hermenegilda and in Manuela, Hermenegilda's daughter, who were loquacious, and betrayed their sentiments even when they didn't dare to express them frankly. They had a typical low-class esteem for small material advantages, with cynicism about all virtue and all so-called higher interests. In the working classes, whose poverty does not come from decay, concern about little benefits and little losses is a sign of thrift: thrift that makes for a modest well-being and for mastery in some honest art. There is no mockery then about superior gifts or unselfish virtues; there is respect for them and ambition to cultivate them. There may be even great illusions about the superiority of superior people. From such illusions my female relations at Tarragona were scornfully free. They imagined that they knew perfectly the corrupt motives and morals of all the rich and the famous. And yet they didn't love the poor or consent to be identified with them. Manuela, whose pension when she became an orphan was only forty pesetas or eight dollars a month, might have married an honest member of the *Guardia Civil* or Constabulary, who had courted her; but he was only a soldier or non-commissioned officer, and she refused. She thereby became chiefly dependent on me, or on what I induced my sister Josefina to give her. I didn't dislike Manuela: her mind was common, and sometimes also her manners, but she was sincere and unprejudiced. You could talk with her as with a man, and though her judgments on people were ignorant and uncharitable, they were hypothetically penetrating: I mean, they showed what such people *might* be. Incidentally, they revealed the quality of Manuela's education and character. She didn't belong to the Intelligentsia, because she had read nothing, but she belonged to the revolutionary party, to the Reds. Since we are all rascals, let us all be rascals at one level, with equal chances to worm our way to a false eminence.

Abortive plan to annex me to it. These principles were not entirely theoretical. Before I left Tarragona, my father and I became aware that there was a plot afoot to marry me to Manuela. It was a repetition of the plot that had succeeded in marrying her father and mother. *Tío Nicolás* could not have been ignorant of this scheme, if not actually the author of it: something that rather lowered my esteem for him, and chilled a little my sense of the kind treatment I had received in his house. He may have thought: What is there wrong in mating these cousins? Why is young Manuela worse than any other girl that Jorge might marry? In the abstract, there might seem to be nothing; at this distance they could have no notion of my real circumstances in America, which made any marriage impossible. Perhaps they counted on keeping me in Spain: counted on my mother's help, without understanding her character.

I hear Sarah Bernhardt. Illness had prevented me from reaching Paris at the time when my steamer friend Mrs. X of Cincinnati, Ohio, was to be there; but I had her address and wrote explaining what had happened, not disguising the disgusting and contagious nature of that illness but calling it small-pox in plain English. Having done the Rhine she was now going to do the Rhône; and as I was also passing that way, I suggested that we should meet in Lyons. Lyons turned out to be a lucky choice, and I spent a week there, not waiting for Mrs. X but going every night to the theatre where Sarah Bernhardt happened to be performing. It was a great treat: *Phèdre*, *La Dame aux Camélias*, *Frou-frou*, *Adrienne Lecouvreur*, and *La Tosca*. The divine Sarah was still relatively young, serpent-like, with her "golden voice" fresh and not too monotonous; and while dramatically she seemed most adequate in *Frou-frou* and *La Dame aux Camélias*, poetically and verbally it was in *Phèdre*, and especially in the passage from *Phèdre* repeated in *Adrienne Lecouvreur*, that she captivated me entirely: and I still repeat to myself at night, as if it were a prayer, that passage and others as nearly as I can after her fashion. It was liturgical: the text spoke as if it were an oracle, and the actress was a speaking statue, and her voice came, ideally, through a mask. In listening to *La Tosca*, on the contrary, in the scene where Mario is being tortured, I found the strain intolerable, and slipped out—being in the pit, near the door—for fear of fainting. This experience led me to understand that there is a limit to the acceptable terror and pity that tragedy may excite. They must be excited only speculatively, intellectually, religiously: if they are excited materially and deceptively, you are overcome and not exalted. The spectacle either drives you away, as it did me, or becomes a vice, an indulgence that adds to the evils of life rather than liberates you from them. Sardou was not a tragedian; he was a contriver of sensational plays.

The end of a travelling acquaintance.   The rest of my journey is described briefly in one of my father's letters: it acknowledges one of mine from Antwerp, whence I was sailing on October 8th.

"Avila, 9th of October, 1883.

.... "I see with great pleasure that you have kept well, that the financial or cash question has been happily solved, and that you have nothing to complain of unless it be having missed your Conquest, who as appears from the letter that I enclose and that I opened to see if it shed any light on your whereabouts, has been playing with you at hide and seek. My cousin Nicolás had already maliciously guessed as much [*lo ha maliciado*], for being a priest he has a keen scent for everything that concerns women. He used to tell me he was sure that you would never find that lady, and attributed the fact to the small-pox. I think that you will not have been overmuch troubled at such a trifle, and that you will not go to look for her in Cincinnati, Ohio, but that you will wait tranquilly for her to send you that tea-cup, bought expressly for you, and the only one that was not broken, seeing that she has sworn not to let anyone use it but you."

The tea-cup never was sent and I never went to Cincinnati, Ohio, or had further correspondence with Mrs. X. Some ten years later, however, I received a visit from a beautifully dressed young clergyman who said he was the Reverend Reginald X of Cincinnati. Only an English military tailor who had been converted could have made a clerical coat look so like the smartest of officers' tunics. I remembered Mrs. X saying how much she hoped that her son would become a "priest"; and putting two and two together I could imagine which way the wind blew in that young man's religious vocation. We talked of seasickness, of the sea, of the British navy, of the Church. I spoke sorrowfully of the state of religion at Harvard, and hoped it was better in Cincinnati. Even the Episcopal Theological School in Cambridge was not traditional and Catholic enough for my taste; nevertheless on week-days when their chapel was almost empty, I sometimes dropped in there for Vespers, if I got back early from my walk and it wasn't yet time for afternoon tea. He smiled and understood my banter perfectly; scoffers were half converted when they laughed at themselves; but when I asked about his mother, as I did repeatedly, his replies were curt and he changed the subject.

XV

College Friends

Essential vs. accidental friendships.
My deeper friendships were all individual. The bond was not due to belonging to the same circle or class or even nation. Chance having allowed us to discover each other, character, quality, and sympathy did the rest. Of such friendships I have mentioned only the two that I formed at school; they had little or no sequel, except in my inner mind. Now I come to others that, by chance, I formed at college; not like those friends I have described as figures in the Yard, where college life had brought us together. These other friends were picked out from that flowing mass precisely because they belonged elsewhere; the Yard where we happened to be did not unite us, nor does the memory of them take me back to the Yard.

Charles Loeser.
First in time, and very important, was my friendship with Charles Loeser. I came upon him by accident in another man's room, and he immediately took me into his own, which was next door, to show me his books and pictures. Pictures and books! That strikes the keynote to our companionship. At once I found that he spoke French well, and German presumably better, since if hurt he would swear in German. He had been at a good international school in Switzerland. He at once told me that he was a Jew, a rare and blessed frankness that cleared away a thousand pitfalls and insincerities. What a privilege there is in that distinction and in that misfortune! If the Jews were not worldly it would raise them above the world; but most of them squirm and fawn and wish to pass for ordinary Christians or ordinary atheists. Not so Loeser: he had no ambition to manage things for other people, or to worm himself into fashionable society. His father was the proprietor of a vast "dry-goods store" in Brooklyn, and rich—how rich I never knew, but rich enough and generous enough for his son always to have plenty of money and not to think of a profitable profession. Another blessed simplification, rarely avowed in America. There was a commercial presumption that

a man is useless unless he makes money, and no vocation, only bad health, could excuse the son of a millionaire for not at least pretending to have an office or a studio. Loeser seemed unaware of this social duty. He showed me the nice books and pictures that he had already collected—the beginnings of that passion for possessing and even stroking *objets-d'art* that made the most unclouded joy of his life. Here was fresh subject-matter and fresh information for my starved aestheticism—starved sensuously and not supported by much reading: for this was in my Freshman year, before my first return to Europe.

Rich friends and my relations with them. Loeser had a tremendous advance on me in these matters, which he maintained through life: he seemed to have seen everything, to have read everything, and to speak every language. Berenson had the same advantage, with a public reputation that Loeser, who wrote nothing, never acquired; but somehow I felt more secure under the sign of Loeser. He had perhaps more illusions, but also a more German simplicity and devotion to his subject. I felt that he loved the Italian renaissance and was not, as it were, merely displaying it. This was then in the future; for the moment it was only a question of reading a few books that he lent me, discussing them, and sometimes going together to the theatre—which was at his invitation. In those days there were foreign companies often playing for a week or two in Boston, French operetta, Salvini, Ristori, and grand opera. I saw everything, and in the first years it couldn't have been at my own expense. It might seem that all my life I have been "sponging" on my rich friends, or even that I have sought rich friends for that purpose. This was not the case: there were plenty of rich people about that I fled from. But with people with whom I was otherwise in sympathy, friendship was naturally more easily kept up and cemented if they had a house where they could ask me to stay, or could invite me to be their guest, partly or wholly, for trips or entertainments that I couldn't afford if left to my own resources. Loeser was my first Maecenas of this kind, and one of the most satisfactory. His invitations were specific, for particular occasions. Only once, when we were looking at some modern pictures, I stopped before one that I liked and said that it was painted as I should have wished to paint. "Why don't you do it", Loeser cried impulsively. "Why don't you stay in Paris and paint? I will help you." But I knew that this was an *ignis fatuus* in the case of both of us: I couldn't give up philosophy and an assured livelihood, and he couldn't commit himself to a responsibility that would have at once become a burden and a source of angry feelings. Ordinarily his favours were discreet, and made for his own pleasure. He never gave me money or presents, nor did any of my other friends. It was simply a question of making possible little plans that pleased us but that were beyond my unaided means. Thus when we travelled together in Italy, I contributed twenty gold francs a day to our expenses, and he, who knew the ropes and the language, made all the arrangements and paid all the bills. He might have been a sort of magic dragoman in my service, spiriting up the scenes and spiriting away the deficits.

Loeser overlooked at Harvard. At Harvard Loeser was rather friendless. The fact that he was a Jew and that his father kept a "dry-goods store" cut him off, in democratic America, from the ruling society. To me, who was also an outsider, this seemed at first very strange, for Loeser was much more cultivated than the leaders of undergraduate fashion or athletics, and I saw nothing amiss in his person or manners. He was not good-looking, although he had a neat figure, of middle height, and nice hands: but his eyes were dead, his complexion muddy, and his features pinched, though not especially Jewish. On the other hand, he was extremely well-spoken, and there was nothing about him in bad taste. To me he was always an agreeable companion, and if our friendship never became intimate, this was due rather to a certain defensive reserve in him than to any withdrawal on my part. Yet in the end, taking imaginatively the point of view of the native leading Americans, I came to see why Loeser could never gain their confidence. His heart was not with them, and his associations and standards were not theirs. He didn't join in their sports (as rich Jews have learned to do in England), he hadn't their religion, he had no roots in their native places or in their family circles. In America, he floated on the surface, and really lived only in the international world of art, literature, and theory.

His habit of hiding. Yet there was something else at work; for, except for my connection with the Sturgises, all those things were true of me, with poverty added, yet I was never expressly excluded from anything in America or at all isolated, except quite secretly in my own feelings, as any poetical or religious youth might have been anywhere. And I found afterwards, when Loeser lived in Florence, that while he knew the whole Anglo-American colony slightly, he seemed to have no friends. For a rich bachelor that was odd; and I suspect that he preferred to keep his gates shut, and prowl about as if a little mad, in his own castle. There was usually a certain vagueness about his assertions and plans, as if he were afraid that people might interfere with him; and when he married, at fifty, a German Jewish pianist, the separation remained, except that his wife sometimes still performed, and with great power, in public or in private concerts. It surprised me, whenever I was at Strong's villa, that Loeser who had a good motor, never came to see me or asked me to go to his house, except once, to see his new tower. This made me doubt whether Loeser had ever had any affection for me, such as I had for him, and whether it was only *faute de mieux*, as a last resort in too much solitude, that in earlier years he had been so friendly. However, circumstances change, one changes as much as other people, and it would be un-reasonable to act or feel in the same way when the circumstances are different. Loeser in any case had shown me Italy, initiated me into Italian ways, present and past, and made my life there in later years much richer than it would have been otherwise. Let him be thanked without any qualifications.

His fancies and illusions. In the 1890's I saw him several times in London. He lived in the Burlington Hotel, behind the Arcade, amid a great lot of leather portmanteaux and hat-boxes. He had become very English, much to my taste; his alien but expert knowledge of how an English gentleman should dress, eat, talk, and travel amused and instructed me vastly; but he didn't seem to have real friends among the English, other than Algar Thorold, son of the Bishop of Winchester, who (twice, I believe) had gone over to Rome. The first time he had essayed to be a Carthusian; but being disappointed and having a relapse, the second time he married and became an ordinary lay Catholic. He lived in Italy, in a truly Italian villa, where I was glad to hear him and his wife speak of Loeser with affection. It helped to relieve the latent uneasiness I felt about my friend. He had sometimes been so dark and inconsequential that I suspected a touch of madness in his nature. He would say and do things that might pass for jokes; but oddities when indulged may become illusions. He maintained that he had two original works of Michaelangelo in his collection: one a rough ordinary *putto* from some fountain or altar, the other a truly beautiful panel in wax, a Madonna and Child (certainly after Michaelangelo's earlier work) with a St. Joseph perhaps less convincing. I am no judge in the matter; but to have discovered two unknown and genuine Michaelangelos, and got them cheap, is certainly a collector's dream, and incredible.

It was with Loeser that I first went to Rome and to Venice: my preference for these two cities, rather than for the Florence so dear to English-speaking people, may be partly due to a first impression gained under his auspices. His taste was selective. He dwelt on a few things, with much knowledge, and did not confuse or fatigue the mind. We reached Rome rather late at night. It had been raining, and the wet streets and puddles reflected the lights fantastically. Loeser had a hobby that architecture is best seen and admired at night. He proposed that we should walk to our hotel. He had chosen the *Russie*, where as he said only Russian Grand Dukes stayed, so that it was just the place for him and for me. We walked by the *Quattro Fontane* and the *Piazza di Spagna*—a long walk: but I doubt that the first loud accents that I heard on arriving at the hotel were those of a Russian Grand Duchess. She said simply: "Oh, my!"

Oddities in Florence. Some ten years later, in 1905, Loeser had a spacious apartment in an old palazzo near the *Uffizi* in Florence. He said he couldn't offer me a room, but had secured a choice one (*choice* was a favourite word of his) for me, quite cheap, in a tower in the *Via dei Bardi*, with a loggia where I might have my breakfast, and wave to him across the river; for he too slept in a tower and had his bath in the open loggia at the top of it. My room was indeed in a tower; there were 149 stone steps with hardly a door to pass on the way up: my choice room did have a bed in it, but the loggia was bitterly cold in those sunless mornings. This didn't matter, however, since there was no breakfast. My woebegone landlady had no idea of coffee, milk, or rolls, and her tea, in an open broken old dish, was half dust. However, I managed. I got up late, and went to breakfast in a good café, read the papers, sunned myself in the *Lungarno*, and by half past twelve was at Loeser's place, where I was expected daily for luncheon. But he said he had no dinner, only a bite of something by the fire in his library. One evening, however, I was invited to this frugal supper, and warned that Mrs. Y, of whom he had spoken to me would be there also. Mrs. Y was the wife of a British officer serving in India, and I had been given to understand that she and Loeser were on the best of terms. "But my servant Antonio", he had added, "doesn't approve of her. I asked him if he was shocked. '*Chè*,' said Antonio, 'she is too thin.' " I found Mrs. Y most amiable, a slender blonde dressed like Botticelli's *Primavera*, hatless, with a work-basket beside her and evidently quite at home. Dinner was ample, served pleasantly at a low table in front of the fire. Apparently Mrs. Y dined there every evening, and I began to understand that practically, if not nominally, she lived in that house. This explained why there had been no room to offer me, and why Loeser never "dined". Why hadn't he simply told me the facts? Did he think I should be shocked like Antonio? Or was he protecting the lady's reputation? But then why let out the secret in the end? However, it was better to be inconsistently secretive than to be mad.

Religious reflections during a mountain tour. ·In an earlier year, when I had been free in the spring, Loeser proposed a walking tour across the Apennines. First we went to Ravenna, which I hadn't seen, and thence to Pesaro where we abandoned the railway and drove to Urbino. From there, sending our things ahead by rail, we walked to San Sepolcro and La Verna. It was travelling as in the Middle Ages, stopping at small inns or at monasteries. At La Verna we found the Franciscan community making a procession in their half-open cloister. The monks were evidently peasants, some of them young yokels fresh from the plough, no doubt ignorant and stupid; and Loeser's modern Jewish standards betrayed themselves in his utter scorn of those mere beasts, as he called them. I wondered if Saint John the Baptist or Elijah might not also have seemed mere beasts; but I didn't say so. Being at once a beast and a spirit doesn't seem to me a contradiction. On the contrary, it is necessary to be a beast if one is ever to be a spirit. The modern Jew recognises verbal intelligence, but not simple spirit. He doesn't admit anything deeper or freer than literature, science, and commerce.

When we were at the top of the pass, after deliciously drinking, like beasts on all fours, at a brook that ran down by the road, we looked about at the surrounding hill-tops. They were little above our own level, but numerous, and suggested the top of the world. "What are you thinking of?" Loeser asked. I said: "Geography." "I", he retorted, "was thinking of God." So that Loeser would probably have reversed my judgment about not apprehending pure spirit, and would have said that the Latin or Catholic is hopelessly materialistic even in his religion, whereas the Jew hears the voice of an invisible God in the silence of nature. Very good: but why not hear that voice also in the silence of beasts or of monks? Perhaps the reason was that the mountains are the skeleton of that land which feeds and surrounds literature, science, and commerce. To the Jew the earth seems a promised land, suggesting the millennium, the triumph of God in the human world. Swine, epicureans, and monks, on the contrary, not being legally edible, seem not only useless for that purpose but positively unclean. This comes consistently enough of regarding God only as a power, the power that conditions our happiness. It is then no metaphor to say that God *dwells* in the mountains or in the whirlwind: their reality is his reality, and their work his work. In science, commerce, and literature you are tracing his ways. And the idea that all these vast and apparently dead forces secretly conspire to direct human history and to prepare the glory of Zion, becomes sublime. But if God were regarded rather as the *end* or the *good* in which happiness might be found, might he not seem to dwell far more directly and intimately in the monk and even in the beast than in commerce, literature, or science?

The young Ward Thoron. At the beginning of my Sophomore year, not in the Yard but in the church of the Immaculate Conception, I made the acquaintance of Ward Thoron, destined to be my closest friend while we were undergraduates. He said in recent years that he was the original of Mario in my *Last Puritan*, and there is some truth in that assertion, especially in regard to his family relations; but I had other far more accomplished models for my young man, and gave him a different education, different motives, and a different career. Ward had not been educated at Eton, but at the Jesuit College in Fordham, New York. He had graduated there at seventeen; and on the strength of that degree he was mechanically and foolishly admitted to the Sophomore class at Harvard. We were in the same class, but he was three years younger than I, and younger than most Freshmen. This, together with his being a Catholic, gave me at once the feelings of an elder brother towards him, and of a sort of mentor. Except that he was at home in scraps of church Latin, he was utterly unprepared for the studies he was to take up; and not coming from any of the usual preparatory schools, he had no ready-made circle of acquaintances in the college, who might have adopted him and steered him more or less safely. Nevertheless, he had a social position much better than mine, and lived in a private house full of boys of good families, with plenty of money to spend. He was never lonely: and this was at once an advantage and a danger.

His relations. His grandparents, Mr. and Mrs. "Sam" Ward, of New York, were persons of high transcendental New England traditions, but at the same time rich and fashionable. Mrs. Ward was an impressive old lady, dressed in obsolete but regal garments and speaking in impassioned accents. "Ah," she would exclaim, "I could

222 Persons and Places

never close my eyes, if I hadn't first opened wide my window and gazed at the stars!" In her youth she had been a colonist at Brook Farm with the social utopians; then she had passed from one Evangelical sect to another, until she finally landed in the Catholic Church. There she found inner peace, but socially she remained militant. She managed to convert her daughters and even her son, but her husband, alas! held on to his heathen idealism and Germanic intuitions; for he too was an ardent spirit, modified by luxurious living and much shrewd knowledge of the world. His grandson sent him an essay of mine on Freewill, which had been printed in a College paper: on which the old gentleman made the penetrating observation that if I ever had anything to say I should be able to say it, that I knew the stock arguments on the subject, and that there were no others.

Not satisfied with converting her daughters, Mrs. Ward insisted on marrying them safely to Catholics, which at that time in her circle practically meant to foreigners. One of these, my friend's father, was a Frenchman who had occupied some post in the Levant; his wife had died; and their children had been adopted by their American grandparents. Ward saw his father but seldom; however, he could speak French easily, and took easily to his Catholic education and his American surroundings. He needed to sail before the wind. Rough seas and contrary blasts were not for him: I think he had no clear object in view that could have justified him in facing them. But given an open course he was clever enough to steer his festive voyage and enjoy himself thoroughly in doing so.

If all is lying everything is true. He once wrote an essay—it was only an exercise in composition, so that the views advanced didn't matter— on the *Art of Lying*, in which he gathered such arguments as occurred to him to prove the advantages of concealing or misrepresenting the truth; and then added that equal advantages could be found in telling it. He felt that he was playing a farce, and there seemed to be nothing else for him to do. Fordham had been a farce, Harvard was a farce also: yet if everything is a farce, the one in which you find yourself acting acquires, for the time being, all the values of reality.

This philosophy, hidden in a boy of seventeen under verbal sparkle and easy manners, but breaking down under pressure into genuine Catholic humility, had everything to please me. It was not even then my own philosophy. I was as convinced as I am now of the steady march of cosmic forces that we may, in a measure, enlist in our service, and thereby win the prize of life in the process of living, without laying any claims to dominate the universe, either physically or morally. But this is a comparatively mature, though very ancient, conclusion; and it is well to become aware in the first place of the uncertainty and blindness of human opinion.

Our brotherly affection. Ward and I didn't move in the same circles; I didn't know his friends nor he mine. Yet there were hours, especially the late afternoon hours, when we were much together, when the crowd were at their sports, in which neither of us took part. In the evening his casual boon-companions would carry him off on their larks, perhaps too often for his tender years. He fell ill; and during a long convalescence, when he was confined to his sofa, I used to keep him company. During those long winter afternoons we read aloud alternately the whole of Tolstoi's *War and Peace* in French. It was no school task; we could talk instead, if there were anything to talk about; and we talked more or less about everything.

Signs that our paths had diverged. I should gladly stop here, and let that moment stand for the true picture of our friendship, when I cared for Ward as for a younger brother, of the same flesh and blood as I, and rooted in the same ultimate loyalties. But these reminiscences are not obituary notices or funeral orations over the past; they are, as far as I can make them, true total views of men and things. Now, on a total view, it seems to me that there was, as the circumstances would lead one to expect, no identity between our respective natures or needs; we were alike only in some external particulars. I realised this suddenly when after two years in Germany, I returned to Boston. Ward, not having received a bachelor's degree from Harvard, had turned to the law, following I suppose his grandfather's advice. By chance I came upon him in Commonwealth Avenue; I was with a friend, and he with two or three young men that I didn't know. On seeing me, he made a loud show of surprise and jocose pleasure, so loud and so hollow that I was taken aback, and the men who were with us noticed my astonishment. Why didn't he come and shake hands with me simply, as if we were alone? Would that have shown that our friendship was too real, and did he prefer to disguise it with an unmeaning halloo, as to an old forgotten school-fellow? However, the incident passed off, with some joke about my having acquired English manners, because when I spoke it was in a voice much lower than his. Shouting was so entirely contrary to my feelings at that moment, that even if I had wished, I couldn't have done it.

The impression that we had moved into different climates was confirmed some years later when after his marriage he invited me to stay with him in Washington. He was living at his mother-in-law's, presiding at the other end of the table, while his wife sat with her sisters at the side, as if they were still children. He took me to see Mr. Henry Adams, with whom he was on very friendly terms. "So you are trying to teach philosophy at Harvard", Mr. Adams said, somewhat in the gentle but sad tone that we knew in Professor Norton. "I once tried to teach history there, but it can't be done. It isn't really possible to teach anything." This may be true, if we give very exacting meanings to our terms; but it was not encouraging. Still, both Mr. Adams' house and that of Ward's new family were luxurious. I got the impression that, if most things were illusions, having money and spending money were great realities. I also gathered that Ward no longer called himself a Catholic, but was more or less affiliated to his mother-in-law's church.

His prosperous career. I have never seen Ward after that visit to Washington. He remained there while I was in America, or in summer resorts that I didn't frequent, and he has never, to my knowledge, been in Europe in the later years. But this material separation was no mere accident; it symbolised a separation in our interests and aims. I recognise the perfect right of anybody to surrender his private inopportune advantages for the sake of others more public and opportune. That is the path of material evolution. But the evolution I desire and appreciate is not of that kind, which changes the character and the ideal pursued. The evolution that interests me is that of a given seed, towards its perfect manifestation. From what I have heard about my friend in his maturity and old age, I gather that he played his part well and had his reward: but it was the sort of success by adaptability in essentials that leaves me cold: so that perhaps nothing was lost to him and me by our separation, and our affectionate relation in youth retains its intrinsic value all the more distinctly by not being followed, as in the case of some of my other friendships, by later contacts that might obscure it.

The Bostonians. Three other men in the Harvard Class of 1886 belonged in the front rank of my friends: Herbert Lyman, Frank Bullard, and Boylston Beal. All three were pure and intense Bostonians of the old school, yet with differences that mark the range that Boston "culture" had at that time. "Culture", with religious and philosophical preoccupations, belonged especially to Bullard. He was a nephew of

Professor Norton, and I might almost say in fortunately delicate health; fortunately, because if he had been thoroughly sound, strong, and athletic, he would have had to go into "business" or into a profession no less businesslike and absorbing, because according to the ruling code, this would have been his duty to society. That was what Herbert Lyman (also potentially rich) was obliged to do all his life. Business, together with music and a semi-administrative interest in King's Chapel, formed the entirely orthodox themes of his moral harmony. This harmony was beautifully achieved; yet it had cost him some renunciations and some moments of difficulty. He would have liked to devote himself to music entirely; but he had neither the great voice nor the exceptional musical genius that would have justified him in becoming a professional musician. Later his health faltered; but he pulled through, to the good age of seventy-seven. Only two years earlier, he was kind enough to make me a visit at Cortina, and seemed to me little changed from the memorable days, fifty-five years before, we had spent together at Dresden. Of these, and of him, I will speak again. I mention him here lest he should seem to be forgotten in my catalogue of College friends.

Frank Bullard and Turner prints. Bullard and I hardly knew each other when undergraduates; but ten or fifteen years later he took to studying philosophy and came to hear some of my lectures. We then established an active exchange of moral and intellectual ideas. The influence of his uncle had led him to collect prints, especially Turner prints. They were very beautiful, and on the frequent occasions when I was a guest at his mother's house, we used to go up after luncheon to his study and look over his treasures. He had also some pre-Raphaelite prints that I couldn't praise so much; but the Turners and the photographed drawings by the old masters found us equally appreciative. It is not true, by the way, that the aerial effects in Turner's landscapes are exaggerated and melodramatic. Nature in England and elsewhere—for instance, in Venice—is often like that, or even more emphatic; and the delicacy with which Turner preserves the special character and melody of the parts in the midst of that violent ensemble, shows a sincere love of nature and life and a devout imagination.

His philosophy. Frank Bullard and his collections did much more to educate my taste than my lectures did to clarify his intellect. He was interested and unprejudiced but, as he said, "bird-witted". His flights were short and flurried. He came to no large clear conclusions; what survived was only an open and ardent spirit. Christianity and Puritanism had here debouched into a sensitive humanity; yet the natural aims of life remained for him miscellaneous and conflicting. The day of fresh decisions and sharp exclusions had not yet dawned.

Boylston Beal.   With Boylston Beal, too, my friendship grew after we had left College. We lived in the same boarding-house one winter in Berlin, and we were constantly together at Cambridge in the early 1890's, he being at the Law School and I a young instructor, and both frequenting the same club. Later he married a cousin of my family, which established another bond. He travelled everywhere and knew the principal languages, and was as much at home in England and in European high life as it is possible for an American to be. During the war of 1914–1918 and afterwards he was Honorary Counsellor to the American Embassy in London, telling the ladies what to wear, the men what to say and how to address royalties and persons possessing complicated titles, by law or courtesy. It was happiness for him to live in beautiful places, among refined people, with simple, graceful, and honest minds; and so it would have been mine if my lot had been more often cast among them. I did have it, in an obscure modest way that perhaps ran deeper, if less sparklingly, than official or fashionable society; but Beal saw the thing in its spectacular as well as in its intimate forms. The spectacular and official side is easier to describe and to talk about, it gives one a glimpse of political history; yet I am sure that it was the quiet and domestic side that he loved and that coloured his mature judgments and opinions.

Our great sympathy, but hardly agreement, in religion and politics.   A proof of this appeared in his attachment to traditional religion—not to his home tradition, but to the Catholic and Anglican. In Rome, where he liked to spend, when he could, a part of the winter, he sometimes would take me to some sequestered little church that he had discovered, where there was a devotional atmosphere. He was not offended by modern images and pictures and flower-pots; he didn't mind if the good nuns furnished their chapels like boudoirs; he felt the pious intention: they gave their best. This is even more Spanish than Italian: a domestication of the mind and heart in religion, and being faithful in small things, rather than coldly despising them and confining religion to morality or to great tragic and cosmological vistas.

In politics also Beal reacted against the denials and abstractions of the reforming zealot, and was a pronounced Tory. I sympathised with all the affections that such a position implied: but I like to open the windows of the mind wider, and to recognise not only the inevitableness of moral mutations, but their fertility. One good thing is destroyed, but another good thing may be made possible. I love Tory England and honour conservative Spain, but not with any dogmatic or pre-scriptive passion. If any community can become and wishes to become communistic or democratic or anarchical I wish it joy from the bottom of my heart. I have only two qualms in this case: whether such ideals are realisable, and whether those who pursue them fancy them to be exclusively and universally right: an illusion pregnant with injustice, oppression, and war.

XVI

College Studies

With my return to Harvard, a fortnight late, from the journey to Spain, my College Studies may be said to have begun. They did not begin well. I had failed in one subject—a half-course in algebra—which I was obliged to pass later, as Freshman work was prescribed and no substitutions were permitted. I had done well enough in the rest of the prescribed mathematics, analytic geometry, which I had had some grounding in at school, and also in the physics, which interested me immensely: and even in the algebra there were points that struck my imagination, as for instance the possibility and advantages of duodecimal notation; our decimal system being founded only on the stupid reason that we have ten fingers and ten toes. If my teachers had begun by telling me that mathematics was pure play with presuppositions, and wholly in the air, I might have become a good mathematician, because I am happy enough in the realm of essence. But they were over-worked drudges, and I was largely inattentive, and inclined lazily to attribute to incapacity in myself or to a literary temperament that dullness which perhaps was due simply to lack of initiation. With a good speculative master I might have been an eager pupil and cried at once: *Introibo ad altare Dei.*

The elective system. I began badly also in not having a fixed plan of study. President Eliot's elective system was then in the ascendent. We liked it, I liked it; it seemed to open a universal field to free individuality. But to be free and cultivate individuality one must first exist, one's nature must be functioning. What was I, what were my powers and my vocation? Before I had discovered that, all freedom could be nothing but frivolity. I had chosen to go on with Latin and Greek, but disregarded the requirements for second-year honours in the classics, because those requirements involved Greek composition, which I wouldn't attempt. I consciously continued my reading as an amateur, not as a scholar. I wasn't going to *teach* Greek or Latin. In this way I illustrated the complementary vices of the elective system: I was a smatterer, because things were arranged for the benefit of professionals.

Lucretius.   So superficial was my study that I hardly remember what Latin authors we read or who was the professor. *I* read Lucretius, in a pocket edition without notes given me by a friend, somewhat pathetically, because he was leaving college. I couldn't properly understand the text, many a word was new to me, and I had to pass on, reading as I did at odd moments, or in the horse-car. But the general drift was obvious, and I learned the great passages by heart. Even the physical and biological theories seemed instructive, not as scientific finalities, as if science could be final, but as serving to dispel the notion that anything could be non-natural or miraculous. If the theory suggested were false, another no less naturalistic would be true; and this presumption recommended itself to me and has become one of my first principles: not that a particular philosophy called naturalism must be true *a priori*, but that nature is the standard of naturalness. The most miraculous world, if it were real, would subdue the teachable mind to its own habit, and would prove that miracles were—as they are in the Gospels—the most ordinary and most intelligible of events. It made me laugh afterwards to read in pedantic commentators that Lucretius abandoned his atomism whenever he was poetical, and contradicted himself in invoking Venus, when Epicurus maintains that the gods do not trouble about human affairs. On the contrary, Lucretius might perfectly well have invoked Jupiter or Fate (as Leopardi constantly invokes Fate); for Fate, Jupiter, or Venus are names for the whole or some part of the life of nature. There is no incompatibility in these various appellations, if they are understood sympathetically as the ancients understood them. They were not gaping phenomenalists, but knew that our senses, no less than our poetry and myth, clothe in human images the manifold processes of matter. By these hidden processes they lived, before them they trembled, the promise and potency of them they sought to prophesy. Matter was the ancient plastic reality of all the gods.

I also took a half-course in Latin composition which I audaciously neglected, "cutting" all the lectures except the first, but doing the prescribed exercises and taking the examinations. I passed with a mark of ninety per cent.

Greek tragedy under Louis Dyer.   In Greek I did as badly as at school. Here again this was not the teacher's fault. He was the amiable Louis Dyer, who had studied at Balliol, married a Miss Macmillan, and later lived in Oxford, where I often saw him. He gave me his *Gods of Greece*, nicely bound, a book that had a great influence over me. Perhaps Matthew Arnold moved in the background and inspired us. But I was thirsting for inspiration, and Greek grammar and prosody didn't hold my attention. We were supposed to read the *Ajax*, but though in this case I went to all the lectures, I didn't study the text. The *Bacchae*, however, was a revelation. Here, before Nietzsche had pointed it out, the Dionysiac inspiration was explicitly opposed to the Apollonian; and although my tradition and manner are rather Apollonian, I unhesitatingly accept the Dionysiac inspiration as also divine. It comes from the elemental gods, from the chaotic but fertile bosom of nature; Apollo is the god of measure, of perfection, of humanism. He is more civilised, but more superficial, more highly conditioned. His worship seems classic and established for ever, and it does last longer and is more often revived than any one form of Dionysiac frenzy: yet the frenzy represents the primitive wild soul, not at home in the world, not settled in itself, and merging again with the elements, half in helplessness and half in self-transcendence and mystic triumph.

My first sonnet on a text from the *Bacchae*.   I have taken for a motto a phrase out of one of Euripides' choruses: Τὸ σοφὸν οὐ σοφία. It was this phrase, in that year 1884, that led me to write my first sonnet, printed a year or two later, and reappearing as Sonnet III in my *Poems*; the first two having been composed afterwards on purpose to frame in the earlier one and bring the argument to a head. I translated the dictum of Euripides in the rather thin and prosaic line: "It is not wisdom to be only wise"; and then, given that sentiment and that rhyme, I built the whole sonnet round them. Even when I wrote it, this sonnet was belated. I was twenty years old, and the sentiment was what I had felt at sixteen. But I still recognised, as I recognise now at nearly eighty, the legitimacy of that feeling.

Changed meaning of the word "faith".   The chief difference is that when, at sixteen or even at twenty, I said "faith", I meant the Catholic faith; and when now I oppose "faith" to reason I mean faith in the existence and order of nature, a faith if you will in rationality or intelligibility of a sort; but I see far more clearly than I did in my youth that pure reason, a reason that is not based on irrational postulates and presuppositions, is perfectly impotent. It is not "smoky" or indistinct: on the contrary, it is mathematically precise, but abstract and in the air. What I had in mind then when I spoke of "knowledge" was the common sense and science of the day, which in fact were uncritically based on animal faith and empirical presumption, and which I, with a solipsistic breath, could at once reduce to a dream, not to say to a nightmare. For that reason I called them "smoky", at once ugly, obscure, and unsubstantial. But it was immature of me to wish, lackadaisically and hopelessly, to substitute a religious myth for that worldly obsession. And the rest of those twenty youthful sonnets pointed out well enough where a mature solution might be found: in obedience to matter for the sake of freedom of mind.

The early William James and his criticism of Spencer.   As to William James on Taine's *De l'Intelligence*, I am not conscious of any intellectual residuum, only of a few graphic memories touching his aspect and ways, which at that time were distinctly medical. He was impatient of the things he didn't like in philosophy; his latent pragmatism appeared only in its negative germ, as scorn of everything remote or pretentious; and his love of lame ducks and neglected possibilities, which later took the form of charity and breadth of mind, then seemed rather the doctor's quick eye for bad symptoms, as if he had diagnosed people in a jiffy and cried: "Ah, *you* are a paranoiac! Ah, *you* have the pox!" I remember his views better in another set of lectures on Herbert Spencer, or rather against him. James detested any system of the universe that professed to enclose everything: we must never set up boundaries that exclude romantic surprises. He retained the primitive feeling that death *might* open new worlds to us—not at all what religions predict but something at once novel and natural; also the primitive feeling that invisible spirits *might* be floating about among us, and might suddenly do something to hurt or to help us. Spencer was intolerable for shutting out such possibilities; he was also intolerable for his verbose generalities and sweeping "principles". There were no "principles", except in men's heads; there were only facts. James did not stop to consider whether this assertion was not itself a principle that might describe a fact.

Worthlessness of Spencer's philosophy.   Herbert Spencer, I think, taught me nothing. I agreed with his naturalism or materialism, because that is what we all start with: the minimum presupposition of perception and action. But I agreed with James about Spencer's theory of evolution: It was a tangle of words, of loose generalities that some things might sometimes suggest to us, and that, said properly, it might have been *witty* to say, but that had absolutely no value as "laws" or "causes" of events. Spencer in his "principles" was an "objective idealist", not a naturalist or a scientific man. James was characteristically masculine and empirical in his wrath at the "scandalous vagueness" of Spencer's ideas. For instance, what did it mean to say that things passed from the indefinite to the definite? Nothing can be indefinite. Make a blot of ink at random on a piece of paper. The spot is not indefinite: it has precisely the outline that it has.* But James, though trenchant was short-winded in argument. He didn't go on, for instance, to consider on this occasion how, if there be nothing indefinite, the notion of the indefinite comes into existence. Suppose that having made a random blot, shapeless as we call it in spite of its perfectly definite shape, I at once folded the paper in two. The blot would become two symmetrical blots, or a larger blot bilaterally symmetrical. It might resemble an oak leaf. It would then cease to have a nameless shape, but would become Platonically or humanly specific. We should say it had a definite shape, one that we could recognise and reproduce. Spencer, if we interpret him critically and progressively, was therefore saying that things change from forms that for our senses and language would not be recognisable or namable into forms that we can distinguish and name. This happens sometimes, not because things grow more definite, but because our senses and imagination have a limited range and can arrest one form of things rather than another; so that the world grows definite *for us* when we are able to perceive more parts of it and their relations. Nature thereby has changed, but not evolved; change is called evolution when sense and language are thereby enabled to distinguish its form better. The notion that nature first acquired form as an animal mind may gradually grow less stupid belongs to the age of fable. Spencer, unlike Lucretius and Spinoza, had no speculative power. He meant to be a naturalist, but language and the hypostasised idea of progress turned him into an idealistic metaphysician.

Spinoza and Royce. I will not attempt to describe here the many lessons that I learned in the study of Spinoza, lessons that in

*Here was a hint of my "essences", given by an unintended shot, that hit the bull's-eye without seeing it. Forms are infinite in multitude and each perfectly concrete. James's radical empiricism was undoubtedly a guide to me in this matter. Also Berkeley's nominalism.

several respects laid the foundation of my philosophy. I will only say
that I learned them from Spinoza himself, from his *ipsissima verba*,
studied in the original in all the crucial passages; as a guide and
stimulus I had Sir Frederick Pollock's sympathetic book, with good
renderings, and not much modern interpretation. It was a work, as
he told me himself forty-five years later, at the Spinoza commemoration
at The Hague, of his youth; and perhaps the science was emphasised
at the expense of the religion. Yet that the object of this religion was
Deus sive Natura—the universe, whatever it may be, of which we are
a part—was never concealed or denaturalised. Royce himself seemed
to suffer less from the plague of idealistic criticism in this case than
usual; for instance, about the saying of Spinoza's that the mind of God
resembled the mind of man as the Dog-Star resembles the barking
animal, Royce said only that this was too materialistic, without caring
or daring to broach the question as to the diffusion or concentration
of that cosmic "mind". The unified cosmic "mind" that Royce posited
would not be a "cogitation" but only a truth, the total *system* of cog-
itations that may accompany the total movement of matter; if it were
one actual intuition it would not *accompany* the movement of matter
but either describe and command it from afar or merely imagine it.
Royce had a powerful and learned mind, and it was always profitable,
if not pleasant, to listen to him: not pleasant because his voice was
harsh, his style heavy, repetitious and pedantic, and his monotonous
preoccupation with his own system intolerable. To listen was profitable
nevertheless because his comfortless dissatisfaction with every possible
idea opened vistas and disturbed a too easy dogmatism: while the
perversity and futility of his dialectic threw one back in the end on
the great certainties and the great possibilities, such as made the minds
of the great philosophers at once sublime and sane.

Inadequacy of Spinoza in ethics.   As I have said elsewhere, I regard Spinoza as the only
modern philosopher in the line of orthodox physics, the
line that begins with Thales and culminates, for Greek
philosophy, in Democritus. Orthodox physics should inspire and support
orthodox ethics; and perhaps the chief source of my enthusiasm for
him has been the magnificent clearness of his orthodoxy on this point.
Morality is something natural. It arises and varies, not only psychologically but prescriptively and justly, with the nature of the creature
whose morality it is. Morality is something relative: not that its precepts
in any case are optional or arbitrary; for each man they are defined
by his innate character and possible forms of happiness and action.

His momentary passions or judgments are partial expressions of his nature, but not adequate or infallible; and ignorance of the circumstances may mislead in practice, as ignorance of self may mislead in desire. But this fixed good is relative to each species and each individual; so that in considering the moral ideal of any philosopher, two questions arise. First, does he, like Spinoza, understand the natural basis of morality, or is he confused and superstitious on the subject? Second, how humane and representative is his sense for the good, and how far, by his disposition or sympathetic intelligence, does he appreciate all the types of excellence toward which life may be directed?

Now Spinoza, my master and model in respect to the first point, does not satisfy me in respect to the second; and I will take this opportunity, since I may not have any other, of clearing my conscience of ambiguity in that respect. The complete moralist must not only be sound in physics, but must be inwardly inspired by a normal human soul and an adequate human tradition; he must be a complete humanist in a complete naturalist. Spinoza was not only a complete naturalist, but, by a rare combination, also a spiritual man, seeing and accepting the place of the human heart in the universe; accepting it not grudgingly or viciously or frivolously, as your worldling does, but humbly and joyously: humbly, in that he asked to be nothing more than he was, and joyously because what he was allowed him, in spirit, to salute and to worship every form of the good. Nevertheless, Spinoza was not a complete humanist. He had no idea of human greatness and no sympathy with human sorrow. His notion of the soul was too plebeian and too quietistic. He was a Jew not of *Exodus* or *Kings* but of Amsterdam. He was too Dutch, too much the merchant and artisan, with nothing of the soldier, the poet, the prince, or the lover. Had he ever read Plutarch? Could he have relished Shakespeare or Racine? Could Virgil or Dante mean anything to him? Now such limitations, deep as they run, do not at all annul the nobility of Spinoza's simple and brave life, devoted to sublime speculation; yet they destroy the authority of his judgment in moral matters. He was virtuous but not normal. He had found his vocation, which it was his right and duty to follow; a high but very special vocation, that made him a model neither for mankind at large nor for man in his wholeness. He was a genius; but as a guide in the spiritual life, he was narrow and inadequate. The saint and the poet are hardly sane or authoritative unless they embody a wide tradition. If they are rebels, disinherited and solitary, the world may admire but cannot follow them. They have studied human nature by looking at the stars.

Old Francis Bowen and his instructive dogmatism. James and Royce were then the "young" professors of philosophy, they represented the dangers and scandals of free thought, all the more disquieting in that their free thought enveloped religion. But Harvard possessed safe, sober old professors also, and oldest of all, "Fanny" Bowen. He was so old that to be old, self-repeating, dogmatic, rheumatic, and querulous had become picturesque in him, and a part of his dramatic personage. He was a dear old thing, and an excellent teacher. Between his fits of coughing, and his invectives against all who were wrong and didn't agree with Sir William Hamilton, he would impress upon us many an axiom, many an argument belonging to the great traditions of philosophy; and when after spitting into the vast bandana handkerchief that he carried for the purpose, he would drop it on the desk with a gesture of combined disgust and relief, he expressed vividly to the eye the spirit in which philosophic and religious sects have always refuted and denounced one another. History sat living before us in this teacher of history. Descartes, Leibniz, and Spinoza would be quoted verbatim, and expounded (especially the first two) on their own presuppositions and in their own terms. It was not criticism but it was instruction. Spinoza was rather beyond Bowen's range; yet even here the words of the master would be repeated, and could be remembered in their terseness, while the professor's refutations would blow by like dead leaves. Unfortunately, old Bowen did not always preach to his text. Sometimes he would wander into irrelevant invectives against John Stuart Mill, who in a footnote had once referred to Bowen (who was then editor of a reputable review) as "an obscure American".

Cloying effect of Palmer's sweetness and idealism. We had another right-thinking and edifying teacher, no less thoroughly well-baked in all his opinions and mannerisms, but younger in years and following a later fashion in philosophy. Professor Palmer practised all the smooth oratorical arts of a liberal orator or headmaster; he conciliated opponents, plotted (always legally) with friends, and if things went against him, still smiled victoriously and seemed to be on the crest of the wave. He was the professor of ethics. His lectures were beautifully prepared, and exactly the same year after year. He had been professor of Greek also, and made anodyne translations from Homer and Sophocles in "rhythmic" and sleepy prose. In his course on English moralists he brought out his selected authors in dialectical order; each successive view appeared fresh, and plausible, but not sensational. They came in a subtle crescendo, everything good, and everything a little better than what went before, so that at the end you ought to have found yourself in the seventh heaven. Yet we, or at least I, didn't find ourselves there. I felt cheated. The method was Hegelian adapted to a Sunday School: all roses without thorns. All defects in doctrine (why not also in conduct?) were stepping-stones to higher things. We began with pungent, mannish violent theories: Hobbes and Mandeville. We passed onward to something more feminine and refined, to Shaftesbury. From this we dialectically reacted, landing in the apparently solid, liberal, political reformer, John Stuart Mill: but no, that was not our divine destination. A breath of higher philosophy somehow blew over us. We levitated; and, we knew not how or why, utilitarianism dissolved, lost in the distant valleys beneath us, and we realised the providential utility of utilitarianism in carrying us so far above it. "Purring pussy Palmer", my sporting friend "Swelly" Bangs used to call him: yet Palmer was a benign influence. The crude, half-educated, conscientious, ambitious young men who wished to study ethics gained subtler and more elastic notions of what was good than they had ever dreamt of; and their notions of what was bad became correspondingly discriminating and fair. Palmer was like a father confessor, never shocked at sin, never despairing of sinners. There must be a little of everything in the Lord's vineyard. Palmer was a fountain of sweet reasonableness. That his methods were sophistical and his conclusions lame didn't really matter. It was not a question of discovering or deciding anything final: the point was to become more cultivated and more intelligent. You could then define your aims and your principles for yourself. I found the authors read in Palmer's course, especially Hobbes, valuable in themselves; and Palmer's methods of exposition and criticism, sly and treacherous as they were, gave me a lesson in dialectic, and a warning against it. I began to understand that the cogency of dialectic is merely verbal or ideal, and its application to facts, even to the evolution of ideas, entirely hypothetical and distorting. If ideas created themselves (which they don't do) or succeeded one another in the mind or in history by logical derivation (as again they don't) evolution might be dialectical: but as it is, dialectic merely throws a verbal net into the sea, to draw a pattern over the fishes without catching any of them. It is an optical illusion.

Use and abuse of dialectic.   Dialectic didn't show its other, its honest, side to me until many years later, when I read Plato and knew Bertie Russell. Honest logicians never apply dialectic to history, and only in play to cosmology. Events are derived from one another materially and contingently. This is no less true when events are mental than when they are physical. It is *external* insights and interests that transform one system of philosophy into another, Socrates into Plato, Locke into Berkeley, Kant into Schopenhauer and Hegel. Each system remains logically and morally stable, like a portrait of its author. A philosophy that is radical and consistent cannot evolve. That which evolves is only the immature, the self-contradictory; and, if circumstances do not permit it to ripen according to its inner potentialities, it withers and dissolves into dust, leaving no progeny. Each fact, each group of ideas, in fusion with other facts, passes into a new natural form, not evolved from the previous forms dialectically, but created by nature out of their matter or ground at each juncture with a fresh spirit. What these "objective" idealists call spirit is simply the force of matter and Mammon, ruling the world; and if they love the world so much and are so well received in it—never crucified in it or martyred—the reason is simple. They are idealists only in technique; in practice and allegiance they are moral materialists and Mammon-worshippers. Like a sanctimonious Satan the idealist sets before himself all the kingdoms of the earth in a false panorama, as if there were nothing in them except what he sees there and covets; and he promises himself the possession and control of all those treasures, if only he will worship himself. Himself he calls spirit, but cheats his spirit and enslaves it to that cruel material world which he thinks he has mastered.

Locke, Berkeley, and Hume.   I also studied Locke, Berkeley, and Hume under William James. Here there was as much honest humanity in the teacher as in the texts, and I think I was not impervious to the wit and wisdom of any of them. Hume was the one I least appreciated; yet Palmer once said that I had Hume in my bones. In reality, whether through my immaturity only, or through James's bewilderment also, I seem to have gathered no clear lesson from those authors or from James himself. Verbally I understood them well enough; they were not superficially obscure; but critically, as to their presuppositions, their categories, and their place in history I understood nothing. Even when four years later I gave that very course, I didn't advance beyond a friendly literary interpretation of their meaning and of the psychological cosmos that they seemed to posit. I hardly questioned their ambiguous units, their "perceptions" or "ideas", but accepted them, as James then accepted them, as representing total scattered moments of "experience" or "life". This was historically just. This philosophy is purely literary and autobiographical. It sees "experience" as composed of the high lights that language and memory find in it retrospectively. It hypostasises the description into the object. But such hypostasis is an indefensible trick of memory, a poetic or mythical substitution of images for events and of verbal for dynamic elements. It is as if I pretended, in writing this book, to have discovered the fundamental reality and total composition of myself, of my family, of Spain, America, Germany, England, and Italy. A monstrous trick of verbal legerdemain, a sophistical curiosity.

Later judgment on their psychologism. The only solid foundation for all my play with this subject was supplied by the sturdy but undeveloped materialism of Hobbes, powerfully supported by the psychology of Spinoza and insecurely by the early medical psychology of James: to which in Germany my passing enthusiasm for Schopenhauer may be added, because by that time I was able to discount the language of a system and perceive from what direction it drew its inspiration. The "Will" in Schopenhauer was a transparent mythological symbol for the flux of matter. There was absolute equivalence between such a system, in its purport and sense for reality, and the systems of Spinoza and Lucretius. This was the element of ancient sanity that kept me awake and conscious of the points of the compass in the subsequent wreck of psychologism. Such wrecks are not fatal. Psychologism lives, and must always live, in literature and history. In these pursuits we are living as we imagine others might have lived, and seeing things as they might have seen them. We are dramatically enlarging our experience. What was lost in that moral tempest was only the illusion that such play of imagination revealed any profound truth or dislodged Nature to put Fable in her place.

Strong, destined to be my life-long friend, comes to Harvard. An event that had important consequences in the future course of my life occurred silently and almost unnoticed during my Senior year. A young man named Charles Augustus Strong—there was already something royal and German about that "Augustus" and that "Strong", though the youth was modesty and Puritanism personified—

came from the university of his native Rochester, New York, to study philosophy for a year at Harvard. As I too was taking all the advanced courses in that subject, we found ourselves daily thrown together, gradually began to compare notes, and to discuss the professors and their opinions; and finally we founded a philosophical club, in order to discuss everything more thoroughly with the other embryonic philosophers in the place. Towards the end of the year we both became candidates for the Walker Fellowship, usually awarded to graduates who wished to study philosophy in Germany. This was a rivalry that I disliked and also feared; because, if I had the advantage of being a Harvard man and better known to the professors, and also of being more glib and more resourceful in examinations, he had the decisive advantage of inspiring professional confidence. When you learned that his father and his brother were Baptist clergymen, you recognised at once that he too was a Baptist clergyman by nature and habit, only that some untoward influence had crossed his path and deflected him from his vocation. He had lost his faith in revelation. Modernist compromises and ambiguities were abhorrent to his strict honesty and love of precision. You mustn't preach what you don't believe.

Contrast in our characters and aims. He turned therefore to the nearest thing to being a clergyman that he could be sincerely, which was to be a professor of philosophy. He was already, in aspect, in manner, in speech, in spirit thoroughly professional. Moreover, for studying in Germany he was far better prepared than I in that he spoke German perfectly. He had been at school in Germany, in a Gymnasium at Güteslohe, and had received that strict training in all subjects which was not to be expected in free America. He was slow but accurate, and his zeal in the pursuit of truth was unflagging. He had the memory and solidity of the head boy of the class. Besides, when you observed him afresh, you saw that he was very good-looking, tall, firm, with curly black hair and noble features. It was only his shyness, reserve, and lack of responsive sympathy that obscured these advantages. Perhaps if he found his proper element and were happy they would shine out again.

Now how about me? Was I professional? Should I ever make a professor of philosophy? Everybody doubted it. I not only doubted it myself, but was repelled by the idea. What I wanted was to go on being a student, and especially to be a travelling student. I loved speculation for itself, as I loved poetry, not out of worldly respect or anxiety lest I should be mistaken, but for the splendour of it, like the splendour of the sea and the stars. And I knew I should love living obscurely and freely in old towns, in strange countries, hearing all sorts of outlandish marvellous opinions. I could have made a bargain with Mephistopheles, not for youth but for the appearance of youth, so that with its tastes but without its passions, I might have been a wandering student all my life, at Salamanca, at Bologna, in Oxford, in Paris, at Benares, in China, in Persia. Germany would be a beginning. If I never became a professor, so much the better. I should have seen the world, historical and intellectual. I should have been free in my best years.

We agree to share a travelling Fellowship for which we were rivals. Now my mother was going to assign me a permanent allowance of $500 a year, the sum that she received from "Uncle Russell" and that symbolically represented the $10,000 she had once received from "Uncle Robert", which she retained and meant to leave to me. The Walker Fellowship amounted to another $500. The two would make a neat sum, yet I knew that in Europe I could easily get on with less. From things Strong had dropped in conversation, I had gathered that he was much in the same case. His father was well off and he too had an allowance. Perhaps he didn't need the whole Fellowship. I therefore did a sly thing. I asked him if he would be willing to agree that whoever of us got the Fellowship should divide it with the other. Then we should both be sure of going to Germany for the next year. He consented at once. I think he liked the idea of having me with him. Our discussions enlivened him. I should serve as a useful pace-maker in the pursuit of absolute truth.

Nevertheless my conscience was a bit uneasy. I felt in my bones that Strong would get the appointment, and I was simply robbing him of half his stipend. So I made a second proposal. Before agreeing to this plan, let us lay it before Professor Palmer, professional moralist and Head of the Department, practically the man who would decide between us. Let us ask him if he thought well of it. We went to see him together. I acted as spokesman, having the readier tongue. I said we supposed we were the only likely candidates for the Fellowship, that we both wanted it very much, and that we both had small allowances from our families, so that we could get on with less than the whole amount of the Fellowship. Would it be a fair thing for us to agree, whoever got it, to divide it between us.

Professor Palmer bit his lips, thought for a moment, and decided to be sympathetic. He saw no objection. The action would be equally unselfish in both of us. I knew it was not unselfish in me, yet Palmer's cant set me at rest. They must have been undecided about the choice in the Committee, otherwise Palmer would not have agreed to the division. Now they would give the Fellowship to Strong knowing that I was to get half the money; so that really they would be voting half the money to me. Not quite satisfactory this, but excusable and rather ingenious.

Far-reaching consequences of this step. I think this is the only occasion in my life when I have done something a little too clever in order to get money. Yet the result might have encouraged a person inclined to trickery, because I not only got what I wanted, but in consequence made a great haul, not exactly in money, but precisely in what I cared for more than for money, in travel, in residence in foreign parts, in a well-paved path open to all sorts of intellectual pleasures. Strong, for a family reason that I shall mention later, gave up the Fellowship at the end of one year. It was then awarded to me for two successive years. Later, Strong went to live in Europe, in Paris, in Fiesole. He had got used to having me to talk with. I was often his guest for long periods; and that division of his $500 let me into a series of favours that I was positively begged to receive. Strong had become rich, he was married and had a young daughter; yet his life was strangely solitary. He was no less bored than when he was younger. He would actually have paid me, as he paid one or two others, to live near him so as to have stated hours for philosophical discussions. He once expressly offered to guarantee me an income of $2,500 if I would give up my professorship and go and live with him in Paris. I didn't accept that offer; I waited before retiring until I had money enough of my own to make me independent; but I did make his apartment in Paris my headquarters for some years; which for me at that time was a great convenience and economy. I had a lodging at will gratis, and I paid for food and service only when I was alone in the apartment or when we dined in restaurants, as we did every evening. At first on these occasions each paid for both on alternate days; later each always paid for what he ordered. Our tastes were becoming more different.

Advantages and difficulties in our partnership. There was always a latent tension between us, because our reasons for living together were mixed and not the same in both of us. In both there was real sympathy up to a point and a real interest in the same philosophical problems and political and social matters; and our views if not identical were co-operative. They played round the same facts in the same speculative spirit. Yet we were not intimate friends. We were more like partners in the same business. And our motive for forming this partnership was in neither of us personal affection but in both only private interest. Strong wanted a philosophical friend to talk with; at first mainly for the sake of company and stimulation, later rather in the hope of enforcing his views and confirming himself in them by convincing some one else of their truth. I, on the other hand, wanted a material *pied-à-terre*, a place and a person or persons that should take the place of a home; and Strong offered these in a most acceptable form, especially when he lived in Paris. He was free from almost all the bonds from which I wished to be free; he was less entangling socially and politically than such attachments as I might have found in Spain or in England. Besides, I lived with him only at certain seasons, seldom longer than for a month or two at a time; and there was no pledge that our arrangement should be permanent. In fact, I constantly went off by myself, to Spain, to Oxford, to Rome, or even to other lodgings in Paris: because I found writing difficult, both materially and psychologically, when we lived together. His hours were inflexible, also his determination to revert daily to the same discussions; the limitations that had become tyrannical over him became tyrannical over others also. In this way, while the friendliness of that division originally made by us of the Walker Fellowship accompanied us through life, the mixed motives that had prompted it accompanied us also. Strong was always being cheated, and a victim that complained at not being victimised enough; and I was always being punished by a sense of unnecessary dependence and constraint, when it was freedom and independence that I had sought.

Happy conclusion of my undergraduate life. These observations anticipate events that lay far in the future. For the moment I was plunged in work, more wholeheartedly perhaps than ever again, because I saw my future and my studies in an undivided prospect: my whole inner life would lie in those studies, while those studies in turn would determine my career. And my bad beginning as a student at Harvard was redeemed by an honourable end. I received my bachelor's degree *Summa cum laude*. In spite of my mediocre standing in some subjects, my teachers thought that my speculative vocation and my understanding of the great philosophers entitled me to a first place. This was a repetition with a difference of my career at the Latin

School. There I had, as a person, carried the day against a middling record as a pupil; now at Harvard I carried the day against the same handicap by force of personal abilities in a special half-artistic direction.

I didn't wait, however, to receive my degree in person at Commencement. Herbert Lyman took the parchment in charge and brought it to me in Germany. On taking my last examination, I had sailed without knowing what would be the result. I took a German ship, not that I was bound directly to Germany, but that it touched at Cherbourg whence, second class this time, I could travel leisurely to Avila and see a lot of cathedral towns: Caen, Le Mans, Angers, Poitiers, Angoulême, Bordeaux, and Burgos. The expense, stopping one night at each place, was not greater than in going first class through Paris. I was to spend the summer quietly in Avila, and in the autumn to join Herbert Lyman in Dresden and Strong in Berlin.

The curtain drops here, to rise presently on those other scenes.

ADDENDUM

We Were Not Virtuous

I have said that in our mother's estimation we, her children, were not virtuous.

Disappointing children. Why not? Surely at least Josefina and Robert were blameless and a comfort to her as far as their powers went; but, alas, their powers were so limited! I remember on Robert's wedding-day my mother, in purple and black silk, with what black lace she still possessed, driving from our house in Millmont Street to the Church of the Advent—because Ellen, our new sister-in-law, was a most devout Anglo-Catholic. Suddenly tears suffused my mother's eyes, and one or two trickled down her cheek. I think this is the only time in my life that I saw her cry. *"Roberto"*, she said, *"ha sido un buen hijo."* Robert had been a good son. Apparently his career as a good son was now at an end, that is, his dutiful term of office had expired, and she could no longer count on him to be devoted, in the first instance, to herself. As a matter of fact, it was after his marriage that he began to be of real use to her, and to all of us, because he emancipated himself from his superiors in business, who had never liked or advanced him, and became a professional agent for the investment and care of property, his own, ours, and his wife's; and he did this work so well that we, at least, emerged from penury into ease and comfort. But he was immensely ignorant of other things, and correspondingly opinionated. He had the Sturgis limitations, rendered annoying by small faults of manner and speech and a sad want of tact, so that he was not a joy in a family, not even in his own. He was not a joy to poor Ellen, his wife; not that he did anything intentionally unkind, but that, for instance, his eyes would intently follow the servant-girl round the table, if she was at all young or pretty; and that he was president of a so-called Spanish Club (which I avoided like the plague) where he met three sisters, Portoricans, one of whom was such a close friend of his that, when Ellen died, we all feared he would marry her. But he was content with remembering her in his will; for he felt old, very old for his sixty years, and he loved his daughter too much to offend her and reduce her inheritance by a second marriage; and indeed he survived his wife for less than three years. It was no joy, then, that was departing from our house with Robert; it was only a prop that our mother felt she was losing, a familiar person in attendance who would leave a gap. He had been properly devoted; he was tender-hearted and generous, where his sympathies were once engaged; yet in a classical or romantic sense he was not *virtuous*: he was not a beautiful white statue of austerity. No more was poor Josefina, who in the later years became our mother's watchful, anxious slave and perpetual shadow. The sad fact was that, even when our intentions were good, none of us could be satisfactory. None of us expressed to the eye all that our mother would have wished us to express. It was in part the fault of our natures, but in part also the fault of her circumstances, which so much limited our education. She was profoundly genteel, she had a quiet love of finery, and of a distinguished way of living; but that being beyond her means, she was determined to be genteel in her poverty. She renounced very early all desire to seem young, and took to wearing lace caps with pale blue or lavender ribbons, because even if you were elderly and poor it was a duty to be dressed with taste and to have a flower or two on the table, while you did your embroidery or read your novel. But Susana and I, though we had some nice friends, were not inwardly genteel. We were corruptible, fond of fun, given to mockery and ridicule; and we were disaffected. We kept, in our loose, miscellaneous, international attachments, just within the bounds of respectability: but we were distinctly not virtuous.

Points in which there was instinctive sympathy between my mother and me. On the aesthetic side I sympathised more with my mother than did my brother and sisters. It was I that always helped her to rehang the pictures, or rearrange the furniture; something that every now and then it pleased her to do. And I had, like her, an eye for clothes. We bought very few clothes but, according to Polonius' advice, costly as our purse could buy; and they lasted us a long time. I kept them fresh by always changing into old duds whenever I sat down to work, or to be alone in my room, which was most of the time; and this not merely to preserve the presentable garments, but for positive comfort and freedom, like a workman in his overalls or an artist in his studio. The body must be loosely clad—*a sus anchas*— if the mind is to forget it and impetuously lead its own life.

My mother also, like most ladies, at least in those days, changed her dress to go out; and in the street, though not imposing in figure or dressed in the latest fashion, she looked so manifestly *the lady*, that everyone instinctively treated her with deference. She had the secret of final touches, veil, gloves, laces, a half-hidden old brooch or gem that suggested depths more distinguished than the surfaces. Above all she moved silently, slowly but deftly, without hesitation or curiosity, as if carpeting the way as she went. Yet with all these signs of high breeding in her demeanour, she was too indolent or too disheartened to trouble about them in her children. We were innately too inferior and the times too inelegant. Not that she ever said so; for in theory she appreciated nothing but progress and reform; but she made us feel our inferiority and implicitly derided reform and progress by having nothing to do with them. Her notion seemed to be that church, state and society were victims of unnatural tyranny: remove the tyrants, and everything would become perfect of its own accord. That business and wealth might be tyrannical never occurred to her; she regarded them as fountains of pure benefit all round, as were science and enlightenment. She was therefore theoretically content with the nineteenth century, with America, and especially with Boston; and apparently, in such a blessed environment, it was not necessary to do anything in order that everything should be all right. The fact that everyone was hectically "doing things", multiplying wealth, busy with science and organisation, and finding and creating endless pressing problems to solve, she ignored. I think, if she had been pressed, she would have pronounced such intense activity unnecessary, even if she had not ventured to think it dangerous. Could it be silently undermining liberty and corrupting the state of nature? Could it be imprisoning mankind anew? She preferred not to consider such questions, but to live on in Boston, as if it were still the Boston of 1856.

My sisters' difficulties. Automatic happiness in liberty might have seemed easy to us children if we had had plenty of money. The result might have been unexpectedly bad, but at first we should certainly not have objected to our mother's philosophy. It happened that we were poor, and poverty puts liberty in another light. The girls, for instance, had inadequate allowances to dress on, no help, and no hope of an additional sum on special occasions. They had their clothes made at home by a secondrate sempstress (the days of ready-made gowns had not arrived). Our mother's taste and her skill in needlework could have served excellently to give hints and to inspire interest; and the girls might have learned to work with pleasure for their own benefit. But nothing was done; and Susana had to go into society looking rather shabby, while Josefina, being plain and shy, preferred not to go at all. Young girls, our mother said, ought not to care for admiration, and everyone must be contented with his lot.

A lesson in morals. I remember one day at luncheon when I was a boy (it must have been a Saturday or Sunday, for on other days I reached the house at half past two, and lunched alone) we had finished a rather insufficient repast, and there was one odd piece of cake left in the silver basket. I asked if I might have it. "*No*," said my mother, "*es para los pajaritos*, it is for the little birds." And presently, though it was by no means a fixed habit of hers, she opened the window and spread the crums out for the sparrows. She did not care for sparrows, she never watched them or tried to tame them; and that day, having performed her act of zoological benevolence, she closed the window at once, and went upstairs to sit as usual in her own room. She had never troubled her mind with municipal affairs, and probably had not heard that people were complaining of the pest of sparrows, which was driving other more interesting birds from the parks. Yet I am sure that in her silence she felt that she had given me a lesson in justice and in universal love. She had kept the cake from her son and given it to the sparrows. She was a liberal in politics.

A non-affectionate home. In respect to both my parents, whom I am proud of as persons of marked character and philosophic conformity with fate, I feel a certain strange distance, as if my bond with them had not been close and physical, but somehow accidental and merely social or economic, as with a schoolmaster or a school matron. By adding memories of early childhood and certain hereditary traits—for in some things I exactly reproduce my father and my mother—they may be turned into the semblance of interesting grandparents, imposing persons in the background, vividly remembered, but who were too old and faded to lead, or to count in shaping one's vital interests. A real father in my case was lacking, and the real mother was my sister Susana. This fact, that my sister took on the higher duties and influence of a mother over me, initiating me into religion and society, caused my mother to seem a superimposed and rather hostile power; for in her apparent passivity she retained absolute authority in matters of discipline and money. She was not meddlesome, she left us for long stretches of time to do as we liked; but then suddenly the sword would fall, pitiless, cold, and surgically sterilising, to cut off our tenderest tentacles for our own good. I could shrug my shoulders at this high control, because I was not passionately wedded to what I was doing in any case, and could view this interference sardonically, without in the least modifying my inner allegiances; I could even sympathise with my mother's intelligent firmness, granting her ideal of Victorian virtue and bourgeois eminence; but the others suffered. They demanded a sympathy that they never found, and they hadn't the strength of will to laugh at the tyrant precepts as I did, while momentarily bowing to the physical necessity of obeying them. In me, my mother saw and dreaded an equal; not an equal, of course, to what Pepín would have been, or even to what I might have become if I had been virtuous; but an equal to her in independence of will. In the others, who trembled more before her, she saw only an inferior endowment. By them virtue was missed, not intentionally but through a helpless vagueness, or through their incapacity to resist contagion, now from outworn religions and now from vulgar friendships. Such feebleness of soul could not be positively blamed, as could a deliberate alienation from virtue in mockery and self-indulgence; but was it not even more discouraging? Alas, we were not Catos or Brutuses or Portias! But how *could* we have been? Our mother was heroic; but Papa George, though virtuous, was limited, and Papa Santayana, though no fool, positively *liked* to be limited and perhaps wasn't quite virtuous.

1. An oil portrait of Susana and
Santayana painted by his father,
c. 1866–67. By permission of Richard
C. Lyon.

2. Santayana's Harvard class photograph of 1886. By permission of George Santayana Papers, Rare Book and Manuscript Library, Columbia University.

3. A charcoal sketch by Andreas Andersen, 1897, one of Santayana's favorites. By permission of the Houghton Library, Harvard University.

4. Santayana at the Lymans', *c.* 1889.
By permission of Harry Ransom
Humanities Research Center, The
University of Texas at Austin.

5. Santayana in Hamburg, 1907. By
permission of Harry Ransom
Humanities Research Center, The
University of Texas at Austin.

6. Santayana in 1898 at the Delta Phi
Club. By permission of Harry Ransom
Humanities Research Center, The
University of Texas at Austin.

7. Santayana in 1918. By permission of Harry Ransom Humanities Research Center, The University of Texas at Austin.

8. Santayana in Avila, *c.* 1919–25. By permission of *Piedra Cabellera* (Avila).

9. Santayana in Rome in 1936. By
permission of Harry Ransom
Humanities Research Center, The
University of Texas at Austin.

10. Santayana in the Blue Sisters clinic
in Rome, *c.* 1948–52. By permission of
George Santayana Papers, Rare Book
and Manuscript Library, Columbia
University.

11. The Philosophical Club at Harvard.
Santayana as president, seated in
center. By permission of Harvard
University Archives.

12. The O.K. Club, 1886. Santayana
seated, second from right. By
permission of Harvard University
Archives.

13. The *Lampoon* staff, Santayana
standing in back row, third from left.
By permission of Harvard University
Archives.

14. The *Harvard Monthly* staff,
Santayana standing, at left. By
permission of Harvard University
Archives.

15. The Hasty Pudding play
c. 1884–86, cast in costume. Santayana
(in a white dress) is seated in chair,
third from right. By permission of
Harvard University Archives.

16. Augustín, Santayana's father, a self-portrait. By permission of Richard C. Lyon.

17. Josefina, Santayana's mother, *c.* 1890. By permission of Harry Ransom Humanities Research Center, The University of Texas at Austin.

18. Susana, Santayana's half sister, 1892. By permission of Harry Ransom Humanities Research Center, The University of Texas at Austin.

19. Robert, Santayana's half brother. By permission of the Houghton Library, Harvard University.

20. Santayana, his half sister Josefina,
and family friend Mercedes Escalera in
Seville, 1914. By permission of Harry
Ransom Humanities Research Center,
The University of Texas at Austin.

21. Celedonio and Susana Sastre in
Avila, *c.* 1915. By permission of Harry
Ransom Humanities Research Center,
The University of Texas at Austin.

22–25. Santayana's friends among the Harvard class of 1886. All photographs by permission of the Harvard University Archives.

22. Charles Alexander Loeser.

23. Herbert Lyman.

24. Julian Codman.

25. Warwick Potter.

26. Charles Augustus Strong.

27. Robert Dickson Smith, Jr. (later Robert Dickson Weston-Smith).

28. Robert Burnside Potter.

26–29. Santayana's undergraduate friends during the early part of his teaching career. All photographs by permission of the Harvard University Archives.

29. Joseph Trumbull Stickney.

30–37. Santayana's colleagues during his years as a Harvard professor.

30. Charles William Eliot. By permission of the Harvard University Archives.

31. Archibald Cary Coolidge. By permission of the Harvard University Archives.

32. Charles Eliot Norton. By
permission of the Harvard University
Archives.

33. Barrett Wendell. By permission of
the Harvard University Archives.

34. William Lyon Phelps, 1905. By
permission of Yale University Archives,
Yale University Library.

35. William James. By permission of
the Harvard University Archives.

36. George Herbert Palmer, 1911. By
permission of the Harvard University
Portrait Collection.

37. Josiah Royce. By permission of the
Harvard University Portrait Collection.

38. Boylston Adams Beal. By
permission of the Harvard University
Archives.

39. Robert Burnside Potter in middle
age. By permission of Harry Ransom
Humanities Research Center, The
University of Texas at Austin.

II

XVII

Germany

My imperfect immersion in the German medium.   The impulse that sent me to study in Germany came from America—something for which America is to be thanked; yet the failure of that adventure in my case was connected with its origin. I was too much enveloped in my American (and afterwards in my English) associations to lose myself in the German scene, to learn German properly, and to turn a copious German "spiritual" stream into my private channel. In my Germany there was, and there still is, too much of me and too little of Germany.

Göttingen.   Some recommendation that I have forgotten led me in the early autumn of 1886 to Göttingen, with the idea of learning a little more German than the very little that I knew. I lived in a boarding-house kept by Frau Pastorin Schlote, whose elderly daughter—not the Irma of *The Last Puritan*, who is imaginary—knew English and gave the foreign boarders lessons in German. I learned enough to understand lectures and formal conversation from the first; but there was no one with whom I could begin to talk, and with my dislike of drudgery, I turned rather to deciphering for myself, with the help of a grammar and a dictionary, texts that were worth reading on their own account: *Deutsche Lyrik*, Heine, and *Wilhelm Meister*. I made good progress of a sort, for my own ends, but without thoroughness; and my tongue remained torpid and my inflections inaccurate. "*Sie sprechen sehr nett*" the superior housekeeper said one day when I excused myself, "*die Endungen aber fehlen.*" Two or three months later in Berlin my landlady and her friends one day were discussing me, when her daughter observed that I was in my room and could hear them through the thin door. "*Der versteht ja nichts*" her mother cried impatiently, and went on wondering at my solitary life, that I went out for a walk alone and all the rest of the day sat working in my room. I understood every word perfectly: but in conversation I was helpless; there were no people with whom I cared to talk; and my punishment was that I never learned to speak the language.

Dresden with Herbert Lyman. From Göttingen I went to Dresden, where Herbert Lyman had invited me to join him. I say "invited" because although I paid for my lodging, breakfast and midday dinner, he paid everything else for both of us, our way of living being entirely beyond the means of a student on half a Fellowship. We took a daily German lesson, and a daily walk; and in the evening, or rather in the afternoon—for performances began at five or half-past five o'clock—we went to the Royal Theatre, hearing an opera or a play on alternate nights. The play often was Shakespeare, in the excellent German version. I remember *Julius Caesar* particularly, a play I have never seen done in English, I suppose because it is hardly a play for a star, like *Hamlet* or *Othello*; but the dutiful German State Company performed it with zeal and good judgment. We had an ample feast of Wagner, with Gudehus and Malten: old stand-bys but still adequate, singing and acting with a devout enthusiasm that was contagious. And after the theatre we had another treat that must not go unrecorded: an enormous delicious sweet omelette or *Pfannkuchen*, hot and crisp at the edges in its great pewter platter, followed by bread and cheese and a flagon of beer.

Baroque. Memorable and important for me were these Dresden impressions; and I should include the lesson in architecture taught me by the Zwinger, the Royal Palace, and the Katholische Kirche; a lesson reinforced many years later by the monuments at Nancy. Baroque and rococo cannot be foreign to a Spaniard. They are profoundly congenial and Quixotic, suspended as it were between two contrary insights: that in the service of love and imagination nothing can be too lavish, too sublime, or too festive; yet that all this passion is a caprice, a farce, a contortion, a comedy of illusions.

Grounds of Lyman's liking for me. All these wonderful things, besides the *Madonna di San Sisto* and everything else in the picture gallery, I saw while I stood side by side with Herbert Lyman, an intelligent observer who knew much more than I about music, yet a typical Yankee, cold shrewd and spare inwardly, smiling with a sort of insulated incredulity at everything passionate, as if he lived inside a green glass bottle, warranted an absolute non-conductor. He condemned nothing, yet nothing seemed to make any difference *in him*. Why was he such a devoted friend of mine? We had no special interests in common, and I should not have distinguished him particularly from other kind and correct Bostonians if he had not shown such a marked and constant friendliness towards me. The secret of this was perhaps revealed by his younger sister one day at table in their house *in Beacon Street, opposite the Common,* the place where perfect Bostonians ought to live. The conversation had turned on summer resorts, and I said that I went every year to Europe, because the heat in New England was intolerable. This was tactless of me, since the Lymans had a luxurious ancestral house in Waltham near Boston which it would have been a crime for them not to occupy in summer, no matter what heat they might suffer there. However, I had smiled as I spoke, as if I couldn't really mean what I said. "Oh, thank you," cried the younger Miss Lyman, "we can't say that ourselves, but it's such a relief to hear it!" I expect that I said a good many things that it was a relief for her brother to hear. I was an exciting, a slightly dangerous friend, yet not exactly disreputable, since I was by way of becoming a professor at Harvard. I could be acknowledged and cultivated and invited to the house. Moreover, I had Bostonian connections. My sister was an intimate friend of Miss Sara Lowell, Herbert Lyman's own aunt, his mother's sister! Possibly he had heard of me before he had seen me, and that made such a difference in Boston! If my half-foreign sister was all right, why shouldn't I, at least educated in Boston, be all right also? He had very simple tastes; he liked my comic verses, and would sing them to popular airs; for silly as the words were they could be sung without offence in any drawing-room. Yes, the partiality of the excellent Herbert for me was explicable. Other Bostonians, though they might not share it, could understand it. I was such a relief!

Our tastes united us before our lives diverged. He not only sang a little, but would have liked to devote himself entirely to music. How, in what capacity? As a composer, as a performer, or merely as a critic, like "Billy" Apthorp in the *Boston Transcript?* Music would be an acceptable profession if you could begin by being famous. It was not acceptable if you were to begin at the foot of the ladder, and perhaps remain there. Herbert, who hadn't a great voice or a precocious talent, must therefore go into business. Yet there was no hurry about it. He might go to Germany for a year or two and study music. He would enjoy the Boston Symphony concerts all the more intensely every Saturday evening for the rest of his life. And his German musical holiday might well begin at Dresden. Now I was going to Germany too, where term at the universities didn't begin until the middle of November. Why shouldn't I spend the interval at Dresden? We could then learn German together, and have a good time as well. We had a very good time, but I, at least, didn't learn much German; I learned only what sufficed for my secret purpose—secret I mean even to myself, the purpose on which my heart was naturally set. This was not at all to be proficient in languages or to be a professor of philosophy, but to see and to understand the world. For this purpose our month or six weeks in Dresden was not merely a good preparation. It was a culminating point, one of the happiest episodes in my whole life.

Good things in Germany.   I used at that time to sum up my first impressions of Germany by saying that there were three good things there: the uniforms, the music, and the beer. The formula was playful, yet it might still serve to express my sentiments if its terms were taken symbolically. *Uniforms*—which at that time were ornate and many-coloured, some sky-blue and silver, others white and gold—would stand for discipline and the glory of discipline. *Music* would stand for idealism, understood to mean love of ideal and immaterial things, of pure science and free imagination, and not "idealism" about material things, concealing or falsifying the truth about them. Finally *Beer* would stand for *Gemütlichkeit*, for joy in hearty, fleshly, kindly, homely, droll little things. How very much these three German virtues, when not exaggerated into vices, redeem the human soul from disorder, from servitude, and from spleen!

My first semester in Berlin.   Berlin after Dresden seemed big, modern, and ugly; but modernness, ugliness and bigness were familiar to me. I could live my own life in the midst of them, and so I did here. There were morning lectures with an interval of an hour between them: which I spent at the Museum, or at the Café Bauer over the English papers and a coffee with whipped cream. There was then a full dinner at half past one o'clock, in a restaurant upstairs near the Friedrichstrasse. It was so copious that, although this was my only solid meal, I usually skipped the boiled meat and vegetables, contenting myself with soup, fish, roast meat with vegetables, compote, and salad, and a dessert; washed down with a half-bottle of white wine. The whole expense was three marks, two for the dinner, fifty pfennig for the wine, twenty-five for coffee and the same for the waiter. I always sat at the same table, being one of the first to arrive, was expected, well received, and came to feel quite at home. I had a small room up many flights in the Louisenplatz, with a porcelain stove like a tomb in which a few diminutive cubes of synthetic fuel were buried every twenty-four hours. They did not make the room warm, but kept it from being too cold to sit in, warmly dressed, with a rug over one's legs. My landlady supplied coffee and rolls in the morning, and bread and cheese with a bottle of beer in the evening; so that after a good walk in the Thiergarten I could go home and devote the rest of the day and evening to work, without fear of interruption. At lectures I often sat with Strong, and sometimes with Houghton; they were my only acquaintances that year.

Paulsen on Greek Ethics. Of the four professors to whom I listened Paulsen was the most important: not very important in himself—he was simply an excellent professor—but important for me as a medium and as a model of judicious and sympathetic criticism. This semester he lectured on Greek Ethics, and in the next winter semester on Spinoza. In both subjects he helped to settle my opinions for good. The Greek ethics wonderfully supplied that which was absent in Spinoza, a virile, military, organic view of human life, a civilised view, to keep the cosmic and religious imagination of Spinoza in its proper moral place. The Greeks knew what it was to have a country, a native religion, a beautiful noble way of living, to be defended to the death. They recognised heroically that which Spinoza recognised only descriptively or pietistically: that the power of nature infinitely exceeds and ultimately destroys the power of each of its parts. The Greeks were thereby saved from arrogance without condemning themselves to littleness; for what is greater than beauty, and what more beautiful than courage to live and to die freely, in one's chosen way? The Jews, on the contrary, and even Spinoza with them, fell into both littleness and arrogance: into the littleness of being content with anything, with small gains and private safety; and into arrogance in proclaiming that, in their littleness they possessed the highest good, heard the voice of absolute truth, and were the favourites of heaven. Undoubtedly if you renounce everything, you are master of everything in an ideal sense, since nothing can disturb you; but the Jews never renounced anything that was within reach; and it was rather the Greek hero who renounced half of what he might have possessed, in order that the other half should be perfect.

My philosophy in the germ. I was thus fully settled in my naturalistic convictions; they revealed the real background, the true and safe foundation, for human courage, human reason, and human imagination. These might then fill the foreground *ad libitum* with their creations, political and poetic. Both the Greeks and Spinoza, by a spontaneous agreement, combined the two insights that for me were essential: naturalism as to the origin and history of mankind, and fidelity, in moral sentiment, to the inspiration of reason, by which the human mind conceives truth and eternity, and participates in them ideally.

Ebbinghaus on William James.   Besides Paulsen I heard Ebbinghaus who even asked me to his house, showed me his first fat baby and talked about William James, of course eulogistically, but with fundamental reservations, as for instance, on the question of free will and responsibility, on which he said *"Das hat er eigentlich nicht durch-gedacht."* This seemed rather a scholastic judgment to pass on James. He had thought and thought on that subject; yet he hadn't thought himself out of his half impulsive, half traditional horror of determinism, not because he couldn't think the argument out, but because, like Bergson, he didn't trust argument where he had intuition. Of course Ebbinghaus, whose training was scientific, knew that intuition is not a guide to matters of fact. James, however, was no draught-horse patiently pulling the scientific barge along a placid academic canal; rather a red Indian shooting the rapids with spasmodic skill and elemental emotions. To Ebbinghaus it seemed that a professor's business was to trudge along the governmental towpath with a legal cargo, and I agreed with him technically much more than with James; but he was less interesting as a man and less challenging as a thinker.

Gezycki and the weakness of English ethics.

•

Scientifically fitted.   I don't know for what reason I heard some lectures and took a seminar of Gezycki's, doubtless some recommendation from America, because Gezycki, who was a cripple, had emotional sympathies in reforming and free religious quarters in the Anglosaxon world. He defended English ethics rather than explained them; and his seminar on Kant's *Critique of Practical Reason* had no historical or critical value, but merely the interest of a pathetic personal cult of human happiness clung to passionately by an unhappy man. He too spoke to me of William James and of William James's brother-in-law Salter, who was a lecturer for the Ethical Culture Society. He was interested in James on the moral side, yet without spiritualistic leanings; and perhaps I may have learned from Gezycki to see that it is not *moral* to be romantic. This fact, for Gezycki, refuted romanticism; but for me it merely proved that the afflatus of romanticism belongs to the gnostic religions. It is a vital impulse expressed in fantastic assertions about the world; not, what Gezycki's heart desired, a social and personal discipline to increase human happiness and abolish suffering.

My Hellenism in morals. For me, at that time, all this was of little account. What counted was Greek ethics, summed up in the stories that Herodotus tells about Solon, explaining the nature of happiness to the benighted Croesus. A string of excited, fugitive, miscellaneous pleasures is not happiness; happiness resides in imaginative reflection and judgment, when the *picture* of one's life, or of human life, as it truly has been or is, satisfies the will, and is gladly accepted. Epicurus had a different notion of happiness from that of Solon, but it was just as much a form of wisdom, a choice among possible lives; in neither sage was it a calculus of quantitative pleasures and pains. Epicurus renounced most of the things called pleasures, for the sake of peace, equanimity, and intelligence, and Solon's heroes renounced life itself for the sake of a beautiful moment or a beautiful death. The extreme of classical heroism here becomes romantic; because the most romantic career, if deliberately chosen and accepted without illusion, would be a form of happiness: something in which a living will recognised its fulfilment and found its peace.

I prove impervious to German inspiration. After that first semester the wind was taken out of my sails for study in Germany. Strong and I had gone to England for the holidays; but I staid in Oxford, and he joined other friends in Paris, neither of us returning to Berlin for the second semester. This was not dereliction on our part: we both had something better to do. Why hadn't someone warned us not to go to Berlin, but to choose some smaller place where there might be more unity of spirit in the teaching and in student life? Was there no such place at that unlucky moment? Were there no inspired philosophers then in Germany? Was there no enthusiastic romanticism and no *Gemütlichkeit?* For me it is a source of eternal regret to have missed the enrichment and the lesson that fusion with German life, in my youth, might have given me. Nobody gave me clear advice in the matter, nor did Strong, who needed it less, seem to have received it, or to feel the danger we ran of wasting our time. He gave up the Fellowship for private reasons, and I, to whom it was then assigned, knew of nothing to do but to return to Berlin. All was changed there for me. Instead of keen curiosity and expectation, instead of delight at the freedom of thought and breadth of sympathy shown by my new professors, I was absorbed in other impressions and attachments. I had found England infinitely more interesting and stimulating than Germany; I had been again in Spain, even to Gibraltar, to receive my sister and had left her at my father's in Avila. I see now that I ought

260 Persons and Places

to have made a fresh plunge, a bold decision, gone to Marburg or Jena or Heidelberg or Bonn, seen only Germans, compelled myself to master the language, and lived, as during my first semester, an austere poor student's life.

At the time, however, I was will-less. Beal persuaded me to go to the pension, kept by an Englishwoman, where he was living, and where everyone was English or American. Mechanically, I went again to hear the same professors. Paulsen was lecturing on Spinoza: a great treat, but essentially not a new light. I dropped in to listen to other lecturers occasionally, in their public courses: Wagner on political economy, Lasson on Fichte, Deussen on Schopenhauer and the Indians. I took a course under Simmel on "Ten Different Interpretations of the Essence of Kant's *Critique of Pure Reason*"; a clever series of criticisms, producing at least in my mind nothing but amusement and confusion. I was living in Babel. I felt no special inspiration, no guiding purpose, except the engagement involved in holding the Fellowship. Not that inwardly my devotion to philosophy was impaired. It remained my one all-embracing interest, not indeed as a science, only as a balance of mind and temper, in which all the sciences and arts should compose as true a picture as possible of nature and human nature. My quandary was not inward, it didn't concern my philosophy; it concerned only my academic position and possible career. And from that point of view, this German experiment had been a failure. I was wholly incapable of taking a Doctor's degree in Germany. The only thing for me to do was to return to Harvard and take my Doctor's degree there, where I was at home and sure of my ground. I knew German enough to write my thesis on a German subject, if I might write it in English. Then, unless a place as teacher were offered me somewhere—I hardly thought of Harvard itself—I could go to the Institute of Technology and study architecture.

I return to Harvard to take the Doctor's degree.   I wrote to the Harvard authorities explaining my position, saying I was coming back, and asking to have my Fellowship renewed as for a resident graduate. There was some hesitation about this point, but in the end I got the appointment. It was not materially indispensable to me, as I meant to live at my mother's in any case, but gave me more lee-way. I began that year to save, and to possess a little capital. In other words, I began to prepare for my retirement from teaching before I had begun to teach.

Later trips to Germany.   From ten to twenty years later I made several holiday visits to Germany. They were in part acts of contrition for my youthful waste of opportunities, yet I should hardly have made them simply with that idea. The last of these visits I called a Goethe pilgrimage, because I went expressly to Frankfort and to Weimar to visit the home of Goethe's childhood and that of his old age. I was then preparing my lectures on *Three Philosophical Poets*, of whom Goethe was to be one. Even that, however, would probably not have induced me to revisit Germany had I not meantime formed a real friendship with a young German, Baron Albert von Westenholz.

Westenholz.   Westenholz was one of my truest friends. Personal affection and intellectual sympathies were better balanced and fused between him and me than between me and any other person. I made three trips to Hamburg expressly to see him, and he once joined me in London and again at Amsterdam and in Brussels, but travelling ultimately became impracticable for him, on account of his health and hobbies; and I never could persuade him to come to Italy, where we should have found so many themes for enthusiastic discussion. But we carried on a desultory correspondence, and he never lost his interest in my philosophy and in my books. Not that he was in any sense my disciple or surrendered his independence of judgment. His liberal Lutheran background and many-sided studies gave him independent points of view, and his attainments were in many ways wider than mine; so that, for instance, when in the later years I began to read New Testament criticism, chiefly in Loisy, he guided me very usefully to various German authorities on the subject. He always maintained an "Evangelical" conception of Christ very different from mine, which is Gnostic and free from all claims to be historical. He was too dutifully *gebildet*, too indoctrinated, to be as sceptical as I am; and that difference lent spice to our discussions, especially as he, with his lingering illusions, was the younger man and I, the mentor, was the cynic. When my young friends are "gooder" than I, I respect and love them, but when they are less tender than I towards tradition, I feel that they are uneducated and stupid. I could never accuse Westenholz of being stupid or uneducated: but I felt to the end how *German* he was, how immersed in learning and inclined to follow a sect, without much capacity for laughter.

His father had been a partner in a family banking house established in Frankfort and Vienna, originally perhaps Jewish; but my friend's mother was the daughter of a Burghermaster of Hamburg, with the most pronounced Hanseatic Lutheran traditions. The bank had a branch in London, and young Westenholz had served his apprenticeship there and learned to speak English perfectly. But he never entered the firm: his health was far from good; he suffered from various forms of mental or half-mental derangement, sleeplessness, and obsessions, which however he himself diagnosed with perfect scientific intelligence. By way of a rest-cure, he was sent on long ocean voyages; was wrecked off the coast of Brazil, and later turned up at Harvard where he was brought to see me.

Origin of our friendship. I was then, in 1900–1905, living at No. 60 Brattle Street, and had my walls covered with Arundel prints. These were the starting-point for our first warm conversations. I saw at once that he was immensely educated and enthusiastic, and at the same time innocence personified; and he found me sufficiently responsive to his ardent views of history, poetry, religion, and politics. He was very respectful, on account of my age and my professorship; and always continued to call me *lieber Professor* or *Professorchen*; but he would have made a much better professor than I, being far more assiduous in reading up all sorts of subjects and consulting expert authorities. Before he left Cambridge, it was decided that I should visit him in Hamburg: I was to stay for a night at their town mansion (in an extensive park facing the *Alster*) to pay my respects to his invalid mother and his sister—a good many years older than he; and then he would carry me off to a little hermitage he had for himself in the woods, absolutely solitary, without even a carriage-road leading up to it.

My visits to Hamburg. Hamburg was not an inconvenient place for me to reach, since in those days I often sailed in the Hamburg steamers, because they were the first to have single cabins, deep in the centre of the vessel, and well-ventilated, so that I could hope to avoid seasickness, and to enjoy privacy. With these things secured, I was glad of a longish voyage, and instead of landing at Cherbourg or Southampton, I could easily go on to Cuxhaven and Hamburg: and the same convenience naturally existed for the return voyage. Our friendship became intellectually closer in later years, without seeming to require personal contacts; and I never went to Germany again after those external conveniences ceased to make the journey easy and as it were optional.

His obsessions. As for him, his impediments were growing upon him. Fear of noise kept him awake, lest some sound should awake him; and he carried great thick curtains in his luggage to hang up on the windows and doors of his hotel bedrooms. At Volksdorf, his country hermitage, the floors were all covered with rubber matting, to deaden the footfalls of possible guests; and he would run down repeatedly, after having gone to bed, to make sure that he had locked the piano: because otherwise a burglar might come in and wake him up by sitting down to play on it! When I suggested that he might get over this absurd idea by simply defying it, and repeating to himself how utterly absurd it was, he admitted that he might succeed in overcoming it; but then he would develop some other obsession instead. It was hopeless: and all his intelligence and all his doctors and psychiatrists were not able to cure him. In his last days, as his friend Reichhardt told me, the great obsession regarded bedding: he would spend half the night arranging and rearranging mattresses, pillows, blankets and sheets, for fear that he might not be able to sleep comfortably. And if ever he forgot this terrible problem, his mind would run over the more real and no less haunting difficulties involved in money-matters. The curse was not that he lacked money, but that he had it, and must give an account of it to the government as well as to God. And there were endless complications; for he was legally a Swiss citizen, and had funds in Switzerland, partly declared and partly secret, on which to pay taxes both in Switzerland and in Germany; and for years he had the burden of the house and park in Hamburg, gradually requisitioned by the city government, until finally he got rid of them, and went to live far north, in Holstein, with thoughts of perhaps migrating to Denmark. A nest of difficulties, a swarm of insoluble problems making life hideous, without counting the gnawing worm of religious uncertainty and scientific confusion.

His unclouded intelligence. The marvel was that with all these morbid preoccupations filling his days and nights Westenholz retained to the last his speculative freedom. Everything interested him, he could be just and even enthusiastic about impersonal things. I profited by this survival of clearness in his thought: he rejoiced in my philosophy, even if he could not assimilate it or live by it; but the mere idea of such a synthesis delighted him, and my *Realm of Truth* in particular aroused his intellectual enthusiasm. In his confusion he saw the possibility of clearness, and as his friend Reichhardt said, he became sympathetically *hell begeistert*, filled with inspired light.

We celebrate
his sister's
thirty-third
birthday.

If this cohabitation of profound moral troubles with speculative earnestness was characteristically German, so was the cohabitation of both with childish simplicity. I was told one morning that that day was Fräulein Mathilde's thirty-third birthday. Where should I go to get some flowers or bon-bons to offer her with my congratulations: embarrassed congratulations, because if she had completed another year of life and that were so much to the good, it was less so that she had already completed thirty-three of them. But no; it was Sunday, and all shops were closed. I was genuinely sorry, because I am naturally remiss at paying compliments and attentions and giving due presents, and when an occasion presents itself boldly, I am glad to be forced to do the right thing. "If you really want to give her a pleasant surprise, write her a birthday poem", said Westenholz, seeing my perplexity. So I retired for an hour to my room and produced some verses, in which I congratulated the poor, the Baronness, Albert, and their friends on the prospect of having the *good* Mathilde (for she wasn't beautiful) with them for another year. The verses were worthless, but they had enough foundation in truth to serve their purpose. Mathilde really was all goodness, as Albert was too, only that he had intellect and madness to complicate the goodness.

In the afternoon, after a solid early dinner at which the Baronness was wheeled in a hospital litter to the table (for she insisted that she was too ill to sit up), brother and sister put their heads together to decide how they should celebrate the occasion; and it was decided that we three should go to their old house in the city, and take the dolls and the doll-furniture out of the boxes, and arrange everything in the dolls' house just as it used to be. Their old house was that of their maternal grandfather, who had been Burghermaster of Hamburg, belonging now to an uncle who wasn't living there for the moment. It was in the old town, near one of the churches with a high green steeple, and itself lofty and gabled; but we hurried up many flights of stairs as if treading on forbidden ground: I should have liked to see the rooms, but foresaw the difficulties in opening windows and conciliating care-takers that would be involved in a visit of inspection, unauthorised by the owner; so that I too hurried guilty-like to the garret, under a vast pitched roof, where evidently we might forget that we were interlopers. The boxes were opened; the dolls, the furniture, the crockery, were all distributed among the rooms of the immense dolls' house, each precisely where it belonged. The names of the various dolls were recalled, and in rapid German that I wasn't expected to listen to, sundry comic incidents of childhood were referred to and enjoyed for the hundredth time. Then, dutifully, everything was buried again in the boxes, to be resurrected perhaps when Fräulein's thirty-three years should have become forty-five.

Varying conflicts between the heart and the intellect. This joy in simplicity, this nostalgia for childishness, in highly educated, rich, and terribly virtuous people surely is thoroughly German: and doesn't it mark some radical false turn, some organic impediment, in their history? But let me not generalise. Westenholz at any rate was avowedly morbid and abnormal; without being deformed, he had all the pathos and intensity that go with deformity; jealousy and vanity, in professing to judge and to dominate everything from above; great intellectual ardour and display of theory; with genuine delight in the simplest pleasures beneath, and temptation to the crudest vices. It would be a false diagnosis to call him an old child, a pedant whose brain had grown like a pumpkin, and left the heart rudimentary. His heart was not rudimentary, it was large and nobly developed; but the intellectual life accompanying it was not developed out of it but borrowed, foreign, imposed by alien circumstances and traditions; and for this reason, there was relief and joy in reverting from it to homely things. *Los von Rom* is a very different cry in Germany from what *No popery* was in England. In England the King, the prelates and the nobles felt ripe to be their own popes. They wished to graft their culture on their instincts, and their instincts were mature enough to breed a native culture, admirable in those matters that touched English life—the home, the feelings, sports, politics, and manners, trade also and colonial conquests, but fragmentary, poor and incoherent in speculative directions, precisely in proportion as they receded from the manly arts of the native man. But in Germany the expression of the native heart had remained rustic and violent; *los von Rom* was a disruptive cry, expressing in intellectuals an anarchistic impulse, and a rebellion against all control; whereas the princes and theologians and learned men who restrained that rebellion, and imposed a strict discipline on the people, imposed something alien and artificial, imposed officialism, pedantry, or insane vanity. The heart might be free from Rome, but was enslaved to something far poorer and more acrid; so that a return to the heart became a reversion to childhood or to rusticity.

XVIII

London

The desire to
see England
satisfied
at last.
The Germany of 1886 had liberated, it had not enamoured me; and at the age of twenty-three a young
man needs to be enamoured. A siren, however, was not
far off, across the North Sea. After our first semester at
Berlin, Strong and I decided to spend our holiday in England, and
took ship at Bremen for London. It was a nasty voyage in a smallish
German Lloyd steamer, an excellent cathartic to clear away all obstructions and leave a clean and keen appetite for something new.
Regarding England I had favourable preconceptions derived from my
father. It was in his opinion the leading country, the model country,
for the modern world; and although this eminence might be patriotically
claimed by Americans for America, it was not then possessed by their
country even in material things of importance; while in literature and
philosophy, as well as in the art of living, the autarchy of the New
World was that of the log-cabin: you might like roughing it and camping
in the woods, but that did not create a new civilisation.

In approaching England I felt the excitement of a child at the play,
before the curtain rises. I was about to open my eyes on a scene in
one sense familiar, from having heard and read so much about it.
There was keen intellectual curiosity to discover the fact and compare
it with my anticipations. There was my youthful hunger, still unap-
peased, for architectural effects, and picturesque scenes in general;
and there was a more recent interest, destined to grow gradually
stronger, in discovering and understanding human types, original or
charming persons. And where were these more likely to be found
than in England?

The English
a decent
people.
On our second evening from Bremen we had anchored
in the Thames and were to go ashore at Tilbury in the
morning. Meantime, the customs officers came aboard
to examine our papers and our luggage. We were almost the only
first-class passengers; and it was without the least hurry, and almost

in silence, that we laid our passports on the cabin table before the two quiet officials who had sat down there. Quiet they were, well-spoken, laconic, yet civil; half business-like and half deferential, as if in the first place they recognised us for gentlemen, and as if in general they were respectful towards other people's privacy and peace. Perfectly ordinary men like policemen; yet how different from any customs officials that I had ever come upon in Spain or America, in France or Germany! What *decent* officials! They didn't seem to suspect us of lying or cheating, and showed no tendency to brow-beat or deceive us with rigmarole and loudness. A national note, firmness beneath simplicity; a *decent* people, not very perceptive, a little stolid, decidedly limited, but sound, trained, running easily in the national harness. And this among the common people, when not misled. I was glad of this first impression; and it was curiously confirmed in my first journey to Oxford, in a third-class carriage. It happened to be full, five persons on a side, yet nobody said a word; or if any word passed from one to another, it was so brief, and so low in tone, as to disturb nobody else. Not genial, other nations might say, not friendly or human; but I felt that it was truly friendly, since it was considerate; it showed aptitude for getting on together, political aptitude, precisely because it let everyone alone, allowed them their place, and didn't blame them for existing even if their existence were a bit inconvenient.

London streets in 1887. So much for public manners, the best in the world; but soon I had a glimpse of the private feelings that might go with those manners in humble and ordinary people. We went to a boarding-house that Strong had heard of in Notting Hill, a remote place for the sightseer, but correspondingly cheap and *decent*, besides having the incidental advantage of involving long drives on the tops of 'busses, often (since we started at the start) on the front seat, only a little above and behind the driver's box, with whom a word might be exchanged occasionally, and whose powerful horses and skilful driving through the dense traffic might be admired. It was six miles, an hour's drive, to the Bank; and in that cool misty season, with the sun high, but coppery and shining dubiously through the grey atmosphere, the swarming city, still moderately uniform in the character and the height of buildings, offered a scene of inexhaustible interest, justifying the humour of Dickens and Cruikshank, as well as the gentility of Thackeray. Everything seemed ready to be etched, from the broken-down old women in black bonnets selling matches at the corners, to the black and white harmonies of St. Paul's and the churches in the Strand, poetic to see looming in the distance, and interesting to study on a nearer approach. Yet here doubts began to assail the mind, concerning the solidity of England in subtler matters of taste and allegiance, doubts confirmed by the then brand-new Law-Courts. This Italian architecture of Wren's, this Ruskinian Gothic, were foreign here: they were whims, they were fashions, they were essentially shams. But the function of shams in English society is a large subject, and I shall revert to it often.

Moral atmosphere of a Notting Hill boarding-house. At table in Notting Hill one of the inevitable solitary elderly ladies explained to us how much they all loved Longfellow: he was a household poet in England no less than in America. I replied that I was not surprised to hear it; but that in America his vogue was beginning to pass away; at least we poets, at Harvard, never read anything written in America except our own compositions. As for English poets we admitted nobody less revolutionary than Swinburne or less pessimistic than Matthew Arnold. If the lady had been an American and younger, she would have said I was horrid; being English and old she silently thought so, and merely repeated gently, that in England they loved Longfellow best.

There was also at table a modest well-set-up young man, a clerk, who betrayed some interest in philosophy or, as I soon gathered, in religion. On that footing we became friends at once: I have always found it easy to form casual friendships, especially with Englishmen. He said he belonged to the Church of the Apostles, commonly called Irvingites. Should I like to go to one of their services? Very much: and on the next Sunday he conducted me to a church like a Roman basilica, with an apse, quite orthodox mosaics, and a semicircle of living apostles in stalls, wearing white smocks, and looking like a row of butchers, except that butchers seldom have long beards. The sermon informed us that it was not necessary to die. The Day of Judgment had long since come, and people were constantly being caught up to heaven alive, perhaps as they walked the streets, or through the chimney. My friend gave me no further evidence of this phenomenon; but I saw (which was what interested me) that for him these absurdities furnished a happy interlude in a drab life, a peep-hole into fairyland, a little secret, unsuspected by the world, to keep up his self-respect, and cast a ray of supernatural hope into that small room in the third floor back, which might prove any day a jumping off place for a flight to heaven. By some chance his need of faith had attached him to the

Irvingites; had his connections and education been more fortunate he might have become a High Anglican or Catholic; and his case showed, as it were under the microscope, the mechanism of conversion in higher spheres.

I take lodgings in Jermyn Street, Saint James's. After two or three weeks at Notting Hill, spent in seeing everything in London that the guidebook recommended, Strong unexpectedly announced that he was obliged to join some family friends in Paris. He had evidently fresh money to spend, or was invited: I was not able or inclined to accompany him. Paris suggested a different side of life, and greater expenses; besides, I was intent on continuing my explorations in England and extending them at least to Oxford. Strong had dutifully kept me in the strait path of the earnest sightseer, visiting historic spots and notable monuments in the order of their importance and instructiveness, from the Tower to Madame Tussaud's. But when I was left alone, I began to live on a different plan, which I have followed when possible in all my wanderings. I moved to lodgings in Jermyn Street, Saint James's, No. 87, a house to which I was faithful for more than twenty-five years, and abandoned only bowing to *force majeure*. First Miss Bennett, the genial motherly landlady died; then her younger sister, a widow, married Colonel Sandys, who had long occupied the first floor. On arriving one year I noticed a change in the aspect of the house. The front door was painted a well-varnished dark green, with shining brass knocker and door knobs; there was a fresh thick door-mat, and when I rang the bell, though the man was the same familiar valet, he seemed much more spruce, and even a bit embarrassed in his conspicuously clean linen. The same lady, he explained, still lived here, but the house was no longer an hotel. And he politely presented me, on a solid silver tray, the letters that had arrived for me. There was nothing to do but to look foolish, and say, "Oh, indeed—I see—thank you", and get again into my taxi—it was already the age of taxis—and vaguely tell the driver to go somewhere else—anywhere—to the British Hotel a few doors beyond. But neither at the British Hotel nor elsewhere did I ever feel at home again in London lodgings; and this circumstance contributed to make my stay there always shorter and shorter.

My life there in later years. Miss Bennett's was not a luxurious house, and I never took more than a single room there, and breakfast; yet though not a very profitable guest, I was a constant one, and always seemed to be welcome. I would even leave a hat-box there from year to year, as a sort of pledge, to get rid of the useless burden of a top-hat in the rest of my journeys. The full savour of the London of my youth, in the 1880's and 1890's, clings to my memories of Jermyn Street. I usually came down at nine or half-past to breakfast in a small back room on the ground floor, always on bacon and eggs and *The Morning Post*. Sometimes another lodger would be there too, but not often; and then we politely ignored each other's presence, concentrating each on his own tea-pot and toast-rack and dish of marmalade, and on his own newspaper, which in the other man's case was likely to be *The Times*. In the early days I preferred *The Standard*, because it was the Anglican clerical paper, opening to me the side of English life that interested me most; and when *The Standard* stopped publication, I took up *The Morning Post*, until that too succumbed to the flood of vulgar journalism. After that, I subscribed to no English newspaper; the continental press could inform me sufficiently about gross events, and I could always procure single copies of *The Times*, if there was anything of special importance.

The fire, in Miss Bennett's breakfast room, was the only common interest between the other lodger and me. Neither of us would attempt to monopolise it; we both kept at the distance that good form required. It would have been beneath us to huddle up close to it, as if we were ignominiously suffering from cold; yet we took good care not to retreat to such a distance as to abdicate the right to the best place, if we had come early and secured it. The best place then exalted the person who occupied it, and to preserve his Rights had become his Duty. I was being initiated into the secret of British politics.

Daylight aspects and night sounds. In those days Jermyn Street preserved the character of a quiet and correct street in the heart of Saint James's. No. 87 was directly opposite the pleasant red brick church with its pleasant trees, that made a green landmark, and with the pleasant broad face and pleasant chimes of its clock, that told you the hours. At night, lying warm in bed with the window open, I also liked to hear the patter, as of a child's drum, on the probably wet asphalt, as each hansom-cab, noiseless as to its wheels but *quadrupedante sonitu* as to its horse's hoofs, drove up the street, and drove away again, in a brisk diminuendo.

The spirit of London as a spectacle. It was precisely to the inveterate stranger in me that London had mightily appealed. All those hollow principles and self-indulgent whims of a decadent age had merged in the English gentleman into good form and sly humour; and in the Cockney they were reflected in his goodnatured derision and comfortable jollity. The spirit of London seemed remarkably mellow and rich in experience; for that very reason leisurely, gently mocking, not miscellaneously eager and hurried, like New York, nor false, cynical, and covetous, like Paris. Not that great things have happened in London; it has no such memories as Rome or Florence; but being a commercial city, a port, and the centre of a colonial empire, it has encyclopedic contacts, and means of knowing the world at a distance without being much disturbed by it in its own back-parlour. There is therefore balance in its omniscience, and a wise perspective in its interests. Experience fosters both affection and unconcern; and we are lucky when the affection settles down upon what is near, and the unconcern upon what is distant and irremediable, with a subtle amusement at both. This seemed to me to happen in the typical Londoner, and it made him an engaging person.

London had always responded to a rather youthful interest of mine, the interest in streets, in clothes, in manners, in curious architecture; also to my pleasure in casual acquaintances and small explorations. These human episodes enlivened the landscape and made particular spots memorable that would otherwise have been merged indistinguishably in the motley scene: yet it was the aerial landscape, always evanescent and always picturesque, that fed the spirit, as the cool moist air expanded the lungs. I loved the Parks, — St. James's with its suggestions of by-gone fashions and a smaller town; Green Park, spacious and empty, like a country common; and Hyde Park above all, with its fashionable pedestrians and riders, its horses and carriages, and its band concerts; all easy to turn one's back on, for the sake of a long solitary walk. Yet these pleasures presupposed summer and fine weather. It was a setting for a holiday, not for a life. I never studied in London or read in the British Museum (as I did in the Bodleian) or gathered books, or made lasting friends. I visited nobody, not even the Sturgis connection; I was, and I liked to remain, an unrecognised wanderer.

The London stage.   Even the theatres seldom attracted me. British plays are anodyne, transparently moral or sentimental or intellectual; that is to say, not spontaneous products of the imagination. I think it must have been Protestantism that so completely extinguished Elizabethan genius. When the theatres were reopened at the Restauration, writers and audiences were utterly cut off from the healthy current of national life, and from the great classic and poetic tradition. They cared only for wit and satire and the evil pleasure of scandal. Now the wish to be edified has been added; but that limits the already slight range of the plays, without infusing into them anything poetical. The acting, too, is awkward and uninspired; the players are interested in themselves and not in their parts, and so are the audiences. Everything is modish, affected, trivial, and amateurish. Earlier, in the days of Irving and Terry, the stage production had been an object in itself. Elaborate scenery and costumes were designed to bring some historic epoch to light. Taste was pre-Raphaelite; the stage resembled the Arundel prints after Pinturicchio that I had had in my rooms in Brattle Street. That fashion had passed when I was much in London, but the taste had not died in me, when the Russian ballet made its appearance. Here imagination and passion had fallen back upon first principles. Aestheticism had become absolute and violent, the appeal to the exotic and dream-like scorned to be accurate or instructive and was content to be vivid. Nor was elegance excluded, but it figured only as one *genre* among many, just as it does in Shakespeare and in real life. Delicacy was cultivated in its place, yet the way was left open in every direction to strength, to passion, to nature, and to fancy. I wonder if Shakespeare could not be turned into Russian ballets to advantage: or into a kind of opera-ballet, in which the more important speeches could be introduced in recitative into the music. Aristophanes also might lend himself to such treatment.

Nature, comfort, and liberty preferred to art. It was only on rare evenings in London that I dressed or dined with friends or went to any show. I tasted the specific quality of the place better when I strolled about alone, dined in some grill room or in some restaurant in Soho, or walked out over the bridges to watch the evening glow reflected on the river. England preserves the softness and verdure of the country even in the city; and London, the densest of Babylons, is everywhere turned into a landscape by the mist, by the cloudracks, by the docks and shipping towards the East, by the green reaches, the fields, the boating crowds towards the West. It thins out and becomes rural imperceptibly in its immense suburbs, and not always vulgarly; there are royal preserves and stately seats in all directions, Woolwich steps down grandly to the sea, and Kensington Palace and Hampton Court lead nobly towards Windsor Castle. This instinct to merge town and country in one limitless park, and never to lose sight of a green field, an overhanging tree, or an impenetrable hedgerow, no doubt renounces architecture on the grand scale. The city remains a conglomeration of accidents, of incongruous whims and private rights huddled together. The roads turn and wind round the freehold cottages and jealously fenced gardens, and comfort is never sacrificed to symmetry. Yet in neglecting grandeur the Englishman remains jealous of his dignity, and also of his privacy. He plants his neighbours out, if he possibly can; the comforts he exacts are simple; too much luxury would be incompatible with quietness and liberty. Even in the great respect that he shows for wealth and station he honours freedom rather than power. Your rich man can do as he likes, and can live as he chooses. Then the liberty that is a sham in public becomes a reality in private.

The commercial essence of London. To the classic mind landscapes are always landscapes with figures. Even the desert, the sea, or the stars draw all their magic from the solitude or the secret companionship that the soul feels in their presence. So the aspects of a town borrow their quality from the life that they suggest, market, temple, fortress, or garden. London is essentially a commercial city. Everything about it hangs upon that fact, even the golden mist and the black fog that make its beauty and its monstrosity; for they are effects of occupying a watery place near the corner of an island, ideal for shipping and in the midst of sea routes, and of being able at the same time to burn prodigious quantities of soft coal. Civilisations and towns created by commerce may grow indefinitely, since they feed on a toll levied on everything transportable; yet they are secondary. However much they may collect and exhibit the riches of the world they will not breed anything original. Their individuality and excellence, no less in Venice than in London, will be the fruit of accidents, of converging influences and borrowed traditions. If an Englishman set out to be a *great* man, a genius, a saint, or a responsible monarch, the devil would soon pocket him. It is only the *rich* Englishman that can truly prosper in England. Like the Lord Mayor of London he can dress up in a traditional costume, and receive Royalty and all other grand people at his feasts. He can repeat the consecrated platitudes, and drink the approved wines; and in his hours of obscurity and thrifty labour, he can revise accounts, poke his library fire, drink tea with his buxom wife, and send his sons to Eton or Harrow. Commercial communities in this way accumulate great treasures and hand down admirable institutions; yet in them the whole exists only for the sake of the parts and their greatness is only littleness multiplied. They become museums, immense hostleries, perpetual fairs. Society will be nowhere brisker or more various. Everything that money can buy will be at the command of those that have money. The dandies and snobs will lead the aristocracy; fashion will nowhere be more splendid and more respected, and misery nowhere more squalid. The metropolis will overflow with life gathered from the four quarters of the heavens; it will never be a fountain of life.

As to the fish swimming about in this whirlpool, I could infer from my American experience of a society even more commercial and casual, that they had individual souls and personal histories; and I had learned in Dickens something about such souls in the lower classes, the Sam Wellers and the Mrs. Gamps, and among the merchants and lawyers, for whom London was all in all. These are not classes in which a stray foreigner like me would be likely to make acquaintances; and a metropolis is not like a ship or a college, where prolonged contact with the same persons discloses their individualities even to the least sympathetic stranger. Yet in the classes with which intercourse was easier for me, I did pick up various acquaintances; and some of those figures have remained pleasantly painted in my memory.

Life of pleasure in the West End. One day in Jermyn Street, when I had breakfasted in bed and came down nicely dressed about noon, fat Miss Bennett, who was arranging the flowers in a row of little vases in the narrow entry, smiled in her motherly way as she made room for me to pass, and said: "You have been doing the young lady this morning, sir." Yes: though I was no longer a young man (this was in 1901) I had had a momentary lapse into fashionable life, and was going to take a turn in the Park before lunching at Hatchett's; and I confided to her that the previous evening I had been dining at the Savoy with two young officers of the Guards. It had been as far as possible from a debauch—I will describe it presently—but it had thrown me back into the mood of 1897, when I had known a knot of young men about town, acquaintances made in Cambridge; not all English, for there was an Australian and a Frenchman, and for that reason all the more knowing and entertaining. At that time (in my holiday year at King's and in Italy) I had been wide awake; but now I had entered a somnambulist tunnel, when the engines worked and the wheels made a more furious noise than ever, but when the spirit was suspended on the thought. When shall we come out again into the light and air? The two Guardsmen brought a glimpse into the open, not promising but suggestive. They knew nobody in my world,

I knew nobody in theirs. Yet I, at least, was never more in my element than when I was far from myself. How did I know them?

Two old Etonians. We were waiting on the pier at Southampton in the previous September for the German liner that was to convey us to America. Fog had kept her from making the port on time. In standing about the steamer-office, waiting for information, I noticed two young Englishmen, tall, well dressed, good-naturedly accepting the accident of being sent to dine and to spend the night at a local hotel, and being correspondingly delayed in their arrival in New York. They evidently didn't care. They were not going to America on business: I wondered what they were going for. For nothing, perhaps, to spend the time, to see the Rocky Mountains, or to look for heiresses. There was an air about them, of being thoroughly equipped, perfectly trained and hardened, thoroughly competent to do anything, and not knowing what on earth to do.

Amenities at sea. The next day on board, when the chief steward had found a place for me in the dining-room, there were the two young men, directly opposite me at the same table. Their casual conversation was not audible to me: they were English. After a day or two, however, in passing the mustard or the salt, we began to exchange a few phrases, and gradually came to joining forces on deck or in the smoking-room. The smoking-room was my place of refuge in transatlantic steamers, when I was not walking on the lower deck, which was clear of chairs, nearer the water, and comparatively deserted, allowing freedom of movement as well as of mind. When I had taken my exercise, and wished to sit down, I looked for a comfortable corner in the smoking-room. The smoking-room was the one place sure to be well-ventilated; there were deep leather chairs or benches where I could read at ease or even write in a notebook. The crowd and the hubbub didn't in the least disturb me, since I wasn't asked to attend to it. Here I could have tea, and here sometimes my two new friends would join me, and would explain incidentally that they were simply on a tour, curious about America and apparently entertained by what I said of it. They were eventually coming to Boston, and I rashly offered to show them the sights of Harvard.

Nothing to show at Harvard. Rashly, I say, because when they turned up a month or two later, it puzzled me to think what the sights of Harvard were. These young men didn't want to see the Stadium (then a novelty) nor the glass flowers. The Yard was leafless, muddy, and at its ugliest, and I no longer lived there but in Brattle Street, not in rooms worth showing. Nor had I any longer any interesting friends that I could have asked to meet them at tea. So I frankly confessed my predicament and took them to see Memorial Hall with the panorama (and smell) of a hundred tables and a thousand men at dinner—for it was already six o'clock. They said it looked like Sandhurst. Evening had already come, and there was nothing to do but to walk back to Main Street and to the electric car that would take them back to Boston. By way of apology for this futile afternoon, I sent two books to their ship to entertain them on their homeward voyage: my *Interpretations of Poetry and Religion*, then just out, for A, the one who seemed more intellectual, and Flandrau's *Diary of a Freshman* for the other, B, who was apparently simpler and younger. I knew that the first book was too serious and the second too frivolous, but perhaps between them they might represent the winds blowing at Harvard.

Nothing to show me in London. When I dined with them the next summer in London, I felt that they had asked me to the Savoy because they were in much the same predicament that I had been in when I took them to the gallery of Memorial Hall: they wanted to be civil to me, but they had to invent a way. The food was excellent—all cold, by a caprice of B's—and they spied well-known people at some of the other tables, whose names they whispered with smiles: but they might have dined more pleasantly and cheaply by themselves at the Guards' Club, to which strangers were not admitted. The evening was clear, and they proposed walking back to Pall Mall, exactly what my instinct would have prompted me to do. This undercurrent of common tastes was what established pleasant relations between them and me, in spite of completely different backgrounds. When we reached Pall Mall, I knew they were making for their club; I therefore said good night and turned up through St. James's Square, reflecting on what a tax it is to entertain strangers, even for people enjoying every advantage in the heart of London. Besides, three, except among very intimate friends, is not a propitious number for conversation: it renders sympathies shy to show themselves and interesting subjects hard to follow up. To cement a new friendship, especially between foreigners or persons of a different social world, a spark with which both were secretly charged must fly from person to person, and cut across the accidents of place and time. No such spark had seemed to pass between these young men and me; and yet I was sure, especially in the case of B, that a latent sympathy existed unexpressed: and the proof of it appeared not many days later. B wrote asking me to dine with him again, without dressing, in the most singular of places for dining—in the Bank of England. He happened to be for the moment the officer commanding the guard at that place; and this officer had the privilege of inviting one person to dine with him, and of drinking one bottle of claret and one of port. Would I come?

Dinner at the Bank of England. It was raining hard on the appointed evening and when I told my cabby to go to the Bank—the Bank of England—the fellow almost laughed in my face, but in a moment recovered his professional gravity, and observed a bit quizzically: "Bank, sir? Bank will be closed, sir", evidently doubting whether I was a little mad or excessively green. I said I knew it was closed to the public, but went there by special appointment; and I jumped in resolutely, and closed the doors. My man started, driving at first rather slowly, but being once in for it, gained courage, and drove smartly the rest of the way. When I had got out and paid him, I noticed that he lingered a moment. His curiosity wasn't satisfied, without seeing whether people ever got into the Bank of England at eight in the evening.

The policeman at the door, on the contrary, understood everything, said "This way, sir", affably, and hurried me across the court faster than I could have wished, because the scene was wonderful. In those days the court you first entered was surrounded by pavilions no higher than the blank outer wall; various cross-lights from archways, doors, and windows were caught and reflected by the wet pavements and casual puddles, or lit up bright patches of scarlet or brass or shining white belts in the groups of soldiers, hard to distinguish under that black sky, who lounged in the doors or huddled for shelter under the eaves. I thought of Rembrandt's *Night Watch*; but this scene was more formless yet more alive. Here everything trembled, water trickled and sparkled over all; and in the darkness itself there was a sense of suspended animation among ambiguous shadows that would yield for a moment to recognisable reality, when a face lifted or an arm moved or a voice spoke some commonplace word.

The room into which I was ushered had a dingy Dickensian look of solidity grown old-fashioned and a bit shabby. There was a walnut mantelpiece with a small clock and two candlesticks without candles; heavy black walnut chairs, with horse-hair bottoms, and a table set unpretentiously, with thick white plates and thick glasses. But there was a pleasant fire in the grate, and the rather superannuated butler served us an excellent absolutely English dinner: mock-turtle soup, boiled halibut with egg sauce; roast mutton; gooseberry tart and cream, and anchovies on toast; together with the two bottles of wine already mentioned. Too much food, you might say; but in the English climate, distressing to the lazy but friendly to the active man, after a long day of pacing the streets in rain and shine as if you were pacing a deck, all that food was appetising. The old butler knew that it was just right, whatever notions the young officers of today might have got into their heads. One had to put up with them; but he was conscious of the whole authority and weight of the Bank of England backing him up. Where would the Army be without the Bank? Nowhere.

The troubles of youth. The good claret and port were left entirely to me. My poor friend was under the doctor's care and could drink only milk. He seemed very young and very dejected, in his white flannel shirt and sporting jacket, while his red and gold tunic and his huge bearskin lay on a chair, waiting to be put on at eleven o'clock for the evening inspection, when I should have to leave. He told me frankly the cause of his indisposition, and we had a friendly philosophical talk about the troubles of youth—the chief of them being that youth cannot last. This fatality casts its shadow before it and makes the young dissatisfied with youth, although what will follow will probably be no better. My two Guardsmen were apparently thinking of resigning their commissions; something that surprised me a little in the case of A, who I knew had made a special study of gunnery. As for B, soldiering was what any obligation is for the vaguely young— a constraint with some compensations. He was bored in the army: but the devil of it was, what to do afterwards. Pity he hadn't found an American heiress; he would have been quite happy as a country gentleman, with nice horses and nice children. Perhaps he would have preferred an English heiress, who wouldn't have wanted to rush back to New York every winter; or perhaps he was already in love with someone who was not an heiress, and who drove him to foolish adventures in the vain effort to forget her. I was sorry for the poor chap. Most enviable of men, I should have thought him, in his person and surroundings; yet for that very reason he seemed to have no future. The garden that had bred him, having seen him bloom, had no further use for him. It is indeed in the nature of existence to undermine its best products, and also its worst. This may be an acceptable reflection to the philosopher, who dwells in the eternal, but not for the fatted calf being led to the slaughter.

To the slaughter he was being led without suspecting it, like any placid wreathed bullock marching to the sacrifice. His generation had just endured the carnage of the Boer War, but that of 1914 was approaching. After all this was the traditional calling of his class, but in a simpler, smaller, clearer phase of society, when there could be chivalry in the master, and devotion in the servant. Now all *that* was outmoded, and the ethics of it sounded hollow. The gentleman no longer felt at home in the saddle or in the field; he was no longer the ruler of his land and his country: he was a tax-payer submerged and forced to sell his estates by the very war that he helped to wage. Nor could he escape by becoming a plain citizen. Slaughter would continue, slaughter now by the indistinguishable million. It would be a question of victims without a vocation to die, conscripts and mechanics buried by chance in an avalanche of missiles.

Noblesse oblige. Our conversation was interrupted by a knock at the door. The sergeant came to report that one of the men had been taken ill. "Get a cab—a four wheeler would be better,"— my friend said thoughtfully, "take him to the barracks and bring back another man", and he gave the sergeant some money for the fares. "Doesn't the government", I asked, "pay little items of this sort?" "Oh, I suppose I might charge it, but it's hardly worth while. It doesn't happen very often." He spoke in his habitual tone, half resignation half amusement; but I suspected an impulse beneath to look after his men personally, and to let them feel that the imperturbable air of an officer didn't exclude a discerning good will towards his soldiers. The ethos of an aristocratic society, I perceived, is of a very high order. It involves imaginative sympathy with those who are not like oneself, loyalty, charity and self knowledge.

It seemed a good moment to say goodnight, without waiting for the hour when I should be asked to leave. The rain had ceased; many of the lights in the court had been put out; the place seemed emptier and more ordinary than before. When the ponderous doors had been closed after me, I looked at my watch. It was half past ten. The pavement was wet, but I had on thick boots. Why not walk back the whole length of Fleet Street and the Strand? If I had melancholy thoughts, the cool moist air and the pleasant exercise would transform them. Scattered lights revealed only nebulous spaces, as the stars do in the sky, save where a few stragglers loitered in the glare of the

theatre entrances. Morally all things are neutral in themselves. It is
we that bathe them in whatever emotion may be passing through us.
That singular evening at the Bank of England remains for me a picturesque image, lurid, cynical, yet on the whole happy.

A second chance meeting.   Thirteen years later, in July 1914, I was on my way
for a short visit to England with a return ticket to Paris
in my pocket, good for three months. As soon as I got
into the boat at Calais, I prudently hastened to have a bite in the
cabin before we left the dock; that, with a useful medicine that I had
learned to take, would help me to weather the passage. I was having
my cold meat and beer at one end of the empty table, when a steward
came to ask me if I was Mr. Santayana — or something that represented
that sound. The gentleman at the other end had sent him to inquire.
I looked up, and in spite of astigmatism and nearsightedness in me
and the ravages of ten years in him, I recognised my young Guardsman.
I nodded assent to him, and immediately gulped down the rest of my
beer and went over to say how-do-you-do. But I couldn't stop; he
knew I was a bad sailor; and I must go and find a sheltered spot on
deck. I would look for him there later, weather permitting, or in any
case at Dover. But I didn't look for him: on the contrary I chose a
nook on the lower deck, in the second-class portion, wrapped myself
up in great-coat and rug, and weathered the passage undisturbed and
without accident. At Dover, however, I found him standing before the
train that was to take us to Charing Cross. We exchanged a few words.
He was going home, he said, to rejoin his regiment. He was with
ladies. The ladies were already in the carriage, and looked as if they
might be his mother and sister or his wife and mother-in-law. In any
case, they would certainly prefer to travel by themselves, and I discreetly
got into another compartment.

Decorum est pro patria mori.   We had each other's addresses. Perhaps if I had known
I was to remain in England for five years, or if he had
known that he was to die in five months, it might have
occurred to one of us to write; but neither of us did so. It was better
not to force a renewal of our acquaintance. Our paths were divergent,
neither of us was any longer young, and it had been his youth and
that very divergence that for me had made our acquaintance interesting.
There would no longer be anything strange in his being unhappy. He
had lost his good looks and his mocking pleasure at the ways of the
world. Although still a soldierly figure and distinguished, he was now

yellow, battered, and preoccupied. I rather suspect a wife and children didn't exist; if they did, his end, for them, may have been a tragedy. But for a bachelor tired of knocking about and doing nothing in particular, a gallant death was a solution. It placed him becomingly in the realm of truth and crowned the nonchalance of his boyhood.

The first Zeppelin raid. It was on this trip, in July 1914, that I found 87, Jermyn Street, "no longer an hotel"; a trivial circumstance in itself that still marked the end of my pleasant days in London. I was there henceforth only on the wing, as at a centre from which to visit my friends in the country, or go for a season to Oxford or Cambridge. I was at Cambridge, at the Red Lion, in the first days of that August, when war broke out; and I was again in London, at rooms I often took afterwards at 3, Ryder Street, when one evening, as I was going to bed, I heard a great crash. They must have dropped a heavy tray of dishes in the pantry, I thought: but presently came another crash very like the first, and then other detonations: it was the first Zeppelin raid. I put on again such clothes as I had taken off, and went down into the streets. It was not late, hardly eleven o'clock; and the people about were naturally excited and communicative. I went as far as Piccadilly Circus, from whence I could see, towards the east, the glare of distant fires. One corner shop in the Circus had been smashed: I suppose that was the first great noise that I had taken for broken crockery. The next evening many people waited late in Hyde Park, to see if there would be another raid; but nothing occurred. Nevertheless here was now another reason for not staying in town, and I soon moved to Oxford, favourably placed, from the point of view of safety, in the very middle of England, not yet an industrial town, and the proverbial seat of quietness, religion, and study.

I renounce all thought of living in London. The moment when I lost my pleasure in London was the very moment when I was at last free and might have settled down there, as would be natural for an unattached man who writes in the English language. Moreover, unlike most foreigners, I was perfectly happy in the English climate and the English way of living. They were a great relief from America in softness and dignity, and from the Continent in comfort and privacy. Yet a somewhat mysterious contrary force prevented me from making the attempt. Perhaps it was my age. I was fifty, and the prospect backward had begun decidedly to gain on the prospect forward. For the future I desired nothing fixed, no place in society, no circle of prescribed friends and engagements. Decent human relations, certainly, with whatever persons I might come across, which might include stray poets or philosophers, or agreeable ladies, for instance, like "Elizabeth". But they should come and go, and I should be free always to change the scene and to move into another sphere. For constant company I had enough, and too much, with myself. A routine had established itself in my day, which I could carry with me wherever I went; it gave me abundance of private hours, and for relief and refreshment, I liked solitude in crowds, meals in restaurants, walks in public parks, architectural rambles in noble cities. To have become simply an old bachelor in London would have been dismal and monotonous. Acquaintance with varied and distinguished people, which London might have afforded, didn't in the least tempt me. The intellectual world of my time alienated me intellectually. It was a Babel of false principles and blind cravings, a zoological garden of the mind, and I had no desire to be one of the beasts. I wished to remain a visitor, looking in at the cages. This could be better done by reading people's books than by frequenting their society.

Mrs. Arthur Strong's husband. With few exceptions, nobody of consequence in London knew of my existence. Even my publishers, except old Mr. Dent, remained unknown to me, as Scribner had remained unknown in New York. I can remember only one literary man that (through Loeser, I believe) became a sort of friend of mine: and then it was his wife rather than himself that was eventually well known to the international public: but my London friend was her husband, Arthur Strong. He was at that time librarian to the House of Lords and was believed to get up the facts for the Prince of Wales' speeches. He had been originally librarian to the Duke of Devonshire, with whose house he was said to be connected somehow *sub rosa*: and his wife's origin also was spoken of in whispers, no doubt baseless, to the effect that she was a daughter of Napoleon the Third.

Her aspect. She was a large woman, with bold pseudo-classic features, like a late-Roman statue of Niobe; and when I saw her in their house in London, she looked like a figure by Burne-Jones that had walked out of the canvass: great heavy eyes, a big nose, a short upper lip, and full richly curving lips, over a conspicuous round chin. But the most characteristic thing about her was the neck, long, columnar, and extremely convex in the throat, as if she habitually yearned forward and upward at once. She was also, at that time, pre-Raphaelite in dress. I remember her one day at luncheon in green cotton brocade, with a broad lace collar, like a bib, drooping over it. She was silent, and let her husband talk. Perhaps her thoughts were far away from him and from me. She was destined to become a Catholic and an authority in the history of Christian art, especially Roman archeology of the early centuries: and when I came across her once at the Berensons' in Florence, she did not recognise me or seem to remember that I had several times been her guest in London.

His mind. With Arthur Strong's mind I felt a decided sympathy. He was very learned in important but remote matters, such as Arabic literature, and his central but modest position in the great world gave him a satirical insight into affairs, and he summed up his inner solitude in pungent maxims. He reminded me of my father. Through the Moors he had good knowledge of Spain also: and he said something about the Spanish mind that has given me food for reflection. "The Spaniard", he said, "respects only one thing, and that is—", and he raised his fore-finger, pointing to heaven. There is no power but Allah: he is omnificent, and all appearances and all wills are nought. It is quite true that no genuine or reflective person in Spain trusts anybody or is proud of himself. He may be vain and punctilious, but that is play-acting: he thinks that pose is set down for him in his rôle: but inwardly he knows that he is dust. This is the insight that I express by saying to myself that the only authority in existence is the *authority of things*. I like the irony and the blessedness of this: that since only *things* have any authority there is, *morally*, no authority at all, and the spirit is free in its affections. Is this what the Moslems really feel? At any rate something keeps them (and me) from hurrying and fussing and being surprised. It is better to put up with things than to be responsible for them. We may leave responsibility, like vengeance, to God who made us and made the world and seems not to be disturbed at the result.

America judged by inapplicable standards. At the antipodes of this subject lay another that Arthur Strong sometimes touched upon: America. After discovering tentatively that I had no illusions in that direction, he would say quietly, but incisively, "America is the worst thing there is." I think he had never been in America and judged it only by its influence, which from the point of view of the House of Lords or of Moslem quietism is certainly devastating. But influence is something accidental and extraneous: it depends on the existence, sensibility, and native direction of the outsider. You might be perfect in yourself, and be the worst of influences upon all the interests that your perfection excluded. Arthur Strong was extremely sensitive, a sort of aged Lionel Johnson; and sensitive Englishmen in those days, while they began to feel the influence of America physically, simply detested it morally. They did not perceive how much their own influence on other nations was of the same sort. They only felt how utterly the dignity and sweetness of English life would be lost if, as seemed too possible, it should be Americanised. Therefore America seemed to them the worst thing in the world, while it seemed the best thing in the world to its own inhabitants.

Arthur Strong was sallow, small, and thin. He did not feel the perennial elasticity and resilience of nature, and the adaptability of mind to matter, whatsoever form matter may take. He feared that the cause of mind might be a lost cause. Americans, who know how to keep their organisms sound, as military and commercial Englishmen do also, have no such fear. They assume that the appropriate form of mind will follow automatically. Perhaps they possess that form of mind already, and see no use in any other. Why should the Arthur Strongs object?

Logan Pearsall Smith's family. There was another member of the intelligentsia in London with whom later I sometimes discussed this subject. It preoccupied him intensely; and though his judgments were deliberately good natured, I think he suffered from being an American as from an incurable disease. Of late years he has explained himself very well in his memoirs, entitled *Unforgotten Years*. I came upon him from two sides: Bertie Russell had married one of his sisters, and Berenson eventually married the other. It was Bertie that first introduced me to his wife's family, Quakers from Philadelphia long resident in England. In the name of his parents-in-law he wrote asking me to come to Friday's Hill, a place they had taken in Haslemere. I went, and found myself in an odd society. Old Mr. Smith, prosperous and proprietor of a thriving factory, had been also a Quaker preacher, and no less successful in saving souls than in making money; but, alas, in the midst of his apostolate he had lost his faith, and was at a loss how to reply to his trustful converts when they came to him for further guidance along the narrow path. "Don't tell Mrs. Smith," he said to me while showing me his garden, "but I am not a Christian at all. I am a Buddhist." And he pointed to what he called his Bo Tree, a great oak, in the midst of which he had had a glass house constructed. We climbed the ladder into it, a single small chamber with a black horsehair lounge and a small bookcase, filled with little old-fashioned

American books, among which I spied *Prue and I,* a novel by our "Aunt Sarah's" son-in-law, George William Curtis. I had expected the Dhammapada or the Upanishads. Vain flight of the American puritan to softer climates! He carries his horizon with him, and remains rooted at home.

Mrs. Smith too had been a preacher, and she remained a Quaker in as much as she continued to advocate simplicity of life and to call her children "thee"; and although she had abandoned the belief in hell, she went on preaching and feeling the immense importance of rescuing oneself from perdition: for as she wisely thought, there were bad enough hells on earth from which people needed to be saved. However, with a resignation that had a touch of defiance and warning in it, she put up with the unregenerate views of her children, and of the world at large.

Hybrid marriages.   It was strange to see Bertie, and even his brother, who turned up one day for luncheon, in that American Quaker family, and to hear those girls speak of the latter as *Frank,* which I never heard any of his friends or his wives do. But the Russells never knew themselves or their proper place in the world: that was a part of their mixture of genius and folly. I myself felt out of my element in the Smith family, yet was destined to come upon them all my life long in various ways. They not unnaturally thought of me among their class of expatriate Americans and members of the Intelligentsia: only Mrs. Berenson, who had motherly insights and had been married to an Irish Catholic, understood me a little, and perceived how unwillingly and deceptively I had come to fall under those categories. However, I have much to thank the Smiths for. They formed a lively band in the carnival, and led me into other bands in the masquerade, which I should hardly have joined of my own initiative.

"Michael Field".   At Haslemere, for instance, they took me to visit "Michael Field", whose identity and whose poems I had never heard of. Michael Field was a pseudonym for two ladies, aunt and niece, who were linked together by the tenderest affection and by a common inspiration of the classic Muse. They had been forewarned, they may have read up my poetry expressly: in any case, they awaited me as if I had been Orpheus approaching lyre in hand towards their bower. The aunt stood at the door, serene but intense; dressed in rich black lace; I noticed a preciously bound small volume in her hand and pink roses in her bosom. The niece kept somewhat in the shadow, as if too young to be more than silent and curious.

On the tea-table there were red and green apples in a golden basket, and under the table a large dog, with a wonderful coat of long silken bronze-coloured hair. Unfortunately the dog couldn't travel, and would die if they left him: for that reason they were prevented from ever going to Italy and Greece. But what did that matter, when they had Greece and Italy in their hearts? They didn't say so in words, but words in such a case were superfluous. Everything breathed inexpressible tenderness and silent passion.

A glimpse of Henry James. Some years later the Smiths introduced me to a better-known personage: Henry James. Bertie and his first wife had then been divorced, and she and her brother lived together in St. Leonard's Terrace in Chelsea. By that time Logan Pearsall Smith had developed his amiable interest in my writings, and the Berensons also had shown me the greatest kindness. Now, the brother and sister asked me one day to lunch with Henry James. Those were his last years and I never saw him again. Nevertheless in that one interview he made me feel more at home, and better understood, than his brother William ever had done in the long years of our acquaintance. Henry was calm, he liked to see things as they are, and be free afterwards to imagine how they might have been. We talked about different countries as places of residence. He was of course subtle and bland, appreciative of all points of view, and amused at their limitations. He told us an anecdote about Prosper Mérimée wondering at him for choosing to live in England, and finding that a good background for his inspiration. "*Vous vivez*", he had said, "*parmi des gens moins fins que vous.*" All of us naturally felt the truth of this as applied to Henry James, and each of us no doubt thought it true of himself also: yet how well we all understood, not withstanding, the incomparable charm of living in England!

As for me, apart from the climate and the language, both entirely to my taste, there was the refinement, if not the *finesse*, of English people in all their ways. They were certainly less disinterested than I, intellectually, morally, and materially; and it was not from them that I wished to draw my ideas. But I respected and loved the English psyche, and the primacy there of the physical and moral nature over the intellectual. It was the safer order of things, more vital, more manly than the reverse. Man was not made to understand the world, but to live in it. Yet nature, in some of us, lets out her secret; it spoils the game, but it associates us with her own impartiality. We cannot abdicate that privilege. It is final, ultimate, proper for the funeral oration over the earth: but those who are destined to live in this world had better not hear of it, or if they hear of it had better not take it too much to heart.

Incidental residence at Richmond. Of the London suburbs the only one where I have stayed for any time, besides Windsor, is Richmond. I saw the old Star and Garter at its last gasp; it was being sold and transformed; and while the dinner there was good enough, there was an uncomfortable air of removal. But during the year of the armistice I spent some weeks at the Richmond Hill Hotel; I was waiting to obtain leave to return to Paris. The French authorities made a great fuss about it. Why, if I lived in Paris, had I abandoned *La France* in the hour of danger? The military official evidently suspected that I was not a neutral or an elderly man, but a young coward or a secret enemy. I might have retorted that if I had returned at the outbreak of war, I should only have added another mouth to the population, quite likely to be starved during another siege. But I never protest or argue with persons in authority: instead I produced a note in a fashionable lady's handwriting. It was from Madame de Fontenay, addressed to the Chancellor of the French Embassy, requesting him to facilitate my journey, and including her husband's card. She wrote because I was a friend of the Strongs who were great friends of hers; and they were great friends of hers because they were son-in-law and granddaughter of Rockefeller. Monsieur Rockefeller, she once said to me with decision, was like a king. Her perfumed little letter worked like magic; and I was immediately able to cross the Channel; it was on the very day of the signing of the peace of Versailles.

In Richmond I had not had the comfort of private lodgings, but had quiet and rather nice early Victorian rooms; and for going in to London, as I did often, I liked the top of the busses, now motor-busses, and the long drive over Fulham Heath. On other days Richmond Park was at hand for walks in almost complete solitude. The Terrace, the tea-rooms, the river, and the trippers entertained me after the fashion of the Paris boulevards.

Midshipman Easy. One day I fell into conversation with a young man who was reading a French novel conspicuous in its yellow cover. They all knew French and Italian, he said, in the Navy. He had cruised all over the Mediterranean. Now he was on special leave because his father was on his way to England to try the Kaiser. His father was a Chief Justice in India—Jenkins: I had of course seen the name. Yes: I had certainly seen the name somewhere: I didn't add, over the fishmonger's round the corner. And the Chief Justice and his gallant son were enjoying their holiday for nothing. They didn't after all hang the Kaiser.—Such little casual acquaintances amused me in my travels.

A visit to   I had been in Richmond once before on a much briefer,
Pembroke   soberer, more exalted errand: to visit old Lady Russell
Lodge.   at Pembroke Lodge. Bertie took me there to high tea one evening. There was a beef-steak, and a half bottle of claret exclusively for me. The atmosphere was exactly that of old-fashioned Boston: only the voices and the subjects of conversation were different. Lady Russell at once asked me if I knew *The Bible in Spain*. I had heard of Borrow's book, but unfortunately hadn't read it, so that I was at a loss to make a suitable reply. Soon, however, I was put at my ease by not being questioned, and Lady Russell—her daughter Lady Agatha was present but didn't talk—began to speak about herself and her feelings. The world had moved away from what it was in other days: she never went to London now except to dine with Mr. Gladstone. In fine, a picture of self-confirming but melancholy old age, when the nebula of experience contracts into a single central sun, alone now visible or trusted, and destined soon to be extinguished in its turn.

This visit forms an interesting contrast to the one, already mentioned, which I had made some years before to the Russells' other grandmother, Lady Stanley of Alderley. There I had been taken by the elder brother, here tabooed. I had just returned to London from Oxford, and Russell had asked me to join him at his grandmother's on the way to Teddington, where he then lived. It was a large house in Dover Street, now a club or hotel. The front door, at one end of the façade, opened directly into a large square hall, where I was received by two flunkeys in white silk stockings. When I asked for Lord Russell and gave my name, it was evident that I was expected, for the footman I spoke to said, "Yes, sir. In a moment", and the other instantly disappeared. Presently I saw the youthful figure of Russell himself tripping down the red carpeted grand stairs, and I can see it still, silhouetted against the western sunlight that streamed from the opposite windows above the landing. He was in an amiable mood, seemed to approve of my new clothes and hat and lavender tie, and led me up in the most friendly manner into a long room like a gallery that evidently occupied the whole front of the house. There was a row of windows, with boxes of plants in front of them, running along one side, and opposite a row of cabinets and sofas against the wall, the whole floor between being clear, and with the parquet highly burnished and waxed, so that footing was a bit precarious. At the other end, however, there was a large rug spread, on which stood the tea-table, surrounded by three ladies, and two or three vacant chairs of comfortable and homelike appearance. Lady Stanley, fat, old, jolly, and monumental was enthroned in the centre; on one side sat the Hon. Maud Stanley, her daughter, amiable and middle-aged, and on the other side her granddaughter, Lady Griselda Ogilvie, charming in the latest fashion and smiling with an easy grace. Our visit was as short as it was agreeable, for Russell was always conscious of the due time for catching trains. But it sufficed to leave a permanent impression in my mind, since this is the only glimpse I ever had of a grand house and of good society in London.

The recollection will serve to bring my rambling narrative back to the year 1887, and to the most extraordinary of all my friends.

XIX
Russell

He turns up   Because the windows of my room in Hollis Hall looked
at Harvard.   out directly on the brick path that led from the Harvard
Yard to Jarvis Field, then the college playground; or because, for an
undergraduate, I was thought comparatively articulate; or because I
was a foreigner and known to write verses; or because the guide to
whom the young Earl Russell was entrusted, was a good friend of
mine,* that exceptional nobleman, grandson and heir of Lord John
Russell, was brought to see me, when on being sent down from Oxford
in 1886 he visited America in charge of a tutor. He was the first
Englishman I had ever spoken to or that had ever spoken to me. That
of itself would have made him notable in my eyes; but this Englishman
was remarkable on his own account.

Our first   He was a tall young man of twenty, still lithe though
interview.   large of bone, with abundant tawny hair, clear little steel-
blue eyes, and a florid complexion. He moved deliberately, gracefully,
stealthily, like a tiger well fed and with a broad margin of leisure for
choosing his prey. There was precision in his indolence; and mild as
he seemed, he suggested a latent capacity to leap, a latent astonishing
celerity and strength, that could crush at one blow. Yet his speech
was simple and suave, perfectly decided and strangely frank. He had
some thoughts, he said, of becoming a clergyman. He seemed observant, meditative, as if comparing whatever he saw with something
in his mind's eye. As he looked out of the window at the muddy paths
and shabby grass, the elms standing scattered at equal intervals, the
ugly factory-like buildings, and the loud-voiced youths passing by,
dressed like shop-assistants, I could well conceive his thoughts, and I
said apologetically that after Oxford all this must seem to him rather
mean; and he replied curtly: "Yes, it does." I explained our manner
of life, our social distinctions, our choice of studies, our sports, our

*Herbert Lyman

food, our town amusements. He listened politely, obviously rather entertained and not displeased to find that, according to my description, all I described might be dismissed for ever without a further thought. Then he sat good-naturedly on the floor and began to look at my books—a rather meagre collection in some open shelves. He spied Swinburne's *Poems*, and took out the volume. Did I like Swinburne? Yes, perhaps he was rather verbose; but did I know the choruses in *Atalanta in Calydon*? No? Then he would read me one. And he read them all, rather liturgically, with a perfect precision and clearness, intoning them almost, in a sort of rhythmic chant, and letting the strong meaning shine through the steady processional march of the words. It seemed the more inspired and oracular for not being brought out by any human change of tone or of emphasis. I had not heard poetry read in this way before. I had not known that the English language could become, like stained glass, an object and a delight in itself.

The seed sown.   He staid a long time, until the daylight having decidedly failed, he remembered that he was to dine at the James's. My own dinner was long since cold. He was off the next day, he said; but I must look him up whenever I came to London. I saw no more of him at that time; but I received through the post a thin little book bound in white vellum, *The Bookbills of Narcissus*, by Richard Le Gallienne, inscribed "from R." And William James not long afterwards took occasion to interrupt himself, as his manner was, as if a sudden thought had struck him, and to say to me: "I hear you have seen this young grandson of Lord John Russell's. He talked about you; you seem to have made an impression." The impression I had made was that I was capable of receiving impressions. With the young Russell, who completely ignored society and convention, this was the royal road to friendship.

I join him the next year on the Thames.   When late in March of the following year, 1887, after the winter semester at Berlin, I reached England for the holidays, Russell was not in town, but wrote that he was bringing a boat down from the engineers at Newbury to the boatbuilders in London. They were merely patched up for the journey; it would be a three days' trip, one on a canal and two on the Thames. He feared he couldn't offer me much accommodation and I should have to sleep ashore, but it would be a good chance of seeing the river. It was finally arranged that I should join him on the second day at Reading. Muddy and sordid streets led from the dismal railway station to the Kennet Canal Office where Russell's small yacht, the *Royal*, was to lie for the night. After various inquiries I found my way over a shaky plank (very little to my taste) to a narrow strip of deck surrounding the cabin skylight. There I found my host in conversation with a workman. My arrival was noticed, and I was asked if I had duly deposited my bag at the inn. All being well, I was left to stand about, while the conversation with the workman continued. I stood by for a while and listened; but seeing that the business gave no signs of coming to an end, and was not very intelligible or interesting, I sat on the edge of the cockpit and took to sketching the hulks, masts, and chimneys visible from the river. In those days I always carried a notebook and pencil in my pocket, for setting down sudden inspirations. I had full time for exhausting the dreary beauties of the scene and my small skill in expressing them. At length the worthy workman departed (I suppose his working hours were up) and Russell called me, quite affectionately, slipped his arm into mine, and took me to look at the cabin and the engine-room and the galley, which was also the place where one washed. My ignorant questions were answered briefly, clearly, with instant discernment of what I knew and didn't know about ships. Then we went ashore for tea.

Developing into an engineer.   Russell said he should not have been a peer but an engineer. At the time I thought this a little joke, remembering him reading the choruses in *Atalanta* and wishing to be a parson; but now I see that there was a genuine feeling in it. When he died, one of the notices in the newspapers referred to his "scientific training" and its value in his political career. What was this scientific training? Surely nothing that he acquired at Winchester or Oxford, but what he learned while refitting his steam yacht and talking to workmen, as he had that afternoon. He took up each mechanical novelty as it arose, experimented, became more or less expert. He carved, drove, and steered admirably; he would have made an excellent naval officer and gunner. When he lived at Broom Hall and had a private electric plant, for charging his launch and supplying his light, I remember asking him what electricity was. And he said, "I will show you", and after making me leave my watch at a distance, he brought me close to the large magnet that formed part of the machinery, until I felt a strong pull; and then he said triumphantly, "That is what it is." In one sense, a scholastic and verbal answer; yet there was the scientific humility and peace in it, that is satisfied with dark facts. And there was another side to his pleasure in engineering: the sense of mastery. Matter can be wooed, coaxed, and mastered like a woman, and this without being in the least understood sympathetically. On the contrary a keen edge of the pleasure comes from defiance. If matter can crush us when ignored, it can be played with and dragged about when once caught in its own meshes; and this skilful exercise of compulsion was dear to Russell. When he acted as leader of the Opposition in the House of Lords he was not half so happy or in his element. The peers could not so easily be engineered.

His ways at the inn.   At the inn he began to lavish endearments on the cat, who returned his advances disdainfully, and after purring a little when stroked found the thing a bore and scooted into parts unknown. The barmaid then had her turn for a moment, and would doubtless have proved more responsive; but the other servants had to be spoken to about the tea—tea was very important—and the smiling barmaid and the ungrateful cat were alike forgotten. Tea was a wonderful sedative; and the post and the newspapers were brought in at the same time. Russell opened his letters with the tips of his strong fingers, without haste, without one needless movement or the least unnecessary force. A brief glance usually sufficed, and the letter was dropped, as if into eternal oblivion, upon the floor. But now and then something called for a comment, and then my presence seemed providential. I was invited to observe the stupidity of the correspondent, or the folly of the government, or the outrage it was to have such prolonged bad weather. What did I think of the absurd language of the Scottish housekeeper who asked: "*Will* I light the fire?" And could I conceive anything more annoying than the position of a young man who hadn't yet come into his money and whose grandmother (Lady Russell, not Lady Stanley) was a fool? In all this faultfinding there was nothing really troubled or querulous, nor was there anything merry. It was all serene observation of the perversity of things, the just perceptions and judgments of a young god to whom wrongness was hateful on principle, but who was not in the least disturbed about it in his own person. Was it not his own choice to move in this ridiculous world, where there were imperfect inns and yachts to be refitted and untrustworthy tradesmen and faithless cats and silly disappointed barmaids? What difference could such incidents of travel make to a transcendental spirit, fixed and inviolate in its own centre?

The steam yacht *Royal*.   The next day early we started down the river in the *Royal*. She was a steam yacht of one hundred tons, rigged at sea, I was told, as a schooner, but now mastless. There was a cockpit aft, with a seat round it, and the wheel in the middle; my ecclesiastical mind at once compared it to the apse of a primitive basilica, with its semicircle of stalls and its bishop's throne in the centre, whence the pilot of souls might rise and lay his hands on the altar, in this case, the wheel. Two or three steep steps led below, from this cockpit, into the cabin, which occupied the whole width of the boat and perhaps a third of her length. There were some lockers on either side, and two broad bunks beyond, supplied with red plush mattresses and pillows. The table between had flaps that could be let down, leaving only a ledge some six inches wide running down its length; two other sleeping places could then be arranged on the floor between the table and the bunks: but we were never more than two when I was on board. The cabin was sealed at the end by a varnished yellow bulkhead, decorated with a large barometer and a small clock. To go forward it was necessary to skirt the cabin roof, with its row of square lights, along the edge of the deck. There was a cabin boy who cooked and served our meals quite properly and might well have been called a steward. The two or three other men of the crew I hardly ever saw, even during the three weeks that I spent, the following year, in the *Royal*.

I find my level and my liberty.   At such close quarters I soon began to understand what was expected of me. I was liked, I was wanted, I was confided in, but only when my turn came, when other interests flagged and nothing urgent was to be done. I should not have been liked or wanted or confided in if I had interfered with other things or made myself a nuisance. But as a sympathetic figure in the background, to whom Olympian comments were always intelligible, I fitted in very well. Being an unpractical person, a foreigner, and a guest I naturally accepted everything as it came; and being indolent but meditative, with eyes for the new scenes before me, I was never better entertained than when neglected or busier than when idle. Moreover, I was left free and had my escapades. In later years Russell, who was no pedestrian, liked to plan my walks for me and did it very well. His topographical sense was excellent, and in driving or motoring about he noticed and remembered every nook and every prospect. When asked for directions he liked to give them; it was a pleasure to his executive mind. So the next morning, when we arrived at Windsor and were stopping for some supplies, I was allowed half an hour ashore, and advised to go up to the Castle terrace: but I mustn't loiter, for in all Russell's mighty movements punctuality was absolutely demanded.

A glimpse of Windsor Castle. In the lovely misty sunshine of that April morning, I climbed the outer Castle steps, not without profound emotion. I was treading the stones of Windsor Castle. The Thames valley stretched before me, green and rural, peopled and living. Eton lay at my feet: I could distinguish the great east window of the Chapel, and the wooden turrets. The fields, the trees, the river, glittered mildly in the sun, as if all a-tremble with dew. What homeliness, what simplicity in this grandeur! How modest were these important places, how silent, how humbly faithful to the human scale! If such sweet discipline could conquer the world, why should it not conquer the heart? But I mustn't sentimentalise too long, or my rebellious friend below—horrible thought!—might be kept waiting. Strange that being the heir to so many privileges he should appreciate them so little, and should use the strength that he derived from tradition in deriding tradition and in destroying it.

A mishap. My position as a familiar friend who was not a nuisance was not established without some preliminary slips. One was a slip in the literal sense of the word. Russell had at Hampton, where he then lived, an electric launch for scurrying at a surprising speed along the river. Electric launches were novelties in those days, and with his good steering and perfect serenity, he attracted the admiring attention of the good people in the boats or on the banks. But nature had endowed him with a more surprising ability of another kind. He could walk along the edges and ledges of roofs, and up inclined poles, like a cat. I suppose all boys, except me, have had a desire to do such things, and have tried their hand at them at a certain age, and then abandoned feline ambitions for things more human. But in Russell, for some reason, feline instincts survived, and developed into habits. He performed his acrobatic feats as a matter of course, without training and without comment. He never boasted of them; he only thought it a singular deficiency in others not to be able to do them. One Sunday afternoon we had landed at Richmond for tea, and on our return found the launch removed from the landing—there was naturally a crowd of trippers on that day—and it lay at a little distance from the sloping bank, which didn't allow it to come nearer. For Russell this created no problem. One long boat-hook was turned into a bridge from the launch to the shore, and seizing the other, as a *picador* does his lance, and sticking the prong through the clear water into the sand, he walked calmly and quickly aboard. But how was I to get in? In the same way, of course. In vain did I protest, like Rosencrantz and Guildenstern, that I hadn't the skill. Hamlet said it was as easy as lying. If I had insisted on making them turn about, and wait for their chance to come up to the landing, so that I might step aboard easily, I should have been making myself a nuisance. Seeing my hesitation, Russell said encouragingly: "Come on. Try it. I'll lend you a hand." I knew I should fall in; but I might as well try it, since the only alternative was to wade across, and I must get wet in any case. The pole was rather steep, I had on ordinary boots, not tennis shoes like Russell, and no experience in walking the tight rope. So I took the boat-hook, and gave Russell my other hand. The result was tragic, but not what either of us expected. I fell in, inevitably, but I pulled him in after me; and while I only got my legs wet, he fell in backwards head over heels, with a tremendous splash, which caused great laughter among the Sunday trippers lined up on the shore. There was no danger, even in a complete immersion; two feet of water at most, and a warm summer afternoon. We both climbed in easily; but Russell flew into an indescribable rage. His language showed that the society of working men had not been wasted upon him; or rather that he must have overheard a great deal that no working man would knowingly have said in his presence. Where? Or could nature have endowed him with Billingsgate as it had endowed him with somnambulism when awake? For that inexhaustible flow of foul words and blasphemous curses was somnambulistic: he didn't know what he was saying or why. It was an automatism let loose, as was his acrobatic instinct.

Psychology of the absolute ego. I thought at the time that what maddened him was having been baulked and made a fool of in public; but now that I know him better I believe he had no idea that he was in the least to blame. He felt innocent and injured. It was all my fault for being such an incredible muff. I had ducked him in the Thames and was keeping him wet to the skin in the cool breeze all the way home. His memory for injuries, however, — and he thought everybody injured him — was remarkably short. As soon as he got into dry clothes his wrath subsided. Still, he had been so outrageously abusive, and so persistent, that I was cut to the quick. Not that I minded his words, which I had hardly distinguished and couldn't remember; they had no real application to me and couldn't stick. What I feared was that the sting of his own folly had made him hate me, and that all might be over between us. But not in the least. He didn't understand why that evening I could hardly swallow my food, or why I was leaving the next morning.

No harm done.   There was some difficulty about getting my things to the station. It wasn't far, and I had only a bag, but it was rather heavy. "I'll carry it for you", he said; and he actually did so, most of the way. And he continued to send me little notes, inviting me to this or that, so long as I remained in England; and before long, instead of signing them "yours sincerely," he began to sign them "yours ever". This was not meant for a mute apology, kindness vanquishing resentment. He behaved exactly in the same way with his worst enemies, such as Lady Scott: forgot terrible injuries, and reverted spontaneously to a deeper impulse, which events had obscured for a moment. I accepted all his invitations. My ego was no less absolute than his, and calmer. If he allowed me my inabilities, I could allow him his explosions. That the wild animal and the furious will should exist beneath his outwardly exact and critical intelligence was so much added, a double *virtù*. I liked it and I didn't fear it.

The astonishing thing about this incident was that Russell completely forgot it. Years after, when I once referred to having pulled him into the water at Richmond, he denied it, and didn't know what I was talking about. This again was not a case of legal oblivion, such as lawyers command a man to scatter over his past when he is about to give evidence: it was a genuine blank. A blank, that is, in his conscious memory; for in his inner man the thing must have left its trace, because he never afterwards urged me to do anything to which I was not inclined or taxed me with any defect. He respected my freedom unconditionally and gladly, as I respected his. This was one of the reasons why our friendship lasted for so many years, weathering all changes in our circumstances, in spite of the few points of contact between our characters and the utter diversity in our lives. Neither of us was ever a nuisance to the other.

Russell's Oxford friends.   When I was about to make my first visit to Oxford, I had received four notes of introduction, enclosed in the following letter.

21 Ap. 1887   Ferishtah, Hampton.

Dear Santayana

I find that the number of my intimate friends actually at Oxford is much decreased. Natheless I send you 4 to 1. Burke of Trinity, 2 Jepson of Balliol, 3 Johnson of New, 4 Davis of Balliol.

1. is a friend of 8 or 10 yrs. standing, a good fellow but so terrible reserved that you'll get nothing out of him.

2. is a funny fellow of immoral tendencies & pessimistic affectation. Well worth your visit to make him show off.

3. is the man I most admire, and—in the world, knows every book that is, transcendentalist, genius, and is called affected. The way for you to treat him is to take no notice when he tries (as he will) to shock you. If he discourses, listen: it will be worth while.

4. is a strictly moral Radical Positivist. You may label him with all the —'ists suitable to that combination. He will only talk politics to you but has more heart than he shows on the surface. Still of course he's a Philistine.

Eh voilà!

Yours sincerely,
Russell

Write to me in about a week.

Burke.   Number One in this list was not number one by accident. Perhaps I got nothing out of him, but I liked him very much. He was sensitive and brave. You felt that in some way he must have suffered a great deal. Had it been bad health, family quarrels, love, or perhaps some disgrace? He was Irish, but Protestant, very Protestant in a profound, silent unhappy way. Intense moral feeling, intense sense of the difference between the better and the worse. He had been with Russell at a private school, and had a good education, but felt very Irish, and perhaps regretted that his money came from a brewery—*Burke's Ales, Stout & Porter*. We talked chiefly about Russell, whom he cared for; but caring didn't modify his strict standards, and while he could forgive Russell's commonplace peccadilloes, when it came later to his treatment of the Billings girls, whom Burke knew, he became intractable, and broke with him. As I wasn't going to desert Russell for that, or for anything, Burke and I ceased to keep up our acquaintance. I believe he died young.

Jepson.   I found Number Two in comfortable not very academic
            lodgings, the best available no doubt, yet hardly worthy
of his ornamental person. He was not really good-looking, but his hair
was yellow, parted in the middle and carefully waved, like a ploughed
field. He said his life was devoted to the culture of it. Incidentally,
however, he had accomplished a greater thing. He had already, at
twenty, doubled human knowledge in one of the sciences, the science
de modis veneris. There had been forty modes before, now there were
eighty. He didn't show me the classic designs for those forty modes;
they are probably not extant; nor did he reveal the secret of his new
variations. I was sceptical, and Jepson didn't interest me. Thirty years
later he and his wife came for a week-end to Telegraph House when
I happened to be there. He was no longer silly: he had written novels,
and seemed rather commonplace. He still had vestiges of the same
cultivated hair, but silver, alas, mingled with the faded gold. I rather
wondered why Russell, who had given up most of his old friends, still
kept up with Jepson. Or was he a literary friend of Elizabeth's, who
was also a novelist? No, said our hostess; they were Russell's friends.
He had an affair with Mrs. Jepson. This suggestion surprised me.
Elizabeth ought to have known; but she was beginning at that time
to hate her husband, and hatred is a great deceiver.

Lionel   Number Three was then in his first year at New Col-
Johnson.   lege. He had rooms at the top of the new buildings
overlooking Holywell. Over the roofs of the low houses opposite, the
trees in the Parks were visible in places, as well as the country beyond:
and pointing to the distant horizon Lionel Johnson said sadly: "Everything above that line is right, everything below it is wrong." These
were almost the first words he spoke to me, and they formed an
admirable preface to a religious conversion.

His   He was rather a little fellow, pale, with small sunken
appearance   blinking eyes, a sensitive mouth, and lank pale brown
and pose at hair. His childlike figure was crowned by a smooth head,
the age of   like a large egg standing on its small end. His age was
twenty.   said to be sixteen, and I readily believed the report. His
genius was of the kind that may be precocious, being an inward protest
against external evidence; and his aspect, though thoughtful, was very
youthful: yet his real age seems to have been twenty, only a year and
a half younger than Russell and three years younger than I. He said
he lived on eggs in the morning and nothing but tea and cigarettes
during the rest of the day. He seldom went out, but when he did it

was for a walk of twenty miles in the country; and on those days he dined. There was also conspicuous on a centre table a jug of Glengarry whiskey between two open books: *Les Fleurs du Mal* and *Leaves of Grass*. Two large portraits hung on the wall: Cardinal Newman and Cardinal Wiseman. When he was of age he intended to become a Catholic and a monk: at present his people, who were Welsh, objected. This intention he carried out in part; but instead of becoming a monk he became a Fenian; for at the same time that he was converted from a legal Protestant to a legal Catholic, he was mystically transformed from a Welshman into an Irishman. It was the same thing, he said, being Celtic. Perhaps too being Irish was closer to his inner man, and certainly more congruous with Catholicism and with whiskey.

The "insubstantial fabric" of his mind. Our acquaintance was never close, but it seemed to gain in interest, for both of us, as it receded. Some years later he honoured me with a poem *To a Spanish Friend*, beginning with the words "Exiled in America", and ending with an exhortation to return to Saint Theresa and her "holy Avila". I returned often, and should gladly have grown old in that atmosphere, yet not in order to indulge the impulse to dream awake: rather in order to remove the pressure of reality (of which I was only too well aware) and to leave my reflection free to survey that reality fairly, at arm's length. Lionel Johnson lived only in his upper storey, in a loggia open to the sky; and he forgot that he had climbed there up a long flight of flinty steps, and that his *campanile* rested on the vulgar earth. The absence of all foundations, of all concreteness, of all distinction between fiction and truth, makes his poetry indigestible. I see that it is genuine poetry—an irresponsible flux of impassioned words; and his religion too was genuine religion, if we admit that religion must be essentially histrionic. Let everything that comes, it says, be to thee an Angel of the Lord; embroider upon it in that sense, and let the vulgar world recede into a distant background for an endless flapping of angelic wings and chanting of angelic voices. The age had given Lionel Johnson enough verbal culture and knowledge of literature to raise his effusions in that angelic choir to a certain level of refinement and fancy; but he was not a traditional Catholic, accepting good-naturedly a supernatural economy that happened to prevail in the universe, as political and domestic economy prevail in one's earthly fortunes. Nor was he a philosopher, enduring the truth. He was a spiritual rebel, a spiritual waif who couldn't endure the truth, but demanded a lovelier fiction to revel in, invented or accepted it, and called it revelation. In part like Shelley, in part like Rimbaud, he despised the world and adored the unreal.

A fundamental transcendentalism and humanism. Had that first saying of his to me, that everything above the horizon was right and everything below it wrong, represented his primary and constant mind, he might have become a monk as he had intended; because that is the foundation of Christianity. There is a divine world *surrounding us*; but there is sin and damnation *in us*. Lionel Johnson never seemed to me to feel this, as for instance St. Paul and St. Augustine felt it. What he felt was rather the opposite, that everything within him was right, and everything outside wrong; and if he made an exception of the blank sky, this was only because he could fill it at will with his poetry. In other words, he was a transcendentalist and a humanist; for that reason he seemed a prophet to Russell; and at bottom nothing could be more contrary to Christian humility and to Catholic discipline. I know that an effort has been made to represent him as a saint, hushing the sad reality: it is part of the general practice of bluff, silence, and the *claque* in journalistic criticism. Let me give some grounds for a contrary opinion.

How expressed at eighteen. Russell, who was faithful to the inspired friend of his school days and completely ignored his conversion and Catholicism, published a collection of Johnson's letters from Winchester, written when he was seventeen or eighteen years old. Here are some extracts:

"I do not love sensuality; I do not hate it; I do not love purity; I do not hate it: I regard both as artistic aspects of life."

"A man's life is not his acts of profession: drills, sermons, death-beds, stone breaking are not life, but accidents of life; the life is the sunsets we worship, the books we read, the faces we love."

"I tell you, be happy, for that is to know God; be sinful, for that is to feel God; be all things, for that is to be God."

"At my worst moments I see myself Archbishop and Poet Laureate, at my best I don't see myself at all, but merely God and other men and the world and my dear art."

"I think that my earlier scriptures were the spiritualised expression of my life-long faith—I adopted the language of convenient morality to apply it to the immoral doctrines of my personal gospel."

At twenty-one. After three years at Oxford, Johnson had developed an element of banter, and favoured me with the following letter:

August 2nd [1888]

Hunter's Inn,
Heddon's Mouth, Barnstable.

My dear Santayana

Forgive my not writing earlier: I have been for weeks a wanderer, with letters chasing me about the world in vain.

I wish I could be in Oxford in August; but only, be sure, for the sake of meeting you. Unhappily it is impossible. I am bound, hand and foot, to a "reading party" in an obscure corner of Devonshire; and see no prospect of escape. Can you not find your way to our pastoral retreat? or be in Oxford in October? You will not go back to our dear America just yet, mon ami?

Berenson charmed Oxford for a term, and vanished: leaving behind a memory of exotic epigrams and, so to speak, cynical music. It was a strangely curious time. He is something too misanthropic: but always adorable.

I missed Russell lately by four hours: you know we have not met for many a year, almost. I incline to think it time for his drama of life to become critical in some way: at least, beyond disregarding all unities of time and space he does not appear to progress. This morning is very hot; the sea sparkles; Plato is beautiful; the world very charming; but why go to America? Come to Oxford in October and learn of me how to live on nothing with nothing to do. I intend to teach Berenson: and neither of you shall set foot again in Boston, that Holy and self-satisfied city.

Do you read Shelley still, and have you renounced that stage devil, Byron, and all his works, except Don Juan? Kegan Paul, whom you met, asked me the question concerning you the other day. Ach! there is always Keats.

When next you hear from me you will probably hear that I am a Jesuit novice or a budding Carthusian or some such an one. Anyway, the Church will probably have claimed her own in me. But just now I am lazy and fond of life this side of death.

Will you let me know your movements? And pray think out ways and means to see us all before you go to the Land of the Lost, and leave us desolate!

Yours very sincerely,
Lionel Johnson.

This was written at the moment when the vogue of aestheticism, pessimism, pre-Raphaelitism, and amateur Catholicism was at its height. The superior young mind was bound to share these affectations, but might save itself by a mental reservation and a pervasively weary, all-knowing, and all-mocking tone. Was Lionel Johnson laughing at Jesuits and Carthusians, at Plato, Shelley, and Keats, no less than at Berenson and me? Or had something or somebody, Shelley perhaps or the Jesuits, really taken him in? I have no doubt that sincerity existed somewhere beneath all these poses, but the exact place of it is hard to discover. Russell at that moment, in the drama of his life, was making rapid progress in the direction of Byron's Don Juan: he had fallen into the clutches of a mature adventuress, who was marrying him off to her daughter. In what direction was Lionel Johnson's sincere drama progressing?

And at thirty. I am not writing Johnson's life or Russell's or even my own, but only picking out such points as interest me now in my personal retrospect. I saw Lionel Johnson in later years only at long intervals and found him each time less accessible. My last glimpse of him was in the summer of 1897, in Russell's rooms in Temple Gardens. It was a tragic spectacle. He still looked very young, though he was thirty, but pale, haggard, and trembling. He stood by the fireplace with a tall glass of whiskey and soda at his elbow, and talked wildly of persecution. The police, he said, were after him everywhere. Detectives who pretended to be friends of his friend Murphy or of his friend MacLaughlin had to be defied. Without a signed letter of introduction he could trust nobody. He had perpetually to sport his oak. As he spoke, he quivered with excitement, hatred, and imagined terrors. He seemed to be living in a dream; and when at last he found his glass empty, it was with uncertainty that his hat sat on his head as with sudden determination he made for the door, and left us without saying good night.

Echoes of his inner life in his poetry. I never saw him again, but he still lived for five years, and there may have been important changes in him before the end. Nor do I profess to have fathomed his Celtic inspiration or his Celtic Catholicism. He says in his lines on *Wales*:

> *No alien hearts may know that magic, which acquaints*
> *Thy heart with splendid passion, a great fire of dreams,*

and I am willing to believe him. But to my prosaic apprehension, he remains a child of premature genius and perpetual immaturity; and I cannot forget what Oscar Wilde is reported to have said of him, that any morning at eleven o'clock you might see him come out very drunk from the Café Royal, and hail the first passing perambulator. Yet I should be the last to deride the haze in which he lived, on the ground that Bacchus had something to do with it. Bacchus too was a god; and the material occasion of inspiration makes no difference if the spirit is thereby really liberated. Lionel Johnson lived in the spirit; but to my sense his spirituality was that of a transcendental poet, not that of a saint. His mind was subjective in its presuppositions or in the absence of all presuppositions; so that after reading him through you are aware of a great wind of passionate language, but not of what was said or of what it all was about. And this vagueness was hardly due to absorption in something higher, because it did not liberate him from everything lower. So at least he tells us in *The Dark Angel*:

> *Because of thee, no thought, no thing*
> *Abides for me undesecrate. . . .*
> *Of two defeats, of two despairs,*
> *Less dread a change to drifting dust*
> *Than thine eternity of cares.*

And if we ask what the alternative to these two despairs may be, and what will issue from the triumph that he still hopes for, we find nothing positive, nothing specific, but only transcendental spirit, still open to every thought and to every torment:

> *Lonely, unto the Lone I go,*
> *Divine, to the Divinity.*

These words are the words of Plotinus and of Christian mystics; but here we do not feel them to be backed by either the Platonic or the Christian scheme of the universe: they are floating words. Even the firmness and constructive power of the Catholic faith could not *naturalise* Lionel Johnson in the Catholic world. The same emotional absolutism, the same hatred of everything not plastic to the fancy, which drove him from Victorian England into Celtic poetry and Catholic supernaturalism, kept him from accepting definition and limitation even there; he could not deny himself other dreams. As he writes in *Gwynedd*:

> *We will not wander from this land:* [Wales]
> *Here distress*
> *Dreams, and delight dreams; dreaming we can fill*
> *All solitary haunts with prophecy,*
> *All heights with holiness and mystery;*
> *Our hearts with understanding, and our will*
> *With love of nature's law and loveliness.*

The last two lines may seem to contradict what I am saying; but I quote them in order to be fair. Understanding, with love of nature's law, if it were real understanding of the true law of nature, would stop all that dreaming, or reduce it to wasted time and gratuitous trouble, as he himself says in *The Dark Angel*, already quoted:

> *Because of thee, the land of dreams*
> *Becomes a gathering place of fears:*
> *Until tormented slumber seems*
> *One vehemence of useless tears.*

But the word nature, in a Celtic poet, does not mean what it meant to Lucretius, nor understanding what it meant to Aristotle, nor law what it meant to Newton. These words mean rather landscape, divination, and magic; as in the first line quoted, where he says he will not leave *this land*, he means the *soul* of this land, which is the land of dreams.

A congenital refusal to endure the truth. The passionate need of sinking into these dreams, and defying the false world that pretended to be more real, seems to me to have been the secret of Lionel Johnson in all his phases. It was what made him a pagan or a Buddhist at Winchester, a Baudelairean Catholic at Oxford, and a Fenian conspirator in London. In his verse he could modulate those dreams lyrically, but not logically, morally, and historically as the Church had modulated her original inspirations; and he dared to take them, as the Church did hers, for revelations of the truth. But his dreams had no such application to the facts and sorrows of life as had the Christian faith. Their passion remained dreamy, weak, and verbal, and he perished not a martyr to his inspiration, but a victim of it.

Russell's transcendental sentiments. Now to return to Russell. In their adolescence both he and Lionel Johnson had revelled in transcendental liberty: but Russell was strong, and exposed to the dangers and vices of strength, as Johnson to those of weakness. Russell had no gift of fancy: he had to be satisfied with the vulgar plots that real life furnishes willy nilly to the spirit; and he sank into them desperately, without discrimination and without taste. Yet his strong intelligence, rather conventional in worldly matters, remained conscious that it was being deceived. This early transcendentalism was not apparent in him; his wives, I expect, never understood that it was there; yet I think it helped to make him reckless in choosing and in divorcing them. For him it was all a desperate and worthless gamble in any case. Any lust, any convenience, any enterprise, any stale moral or political nostrum would do to play with: the point was to dream your dream out, and to have your way in it.

This is my interpretation: but in a letter written a fortnight before his death—almost the last I received from him—he puts the matter in the following words:

"It is not really the case that Lionel lies in the limbo of almost incredible things. On the contrary, all that is the real part of me and my very extensive external activities are to me of the nature of Maya or illusion. They interest me, they are my job, and I do them, but they are not part of my real life. I am surprised that you should say I minimise my friendship of Lionel, to all intimate friends I have always admitted that he was my dearest friend and the greatest influence in my life, but I seldom take the public into my confidence about my real feelings. I received two great shocks in my life; the first being when Jowett sent me down. My rage and mortification at being so wronged produced a bitterness and permanently injured my character. Finally, when Elizabeth left me I went completely dead and have never come alive again. She never realised how I worshipped and loved her, and how I idealised what is in essence a worthless character, and her light-hearted cruelty killed something in me which has never revived. Since 1918 I have had neither ambition, nor enthusiasm, nor interest, nor will to live, and I ascribe my bad heart entirely to the year's anguish I suffered after she left me and her betrayal with a kiss of Judas. Still, as you say I obliterate my feelings so easily, no doubt you will not believe this."

My belief in their sincerity, both in him and in Lionel Johnson.

No: I didn't believe *all* this; the words about Elizabeth didn't ring true in my ears. But I believed and believe what he says about Lionel Johnson, which is what concerns me here; and I can also credit his living "dead", precisely when he was a member of the Government, busy, and rehabilitated officially and financially. It would be an experience such as in my own case I call somnambulistic, under which I may be doing mechanically what some people think my best work. He had transcendental insight, acquired in his adolescence (the natural time for it) under the influence of Lionel Johnson; and this common spiritual challenge to the dream of life raised their friendship to a great height and made it constant in spite of all obstacles and external disparities. Neither Johnson's Catholicism and drink, nor Russell's matrimonial imbroglios did justice to their inner man; such commitments were accidents, as was their vulgar politics also; and both knew it. I also divined it in them, but from the outside, and I am glad to have this confession of Russell's, written almost on his death-bed, to buttress my divination. Transcendental rebellion, like that of Lucifer, lay at the bottom of his heart, but buried like a prehistoric civilisation under layer upon layer of ruins. Lionel Johnson could display this spirit lyrically and publish it to the puzzled world in his talk and in his poems; but poor Russell had only his ruins to display and to be judged by most unjustly, ruins of passions that had hounded him through life like a succession of nightmares, and had made the gossips call him "The Wicked Earl".

Circumstances of Russell's quarrel with Jowett.

The first of these ruins came with the great shock he speaks of in this same letter, of being sent down from Oxford. It happens—it was a mere accident—that the innocent first cause of this shock was Lionel Johnson himself, the inspirer of the bold spirit that was buried under it. For in this matter a proper discretion has led everybody, including Russell himself, to keep the name of Lionel Johnson out of the public ear. Jowett's action was ascribed to the discovery of "an improper letter" written by Russell, a letter never produced or quoted when he was accused of it. Was it improper in its words, in its ideas, or in its proposals? Only the last could have justified the action taken, because improper words and ideas are universally current in the talk of very young men. But what could have made Jowett assume that the alleged letter contained any improper proposal? For it was not Jowett that had seen the letter, but the Vice Chancellor: and why did

Jowett open the subject with the Vice Chancellor at all? Because he
had had a stormy interview with Russell previously on quite another
point.

This was Russell's first year at Balliol, and Lionel Johnson, who was
still at school in Winchester, had come up to Oxford for the day to
see him. Somehow he had missed the last train to town, and had
spent the night in Russell's rooms in the College. This being against
the rules had been reported by the "scout" to the Master; and Russell
was summoned to explain the matter. An evil spirit must have inspired
Jowett or Russell on that occasion, or probably both, for neither behaved
reasonably. Jowett began by frowning and looking suspicious, and said
that Johnson was *too young* to be Russell's *natural friend*. On this, instead
of replying that Johnson was much older than he looked and only a
year younger than himself, Russell flew into a rage, assumed a lofty
tone, declared that Johnson was his intellectual and moral superior,
and defied Jowett to prove anything against him. This naturally increased Jowett's irritation, if not his suspicions; he consulted the Vice
Chancellor, who then remembered "an improper letter", and with
this corroboration, without any further investigation or hearing, they
sent Russell down for one year, to allow his resentment and their own
scandal mongerings to blow over. But Russell's wrath was absolute
and unyielding. He had been wounded in his tenderest spot, and he
took his name off the books, and abandoned the University. Had Lionel
Johnson not been involved, I think Russell would have returned to
Oxford. Jowett would have taken pains to reconcile him, as he eventually tried to do, and Russell's whole life might have run a smoother
and more reputable course.

Its unfortunate effects.   In regard to people's reputations the polite world is
at once cynical and good-natured. It believes the worst
and acts as if nothing were amiss. But this compromise lasts only so
long as the man keeps his head above water legally and financially.
Let him make himself embarrassing by washing his dirty linen in
public, or let him lose his money in the process, and the polite world
will turn its back on him. This happened to Russell; what damned
him was not the things of which he was accused, which were false or
trivial, but his own perverse way of wasting his opportunities. He
fought the whole world heroically for the sake of trifles, using all
available legal machinery for arbitrary ends, often as ill-chosen as his
wives; and in his inner solitude, he sank sternly into petty vices which
gave him infinite trouble and no pleasure. At the end he seemed to

have lived down his early misfortunes and later errors, and to be accepted, at least in advanced circles, as a man of remarkable gifts; and yet it was at that time that he was most unhappy, and most blinded inwardly. In his life the transcendental spirit had passed *un mauvais quart d'heure*.

A visit to Winchester.   But let me return to the pleasant summer of 1887, when under his auspices I first felt the full charm of England. His last invitation before I left for Spain took me to Winchester. He was staying at his old Housemaster's for the School celebration of the Queen's Jubilee, and he took a room for me at an inn. In this way I had the advantage of being guided, introduced, and shown what there was to see, and also the advantage of being left alone so as to see it. This was my first acquaintance with an English public school. Externally the flint walls and low buildings prepared me for mediaeval austerity; but at the Commemoration service in the chapel it was the soul of modern England that stirred under those Gothic arches and windows, and knelt or sang in those monastic stalls. Deeply moving was the singing by the whole school in unison of *God Save the Queen*, all the verses, under the spell of restrained emotion: fifty years of safety and glory behind, and before, for those young spirits, the promise and the uncertainties of a broad future. This was more than ten years before the Boer War, before the first hint of difficulty and limitation in British dominion. Nothing as yet impaired the sense of a glorious heritage committed to the care of the rising generation, to be maintained and enriched indefinitely. The pride of earth merged delusively and overpoweringly with the will of heaven.

"Mrs. Dick".   We lunched with one of the masters, Mr. Richardson, whose amiable wife seemed to have a mother's heart for all the boys, and among them for Russell. She instantly perceived that I cared for him and became friendly and confidential. Winchester was the only place where he was loved. Ten years later, when I went with him there again for a hearing connected with the trial of Lady Scott, Mrs. Dick, as she was called, said to me: "We would all perjure ourselves for him." The act was hardly necessary, but the readiness showed the right spirit. Justice is before the law, moral reality above moral shams; and in that trial everything was a sham, and yet substantial justice was done in the end. It is the English way.

Youthful religiosity.   In the evening I went again to the chapel. This time I was alone, and from my corner I drank in the memorable spectacle, more memorable for being something usual and the crown of every school day. The boys were less restless at that hour; fatigue and darkness cut off distractions; the spirit of the place, the language of the prayers, had a chance of attuning the senses to their ancient music. That everything external was perfunctory rather helped something internal to become dominant. I saw some boys bury their faces in their folded arms, not (it seemed to me) affectedly, but as if seeking solitude, as if fleeing to the wilderness, carried by a wave of juvenile devotion. How well I knew that plight! Adolescence, in its pregnant vagueness, casts about for some ineffable happiness in the fourth dimension. But how admirable the setting here to give a true pitch to those first notes! This simplicity in wealth protects from vulgarity, these classic poets, when grammar and ferrule are forgotten, leave a sediment of taste and soundness in the mind, and these reticent prayers, with their diplomatic dignity and courtesy, leave it for the heart to say the last word. It is all make-believe, as sports are; but in both those dramatic exercises there is excellent discipline, and the art of life is half learned when they have been practised and outgrown. What has been learned is the right manner, the just sentiment; it remains to discover the real occasions and the real risks.

His trip to the Mediterranean. In Avila, late in September, I had word from Russell, at Toulouse. "The little 'Royal' is now not far from the Pyrennees . . . We shall be at Marseilles in a week or 10 days & stay there a fortnight. I shd. be only too much pleased if you would join us there on route for Naples." His notions of travel and of foreign parts were those of the British naval man that he ought to have been. To go to Spain you took ship to Lisbon, and to get out you took ship at Barcelona for Marseilles. He was bringing the *Royal* over the *Canal du Midi* from Bordeaux to Narbonne, and back over the *Canal de Bourgogne* from Marseilles to Havre. The yacht was too small for the high seas, and her draught just not too great for those inland shallows. Naples and Sicily had been familiar to him in his childhood; he had spent long seasons there with his parents; but intervening places had little hold on his imagination. My way of travelling from one cathedral town to another he called "getting lost among the railways". Naturally, joining the *Royal* in the Mediterranean was impossible for me, living as I did on a Harvard Fellowship for study in Germany. But his lordship took another view of the matter. "What you say about reading sounds nonsense," he wrote in October. "I should say a 'travelling fellowship' meant <u>travel</u> & keep your eyes open, not settle down in a hole to mug." But before the end of

November his own spirits had flagged. He was at Civitavecchia, and wrote: "We have had vile weather—rain, cold, and lots of wind & sea: and tho' the little boat has behaved wonderfully, you would scarcely have appreciated it. . . . Thynne left me at Savona, Roberts never came, Jepson leaves me here . . . I shall probably lay up the 'Royal' at Naples, and come home about the New Year." In May, however, he was back in Italy, coasting from port to port after the fashion of the ancients. "I wish you would join me at Marseilles for the canal journey thro' France", he wrote, "as I shall be quite alone, & it will be a trip than wh. there could not be [anything] more pleasant or more lotus eating."

I join the *Royal* homeward bound on her inland voyage. By that time I had given up all hope of profiting by a longer stay in Germany, and had decided to return to Harvard to complete my studies for the doctorate. I would spend my last summer at Avila; but on the way, why shouldn't I join Russell, not at Marseilles but somewhere on the Rhône, and go with him as far as Paris? This was arranged, and I met him at Valence, early in June.

It was an inland voyage of three weeks, up and down innumerable locks, through a country wilder and more deserted than I should have thought existed in France. The rivers, whether flowing southward or northward, were wider and swifter than they seem when looked at from the banks, and seen as pictures, not felt as powers. The banks too, for the most part, without being mountainous, looked strangely primitive and unkempt. Such they must have been when Caesar and his Gaulish chieftains took them for boundaries, or forded them with warlike cries. In sympathy with those rude predecessors (or because my razors were dull and toilet on board difficult to manage) I let my beard grow: an experiment that I repeated twenty years later, much in the same spirit and ultimately with the same negative result. Being primitive and "natural" does very well when it is inevitable and unconscious; but it is a mistake and a perverse affectation when it is intentional. I shaved again that summer as soon as I got to Paris and to a decent barber; and I shaved again in 1912 when I left Harvard and began life afresh as an elderly gentleman of leisure.

Sham assurance on slippery ground. Russell spoke French readily and not incorrectly, with a strong English accent; and when speaking it he put on an air of genial assurance (rather American, I thought) entirely absent from the quiet precision of his usual con-he did the same when he spoke in England in public. It was the second thickness of the veil of Maya wrapping and smothering his transcendental self. The first layer of illusion or shamming plunged him into the business of this absurd world; the second turned him into a sort of Low Church Evangelist or middle-class Browningite or unscrupulous lawyer, smilingly and victoriously proving the truth of some palpable lie. He was said to be an excellent debater; but Lord Curzon was also said to be an eloquent speaker; and when once I heard him speak in the House of Lords, on an Indian question which he ought to have known at first hand, he was so platitudinous and partial in his matter and such a bad actor in his manner, that I could hardly believe my ears. One of the French ministers under Clemenceau, at the end of the war, at a luncheon given by the de Fontenays, had the same incredibly vulgar way of repeating party slogans with a false intonation, like a school boy declaiming badly. I can explain it only by the degradation of taste and intelligence produced by partisan propaganda. People will shout under the spell of convention things they would shudder to hear in their waking moments.

Character of his friendship. Two men in their early twenties, eating and sleeping for three weeks in the same cabin, seeing the same sights and living through the same incidents without one moment of boredom, without one touch of misunderstanding or displeasure, could not but become very good friends. But we were predestined friends before, in fact, ever since our first acquaintance; and I don't think this trip through Burgundy made much difference. Friendship in any case didn't mean for Russell what it meant for me. There was no dramatic curiosity in it for him, no love of speculation and unanimity. He cared nothing about what other people might be in themselves or in their feelings and careers; nor did he have the least need of unbosoming himself. He was frank enough and didn't take pains to disguise facts in his own life, when the interest of the moment led him to refer to them. In that way, during his lawsuits, he told me many secrets by implication; but he never set out to relate his affairs expressly, for the sake of communication and sympathy. On the contrary, I think he revelled in secrecy. By this time, in France, he already had secrets that he didn't tell me, which I think had not been the case in England the summer before. Thus he said once that he might try his luck at Monte Carlo *again*. I knew nothing of his having been there at all; but I now gathered that he had probably lost a good deal at the tables.

Broom Hall,   The atmosphere of mystery had become thick, how-
Teddington.   ever, when I joined him again in England in August. He
had now taken what might be called a mansion, Broom Hall, Teddington, with great old trees and a spacious lawn sloping gently down
to the water's edge. The dark red brick house at the top, also spacious,
without being large, had a quiet old-fashioned air. The place might
have seemed a little sad; but Russell was then bent on boating in the
Thames and despised fashionable society. For him it seemed to me
perfect. It was dignified enough to make a home of so long as he was
a bachelor, where he could have his books and family heirlooms
properly placed, and at the same time keep the *Royal* and the electric
launch at hand in his private dock. This prospect pleased him, and I
found him engrossed in putting in the electric light, and other domestic
arrangements.

Domestic   Broom Hall has acquired in my mind an ominous
complications.   aspect, like that of a smiling landscape about to be overshadowed by lowering clouds. Here were treasures piously gathered,
as if Russell meant to pick up the threads of his family traditions and
of his own chosen interests. Here were his father's books, many of
them uniformly and richly bound, lining the upper shelves; not probably
to be much read, for they were too intentionally edifying in their
virtuous adherence to a pure old-fashioned liberalism. Yet they seemed,
by their mere presence, to shed, as if they had been ikons, the simple
and ardent spirit of the young Lord Amberley, for whom his son
retained a profound affection. Lower down were ranged school classics
and the latest scientific and engineering manuals, to keep his yachting
and mechanical tastes enlightened and allied to public and intellectual
interests. Yet all this, compared with his masterful person, seemed
rather a false background, put there according to plan and intention,
but disregarded in the talk of the day. Sometimes, indeed, a paragraph
from some address at the Royal Society would be read aloud for my
benefit or some ponderous platitude, maliciously, from *The Times.*
Something else, however, would blow in, something less definite but
more alive, a breeze from the climes of Venus, a call from the open
that made those walls and those relics seem strangely sombre and
frigid. I saw only a casual intrigue; but something more serious and
fateful lay hidden behind which later was revealed to me.

As it was, I sailed for America with vague misgivings, and even
wrote some verses on Broom Hall that I soon destroyed; yet a phrase
or two linger in my memory that seem to have been prophetic. I

praised the aspect of the place, then added, *Worse follows better: the wreck of boyish faith and boyish love.*

He announces his engagement. The next summer I remained in America, preparing my first course of lectures at Harvard. There I received the following letter.

23 July 1889	Broom Hall Teddington

Dear Santayana

    I am now replying to your letter of May because I have found an answer to your query when the state of lethargy would cease. It has ceased and for the most commonplace of reasons. I have met a young woman and fallen in love with her! and soon I shall be a married man. Could a happier eventuality have occurred? Did I not often say that marriage was my best hope of salvation, only the trouble was to come across anyone I cared about? . . .

    Though no doubt the thing is common enough and may be seen every day, still the difference is that the touch of a warm human love has come to *me*, and swamps and sweeps away all cobwebs and ash-heaps in my brain. All my friends & relations say they would not know me. If I ever told you I was satisfied with my situation before, it was a lie & a mere vain attempt to deceive myself.

    Write to me and let me know if you will ever be in England or if we must wait till we go to the States to meet you.

> Ever yours
> <u>Russell</u>

    My appointment at Harvard having been renewed I took a fast steamer in the following June and was in London before the end of the month. There I found the following note awaiting me:

16 June 1890	Walton

Dear Santayana

    I am so glad to hear you are coming over. I enclose my new address: I am just moving. I shall be so glad to see you & hope you can give me a whole week . . . Name your own time as I must not miss seeing you. I am so sorry you have only a few days in England. Write me a line as soon as you get this.

> Ever yours
> <u>Russell.</u>

Mystery of a bridegroom without a bride. His new address was Amberley Cottage, Maidenhead. Odd that a newly married man should not mention his wife and still say "I" and not "we": but Russell was said to resemble Merideth's *Egoist*, and perhaps this was a sign of it. When I reached Maidenhead I was met by a little cart with a white pony: here at last was the feminine touch. We drove into a region of newly built villas in small squares of land with young hedges and little trees in curl-papers, and stopped at a flimsy particoloured "cottage", with a shallow tin verandah and the look of never having been lived in. I regretted the lovely lawn and trees and the stately symmetry of Broom Hall: but no doubt the new Lady Russell was "modern", found Teddington impossibly dull and unfashionable, and thought it better to remove Russell from his old associations. Yet why choose this vulgar place? No view, no privacy, no glimpse of the river: a colony of hen-coops in a waste field.

But where was the new Lady Russell? No sign of her in the house, which was almost unfurnished. Even Russell's "office" was bare and carpetless, I saw only a desk, two leather armchairs, and on the mantelpiece a single framed photograph: an oldish but strikingly handsome woman in a ball gown, with great eyes and other conspicuous charms: might have been an emotional actress or a prima donna. It could hardly be Russell's wife: he had spoken of a *young* woman. He noticed that I was examining the photograph attentively and said: "That is Lady Scott."

The explanation. Lady Scott was his mother-in-law. As I gathered later piecemeal during the various lawsuits that ensued, she was the daughter of a country parson and had run away to Paris when still a girl, with a wild young baronet named Sir Claude Scott; they had been married but unhappy, and she had long been a grass widow, with an uncertain income, scouring the borderland between the *monde* and the *demi-monde*. She then lived at Bray and fished in the boating region of the Thames. When she learned that a young and unmarried earl had taken a house not very far from hers, she soon found the means of making his acquaintance. She had a daughter, Mabel Edith, not so handsome as herself but presentable, and brought up like a lapdog amid false luxury and false gaiety. Here was a chance of settling Mabel Edith for life.

If you should read Russell's letter of the previous July, quoted above, without any preconceptions, would you detect anything wrong or queer about it? I think I should have suspected the rhetoric about a warm human love that had made him a new man. But Russell had really undergone a change, "the touch of a warm human love"; only the object of it had not been Mabel Edith. It had been her mother. Or rather, not so much the object of love as the guide to love; for it had been the half motherly half wifely love of a mature woman for a young man physically susceptible but morally crude and insensible. She had overwhelmed him—their letters prove it—in a torrent of effusive sympathy and affection. He had never known a mother's love: "Mrs. Dick's" had come the nearest; but now such a love enveloped him, mixed with all the arts of sensuous seduction and worldly-wise prattle of a woman that had been beautiful and was still appealing. It had been a feast of sincerity, of sympathy, of abounding endearments such as he had never known or dreamt of. Lady Scott had persuaded Russell that the way to make him and her friends for life, and guardians of each other's happiness, was for him to marry Mabel Edith. Mabel Edith was insignificant, but she was not less attractive than the housemaids and the lady-secretaries that could so easily seduce him. He would marry her.

Moral emotions of the disreputable. Persons of strict morals and limited experience might well cry: Scandalous, monstrous, impossible! What mother would so outrage and deceive her innocent child? Yet in this case the innocent child never complained of her mother: the two remained perfectly united in feeling and policy until death. To pass on Russell to Mabel Edith was, in the eyes of the latter, an act of foresight and love on her mother's part. Wasn't she marrying an attractive and important young man? Didn't she become a Countess? And if the match didn't turn out well, what marriage in the Scotts' social circle had ever turned out well? That would be bad luck, or other people's fault: and Mabel Edith could always sue for divorce, with a tidy alimony. Of course this match couldn't turn out well; and if Lady Scott didn't foresee it, I think her blindness could be due only to the fact that she was in love with Russell herself and in such a welter of emotion and excitement that she was incapable of clear observation or judgment. But poor Mabel Edith—I can't help being sorry for her—very soon discovered the mistake they had made. Russell as a husband, Russell in the domestic sphere, was simply impossible: excessively virtuous and incredibly tyrannical. He didn't allow her enough money or enough liberty. He was punctilious and unforgiving about hours, about truth-telling, about debts. He objected to her friends, her clothes, and her borrowed jewels. Moreover, in their intimate relations he was exacting and annoying. She soon hated and feared him. One day she couldn't endure him any longer and ran home to her mother, crying like a frightened child. Her mother clasped her to her bosom, petted her, soothed her; and they began to consider, with their solicitors, how best to get money out of Russell. That loving a man passionately and getting money out of him should go together was no paradox to Lady Scott. It was her ideal in life.

Such were the events, at least as I conceive them, that had caused me to find my friend no longer in the pleasant retreat of Broom Hall, but camping out in an ugly half-furnished villa in a new jerry-built quarter of Maidenhead, without his bride, but with her mother's portrait on the mantelpiece. He was already threatened with two nasty lawsuits: one brought by Emma Billings, for breach of promise of marriage, and the other by Mabel Edith, for a legal separation on the charge of cruelty.

The case against Russell. I had seen enough at Broom Hall to know that in the case of Emma Billings, Russell had something to hide: it was a common seduction, but aggravated by his old relations with the family and by the oddity of some of his demands. Russell was aware of this, and settled the matter out of court; yet a field remained open here where the Scotts might still sow rumours and insinuations. The Oxford scandal was another such field; and both, in a corrupt society, could be used to corroborate the charges of cruelty brought by Mabel Edith. These charges were ridiculous in themselves, except where they touched the intimate relations of the wife and husband: and here they were so embarrassing to describe and so impossible to prove, that they could serve only to arouse prejudice.

Position of his accusers. Lady Scott had planned something heroic: to give Russell up as a lover, resign him to her daughter, and keep him only as a dear, dear son and as a source of income. When Mabel Edith spoilt everything by leaving him and declaring war to the knife, her mother's friendly relations with him were not interrupted. "Lady Scott", he wrote, "accompanied me to Winchester on a visit to Mrs. Dick & got rather pitched into by her." No wonder; but he seems to have regarded the two matrons as his two godmothers. Lady Scott in fact always hoped for a reconciliation, and both mother and daughter kept writing him begging letters. If he proved so heartless as to refuse them all funds, what could they do but threaten? Make peace with us, they said; give us an allowance, or we will ruin your reputation. You are driving us to this against our will, and you know what lovely cues you have given us. Lady Scott felt grievously injured that Russell shouldn't understand her or remember how much she had always loved him.

The facts. As to the facts, I think I know, in outline but not in detail, exactly what they had been in Russell's earlier years. He had sown his wild oats; yet not after the manner of an ordinary rake. Gaiety was not one of his virtues or of his dangers: he was never drawn into the revelries of boon companions or of loose women. His adventures had been relatively few and obscure. He entered upon them coolly and deliberately, with certain superior preconceptions: first, a general claim to absolute liberty, and then a familiarity on the one hand with the classic poets and on the other with the life and mind of the working classes. He would talk with them endlessly, always keeping his distance, but feeling that he was virtuously democratic. This opened the way to relations that did not always remain virtuous. At school his morals were those of the typical big boys' code, no strict chastity and some bravado; but he was not exceptionally vicious or dangerous, else he would never have been appointed house prefect. His friends were the bolder spirits, and sometimes free in their talk and even in their conduct; but they were not chosen for any personal attractiveness. There was never anything soft or erotic in his relations with them; and with Lionel Johnson, his bosom friend, he moved in a nebulous revolutionary Shelleyesque heaven: they might have been two Polish poets planning a fresh creation of the universe.

The idea of paederasty, suggested by Jowett in an unhappy moment and become common talk later through the notoriety of Oscar Wilde and other aesthetes, though it had fallen within Russell's horizon in boyhood, was entirely contrary to his free inclination, as his career abundantly proved. He was not at all aesthetic; that was one of his limitations; and in his love-affairs the only abnormality was rather an excessive dominance of the primitive male impulse to be masterful, despotic, and polygamous.

The results. Thus Russell, at the age of twenty-five, found himself with his back to the wall, and obliged to defend himself in public against scandalous accusations. He was victorious in his two principal trials; but in the meantime he had delapidated his fortune and forfeited his place in the polite world. This was a greater misfortune than he thought it, because whenever he found himself opposed by a ruling convention, he comforted himself with the assertion that he was right and the convention wrong. This self-righteousness only made matters worse; he felt deeply injured, and alienated himself all the more from a world that was less offended than he, and would easily have taken him back. There is nothing sacred about convention; there is nothing sacred about private passions or whims; but the fact that a convention exists indicates that a way of living has been devised capable of maintaining itself. I had no more *respect* for the polite world than Russell had, and that was the ground of my sympathy with him: for if convention has the advantage of possessing the field, rebellion against convention has the advantage of springing afresh from the heart, the ultimate judge of everything worth having or doing. Yet a young man with a brilliant career open to him in the world is a fool to flout public opinion, even if he secretly despises it. Peace with the polite world is all important for one's comfort and euphoria so long as one lives in the polite world.

Luckily Russell's rebellions were not total or radical. They were in fact hereditary, and those of a vast movement long afoot in modern times. He was therefore able to pass into what might be called the anti-polite world, and to play his part there. The Labour Party could take his sermons in gaol at their word, and the verdicts of Courts in his favour as final. They could regard him as morally rehabilitated, and could mend his fortunes by including him in the Government. But Russell was never more desperate than in those last years. British society is sustained by "created interests", that is to say, by vain commitments into which people have been led unawares, but which it would be too disturbing now to abandon. The farce must be kept up, and it becomes a point of honour to drop dead at last upon the stage, in all one's paint and feathers.

XX
Changes in Avila

Avila again my centre. When after three years, in July 1886, I returned for the second time to Avila, my arrival had been duly announced by letter, for a suitable hour in the afternoon. My father and Don Pelayo were at the station to receive me, and everything at the house was as I had left it. There were no explanations to make. Even my old aunt María Ignacia knew that I was going to Germany to study philosophy. I was to be a professor abroad, or if not a professor, an architect. There was no question any longer of a career in Spain; I was too old and too much expatriated by my English language and my American associations. On the other hand I came to Avila with a sense of coming home, and with the intention of always returning there. Official life would carry me out of Spain, as it had carried my father; but so long as he lived, he would be my natural centre. While a student, I should spend my longer holidays with him; and I vaguely foresaw, what has not proved altogether unlike the truth, that I should spend my old age very much as he did, perhaps in Avila, with another Don Pelayo for company.

I find another cousin married to Rafael Vegas. The next day my father said we must go to see my cousin Elvira, daughter of his brother Nicolás, my godfather; she was now married and living in Avila. And married to whom? To Rafael Vegas, the same who had been the husband of my other pretty cousin, the unfortunate Antoñita. In the interval of some fifteen years, naturally Rafael had not lived alone, but had married and buried his third wife. He was still the same peacock, though some of his plumes were now white, and when he wedded Elvira people shook their heads. He was a bluebeard, and this poor young girl would die of childbirth within a year, like Antoñita, and leave the old libertine, with his taste for dainty morsels, to gobble up some fifth victim. But the gossips this time were wrong. They didn't suspect the equal capacity of the fair Elvira, as yet unrevealed, for shedding yearly husbands. I have never heard of such a wealth of legal couplings as there were in her matrimonial circle. She was the fourth wife of her first husband, the second wife of her second, and the third wife of her third. She would remain each time childless, quietly smiling, and readier than ever to marry again.

A pleasing Though short and fat, Elvira had a pronounced fem-
person. inine charm. There was something calm, friendly, and sound about her person. Her clear white skin and no less clear brown eyes and soft curly brown hair gave her an air of neatness. She was *simplex munditiis*; and in spite of domestic duties, even at the times when she was poorest, she was always scrupulously clean. Her small hands moved nimbly and touched pleasantly; and she had a way of folding a scarf or shawl round her exuberant bosom that expressed happiness, grace, and almost humour. It was in the breast that she was most developed; the rest of her figure, though plump, seemed in comparison well-turned and almost tapering. She moved well; and when she was prosperous and suitably dressed—her third and last husband was a banker—she had the free and sure air of a lady. She ought to have been a lady, being born the daughter of an army officer who ought to have been a gentleman; and her Andalusian mother, whose name was Engracia or Grace, also had some pretensions to breeding or at least to luxury. But this only made her the more dissatisfied with her lot, her skin the yellower and her voice the shriller; and my maiden aunts, who resented her superior airs, used to say of their brother: "*Engracia le ha caido en gracia, y se ha desgraciado*", which might be translated theologically by saying that Grace fell upon him and he was lost. The lady no doubt had a bad temper and could not forgive herself for being less brilliant than a sister of hers who had gone on the stage, who sang in light opera, married a rich man, became a widow when still young and good-looking, and lived luxuriously with her four children in Malaga, in an apartment like a *bonbonnière*, where I visited her in 1887. These were Elvira's "rich" relations, from whom she got her ideals of elegance and coquetry; yet by nature, like her father and mine and all true Castilians, she possessed a rather detached and sceptical philosophy, one that teaches us that all conditions are bearable, all dignities trumpery, and wisdom simply the gift of making the best of whatever is thrust upon us.

Elvira at my Rafael always had lived from hand to mouth, appar-
father's. ently prosperous but without any roots. His unexpected death left Elvira penniless, and she had to go and live with my father, in his poor man's house; for in spite of his own very modest means,

he was the stay and refuge of his whole family. This was the young widow's hibernation, and lasted several years. Whenever I came back to Avila, I found her established at my father's as one of the family, at times with Susana, usually alone. She seemed resigned, disillusioned, and cheerful. It was not at this time that she thought of perhaps marrying me. I was too young, a mere student from Germany, insignificant in comparison with her late pompous husband, who always took the lead in any circle, and knew by heart all the tricks of a country lawyer and an elderly ladykiller. But we got on very well together. I perceived that a year's life with Rafael, while it had left her without a shred of innocence, had neither disgusted nor corrupted her. She took the whole concealed side of life calmly, sensibly, without horror or curiosity; she had instinctively seen how tiresome it is; and we were able to talk about everything satirically, like two old cronies for whom the world has only a speculative interest.

She rejects an army captain risen from the ranks. She was not in those days without an earnest suitor, though she never accepted him, even as a *novio*. He was an excellent person, about forty-five years of age, but common; a cavalry captain who had risen from the ranks, whose name was Don Cándido. He was riding-master to the small garrison of the town, and gave me—as an indirect attention to Elvira—the only riding-lessons I ever took. They were of little use to me; I am not built for dancing or riding, and a foretaste of my necessary clumsiness at such things makes me avoid them. If I could ever have become good at them it would only have been, as in the case also of mathematics, if I had found an intelligent master who should have begun by explaining to me the *principles* of the thing, not an empirical practitioner like honest dull Don Cándido who could only tell me to stick to the saddle and to go ahead.

But accepts an old man and soon becomes an independent and expectant widow. But sticking to the saddle is not enough to please the ladies, and he never got ahead with Elvira. Somehow, however, she attracted the notice of a retired shopkeeper—let us call him merchant—a worthy and childless widower, who asked her to become his wife, as she sensibly did, foreseeing that he would soon leave her a little money, enough to make her independent. This happened almost at once; and then she took a small flat, in an *entresol*, overlooking the busiest street in the town. Sitting by her balcony, she was little above the heads of the passers-by. Everybody saw and admired her, demurely sewing between her flower-pots; and she saw everybody and everything that passed, and through her maid or her own explorations she could learn everything that happened. It was a pleasant nest; and when I occasionally went to see her there, although we could hardly have the long unintentional conversations of the days when we lived in the same house, I became aware that she was considering the possibility of marrying me. She had no notion of geography or of foreign languages or foreign life; and seeing that I was well dressed and travelled about comfortably, she imagined she might live pleasantly in "America", that is, in Habana, on fifteen hundred dollars a year, which was then my salary. Probably she supposed that my family were rich and that I should have a share in their fortune.

The expected arrives. It was not necessary for me to undeceive her on these points; my stay in Avila was short; and when I returned in a later year, I found that a far more desirable suitor had presented himself and been gladly accepted. He was her neighbour, and doubtless from his own balconies on the first floor over his banking-house, he had watched her agreeable face, at her window, and been assured of her simple and quiet life. His second wife had recently died, leaving an infant in arms, his only child. What better mother than Elvira could he provide for it, or more blooming partner for himself?

Also the unexpected. In October, 1905, I was in Avila, having a year's leave of absence from Harvard, and being on my way to Egypt, Palestine, and Greece. The procession of *La Santa* passed Elvira's new house, and I was invited to see it from her windows. Two agreeable nieces of her husband's also were living there; the husband himself was gracious and well-spoken; we discussed the King's English marriage, then just announced, and I duly admired the fat and rosy baby. It was a picture of domestic happiness, dignity, and peace. But letters reached me that winter while I was in the East, announcing a rather strange and melancholy coincidence. Elvira had mysteriously fallen ill, and her husband also, and lying in separate rooms the two had died on the same day.

Elvira was not religious or romantic. Such a sudden fall of the curtain on a scene of decent well-being fits well with her person, her character, and her ideas. Her life had been thoroughly reasonable, frank, and mediocre. After a Chinese fashion, it was philosophical and sufficient.

Susana
comes to
live in Spain.

The great event for me in Spain occurred upon my third return, in 1887, when after my memorable first sojourn in England, and a quiet month or two at Avila with my father and Elvira, I went to Gibraltar to meet Susana. That Susana should henceforth be in Spain (for I was sure she would never return to America, although she sometimes spoke of doing so "for a visit") weighted that centre of gravity decisively in my planetary system. It gave me an added reason for returning there often, and solved the problem of residence whenever I returned. For her, however, it was not a sufficient solution. She needed to be enthusiastic and she needed to be comfortable, and Spain was neither. Not that she had any feeling but affection for Spain, and loyalty to it even in those unhappy days; but now she was herself unhappy, and Spain didn't help her. Still, on the religious side the change of atmosphere was a relief; it removed the sense of tension under which she had so cruelly suffered; and this not merely externally or socially. I think that slowly, by living in Spain, her personal religious life was normalised, reduced to its healthy human function, and cleared of anxiety and bitterness.

Small
discomforts
and large
disappoint-
ments.

On the social side, Susana was adaptable, and always took a healthy interest in the present. When in America she hadn't missed Spain, and now again in Spain she didn't miss America. Her good spirits in Boston, in the earlier days, had flowed from fun and comfort. When now she spoke of Boston society, she laughed at it for being so full of false pretenses and of unnecessary points of pride. These were things that her Catholic discipline had taught her to put away. The only American memories that she seemed to idealise touched little luxuries and creature comforts: warm houses, bathrooms, table manners, ventilation, and *silver* knives, as she credulously called them, for the fruit. Her constitution was soft and frail, in spite of her robust appearance, and she suffered disproportionally from minor irritants: tobacco smoke, lights in the eyes, the crude scent of mutton, sourness even in good strawberries. She was weary, these trifles disturbed her physical peace, and made her seem less amiable than she was by nature. For in regard to people, though retrospectively critical enough, she was spontaneously sympathic. Strangers, especially ladies, who saw her for the first time or had only occasional interviews with her, almost invariably liked her very much; but the value of such sympathy was only social, and left her daily life empty and dull. The fundamental difficulty came neither from Spain nor from America, neither from her friends nor her family. It came from the fact that she was thirty-six years old, and unmarried.

Susana's excursion with my father to the tomb of Santa Teresa. Between my father and Susana there was an old mutual affection, and they attempted for a while to live up to it. For instance, Susana wished to make a pilgrimage to the tomb of Santa Teresa; but Alba de Tormes, where the saint is buried, was almost inaccessible, except on horse-back or rather on mule-back. There was a road of sorts, but no public conveyance, and a private carriage would have involved too much expense. My father, being a good pedestrian, was willing to walk there and back; and for Susana he conceived the plan of hiring a country waggon, with a mule and a *mozo*; a mattress could be spread out in the cart, which had a round canvas top; and there Susana could sit or lie down during the longer stretches. It was rickety, hard, and not very restful; and they would have to spend one night in whatever *posada* they could find at Alba; but they managed it. The excursion remained a memorable jaunt for him, and an act of piety or of penance for her: and there were no unpleasant effects, except that in Avila she acquired the nick-name, *la pelegrina*, which became capable of unkind interpretations.

Imperfect sympathy with Mercedes. For a few days old affection and present good intentions could carry off the comedy between step-father and step-daughter; but it couldn't be kept up permanently. He was too old, crotchety, and poor; she was too much wedded to those religious opinions which directly or indirectly he was always attacking. Nor was there any need of keeping the thing up. She hadn't come to Spain in order to live with him, but rather with Doña Victorina and Mercedes. They had a flat in Madrid and a little house by the seaside, near Vigo, for the summer. Here there was no religious quarrel. Doña Victorina was pious, and Mercedes was more than pious: not only daily mass and communion, but apostolic labours in evening schools for working men in Vigo. Mercedes also had social position and, like Susana, had basked in the smiles of royalty; often visited the Infanta Isabel, and sometimes Queen María Cristina and even Queen Victoria Eugénie. Nevertheless, although in speaking to me both sides were naturally discreet, I could feel that between Susana and Mercedes there was no real sympathy, not even in religion. Mercedes was immensely spontaneous, pagan, superstitious, over-flowing with devout sentiments, in diplomatic relations with the court of heaven even closer than with the court of Madrid. Susana was theological, instructed, theoretical; she justified her sentiments first and then, perhaps, she felt them. Mercedes was all initiative. In religion Susana had no initiative; she had sympathy only with things already afoot. She was at once imitative and satirical; because after mimicking involuntarily something that others were doing, her own disposition and intelligence reasserted themselves; so that she, like me, played a double part in her tragedy: she was one of the characters and also the chorus. And, unlike me, she had executive impulses that must have clashed with those of Mercedes. When she joined a movement, she wanted to manage it. When she joined a family, if it were not possible or proper for her to rule it, she couldn't rest there. Cohabitation with the Escaleras was therefore never a real solution. Susana said that Galicia in summer didn't agree with her: the verdure and dampness brought on her New England "hay-fever". She preferred Avila.

Quarrels and jealousies.   Yet Avila, secluded as it might seem, was a microcosm, with all the problems of a world. Besides the tension with my father, there was soon an open quarrel with Elvira. The two hadn't the same breeding; Elvira wasn't pious, she had been the wife of an old rake, Susana found her unprincipled and coarse. Elvira on her side whispered things about Susana that oughtn't to be whispered and attributed motives that oughtn't to be attributed. It became impossible for my father's two guests to remain together. Elvira couldn't be sent away; she had nowhere to go, and no money. Her rich aunt in Malaga, on the first Christmas after Rafael's death, had sent a large box of raisins and other sweets to console her niece, who was so fortunate as to have a dear old uncle to live with in her widowhood; but on the second Christmas, when Elvira hoped to be invited by her dear rich aunt to go and live in Malaga, no present arrived and there was stony silence. It was therefore Susana, being independent, who had to leave. In winter, in any case, she was to join Doña Victorina and Mercedes in Madrid; the parting from my father therefore had nothing tragic about it; and Elvira automatically remained with him, uncriticised and blooming alone. But where should Susana spend the following summer? With Doña Victorina and Mercedes in Galicia, when she was a free American and preferred Avila? She wasn't going to allow an ill-bred ill-natured woman like Elvira to upset her plan of life or control her movements. She would spend that following summer in Avila, in another house.

There were two quiet and agreeable elderly sisters, old friends of Susana's, whom we called *las de Madorell*, one of them a widow with two daughters. The elder daughter, Monserrat, had lately been married. They had room for Susana in their house and would be really glad of her company, much more entertaining than their own, and of the generous contribution she would make to their little budget. There was only one objection—a foolish one. *Las de Madorell* lived in the same street as Don Celedonio Sastre, an old flame of Susana's, now a widower. Evil tongues would say that she came to live in that street so that Don Celedonio should not be able to forget her existence and her proximity. Such nonsense had to be disregarded: but Providence had mysteriously designed the means of defeating such gossip before it arose. Monserrat unexpectedly died, leaving two little girls, one just born, the other a year older. Their grandmother, one of the Madorell sisters, would go to look after them, leaving still more room for Susana in the house, and would establish a sort of continuity, almost a union, between the Madorells' household and that of Monserrat's disconsolate husband.

A military admirer.   This husband, now a widower, whose name was Bringas, thus became a second widower in Susana's immediate neighbourhood; and this to some purpose. Bringas was an army man and a professor in the Military Academy in Avila. Of the various Military Academies this was the most modest, preparing cadets for the Commissariat; but this involved in the professors somewhat wider and more business-like knowledge than infantry or cavalry officers were expected in those days to imbibe: supplies and transport were at once scientific and commercial matters. Bringas accordingly had a rather wide acquaintance with international affairs, industrial as well as political; and from the first he had naturally found much to talk about with Susana, fresh as she was from twenty years' residence in the United States. I believe he was an intelligent as well as a kindly man; but all that I may have heard him say was obliterated in my mind by the image of his person and his extravagant gesticulations. He jumped about and waved his arms like a puppet on a wire; and he proved the absurdity of this, or the impossibility of that, with so much emphasis and victorious joy, that you forgot entirely what the joy and the demonstration were about. He was a thin nervous man, I daresay very strong, with a thin black beard and bright black eyes: most lively, but most restless, and I should have thought most tiresome. Yet those who knew him well were greatly attached to him; and I think Susana liked him, liked him better, perhaps, than she did Celedonio, but also feared him more, and felt less secure in his presence. In Celedonio there were no possible surprises, he was older and thoroughly consolidated, in mind and body. Bringas was a jumping-jack, an electrical apparatus. Who could tell what he might do next?

Peace without victory. The sympathy that grew up in these circumstances between Bringas and Susana was obvious to everybody: it was obvious to me whenever I saw them together; and it was known to Celedonio; so that the presence of Susana for one summer in his street, far from seeming an advance toward him on her part, proved a cause of jealousy. A passing cause: because before the next year Elvira had married her second husband; then Susana returned to live at my father's, and ultimately Bringas married his deceased wife's sister, who had always secretly cared for him. The storm in the Avila teapot had cleared, and Susana's future remained to be determined by undisturbed reason.

Susana's marriage. I call it reason, because reason in my philosophy is only a harmony among irrational impulses; and the hesitating, much meditated, troubled course that Susana now took was rational only in that sense. She decided to marry Celedonio. In their difficult negotiations it was agreed that the wedding should take place *after* that of Celedonio's daughter, who was the eldest of his six children, and had been for some years at the head of his household. Obviously, it would be unpleasant for her to be superseded there by a half foreign step-mother, with money of her own. The five boys wouldn't mind so much; they might even see the advantages of the change: they would have better food, more interesting talks, and perhaps a few lessons in English at home gratis. But Celedonio had the selfishness of lazy power. Without being ambitious or meddlesome, he was insensible to the desires of others. His daughter had a *novio* of whom he didn't approve. He desired her to marry another man, whom she didn't like. He would not force her, of course; he was no tyrant; but he wouldn't allow her to marry the other man. His own marriage was thereby postponed or would have had to be given up; but that his dignity wouldn't permit. And he persuaded Susana to consent to their marriage *before* that of his daughter. If on trial, step-mother and step-daughter couldn't get on, that would be an added incentive for the girl to be reasonable and marry the man that pleased her father. And this wasn't the end of Celedonio's selfishness. Far from hastening his daughter's match, when trouble began between the women at home, he put off any settlement. He liked to have his only daughter at home, as well as his new wife. She could do him all sorts of little services, as of old, that were not to be expected of Susana; and she could look after the boys in the old slip-shod economical way, and let Susana play the sultana, growing fat and indolent, in quite separate apartments. The result was that Celedonio found himself the master of two households, actually on two separate floors, his wife's and his daughter's. When definite disputes arose, he settled them judicially, like a Roman father; and he pretended not to notice the daily friction, the estrangement, the grievances that grew worse every year. His daughter was condemned to die an old maid, and his wife never to feel identified with her new family or to secure their affection.

She ends by establishing her position. Only in the later years, after her step-daughter had died and several of the boys were married, did Susana's position become less unpleasant. She had more money than at first and kept a part of it from her husband. This Yankee insistence on individual rights was a sort of revenge for not being accepted and appreciated as she deserved; but in the end it redounded to the advantage of Celedonio's family. In old age he became stingy, and he had always been insensible to his children's wishes and needs: the result was that they had hardly enough to live on. It was then Susana that came to the rescue; and the boys' wives were grateful. They called her *mamá*, as the boys had never been allowed to do by their sister; and they brought up the grandchildren to speak well of her and to respect her.

My quarters at my brother-in-law's. Celedonio was a landlord on a small scale, as well as a lawyer, and possessed a farm at easy riding distance from Avila and a house in the town; but his chief occupation was to be agent for two or three greater landlords who had estates in the province, and lived elsewhere. His house stood on the better side of the town, a little beyond the walls, and had a wide view over the *Valle de Amblés*. For me now it became a sort of summer home. Towns in these parts are cooler than the country. Thick stone walls and courtyards overhung with galleries protect from the merciless sun, while the keen mountain air blows through and keeps the lungs and the spirit fresh. Here my father's books, in their old bookcases, and various portraits painted by his hand, as well as odd things of my own, were collected in two little rooms to the left of the street entrance or *portal*; and this apartment was called *el cuarto*

de Jorge. There I was entirely independent, with a door into the open
court, and two barred windows on the square. To those bars sometimes
in the early morning some passing peasant would tie his donkeys. I
could hear the vendors' cries, and the bells ringing not very melodiously
for mass, or tolling for the dead. I could also overhear various conversations of the passers-by, or of old women who stopped to gossip.
I was in the old world; I might have been in the seventeenth century.

The house   On the other side of the street entrance there was a
and the life   large room, now a coach-house and lumber-room, that
in it.   must have been originally the hall or countinghouse,
where the master sat and received his tenants or clients and carried
on his business. In a restoration it would have made the best room
in the house: an excellent library or billiard-room, according to the
taste of the proprietor. Behind this lay the court, paved in large irregular
stones and stretching, on the ground floor, from wall to wall the whole
width of the house; but the stone stairs, open to the air, led up on
one side to an overhanging gallery, supported by a few stone pillasters,
that ran round three sides of the court on the first floor, and left only
a central square open to the sky, with the tiled roof sloping from all
sides inward, so that during a heavy shower the water came splashing
and roaring down as in four little cataracts upon the stone pavement.
This ground floor was not the ground floor at the back: the sharp
declivity of the land here turned it a second storey. There was a central
deep room, the family sitting-room, and two smaller rooms, one on
each side. The central one had a large alcove, with two beds, where
Celedonio and Susana slept: one of the smaller ones was his office
and the other her dressing-room. Upstairs the house was again divided
by the court into two distinct portions. In front, looking out on the
square, was a suite of five rooms, occupied by Celedonio's daughter,
and her aunt, her mother's maiden sister, who had been left alone,
and had become a member of this family. She was a delicate quiet
person, and rather a blessing, since she behaved well and kept her
niece company. In the back part of this floor were some new additions
made by Celedonio: a large dining-room with a splendid outlook, a
kitchen, and several other rooms for the boys and for the servants.
We had breakfast,—chocolate and a large roll cut into long strips,
and perhaps a glass of milk in addition,—each in his own room; and
dinner was at two, or whenever Celedonio had finished his business
in his office. After dinner the family dispersed immediately, and often

Celedonio also went down stairs to interview somebody who came on business.

Tête-à-têtes   Susana and I would usually sit for an hour or more
with Susana.   *de sobre mesa*, and if we were alone, would sometimes drop into English. But I didn't like this, unless reminiscence of Boston made it appropriate. Susana's Spanish was better than mine, but her English was worse, partly because of disuse, partly because she had adopted indiscriminately all the ways of speaking that she had heard, and some of them were dreadful. The best conversations we had, however, were in the evening after supper, in the earlier years. Supper was nominally at half-past nine, sometimes later, and Celedonio would immediately go to bed and fall asleep. The boys went to the Mercado Grande, where the élite of Avila walked and sat on summer evenings, sometimes to the primitive music of the town band. Then Susana and I could sit by the open balcony in the *sala*, admiring the extraordinarily brilliant starry sky, enjoying the cool of the night air, and discussing the past, the present, and the future. On the eternal we seldom touched. Her religious zeal had become wiser, she let God look after his own interests, and didn't worry any longer about other people's salvation.

My walks.   The only entertainments for me during these many
                    seasons in Avila were my long afternoon walks. At first Rafael, one of the boys, used to accompany me. He was sensitive to poetry, to religion, and to the arts, without having much technical knowledge; but his feeling was genuine and uncontaminated by any passing fashion. In 1905–6, when I was lecturing at the Sorbonne, I invited him to come and spend a month in Paris. He came: and I remember one day in the Louvre, when I pointed out some Luca della Robbia reliefs, his sudden interest, and the simplicity with which he took out a note-book and pencil, and made a sketch of one of the pieces, with a note of the colouring. "When I get back to Zorita" (his father's farm) he said, "I will make one like that." Later, in Avila, however, I usually walked alone, and reduced myself to modest elderly circuits. The shortest and most obvious was to go round the city walls, down by the Rastro to the river, then up the old road skirting the north wall closely as far as San Vicente, and then home by the Cathedral apse and the Mercado Grande. This walk—a question of less than an hour—had something that especially recommends itself to my heart and lungs. The ups are sharp and short, the downs gradual and long drawn out. You are stimulated at moments to a little climbing, and you are insensibly propelled and aided in the long stretches. My father's

favourite walk, up the *carretera* to the *alto de Vico* and back, had the disadvantage of a slight rise all the way out; also that of occasional dust and passing muleteers and pedestrians. I preferred pristine solitude. Such was to be found by following the river downward, as far as the dam at the electric power station; it was a path amid great boulders, with varied effects of foreground and distance. But it meant coming up-hill all the way home; and the same objection kept me from often choosing the road to Toledo, though the scene was pleasing and I came out into the country at once, without passing through the town. In the end I discovered something unexpected: that the footpath along the railway-line going towards Madrid made an excellent promenade. There were no trains either way at the hour when I went out; and the rocky slopes upward on one side, and the ravines downward on the other, gave you the sense of being in the mountains, as in fact you were. There were also more trees and grass than usual in these highland moors, where the earth is dressed prevalently, like the religious orders, in browns and greys. Avila, though it supports life, looks enough like a desert to symbolise the desert that the world is for the spirit, in spite of the crowd and the pressure there. In both you may come unexpectedly upon scattered flowers or herbs of the sweetest smell; and I treasured the double monition of that bare and austere landscape, and of those sombre yet glittering altars.

A new phase in my family relations. Those pleasant seasons in Avila were interrupted for me by the war; and when I returned in 1919, after five or six years' absence, though the places were the same the persons were somewhat altered. We all were growing old. I in particular had been deeply affected, not only by the war but by a thorough review and digestion of all my English and American experience. I had written *Egotism in German Philosophy*, *Soliloquies in England* and *Character and Opinion in the United States*. Not being able to fix my thoughts on abstract matters, I had read Dickens, and learned to love that humbler side of English sentiment and virtue. Without so much as asking for a reason, my heart had been entirely on the English side in the war. At Avila, everybody's sympathies were entirely on the other side; and this antithesis rather disconcerted me. My Spanish, too, from disuse had become less fluent. There had been deaths in the family; the daughter, her aunt, and one of the sons. These things somewhat narrowed the field of talk and embittered it. I asked myself why I should still come here, if it were not to be a pleasure all round.

I play the affectionate great uncle. Yet there are attachments to persons and places that hold us even when they give us pain; and I found, at least the first year, a new pleasure here and a new attachment. Pepe, the youngest of the sons, had been married before the war and he now had two little boys, five and four years of age, who became my companions. Not for walks, naturally: but they would come into my room in the early afternoon and we would amuse ourselves painting pictures. When this vein was exhausted, I got a toy theatre, with various stage-settings and card-board figures; and with my old box of water-colours at hand I was able to make other figures, and to reproduce one of the plays in which Susana had acted in her girlhood (our sister Josefina remembered the text) and also one or two Russian ballets, that I had seen in Paris or London. We had one dress performance, to which the whole family was invited; and the preparations and rehearsals amused the little boys and amused me even more for days and days. These were not pastimes that could last long. When I returned in a later year the elder boy was not at home. He had been sent, probably for religious instruction, to an uncle, his mother's brother, who was a priest; and with the younger boy, Roberto, alone, we couldn't revive the old interest. But we read a book of Mother Goose, which they had; and although the child didn't learn much English, I learned sometimes how profound was the difference between modern English and Catholic breeding. Roberto was a sensitive and high-spirited boy; and when I translated for him the lines about Little Jack Horner and the Christmas pie, he felt the *fun* of it perfectly, until having stuck in his thumb and pulled out a plum, Jack Horner says, "What a good boy am I!" Instead of laughing at this, Roberto blushed, seemed a little embarrassed and doubtfully amused, as if he had heard something very improper. What a shocking, incredible thing, he thought, for anyone to say! So deeply had the lesson of Christian humility penetrated into this society, that it seemed scandalous even as a joke to imagine a greedy boy praising himself or congratulating himself. Even one's relations were never to be praised or boasted of. You might expatiate on how much you loved them: this was a source of care, a constant danger of great suffering, for you; it was not a virtue either in you or in those you loved. It was one of your trials, almost one of your sins. You were a bundle of imperfections. You might laugh or you might grieve; you never could have anything to boast of.

The young Roberto, named after my brother.   This boy Roberto had been so named after my brother, who had made at least two journeys into Spain, first with his whole family, then more wisely alone. He had been taken ill there, and stayed longer than he had intended. He had been with Mercedes to Galicia, and much delighted with her circle, in which, as I once counted it in Madrid, there were twenty-seven women and not one man. My brother Robert seemed a complete Yankee. He had no knowledge and no feeling of what Spain represents in history and in morals; but with Spanish women he returned, as it were, to a forgotten paradise. He was generically fond of the sex, of no matter what nationality; but Spanish women held him suspended in a special way between respect and desire; and far below his crude conscious level something in him responded to Spanish love and Spanish religion. This secret need—unknown even to himself—had inspired him with a great sympathy with Pepe, who wished to be married but was prevented by his father's opposition; and Robert succeeded in bringing Pepe's wedding about, partly by expostulating with Celedonio, going so far as to call him a tyrant, and partly by generous gifts of his own to help the young couple. It was in gratitude for this action of Robert's that they had named their second son Roberto.

Light shining in the darkness.   My brother didn't live to see the destiny of his namesake; it was I who watched it from a distance with a special interest. Roberto was fond of books and of all sorts of knowledge, reminding me of my boyish pleasure in geography and travels. He, like his brother, was also religious; they were among the first to catch the new wave of hope and enthusiasm for the moral regeneration of Spain. They joined the *Falange*, fought in the civil war, and Roberto, after being twice wounded, was killed at the end, within sight of victory. It is at once sad, bitter, and amusing to think how little my brother Robert, and the hundred million like him in America, could have understood this little tragedy, the fruit in one way of his overflowing good will and kindness.

Farewell to Spain.   I watched all this, as I say, from a distance, because after Susana's death in 1928, there was little occasion or propriety in my imposing myself on Celedonio's family. I went that summer to Galicia, to see Mercedes and my sister Josefina; also to see something of that corner of Spain, which was new to me. I even passed through a corner of Portugal, taking the fast train from Paris to Oporto, and thence to Vigo by a secondary line; and on my way back I visited Santiago de Compostela, La Coruña, Leon, and Palencia, studiously avoiding Avila, because I knew that the state of Celedonio's mind was unfavourable, and I wished to avoid unnecessary discussions. He was nearly ninety, full of crotchets, and bent on delaying the execution of Susana's will. He died, however, before the next summer; and then I did go to Avila, for the last time, to settle Josefina's affairs and also my own. This I managed without great difficulty. I gave my father's house, built by John Smith, to the Sastre brothers. For many years they had been collecting the rent of it for me, and this was only a small acknowledgement of their friendliness and of the prolonged hospitality of their family, which had been a cause of great joy to me. Besides, I persuaded Josefina to sign a letter—a formal will covering her American property had been signed in Vigo the preceding summer before the American consul—asking her executors to give suitable legacies for life to Mercedes, the Sastre brothers, and some other friends of hers in Spain. Having thus burned my ships and cleared my conscience in regard to business duties, I said farewell to Avila and to Spain, no doubt for ever. I shed no tears. I retained within me all that I wanted or could ever now enjoy in Spain. I cut off only useless repetitions and disappointments.

Last days of my sister Josefina. My sister Josefina, who was seventy-seven years of age, died the next winter, peacefully, without pain, and without moral worries. She was not without a certain shrewdness in small matters, but vague and indifferent in most directions. After Susana's death, they found means of reconciling Josefina to the Church: Susana had been, curiously enough, the great obstacle to her sister's faith: Josefina didn't want to be dominated. But the ladies in Avila, who were pious without being aggressive or punctilious, won her over with soft words; and they told me that the Dominican who heard her confession said that he thought she had never committed a mortal sin in her life. Perhaps not. He saw that she was like a little child, docile or rebellious according to the tact of her elders, but irresponsible. Some lines from I don't know where stick in my mind, for describing her perfectly:

> *Elle est morte et n'a point vécu.*
> *Elle faisait semblant de vivre;*
> *De sa main est tombé le livre*
> *Dans lequel elle n'a rien lu.*

Trials and projects in Susana's old age.

Susana, who had lived intensely and had made brave, desperate ventures more than once in her day, could not hope for such a tranquil end. When time and death had solved the worst difficulties of her married life, and she might have expected to reach port in calm weather, a new and unforeseen trouble overtook her. Celedonio, who had never been considerate, became morose and intractable. At the same time, he became helpless. There arose a chronic resentment between them. The only comfort was that now his family were on her side; for it was the sons that suffered most from their father's obstinacy and niggardliness. Susana no longer slept in the other bed in Celedonio's alcove: one of his sons slept there, in case his father required help during the night. Susana had a bed in her dressing-room, which looked out into the broad country. She could sleep in a well-ventilated apartment. And she could keep her savings, as much as twenty thousand dollars, safe in a concealed drawer, unknown to her husband. And her thoughts would run—was it wicked to let them do so?—to the time when Celedonio would have disappeared, and she could restore the house next door—not this house, which had too many disturbing associations—to live in comfortably in her last days, with me and Josefina and the eldest of Celedonio's sons. Wouldn't he, I asked her, prefer to join one of his married brothers? No, said Susana, because in his brother's household he would have to pay his share of the expenses while at his step-mother's he would get board and lodging for nothing.

Architectural dreams, as in our first days in Boston, again would bring us together. Should the court-yard have a glass roof? I said no. The duke of Valencia had put one into his restored palace because he was an Andalusian; and in Seville the *patio* was the family living-room in winter as well as summer, and they wished to be protected from the cold and rain. But in Avila no one would think of sitting in winter in a court-yard; the open air, on the south side of some great wall, was the place for sunning oneself; and a glass roof spoilt all the architectural effect and poetry of a *patio*. But Susana said the galleries would be terribly cold in winter for passing from one room to another. That, I retorted, could be prevented by glazing the upper galleries, leaving the court and the lower gallery open to the sky. A glazed or even walled upper gallery was a characteristic and picturesque feature in mediaeval houses. She might have that next door, and be both comfortably and artistically housed.

The tragic incompleteness of life. Celedonio must have surmised that, with various degrees of impatience, Susana, his sons and especially his sons' wives were waiting for him to die. Not a pleasing thought to hover over your pillow. And your retort in old age can hardly be to grow amiable and generous, so that everybody shall love you and wish you a long life. That is not feasible. The natural retort is to revenge oneself by growing more disagreeable and more miserly, and by straining every nerve to live longer than people expect. The sweetest triumph would be to survive all these younger people who wish to bury you. And Celedonio, as far as Susana was concerned, enjoyed this triumph. When I last said goodbye to him, "until next year", he shook his head, and muttered that he wouldn't survive that winter. He did survive it; but Susana, who was standing by and not thinking of dying so soon, did not survive it. She had never been really strong. At one time she grew enormously fat, then later lost flesh and seemed less unwieldy; but she suffered from physical and moral disharmonies in her nature, and never was or could be thoroughly resigned or content. The house next door was restored by one of her stepsons with her money; and the same pile of banknotes kept so secretly in her drawer served another step-son to restore the house she had lived in for thirty-five years, in comparative shabbiness and discomfort. She and I never had our architectural domicile together; and she never enjoyed the sense of having found her true place in the world and of having won the esteem and gratitude of those who surrounded her. The bar sinister, as it were, of divided allegiances and of incompatible demands always cut across her fairest prospects.

Susana was a Sturgis. Like many of the Sturgises she had good looks, good humour, enthusiasm, love of society, and love of fun; and like the best of them, such as her Aunt Sarah, she had also an intrepid instinct of leadership, and could direct her passionate interest to some ideal and public end, in her case, towards the Catholic Church. This was not an effect of special intellectual or mystical insight into religion; the Sturgises were not naturally religious. It was an effect of contagion: she easily caught any ambient enthusiasm, and held to it more innocently perhaps and longer than those from whom she caught it. At the same time, she needed social support and sympathy. It would have been agony for her to be alone with Allah. In order to flourish she required benign and congenial influences. Had these been more prevalent in her life she would have been universally loved and admired. Her mind would have been enlarged and refined; whereas in her continually difficult position she could hardly avoid the irritability and the unjust judgments of the unsatisfied. Yet this ran counter to her nature; I, to whom she had always shown her best side, could feel the warm affection beneath her partisanship, and the comedy behind her illusions. She couldn't bear to let the good and the beautiful slip by unrealised. Hence her impulse to dominate and to manage. That which grieves me now in her destiny is not so much what she missed as what she suffered. It is a shame that she should have suffered, when she was created to love, to laugh, and to enjoy.

XXI

Younger Harvard Friends

A grandson
of "Aunt
Sarah". One evening in the autumn of 1889, when I was stammering my first lectures in philosophy, there was an unexpected knock at my door in Thayer Hall; and on opening, I saw before me a young man of middle height, with dark hair and a smiling mouth, who said: "My name is Barlow, and my mother has asked me to come and see you." Two simple facts, baldly stated, with an air betwixt sheepishness and mockery, and conveying everything that I needed to know. Here was a Sturgis. His mother, whom we called Nelly Barlow, was the prettiest of "Aunt Sarah's" four daughters, and had married a rough diamond, General Barlow, fresh from the Civil War. This young man was Bob, their eldest son. I don't remember the rest of our conversation that evening, but we had no lack of subjects, knowing perfectly who and what we both were, and being equally at home in Harvard. I perceived at once that Bob had an acute realistic mind; he didn't mince matters; and his way of talking might have seemed brutal, but for a certain background of refinement and indifference that kept it from being conceited or aggressive. We are all fools and poor devils, he seemed to be saying, and we might as well put up with that fact.

Some years later, I saw his father at their house in New York, where after looking at his son's head and at mine where the hair was getting thin, he observed dryly: "The trouble with you young men is that you are rotten before you are ripe." A conspicuously pretty mother and a conspicuously gruff father explained the character of their first born. Bob was a satirical lover of the frail sex, and frequented all levels of female society, approaching the dear creatures with a cold eye but with gallant inclinations. He allowed himself no exclusive passions, and remained a bachelor all his life. He particularly liked Paris, the French language and the French stage, about which he knew more than does the ordinary tourist. He was rather well-read, with a relish for the sayings of wits, rakes, and cynical philosophers. Boldness pleased him in thought and in war, no less than in love; any man of character had his respect who dared speak the truth and shame the hypocrites. With this taste, sharpened and fed by legal practice, for he became a lawyer, went a certain gentleness of aspect and manner, equable, lazy, and a bit sleepy. You saw in him the child of a beautiful woman who lived to be over ninety; and he himself, though not positively good-looking, had the placidity of a privileged person, round whom everything was expected to revolve without demanding any special effort. He led a life of pleasure with apparent indifference, not to say melancholy, and he might have appeared somewhat weak or disappointed had he stood alone.

Bangs & Barlow. But Bob Barlow never stood alone. He was one of a pair, like statuettes for the mantelpiece. His mate, however, was no shepherdess, but a big, heavy, jolly man named "Swelly" Bangs, once centre of the 'Varsity football squad, and later an imposing judge. Nobody spoke of Barlow and Bangs, everybody said Bangs & Barlow, as if they had been a firm of lawyers in Dickens, and Bangs the senior partner. But, though both lawyers, they were not partners, Barlow having lived at first with his parents in New York, while Bangs was faithful to Boston. Bangs was simply the greater weight, the more obvious presence, with the more emphatic voice and the more aggressive opinions. What in Barlow was an innuendo, turned in Bangs into a crushing dictum, as if he were about to sentence the prisoner to the gallows. Both friends had the mentality of the eighteenth century, and Bangs might have reminded one of Dr. Johnson, save that he banged most softly, with an air of the fine gentleman; for "Swelly" was a man of fashion. My first sight of him was when I was sitting in my lecture-room, waiting for the usual seven minutes to elapse before beginning; and, the place being almost empty, I noticed a new person, dressed in a yellow Norfolk jacket with a large plaid, come in and deliberately choose a seat at the back of the room. He then produced a small leather ink-stand and *a quill pen*, for the improbable purpose of taking notes. I don't think he came again; but on mentioning the apparition, I was informed that "Oh, yes, he was well-known. It was Swelly Bangs." Neither he nor Barlow were especially my pupils, or much given to technical philosophy. The bond between them and me was of another kind. It was what I might call the sporting mind, unbiassed intelligence, spreading freely from youthful curiosity to the interests of the world in general, including the adventures of the philosophers: a sporting mind found in the old wits, in Montaigne and

Voltaire, in Hobbes and in Dr. Johnson, but seldom found anywhere nowadays, least of all in America.

Suppers at   Bangs & Barlow sometimes took me to supper at a
The Spee.   club they belonged to called popularly *The Spee* and of-
ficially the Zeta Psi. The dining-room resembled an old-fashioned ship's cabin, narrow, low, with sides and ceiling all panelled in wood, and a cushioned bench running round the wall. A narrow long table occupied the space between, so that dishes had to be passed along from hand to hand, till they got back to the lower end of the table: and I think there were nautical lanterns for the lights, and other little suggestions of the sea. A pleasant setting for my fancy: confinement and comradeship in the midst of a boundless wilderness, and freedom of mind without the peril of losing one's physical balance. The company, the tone, the yarns, and the songs, if not literally nautical, yet had the mannish character proper to a band of young spirits, escaping, in sport or in earnest, from the conventional world to sea or into the wilds. Bangs himself used to recite a whaling story, always called for on these occasions, which proved how a ritual gains by repetition. Everybody knew it by heart, and sometimes recited it in chorus. It was called, "Cap'n Sims, thar' she blows!" It was full of dialect and local colour; and I still remember Captain Sims' praises of salt pork. Other victuals, he said, leave you half hungry, but salt pork "lays there a-nourishing of you for days and days". The supper, however, didn't conform to this ideal, but was apt to include scalloped oysters and a welsh rarebit, with excellent drinks, both hot and cold. It was a some-what freer and rougher society than I had known in my own college days, but I liked it immensely and didn't feel out of place in it. Being a little older than the others and a teacher in the College, I wasn't expected to contribute to the entertainment, nor had I any gifts in that direction. I might sometimes say a *bon mot*, but I could never tell a good story. Nature thus helped me to be discreet in all my relations with younger people and to preserve a certain propriety of language which the youngsters respected and didn't seem to dislike. At any rate, I was asked repeatedly to *The Spee*, where Bangs & Barlow were always my hosts. My position in these undergraduate circles was like that of the prefect in *"Le Monde où l'on s'ennuie"*, then a well-known comedy, when the duchess, going in to dinner on the prefect's arm, sighs that he won't be able to tell tales about the government, and he replies, "No, madame; but I may listen to them." So I was able

to listen to "Cap'n Sims" and to much else, without either forgetting my status or spoiling the fun.

An excursion to Cape Cod. The Bangs family had a country house near Wareham, in the flat sandy region of Cape Cod, and during one Easter vacation, "Swelly" had an angling party there, in which I was included; for though I had never held a rod in my hand, and never meant to, I was notoriously content with looking on; and the nominal duty was assigned to me of opening the baskets and laying out the food for the luncheon in the woods. The woods are rather meagre and scrubby in Cape Cod; but there was moss and rock enough by that sluggish little stream to sit down with comfort, and trees high enough to produce an illusion of being embowered. And we camped out pleasantly at the house, which was closed except for a care-taker, and cooked our own food by a roaring wood fire after our exhilarating day in the fresh air. It was on this occasion that I wrote some lines on *Cape Cod*, of which the poet William Moody said that there for once I had been inspired. But that inspiration came only by the way, as on returning we skirted a beach in the gathering twilight. Cape Cod in general has the most cheerful associations in my mind.

A grandson of Russell Sturgis. For here too, at Cotuit, appropriately enough, lived the Codmans; and it had been in the summer of 1889 that I had staid there, forming an affectionate friendship with the whole family, and in particular with Julian, the youngest son. The mother, whom we called "cousin Lucy", was a daughter of the great Russell Sturgis of London, by his first marriage; and although she had married a Bostonian, a somewhat English atmosphere permeated the household, its habits, its speech, and its sentiments. The family were Episcopalians, though not yet Anglo-Catholics. This was not really backsliding towards superstition, as Old Boston might think; everybody knew that Bishop Brooks was as liberal as any Unitarian, only nicer; and Julian, though apparently merely a rather short but well-built and good-looking young man, with excellent unaffected manners, had imbibed secret religious feelings; not so secret, however, that I wasn't perfectly aware of them. I liked those feelings. They were ballast, good for a young man of family who might otherwise dance too lightly on the summer waves.

Poetry readings. The always agreeable Julian also had a feeling for poetry, which (like me, if less speculatively) he merged in religion: poetry especially of the Victorian sort, perspicuous, highly aesthetic, elevating, yet disillusioned. That disillusion should be elevating was nevertheless a mystery; because after all it wouldn't do not to play the game. Pessimism was allowed, when it was sincere, but the matter simply remained in suspense, for a solution to be found later. With this happy turn of mind, Julian became the life of my "poetry bees", as he called them, when half a dozen of his friends would come to my room in Stoughton in the evening, to beer or hot Scotch whisky, and poetry: most often Keats, but often also Shelley, or Shakespeare's sonnets and songs. Without Julian's tact and fidelity the others (except Warwick Potter) would hardly have proved constant: but he gave the thing such a good start and chose the participants with so much tact, that the pleasant practice lasted for years. Harvard social distinctions, not founded on wealth, breeding, or attainments, had to be understood and respected if anything of this kind were to be "a success". For instance, I had a friend who was himself a poet, exceptionally cultivated and educated by his father (an unemployed teacher) to perfection: Joe, or, as he preferred to call himself, Trumbull Stickney. I once tried to introduce him into our readings; but no, it wouldn't do. Julian confidentially informed me that "the others didn't like him". Why not? Because he had mentioned the sunset and called it "gorgeous". I understood that he was too literary and ladylike for Harvard: and I myself found him more companionable later in Paris, where my memory prefers to place him.

A revival eighteen years later. Many years later, in 1910–11, I revived these poetry readings, but almost as if they were a university "seminar". We met in the afternoon, regularly once a week, and read only Shelley, from beginning to end, except *The Cenci*. Julian's mantle, on that occasion, had fallen on the worthy shoulders of Conrad Aiken. He was the soul of the party; and we were too sensible, and too intent on our poet, to note particularly who took part. Friendship was not a prerequisite or a necessary result; for me the thing had an ulterior use, in that it led me to write my essay on Shelley.

Julian Codman at college and after. Julian was a great comfort to me in those earlier days: reconciled me to being again at Harvard without my old friends, and gave me fresh information, judicious and never uncharitable, about things and persons in that little world. He had no fads, no vices, no prejudices, no faults. A little negative, you might say: and description can hardly do him justice.

He was amiable, but having no special gifts, he lost distinction as he lost his youth. To have remained at forty or fifty as socially perfect as he was at twenty would have required one artificial aid: plenty of money. He would have known how to combine, in a generous establishment, material, intellectual, and social pleasures; his legal profession would not have left him without sufficient leisure, and his house would have been a Mecca for all his friends. Even as things were, I was always happy in his company. At Harvard he had been my best guide to the rest of the student world, graduate and undergraduate, and the friendliest person in it. Our nominal relationship through the Sturgises covered a real affinity. He was a young man of the world, and made no bones of differences in age, background, religion, or nationality. We laughed at the same things, and we liked the same things. What more is needed for agreeable society?

A grandson of Emerson. On the same sandy coasts of Cape Cod I repeatedly visited another young friend, Cameron Forbes, at Naushon, an island in Buzzard's Bay that belonged to his grandfather, Mr. John Forbes, a personage who had played an important part, financially, in the remote times of the Mexican War and the annexation of Texas and California. "Cam", as he was called, inherited from that grandfather, as well as a prospective fortune, an aptitude for affairs and for public life. He was not a youth to waste his time lounging in clubs, nor was he particularly absorbed in books; when he had a free day he would escape from Cambridge to his family farm or estate or settlement in Milton, where there were horses and woods and crops and buildings to inspect and to look after. At Harvard his most urgent occupation was football, not only the practice of it but the theory, and he eventually became coach to the 'Varsity eleven, which that year, by what seemed a miracle, won the Yale Game.

All this sounds rather remote from my meditative idleness; but Cam had another grandfather. He was also the grandson of Emerson. That heritage was no less real in him, though less apparent: or rather, it appeared in him negatively, as a saving check or divine inhibition. It kept him absolutely removed from playing the rich young man. Simplicity, rusticity, hard work, and public duty held him fast bound; yet as with Emerson, so in him, this severity was practical more than imaginative. Imaginatively he could escape from business as gladly as, in life, he fled from luxury. There was no moral hesitation, no temptation to be soft: his whole life, in spite of uncertain health, was devoted to affairs, to politics, to administration; he was at one time

Governor of the Philippine Islands; and I heard that in his old age, still a bachelor, he lived in his grandfather Forbes's house in Naushon, surrounded by his brothers' families, and most affectionately playing the patriarch. Nevertheless, transcendentally, I think he was haunted by the suspicion that all this ado was terribly unnecessary, just as football, if you think of it, is terribly unnecessary; and instigated by that qualm, he would sometimes draw me aside, and talk about rather intimate matters. He was not one of my little circle; but trusted that my experience and philosophy would enable me to understand in him that which he himself hardly understood.

Cameron Forbes and his philosophy of life. One day, for instance, he showed me some verses of his, about a young man dreaming that two goddesses, Life and Death, appeared to him and offered him their respective gifts: a sort of Puritan Judgment of Paris. The young man listens to their respective boasts and respective promises, and then says: I will choose Life, but on one condition: that I may afterwards reverse my judgment, and choose Death.

The verses were not well composed, and I doubt that Cam has written any others; but the thought was so original, so wise, and so courageous, that nothing in Emerson has ever pleased me more. Think what an incubus life would be, if death were not destined to cancel it, as far as any fact can be cancelled! That is the very image of hell. But natural life, life with its ascending and descending curve, is a tempting adventure; it is an open path; curiosity and courage prompt us to try it. Moreover, the choice must have been made for us before it can be offered; we are already alive, and a whole world of creatures is alive, like us. The first question is therefore what this world may bring to light, for others and for ourselves, so long as it endures. Therefore the preference for life is, as Cam felt, a duty, as well as a natural sporting impulse; but it is a conditioned preference, and something deeper in us than any casual prompting transcends that preference and is fortified by being able to transcend it.

Points borrowed in *The Last Puritan*. Various traits, major and minor, belonging to Cam Forbes were appropriated by me for the hero of *The Last Puritan*. In the first place, the relation to his father, the atavism of Puritan blood asserting itself, affectionately and kindly, but invincibly, against a rich father, a sportsman, and a man in whose life there was something vague and ineffectual. I didn't know Mr. William Forbes well, nor much about him; but he was present and played the host the first time I went to Naushon. We had champagne every day for dinner: something so entirely contrary to Cam's instincts or possibilities, that when I went to Naushon the second time, with a party of young men from Harvard, Cam commissioned one of us to provide the drinks: even to think of them or order them repelled him. Yet it was a purely private and inward protest: his conscience allowed him to pay for the drinks of others. But my Oliver is no portrait of Cam or of anyone else, although many of the details are drawn from life in various persons. I meant the divine vocation in Oliver, though unrecognised, to be radical and devastating; there was nothing so definite in Cam, who was able to live the expected life and to make a "success" of it. And I also gave Oliver a better education and more ability than Cam ever had, and a greater sensitiveness to the equal rightness of the gay world and the religious world from which his own destiny had cut him off.

Weh dir, dass du ein Enkel bist!   Here are three young men (excluding Bangs) who were grandsons, not as we all are, but essentially, so that being grandsons dominated their characters and their whole lives. In other words, they illustrated the decline of an age—the age of the great merchants. They were in one sense its ripe fruits, but in another marked the dissolution of that economy, its incapacity to maintain itself for more than three generations. Two of my friends never married—a rare and almost discreditable thing in their world— and the third died rather young and left, I believe, only one child. Either their fortune was inadequate, or their virtue was inadequate, or their health and stamina were inadequate. Gently, or sadly, or cynically they had to bow themselves off of the stage. But this decline regards only a phase of society, not the life of society as a whole, which in New England was growing richer and more vigorous as it passed out of the period of great merchants into that of "big business" and was merged in the vast American vortex. These grandsons, these essential descendents, couldn't merge in it. They were not hardy enough, not crude enough, too well aware of what they would miss. They were not Babbitts.

Howard Cushing and his happy disposition.   Apart from any possible affinity to Babbitt, good sense and good nature (as in Bangs) kept the majority of well-bred Bostonians from being merely grandsons; and in some there was pure individual spontaneity and the certainty of having a fixed vocation. This was the case at that time with another young friend of mine, Howard Cushing. When an under-graduate he was already a painter, and sure that he would never wish to be anything else. The whole world was there before him for a model, and he would never tire of catching poses and distinguishing colours. He was not poor, he spoke French fluently (his mother belonged to an old French family in Louisiana), and he was at home in all countries, but never happier than in his own. He loved what he called the *fearless look* and character of Americans; and his nature was so aristocratic (like that of Thomas Jefferson) that he could feel and actually be perfectly free, even in a democracy. What the crowd did and what the crowd thought was a splendid subject to observe, if not to paint, like scenes from the French Revolution or the martyrdom of early Christians: it was all delightfully full of colour and character. Yet what in the end he painted with most pleasure was the wonderful golden-red hair of his young wife and of his little children. He was domestic, all affection and simplicity, and something of his painter's art seemed to overflow into his surroundings, wherever he might be, and turn them into a picture.

"The Club".   I should hardly have known these younger men, or known them so intimately, but for what we called "the club". In my undergraduate days three of my best friends, Ward Thoron, Herbert Lyman, and Boylston Beal, who ought to have been invited to join some club such as that to which Bangs and Barlow later introduced me, found themselves left out in the cold; and it occurred to them to found a new club of a socially superior kind, less popular perhaps, and less athletic, but more distinguished. They invited me to join them; but clubs, with assessments and inevitable incidental expenses were then beyond my slender means. That club had now amply fulfilled its promise; it had gathered together stray young gentlemen not duly appreciated by their contemporaries, but interesting in themselves, some rich, others clever, still others simply agreeable. Julian Codman, Cam Forbes, and Howard Cushing belonged to this club. It then (1890) occupied a wooden house in Mount Auburn Street, and was called officially the Delta Phi, or more familiarly "The Gas-house", because all its windows would be lighted up at once by the electricity that was then a novelty; so that it was called "The Gashouse" because of the absence of gas. Yet the nickname stuck, and could be interpreted to refer to the brilliancy of the members' minds, or the vanity of their speech. My contemporary, Beal, who had spent some years in Europe, was still studying at the Law School, and came daily to this club; and I suspect that it was he that suggested that I might now be made an honorary member. This was done, and I soon became an *habitué*, and picked up many a stray meal there, not having a regular eating place. There was another graduate, besides Beal, to keep me in countenance, Billy Woodworth, who was an Assistant at the Agassiz Museum, and an excellent cook. He would sometimes preside at supper, producing a dish of his own invention; and his conversation opened to most of us new perspectives, scientific and social: for he was a Californian of the freest type.

The Potters.   It was at the club that I formed the most unclouded and heart-felt of my American friendships, that with Bob and Warwick Potter. Of Bob I will speak later; he was in the class of 1891, and in his last year at Harvard he was preoccupied with his future. He was as much an architect by vocation as Howard Cushing was a painter, and they were both full of the studies they were about to make in Paris, at the Beaux-Arts or at Julien's. But Warwick, who was in the class of 1893 and died at the end of that year, was for the two previous winters my constant companion, and also pupil; and it was at the club, in our poetry-readings in my room, and in our walks that I insensibly came to think of him as a younger brother and as a part of myself. I didn't know how much attached to him I was, until I heard the unexpected news that he had died on board Edgar Scott's yacht in the harbour of Brest. He had been terribly seasick, and the seasickness had provoked an attack of cholera that had proved fatal. It seemed a new kind of blow, not violent, not loud, but strangely transforming. A gradual change due to many converging causes was going on within me. A twelvemonth before, my sister Susana had been married; that summer my father had died; and the death of Warwick now came to accentuate the effect of these mutations and to make me aware of their meaning for my spiritual life. I shall return presently to this my *metanoia*. Nothing apparently was much changed in my surroundings, opinions, or habits; yet the whole world was retreating to a greater distance and taking on a new, a more delicate colouring, as if by aerial perspective. I realised that it was not my world, but only the world of other people: of all those, at least, and they were the vast majority, who had never *understood*.

Goodness and laughter.   I have already said something about Warwick in comparing him to my early friend Bayley: they were both good, or rather loved and understood the Good: for they were both too young to have been tried in the furnace and proved to be pure gold. But I felt that they were pure gold. There was an important element in Warwick, however, that didn't appear in Bayley: Warwick was full of laughter. Now laughter, as I have come to see in my old age, is the innocent youthful side of repentance, of disillusion, of understanding. It liberates incidentally, as spiritual insight liberates radically and morally. Susana also was full of laughter; it was the deepest bond between us. By laughing together we could erase the traces of any divergence or failure of sympathy. At the same time, Susana, like Bayley and Warwick, was devout; this marked their sensitiveness to the Good, their capacity to worship. Those were the two prerequisites, in my conception, to perfect friendship: capacity to worship and capacity to laugh. They were the two windows through which the mind took flight and morally escaped from this world.

Character of Warwick Potter.   Warwick was not clever or specially good at his lessons: had he become a clergyman, as he rather expected, his scholarship would have been his weak point, and his theological ideas would have remained vague and verbal. Yet he was very well educated after the manner of ladies (which is rather the Groton manner); he had heard of everything, knew the points of the compass in morals and history, and had good taste in English literature. He also had good taste in choosing his friends and in judging them; and his intimates were not of his own type: they were not good pious boys, but captains of crews and owners of yachts; young men who had experience far beyond his own innocence. He was not out of place in their society, as he was not in that of his masters at Groton or in mine. Though young for his age in experience, he was intellectually merry and without prejudice, and laughingly open to every interesting fact or idea — a trait that youth ought to possess but that is really the sign of a rare maturity. You could sit with him by the fire, over a mild whisky and soda, until the early hours, discussing Falstaff and Prince Henry, or the divinity and humanity in Christ, or the need of arms to give strength to letters. Both are needed; and the whole world is needed, and a complete life, to give strength to friendship.

Evanescence of friendship.   These relations of mine with younger spirits were all cut short by early separations. That was in the nature of things, because friends should be contemporaries. But I was divided from my contemporaries by initial diversities of race, country, religion, and career; and in spite of those barriers, my old friends kept their place in my affections and interest to the end.

Modern life is not made for friendship: common interests are not strong enough, private interests too absorbing. Even in politics, colleagues are seldom or never friends. Their ambition, being private and not patriotic, divides instead of uniting them. Nevertheless, I continued to have young friends, very nice young friends, all my life: a little ghostly and evanescent, but agreeable. As widowers proverbially marry again, so a man with the habit of friendship always finds new friends. I had many more at Harvard: I will speak of some of them among Americans in Europe, since it was usually in Europe that our acquaintance could first become companionship; but it would be monotonous to repeat story after story, all with the same moral, and in the same landscape. Harvard had nothing essentially new to offer or to awaken within me, after I returned from King's College, in 1897: the following fifteen years that I remained a professor were a somnambulistic period, interrupted only by the waking dream of a journey to Egypt, Palestine, and Greece. Persons yielded in interest to places; and having chosen a place for the time being, I lived as best I could with the human souls that inhabited it. Not at all in bitterness; not with any painful sense of disappointment. My old age judges more charitably and thinks better of mankind than my youth ever did. I discount idealisations, I forgive onesidedness, I see that it is essential to perfection of any kind. And in each person I catch the fleeting suggestion of something beautiful, and swear eternal friendship with that.

XXII

Boston Society

Clannishness
and culture
with a basis
in trade. When in the year 1858 my mother heroically fulfilled her promise to her late husband and first went to live in Boston, she knew what she was doing, for she had spent some months there two years before and had made the acquaintance of all the Sturgises and their friends. And yet I think she had expectations that were never realised. If not for herself— since she had lost all interest in society—at least for her children, she pictured a perfect amalgamation with all that was best in Boston. This amalgamation never occurred. I have described the difficult position that my sister Susana found herself in, and her ultimate return to Spain; and my brother Robert, though a thorough American in all externals, never made a place for himself in good Boston society. This society, in my time, was on the one hand clannish, and on the other highly moralised and highly cultivated. The clannishness was not one of blood; you might almost say that all the "old families" were new. It was a clannishness of social affinity and habit; you must live in certain places, follow certain professions, and maintain a certain tone. Any adaptable rich family could easily enter the charmed circle within one generation. Money was necessary, not in itself, but as a means of living as everybody else did in good society; and those who became too poor, fell out in one generation also. As to the other characteristic, of being cultivated and high-principled, it was not indispensable for individuals already in the clan; but it was necessary to the clan as a whole, for a standard and a leaven. I suspect that the lack of those qualities may have dissolved the society that I speak of, and allowed it to become indistinguishable from the flowing mass of the rich and fashionable all the world over.

Conversation in society, for me at least, was almost exclusively with ladies; but whenever I found myself by chance among elderly men, as for a while after dinner, I became aware of living in a commercial community. Talk reverted from banter to business worries, if not to "funny stories". The leaders were "business men", and weight in the business world was what counted in their estimation. Of course there must be clergymen and doctors also, and even artists, but they remained parasites, and not persons with whom the bulwarks of society had any real sympathy. Lawyers were a little better, because business couldn't be safeguarded without lawyers, and they often were or became men of property themselves; but politicians were taboo, and military men, in Boston, non-existent. Such persons might be occasionally entertained, and lauded rhetorically in after-dinner speeches; but they remained strangers and foreigners to the inner circle, and disagreeable to the highly moralised and highly cultivated Bostonian.

My marginal position in Boston.   My contacts with this society were neither those of a native nor those of a visiting foreigner; nor could they be compared with my relation to Harvard College, where I was as much at home as anybody, with a perfectly equal and legal status. In order to have slipped no less automatically and involuntarily into Boston society, I should have had to go to a fashionable school, and my family would have had to occupy the position that I imagine my mother had dreamt of. As it was, I skirmished on the borders of the polite world on my own merits, and eventually limited myself to a few really friendly families. Yet at first my lot fell, as was natural, within the circle of the Sturgises, especially of the children and grandchildren of Russell Sturgis of London.

In the summer of 1889, when living at my mother's in Roxbury and preparing my first course of lectures, I received an invitation to spend a few days at Manchester-by-the-Sea, with Russell Sturgis, Jr., and his family. I had never seen this elderly cousin, or any of his younger children: only once his eldest son.*

---

*This had been in the year 1876, when I was twelve years old. Robert and I had gone to Philadelphia to see the Centennial Exhibition. I remember only two things seen in Philadelphia, both architectural: the Fine Arts Building, and the odd features of the typical Philadelphia houses: the white wooden shutters outside, and the ingenious arrangement of the stairs, making a bridge between the body of the house and a long wing behind, entered from the landing. The stairs could be lighted through a large window at the side, and the wing would supply various rooms, the dining-room especially, half way between one storey and another of the house proper. For some reason, on our return, Robert wished to stay in New York. Young Russell Sturgis, 3rd, then nineteen years old, offered to look after me on the way home. We travelled by the Sound Boat—another interesting discovery in construction—a vast flat-bottomed steamer with a hall in the middle, surrounded by galleries and rows of little doors to private cabins. If we had only been quadrupeds, we should have fancied ourselves in Noah's Ark.

Russell Sturgis, Junior. From Susana's satirical gossip of years before I had learned something about her Cousin Russell. He was very Evangelical, distributed tracts entitled "Do you love Jesus?" and would send us Christmas cards—he never came to see us—wishing us joy and "one more year of leaning upon Jesus' breast." There was always some religious motto printed on his note-paper, which once happened to be "Ye are bought with a price"; and he having inadvertently written to Judge Gray on that paper, his letter was returned as a libel by the insulted magistrate. Apart from his Evangelical work "Cousin Russell" seemed to have no occupation; and he was known to have spent the winter at Manchester-by-the-Sea for economy, which precluded daily attendance to business, if he had had any. He may also have thought that on moral grounds, as a discipline and a tonic, a winter in the bleak country might be a good thing. The kindred points of heaven and home might there seem more precious than ever. We are always so near the abyss, and the wintry ocean might remind him of it. But why suddenly ask me to stay at his house, when he had never seen me and there was no real bond between our families? Had he heard that I was about to begin teaching at Harvard? If I were the right sort, might I not prove a useful acquaintance for his younger sons, who were younger than I? And if I were not the right sort, why shouldn't he prove a saving influence over me?

Small-Boys' School for grown-up people. When I turned up, I don't know what his first impression may have been; he and the whole family were certainly very kind. They seemed to accept me as an adopted relative. But gradually my defects must have become evident. No, I didn't swim, and I'd rather not take a dip in the sea before breakfast, as he and the boys did every morning even in winter. I didn't say so, but it cost me an effort to be shaved and dressed in time for the inevitable family breakfast. Lazy, soft, luxurious young man, and a *poor* young man, too, which makes vice so much worse and so much less excusable! However, these thoughts were as yet only in embryo. I got down to breakfast in time—a very nice breakfast, all sorts of hot things, not unwelcome when one has got up early—but after it there was a strange, awkward silence; everyone was standing and no one leaving the room, except to move into the drawing-room which was separated only by a screen. The servants now came in, and stood uncomfortably in a corner. There were to be family prayers! They were *after* breakfast, as "Cousin Russell" afterwards frankly explained, because if they had been *before* breakfast, everybody would have been late or would have missed prayers altogether; but *after* breakfast, there you had them all, and no escape. Filled and soothed as I was by that abundant oatmeal, I rather liked the idea of prayers. I should have a peaceful quarter of an hour, speculative, digestive, and drowsy. Chairs, big and little, were arranged in a circle round the room. In lieu of ecclesiastical objects, the broad sea and sky were visible through the long open windows. We might enlarge our thoughts, while "Cousin Russell" read a chapter of the Bible, not at all in a clerical voice, but familiarly and dramatically, to bring out the good points, and make us feel how modern and secular it all really was. The book closed, he rose and we all rose automatically to attention — he had been a major in the Civil War — we executed a sharp right-about-face, fell on our knees, and buried our faces in the warm chair where we had been sitting. He recited, and the rest half murmured, the Lord's Prayer, with some other short things from the Prayer Book, and a benediction. Then we all rose again, the servants disappeared, and a programme of healthy pleasures was announced for the rest of us for the morning. In the afternoon there would be an excursion, and in the evening (not pre-announced) there were to be parlour-games.

I prove recalcitrant and am not further evangelised. Never having been in an army, in a nursery, or in an Evangelical family, I found all this rather odd and exacting; but I was out to learn something of the world, and this was a part of it. On that occasion, for two or three days, I tried to do my duty; but duty in my ethics means a debt, an obligation freely undertaken; and I saw at once that I was unfit to live under a free government, where other people voted as to what I should do. My unfitness must have transpired, for I was never asked again to Manchester-by-the-Sea, nor should I have been tempted. When later I knew how the other children of "Uncle Russell" lived in England, although, as I was informed, all had equal fortunes, this family seemed to belong to a different social class. Among the truly noble, as for instance in Spain, there was grandeur without much luxury or comfort; under the plutocracy, in which "Cousin Russell's" English brothers moved, there was luxury without grandeur; and in the *bourgeoisie*, which "Cousin Russell" himself had joined, there was comfort without luxury. Comfort, in his case, was stiffened by Spartan and athletic austerities, yet in sentimental directions he was soft enough. He was pleased with his appearance, being well-built, portly, with fair side-whiskers that flew backward as he marched about; and of a summer evening he and his wife would stand embraced by the window, gazing alternately at each other and at the sunset over the sea. I knew this was a form of evening prayer, a wordless *Angelus*, and I stood discreetly aside.

The Codmans.   At about the same time I made a first visit to another of "Uncle Russell's" children, "Cousin Lucy Codman" and her family, at their country house at Cotuit in Cape Cod. It was a much softer, sandier, flatter, poorer region than the Massachusetts "North Shore", with few summer residents, and little but scrub pine woods, straggling farms, and ghostly gaunt natives who "made remarks". On the other hand the Codmans, in spite of their name so appropriate to Cape Cod, seemed almost to be living in England, with all the freedom, largeness, and tact of good society. You were taken for granted, put at your ease, made materially and morally comfortable. Conversation was spontaneous, unpretending, intelligent; you could talk about what interested you—if you did so with discretion, and briefly; and you were not asked for your opinion on things you cared nothing about. The house was agreeably furnished, not over-furnished: there were flowers, a little music, enough wit to make express entertainments unnecessary. The father and the two elder sons were away—kept in Boston by their work; but the youngest son, Julian, sometimes took me out sailing in a cat-boat in very smooth water, a peaceful somnolent amusement very much to my taste. He was destined to become the most confidential of all my young friends in the following years, and I have already described him, his career, and the perfect sympathy there was between us. Julian, with the cat-boat, comes under the head of friendship, not of Boston society: and it was not on his account that I was invited to Cotuit.

I am introduced to Howard Sturgis.   I had been expressly summoned in order that I might make the acquaintance of Howard Sturgis, "Cousin Lucy's" youngest brother, who might well have been her son, being then thirty-three years of age. Howard, too, comes properly under the head of friendship, since I began the next year to make him almost yearly visits, sometimes reduplicated, at his house in Windsor: but since I first saw him in America, and it was my Sturgis connection that established a kind of family intimacy between us, I will say something about him here.

He had been his mother's darling and pet.   He had come to America for a complete change of scene, hoping it might help to heal the wound that, in his excessively tender heart, had been left by the death of his mother. She had not been, from all I have gathered, at all a remarkable woman, but luxurious and affectionate, surrounded in London by a few rich American friends, especially the daughters of Motley, the historian, who were married to Englishmen, and beyond them, more by hearsay than acquaintance, by the whole British aristocracy. Howard had been her last and permanent baby. The dear child was sensitive and affectionate, with abundant golden hair, large blue eyes, and well-turned chubby arms and legs. Her boudoir became his nursery and his playroom. As if by miracle, for he was wonderfully imitative, he became, save for the accident of sex, which was not yet a serious encumbrance, a perfect young lady of the Victorian type. He acquired a good accent in French, German, and Italian, and instinctively embraced the proper liberal humanitarian principles in politics and history. There was an absolutely right and an absolutely wrong side in every war and every election; only the wicked, selfish, and heartless still prevented the deserving from growing rich, and maintained an absurd and cruel ascendency of birth, superstition, and military power. These were the sentiments of the Great Merchants, economists, and reformers of the earlier nineteenth century, and Howard would have embraced them in any case because they appealed to his heart, and his feminine nature would never have allowed his intellect, no matter how keen, to do anything but defend his emotions. When women's opinions waver, it means that their hearts are not at rest. Let them once settle their affections and see their interests, and theoretical doubt becomes impossible for them. Howard's affections and interests were inextricably bound up with the liberal epoch; and no evidence would ever have convinced him that this was the only ground for his liberal dogmatism.

His feminine tastes and automatisms.   This was not all that he imbibed from his mother's circle. He was not only imitative, but he also had a theory that there was nothing women did that a man couldn't do better. Pride therefore seconded inclination in making him vie with the ladies and surpass them. He learned to sew, to embroider, to knit, and to do crochet; these occupations were not only guiltless of any country's blood, but helped to pass away the empty hours. He became wedded to them, and all his life, whether he sat by the fire or in his garden, his work-basket stood by his low chair. His needlework was exquisite, and he not only executed gorgeous embroideries, but designed them, for he was clever also with the pencil. Imitation, or a sort of involuntary caricature, sometimes went further with him. He would emit little frightened cries, if the cab he was in turned too fast round a corner; and in crossing a muddy road he would pick up the edge of his short covert-coat, as the ladies in those days picked up their trailing skirts.

My psychoanalytic explanation of them. Some of these automatisms were so extreme and so ridiculous that I can't help suspecting that there was something hypnotic or somnambulistic about them. He was too intelligent and too satirical to have done such things if he could have helped it. There may have been some early fixation at work, probably to his mother, of the kind that induces dreams, and develops into grotesque exaggerations and symbolic fancies. He mimicked people, sometimes on purpose, but often involuntarily; and his imagination penetrated their motives and thoughts, as his novels show, not necessarily with truth, but plausibly and with an endless capacity for extensions. He may have been at times the victim of this dramatic fertility in his own person, and found himself playing a part, that the real circumstances did not call for.

His gifts and his education. He had not yet written his best novels, only an ultra-pathetic story about a little boy "Tim"; but one morning we found him sitting in the porch outside the living-room, on one of the wicker chairs with red-cotton cushions that adorned it, and that he copied later in the addition made to Queen's Acre; and we found him armed, not with his usual work-basket, but with a red leather writing case, and an absorbed and far-away air. He was writing poetry: verses about the loss of his mother. We asked him to read them: he would not have brought them down-stairs if he had wished them to bloom and die unseen. He read them very nicely, without self-consciousness or affectation: the sentiment was intimate, but the form restrained and tactful.

Courage and distinction will save a man in almost any predicament; and Howard had been at Eton, where he acquired distinction and showed remarkable courage. Sending him there must have been a last desperate measure insisted on by his brothers, to cure him of his girlishness. A cruel remedy, it might seem, as if he had been sent to sea before the mast. Why hadn't his father and mother corrected him sooner? His father's mind had been growing feeble, and his mother probably thought him sweeter as he was. After all, too, they were Bostonians; and would it have been *right* to correct dear little sweet Howard for girlishness, when girlishness wasn't *morally wrong?* Let him go to Eton, properly safeguarded, if his brothers thought it absolutely necessary. And this heroic remedy didn't prove in the least cruel, or in the least efficacious. Young Howard calmly defied all those school-boys with his feminine habits and arts, which he never dreamt of disguising. He was protected by his wit and intellectual assurance; while his tutor, Mr. Ainger, author of the *Carmen Etonense*, and the two Misses Ainger, adopted him and screened him from the rude mob. Besides, Howard attracted affection, and however astonished one might be at first, or even scornful, one was always won over in the end.

After Eton, Trinity College, Cambridge, was plain sailing, and con-firmed his humanitarian principles and aristocratic habits. His studies don't seem to have been serious; but he remembered what he had read of *belles-lettres*, just as ladies do. He had even dipped into Berkeley's philosophy and had laid it aside, not unwisely, as an academic curiosity. To see interesting people, or at least fashionable people, and to hear about them, made his chief entertainment later. Of course he had travelled abroad, and seen everything that everybody should see; he remained old-fashioned, without pre-Raphaelite affectations, in matters of art. His novels were exquisitely felt and observed, full of delicately satirical phrases, and not without an obvious moral aimed against domestic prejudice and social tyranny: but his writing had hardly force enough, either in style or in thought, to leave a lasting impression.

Queen's Acre and "The Babe". In what he felt to be his homeless plight, he had looked about for a house, and had finally taken a small one, with a nice garden, on the outskirts of Windsor Park. Its name had been Queensmead, but there was a Kingsmead next door, and seeing that the land was little more than an acre—at least the part of it visible from the house—he re-christened it Queen's Acre, familiarly and ironically abbreviated to Quaker. The nearness of Eton, and of the Aingers, had attracted him, for as often happens, he retained a much greater affection for his school than for his College or University. In those first years his garden and his table were often enlivened by groups of Eton boys. To some of them he gave pet names, such as The Lion, The Bear, or The Babe; this last being Willie Haines Smith, a distant cousin of his, who became his adopted younger brother and companion for life.

The Codman girls.   All this lay in the future, and in England. For the moment, at Cotuit, although Howard was the guest of honour, the ruling spirits were the ladies. There were two daughters, both in the early twenties. Something, I hardly know what, seemed to designate the younger one, Susie (another Susie!) as the one in whom I ought to be particularly interested. She was good-looking, slight, with dark hair and frank manners, intelligent, and keenly critical in moral and artistic directions. I never discovered how far her principles were religious, how far philosophical, but she seemed not to mind my Mephistophelean character; and this was perhaps the ground on which the chorus chose her for my special friend. When, however, I thought the matter over—quite speculatively and calmly, because marriage was out of the question for me—it seemed that I might have preferred the elder sister, Nannie. Nannie would have been safer. She was also, as a woman, more the kind of woman that contents me, in whose presence I can feel the glow of trust and of happiness. She was a trifle stout, placid, motherly, with beautiful long abundant chestnut hair and a sober settled judgment. I somehow felt that, without the least flutter of pretended interest, she liked me better than Susie did. Susie, if she had come to care for me, would have been unhappy, but Nannie in the same case would have been serene. She would also have made a wiser and less anxious mother: but that is not a young man's reason for falling in love, or even for choosing a wife. Choosing a wife was the last thing that I was thinking of; yet it was expected that this should be a young man's guiding interest, and that my attentions should be directed to Susie. Certainly it was with Susie that I found myself most often talking; she seemed to take a lively interest in the things that occupied me: not technical philosophy, but views of life and nature in general, and political questions. Yet if we had carried discussion further, we should not have agreed. She would have discovered that I had a wicked mind. Whereas Nannie, if she had discovered it, wouldn't have troubled so much. She would have said that it didn't matter what a man thought he thought, provided he was decent. She was in the line of psychic health and knew, without knowing it, that consciousness is an "epiphenomenon".

Match-making in vacuo.   This delicate question, never spoken of, was left hanging in mid-air, until years later, when one day Julian deliberately asked me why I didn't marry. I replied that I wished to be free and didn't intend to live always in America. Whether Julian's mother had prompted him to ask that question, I don't know; perhaps not, since she had no reason to desire me for a son-in-law, and her daughters, on approaching the age of thirty, made reasonable and more suitable marriages. Yet, out of sheer kindness, she seems to have taken an interest in my happiness, as she conceived it ought to be; for she took pains to tell my mother, whom she seldom visited, *how strongly she felt* about certain things; one of which was the *sad mistake* that a poor young man made sometimes in backing away from a rich girl, simply because she was rich, when they sincerely cared for each other. This arrow was of course aimed at a particular target, but couldn't regard "Cousin Lucy's" daughters, since they were not rich; so far from rich, indeed, that a poor young man couldn't have married them, no matter how often he had popped the question and been accepted. It would have meant a long engagement, with an eventual descent into another level of society.

The uprooted should never marry. I think I know what "Cousin Lucy" had in mind. She was spinning a romance out of a nascent sympathy between a certain distinguished heiress and me; it never went beyond agreeable conversations about books, operas, plays, and travels, merely at dinners and other social functions. Had I been in love with her, and pressed my suit, she might have made the mistake of accepting me, to the consternation of her numerous relations; but I didn't allow myself to fathom the question whether I was in love with her or not. The barrier was not her person nor the fact that she was rich; this fact was precisely what might have encouraged me, because I should not have been imposing any material sacrifices upon her; but she would have been imposing upon me her whole background, her country, her family, her houses, her religion. Not that I had any fault to find with these things *for her*; but a *déraciné*, a man who has been torn up by the roots, cannot be replanted and should never propagate his kind. In the matter of religion, for instance, I found myself in this blind alley. I was not a believer in what my religion, or any religion, teaches dogmatically; yet I wouldn't for the world have had a wife or children dead to religion. Had I lived always in Spain, even with my present philosophy, I should have found no difficulty: my family would have been Catholic like every other family; and the philosophy of religion, if ever eventually discussed among us, would have been a subsequent private speculation, with no direct social consequences. But living in a Protestant country, the freethinking Catholic is in a socially impossible position. He cannot demand that his wife and children be Catholics, since he is not, in a controversial sense, a Catholic himself; yet he cannot bear that they should be Protestants or freethinkers, without any Catholic traditions or feelings. They would not then be his wife or children except by accident; they would not belong to his people. I know that there are some who accept this consequence, even pretend to have become Protestants, and bury as deep as possible the fact that they were born Catholics or Jews. But I am not a man of that stamp. I have been involuntarily uprooted. I accept the intellectual advantages of that position, with its social and moral disqualifications. And I refuse to be annexed, to be abolished, or to be grafted onto any plant of a different species.

My taste for society. This feeling was absolutely fixed in me from the beginning, but didn't prevent me from liking the Boston ladies, though I never courted any of them. I liked the elegance, the banter, the wit and intelligence that often appeared in them; I liked to sit next to them at dinner, when conversation flowed more easily and became more civilised in the midst of lights and flowers, good food and good wines. The charm of the ladies was a part of that luxurious scene, of that polite intoxication; for me it was nothing more. But people didn't understand that this could be all; even my sister Susana didn't understand it and more or less seriously looked about for someone with whom to pair me off. This was when we were children; later, when I began to find my real affinities, Susana had returned to Spain, and perhaps had seen that I had no thought of marrying anyone in Boston, not even among the Catholics.

Social divorce in domestic union. My real affinities were with three or four elderly ladies, who never appeared off the social stage, and who like me were more or less spontaneously playing a part, as it were, in public, while their real and much less interesting life lay hidden beneath, like the water-supply, the drains, and the foundations of their houses. They were all childless, or had lost their children, and their husbands, when living, either didn't appear at all in the same scenes, or played a subordinate, comic, errand-boy part in them. The invisible husband might be, in his own world, an important person, esteemed as much or more than his wife in hers; but like royal spouses occupying opposite wings in a palace, they had their own exits and entrances, their own hours and their own friends. This was the case with two leading ladies in the Boston of my time, Mrs. Gardner and Mrs. Whitman. Often as I lunched and visited at Mrs. Gardner's, both in town and country, I hardly ever saw her husband;

and it was only after years of acquaintance with Mrs. Whitman that once, at a week-end party by the sea, I caught sight of Mr. Whitman: not that he was living in the house or belonged to the house-party, but that he had come, as if by chance, in his yacht, and had looked in upon us.

Mrs. Gardner. These two ladies had individual vocations; their husbands had their own position, their own work, and their own friends, and having ample separate means they amicably cultivated separate gardens. Mrs. Gardner was not a Bostonian: her vocation was to show Boston what it was missing. Instead of following the fashion, she undertook to set it. It wasn't followed; Boston doggedly stuck to its old ways and its old people; yet it couldn't ignore Mrs. Gardner; her husband was an old Bostonian and always countenanced, supported, and (invisibly) stood by her; and she had an indefatigable energy and perseverance that, in spite of all murmurs and hesitations, carried the day. When she became a widow and built her Venetian palace in The Fenway, as Egyptian monarchs built their tombs and went to live in them, she became an acknowledged public benefactor. Criticism was hushed: and there was something moving in beholding this old lady, whose pleasure it had been to shock, devoting herself more and more modestly to preparing and completing her museum, to be left to the town that she had startled when younger, that had long looked at her askance, and that she was now endowing with all her treasures.

Her ambition and her achievement. What her inner life may have been, her religion (she was outwardly a very High Church Anglican) or her sentiments regarding Boston, her husband, or the child she had lost, and regarding the works of art and the artists that she devoted herself to collecting, I do not know: but it is easy to perceive the figure that she wished to cut in the world. She modelled herself on the great ladies of French and Italian society, as she had seen them in her travels or during her residence in Venice. She was far from beautiful, but she knew that this was no obstacle to dressing magnificently and boldly, or being positively alluring; her clothes (for the evening) filled Boston with alarm and with envy. She was not of good family, although professedly related to the royal house of Stuart; but she gave Boston a lesson in being aristocratic, and surrounding herself with interesting people, strangers, artists, musicians, and anyone who was either distinguished or agreeable. If the old Bostonians didn't like it, they needn't come; but they came, if they were asked.

Her museum. She followed the fashion of the 1890's in collecting real or alleged works of the Old Masters, and also of some modern painters; but here the state of society in the twentieth century and in America prevented her from collecting as an aristocrat might, for his own pleasure, to enhance the surroundings of his life and the heritage of his family. She collected to collect; and such collections can have only one end, a public museum. This fatality, imposed by circumstances, worked a slow and subtle change in her bearing and in her satisfactions. She became an agent for her own museum. At least, so she seemed in her public capacity, for by building her museum she became a public character: but her personality never was quite transformed. I may say that I have never really seen her collection; for she would insist on showing me everything, instead of letting me—as a true *grande dame* might have done—ramble about without her and study what caught my eye; and when she showed her treasures, she would tell something about them, where she found them, or their history, and there would always be the personal play of conversation between her and her guest: so that the guest had a charming half-hour with her, but never *saw* any of her things. I should have bought a ticket and gone to her Museum on the days when it was open to the public; but I dislike museums and never did so, especially as I heard that sometimes she walked about even on public days and acted as cicerone. Her palace and her pictures had become the last costume and the last audacity by which she would vanquish old Boston.

Her virtues. Mrs. Gardner, though she defied prudery, practised the virtue most difficult for a brilliant woman in a hostile society: she spoke ill of nobody. She joined kindness to liberty; and she played the queen and the connoisseur with so much good nature that in her masquerade she was aware of no rival, while in the real world she scattered substantial favours.

Mrs. Whitman. More in the spirit of Boston, more conscientious and troubled, was Mrs. Whitman. Not content merely to love the fine arts, she became an artist and designed stained-glass windows. There were echoes in her of Transcendentalism, but no longer imageless or countrified. It had become symbolical, ritualistic, luxurious. I remember the high wax candles, as on an altar, decorating her dinner-table. She didn't make a point of entertaining itinerant artists or other celebrities; but devoted herself to instilling the higher spirit of the arts and crafts into the minds of working girls. Our good works, alas, are often vainer than our vanities. "What did Mrs. Whitman talk to you about?" somebody asked after a lecture. And one of the girls replied: "She said that art was green." It is true that Mrs. Whitman was partial to that colour, and Mahomet expressed the same preference, for an easily assignable reason; but when we express preferences, though we may diffuse those preferences by mere suggestion or hypnosis, we incite others to express their contrary preferences, and to nurse every preference, instinctive or imposed, out of pure doggedness.

The arts killed by aestheticism. This is not an incitement to learn, but to be content with not learning: the great temptation of freedom. Mrs. Whitman's lecture, in the case of that working girl, was a complete failure. If she had reported the *explicable* fact that Mahomet thought green the most beautiful of colours, or the very type of the beautiful, something might have been gained; because the working-girl's casual preference for pink or for blue would have been not merely challenged but undermined. For if Mahomet loved green, because he constantly travelled through deserts, looking for the palm-trees of some oasis, what desert are you, poor working-girl travelling through, that causes you to long for pink and blue ribbons? If you reflect upon that, the apparently inane conclusion that art is green, might acquire a pregnant meaning. Art would appeal to the mind in general as the colour green appealed to the eye of Mahomet, and for similar reasons. We must consider human nature and the radical predicaments of the living arts if we are to recover definite taste or artistic power. The aestheticism of the nineteenth century was a symptom of decay, aggravated by the pathos of distance.

She graces a philosophical supper given by William James. Mrs. Whitman was a great friend of William James. They had similar impetuous perceptions and emotions, a similar unrest, and a similar desire to penetrate to the hidden facts, the submerged classes, the neglected ideas, unpleasing to the official world. The generosity in all this was evident: less evident was the fruitfulness of it. The field was vague, and so was the mind of the reformers. One day James asked me to come to a supper that he was giving for his more advanced pupils, about thirty of them. Mrs. Whitman was coming. He wished me to come too—without dressing, of course—and help Mrs. Whitman to feel at home. And I was placed at her right hand, James sitting opposite, in the middle of the other long side of the table. Neither Mrs. James nor any other member of the family was present: it was to be a philosophical conclave, a semi-religious semi-festive mystery. Why did James conceive such a supper? Out of kindness, to be hospitable and fatherly towards his disciples. But why did he ask Mrs. Whitman, or why did she wish to come? Mrs. James could have been equally hospitable and kind. Perhaps it was not from the young men's point of view, but from Mrs. Whitman's, that he saw the desirability of inviting her. She was interested in diffusing high aspirations among the people: here she would see a chosen group of ambitious young men, and perhaps scatter some good seed, or get some hint or some encouragement in her work. The young men were of course impressed, some of them no doubt dazzled, by James in his own library, walled completely with books, save for his father's portrait in oils over the mantelpiece, and by the lordly supper—with a touch of the *Kneipe* about it, for we all had beer, except Mrs. Whitman. For her a half-bottle of champagne was provided, which, as James said, would not be good for the rest of us. Above all they must have retained a striking image of Mrs. Whitman, beautifully dressed, not in an evening gown, but in a green velvet bodice with long sleeves, delicately set off by gold braid, an ample white silk skirt, and a large bunch of violets. She was not particularly beautiful, nor the opposite (as Mrs. Gardner was), but she had that vivacity and intelligence, added to the discreet arts of the toilet, that keep French ladies from ever looking old. I doubt that she said anything that any of those young men would note or remember. I had been summoned expressly to entertain her, and spare her the effort of having to make talk with shy uncouth youths all the evening; for there were no speeches. In philanthropic and propagandist directions I doubt that anything was accomplished: but the feast was rather beautiful in itself, and certainly cannot have been forgotten by any of those who were there. It was an instance of the manner in which those two distinguished spirits, William James and Mrs. Whitman, failed to diffuse their intended influence, and yet succeeded while failing: for they added something pleasant and pure to the world.

Two exceptional Bostonians.

•

Judge Holmes.

As to the male element in Boston society, it would perhaps be better for me not to say anything. I knew few of them well, because most of my friends, even at Harvard, were not Bostonians, and those who were Bostonians were seldom seen at parties. The men went there to see the women, and were like fish out of water in

368 Persons and Places

regard to one another. Besides, Boston society was dominated by the very young, except in staid elderly circles that met only at dinners. Sometimes, being a conveniently unattached bachelor, I was honoured by an invitation to small parties of that sort, at houses where I was not intimate. On such occasions I might make the acquaintance of representative elderly men, or hear them talk, when conversation became general. One distinguished Bostonian that I came to know in this way was Judge Holmes. His wife never went anywhere, and he, still rather youngish with a sweeping blond moustache, would play the bachelor. One day—this was at Mrs. Gray's, who had been a Boston "beauty"—he said he didn't like to walk in Beacon Street. Every door seemed to him the tombstone of a dead love. This was one direction in which the Justice unbent; but his mind was plastic also in speculation. Being an exceptionally successful man he could be pessimistic in philosophy, and being an old Bostonian he could disinterestedly advocate democratic reforms. After I had left America, he surprised me by writing in high terms about my *Winds of Doctrine*, especially the first page in which there is nothing not commonplace except perhaps the tone in which moral and political revolutions are spoken of, as natural episodes in a transformation without end. It is or it was usual, especially in America, to regard the polity of which you happen to approve as sure to be presently established everywhere and to prevail for ever after. To have escaped this moralistic obsession, at least for a moment, evidently was a pleasure to Judge Holmes. He had a really liberal, I mean a truly free, mind.

And Roger Wolcott. There was another local celebrity whom I once heard discourse about politics at a dinner, not in a set speech, but in ordinary conversation. Everybody else stopped talking in order to listen to him because, by a rare exception in his class, he had gone into politics and been governor of Massachusetts. His name was Roger Wolcott, and in his young days he had been regarded as the handsomest man and the greatest beau in Boston. He was attacking the New York *Nation*, a weekly paper which I always read. Its politics were radical, but the book reviews were written by professors, often professors of foreign languages, about subjects that interested me. The views of the professorial class, or intelligentsia, are naturally literary and captious; Roger Wolcott, as a man and as a practical politician, detested them. He said *The Nation* had a very bad influence in the country, especially among the young men. It gave them a false idea of what government was and ought to be. It made them ignorantly critical, supercilious, unpatriotic. As far as I remember, Wolcott didn't go beyond bare denunciation; he was probably not speculative, like Judge Holmes; and he might seem to have been guided merely by club spirit or esprit-de-corps like so many Lodges and Greek Letter Fraternities that flourish in America, without representing any genuine public interests. On the other hand, his experience may have given him some true intuition of the fated movement and destiny of his country, and his "stalwart" politics may have been only a vulgar cover for something heroic: I mean, for the courage and pride of sharing the life of his country, in soul as well as in body.

XXIII

Americans in Europe

Circum-stances ally me with Americans in Europe. More than with any other class of people, fate has associated me with Americans in Europe. Even when I was still living in the United States, it was people at home in Europe, socially and morally, that most readily became my friends. Not that being at home in Europe or at home in America counted in itself in my true friendships. That which counted in that case was exclusively the individual man or woman, the body and the soul. A field of action and thought was essential, but only as a language is essential for conveying a thought: for when the thought is absorbing, the language is not noticed, and seems indifferent. Yet a common language, a common social and moral idiom, becomes in itself a great bond when you are travelling in strange places, among people with whom you cannot communicate. The common language draws you together, even if what each will say may eventually not prove important or acceptable to the others.

Now with Americans in Europe I had a common field of experience, a common social and moral convention and we were for the moment in the same boat. A travelling acquaintance may of course disclose a vital affinity: but I think this was not the case with any of my American friends in Europe: either no vital affinity existed or we had discovered it in America, and it was independent of all accidents of residence. With converts of any kind, with American women married to Eng-lishmen, with expatriates, with aesthetic souls that fled from America because the voices there were too rough, I never had much sympathy. It was persons who were thoroughly European or thoroughly American that held the first place in my esteem. In my esteem, but not in my life. In my life the foreground was filled with Americans in Europe.

Strong marries Miss Bessie Rockefeller. This appears emphatically in the case of Strong, the only person not of my kindred with whom I have lived, on and off, for years. I have described the origin of our friendship and its not altogether satisfactory result. Why did Strong live in Europe at all? It would require more knowledge than our life-long acquaintance has given me to answer this question properly: there are mysteries involved, and Strong was more than reserved, he was inhibited, in regard to his private affairs. I can only point to the gross facts: he had been at school in Germany; he very naturally wished to return to Germany to study philosophy; and, then, when from Germany we had gone to London for our holidays, in the spring of 1887, he one day announced that *it would be best* for him to leave me and go to Paris to join his father who was there with a party of friends. This sounded dutiful and pious enough; it was not for me to ask any questions, nor did I suspect any mystery. But a month or two later I received a letter, saying that he had been travelling with Mr. John D. Rockefeller and family, that he was engaged to be married to the eldest daughter, Bessie; that they were all coming to England in June; and that Mr. Rockefeller invited me to join them, on the day of Queen Victoria's Jubilee, to view the procession from a room he had engaged in Buckingham Palace Road. Not a word more. Had the pious rogue been engaged all the time to this fabulously rich heiress, when he generously consented to divide the Walker Fellowship with me? I can hardly think so. It must all have been a machination behind his back. His father and Mr. Rockefeller, eminent Baptist elders, had thought *it would be best* to settle these young people safely and happily for life, before they got any foolish notions into their heads. Old Dr. Strong (who was himself becoming a financier, had a red nose, and liked good dinners with plenty of champagne) saw a brilliant future assured for his son: and this marriage would rivet Rockefeller even more tightly to himself and to all Baptist institutions; while Rockefeller saw his daughter, his favourite child, whose future gave him some anxiety, safely settled with a good-looking, high-principled young man, sure to make her happy, and with his studious habits and mild disposition never to separate her from her father, either in place of residence or in sound Christian sentiments. The young people were willing enough. Both were probably profoundly bored and with a blank future. To be married was a new idea. It gave them something almost exciting to think about and to do.

In his old age Strong sometimes amused himself by writing "poetry". The most interesting of these effusions recounts how he loved five times, and Bessie, his wife, is one of these lady-loves, but evidently not the one secretly preferred. From this and from other indications I gather that he *thought it would be best*, after having been obliged by his conscience to resist the higher Baptist powers in regard to his religious allegiance, not to resist them in this, that seemed a reasonable proposal. People would think it a piece of incredible good fortune, but somehow for him it was sad.

The Rockefellers at the Queen's Jubilee. In Buckingham Palace Road, on the appointed day, I was duly introduced to the great millionaire, still a dapper youngish man with cordial American manners, and to his daughter Bessie, not at all the blushing bride, but the image of vigorous health and good sense, nice-looking, frank, and with manlike college airs, for she was fresh from Vassar. Our conversation corresponded, and was nothing but commonplaces helped out by smiles. Little did I suspect that I should never have a chance to talk with her rationally again; for even when I staid in later years at her house, I hardly ever saw her. She was always, as they put it, in delicate health, which was a euphemism for not being in her right mind. It was to be Strong's destiny to become a sort of guardian or watchman over his invalid wife. At Compiègne, during her last years, he would see her for ten minutes in the morning, and for ten minutes again in the evening, each time bringing her a picture postcard to talk about. He had a great collection of them in stock, and dealt them out, as if just discovered, two each day, for her to put in her album.

Later conversations with Rockefeller. Ten years later, when I was at King's College, the Rockefellers invited me again to see the Queen's procession, when she drove to the service in front of St. Paul's in thanksgiving for her sixty years' reign. This time we were in a room in Piccadilly; and the sight so absorbed me, with its vast historic and political suggestions, that I don't remember Rockefeller being there at all, or any of the other guests. On another occasion, however, when I went to spend a holiday with Strong at Lakewood, New Jersey, I had a capital opportunity of learning some of the great capitalist's characteristics; for the house was his, he had only lent it to his daughter and son-in-law, and at that time he was living in it, in order to be near his private golf-links, where his own larger house had been closed for the winter. I saw him only at table; but as Strong was a silent man, and his wife was ill upstairs, it was practically with me that Mr. Rockefeller had to talk. He played golf assiduously, always alone, matching his record on one day against his record on another; just what the saints do when they daily examine their conscience and consider whether they have developed any new sins, or been carried by the grace of God one step forward towards perfection. Such was probably also the interest dominating Rockefeller's chase after millions. He was beyond comparing himself with his competitors; he compared himself with himself.

The prophet of monopoly. One day when I had mentioned Spain, he asked me, after a little pause, what was the population of Spain. I said I believed it was then nineteen millions. There was another pause, this time rather longer, and then he said, half to himself, "I must tell them at the office that they don't sell enough oil in Spain. They must look the matter up."

I saw in my mind's eye the ideal of the monopolist. All nations must consume the same things, in proportion to their population. All mankind will then form a perfect democracy, supplied with rations from a single centre of administration, as is for their benefit; since they will then secure everything assigned to them at the lowest possible price. This was not a subject for me to broach with Rockefeller; but I ventured a hint in another direction, which I don't know whether he caught. In Avila, for I couldn't speak for the whole of Spain, we had passed from olive oil and candles almost directly to electricity. Gas we had never known, but petroleum had been used in cafés and shops, and perhaps in one room in each house, in a lamp over the centre table, under which burned the charcoal *brasero*; but even in Avila the electric bulb was beginning to supersede it. The world changed rapidly, when we once set it changing. Yet the Standard Oil Company had no cause for alarm. Motors were coming in, and petrol would be more in demand than ever.

The self-made man. Another day, in the act of sitting down at table, as if he had something important on his mind, Mr. Rockefeller formally addressed his son-in-law. "Charles, I heard that you had been buying a cord of wood, and I went down to the cellar to look at it. *That* isn't a cord of wood. When I was a young fellow I used to cut a cord of wood, and I know what it looks like. I don't need a tape-measure to measure it with. They are cheating you."

Poor Strong said nothing, and I, trying to be sympathetic, observed that sometimes, when values changed, dealers found it simpler to reduce the measure than to raise the price. As a baker's dozen is more than twelve, so a conventional cord of wood today at Lakewood might be less than a natural cord of wood in Mr. Rockefeller's boyhood. Besides, things come to seem smaller as we grow bigger; and wasn't it possible that a part of the wood might have been burned already? My wisdom, however, seemed to fall flat and we talked of something else.

His extraordinary aspect. Rockefeller himself had changed surprisingly to the eye. From looking much younger than he must have been in 1887, he now looked immeasurably old. He had lost all hair, eyebrows and eyelashes included, and wore a pepper and salt wig decidedly too small for him. His skin, too, was curiously wrinkled, and he was elaborately wrapped up for his long day on the golf-links. But I understood that he remained the active head of his Company, and had a private wire to his office for receiving information and giving orders.

Strong and his wife find French surroundings agreeable. Strong's marriage had been arranged in France, and after it, it was in France that he and his wife lingered. They learned French conscientiously, and to become perfectly fluent, they agreed always to speak French together at table. This habit grew upon Mrs. Strong, until she refused to speak English at all; and when I last saw her, both she and Margaret, then about ten years old, had French nurses and would speak nothing but French. This hobby, and the habit of constantly returning to France, had not been adopted deliberately. Strong was as firmly convinced of the wisdom and duty of living in his own country as were his family and the Rockefellers; but the state of his wife's health and spirits seemed to demand a frequent season abroad, and later his own health and spirits seemed to demand it also. He had not given up his intended profession, and for one year was instructor in psychology at Cornell. Here his wife's health again interfered, and that position was given up. They would live at Lakewood, and he would become an associate professor—this could be easily arranged by Mr. Rockefeller—at Columbia. Nevertheless, they were almost always in France; and Strong became attached to a limited but well-chosen group of resorts, to which he introduced me: Versailles, Saint Germain, Fontainebleau, Compiègne, Aix-les-Bains, and Glion in French Switzerland. To two of these, the first and the last, I often returned alone in later years, finding them quiet and inspiring.

Phantom professorship at Columbia. After his wife's death, Strong made a heroic effort to settle down in New York. He took a flat in an apartment house with a general restaurant, in Fifth Avenue, and a governess for Margaret; and he undertook his proposed teaching at Columbia. In his eagerness to begin work, he arrived on the first morning rather early at his lecture room. As yet there was no one there. He would have a moment to rest, and to look over his notes, recalling the chief points to be made in due order, before the students began to come in. When he looked at his watch again, the appointed hour had arrived, but still no students. It was customary to allow five or ten minutes for them to straggle from one lecture-room to another. Five minutes, ten minutes passed, and not a soul. Was nobody taking his course at all? He must not be precipitate. There might have been some mistake about the room. He would wait another five minutes. At a quarter past the hour, he resolutely gathered up his papers, put on his coat and hat, and thought of the Apostles bidden to shake the dust from their feet. But resentment and mortification, if he felt them, were soon buried deep among forgotten dreams. The feeling that rose to the surface was one of relief. He made his way to the College Office. There he explained to the clerk that he was Professor Strong. Could they inform him if anybody had elected his special course in psychology? They would see. They had a list of all elective courses, with the number of students that had chosen each. No: there was no tally against that special course in psychology. Perhaps it was rather a graduate course. They would let him know if there were inquiries about it.

On his way home the feeling of relief gained upon Strong. He had done his duty. His important but neglected theory of perception, more accurate and scientific than any other, could be better explained in a book than in lectures to beginners. Now he could devote the winter to that necessary task. For the sake of his work, he must be careful about his health. His mind always worked better in a mild climate. He would stop at the up-town office of the Italian Steamship Company and engage cabins in their first boat for Naples. That old convent above the road to Amalfi would be a place to suit him perfectly: quiet, sunny, simple, and healthy.

He takes an apartment in Paris. Italian food and habits, however, proved less favourable for work than he had hoped. The demon that pursued Strong everywhere was *ennui*. In Paris, at least, he could, as he put it, "attend the Comédie Française"; and every day he could sit for an hour or two in front of a café, *la Régence*, *les Deux Magots*, or *la Closerie des Lilas*. That made a little change of scene; and sometimes American acquaintances would come and speak to him. Finally he took an apartment on the third floor at Number 9, Avenue de l'Observatoire. The place was clean and quiet, no passing, and nothing but sky and a wall of trees visible from the windows. The *salon* had been decorated in the style of Louis Seize, with silk panels, but Strong ordered the silk to be removed and the panels painted a dull white, to match the mouldings; and he "purchased" English furniture at Maples', of the sort usually covered with gay chintz, to which he was not accustomed. He had it covered instead with a strong reddish-grey stuff to match the curtains; and a great walnut bookcase was made to run along one whole wall. The room was brilliantly lighted by its three large windows, yet somehow seemed sad and unfinished. Strong hadn't the secret of making himself comfortable, and here, as at Fiesole later, he was always thinking of going somewhere else for a change.

To tell his whole tragic history, and that of his daughter would require volumes, with profound knowledge of families and circles that I have never frequented. It would carry me too far from the persons and places that have left vivid images in my mind. I therefore bequeath the subject to any novelist that it might tempt; for it would be a great subject. As a mere hint, however, of the perspectives to be disclosed, I will describe a single episode that I happen to have witnessed.

The aristocracy opens negotiations for marriage. Strong, and even more his daughter Margaret, were condemned to move within the magnetic field of the Rockefeller millions. Not a few roving atoms, positively electrified, circled and buzzed within it. Among Margaret's Parisian friends were the Marquise de l'Enfernat and her daughter. The Marquise had little money and only one son, already the Marquis and as yet unmarried. One day we had word that she was coming to see Monsieur Strong—he was laid up with paralysis of the legs—for an important consultation. Her daughter accompanied her, but at once carried Margaret off to some concert or to some dress-maker's, so as to leave the elderly people unembarrassed in discussing business. Strong had expressly asked me to remain. When tea had been served, Madame de l'Enfernat, with a perceptible air of addressing the public, began to speak of her son. "We have", she said, "the most satisfactory reports of his work in Poland. You know, Messieurs, how much the government appreciated his services during the war. He is a young officer of intrepid character, with a quick temper and an iron will. He was invited to accept a very difficult, a very delicate post, the command of a company of criminals. His success with them was extraordinary. They became like sheep under him in camp, and like wolves in the battle-field. Men's energies, he thinks, should never be suppressed, no matter how violent. They must be turned into the right path. *Voilà tout!* What a lesson for his future wife, if she only could learn it! Now in Poland he has a task no less difficult, and he is meeting with equal success. Not criminals now, cadets. Cadets who have imbibed, under evil influences, wild notions of liberty. What is liberty? It is taking the wrong path whenever you choose. Yet my son inspires them with respect. He shows them the invincible order that God has established in the world. They learn to obey. They learn to command. Ah, he is a disciplinarian! Yet this severity in him goes with the tenderest heart, when once his heart has been touched. I, his mother, can assure you of it. He has been a good son. And they say a good son always makes a good husband."

Here Madame de l'Enfernat paused, sipped her cup of tea, nibbled the edge of a small cake, liked it, gobbled the rest of it, drank more tea, and proceeded.

"I regret that my son should have been called away before he could pay his respects to you, Monsieur, and to our dear Margaret. He knows through us how pretty, how simple, how charming, how exquisite, and how appealing she is. A man of bold spirit and high temper, a man of action, especially loves gentleness and sweetness in woman, and I think that a young girl like Margaret could not help admiring his soldierly qualities. Her tastes are as yet a little vague, and in the firmness of his character she would be relieved to find the natural solution to her indecision."

But lays down high and mighty conditions. Here again the Marquise made a short pause, and then turned to me with evident premeditation.

"You, Monsieur," she said in a conciliatory tone, seeing that Strong hadn't at all melted, "being Spanish, must be a Catholic?"

"Yes, Madame, we are all still Catholics in Spain, at least nominally. But you know the character of this epoch. Most of us have lost our faith."

"Ah, I know it well. That is an effect of men's vices. It wears off. You will return to us some day." And glancing at me to estimate my age, she added smiling, "You will return soon." Then, addressing Strong again, she went on.

"Ah, faith is so important! Without the faith, the family has no stability, no union, no security. No one recognises any obligation. Everyone is divorced. When public morality is so relaxed, there remains no law except within the Church. We must all be faithful children of the Church. Without that safeguard, no prudent man can venture to found a family."

At this point the bell rang, the young ladies returned from their outing, and almost immediately Madame de l'Enfernat and her daughter took their leave. No distinct proposal had been made. The lady hadn't come to ask for Margaret's hand, as we had expected. She had come to lay down a prior condition, namely, that Margaret should become a Catholic. This was not altogether a gratuitous suggestion. Margaret, when she had a Catholic governess, had shown a marked inclination to the Church, and still felt no hostility to it, only an incorrigible vagueness about everything. The whole affair lapsed; and it was as well. Her proposed family, as I discovered by accident, were already making merciless fun of her behind her back.

Bob Potter and his wife in Paris.   I have mentioned that Bob Potter, when in the summer of 1892, I staid with his family at Bar Harbor, was preoccupied with a love-affair and with his approaching departure for Paris, to study at the Beaux-Arts. A little more than a year later, after the death of Warwick, both matters were happily settled, and I went to New York for his wedding. The bride's father, Mr. Nicholas Fish, had been for years American Minister at Brussels, and there his only daughter had been educated, learning to speak French and German perfectly. With these accomplishments, with the outlook that a diplomatic circle always opens out, and with her own quick intelligence, she had become an unusually charming person; and her ambitious parents expected that she should make a brilliant match. But she fell in love with Bob Potter, quite intelligibly, for he too was unusually *distingué* for a young New Yorker, but, alas, the Fishes thought him penniless: he had only just money enough to smoke good cigarettes. This, to the young lady's romantic mind, seemed quite enough for their conjoint happiness, and she threatened to run away with her lover to Paris, if they refused to consent to her marriage. The matter was compromised by arranging for a quiet wedding in the house, with no promise of an allowance from the Fishes for the future. Something nevertheless was allowed her; and eventually, her only brother having fallen in the Cuban war, Mrs. Potter inherited her parents' fortune.

Our journey together through Italy.   During the following years, I saw the Bob Potters only rarely in Paris, as I could be there only in transit; but these interviews sufficed to show me that, in this case, the marriage of a friend, far from being an obstacle to

further good-fellowship, was an aid to it, because Mrs. Potter proved
to be as good a friend as her husband. In 1897 we arranged to make
a trip to Italy together; and Mrs. Potter secretly took Italian lessons,
so as to be able to rescue us helpless men in all our linguistic difficulties.
I had been in Italy two years earlier with Loeser; and this second
journey with the Potters, partly over the same ground, showed me
how important the human element is in our supposedly abstract interests. I saw Venice and Rome, and the pictures everywhere, in a
new light. Bob was a professional architect, with French training: he
was dazzled by the picturesque and somewhat religiously moved by
the primitives; that was his Anglosaxon side; but he was shocked by
the false façades of the Baroque churches; they were stage settings,
allowed to exhibit their shabby side. Yet in persons, as I would tell
him, he appreciated the charm and dignity of clothes, which were all
façades and *postiches*. Why shouldn't buildings, with their meagre material
framework, expand also into decorative cloaks, ruffs, and *panaches*?
There was a kind of homage to the eye and to the ideal, in such a
seemly masquerade. It presented what it would fain be, and what it
thought worthy of your attention. To seem less grand would have
been less courteous.

The interplay of taste and knowledge. Bob taught me less about the arts than Loeser did; his
knowledge was more limited. Like his wife's notion of
elegance, it was exclusively American and French. But
he taught me a great deal in matters of taste, because
as appeals to taste, as charming images, he appreciated all sorts of
perfection. The only difficulty here was the resulting sense of frivolity
and anarchy. The world became a carnival of butterflies. Insight didn't
penetrate to the organic, moral and physical, energies that were expressed in each type of perfection, and that determined its rank and
dignity in the real world. To have insisted on this vital background,
however, would have destroyed the purity of taste, its aristocratic
independence; and there is a subjective root to immediate pleasure
in form and harmony just as profound as the roots of the arts in the
public world; more profound, even, because the public world itself
takes shape only in obedience to the private capacities of the people
that compose it. The appeal, in a liberal mind, must ultimately be to
pure taste, to instinctive preference; and when Bob Potter, so very
tall and thin, so refined and so embarrassed, said *pfui!* or when he
was religiously silent and evidently moved in the presence of something
exquisite, my own load was lifted, and I saw how instrumental were

all the labour and history of man, to be crowned, if crowned at all, only in intuition.

Students in Paris.   In 1896–7, when I was at King's College, some Harvard friends studying at the Beaux-Arts asked me to spend the Christmas holidays with them in Paris, at No. 3, Rue Soufflot. They could offer me a room, and I might contribute my share to the cost of their common table. It was a pleasant way of seeing something, and hearing more, of student life in the Quartier Latin; and topographically and linguistically, it helped to make me feel at home when I went later to live there with Strong.

Lawrence Butler.   The young men at the Rue Soufflot were only club acquaintances; later I had a real friend, Lawrence Butler, also at the Beaux-Arts, whom I often saw and visited, before and after, in America, although always, as it were, in the character of an American in Europe. It was in mid-ocean, in June 1895, that I made his acquaintance, when he was perhaps nineteen years old. I heard that he had fallen down the steep and curving stairs that led below to the cabin, and had sprained his ankle. When two or three days later, I crossed him in that very place, I spoke to him. He was getting on, he said, and could move about with a crutch. This was the beginning of a very long and very satisfactory friendship. He was a well-bred youth and always kept his place as a *young* friend even when no longer very young; and this discretion on his part turned the difference in our ages from a difficulty into a pleasure. He asked me to stay at his house, and introduced me to his family, especially to his mother and his favourite aunt, wife of Stanford White, the architect. He became an architect himself, though somewhat casually as to the practice of his profession; and this was a double bond, because his knowledge fell in with my tastes and his leisure with my habits.

How privileges become impediments.   His interest in building was human, domestic, proprietary: he was always thinking of *living* in his houses and *praying* in his churches. For beneath the surface, which was a sort of helpless fashionable herd-instinct, there was natural piety in him. He was affectionate and he was religious. I could be happy in his company. I used to tell him, and he agreed, that he ought to have been an English country gentleman. In Long Island, where he lived and where his mother's family had a sort of estate (since Smithtown and Garden City had been originally their land) things were too changeful and urbanised. There was no room

for a landlord: there was only a land company. Nevertheless he had
an ample house in the midst of woods, far from all others, and even
a toy Cathedral in Garden City, which he looked after with special
care. And his somewhat inarticulate inner man had another outlet.
He sang very well: at least, he had a good tenor voice that promised
great things, and that he took pains to cultivate, as he took pains to
study architecture. In Paris Jean de Reszke gave him lessons, telling
him to sing out and to shout—which was exactly what he could have
done well and heartily; but those lessons were only occasional, and
ordinarily his teacher was an old woman, evidently once an accomplished singer, but now good exclusively for phrasing and method.
Between the two, Lawrence made no progress: at least, that was my
opinion. But when many years after I asked him if he still sang, he
said, Oh yes, and sang several things for my benefit, all French. Now
his French was good enough for a foreigner in the Quartier Latin; but
enlarged in singing, it turned out not to be pure and native enough.
And there was another point in which I think he had been misguided.
He said he had improved in expression. He meant that he could now
sing pianissimo—just what Jean de Reszke had intuited would not be
his forte. It was dreadfully artificial. What a pity that a man who was
full of real emotions, should attempt to coax and simulate emotions
that he didn't feel! Such mistakes come from international and inter-
racial confusion. Lawrence could sing hymns and glees and hunting-
songs; he couldn't sing malicious French trifles. His architecture and
his religion also fell between two stools. He couldn't be either a designer
of sky-scrapers or a true continuator of classic building; he couldn't
be a freethinker, and he couldn't become a Catholic. He was also fond
of sports, and good at them, though not a champion; but in America,
after early youth, only champions were felt to have justified their
avocation; and sport survived as a means of entertaining great crowds
of spectators or of readers of the sporting pages in the newspapers.
As if he had felt that he still limped from that early sprained ankle,
Lawrence Butler never married. His essentially affectionate nature was
left to wither in philanderings or in scatter-brained plutocratic amusements. Like my poor Oliver Alden—to whom he contributed some
traits—he petered out.

Moral immaturity of the times.   Petering out, which was almost universal among those
of my friends that had artistic or intellectual pretensions,
was not always due to the materialism of the age, or to
other untoward circumstances; not always even to being smothered

in circumstances ironically too favourable. The cause seemed sometimes to be innate: dreaminess or somnambulism in a soul too vegetative to resist transformation or to transform anything else into its own image. Is it the fog of the North? That is what Nordics seem to think when they flock to the South for inspiration. They are then initiated into southern sensuality, as if into a warmer mysticism; but that doesn't enable them to accomplish anything definite. Is it immaturity? Perhaps we might say so, in a complimentary sense. Externally, in action and learning, they may be more than competent, they may be pedantic; yet there may remain undeveloped resources and potentialities within them; so that they feel always unsatisfied, reject all finalities, and elude all discipline.

Conrad Slade. The most Nordic of my American friends was so Nordic, that he seemed an American only by accident. When he went home, everything seemed to him unnecessary and inhuman; and he was content to live in Paris among poor artists and working people, with none of the comforts or social pleasures among which he had been bred. His father, Dr. Slade, was a well-known Boston physician; but his mother was a Fräulein Hensler; and whatever Scandinavian tallness, blondness, calmness, vagueness, and migratory instinct may have been latent in her, must have been concentrated in her son Conrad. He was very good-looking in the expressionless statuesque manner, rowed with the 'varsity crew, and allowed himself to do as others did around him; but inwardly he was extraordinarily solitary and independent, as if he still lived among the fiords. He had warm poetic passions, very un-American: no scruples, no tipsy gregarious impulse about indulging them, and no ribaldry. It all seemed to him a wonderful work of nature, like the revolution of the stars; and leading afterwards what in Boston would have passed for a most irregular life, he preserved an air of perfect purity and serenity, his blue eyes as clear and his thoughts as speculative as ever.

Humble amours and aesthetic speculation. At Harvard, for some instinctive reason that I won't attempt to fathom, he became attached to me, and told me his love-affairs, which were, as poetry should be: simple, sensuous, and short. He didn't move at all in Boston society. His lady-loves were mature prima-donnas, or country lasses, or city waifs. In Paris, where he went at once in the hope of becoming a sculptor, he grew comparatively domestic and monogamous, following the ancient dictates of nature. He wandered, when the spirit moved, through Italy and Greece, and southern France, always with the eye of an artist and a prophet, seeking to divine the secret of the beautiful. In time he became a devout admirer of Renoir, who he said was the greatest painter since Rubens: for he himself had dabbled in painting more than in sculpture, without visible results in either, but with much subjective deepening of sentiment and perception. He could never explain to me in words what was the merit of Renoir and the other moderns; the merits I could discern in them were evidently not to the point. About Greek art he did give me a hint, that my knowledge is too superficial for me to follow out or to test. It concerned the priority of the skeleton and the movement in figures: the visible detail, even the visible outline, was to *grow* out of the attitude, not merely to catch it, as in a modern caricature. In that sense, he made some designs in silver-point after Greek coins, which seemed to me truly classic in spirit. It is the dynamic symbol to the mind, conveyed by means as simple as possible, that works the miracle: as to the detail of the image, the eye itself is inattentive, and the artist wastes his science.

Esser beato nega ai mortali il fato. In later years Slade was an impressive figure, tall, calm, stately, bald, with a great curly yellow beard, with grey hairs in it; he looked like Leonardo da Vinci. The only change in his mind was a new, natural, and fixed affection. He had had a little boy, and was wrapped up in the child. Then stepmotherly nature smote him in his tender spot. The boy developed a disease of the bones; the doctors said it might be cured. I was never told of the end, and heard only of the child being wheeled about in his bed from one sunny beach to another, in the hope that the rays of the sun might penetrate to his crumbling bones, and heal him.

Andrew Green. Another American expatriate of marked personality, though not an expatriate in Europe, differed from most of my friends in being a Westerner, in having read my books, and in our acquaintance having been cemented not so much in youth as in mature years. Andrew Green had been my pupil in College, and I had once asked him, seeing how good he was at field sports, why he didn't go in for football or rowing. He replied that he cared nothing for sport of any kind, and only did his high jump and his broad jump for a private reason. Not then, but years later, he told me what that reason had been. He liked to belong to the athletic squad because at the training table he could see his friend Richmon Fearing every day, whereas otherwise they would never come across each other. This was because Fearing was a swell and Green an outsider. I knew what that meant in College; and the interesting thing was Green's supreme contempt for such barriers and his deliberate way of surmounting them when he thought it worth while.

His self-reliance and clear will continued to show themselves later. He went into business in Chicago expressly to make money quickly and to escape from business, exactly as I went into teaching, but more successfully; for in a few years he had made his little pile, went alone to China, and hired a junk to live in, while he sailed leisurely up and down the great rivers and explored the wonders of that country. Moral contrasts, moral liberty: aesthetic contrasts, aesthetic potentiality *ad infinitum.* No wonder that he read my books and understood them! Yet that was only the critical side of my philosophy, which people in my day could appreciate, even if they didn't trust it. That which escaped them, and probably escaped Green, was the deeper presupposition, without which all criticism would be futile: the need of singleness of mind and complete loyalty to the particular virtue possible to each age and to each individual.

The superstition of Mammon-worship. What monstrous selfishness, I hear the Bostonians saying, to drop your work, never to think of the needs of others, and to run away to hide and to lead a useless life of idleness at the antipodes! Yes, Green and I were unmitigated egoists: we thought before acting. We asked what the needs of others really were, and whether we were doing them any good. Had we been conscious of doing great good, as the Bostonians were, that feeling would have filled us with reflected happiness and zeal, and we should have gone on doing it. But were business men in Chicago or professors of philosophy at Harvard working for the good of others? Weren't they working to make money or to propagate their views? Weren't they invading the public aggressively, with their enterprise or their propaganda, to satisfy a private ambition? Philosophy is not a useful science, like mathematics, requisite for engineers. It is a remnant or an echo of prophetic inspirations launched in antiquity into an ignorant world, and it perpetuates the Babel there. And as to business, if this meant the exercise of a needful profession with the necessary moderate compensation, the business man might plod on like any other artisan under a just consumer's economy. But business enterprise and free speculation are not in that class; at best they are instances of the producer's economy, which by chance may launch something valuable, or reorganise economic machinery to the ultimate public advantage; but essentially they are private adventures prompted by private ambition.

A blond Othello and a dusky Desdemona. With his strong satirical intelligence and his strong aesthetic sense, I have no doubt that Green's inland voyage in China was profitable to his mind: but it was not a career. He needed a career; he was not an ornamental young man with an ornamental culture in an ornamental society. By way of settling down, he went to the British West Indies and undertook fruit-growing. Incidentally he found there an original solution to the problem of love and marriage. He formed an uncloudedly happy union—with a negress. This was no mere tropical interlude or sensual captivity. The lady—he showed me her photograph—was a slight little thing, not darker than some white people, and he had the greatest respect for her native wisdom and even for her literary taste. He regretted not taking her with him on his travels, but she would not have been admitted to the hotels, not at least in the United States. They had a son; and a problem arose as to his education. Green wished to have him educated in France; he liked that type of training, and if the boy showed promise he might remain in France, where there was no official prejudice against mixed blood. Otherwise, he might come back to the West Indies and inherit the farm.

All was not well, however, in that tropical paradise. Green's fruit was exceptionally good, but couldn't find a market. The United Fruit Company with its steamers wouldn't accept it: there wasn't enough of it, and it wasn't packed in the popular way. The public preferred insipid standard fruit in great beds of cotton wool to luscious special fruit in smaller baskets. Here was the tyranny of the distributor's economy persecuting the independent American in his Eden.

Joe Stickney. I have commemorated many American friends, and not one man of letters, not one poet. The poets and the learned men remained for the most part in the category of acquaintances. There may have been a professional feminine jealousy between us that prevented a frank and hearty comradeship. Yet I have been keeping in reserve a learned friend and poet for whom I had a great admiration, although I am not sure that it was returned, except by a certain dutiful respect for my age and for the sphere of my interests. We lived in the same garden within the same wilderness, but not with the same emotions. I cared for the garden, and he respected the wilderness. I have mentioned him before, among my younger Harvard friends: Joe or (as he afterwards called himself) Trumbull Stickney.

Classical learning and romantic faith.   It is not at Harvard, however, that I like to think of him, either when he was an undergraduate or when some ten years later he returned there to teach Greek. I remember him with more pleasure in Paris during that long interval, when he bloomed freely under all sorts of influences stimulating to the spirit. In his nice lodgings overlooking the quiet side of the Luxembourg gardens, or in long walks along the Seine, he would reveal his gradual change of allegiance from classic antiquity to something more rarefied yet warmer, more charitable, closer to the groping mind of our day, to the common people, and to the problem of America. He had been privately educated, his Latin and Greek were not of the slovenly kind that passed muster at Harvard, he spoke and wrote French beautifully. Yet except for his friend Henri Hubert, who was an archeologist and very like a German, I don't think he felt in the French the sterling qualities of his own people, nor could he tolerate the English: he was too impatient and too subtle to put up with their slow mental tempo and their moral assurance. I could never bring him to do justice to Spartan or Roman virtue. He found it brutal and stupid. I think he distrusted me also for being a materialist, not so much in theory, for we never discussed that, but in my constant sense of the animal basis of spirit, and my disrespect for any claim on the part of spirit to govern the world. He feared me. I was a Mephistopheles masquerading as a conservative. I defended the past because once it had been victorious and had brought something beautiful to light; but I had no clear expectation of better things in the future. He saw looming behind me the dreadful spectres of truth and of death.

Our leaning towards Indian philosophy.   I wonder if Stickney suspected, when he shuddered thus at my philosophy, that he was helping to quicken in me the immense sympathy that he felt for the philosophy of India. When he died, his friends very kindly asked me if there were any book of his that I should like as a memento. I had vivid mementoes already: a lovely little edition of Virgil that he had given me and that has filled many a vacant half-hour, always with thanks to the giver; and also his own doctor's thesis on *Les Sentences dans la Poésie Grecque*, which was an attack on rhetoric, and gave me a constant warning of the dangers I ran in that direction. Still, for a further memento, I asked for his copy—which he had once lent me—of Gade's *Die Samkyaphilosophie*. The gist of these Indian studies was given also in one of Stickney's most interesting poems. A Hindu finds himself in ancient Athens, bewildered by the noise of trade, politics, and war, elbowed aside by the rude youths, forsaken and starving. At last in a quiet lane he knocks at a modest door. It is opened by a venerable old man. The stranger is introduced into a walled garden, his bowl is filled with pure rice, and he is left alone to meditate by the trickling fountain. The old man was Epicurus.

His premature end.   Stickney died comparatively young. When he returned to Harvard I was expecting to leave, and perhaps less interested in the life of the place than I had been in the old days, while he was busier than in Paris and preoccupied with matters not within my horizon. In any case, we seldom saw each other. When by chance we met, I felt that my society disturbed him. This would not have troubled me in itself or on my own account. I was hardened to the eclipse of friendships, and observed it without bitterness. The sun and the planets have their times for shining: we mustn't expect them to be always in our hemisphere. Yet something else did distress me in Stickney, quite for his own sake. I felt that he was forcing himself to play a part, a painful part like that of a convert who tries to live up to his new faith and to forgive his new associates for unintentionally wounding him at every turn. It is tragic in such cases to look back to the lovely familiar world that one has abandoned for being false or wicked, and to seek in vain for compensations and equivalents in the strange system that one has decided to call good and true. So Newman must have suffered when he became a Catholic. When would the ivy mantle these new brick walls, or the voice modulate the Latin liturgy as it had done the English? In some such case I imagined Stickney to find himself, now that he was back in America. His conscience had compelled him to swear allegiance to his country and to his work; but he was not at home; he had always been an exotic, warmed and watered in a greenhouse; and the harsh air and tough weeds of his native heath tried him severely. Perhaps the suffering that he endured was not due to any such moral disharmony: this may be merely my supposition. It may have been simply overwork, and the beginnings of the tumor in the brain that was about to kill him. Still that tumor itself was a sign of maladaptation. The too delicate plant, that had already flowered, couldn't endure the change of soil and of temperature, and bred a parasite that choked it.

XXIV

Official Career at Harvard

I write a dull thesis for the Ph.D. On my return to America in 1888 I at once consulted Royce as to my thesis for the doctorate, and suggested for a subject the philosophy of Schopenhauer, because Schopenhauer was the German author that I liked most and knew best. The wise Royce shook his head. That might do, he said, for a master of arts, not for a doctor of philosophy. Instead, he proposed Lotze. I had read Lotze's *Microcosmos* and liked a certain moderation and orthodoxy that pervaded it, without deeply respecting its principles or its conclusions. Lotze was a higher form of Palmer. But Royce said that his other books were more technical and his metaphysics rather Leibnitzian. That sounded better. I agreed, procured the complete works of Lotze, and set to work to read, digest, and annotate them, composing a running summary and commentary, out of which my thesis might be afterwards drawn. It was a pleasant task, not at all brain-racking. I was soon absorbed in it, living in complete retirement at my mother's in Roxbury. For exercise I would walk to Boston or to Cambridge. I went to weekly seminars, admirable stimulants, given by James and Royce. James read to us from the manuscript, chapter by chapter, his new *Principles of Psychology*; while with Royce we read Hegel's *Phaenomenologie des Geistes*.

I wish now that my thesis might have been on Hegel: it would have meant harder work, and it would have been more inadequate; yet it would have prepared me better for professional controversies and for understanding the mind of my time. Lotze was still-born, and I have forgotten everything that I then had to read in him and to ponder. I liked Hegel's *Phaenomenologie*; it set me planning my *Life of Reason*; and now I like even his *Logik*, not the dialectical sophistry in it, but the historical and critical lights that appear by the way. I could have written, even then, a critical thesis, say on *Logic, Sophistry, and Truth in Hegel's Philosophy*. This would have knit my own doctrine together at the beginning of my career, as I have scarcely had the chance of doing at the end. My warhorse would not have been so much blinded and hidden under his trappings.

I am appointed instructor for the year 1889–90.   My dull thesis on Lotze was duly accepted, and I was told that I was the most normal doctor of philosophy that they had ever created. Retrospectively, I may have been, because most of their candidates had been lame ducks; but prospectively, as a doctor who teaches, I was to prove unsatisfactory and irregular. They may have suspected as much; but they were kind masters and not in a position to make great demands. They accepted me thankfully in spite of my lack of a vocation for teaching; and at once a place was made for me among them. James wished to relieve himself of his course on Locke, Berkeley, and Hume: I was invited to give it for him at a salary of $500. This was an opening, and in itself a boon. With my allowance I should have $1,000 for the year. I could return to live in the Yard and (if the appointment were renewed) I could go to Europe for the summer.

On the second day that I met my class, of three or four pupils, the door unexpectedly opened and in walked President Eliot, as straight and solemn as Hamlet's Ghost. I got up from my chair, confused but without saying audibly, "Angels and ministers of grace defend me." Eliot said dryly: "Professor Bowen has resigned. Only three students had elected his course on Descartes, Spinoza, and Leibniz, but we don't like to suppress any course that has been announced in the elective pamphlet. I therefore have come to ask you if you would be able and willing to give that course also, in addition to this; and the payment would be the same, another $500." I replied, quite reassured: "Thank you very much. May I have until tomorrow morning to think the matter over, when I will call at your office and give you the answer?" He said that would do perfectly, and looking somewhat less ghostlike he took his leave.

I don't know how clear the rest of my lecture on the life of John Locke may have been; but somehow it came to an end; and it was easy for me, once alone and fortified with a little food, to decide that I could manage to give that other course also. I should have one lecture a day at a convenient hour in the morning. The professors whose place I was taking were old rogues and had chosen eleven o'clock, the best hour for teaching: because it gave you an hour or two before your lecture to think over your subject and look up any necessary point, and luncheon not long after. Personally that pleased me; but professionally—and I now had a competitive profession—it was disadvantageous because that hour was occupied by half the favourite courses for undergraduates. However, a small class with graduate students in it, was perhaps best for a beginning. It reduced the physical strain, as well as the already small distance between the teacher and the pupils. We could philosophise together. And financially I was set at ease. If things went on like that, I could satisfy all my tastes and requirements.

I lecture badly to very small classes. I am told that in my first years I was a very bad lecturer. Certainly my talks were desultory, not rich in information, and not well arranged for taking notes. My interest was never in facts or erudition, but always in persons and ideas. I wished to rethink the thoughts of those philosophers, to understand why they took the direction they took, and then to consider the consequences and implications of taking that direction. At bottom, I was always discovering and developing my own philosophy. This at first was inarticulate, latent in me but not consistently thought out; and I can well believe that my pupils didn't understand it, and gathered only vague notions of the authors I discussed: for I doubt that the texts were much studied directly in those days at Harvard: the undergraduates were thinking only of examinations and relied on summaries in the histories of philosophy, and on lecture notes. Nevertheless, even at the beginning, my pupils were attentive and friendly; and eventually my way of thinking had some influence on some of them. If they had read the texts assigned, their time on the whole would not have been wasted.

Understanding versus information. I think, however, that lectures, like sermons, are usually unprofitable. Philosophy can be communicated only by being evoked; the pupil's mind must be engaged dialectically in the discussion. Otherwise all that can be taught is the literary history of philosophy, that is, the *phrases* that various philosophers have rendered famous. To conceive what those phrases meant or could mean would require a philosophical imagination in the public which cannot be demanded. All that usually exists is familiarity with current phrases, and a shock, perhaps of pleased curiosity but more often of alarm and repulsion, due to the heterodoxy of any different phrases.

Disintered interest in speculation. It may be conceit on my part but I think I was the only free and disinterested thinker among the Harvard philosophers. The others were looking in philosophy either for science or for religion. They were as tolerant as I, or more so, of differences in opinion; but only as you are tolerant of all the kinds and sizes of shoes in a shop window. You are willing to have all varieties of shoes offered for selection; but you look for a single pair of shoes to choose for yourself, to pay for, to own, to wear, and to wear out, or to be buried in; and you examine that vast assortment anxiously, conscientiously, with an unquiet mind, lest you should choose the wrong pair. Those liberal minds were thirsting for a tyrant. I, being a materialist, cynic, and Tory in philosophy, never dreamt of rebelling against the despotism of nature; and I accepted having feet, ugly and insufficient as they might be, because it would be much worse not to have them. But as to shoes, I have and mean to keep a free mind, and would willingly go barefoot if it were convenient or if it were the fashion. So I believe, compulsorily and satirically, in the existence of this absurd world; but as to the existence of a better world, or of hidden reasons in this one, I am incredulous, or rather I am critically sceptical; because it is not difficult to see the familiar motives that lead men to invent such myths. So I survey all those high-heeled ladies' shoes and all those invalids' fur-lined slippers with a smile: I might have worn the first once in some masquerade, and may yet wear the second in my decrepitude; but they are accidental paraphernalia. So are all systems of philosophy, so are all logical languages, so are all categories and images of sense. The study of them is a part of the humanities, initiating us into the history of human life and mind; it is not the pursuit of science or of salvation.

A university may teach the history of philosophy: to teach any one philosophy is to embrace a sect.   This divergence between me and my environment was not merely one of opinion: it interfered with my career and with the natural growth of my mind. President Eliot, who was an anti-humanist, once said to me that we should teach *the facts*, not merely convey *ideas*. I might have replied that the only facts in philosophy were historical facts, namely, the fact that people had or had had certain ideas. But of course, I only smiled and took note of *his idea*. The history of philosophy is the only philosophy that should be taught in a university. *Systems* of philosophy are taught only by sects or by individuals setting out to be prophets and to found a sect. I now have a system of philosophy, which I hadn't dreamt of then, although the reasons for it lay all in me; but this system is not intended to found a sect and will never do so. It aspires to be only a contribution to the humanities, the expression of a reflective, selective, and free mind. But I was living among sects, or among individuals eager to found sects; and I should have seemed to them vague and useless if I had been merely a historian and critic in philosophy. I was expected and almost compelled to be "constructive" or "creative", or to pretend to be so. Or as they put it, I must take up some special subject: physiological psychology (supposed to be a science) or Greek philosophy, if I trained myself to write a history like Zeller's. A man must have a "specialty".

I am led to write a book on "Aesthetics". I was a kind of poet, I was alive to architecture and the other arts, I was at home in several languages: "aesthetics" might be regarded as my specialty. Very well: although I didn't have, and haven't now, a clear notion of what "aesthetics" may be, I undertook to give a course in that subject. It would help to define my status. I gave it for one or two years and then I wrote out the substance of it in a little book: *The Sense of Beauty*. The manuscript of this book went from local publisher to publisher, and was rejected. I had given up all expectation of getting it published when Barrett Wendell, always friendly to me and the humanities, sent me word that he thought Scribner would accept it. I sent it to Scribner, it was printed and did not prove a financial loss to the publisher, although it had neither a large sale nor a warm reception from the critics. However, it was a book, *a fact*; and it established pleasant relations between me and Scribner which have lasted for fifty years.

I hang on at Harvard precariously but not unpleasantly. My sham course in "aesthetics" had served its purpose and so had my little book. Although looked at askance by the President, I was reappointed year by year, and then for three years at a time, with a salary of $1,500 and a seat in the Faculty, which I seldom occupied. My life and pleasures were still those of a student; I lived on intimate terms with a knot of undergraduates; I went to "parties", chiefly dinner parties in Boston. In time I undertook another "constructive" or "creative" course entitled "philosophy of history": this title attracted larger numbers, perhaps thirty men, many of them Jews; and it prepared the ground for my *Life of Reason*. But what then most enticed me in philosophy was Plato, and I had always had a great respect for Aristotle, especially for his *Ethics* and *Politics*; and out of these, with the help of a glance at Bacon, Locke, Montesquieu, and Taine (authors that my pupils could be expected to read a little) I composed my lectures on the "philosophy of history", which for me meant no providential plan of creation or redemption, but merely retrospective politics; a study of what had formed the chief interests of mankind in various epochs. Religion—my strong point in history—naturally came in, and I treated it, I think, without giving offence in any quarter.

At length I provoke a crisis. In the winter and spring of 1896 I became convinced that the time had come for calling a halt. I had been an instructor for seven years: should I ask for promotion or look for another place? In my private life too there had come a crisis: my young friends had become too young for me, and I too old for them; I had made a private peace with all religions and philosophies; and I had grown profoundly weary of polite society and casual gaieties. Then it chanced that at the English Cambridge they had established a new category of "advanced students", and Lowes Dickinson and Nathaniel Wedd, of King's College, had suggested that I might be admitted there. Here was an opportunity to break away from my second college life, already too much prolonged, yet continue my academic career, study Greek philosophy, live awhile in England, and in the holidays revisit Italy more at leisure than in 1895. I therefore asked Eliot for a year's leave of absence without a salary, after which I would return to Harvard for one more year; and then, unless I were appointed assistant professor, I should look for a place elsewhere.

A new start on my own terms. This project was carried out. When I returned to America in September 1897, I settled down at my mother's, now no longer in Roxbury but in Longwood, within walking distance of Harvard. Electric cars were also available. It was a most economical way of living, practically with no expenses, except for luncheon, fifty cents, at the Colonial Club. My relations with undergraduates and with Boston society, although renewed, were renewed on a new basis. I no longer played the familiar companion or the young man about town. I was simply an elderly mentor or an occasional guest. I began to give a new course, Philosophy 12, on Plato and Aristotle in English, which remained my chief subject, until almost the end. I lectured on the *Republic*, the *Phaedrus*, the *Symposium*, the *Phaedo* and the *Nicomachaean Ethics*. These books were assigned to be read in translation; and the essays submitted to me upon them by my pupils, usually not twenty in number, were sometimes excellent. I have given an imaginary fragment of one of them in *The Last Puritan*.

I become Assistant-Professor in 1898 and Professor in 1907.

Early in 1898 I was appointed assistant professor for five years, at $2,000 a year. When this appointment expired, it was renewed on the usual terms; but it actually ran only for four years, when at last I was made a full professor, with a salary of $4,000. Moreover, two of those four years, 1904–1906, I spent abroad: the first, a sabbatical year, in Italy and the East, the second at Paris, as exchange professor at the Sorbonne. This second lap of my assistant professorship was therefore much pleasanter and more varied than the first; and the last lap of all, during the four and a half years of my active professorship, also passed imperceptibly: I knew they were the last lap, and the exhilaration of finishing the race, even if not with an outward victory, was an inward comfort.

Yet remain secluded and independent.

My official career at Harvard was thus completed without a break. When I resigned my professorship, my name had figured in the Harvard Catalogue, in one capacity or another, for thirty years. Yet that long career had been slow and insecure, made in an atmosphere of mingled favour and distrust. My relations with President Eliot and with other influential persons had always been strained. I had disregarded or defied public opinion by not becoming a specialist, but writing pessimistic old-fashioned verses, continuing to range superficially over literature and philosophy, being indiscernibly a Catholic or an atheist, attacking Robert Browning, prophet of the half-educated and half-believing, avoiding administrative duties, neglecting the Intelligentsia, frequenting the society of undergraduates and fashionable ladies, spending my holidays abroad, and even appearing as a witness in the disreputable Russell trial. At the same time, in private, I had breathed the pleasantest airs of sympathy and friendship. My philosophic colleagues had supported me, my old friends had been faithful, appreciative, and always hospitable, my new friends had multiplied in numbers and influence, my books, though received coldly at first, had attained a certain reputation. I was still disliked, but I was swallowed.

Character of Eliot's administration.

Harvard, in those the waning days of Eliot's administration, was getting out of hand. Instruction was every day more multifarious and more chaotic; athletics and college life developed vigorously as they chose, yet not always pleasantly; and the graduate and associated Schools worked each in its own way, with only nominal or financial relations with Harvard College. In public opinion a reaction was beginning to appear;

but it had not taken visible form before the change of Presidents. Government was monarchical; but a monarch can hardly decide everything on his own initiative; he depends on vested interests and traditional advisers for his policy, and on committees and agents for carrying it out. Eliot, autocrat as he was, depended on the Fellows, half a dozen business men in Boston who were the legal proprietors of Harvard, and especially on one of them, the Treasurer, who managed the vast investments of the Foundation. He was also somewhat controlled by the Board of Overseers, elected representatives of the graduates. All this formed an immense tangle of disconnected activities: the President was driving not a four but a forty-in-hand. Most numerous and stately, but tamest, in this working menagerie was the Faculty of Arts and Sciences. Although a member of it, I hardly knew what were its attributions or privileges. The most interesting and clearest business of the meetings was to hear what the President might tell us of the action or prospects of the moment; and it was from him that any likely measures emanated. Sometimes, very rarely, there was clear opposition or even a hostile vote. That might produce a postponement, but could hardly arrest the movement of reform that he had undertaken in the interest of democratic arrangements and quick returns. Education meant preparation for professional life. College, and all that occupied the time and mind of the College, and seemed to the College an end in itself, seemed to President Eliot only a means. The end was service in the world of business.

Practical futility and moral function of Faculty meetings. The Faculty meetings were an object-lesson to me in the futility of parliamentary institutions. Those who spoke spoke badly, with imperfect knowledge of the matter in hand, and simply to air their prejudices. The rest hardly listened. If there was a vote, it revealed not the results of the debate, but the previous and settled sentiments of the voters. The uselessness and the poor quality of the whole performance were so evident, that it surprised me to see that so many intelligent men—for they were intelligent when doing their special work—should tamely waste so much time in keeping up the farce. But parliamentary institutions have a secret function in the Anglosaxon world, like those important glands that seemed useless to a superficial anatomy. There is an illusion of self-government, especially for members of the majority; there is a gregarious sense of safety and reassurance in being backed, or led, or even opposed by crowds of your equals under conventional safeguards and guarantees; and there is solace to the vague mind in letting an anonymous and irresponsible majority be responsible for everything. You grumble, but you consent to put up with the course that things happen to take. It is not as if the ruling party had intended the result: they gave a little push, and evolution has done the rest.

My single intervention and its remote echoes. The Harvard Faculty was not divided into parties. Being appointed by the President, who was the irremovable executive, they were more like officials naturally respectful to their chief; but some of them had personal views on education and public policy which they couldn't refrain from airing in voting on the President's reforms. I seldom went to the meetings, and spoke only once, when asked a direct question touching a degree to be granted out of course to an absent undergraduate, Bayard Cutting, who had left college to be private secretary to the American ambassador in London, and had written a thesis on David Hume as a substitute for his unfinished work. I had read the thesis, and gave my opinion on it. The degree was granted. Bayard Cutting had been one of my young friends at the time when, to my sense, they were birds of passage. He married Lady Sybil Cuffe, who after his death lived in the Villa Medici, close to Strong's villa, at Fiesole. Their only child, Iris, who herself lost her only child, wrote a book on Leopardi, for which she asked me to supply a "Foreword". It is a strange sadness that hangs for me now over all that history. An international Intelligentsia adrift amid unsuspected currents and wrecked one by one on the reefs of El Dorado.

Harvard not a social unit. Did the members of the Harvard Faculty form an intellectual society? Had they any common character or influence? I think not. In the first place they were too much overworked, too poor, too much tied up in their modest homes. Nor had they had, like old-fashioned English Dons, a common education, and written Latin hexameters and pentameters. I believe there were some dinner clubs or supper clubs among the elder professors; but I never heard of any idea or movement springing up among them, or any literary fashion. It was an anonymous concourse of coral insects, each secreting one cell, and leaving that fossil legacy to enlarge the earth.

My friends in
the teaching
body:
Archibald
Cary
Coolidge.
Beyond my philosophical colleagues I hardly had any acquaintances among the professors, except Professor Toy, because of his wife, who was a friend and frequent hostess of mine for many years. Even among the younger teachers I had few friends. One, however, stood in a position very much like mine, in that teaching at Harvard was for him a sort of expedient, rather than a chosen profession, and that his interests, and the subject he taught touched European history and politics. "Archie" Coolidge, as he was called, had been booked for a diplomatic career, and was actually secretary to some legation, I believe in Vienna, when for a private reason he threw up his post and returned to Boston. He had been engaged to be married, and the young lady, in his absence, had changed her mind. The poor man, who was deeply in love, lost his head completely, and thought that by personal protestations he could bring her round. Unfortunately, Archie's person was his weak point. He had family, money, intelligence, experience, and accomplishments, spoke even Russian, and had travelled all over the world. When I once asked why he was going to Kamschatka he replied, "I haven't yet been there." But in his physique and manner, though there was nothing markedly wrong, he seemed not quite normal, as if nature had put him together carelessly, with insufficient materials, and had managed to make him go, but only by fits and jerks. And his mind, too, while well stocked and perfectly reasonable, seemed somehow thin, as if there were no central sun in it, no steady light and centre of gravity. Anyhow, his return only made matters worse; he had left his post without excuse or permission and couldn't resume it. To fill up his time and try to distract his mind from his terrible disappointment, people suggested that he should teach for a while at Harvard. In these circumstances, he came to live in Cambridge, ate at the Colonial Club, and gathered a circle of young friends about him, who were often my friends too. In these ways we were thrown together. We had a common *milieu* at Harvard and a common outlook into the great world, and his wider information always lent interest to what he said; but whether because of diplomatic reserve or of pure intellectual innocence, he never betrayed his deeper allegiance in politics and morals. American diplomacy was as yet innocent, an entertaining sport or holiday for home politicians; at most a little commercial or missionary enterprise might be connected with it. My relations with Archie Coolidge therefore remained always pleasant and unimportant.

Professor Norton. Of the older Harvard worthies I was on good terms with two, Charles Eliot Norton and William James. They were perhaps the most distinguished, but not the most trusted; they too had had to be swallowed. They too, although in my time their position was established, had seemed at first questionable and irregular. Norton, with ten generations of local magnates behind him, had his inspirations and sympathies far away. He worshipped Greek art, he worshipped Christian art, he loved refined English life. He spoke rarefied English. He loved Turner and Ruskin. His personal friends were Burne-Jones, Carlyle and Matthew Arnold. To me he showed the most exquisite paternal kindness. He encouraged and praised me whenever he could do so conscientiously: when he wished to warn or admonish me, he did it through his nephew Frank Bullard, who was one of my best friends. He feared that I lived too much among dreams. When my extravagant drama, *Lucifer*, was published, I of course sent him a copy: and in thanking me he said that the value of it, in its substance, could not be known for the present, but that the versification was that of a master. This was flattery; but not absurd flattery from an old man with Victorian standards in literature. "Versification" was the right word in this case, for mine is not what English-speaking people now call poetry: it is not a dissolution and fresh concretion of language. Verbally it is ordinary speech made rhythmical and harmonious. Where I break through convention, whether in verse or prose, is in my themes or sentiments, as here in *Lucifer*. Norton very modestly and prudently refused to judge on this point. He was not at home in metaphysics or religion; the dissolution of common sense and fresh concretion of myths seemed to him, I suspect, a waste of time. Here he had the prejudices of a positivist; yet he was cultivated and courteous enough to conceal them when speaking to a young man, like me, who possessed imagination without trusting it to reveal truth. My scepticism reconciled him to my mythology, and made him more benevolent than he might have been to a fanatic; and he was always benevolent, even when grieved.

His distress at the drift of public manners and opinion. At the funeral of C. C. Everett, an old professor at the Harvard Divinity School, a Unitarian and a Fichtean, I happened to join Norton as we came out. "All this", he said with his usual sweetness, "must make a sad impression on you." I admitted that of course death was sad, but my acquaintance with Everett had been very slight, and it was not, at his age, a loss to our philosophical forces. "I don't mean the death of Dr. Everett. He was a good man, but he had no intellect-u-al power" (Norton pronounced with this extreme accuracy, but easily; and the habit sometimes gave a satirical force to his words). "What I meant", he continued, "was this survival of superstition among us. Mr. Cruthers has compared Dr. Everett to an eagle." Cruthers was the Unitarian minister in Cambridge, and couldn't help being saturated with complacency and with unctuous flattery of everything mediocre: but he was hardly superstitious. To compare that old theological or antitheological professor to St. John was absurd or if you like blasphemous; but the primary evil was the insensibility to St. John, not the obituary fulsomeness about Everett. Fulsomeness and complete lack of perspective had become habitual in American appreciation of Americans. There was a conspiracy of flattery; free lances were sometimes broken against it, but the phalanx might be expected to sweep the field, and to form public opinion. This, I think, was what made Norton sad.

His speech at a dinner for John Fiske. Norton was president of the Tavern Club, which occasionally gave dinners in compliment to some person not a member. I recollect two such occasions on which Norton presided, and made the inevitable complimentary speech. Here he ran serious danger of falling into the "superstition" that saddened him in others. But he had a means of safety; he was not without wit, a mild irony that saved him from platitudes. One dinner was in honour of John Fiske, a local disciple of Herbert Spencer, who had passed from popular science to history, and published first a book on *Cosmic Evolution* and later a *History of the United States*. Norton, in his speech, after paddling about as is usual in the back waters of anecdote, said that Fiske had been an industrious author. "I wish his style had been a little chastened;* but the substance has been solid. He began by giving us a history of the universe; he proceeded to give us a history of the United States; and we may hope that in this upward progress he may end by giving us a history of Cambridge, Massachusetts." The distrust of speculative pretensions, the positivism, the love of home and country (which was profound in Norton, and the cause of his melancholy) were all expressed in these words, with which he ended his speech.

---

*Norton said "chassened", doubtless to indicate that the word means castigated and not made chaste.

And at one for Rudyard Kipling. The other dinner was in honour of Rudyard Kipling. Hard luck for Norton, I thought at first; why hadn't he pretended to be ill, and let someone else praise what must be odious to him? But not at all. Norton was quite happy, not in his remarks, but in his mood. He had known and liked Kipling's mother, and he was prepared *a priori* to accept the bard of imperialism as a distinguished lover of humanity. Kipling sympathised with the Hindus; he was democratic; a glib prophet with warm feelings and popular rhythms; and Norton was so saturated with morality that when anything seemed to him morally right, he couldn't notice whether it was vulgar. That which seemed paramount in Norton, his fastidious retrospective nostalgia, was in reality secondary. Fundamental still was his fidelity to the conscience of his ancestors.

William James: He inspires trust but creates insecurity. Concerning William James, I have made sundry scattered observations for the public, without attempting a fair total portrayal of the man or of his philosophy: neither he nor his philosophy lent themselves to being summed up. But here, where I am portraying only my own impressions, I may add a word more about the feelings that he excited in me. I trusted his heart but I didn't respect his judgment. I admired his masculine directness, his impressionistic perceptions, and his picturesque words. I treasured his utterances on the medical side of things, such as that the best way to understanding the normal is to study the abnormal. All this belonged to his independent, radical, naturalistic temper, to his American sense of being just born into a world to be rediscovered. But he was really far from free, held back by old instincts, subject to old delusions, restless, spasmodic, self-interrupted: as if some impetuous bird kept flying aloft, but always stopped in mid-air, pulled back with a jerk by an invisible wire tethering him to a peg in the ground. The general agreement in America to praise him as a marvellous person, and to pass on, is justified by delight at the way he started, without caring where he went. In fact, he got nowhere; and for that reason his influence could be great and beneficent over those who knew him, but soon seemed to become untraceable in the confused currents of the world. I, for instance, was sure of his goodwill and kindness, of which I had many proofs; but I was also sure that he never understood me, and that when he talked to me, there was a mannikin in his head, called G. S. and entirely fantastic, which he was really addressing. No doubt I profited materially by this illusion, because he would have liked me less if he had understood me better; but the sense of that illusion made spontaneous friendship impossible. I was uncomfortable in his presence. He was so extremely natural that there was no knowing what his nature was, or what to expect next; so that one was driven to behave and talk conventionally, as in the most artificial society. I found no foothold, I was soon fatigued, and it was a relief to be out again in the open, and alone.

James, Palmer, and I on the annexation of the Philippines. The feeling of walking on the quicksands became almost worse when what he said was in harmony with my feelings than when it was opposed to them. If he talked about ghosts, I didn't care what turn his fancy might take; he would surely be graphic if he described those ghosts dramatically, and he would not in the least disturb me if he suggested that they might now be stealthily gliding behind our chairs. When, on the contrary, he said something that seemed to corroborate my own sentiments, I feared a trap. Let me describe one instance. One afternoon in the autumn of 1898 we were standing in Palmer's library after a brief business meeting, and conversation turned on the terms of peace imposed by the United States on Spain after the Cuban war. James was terribly distressed. Addressing himself rather to Palmer, who was evidently enjoying the pleasant rays of the setting sun upon his back, and the general spacious comfort of his library (he then lived in the old President's house at the corner of Quincy Street), James said he felt that he had lost his country. Intervention in Cuba might be defended, on account of the perpetual bad government there and the sufferings of the natives. But the annexation of the Philippines, what could excuse that? What could be a more shameless betrayal of American principles? What could be a plainer symptom of greed, ambition, corruption, and imperialism? Palmer smiled approvingly, yet he saw the other side. Every thesis had its antithesis; the synthesis would be ultimately for the general good, and the course of history was the true Judgment of God. Those were not his words, but his little vague commonplaces could be so interpreted by anyone behind the scenes.

Folly of expecting a European soul to animate an American body. As for me, I couldn't help resenting the schoolmaster's manner of the American government, walking switch in hand into a neighbour's garden to settle the children's quarrels there, and to make himself master of the place. Yet that has been the way of the world since the beginning of time, and if anything could be reasonably complained of, it was the manner of the intrusion rather than the fact of it. For me the tragedy lay in Spanish weakness rather than in American prepotency: Uncle Sam would have continued to regard all men as free and equal, if all other men had looked as strong as himself. Yet Spanish weakness comes only of Quixotic frailty, due to a tragic and comic disproportion between the spirit and the flesh. The resources of the country and people would not be materially contemptible if they were wisely husbanded, and devoted to developing at home, under native inspiration, an austere, passionate and intelligent life for the soul. The Spanish empire overseas was glorious enough, and the end, harshly as it grazed against my family memories, seemed to me almost a relief. I am not one of those who dream of a Spanish America subject in future to the influence of the mother country. Let Spanish America, I say, and let English America, be as original as they can; what is best in Spain, as what is best in England, cannot migrate.

Spanish resignation. I was therefore much more at peace about this pathetic war than was William James, or than was "Aunt Sarah", whom I had visited in the previous June, on my way to Europe. She, the mother of the heroic Colonel Shaw of the Massachusetts coloured regiment, even before there was talk of the Philippines, was scandalised at McKinley. A large American flag was hanging in the street opposite her windows. "I wish I could pull that down!" she cried, condescending a little, perhaps, to my Spanish sympathies, but chiefly moved by the betrayal, as she thought it, of true American principles. "No, no," I protested, "the thing is sad for Spain, but was inevitable sooner or later. McKinley is only yielding to *force majeure.*" Nor was I alone in this feeling. When the armistice was announced, I ran down to Avila from Paris. As we approached the frontier a merry crowd of young trippers, well-dressed men and girls, filled the train with laughter and shrill cries: they were Spanish people on an excursion to San Sebastian for the bullfight. At Irún I was not even asked for my passport. And in Avila I found everybody as resigned and sadly philosophical as I, or as any ancient sage.

James a metaphysical romancer. Why was William James so much upset by an event that the victims of it could take so calmly? Because he held a false moralistic view of history, attributing events to the conscious motives and free will of individuals; whereas individuals, especially in governments, are creatures of circumstance and slaves to vested interests. These interests may be more or less noble, romantic, or sordid, but they inevitably entangle and subjugate men of action.

The leaders couldn't act or maintain themselves at the head of affairs if they didn't serve the impulses at work in the mass, or in some part of it. Catastrophes come when some dominant institution, swollen like a soap-bubble and still standing without foundations, suddenly crumbles at the touch of what may seem a word or an idea, but is really some stronger material force. This force is partly that of changing circumstances, partly that of changing passions; but passions are themselves physical impulses, maturing in their season, and often epidemic, like contagious diseases. James, who was a physician and a pragmatist, might have been expected to perceive this, and did perceive it at moments; yet the over-ruling tradition in him was literary and theological, and he cried disconsolately that he had lost his country, when his country, just beginning to play its part in the history of the world, appeared to ignore an ideal that he had innocently expected would always guide it, because this ideal had been eloquently expressed in the Declaration of Independence. But the Declaration of Independence was a piece of literature, a salad of illusions. Admiration for the noble savage, for the ancient Romans (whose republic was founded on slavery and war), mixed with the quietistic maxims of the Sermon on the Mount, may inspire a Rousseau but it cannot guide a government. The American Colonies were rehearsing independence and were ready for it; that was what gave the declaration of their independence timeliness and political weight. In 1898 the United States were rehearsing domination over tropical America and were ready to organise and to legalise it; it served their commercial and military interests and their imaginative passions. Such antecedents and such facilities made intervention sooner or later inevitable. Domination was the implicit aim, whatever might be the language or even the thoughts of individuals. William James had not lost his country; his country was in good health and just reaching the age of puberty. He had merely lost his way in its physiological history.

I could sympathise with him as a will, but not as an intellect.   James's displeasure at the seizure of the Philippines was therefore, from my point of view, merely accidental. It did not indicate any sympathy with Spain, or with anything in history that interests and delights me. On the contrary, it was an expression of principles entirely opposed to mine; much more so than the impulses of young, ambitious, enterprising America. These impulses may ignore or even insult all that I most prize, but they please me nevertheless for their honest enthusiasm and vitality. James himself, like a good American, was full of honest enthusiasm and vitality, and besides was sensitive, learned, and a perfect gentleman. In him too I sympathised with the initial phases and moral promptings of his thoughts. The bird flew up bravely; but when my eye was able to follow his flight, I saw him flutter, and perch, as if he had lost his energy, on some casual bough. His inspiration, even in science, was that of romanticism.

Barrett Wendell.   Less distinguished than Norton or James were two or three stray souls in the official Harvard with whom I inwardly sympathised, perhaps without much personal contact. They too were barely tolerated by the authorities; they had cut peep-holes, as it were, in the sacred tabernacle through which to view the natural landscape. One of these was Barrett Wendell. He belonged to a little group of free spirits, almost of wits, in the Harvard Class of 1877, and had been one of the founders of the *Lampoon*. His affections were local and his ideals conservative. He allowed himself little eccentricities, had tricks of intonation mistaken by many for an attempt to speak like the English, he admired the airs of the early nineteenth century, cared for birth and good breeding, and in literature for mannishness and good form, "rum and decorum", as he once put it, and for tenderness and distinction of feeling. Yet he had no real distinction himself, his mind and his attachments, like his speech, were explosive and confused; there was emotion, often deep emotion, but it broke out in ill-governed and uncouth ways. He was not at all an Anglomaniac; he idealised only the old Colonial proprieties and dignities; he longed for an American aristocracy, not of millionaires, but of local worthies, sportsmen, scholars, and divines. The New England literary men and orators of fifty years before would have satisfied him in respect to their station and manners, but he detested the radical revolutionary turn of their minds. He hated the empty cold self-sufficiency, as he thought it, of Emerson and his friends. They had desiccated and im-poverished the heart; they had made the world less passionate and less interesting to live in. In a word, Wendell was a sentimentalist.

A town wit among professors.   Had he been thoroughly educated and a good Latinist like Dr. Johnson he might have expressed and propagated his ideals to better purpose; as it was, his force spent itself in foam. He was a good critic of undergraduate essays, but not a fair historian or a learned man; and his books were not worth writing. He was useful in the College as a pedagogue, and there was a certain moral stimulus in his original personality. He carried his little person jauntily; wore spats and a red beard; when walking he would brandish the stick that (like me) he always carried; and when sitting down and lecturing, he would perpetually twirl the signet at the end of his watch-chain. Something admirable was wasted in him. The age made it impossible for him to do well what he would have loved to do.

Why should such a man ever dream of becoming a professor? His case, I imagine, was not unlike mine. He happened to have his pigeon-hole in Boston, he was not rich, he liked to browse upon *belles lettres*; why not teach English composition and literature at Harvard? But with science and President Eliot in control, would Harvard accept his services? It was long very much in doubt. With time, however, Wendell had become a familiar figure, an object of universal smiles and affection; and when the official guillotine was ready to fall, public sentiment wouldn't allow it. Indeed, in what remained of the old-fashioned college, Wendell's was useful work. He devised and carried out the plan of reading and revising hundreds of "daily themes", each on a half-sheet of note-paper: a voluntary exercise in writing, feeling, and judging of all things like a gentleman. You learned nothing, except what to think about what you happened to know. If the effects of this training could spread and assert themselves against the self-confidence of the illiterate, a great change would appear in the tone of American publications. A change of tone there has certainly been in the last thirty years; and who knows how much of it may not be due to Barrett Wendell?

We both loved   I seldom came across Wendell in Boston, but he was
aristocratic   an inevitable speaker at Harvard meetings and dinners.
liberty.   Yet I think that silently we essentially understood each other. We were on the same side of the barricade. More than once he took some step, quite without my knowledge, to do me a kindness. Perhaps the most tangible sign of this sympathy between us was our common affection for Harvard, for the College, not for the University. We knew that the traditional follies there prevalent were the normal, boyish, almost desirable follies of youth; and that the *virtù* there fostered and admired was genuine *virtù*, not perhaps useful for anything further, but good and beautiful in itself. We both desired to screen those follies and to propagate that *virtù* against the steam-roller of industrial democracy. We were not asking much; for these were precisely the follies and the *virtù* that democracy, if liberated from the steam-roller, would cultivate of its own accord. What we deprecated was only that this spontaneous life of the people should be frustrated by the machinery of popular government and of unorganised private initiative.

"Charley" Copeland.   A more pathetic servant of popular joys, humbler than Barrett Wendell and more openly sentimental, was my neighbour for years in the Yard, and although I seldom saw him, I was always vaguely aware of his beneficent existence round the corner. He was known as Charley Copeland. An artist rather than a scholar, he was a public reader by profession, an elocutionist; he could move his audiences by declaiming, with disciplined voice and restrained emotion, all the most touching or thrilling popular selections from the Bible to Kipling. This was a spiritual debauch for the hungry souls of the many well-disposed waifs at Harvard, living under difficult conditions: and these Copeland made his special friends. Apart from his readings, he took pains to thaw out the most timid and warm them at his fire, materially and morally. He was the poor boy's providential host and inspirer, doing for the forlorn and disinherited what Norton did for those who were, or ought to have been, already somewhat cultivated, or what Palmer did, more speculatively, for the intellectual proletariat. This task of attracting the mass into the vortex of public interests, which at Yale was done by college organisations, at Harvard was done in these discreet ways by individual philanthropists, more from above and more tenderly, but I fear less successfully: because these contacts, for the majority, left only stray memories, without establishing permanent impersonal interests. Copeland was not left without his reward in the esteem and affection of a particular circle, and of scattered admirers, yet his charitable work for the College remained for years without official recognition. It was only under President Lowell that he was made a professor.

Pierre la Rose.   Somewhat in the margin of Harvard lingered also for a time my friend Pierre la Rose. He too was connected with the English department; but he pieced out his work there by planning restaurations of old houses, or decorating and refurnishing them. He had excellent taste, not too servile or pedantic about the style of any period; his joy, I think, would have been like mine, in bolder decorative effects, such as we were regaled with later by the Russian ballet. He was expert none the less in distinguishing the merits of classic and severe styles, and of the corresponding literature, particularly the French. Unfortunately there was nothing classical or severe about his own figure; he was not looked upon with favour by the undergraduates of his own time, except by other exceptional persons, like Trumbull Stickney, with whom he used to play classical music, for he also had some talent in that direction; but later, local prejudice against him was vanquished by his pleasant conversation, discretion, and varied knowledge. I found him, in my later Harvard years, the most sympathetic of friends. We often sat at the same table in the small room at the Colonial Club, and if the food was negative, we had a bottle of claret, and not only Harvard, official and unofficial, but the whole literary and political world, for our intellectual bill of fare. He would have made an excellent permanent Tutor in a genuine college, not only in English composition, but in French and in comparative literature, as well as in the history of the fine arts; and had President Lowell's "Houses" existed in the 1890's, he would doubtless have made a place for himself there. He had a quiet, well-informed, unexaggerated devotion to all charming things, a devotion that teaches by contagion, and awakens a taste for what is worth loving.

William Lyon Phelps.   I had a hearty academic friend also at Yale; and when I say that it was William Lyon Phelps, those who knew him will understand the reason, because he was the hearty friend of everybody. He had come to Harvard when a graduate student to study early English under Professors Child and Kittredge, not to speak of Barrett Wendell, whose hearty friend he instantly became, in spite of the contrast in their idiosyncrasies. My friendship with Phelps would not have become so warm, at least on my side, but for the place and moment in which it was cemented. In 1892, he had returned to Yale, become an instructor or professor there, married, and settled in a nice little house where he was immensely happy, and where there was a spare room for a guest; and knowing my recently acquired taste for contemplating athletic contests, he asked me to come and visit him and his wife for the Harvard–Yale game. I knew nothing of Yale, which for a Harvard man was a half-mythical half-hostile invisible object. Here was a capital chance to unveil the mystery, and see something of Yale from the inside. And I didn't go alone. Warwick Potter, who had a Groton friend at Yale, arranged to come with me; but we parted on reaching New Haven, each being met and carried off by his respective host; and we had entirely different aspects of Yale to describe, as on the Sunday afternoon we travelled back to Cambridge.

Yale wins my heart.   That was at the high tide of my second College period. Teaching philosophy had become a decent means of livelihood, and was not yet a burden; I was not pledged to it, and was writing nothing but poetry. Yale, seen under the enthusiastic guidance of my *cicerone*, seemed a most living, organic, distinctive, fortunate place, a toy Sparta to match our toy Athens at Harvard. I liked it very much: what is more, I *believed* in it. That was the direction in which the anonymous gregarious mind of America could be sympathetically brought to become distinct and integral. Harvard liberalism tended, on the contrary, to encourage dissolution, intellectual and moral, under a thin veneer of miscellaneous knowledge. Phelps was naturally pleased at seeing me so sympathetic. Not considering that I was fundamentally a Spaniard and a Catholic, he thought he had converted me to muscular Christianity; and in fact he had converted me to something Christian, namely, to charity even towards muscular Americanism.

The Yale that Phelps showed me was the official Yale, yet the officials seemed to be of an extraordinarily informal, varied, and youthful type. Phelps himself had these characteristics; and his wife added a gentle harmonious treble to his spontaneous barytone. I was keyed up by them to such an appreciative mood that I liked even the Y.M.C.A. I felt that it was not meddlesome, but truly friendly and helpful; and this was not the only time that I felt this among the Evangelicals. Mrs. Palmer, for instance (unlike her husband), inspired me with immediate confidence and respect. I was sure that she was honestly a friend of life in others, even when their life was not at all like hers; and when still at school I had discovered the same gift of steady charity in the much-loved Bayley. The great point was that these people should not be themselves flabby or sentimental or followers of Rousseau; then their charity might be a true virtue, not a licence for their pet vices.

Friendship by violence.   Phelps was irresistible. His every word was a cocktail, or at least a temperance drink. He made you love everything. Even if you were not naturally genial, you found you were his friend, almost his intimate friend, without having in the least expected it. Whether this mesmerisation should be altogether welcome to a moralist I am not sure. I suppose (when Phelps was not present) the most hearty optimist might distinguish degrees of delight. He might say: I delight in bread, but I delight more in bread and butter, and still more in cake; and I delight in a *baba-au-rhum* even more than in dry cake. Yet if you allow yourself to make these odious comparisons, you cast a shadow of inferiority over all delights except the greatest. You might even suspect that the greatest might some day be overshadowed, and that you might mysteriously find yourself preferring not to eat anything. Life, and the morality that regulates life, seem to require discrimination. They would relax, they would positively dissolve, if delight were spread indiscriminately over an infinite miscellany of commonplaces, and there were nothing that you didn't love, nothing that you invincibly hated. So that perhaps the irresistible Phelps would have been too much of a good thing for all the year round; but for an occasional visit to Yale, or an occasional afternoon in Paris (where he and his wife often turned up) he was all Browning in a nutshell, and the better for that compression.

The fallacy of loving everything. It is an error into which too much domestic luxury has led American taste, that all bread should be buttered. When eaten alone, bread is improved by a little butter or a little cheese, to lend it softness or savour, but when bread itself is an accompaniment, butter is out of place. It only adds grease to the greasy sauces and cloys the meat that it might have saved from cloying. So with moral enthusiasm. Great, solid, fruitful excellence should provoke it, not mere existence. Existence is something haphazard, and a great risk: the possibility of something good, with the peril of many evils. Phelps complained that in my *Last Puritan* there was not a single *good* person. I thought Oliver, the Vicar, Irma, and several of the minor characters decidedly good people, and many others good enough as this world goes; but none were *merely* good, because goodness is an attribute and not a substance. To be good morally you must first be distinct physically: you must not be an anonymous It. The trouble with the goodness that Phelps wanted and possessed was that it was not distinguished. It seemed to me at Yale as if enthusiasm were cultivated for its own sake, as flow of life, no matter in what direction. It meant intoxication, not choice. You were not taught to attain anything capable of being kept, a treasure to be laid up in heaven. You were trained merely to succeed. And in order to be sure to succeed, it was safer to let the drift of the times dictate your purposes. Make a strong pull and a long pull and a pull all together, for the sake of togetherness. Then you will win the race. A young morality, a morality of preparation, of limbering up. "Come on, fellows," it cried, "let's see who gets there first. Rah, rah, rah! Whoop-her-up! Onward Christian Soldier!" Irresistible as Phelps was, for the moment, my nature reacted against that summons. Before I cry onward, I would inquire where I am bound. Before I take up arms, I must know in what cause. Before I call myself a Christian, I must understand what Christianity is and what it would impose upon me. Does it cry to me, as at Yale, "Come on, fellows! Let's see who gets there first!" "There", for a Christian, used to mean yonder, above, *Jenseits*, heaven; but when this world has become so lovely, and effort and work are a crown in themselves, the struggle becomes a crab race, and the real winner is he who runs for ever and never gets there at all. As Emerson said, "If God is anywhere, he is here", so this modern Christian should say, If heaven isn't here, it's nowhere. A conclusion that in some sense I should be willing to accept, only that I shouldn't call it Christianity: rather Epicurean contentment in being an accident in an accident.

I lecture at other colleges. My visits to Yale were unofficial, but I was asked to give odd lectures at most of the other New England colleges, and always did so with pleasure. My hosts were kind, the places, with my early memories of the Latin School and of simple old Harvard, were pleasantly reminiscent, and the intellectual atmosphere was honest and unpretending. I also gave lectures at Columbia, where the professors of philosophy took a professional interest in my views, such as in general I expect nobody to take: only perhaps a momentary pleasure in some phrase or in some bit of literary criticism. This was what came to me, by way of incense, from the female audiences that I often addressed at Radcliffe, at Wellesley, and in other women's colleges. At Bryn Mawr, a comparatively fashionable place where I spoke in the chapel, I overheard, as I came in, a loud and disappointed whisper: "He is bald!" and at Berkeley, where the summer school seemed to have no men in it, a lady observed that I had "a mellifluous voice", but that she "didn't like my logic". In the Middle West I was more honoured, even giving once the Baccalaureate Address, and at Wisconsin being welcomed twice and receiving an honorary degree. The moral and intellectual atmosphere everywhere in the United States seemed to be uniform: earnest, meagre, vague, scattered, and hopeful. After I left America, however, I gather that a sharp change occurred, introducing more variety, more boldness, and greater achievements.

Exchange professor in Paris. My academic career also had an unexpected extension to Paris. At Harvard, during my last years, there was a rich and isolated student named Caleb Hyde, interested in French literature. On graduating he founded an exchange professorship between Harvard and the Sorbonne, lectures to be in English at Paris, and in French at Cambridge. Barrett Wendell was the first appointed at Paris; and when I was in the East, during 1905, I received an invitation to be his successor. It was most opportune, giving me two years' holiday instead of one; for being in training as a lecturer at that time, and counting on an intelligent audience in Paris, my work there would be easy, and three parts pleasure. So it proved. Never have I talked to so *open* a public—I mean in a course of lectures; singly, I have found an equal openness once or twice in England. Yet, after Wendell, I was a sad disappointment to Hyde and, I suspect, to all the officials concerned. For I avoided seeing anyone, presented none of the letters of introduction that Hyde had sent me by the dozen, and lived in my hotel just as quietly as if I had had no academic duties. I had a reason for this, besides my love of obscurity. The tendency to give a political colour to this lectureship repelled me for two reasons: one, that I was not an American, and was presenting myself, as it were, under false colours; the other, that the political propaganda desired was contrary to my sympathies.

Sham appreciation of lectures in foreign languages. In spite of my avoidance of contacts, I came involuntarily on various little manifestations of the sham and corruption that prevailed in the official world. The most simple avowal of it was made by the Rector of the University of Lille, when on the provincial tour that formed a part of the lecturer's programme, I presented myself and expressed my readiness to give, at his discretion, one or two lectures in English. He raised his hands to heaven, and said quickly: "*Une seule! Il ne faut pas abuser de la fidélité de l'auditoire.*" It was fidelity enough in an audience to sit through one lecture, without running away. In Paris, in fact, the doors were always open, and slamming, with people coming in late or going away early. I was told of a group of students that peeped in one afternoon. "*Tiens. C'est en anglais. Filons!*" said the leader, and they all disappeared. This freedom was a little disturbing, yet served to emphasise the sense of security given by the little nucleus of listeners who always came early, smilingly staid to the end, and evidently understood everything.

A sectarian government. Before I set out on my tour of the provincial universities, I had a glimpse of French government behind the scenes. A young man in a shining red motor burnished like sealing-wax turned up at the Foyot, where I lived, and said they wished to speak to me at the ministry of public instruction, and that he would drive me there. I was received by the director of some department, who rang the bell and said that Monsieur so-and-so would explain to me the nature of a request that they desired to make of me. I bowed, said *au revoir, monsieur,* and followed the secretary into an inner room. This secretary was obsequious, yet in himself, had he been dressed in oriental garments, would have been impressive and almost beautiful. He had a pale complexion, large calm eyes, and a long silky black beard falling in two strands. We sat down. He said, with an air of mystery, and perhaps some embarrassment, that in the list of universities that they had selected for me to visit, they had included Lille. Now, there was a special circumstance about Lille to which they wished before hand to call my attention. At Lille there was also a Catholic Institute. If, going as I did under government direction, I should also address the Catholic Institute, it would cause comment which they desired to avoid. For that reason they had troubled me with this little matter; and they hoped I should understand the position in which they were placed.

I replied that I understood it perfectly; that I had never heard of the Catholic Institute at Lille, had no relations with French Catholic circles, and certainly would not repeat my lectures at Lille or elsewhere, even if, as was most unlikely, I should be invited to do so. In fact, the Catholic Institute was as oblivious of me as I was of it. But these precautions of the ministry, and the stealthy hushed tone of them, taught me something of the spirit of the French government. It was not national, but sectarian. It was afraid that a foreign lecturer should repeat to Catholic students what he had been sent to say to Government students. Apparently—though they payed me nothing, for it was Hyde that payed—they felt that, while I was under their auspices, I was pledged to their policy. If I had known this, or had thought it more than an absurd pretension, I should never have stepped within the Sorbonne.

Bombast at   The last university I visited was that of Lyons, and
Lyons.   there pomposity was the order of the day. Everyone was pining for the blessed moment when they should at last be transferred to Paris; but meantime they would pretend that Lyons was the light of the world. I was asked to dinner by the Rector; he said nothing about *sans cérémonie,* and luckily I dressed, for it was an official banquet, forty men, and only one lady, the Rector's wife, in full regalia, next to whom I sat, with the Rector opposite. At the end, with the champagne, my heart sank, for I foresaw that I had to make a speech— my first and last speech in French. Luckily the Rector was very eloquent about the twin republics across the sea, both enlightened, both humane, both progressive, both red white and blue. I had time to think of

something to say. I had been hearing and speaking more French than usual, and I managed, not without faults, but decently, to express my thanks and to praise the young French universities—younger than Harvard—that I had been visiting. But I also said that, although I was not myself an American, I would convey the friendly sentiments expressed by the Rector to my friends at Harvard, who I knew were inspired by the same feelings. When I said I was not an American, which I did at the beginning, not at the end, I had one of the happiest moments of my life. I saw the cold douche playing on the startled nerves of all those official hypocrites and toadies, who hated all foreign countries and ridiculed America at every turn, yet licked the dust before anybody that they hoped they could get money from. Having relieved my conscience, and given them a lesson, I went on more sympathetically and ended without eloquence but with decency. "*Vous avez eu des phrases*", said one of the guests to me afterwards, "*qui n'étaient pas d'un étranger.*" Quite so: the accent may not have been Parisian, but the sentiment was not foreign because it was human and sincere. We all move together when we pursue the truth.

Richard is himself again. The last echoes of my official career were posthumous: the professor was dead, the man revived, spoke in the professor's place, and spoke in England. These were all written lectures, and most of them were published in *Character and Opinion in the United States*. Together with *Egotism in German Philosophy* and *Soliloquies in England* they mark my emancipation from official control and professional pretensions. There was no occasion to change my subjects, to abandon even technical philosophy or my interest in academic life and in the humanities. But all was now a voluntary study, a satirical survey, a free reconsideration; the point of view had become at once frankly personal and speculatively transcendental. A spirit, the spirit in a stray individual, was settling its accounts with the universe. My official career had happily come to an end.

40. Lionel Pigot Johnson, 1885. By permission of Bruccoli Clark, Inc.

41. Baron Albert von Westenholz, *c.* 1910. By permission of Harry Ransom Humanities Research Center, The University of Texas at Austin.

42. John Francis Stanley, second Earl Russell. a. At "T.H.", *c.* 1915. b. In 1890, at the time of his first marriage. By permission of Harry Ransom Humanities Research Center, The University of Texas at Austin.

43 and 44. Lady Scott and Countess
Mabel Edith Russell, first wife of Earl
Russell, in an 1897 court reporter's
sketch, drawn at the time of the libel
trial between Russell and the two
women. By permission of the Trustees
of the Boston Public Library.

45. Countess Marion ("Mollie") Russell,
second wife of Earl Russell, after a
speech for votes for women, c. 1905.
By permission of Harry Ransom
Humanities Research Center, The
University of Texas at Austin.

46. Countess Mary Annette
("Elizabeth") Russell, third wife of Earl
Russell, with one of her dogs, *c.* 1933.
By permission of The Bertrand Russell
Archives, McMaster University.

47. Robert Bridges, 1912. By
permission of Bruccoli Clark, Inc.

48. Bertrand Russell, 1916. By
permission of The Bertrand Russell
Archives, McMaster University.

49. Bernard Berenson, *c.* 1900. By permission of the Harvard University Archives.

50. Avila, the town and its walls, at
the end of the nineteenth century. By
permission of The Mayor of Avila.

51. Apse of the Cathedral of Avila. By
permission of Mrs. Margot Cory.

52. The Alcazar Portal, Avila c. 1853.
By permission of The Mayor of Avila.

53. Beacon Street, facing Beacon Hill.
By permission of the Trustees of the
Boston Public Library.

54. The Church of the Immaculate
Conception, Boston. By permission of
the Trustees of the Boston Public
Library.

55. The old Boston Public Latin School
on Bedford Street, *c.* 1860. By
permission of the Trustees of the
Boston Public Library.

56. Harvard Yard seen from #7
Stoughton Hall, 1896. By permission of
Harry Ransom Humanities Research
Center, The University of Texas at
Austin.

57. Santayana's room at #7 Stoughton
Hall, which he occupied from
1890–1897. By permission of Harry
Ransom Humanities Research Center,
The University of Texas at Austin.

58. King's College Chapel, Cambridge, the West Front. By permission of Mrs. Margot Cory.

Fragments
of
Autobiography

My Place I Time & Ancestry

A document in my possession testifies that in the parish church of San Marcos in Madrid, on the first of January, 1864, a male child, born on the sixteenth of the previous December, at nine o'clock in the evening, at N.º 69 Calle Ancha de San Bernardo, was solemnly christened; being the legitimate son of Don Agustín Ruiz de Santayana, native of Zamora, and of Doña Josefina Borrás, native of Glasgow; his paternal grandparents being Don Nicolás, native of Baddúmès, in the province of Santander, and Doña María Antonia Reboiro, native of Zamora; and his maternal grandparents being Don José, native of Reus, Catalonia, and Doña Teresa Carbonell, native of Barcelona. The names given him were Jorge Agustín Nicolás, his godparents being Don Nicolás Ruiz de Santayana, and Doña Susana Sturgis; "whom I admonished", writes Don Joaquín Carrasco, who signs the certificate with his legal rúbrica or flourish, "of their spiritual relationship and duties". ①

A shrewd fortune-teller would have spotted at once, in this densely Spanish document, the

---

① Original Spanish in a note (for the eventual book: no note if published in a magazine).

59. Sample of Santayana's handwriting.
By permission of George Santayana
Papers, Rare Book and Manuscript
Library, Columbia University.

III

XXV

A Change of Heart

Absolute spirit irrespon- sible.   If a man were a wild spirit without a body or a habitat his philosophy might harmlessly change at every moment, and he might well pride himself on changing it often and radically, so as to display fertility of spirit and enjoy an inexhaustibly rich experience. Being absolutely free and unfettered by circumstances, why should he stick to any particular principles or ideas and waste his time repeating himself like an idiot or a cuckoo?

I feel myself a creature of place and time.   It happened in my case, however, that I reached the age of reflection in Avila, a little walled city, where old people, old churches, and barren grey moors strewn with prehistoric boulders filled my mind from the first with a sense of antiquity. Nor did reflection later, in the New World, lead me seriously to think myself, or anyone else, a disembodied spirit. On the contrary, it seemed to me evident that no discoverable mind can ever have existed except in a body, so that by the presence and action of that body it might give signs and leave memorials of its passage. Then the past might be partly recalled on occasion, not as a vain dream, but as an experience and a lesson still applicable to a moderately stable world. Moreover, this stable world might contain other living bodies, similar to one's own; and their action and gestures, by mimicry, might instantly suggest to us desires and intentions an- imating those creatures, and rendering them sympathetic or hostile to ourselves; and so a moral world, practical and social, would become, for our imagination, the theatre of our action, and a roughly valid representation of the forces actually playing upon us and determining the weal and woe of our lives.

Free spirit lusts wherever it blows.   On the other hand, the true romantic genius who today cries to the West Wind "Be thou me, impetuous one!" will cry no less exultantly tomorrow to become the East Wind for a change: although in infinite vacancy it might be hard to find the difference. A truly free spirit will never repent, as Faust never repents; he cannot revert to his true self, since he has no particular self to revert to. He must simply go on, as transcendental spirit actually does, from one fresh incarnation to another, in and out forever of every living thing. He must will everything, do everything and suffer everything, but his spirit can never die: at least it can never prevent itself from being born again. It must lust for ever after the Eternal Feminine, or to put it more crudely, after the female of every species.

My conscience easy but my intellect distracted.
As for me, not only my body but my rather special and difficult relations to persons and places seemed clearly imposed facts; and in that setting my personal tastes and feelings became early apparent, and caused me to feel that I lived in a kind of solitude, not transcendental and spiritual, but decidedly solitariness in a crowd and foreignness among very distinct people. My preferences were clearly marked and out of harmony with my surroundings and, as I soon felt, with my times. But conceit, or firmness of disposition, kept me from suspecting that I ought to change my allegiances, and think and feel, play and work, as did the majority. Nor did I feel any impulse to contradict them or blame them. I had nothing to complain of, but I preferred solitude.

There was therefore no occasion for me to suffer moral revolutions or undergo any radical change of heart. My interest in religion had never been agonising, only speculative and devotional. Nothing in me called for any conversion, or *metanoia*. Time might transmute, without erasing, my first opinions and affections; I might wish to change my surroundings and my way of living; I never undertook to change myself. I regard my occupations and interests somewhat as an actor regards his various parts or a painter his subjects. That a man has preferences and can understand and do one thing better than another, follows from his inevitable limitations and definite gifts: but that which marks progress in his life is the purity of his art; I mean, the degree to which his art has become his life, so that the rest of his nature does not impede or corrupt his art, but only feeds it.

Two original sins of the spirit: 1st To mistake imagination for reality.
Now in my mental life there have been two great impediments, two congenital vices, two initial temptations: the temptation of the primitive poet to believe his fables, and the temptation of the spontaneous agent to lose himself in his world. The primitive poet falls into that first temptation inevitably: his inspiration is passive

and not an art; he lends credence to his obsessions as to a higher kind of knowledge, and proclaims each new intuition to be a revelation of the truth. The Jews, says Spinoza, whenever they think something, say God told them. Prophets indeed do this explicitly and with full conviction, opposing their sudden intuitions to the current views of mankind. They are even more credulous and absorbed in life than are ordinary people, only in some extraordinary direction. Yet, unlike madmen, good prophets proclaim new ideas that the world can be led to take seriously and to weave into its conventions, at least for a time and in some sect: whence all traditional religions and moralities.

I am naturally incredulous and not a willing dupe of life, either of life in the world or in my own head; yet my imagination is not inactive. I am therefore a sort of prophet at second hand, appreciating the inspiration of others and enjoying it as my own; and for that reason the temptation to mistake it for revelation was in my case never invincible. I have said how my youthful piety was accompanied by an equal delight in geography and in architecture. I had little real contact with any of these things, but pure delight in the form and idea of them. All that I later clearly denied them was the assent due to matters of common knowledge or history: matters of fact important to get right in action, but not especially interesting to the imagination of a poet.

My attachment to Catholicism always poetical. All her life my sister Susana was a little troubled because, as she said, she feared that I was "moving away from God". Yet at heart I was not *moving* at all. I was only *seeing* what a catastrophe the Christian *Weltanschauung* was pregnant with, if you took it for history and cosmology, and not for a symbolic myth. And this intellectual catastrophe would also involve a moral one, in that it implied the exhaustion of an inspiration, the decay of a *Kultur*. It would be comparable to the catastrophe of paganism and of the classic world, tragic but interesting. The idea of such a catastrophe caused no revolution in myself: it was more like a bereavement or a total change of surroundings. I had never *practised* my religion, or thought of it as a means of getting to heaven or avoiding hell, things that never caused me the least flutter. All that happened was that I became accustomed to a different *Weltanschauung*, to another system having the same rational function as religion: that of keeping me attentive to the lessons of life.

Each religion, by the help of more or less myth which it takes more or less seriously, proposes some method of fortifying the human soul and enabling it to make its peace with its destiny. A philosopher may perfectly well cultivate more than one *Weltanschauung*, if he has a vital philosophy of his own to qualify his adoption of each, so as to render them complementary and not contradictory. I had, and have, such a vital philosophy; and the movement of my mind among various systems of belief has tended merely to discover how far my vital philosophy could be expressed in each of them.

Slow dawn of self-knowledge.

•

A motto from Goethe.

My variations therefore never involved rejecting any old affection, but only correcting such absoluteness or innocence as there may have been about it, and reducing it to its legitimate function. So in 1900 I published the result of the gradual transformation of my religious sentiments. Religion was poetry intervening in life. That insight had come to me twenty years before, though not expressed in those words; it had really been native to me and congenial. So when I first went to Germany and began to read Goethe, chiefly as a lesson in the language, my vital philosophy recognised itself at once in the lines:

Ich hab' mein Sach auf nichts gestellt. . . .
Drum ist's so wohl mir in der Welt.

This is perhaps more cavalier-like and jaunty than I was, even at that time; yet the title of this drinking-song is *Vanitas! Vanitatum Vanitas!* and the stanzas describe a gay fellow's discomfiture when he set his heart on money or women or foreign travel or reputation or war; so that when he repeats at the end,

Nun hab' ich mein Sach auf nichts gestellt. . . .
Und mein gehört die ganze Welt,

there is evidently an equivocation in his boast. The whole world belongs to me implicitly when I have given it all up, and am wedded to nothing particular in it; but for the same reason no part of it properly belongs to me as a possession, but all only in idea. Materially I might be the most insignificant of worms; spiritually I should be the spectator of all time and all existence. This implication touched the depths of my vital or congenital philosophy, and for that reason doubtless the refrain of this song became a sort of motto for me at that time. Yet more than ten years had to pass before that implication, on the emotional side, came to expression in my Platonising sonnets; while theoretically I came to clearness about it only in my old age, when I freed "essences" from the psychological net in which we catch them, and distinguished intuition from knowledge.

2nd vice: Intoxication with reality and idealisation of it. Clearer to me in those student days was another point. Goethe's old soldier urges us, if we want to be good fellows, to drown our disappointments in drink. But isn't drink also disappointing in the end? And if it be a solution to drink, in order to forget the vanity of life and incidentally the vanity of drinking, wouldn't it be a better and juster solution to live in general as the world lives, so as to forget the vanity of doing so? Didn't all my American friends endeavour, with a good conscience, to drown unhappiness in work? Wasn't there some intoxication also in wealth, in women, in travel, in fame, and in war? And if drink and comradeship have a good side, which makes them jolly even if vain, have not all those other vanities their good side also? To abuse them satirically, out of spite, because you had expected too much of them, would be merely childish or, if you like, romantic. It would prove you to be moody, ill-bred, and unphilosophical.

Being a philosopher, I couldn't accept a solution not based on the truth. If all is vanity—and I heartily agreed to that—the solution must be built on remembering that fact, not on forgetting it; and if drinking and comradeship have a good side—and I heartily agreed to that too—the solution must recognise the good side of drink, and also of wealth, women, travel, fame, and war. Not being an old campaigner with one leg, like Goethe's soldier, but a young man just beginning to see the sunny side of life; it was more the challenge to drink that appealed to me than the chagrin at having found that drinking didn't pay. I knew that it wouldn't pay, if you gave yourself up to it; I felt no temptation to do that; but without setting my heart on anything the point was to enjoy everything with a free mind.

This was a pretty programme, easy for a boy to draw up; and my antecedent pessimism and religiosity lent a certain reality to the pose. It lay in my nature to foresee disappointment, and never to bet on the issue of any event. Yet without experience of the world, this programmatic distrust remained itself empty and insecure. Genuine detachment presupposes attachment. What can it signify for you to say that you renounce everything, if as yet you have loved nothing? I had been childishly absorbed in religious ideas, and it was a true though bloodless sacrifice for me to wash them clean of all pretensions to historical or material truth; yet I was able to do so when quite young, readily and even gladly, because when I learned to conceive those myths as poetry, their meaning and beauty, far from being lost, seemed to me clearer and more profound than ever.

"Poor soul, the centre of this sinful earth." The problem was not so easily solved when it came to exorcising the world and freeing myself from all illusions about it. The world is not a myth, to be clarified by a little literary criticism. It envelops our substance with a kindred substance immensely more voluminous; it stimulates and feeds from every quarter the concupiscence of the flesh, the concupiscence of the eye, and the pride of life. What can the poor rush-light of spirit, kindled in the midst, do to clarify them? The aspiration and the desire must be accepted for the performance.

My gradual retirement from the world. That nevertheless, as a sentiment, my eventual *metanoia* was sincere, may be seen in the slow change that appeared in my way of living. Old age contributed to it; on the other hand, I had larger means and easier access to the great world, had I been in love with it. But I have ultimately become a sort of hermit, not from fear or horror of mankind, but by sheer preference for peace and obscurity. Fortune has become indifferent to me, except as fortune might allow me to despise fortune and to live simply in some beautiful place. I have cut off all artificial society, reducing it to the limits of sincere friendship or intellectual sympathy. Instead of collecting pictures and books, as I had a tendency to do in the early 1890's, I have distributed my few possessions, eschewed chattels of every kind, a fixed residence, servants, carriages, or anything that would pin me down materially or engulf me in engagements. I have indulged rather freely at certain times in good food and good drink; but I think the glamour of those pleasures was due almost entirely to conviviality, that is to say, to a momentary imitation of friendship. In themselves, when I was alone, food and drink were never important to me. I was almost happier when I could be frugal, as at my father's in Avila, in the Duval restaurants in Paris, in the teashops in London, or now, where I write these words, under the drastic restrictions of war, in the clinic of the Blue Sisters upon the Caelius. I am happy in solitude and confinement, and the furious factions into which the world is divided inspire hatred for none of them in my heart.

Sobering experiences in the year 1893: The end of youth. It should be normal, at least according to the ancients, for a philosopher to reach this moral settlement in old age; but why did the idea and the need of it come upon me powerfully at the age of thirty? There were various reasons. For a poet and a lover of youth the age of thirty is itself a ground for *metanoia*. Being a teacher had been forced upon me by the necessity of somehow earning my living; but being a student was my vocation, and I had been living among students, interesting myself in their sports and their pleasures, and loving their quick and unprejudiced minds. Still this second vicarious adolescence had a rift in it: my sympathy with the young and theirs with me had limits that were growing narrower and sharper. My young friends seemed to me every year younger and younger, more and more standardised and generic. They could no longer be my friends, but only boys at the school where I happened to be one of the masters. That chapter then had come to an end: yet youth, in the world and in the poet's eyes, is perpetual. The platonic transition was therefore at once spontaneous and inevitable, from the many to the one, from the existent but transitory to the ideal and eternal.

The death of Warwick Potter. This transition may be called philosophic *metanoia*. Like the tragic catharsis, it turns disaster into a kind of rapture, without those false comforts and delusions by which religious *metanoia* is often cheapened. This philosophic insight was now brought home to me by the unexpected death of Warwick Potter. Though seven years younger than I, he had been a real friend, and as I now felt, my *last* real friend. I have already mentioned that I was surprised by the effect that the news of his death had upon me. Why did it move me so much? Though he was a general favourite and a long procession of us walked behind the bier at his funeral, there was after all nothing extraordinary about him. The cause of my emotion was in myself. I was brimming over with the sense of parting, of being divided by fortune where at heart there was no division. I found myself, unwillingly and irreparably, separated from Spain, from England, from Europe, from my youth and from my religion. It was not good simple Warwick alone that inspired my verses about him. It was the thought of everything that was escaping me: the Good in all the modes of it that I might have caught a glimpse of and lost.

That of my father. Another event that same year had helped to *disintoxicate* my mind: the death of my father. I had never before seen anyone die, and that in itself is an impressive and sobering experience. We were not at best an affectionate family, and my father had not had severe suffering to endure, yet the circumstances were deeply pathetic. He was seventy-nine years old, deaf, half blind, and poor; he had desired his own death and had attempted to hasten it. The fact that he was my father, whose character and destiny were strikingly repeated, with variations, in my own, called up a lurid image of what my life in the world was likely to be: solitary, obscure, trivial, and wasted. I must not look ahead. Ahead, after youth was gone, everything would grow sadder and sadder. I must look within or above. I must follow the counsel that Beatrice gives to Dante, when she sees him overcome with repentance for his vain life in the world:

Pon giù'l seme del piangere, ed ascolta,*

Drop (false hopes) the seed of tears, and listen. Listen to reason. If the joys of youth and the vision of perfect love have faded from your world, will you allow any baser thing to fetter you there? Let your heart rather follow its true object where that object is gone, into eternity.

My sister's marriage.   A third event, the year before, had struck perhaps even deeper into my conscience. I had seen the illusion in disillusion, the vanity of religious substitutes for earthly happiness. In recording "Changes in Avila" I have said something about my sister's marriage. "Marriage and death and division", said the coxcomb Swinburne, "make barren our lives." Marriage properly makes our lives the opposite of barren; but it was not in the spontaneous ardour of youth, with the prospect of helping to people the world, that my sister had married: she was forty-one years old, and her husband already had six children. Nor was marriage in her case going to separate her from anything or anybody: she had no satisfactory friends or relations, and it was from loneliness that she was taking refuge in the difficult position of step-mother. Nor did her marriage divide her materially from me. On the contrary, it gave me, just when my father's life was closing, a fresh and agreeable home in Avila, where I could make her and her new family long visits. Why then did her marriage displease and dishearten me? Because it seemed, in such unfavourable circumstances, an act of desperation on her part, a redoubled proof of her weakness. She explained it by saying that she needed affection; but a second, semi-foreign wife and a step-mother would surely find

*Purgatorio, XXXI, 46, et seq.

more criticism than affection in her new family. It was not the sweetness of affection actually found that attached her to them, or the prospect of a peaceful home-life. I couldn't help seeing that it was a craving for moral support and social backing in her religion and in her self-esteem: the backing of poor dear old little Avila! This thought distressed me. When she had entered her convent in Baltimore, little poetry or dignity as there might be there, I had admired her courage in showing what seemed such contempt of the world. The material separation between us would then have been complete, but the sense of spiritual sympathy more than outweighed it. Her leaving the convent then was no surprise; she had attempted too much and too late; but her marriage now proved more conclusively that she had no contempt of the world; that her religious enthusiasm itself had been something human and social, and that she, who had given the first impulse to my speculative life, had never had any speculative or mystical insight. She was a Sturgis; and her charm and her ascendency over me had been founded only on her natural warmth, geniality and fun, themselves now less spontaneous and engaging than when she was younger. She still clung to the Church with an intense party spirit, which she developed also in politics; but she couldn't *live* her religion as I *lived* my philosophy. It was too unreal for her human nature.

Is popular Catholicism only a postponed worldliness? This was a sad disillusion for me in regard to the person to whom I was most attached; and it became also in some measure a disillusion about Catholicism. Was Catholicism, in principle, much better than Judaism? Wasn't it still worldliness, transferred to a future world, and thereby doubly falsified? The Jews frankly cared for nothing but prosperity, and their delusion was only that they could make a short cut to prosperity by smashing the Golden Calf and being faithful to circumcision and Sabbaths, or alternately by charity towards widows and orphans. In Christianity the idea of prosperity is abandoned for that of salvation in the world to come; and incidentally there is much aspiration towards spiritual perfection and many a master of it; yet this spiritual discipline is in some sense esoteric; in spite of it the goal, as conceived by the materially pious, remains as with the Jews an impossible security amid impossible splendours. The incidental esoteric discipline, which is all that I respect in Catholicism, terminates in the same inward liberation and peace that ancient sages attained under all religions or under none. The question is whether the paraphernalia of salvation are not in all cases accidental, sometimes pleasing and poetical, sometimes dangerously superstitious; and whether they do not encumber the spirit with other-worldliness.

The solution is to renounce the world as Will while retaining it as Idea. Here, then, were four thoughts merging their currents and carrying me irresistibly towards the same sea: youth was past, friendship had had its day, the future offered me nothing that I cared for, religion and social utopias proposed nothing that I respected. I was driven from the temporal to the eternal, not by any one crisis or conjunction of events, but by the very nature of existence, when this had been honestly faced and frankly admitted. The cry of Ecclesiastes, *Vanitas Vanitatum*, could be re-echoed, and the motto from Goethe about setting my heart on nothing could be retained; but both in a new spirit. At twenty my empty spleen could make a clean sweep of the world beforehand, because nothing in it would last for ever; it didn't occur to me to ask whether lasting for ever would improve anything that was worthless while it lasted. But ten years later, I had travelled. I had learned something of the pleasures and manners of mankind, and for myself I had made some progress in the primrose path of Epicurean wisdom. I had now for ever in my fancy a lovely picture of ancient Greece and a lovely picture of modern England; and having begun by fully admitting that all was vanity, I could not be angry with the primroses for fading or with the path for being short. I accepted them as vain but beautiful, transitory but perfect; and I was no less ready to enjoy them than to give them up. To give them up, I mean, as possessions, as enjoyments, as private hopes; I would never give them up as allegiances. Never should I esteem and love them less because they happened to pass out of my orbit.

In another field, not so strictly personal, I was compelled to accept a rather difficult renunciation. I was a teacher of philosophy in the place where philosophy was most modern, most deeply Protestant, most hopefully new: the very things from which, in speculation, my *metanoia* turned me away. I could never be, I will not say a leader, but even a happy participator in the intellectual faith of my neighbours. Not that I had any hostility to that faith: it was as natural in its place and time as any other, and contained important elements of truth: but it could never be my faith. In the midst of the living, I could live only with the dead. It was a comfort, but a cold comfort, to say that I was living among the immortals.

Losing one's life and saving one's soul. Reacting now against all these closed doors, I found the moral of Goethe's drinking-song cheap and hollow. His old soldier *dishonours* his past, as if his present cynicism and rowdiness could be something better. This is only one more mood, one more incident, and a more vulgar one because there is less courage in it. There was vitality in those human adventures; there is also wit and good humour in laughing now at their seamy side; but it is dishonourable and self-contradictory to forswear your honest loves, past or present. They it is that reveal your true nature and its possible fulfilments; they are the Good, in the modes of it that you can appreciate and unfeignedly worship. There is therefore enthusiasm no less than resignation in an enlightened *metanoia*. You give up everything in the form of claims; you receive everything back in the form of a divine presence.

Painfulness of this solution. This final settlement of the moral problem involved no visible change in my mode of living. I went on teaching and writing, drinking and travelling and making friends; only that now, beforehand and explicitly, these occupations were marked for me with a cross: the sign on the one hand of death and on the other of consecration. Gradual and bloodless as the change was, there was a wrench in it, a passage through dark night. I had become aware that, as a spirit, I was not myself but pure spirit, to whom all selves are mere objects, and all their joys and sufferings so many animal vapours, to be endured courageously and no less courageously dismissed and wiped away. The truth of life could be seen only in the shadow of death: living and dying were simultaneous and inseparable. For, as Emerson has it,

> . . . *this losing is true dying,*
> *This is lordly man's down-lying;*
> *This his slow but sure reclining,*
> *Star by star his world resigning.*

Yet this transit through darkness brought me quickly back into the light, into the pure starlight that transports without dazzling. No part of time is lost in eternity, only the haste and uncertainty of passing from one thing to another. I had not been ravaged by any hostile fate; my heart had simply uttered a warning against its own weakness. It had said to me: Cultivate imagination, love it, give it endless forms, but do not let it deceive you. Enjoy the world, travel over it, and learn its ways, but do not let it hold you. Do not suffer it to oppress you with craving or with regret for the images that you may form of it. You will do the least harm and find the greatest satisfactions, if, being furnished as lightly as possible with possessions, you live freely among ideas. To possess things and persons in idea is the only pure good to be got out of them; to possess them physically or legally is a burden and a snare.

Its inevitable incompleteness.   I know very well that this philosophic salvation is not such as nature or life looks for or can accept: it is only what the truth affords to the spirit. Life and nature do not ask to be saved from themselves: they ask only to run on at full tilt. It is the spirit that asks to be saved from that insane predicament. Yet spirit is an emanation of life, and it is more truly and naturally happy in the first phases of its career than in its final salvation. In the end, when it has understood, and renounced everything, if you ask it whether it is happy, it can reply only as La Vallière replied to the friends who asked her if she were happy in the Carmelite convent to which she had retired: *Je ne suis pas heureuse; je suis contente.* Nature had been muted, but spirit had been freed. In that sense, and under the spell of that profound conviction, I composed the second sequence of my sonnets, using the traditional language and images of love which can render that sentiment best. They belong to a second-rate kind of poetry that in itself has no claim to attention; but here, considered as autobiography, they may be recalled. The key to the whole is given in the one line:

A perfect love is founded on despair.

Metanoia within the passion of love.   This paradox is condensed and rhetorical; to get at the truth in it we must expand it a little and ward off certain misunderstandings. It is not love simply, but only *perfect* love, that includes despair. Love in itself includes hope, or at least a desire to preserve the object of it, to enshrine and defend it. And in regard to the object even perfect love retains this solicitude. It is only in regard to the lover, as a poor human being, that hope must be cut off, plucked up by the roots, if love is ever to become pure, happy, and immortal. The *perfect* lover must renounce pursuit and the hope of possession. His person and life must, in his own eyes, fall altogether out of the picture. Stendhal, in his book *De l'Amour* (which unlike his others pleases me very much), distinguishes four kinds of love, *l'amour-physique, l'amour de vanité, l'amour-goût,* and *l'amour-passion.* The first two are obviously imperfect and impure: they include craving, jealousy, cruelty, fear, folly, and self-degradation. Yet the vital side of physical love cannot be dispensed with, since it is the root of the whole growth and most intense in the *amour-passion*. In the great passion this vital impulse is often diverted from physical lust and jealousy to absolute devotion, heroism, and suicide. It is therefore psychologically not only possible but normal for the passion of love to be self-forgetful, and to live on in the very act of sacrifice and personal despair. So transformed, the great passion becomes worship. And the *amour-goût*, which is more playful and turns the vital element into laughter and delight, also reaches perfection only when all thought of the self, all *amour de vanité*, drops out of it, and it becomes wholly aesthetic, pure joy in beauty and charm. Combine these two elements, the tragic and the lyrical, and you have turned love into a rapture in adoration which seems to me its perfection. It presupposes the total abdication of physical, social or egotistical claims; yet these claims were instinctive in the psyche, and the spirit has either adopted them and repented, or at least felt and understood them in refusing to make them. The passion of love, sublimated, does not become bloodless, or free from bodily trepidation, as charity and philanthropy are. It is essentially the spiritual flame of a carnal fire that has turned all its fuel into light. The psyche is not thereby atrophied; on the contrary, the range of its reactions has been enlarged. It has learned to vibrate harmoniously to many things at once in a peace which is an orchestration of transcended sorrows.

XXVI

King's College, Cambridge

Incidental relations with the English Cambridge.   I first went to Cambridge in 1895, only for the day, being taken there by Russell to see his brother Bertie who, he said, was anxious to make my acquaintance. These circumstances mark, in my mind, the character of my whole connection with Cambridge, wholly different from my connection with Oxford. To Cambridge I went late, on a flying visit, at the suggestion and invitation of a friend, and came away without clear impressions. Bertie was then living in the new part of Trinity, small rooms in a falsely Gothic dormitory that might have been at Harvard. He was very busy; there was a knot of other friends, none of whom I remember distinctly; and I had no time to see the beauties of the place. To Oxford, on the contrary, I had gone eight years earlier, in my first free flight, alone, and with eyes and mind open. I had at once made friends, and learned silently to thread that secluded labyrinth. Officially, I was unknown, and a stray tourist; inwardly, I was perfectly at home. In Cambridge, my friends were all professional. Bertie at once became a Fellow and an intellectual leader.

Thomas Gaillard Lapsley.   Lapsley, a Harvard man of the Class of 1893, later became also a Fellow of Trinity, having written a most learned work on the history of the See of Durham. He spent his life in that College, but kept up his American relations and sympathies with an admirable fidelity. To me he was most hospitable and friendly, although his intense Anglican piety acted sometimes as an ulterior barrier between us. Still, I could tell him whatever I had seen, in Spain or elsewhere, of the too human side of Catholics, and he would relish my naughtiness. Those *Romanists* were so *pagan*, and their liturgy so *incorrect*! He was consumptive, and had never married. For that reason, perhaps, he was on terms of intense friendship with Mrs. Wharton and a host of other American ladies. The doctors commanded him never to skip his daily walk; and he would sometimes come to fetch me in a pouring rain, which I would intrepidly face in his company, although I was not myself a slave to any regimen of exercise or of fresh air, even if heaven fall. He wondered how I could drink wine at luncheon; he drank only in the evening. But I never worked in the afternoon, I only walked or read, which I was never too boozy to do; why then not spiritualise one's midday food with a little liquor? It was precisely in the evening that I liked to sit alone by my fire, and perhaps concentrate my mind on something in particular.

I become an "advanced student" at King's.   It was in a professional capacity, as being an instructor at Harvard, that I was admitted to King's College, in 1896. I was *in statu pupillari*, an advanced student, wore a master's gown (without strings, because not a master of arts of that university) and dined at the high table. Never have I eaten such good food consecutively anywhere else; but it was dinner only: the rest one had in one's rooms. My rooms were first at the corner of Silver Street, and then in Free School Lane: only in the long vacation term, when Wedd lent me his rooms in Gibbs, or the Fellows' Building, did I live in the College. But what a place that was! The front or east room looked out across the Quad toward King's Parade. Over the rather bastard stone screen, you saw a picturesque row of old houses, not decrepit or intentionally picturesque: just the honestly useful, proud, sensitive work of an age of burghers. Each house was individual, but each knew and kept its place with decorum. In the middle of the Quad was a rather diminutive monument to the unhappy founder, Henry VI, adorned with two subordinate figures: Science, as the local epigram had it, turning her back to the College, and Religion, turning her back to the Chapel.

The Chapel exterior.   From my front windows I could see the exterior of the Chapel in violent perspective, the buttresses standing in file, like soldiers with shields, lances, and banners, or like the statue-columns of Karnak. Only a corner of the windows was visible at the top; above which the rough grey wall was crowned with lovely perforated battlements and pinnacles. Away with the pedants who say that battlements should not be perforated! Not, I grant, in a castle, although even there they may be decoratively shaped; but in a church not expected to stand a siege—the walls being all glass—why shouldn't the traditional edging of battlements be retained for beauty's sake? And why shouldn't the compliment be paid to beauty with a frank smile, by opening lights in those mock battlements, as if they were laughing children looking through their fingers? What could be more charming and lovely than the perforated battlements and the eight pinnacles (one especially thick one at the corner, where the stairs wind up) of the Magdalen tower at Oxford? King's Chapel, however, has a grander air, on account of its four solid and lofty turrets. They are almost towers, yet I think more decorative than if they were towers, because more subservient and integral to the nave of the church.

The interior.   And what a church! A Gothic Parthenon in dignity, a chapel only in having no aisles and only one altar; but that is the tradition proper to every temple. We can't have everything or be everything at once; the god of pantheism is a monster; and if we wish to be something perfect we must banish regret for not being anything else. Here we must banish the romantic love of unrealisable things; we mustn't ask for a forest of columns teasing us with alternative irrecoverable vistas; we must renounce a multiplicity of vaults, each higher than the other, and of galleries hanging and looking down over us, as it were, from other worlds. We must renounce the wayside shrine and the screened chapel for our special tombs and our special devotions. In a word, we mustn't dream of cathedrals. This is a Gothic hall, a single chamber, and in that respect like the Pantheon, St. Sophia and the Sistine Chapel. Yet it is Gothic not only in decorative style but in structure and spirit. It is narrow, long, lofty: it draws you on, towards the goal of your pilgrimage, to the place where the altar ought to have been. It is a throne-room for the Risen Christ, to be present in the Sacrament. Here concentration is perfect, the whole court drawn up in order, waiting; only the monarch is late. Meantime the arrangements continue to suggest his presence, and we may study them the more freely while we postpone our acts of homage.

In the first place, it was perhaps not altogether true that there are no side-chapels. There are small chantries between the buttresses under each window, some now used as a vestry; they might have been intended to hold tombs, or even side altars. Yet these chambers are low and walled off, and may be overlooked. That which at once catches and holds the eye is the vault. It is held up, lifted up, as if it could move, like a baldacchino over a procession; it is woven of intricate fan traceries, undulating slightly, without sharp arches, or heavy pendants; the fans open like palmtrees from the piers, and then merge their branches in a chain of diamonds and circles down the flat central part. It is regal elegance, rather than religious mystery that spreads this canopy over us; yet never was perspective more magnetic or vault more alive. We are in the presence of something magical, something sublime.

The screen.   Nor is the Gothic charm of suggestion and interruption altogether wanting. Halfway down the nave there is a screen, with an elaborate organ above, separating us from the choir. This screen has been condemned by many critics, as interfering with the vista; but that seems to me a strange innocence. The *vista* is emphasised, almost created, by the screen: instead of one long monotonous tunnel we have a great vestibule and a great yet only partially visible sanctuary beyond. The vault is uninterrupted; the great series of windows goes round all the way, and we see the central one, with the crucifixion boldly designed, over the altar. But the altar itself, the choir stalls, and whatever else there may be in the chancel, we do not see clearly; and the aerial perspective itself is defined and the whole edifice prolonged, by the presence of that obstacle. I don't say that the organ screen in itself is suitable in style or in colour; I should have preferred a stone one with a great crucifix, as in the Cathedral of Avila; but the presence of a screen, and of a screen high, at least in the middle, is essential to the *living* beauty of the place. Pedants often hanker for a dead beauty.

The glass.   The crowning glory of King's Chapel, however, is the stained glass. I believe the west window, to which one at first turns one's back, is modern, but it is not offensive; all the rest (and for once, they are complete!) belong to the period and are Flemish. Under their spell I once versified my emotion about them, and will not bore the reader by serving it up again cold. I have never studied them in detail, for their technique or the treatment of their subjects; I gazed at them only as luminous tapestry, as accompaniments and accessories; yet over their blue ground and green shadows, their heraldries, and labyrinthine figures, touched with jewel lights, my eye always travelled with pleasure. They served as a sort of opiate; yet the dreams they provoked were all of order, tenderness, grandeur, and peace.

The Backs.   The same qualities that appeared there in a hieratic monument, a relic of the past, appeared smiling and always young if I looked out of my windows on the other side, towards the Backs. The rooms in Gibbs are the noble model humbly reproduced in Holworthy at Harvard; a large square room in front, for receiving, meeting pupils, and dining, and two narrower rooms behind, which in Wedd's apartment were one the bedroom and the other the study.

This study was full of books, especially in Latin, which was Wedd's subject. But the chief attraction was the view: a vast velvet lawn, sloping gently down to the river—here more like a canal—with great avenues of trees and pretty stone bridges leading to the wooded bank and gardens on the other side. Nor was architecture absent in this prospect. To the right the lawn was bounded by the charming garden front of Clare, at once cheerful and stately, decorative and domestic. There was something, as I remember it, particularly warm and amber-like in the colour of its stone; probably the same stone that looked so granite-like in the lower parts of the Chapel, and whitened into silver towards the top. But with colour and aerial quality the English weather plays unending tricks; what you see once you may never see again, yet you may count on soon seeing something new and in some way lovely.

My inner indifference to Cambridge. How was it that my heart was not anchored in King's College, where I had been lodged so grandly and so comfortably, in perfect seclusion yet with everything that I could care for within easy reach? Why have I rather clung to Oxford, where I was never an inmate? It may have been an accident. In 1897 I was not young enough to be assimilated and not old enough to count or to become a centre for a knot of friends. I made few new acquaintances and remained generally unknown. Some of these circumstances were distinctly to my liking and others might have varied with time; yet my feeling when I was at King's was that the birds were not worthy of the cage.*

Oscar Browning. Who were these birds? The Provost—whose name I have forgotten—very civilly asked me to luncheon when I was first admitted to the College, and I never saw him afterwards. There was the antiquarian James—later I believe provost—from whom I might have learned many interesting things, but I never exchanged more than a few words with him. Finally, there was the notorious Oscar Browning. He openly flaunted the banners of gluttony and paederasty, neither of them suitable for a teacher of youth; yet everybody laughed, and the authorities affected a calm indifference. He was obviously a good soul, and kind, but club-footed, fat, self-

---

*The year 1896–7 seems to have been an unlucky one for finding genius at King's. Several literary lights, including Trevelyan, the poet, had just disappeared and several public celebrities, including Keynes, had not yet come up. I believe Bury, the historian, was in residence but I never came across him.

congratulatory, and licentious. His warm affections ranged from Royalty to the lower decks of the Navy. He seemed to be rich; I heard that besides his Fellowship—which was permanent on the old basis—he acted as agent for wine-sellers and launched new brands of choice claret and champagne. The claret he tasted—gratis—every day at luncheon, with a mutton chop, vegetables, and a pudding. His breakfast was no less copious; and before breakfast he had bread-and-butter in bed with his early tea, and a special bottle of ale at 3 a.m. for which he was awakened by an alarm clock. Afternoon tea, for him, required solid accompaniments, after hard daily tennis and a Turkish bath. It was he that had introduced Turkish Baths into Cambridge. Tea by no means took away his appetite for dinner in hall: always a choice of thick or clear soup, then fish, a joint, a hot sweet, a cold sweet, and a savoury, washed down with champagne; and he with Wedd and me were usually the only ones to have the traditional glass of port after dinner in the combination room, on ordinary days; but many others joined us on Saturdays, when there were usually old King's men who came up from London. With all this burden to carry, the O.B., as he was called, seemed always in perfect health and in jovial spirits. Was it genuine happiness, or a bold front put up to hide a desperate misery? He was also, I should have said, an alleged historian; but this seemed to be of no importance.

Nathaniel Wedd. Personal friends at King's I had two, Wedd, and Lowes Dickinson. Wedd, who was a friend of the Russells, was my particular mentor and guide. We sympathised in our pagan satirical view of life. His scholarship and wit were of the Johnsonian stamp. "There", he said once as we walked over the bridge to the Backs, "is where the married Dons have their breeding-holes." I think he was of humble extraction, and accepted a position of Court Fool in the learned world, with licence to say the truth in figurative language. I often remembered Bangs & Barlow when I was with Wedd: it was the same humanism without fig-leaves. Wedd's learning was far wider and more classical, but in his person he was less a man of the world. A little thick-set fellow with a ferreting air, he resembled a woolly lap-dog, only black. His black hair fell over his black eyebrows, and he seemed a picture of pre-historic man. People abroad, he would say, couldn't believe that he was an Englishman. Once when he had mentioned his nationality to a fellow-traveller in France, the Frenchman wouldn't credit it. Irishman, perhaps, or Welshman, but Englishman, *jamais de la vie.* "*Mais si, monsieur,*" Wedd protested in his perfect

French, *"Anglais piu-ah!"* I didn't say so, because Wedd mightn't have liked it, but I think the Frenchman was virtually right. Wedd was no Teuton, no Angle or Saxon or Dane or Norman; he must have been a pure descendent of the few remaining primitive Britons: a Mediterranean race! Hence our good mutual understanding.

A trip through the northeastern counties. The College was not kept open for residence throughout the long vacation; at a certain date in August I had to leave. One of the Dons very kindly gave me a list of towns with interesting churches, in the eastern counties, beginning with Norwich and ending at Durham; a tour in that region, as yet unknown to me, would fill up my time, unless I preferred to return to Oxford where I had spent the previous summer; for paradoxically, being a member of the University of Cambridge I was not allowed to reside in Cambridge out of term, but I might reside in Oxford, term or no term. Wedd, however, had suggested that I might join him at a village near Wark-on-Tyne, by the Roman Wall, and among Roman roads, a good place for long walks; and this decided me to travel northwards, and see something of that part of England. Architecturally, the prevalence of the Perpendicular was rather monotonous, even disheartening; because the Reformation seems to have overtaken most of the Tudor churches before they had clothed their perpendicular bones with the vesture of worship, and they stand bleak and empty, like solitary dead trees. I had seen in King's Chapel the very best that the Perpendicular can do, in its gorgeous intentions; it needs all the colour and all the rich accessories that the commercial wealth of the age could supply, to redeem its spiritual starkness. But at York and Durham, and especially at Lincoln there were lovely relics of the earlier time, the castle-building age, when structure was varied, picturesque, and defiant in itself, without rejecting the splendours that heraldry and religion might introduce into it. Yet somehow the eastern counties, even Cambridge, have less of what I like in England, than have the south and west; they look the wrong way. They are open to the winds and to the thoughts that devastate rather than to those that fertilise and refine.

In Northumberland Wedd and I spent an austere fortnight, in a modest cottage, without baths, with food that only a good appetite could swallow, and long tramps, one day fully twenty miles, over open windswept undulating country. It is the thought of those Roman roads and fortifications, rather than the sight of them, that remains with me. The north is formless; it has spirit in it, wind, but no images that beg to be retained, sculptured, immortalised. Let the north, I say, digest its barren tempests; let it send us only its young men, the raw material of genius, for the south to instruct, to enamour, and to mature.

Lowes Dickinson. In sharp contrast with Wedd was my other friend at King's, Lowes Dickinson. His classicism was not of the rough, coarse, realistic Roman kind, but Greek, as attenuated and Platonised as possible, and seen through Quaker spectacles. I liked his *Greek View of Life*, but it wasn't Greek life as depicted by Aristophanes or by Plutarch; it was what a romantic puritan of our time would wish Greek life to have been. War, lust, cruelty, and confusion were washed out of it. Dickinson was super-sensitive, hard-working, unhappy, and misguided. His gift was for form; his privately printed poems seemed to me admirable; but his subject-matter was perverse, even in those poems, and much more, I think, in his philosophy and politics. He prayed, watched, and laboured to redeem human life, and began by refusing to understand what human life is. Too weak to face the truth, he set himself a task too great for Titans: to shatter this world to bits, and put it together again on a moralistic plan. If at least that plan had been beautiful, he might have consoled himself for his practical impotence by being an avowed poet; but his plan was incoherent, negative, sentimental. It was that no one should suffer, and that all should love one another: in other words, that no one should be alive or should distinguish what he loved from what he hated.

Poor Dickinson came once or twice to America, the first time to give some Lowell Lectures in Boston. It was winter, and he suffered from the cold, as well as from the largeness and noise of the town. I remember his horror when the electric car we were in got into the sub-way, and the noise became deafening; also his misery when one evening we walked across the Harvard bridge, and he murmured shivering: "I have never been so cold in my life." The cocktail, he said, was the only good thing in America. He hated the real, bumptious, cordial democracy that he found there; he would have liked a silent, Franciscan, tender democracy, poor, clean, and inspired. If he could have visited New England sixty years earlier he might have found sympathetic souls at Concord or at Brook Farm. He wouldn't have liked them, reformers don't like one another; but at least he might have imagined that the world was moving towards something better. As it was, he found that it was sliding hellwards with a whoop of triumph.

Henry Jackson. More important for me, and also in themselves, were my friends at Trinity College. Although I was a member of King's, all my work was at Trinity, under Henry Jackson as Tutor, and with Bertie Russell, G. E. Moore and MacTaggart as philosophical friends. Jackson was an influential person, might have been Master of Trinity, the greatest position in the British university world. He was courtly, magnificent in his ample stiff silk gown, hospitable, universally informed, and learned, with the English trick of fathering some childish hobby. He maintained that Plato's logic was the same as Mill's. He was tolerant and considerate about my bad Greek, which I had confessed at the beginning; and he recommended, as I needed a translation to help me in my reading, to get the dialogues we were to read—the *Parmenides*, *Philebus*, *Sophist*, and *Politicus*—in a cheap edition in separate little volumes with the text and a German translation on opposite pages. These little books proved invaluable. They went easily into the pocket, and I could read them anywhere during my walks, or look up again at any time a passage that had arrested my attention. He had published an analysis of the hypotheses about Being that fill the long second part of the *Parmenides*. Without attributing any historical insight to this view, I found it a useful thread through that labyrinth; and it also had an important influence on my philosophy, because it helped me to see that Being, the One, the Many, etc., were names of categories, not of existent things, so that all cosmological theories relying on dialectic (such as that of Leibniz) were sophistical. They played with essences, and thought they were disclosing facts. But there are no necessary facts. Facts are all accidents. They all might have been different. They all may become different. They all may collapse altogether.

A glimpse of Lord Acton. Jackson had splendid rooms in the Cloisters, afterwards occupied by Lapsley, and one day he asked me to luncheon there, to meet Lord Acton. I am not an admirer of celebrities, or curious about them. Obscure people, if they are nice, interest me much more. However, under the circumstances, it was as well for me to go. Lord Acton was a Catholic and a German; I don't know how he came to be an Englishman. He was fat, ponderous, with a full grey beard and an apostolic heaviness. His theory of history was ultra-empirical: anything might happen, and all testimony was acceptable. Miracles abounded everywhere, and the testimony for prophecy, second sight, etc., was overwhelming. But even non-miraculous details seemed to fill his mind and absorb his interest. Having heard that I was at

Harvard, he suddenly turned to me and asked if I knew how a certain movement had been carried out in a certain battle (which I had never heard of) during the American Civil War. The question annoyed me for various reasons. As politely as I could I said that I was born in Spain during that war, that I had heard little talk about it when I went to America, and hadn't studied the history of it. He then went on to explain the point at issue among the various witnesses, and I escaped further interrogation. The vision, I might almost say the smell, of a mind stocked like an old trunk with remnants of faded finery and knicknacks, moved me to sadness not unmixed with aversion. Daily experience, all trivial incidents floating like wreckage in a sea of ignorance, is bad enough: but think of a distinguished mind, consecrated to history, which is one of the Muses, and still remaining in that chaotic state! No wonder that Lord Acton should have felt the need of remaining a Catholic, under no matter what difficulties and sorrows! Not having found any order in the real world, he had to invoke an imaginary world where order should be morally perfect. It is a vendetta of faith against intelligence that perpetuates hostilities.

Bertrand Russell.   Of all my friends, of all persons belonging at all to my world, Bertrand Russell was the most distinguished. He had birth, genius, learning, indefatigable zeal and energy, brilliant intelligence, and absolute honesty and courage. His love of justice was as keen as his sense of humour. He was at home in mathematics, in natural science, and in history. He knew well all the more important languages and was well informed about everything going on in the world of politics and literature. He ought to have been a leader, a man of universal reputation and influence. He was indeed recognised to be a distinguished man, having made his mark in mathematics and logic, and largely inspired the new philosophical sect of "logical realists". Yet on the whole, relatively to his capacities, he was a failure. He petered out. He squandered his time and energy, and even his money, on unworthy objects. He left no monument—unless it be the early *Principia Mathematica* written in collaboration with Whitehead—that does justice to his powers and gives him a place in history.

His personality.   In his physique he was a complete contrast to his brother, a Russell while his brother was a Stanley. Bertie was small, dark, brisk, with a lively air and a hyena laugh. According to some people he was the ugliest man they had ever seen. But I didn't find him ugly, because his mask, though grotesque, was expressive and engaging. You saw that he was a kind monster, that if he spit fire, it was a *feu-de-joie*. For so violent, so merciless a satirist, he made a charming companion. I, at least, was never afraid of him; and he was benevolence itself to the most humble and hopeless intellectual waifs. Though his laughter was savage, it was fed by the subtlest intellectual lights: that was the chief charm of his conversation, added to the sense of security that his faultless memory and universal knowledge gave in regard to any information that he might give. This information, though accurate, was necessarily partial, and brought forward in a partisan argument; he couldn't know, he refused to consider everything; so that his judgments, nominally based on that partial information, were really inspired by passionate prejudice and were always unfair and sometimes mad. He would say, for instance, that the bishops supported the war because they had money invested in munition works; or that the United States government had called out troops, not to fight the Germans, but to support Rockefeller against the strikers. It was for this libel that he was sent to prison; and this wasn't the worst consequence of such rash assertions. They alienated opinion in high quarters, and ruined his official career. "I would go to the stake for that!" he would cry sometimes in summing up a philosophical argument. But going only to Holloway, in the first division, hadn't the posthumous value of martyrdom; and the general feeling that his judgment was unsound and his allegiance misplaced, defeated all his attempts to guide public opinion.

His education. He had been beautifully educated by private tutors at Pembroke Lodge. After the dreadful experience she had had with her elder grandson, who would throw her letters unread into the fire, Lady Russell dreaded the fatal influence of schools: Bertie at least must be preserved pure, religious, and affectionate; he must be fitted to take his grandfather's place as prime minister and continue the sacred work of Reform. Bertie showed me his schoolroom at Pembroke Lodge, and his old note-books on the various subjects that he had studied. It was perfect princely education, but a little like cultivating tropical flowers under electric light in a steaming greenhouse. The instruction was well selected, competently given, and absorbed with intense thirst; but it was too good for the outdoor climate. Moreover, there were obstacles that far from being surmounted were built upon as corner-stones of righteousness and sources of superior light. One was the hereditary liberalism and Low Church piety of the family. Another was Bertie's microscopic intensity, that narrowed each of his insights, no matter how varied these insights might be, lost the substance in the visible image, the sense in the logic of the words, and made him, though he might be many-sided, a many-sided fanatic.

Bertie, Stickney, and Westenholz, the three best-educated persons I have known, never went to school. Bertie, however, did go to the university, and here he made those fruitful contacts that produced his best work and opened to him an academic career. Had he been an obscure and penniless person, such a career might have fulfilled his ambition and determined his path; but for him, destined by his grand-mother to be prime minister and by himself to be an international messiah, academic life was but a preparation or an interlude. His vocation was to reform radically the whole intellectual and social world.

What he might have achieved in politics. I can imagine two ways in which Bertie might have proceeded to prove how great a man it was in him to be. One would have been to carry out his grandmother's plans, get early a safe seat in the House of Commons, moderate his zeal so far as not to denounce bishops, generals, admirals or even Tory ministers, unless he had proofs of their obliquity, and generally to identify himself (as he could well do emotionally) with the official interests of his country. He would not at once or always have been in office. These intervals of leisure would have sufficed for the intensive study and the literary work that were appropriate to a leader of reform; and when his party won an election, he would have been able to exert the power of government for the heroic purpose of diminishing that power. He might have prevented the collapse of the Liberal party, by transforming it into a labour party true to dem-ocratic, anti-military, anti-imperialistic, anti-clerical principles. He might have shown the world whether at least in England it were not possible for a modern civilisation to exist with a maximum of liberty and a minimum of government.

Or in philosophy. The other way in which Bertie might conceivably have become a great man would have been by emulating people like Bacon, Hobbes, Spinoza or Auguste Comte. I don't mean in their doctrines but in their ambition. He might have undertaken an *instauratio magna* of scientific philosophy. He could have done it better than Bacon, in as much as the science at his command was so much more advanced: and the *Principia Mathematica*, a title challenging comparison with Newton, seemed to foreshadow such a possibility. Why, then, didn't Bertie proceed in this course? Or why didn't he choose the other, the political, path?

Fatal traditionalism of this radical. I can judge only superficially, and from a distance. I didn't know him as I knew his brother. But judging by the work that he has actually accomplished, I think that, penetrating as his analysis might be in particular cases, in fundamentals he could never shake himself free from his environment and from the miscellaneous currents of opinion in his day. Except in mathematics, he seemed to practise criticism only sporadically, caught and irresistibly excited by current discussions. His radical solutions were rendered vain by the conventionality of his problems. His outlook was universal, but his presuppositions were insular. In philosophy he couldn't entertain the hypothesis that Berkeley, Hume, and Mill might have been fundamentally wrong. He seemed one day astonished and horrified when I said that the image of the sun as a luminous disc, sometimes (if you squint) with rays round it, was as fictitious and imaginary as the idea of Phoebus Apollo with his golden hair and his arrows. The senses are poets; and a strange allegiance to these imaginary figments kept Bertie's philosophy always inconclusive and unstable. Autobiographically, aesthetically, logically they are ultimates; they are what you confront absolutely when you concentrate and purify your attention; and in a critical analysis of experience Bertie was quite right in distinguishing them and in sticking to them. But they are the fireworks of animal sensation, not the stars of heaven. To turn them into elements in a cosmology, or in a system of ethics and politics seems a blunder of the first magnitude. Animal sensation is sheer dream; only animal faith can lead us to reality. You can't build science out of literature; and the English and Germans, who in their positive science serve material interests and show plenty of hard sense, when they come to interpret science philosophically are crossed by the Protestant and romantic tradition of subjectivism, and end with devout feeling, translating everything into sentimental literature. Bertie at least escaped the fabulous sort of idealism. He almost emerged from psychological physics by composing physics out of logical elements. This was the "logical realism", which he took a leading part in suggesting. But he couldn't carry his suggestion out, because it dies in solipsism of the passing datum; or if you inconsistently grant many data, it dissolves into a multitude of sparks with only logical relations to one another. The universe has become a dictionary of the terms in which we apprehend it.

Streams lost in the sands.   When I was at King's Bertie had just passed from mathematical partnership with Whitehead to apostolic partnership with Moore, and these two had published their *Principia Ethica*, of which Bertie has since abandoned both the principles and the conclusions. Whitehead, though older than Russell, still seemed youngish and clear-headed in those days. He said once, leaning carelessly against the mantelpiece: "There are some questions that can be answered, but they are unimportant; others are important, but they can't be answered." I remembered the wiser saying of Royce, that a question that can't be answered is one that is wrongly put. In his later years Whitehead, whose brother was a bishop and whose son was killed in the war (this is Bertie's explanation of the change in him) has been busy giving vague answers to questions that do not arise in a clear head. Internal liquifaction in his case, like external distraction in Russell's, has spoiled a good mind. Both migrated for a time to America, Whitehead to flatter and be flattered, poor Bertie to earn his living and to be persecuted.

MacTaggart and his good-will towards me.   Less absorbing at the time, but ultimately perhaps more satisfactory, was my philosophical contact with MacTaggart. He was then a very odd person, sidled along the street sticking close to the wall, and half looking sheepishly down; and his absolute Hegelian idealism at that time prejudiced me against him. He had had, I understood, a fantastic tender passion, that made him embrace some foolish illusions. But he must have seen enough in me to wish to save my soul, for he unexpectedly proposed to read Hegel with me, he an adept and I an ill-disposed outsider. It was a great favour to me; and we had a few sittings in the long vacation. We read aloud and discussed the beginning of the minor Logic, in the *Encyclopaedie der Wissenschaften*. I was then refractory to the transcendental point of view, and would continually transfer the matter in hand to the naturalistic plane, which MacTaggart, with some contempt, called *psychological*. Nothing seemed to come of our effort, and we soon gave the thing up. He retained, however, a friendly attitude towards me (as Moore did not); and during my last visit to Cambridge, in 1923, he came one evening to sit next to me at dinner in Hall, and I soon found, when we began to talk about philosophy, that he had discovered that, apart from technicalities, I could be as transcendental as he. Only for me transcendentalism was a deliberate pose, a way of speaking, expressing a subjective perspective; whereas for him it revealed the metaphysical structure of all reality.

He pinned his faith and hope of salvation on what I played with as an optical illusion, rendered harmless by being understood. Why didn't this mockery in me disgust and offend him? I think he was almost content with my doctrines of essence and of truth: indeed, he ought to have been more than content, because I granted much more than he asked for, at least in the case of truth. That evening he quoted to me a line from one of my sonnets:

Truth is a dream unless my dream is true

and said that this was philosophical poetry at its best. The compliment was excessive and most unexpected; but now, on rereading that effusion of my remote adolescence, I can see that probably I then looked to the truth for the sort of *justification of faith* which MacTaggart demanded from the truth now. My imagination had framed a highly poetic, humanistic, supernaturalistic picture of the universe. I felt that it was a fiction; but I said impulsively: "If that fiction isn't the truth revealed, truth can never be revealed to the human heart." Truth was therefore—not really a dream in itself, since no mind was ever to see it—but something which it was a vain dream to look for, or to think we possessed in our philosophy.

Idealism floundering in the eddies of truth. This is what I suspect I felt at the age of twenty; but if so, MacTaggart read into my sonnet something that had never been in my mind—a perfectly legitimate use to make of words that set one thinking. For his own sentiment was different. He was an absolute idealist and could admit truth only as an attribute of opinions, more or less true as they grew more voluminous and consistent. Every philosopher thus had the fountain of truth within himself, and his system would become absolutely true if he could only make it all-comprehensive and perfectly coherent. Learned egotism could not have a more congenial prospect; but in MacTaggart I think there was also another motive force, distinctly not egotistical. Every opinion, in positing a truth to be attained, would remain existentially nothing but a dream, yet each would move truthward if it reappeared enveloped in another dream more coherent and comprehensive than itself. German philosophy is contemptuous of realistic faith in regard to perception or dogma, and of naturalism in morals; but nature takes its ironical revenge, and idealists are often most innocently realistic about society, and domestic, not to say animal, in sentiment. This definition of truth as harmony in dreams is a metaphysical echo of human craving for sympathy and democratic comfort in agreeing with the majority. We go right enough, darling, if we go wrong together!

XXVII

Travels

Dreams of the caged bird.   All my life I have dreamt of travels, possible and impossible: travels in space and travels in time, travels into other bodies and into alien minds. Not having been suffered by fate to be more than an occasional tripper and tourist, I have taken my revenge in what might be called travels of the intellect, by admitting the opposite of all facts and of all beliefs to be equally possible and no more arbitrary. These travels of the intellect helped me in boyhood to overcome the hatred that I then felt for my times and my surroundings; and later they have helped me to overcome the rash impulse to claim an absolute rightness for the things I might have preferred. Ideals are relative to the will. A little change in me would have banished that hatred and reversed that preference. My intellectual travels therefore reconciled me in the end, at least in theory, to the home facts. I could forgive the world everything except the ignorance and arrogance of thinking its condition alone possible or alone right.

In spite of this longing for unexampled things, I have always been a realist about the facts and suspicious of all desiderata and utopias. Your sanguine man who sets forth enthusiastically for El Dorado nurses a secret passion for the happy home. For that reason he is restless in his accidental lodgings and risks everything in the hope of discovering other lodgings where he would enjoy for ever an unclouded happiness. The born traveller, on the contrary, is not pining for a better cage. If ever he got to heaven, on the next day he would discover its boundaries, and on the third day he would make a little raid beyond them. Imagination is potentially infinite. Though actually we are limited to the types of experience for which we possess organs, those organs are somewhat plastic. Opportunity will change their scope and even their centre. The free spirit in us knows that whatsoever may be offered to it is but a reversible accident, and though we are compelled to be absorbed ignominiously in such accidents, yet the interesting side of those accidents for the intellect is only their character and their re-versibility. The precision and variety of alien things fascinate the trav-eller. He is aware that however much he may have seen, more and greater things remain to be explored, at least ideally; and he need never cease travelling, if he has a critical mind.

Aesthetic, satirical, and international influences.   How, being lazy and hating excitements and risks, could I develop this passion for travel? One incentive was aesthetic. I loved picture-books, costumes, theatres, architectural vistas, dialectical perspectives. The har-monies into which accidents could fall were picturesque; they were also ridiculous, and a sense for the ludicrous, a love of laughter, was native to me. A kindred but less innocent motive was satirical. It was not only I, in my silliness, that was laughing at the world: it was the gods that were laughing at it. Its own substance mocked the forms that it took. Not only were events and conventions mere episodes in an endless flux, but they were mechanically produced by forces ir-relevant to our dramatic poses and pert egoisms: they were like patterns seen in a kaleidoscope—a toy of which I was fond. There was a sort of satirical magic in their existence, and the childish impulse was strong in me to turn the crank and see what would come next. A third motive might be found in the antecedents of my family. My father and mother had lived in exotic places. I gathered in childhood that travel was normal and enlightening; it taught us the variety of tastes and standards in the world. My parents were nevertheless most dogmatic in their views and precise in their habits; they rejected almost everything; but this was perhaps the effect of their ill-luck. To me the existence of the things they condemned, such as religion, monarchy, luxury and fashion, was not at all disquieting. On the contrary, those fancy things were fascinating, and a great relief to hear about, in contrast to the dulness of home life. I was glad to allow others to keep their ideals of any sort, provided I was allowed to keep mine. At any rate, in a world where the exotic so abounded, to ignore it would be ignominious intellectually and practically dangerous; because unless you understand and respect things foreign, you will never perceive the special character of things at home or of your own mind. You will make ridiculous claims and assumptions, and you will continually run up against stone walls. *Travel*, therefore, I said to myself, *travel* at least in thought, or else you are likely to live and to die an ass.

Essence of the traveller. So much for the enlightening uses of travel; yet in the philosophic traveller something else is presupposed, without which he would lapse into a frivolous sightseer and his mind into an album of snap-shots and clippings. Ghastly are those auto-biographies that contain nothing but old jokes and old anecdotes. Before he sets out, the traveller must possess fixed interests and faculties, to be served by travel. If he drifted aimlessly from country to country he would not *travel* but only wander, ramble, or tramp. The traveller must be somebody and come from somewhere, so that his definite character and moral traditions may supply an organ and a point of comparison for his observations. He must not go nosing about like a peddlar for profit or like an emigrant for a vacant lot. Everywhere he should show the discretion and maintain the dignity of a guest. Everywhere he should remain a stranger no matter how benevolent, and a critic no matter how appreciative. Were he a mere sensorium, without his own purposes, moral categories and points of reference, he might as well have left those variegated natives to lead their lives undisturbed and unvisited. They would have got on the more comfortably without him, and he the more inexpensively, without them, at home. The traveller should be an artist, recomposing what he sees; then he can carry away the picture and add it to a transmissible fund of wisdom, not as further miscellaneous experience but as a corrected view of the truth.

My moral allegiance becomes definite. Perhaps if in youth I had been able to satisfy my desire to travel, the lack of a fixed background, material and moral, might have reduced me to a vain wanderer. Circumstances prevented. I was tethered, even when I began to cross and recross the Atlantic, to Avila and to Boston, and allowed only an occasional halt between. My real nucleus was this combination, not easily unified. By the time I was free, I was no longer young. The Mohammedan countries, India and China no longer tempted me. If materially I was less attached than ever to any particular spot, morally my native sphere had become definite. I was a child of Christendom: my heritage was that of Greece, of Rome ancient and modern, and of the literature and philosophy of Europe. Christian history and art contained all my spiritual traditions, my intellectual and moral language. There would have been no danger, however far afield I had travelled, of losing my moorings: and foreign things had no meaning for me except as they offered interesting analogies or contrasts for deepening my sense of my ancestral world.

This fidelity of mine to my origins showed itself indirectly even before I was able to choose my way. When in 1887 I went to Gibraltar by sea from Malaga, and saw Mount Atlas, it was the idea rather than the image that arrested me, glorious as this image was; and when I returned there in 1891, this time from America, and crossed to Tangiers with some steamer acquaintances, this first glimpse of something beyond Christendom chilled rather than excited my desire for exploration. This is the more remarkable in that one of those acquaintances was the painter John Sargent. He was then at work preparing his decorations for the Boston Public Library, and intent on finding figures and especially costumes suitable for his Hebrew Prophets; and in Spain he wished to reexamine the dressed wooden images of the Mater Dolorosa, in view of a Madonna that he meant to introduce into his design for the other end of the same hall. His appreciation of these so Spanish images appealed to me. Without being a pre-Raphaelite, he had altogether outgrown Protestant shyness in religious art, and felt the deep passion in it. Nevertheless, we saw nothing in Tangiers that was more than curious: like the customs officers, three venerable old men sitting cross-legged on a raised bench, like a counter, who, having been bribed by my friends' courier, grandly motioned for our valises to pass unexamined. We saw some Jewish houses, not being admitted into the Moslem ones; and while Sargent and the others bargained for all sorts of treasures, I bought a pink and gold cloak, that for years afterwards decorated my wall, and that Sargent said was Venetian stuff woven with half moons expressly for the Oriental market. Two other pictures only remained in my memory of sights in Tangiers, which was then in all its primitive squalor: the marketplace with men, asses, sheep, and camels all lying together on the bare earth, amid puddles and rubbish; and on a slight eminence not far off, a storyteller reciting, like Homer, his military legends (so I was informed) with great calmness and long pauses, to an audience of a few scattered individuals, no less calm and otiose than himself. Yes, here was the antique background to our civilisation, important to remember; but I was sure that if we reverted to it, even as mere students and historians, it would seem tedious, filthy and trivial. In any case, I would let others inquire, and trust to their reports. Therefore, when two years later, I was again at Gibraltar, I let my American fellow-travellers go to Tangiers alone, and spent a meditative day or two seeing what was to be seen from the Rock.

I plan my only real travels.

It was only after ten more years of routine, filled with occupations that leave no memories, that I found myself with two clear summers and one winter before me, for my first real travels. I might have gone to India, China, and Japan, had I been younger and in the mood of the Arabian Nights; but I was middle-aged, and in the mood of Gibbon. *The Life of Reason* was then in the press. What a pity that I couldn't have rested and travelled before writing that book! It would have been richer in substance and purer in form. At least, I could rest now, and hope that the impurities would evaporate from my mind in the fresh air and light of history. My journey would be only over beaten paths, leisurely, comfortable, solitary, towards the fountains of my own past. I would visit, as far as practicable, the scenes where that past took shape and see *in situ* the ruins that remain of it. Perhaps this might help me to distinguish the part of my heritage that is hopelessly dead from the part that still has the seeds of the future in it. European life surely has a hereditary skeleton, an indispensable structure, that must be reproduced, of course with variations, so long as moral continuity and progress remain possible in our world.

A tour in Southern Italy for a curtain-raiser.

The first scene in this drama should properly be Egypt; and from there tradition would bifurcate, one stream running to Palestine and western Asia, the source of our religion, and another stream running to Greece, the source of our art, literature, politics, and philosophy. But the exigencies of travel and of the seasons didn't allow me to take things in strictly historical order. Tourists were not conveyed to Egypt before mid-winter, and there were side-shows, derivative episodes nearer home that might be taken by the way. From Paris, where I had finished and sent off my last batch of manuscript, I went straight to Naples. It was September, still summer, but not unpleasant for a lazy man; and in an upper room at Bertolini's, with a wide view, I spent a few weeks of pleasant repose. I saw what was then visible of Pompeii; nothing of Herculaneum except at the museum; and only the very surface of life in the town. But the atmosphere was already more balmy, more unconstrained, more animal, than in the north; I had moved several degrees towards the equator of the moral sphere. And not merely by way of relaxation; for I went to Paestum, and there saw Doric temples for the first time, symbols of severity, simplicity, harmony, and strength. There was the pure vein to be traced in the quartz of Roman accumulations and grossness; and I followed that vein back to Sicily.

Philosophic reflections at Paestum. Doric purity is not a thing to be expected again in history, at least not yet. It indicates a people that knows its small place in the universe and yet asserts its dignity. In early Christian art there may be simplicity and *naïveté*, but never self-knowledge. The aspiration in it is childlike. For anything like Doric fortitude in the West we must look to the castles, not to the churches; and the castles are Christian only by association. Here then was an ultimate point of reference, a principle of manly purity, to mark one extreme in the moral scale of all human arts, and to give me the points of the compass in my travels. And by a curious chance, during this same excursion to Paestum, I came upon the opposite extreme of the moral scale also, in a form that I have never forgotten. The reader may think it trivial, but I assure him that to me it has the most serious, the most horrible, significance.

Satan at La Cava. At Paestum there was only the railway station and no hotel, but travellers might spend the night comfortably at La Cava, not far away. I had done so, and in the morning was waiting at the station for the train to Naples. The only other persons on the platform were a short fat middle-aged man and a little girl, evidently his daughter. In the stillness of the country air I could hear their conversation. The child was asking questions about the railway buildings, the rails, and the switches. "Where does that other line go?" she asked as if the matter interested her greatly. "Oh, you can see", the father replied, slightly bored, "It runs into that warehouse." "It doesn't go beyond?" "No. It stops there." "And where does this line go?" "To Naples." "And does it end there?" "No, it never ends. It goes on for ever." "*Non finisce mai?*" the girl repeated in a changed voice. "*Allora Iddio l'ha fatto?*" "No," said her father dryly, "God didn't make it. It was made by the hand of man. *Le braccia dell'uomo l'hanno fatto.*" And he puffed his cigar with a defiant resentful self-satisfaction as if he were addressing a meeting of conspirators.

The modern mentality. I could understand the irritation of this vulgarian, disturbed in his secret thoughts by so many childish questions. He was some small official or tradesman of the Left, probably a Free Mason, and proud to utter the great truth that man had made the railway. God might have made the stars and the deserts and all other useless things, but everything good and progressive was the work of man. And it had been mere impatience that led him to say that the Naples line never ended. Of course it couldn't run on for ever in a straight line. The child must have known that the earth is round, and that the continents are surrounded by water. The railways must stop at the sea, or come round in a circle. But the poor little girl's imagination had been excited and deranged by religious fables. When would such follies die out?

Commonplaces that had been dinned all my life into my ears: yet somehow this little scene shocked me. I saw the claw of Satan strike that child's soul and try to kill the idea of God in it. Why should I mind that? Was the idea of God alive at all in me? No: if you mean the traditional idea. But that was a symbol, vague, variable, mythical, anthropomorphic; the symbol for an overwhelming reality, a symbol that named and unified in human speech the incalculable powers on which our destiny depends. To observe, record, and measure the method by which these powers operate is not to banish the idea of God; it is what the Hebrews called meditating on his ways. The modern hatred of religion is not, like that of the Greek philosophers, a hatred of poetry, for which they wished to substitute cosmology, mathematics, or dialectic, still maintaining the reverence of man for what is super-human. The modern hatred of religion is hatred of the truth, hatred of all sublimity, hatred of the laughter of the gods. It is puerile human vanity trying to justify itself by a lie. Here, then, most opportunely, at the railway station returning from Paestum, where I had been admiring the courage and the dignity with which the Dorians recognised their place in nature, and filled it to perfection, I found the brutal expression of the opposite mood, the mood of impatience, conceit, low-minded ambition, mechanical inflation, and the worship of material comforts.

It is essentially perennial but so is the need of escaping from it. In saying this I don't forget that all phases of life are equally natural and spontaneous, and that some animals are furiously busy while others are calm and brave. Each has its troubles and dangers, and each sometimes has its rewards. But I was setting out on my travels with a moral personal interest, not with a scientific one. I wished to clarify and intensify my sense of the humanly beautiful. I wished to measure the distance and the steps between rational life, lived in view of the truth, and blind miscellaneous living. The world has always been filled with the latter; but in classical antiquity collectively, and in modern times individually, there has been an aspiration to look before you live; and this aspiration has left traces of its passage in monuments and maxims that it is my particular desire to understand. These are the maxims and monuments of human wisdom. I had already studied the maxims; now I wished to have a glimpse of the monuments, and a hint of the conditions that had made them possible. On, then, to Sicily.

A glance at Northern Sicily.   It was not yet the season for tourists and at Taormina, my first halt, I found no vehicle at the station, and when at last I got a lift in a local cart, with some difficulty I reached my hotel, where nobody was expected, and I was served a part of my host's supper. Although the weather was good, somehow the place seemed desolate, and it was impossible to fall into the mood of luxurious enjoyment appropriate to the scene. Like Capri, where I have never been tempted to stay, Taormina seems rather a refuge for moral invalids, favourable for a long convalescence or for a slow death. I went on to Palermo. Very like a Spanish provincial city, no doubt with its special charm when you acquired a domicile and corresponding habits; but for me it proved merely the starting point for two excursions: One to Cefalù, for the sea and sunlight and the picturesque, the other to Monreale, for the Byzantine architecture and mosaics. I am no connoisseur or even amateur of the special luxurious arts, carpets, tapestry, carvings, mosaics, iron or silver work. I like it all, as I like stained glass, as an enrichment, as an element in the beauty of something greater; and such things seem to me to require the life to which they belonged, if they are not to seem mere relics, old finery looking a little childish as well as shabby in its neglected gorgeousness. Moreover, for me on this journey, the Byzantine should come at the end, in Santa Sophia.

A look at Agrigentum.   I felt more joyful and breathed more freely, when I passed to the southern coast, and saw something Greek. Agrigentum, in its desolation, left much to the imagination, but stirred it deeply. Not so much the ruins as the magnificent site, as if all the seven hills of Rome had been linked together in a chain, doubled in height, and been made to overhang the forum and the lower town in a broad curve. That vast Acropolis must have been a sublime thing. Outwards, on the convex side, it is a sheer precipice; inwards its horns descend to the plain and make it accessible. One of these horns is occupied by what remains of the town. I climbed to the top, partly by steps. There was a little square, with a café, but no vestiges of the temples that must have stood there; for a reward I saw some large white goats, apparently clean as lambs, browsing among the steep lanes or perched upon the stone enclosures that bordered them. These ancient fortresses, in the long days of peace, must have been very domestic and country-like, little removed from the farms that surrounded them in the simplicity and monotony of their ways. Dull, except for the recurring festivals and the frequent wars, yet well fitted, in both aspects, to fix the character of tragedy and comedy, as the Greeks fixed it, limited, monotonous, liturgical, but intensely felt, profoundly human, wonderfully central and perfect.

Agrigentum was a colony, suddenly rich, like an American mushroom city, short-lived and ruined even more suddenly than it had grown up; but for its day it was enormous, and it gave birth to a great poet-philosopher, the model of Lucretius, and a grander personage, with his tragic end soon enveloped in legend. Both Lucretius and Empedocles are said to have killed themselves, or voluntarily become gods; in any case they saw the world as the gods would; in other words, as we all should if we could surmount our accidental humanity and let the pure spirit in us speak through our mouths. I wonder if a mushroom civilisation, by its very thinness and sudden brilliancy, like fire in straw, may not be easier for the spirit to profit by and to transcend than a more deeply rooted tradition.

A week at Syracuse.   My last halt in Sicily was at Syracuse, where I chanced upon a pleasant small hotel, with views towards the sea, and at once established a routine for the day, which I might have kept up indefinitely. It was already possible for me to lead my chosen life anywhere, provided the material conditions were favourable and unobtrusive. I could have stayed on at Syracuse all winter. I think it was there that I read and despatched the first proofs of *The Life of Reason*. My daily walk usually took me to ruins of the Greek theatre, past what must have been the agora of the upper town in antiquity, where the principal temple remains, turned into the cathedral. This transformation excited my architectural fancy. To turn a Greek temple into a Christian church all you need do is to wall up the peristyle, leaving a window in the upper part of each space between the columns, and then pierce arches in the side walls of the cella. Your interior then occupies the whole or nearly the whole of the temple platform; place an altar where the statue of the god had stood, and you have a complete church: even a great church, if you are prudent enough to retain a narthex before the inner door, and an ambulatory behind the altar. This was not done as I could wish at Syracuse; but the great columns were not walled up so as to be wholly concealed, and the line of the pediment remained visible, if not uninterrupted. The transformation had not been the work of one artist, but of many bishops; yet it allows enough to subsist of the ancient temple to make evident the continuity of worship and the identity of civic function in this edifice for three thousand years.

What surprised me at Syracuse was the slight elevation above the sea of Ortygia, the old castle occupied by the modern town. I had imagined a much loftier citadel, a great marine acropolis; but the defences must have been mainly artificial. There must have been sea-walls as at Tyre round most of the peninsula and great towers and gates upon the isthmus. But today, in walking out towards the theatre or towards the northern quarters where Epipolae extended, you hardly felt any change in height or defensibility. Perhaps my expectations had been raised by the grandeur of the acropolis at Agrigentum; I had to revise my ideal of Syracuse, and remember that the site of Ortygia was chosen, like that of Tyre or of Venice, for being surrounded by water, not for being unscalable from the land: and I began a sonnet that never went beyond the first two lines, which contained all that I had to utter about these places:

> Renowned Ortygia, castle of the sea,
> And Agrigentum, castle of the air.

After this spell of solitude among ruins, I returned to take ship at Naples and found myself in the social bosom of dear old Boston. Mrs. Beal, my friend's mother, was on board with a companion, and it was arranged that I should join the party. I was glad to do so. Mrs. Beal had always been friendly and confidential, I could stand for a while to her *in loco filii*; she, with her courier and maid and companion, would tell me all the facts about everything, and yet leave me free enough to observe them for myself.

Reveries in sight of Crete.   We saw, during a calm voyage, the mountains of Crete, the birthplace of Zeus. Afterwards in Athens, I heard Evans, the archeologist, talk at table about his discoveries there. Tempting, from a distance, to explore those mountains and to study those ruins; yet though I felt the attraction strongly, I nursed no illusions about it and suffered only a theoretical pang at having to renounce it all. In reality, it would have been a terrible bore and far beyond my physical endurance and agility. Yet to read about prehistoric

Crete, excites me always, no matter how imaginative or untrustworthy the author may be. Spengler may dream what he chooses about unknown civilisations, and Racine may render mythology credible and courtly, like the myths in the tapestries of modern palaces. I like to ponder on the wonders of Crete. It was there that Plato, in the *Laws*, thought of founding his ideal city. In such sea-girt mountains I like to imagine it, and I repeat, as an incantation, the words of Phèdre to the son of Theseus:

> *Pourquoi, trop jeune encor, ne pûtes-vous alors*
> *Entrer dans le vaisseau qui le mit sur nos bords?*
> *Par vous aurait péri le monstre de la Crète,*
> *Malgré tous les détours de sa vaste retraite.*

But the monster, though he transforms his monstrosity, is perennial; and it is the pure hero, who might have extinguished monstrosity, that dies young, entangled in the monstrous luxuriance of nature, that pays no heed to perfection.

Modern incongruities. The insults with which time pursues its noblest creations appeared at once in the harbour of Port Said. I knew I was in Egypt, yet I saw nothing but huge iron freight steamers, higher than the shore, and the bustle and sordid confusion of a landing stage and a railway station. However, we were not booked to stay there, and soon found ourselves in a quiet hotel in Cairo. No distinction, no dominant character in that city: a mixture of incongruities. Only one impression, as usual architectural, remains of that week in what was and is a great focus of Mohammedan life: the one or two great mosques that we visited. It was a surprise to me, thinking of Cordova, to see them so high, so majestic. The memory of Babylon and Assyria, or the shadow of the ancient temples in Egypt itself, must have led the Moslem builders to enlarge their scale, and to be imposing; whereas the note I expected in a Mohammedan place of worship was rather that it should be secluded, exquisite, and devotional. However my acquaintance with the religious sentiment of Islam was very slight, and I procured a French translation of the Koran to read during our trip up and down the Nile.

A day alone at Karnak. The flat-bottomed river steamer in which I was to live for a month was comfortable, and the food satisfactory. My cabin was at the end of one of the verandahs, so that I could sit by my open door, which was also the window, and watch the river and the bank undisturbed. I made all the excursions as prescribed except one. We were to stop three nights at Luxor. On the first day I went with the rest to view the ruins at Karnak; but on the next day, when the party was conducted to the Tombs of the Kings—a particularly long donkey-ride with a picnic at the ruins—I seceded. The attraction at the Tombs of the Kings was then merely pictorial: the architecture was not important; while at Karnak I had seen one of the wonders of the world, and I wished to go again, alone and on foot, to see it at leisure. This was my best day in Egypt. I climbed the great pylon; I wandered among the ruins; I lingered in the great hall, trying to evoke an image of what it must have been in its glory; I admired the minor temple with its forecourt of colossal statues serving as columns; but most of all I felt the spell of the inner sanctuary, approached by a sort of labyrinth of passages interlocked, and lighted only by cracks left purposely here and there between the immense blocks of stone that formed the walls and the ceiling. In the inmost chamber there was now nothing: but I could imagine the glittering antique image that must have stood there (like the Virgin of the Pillar at Saragossa, only colossal) which the High Priest, barefoot and duly vested, may have approached with great ceremony perhaps once a year. From all other eyes this inner splendour would have been for ever concealed. How profoundly appropriate, for all its grotesque animal worship and solar myths, this ancient worship was to the real status of man! How childish our metaphysical moralisms and psychologisms seem in comparison!

Advantage of maturity in the arts. For beauty, apart from grandeur and significance, only two or three heads and the temple at Denderah remain in my memory. The treasures of the Kings' tombs had not yet been unearthed, and in any case belong to decorative rather than to constructive art. Denderah, being late (and those heads also, perhaps), reflected Greek influence, and doubtless on that account were easier for me to appreciate. I am not ashamed of liking late styles. They ought to be the surest expression of human taste, since technique has been mastered and accidental mannerisms have been overcome; only the volume and seriousness of inspiration may be wanting, unless the artist is able to transcend and rebuke his epoch, as the tragedians and Socrates and Plato could do in Athens. Then we obtain the maturity of lateness with an early inspiration revived as philosophy or religion.

The Pyramids and the lesson of Egypt. Of course we went to the Pyramids. The tourist talk and the tourist foreground dominated; the great question was whether we should ride or not ride a camel, ascend or not ascend the great pyramid, pulled up at each step (four feet high) by an acrobatic Arab; and little grinning English Tommies were crawling over the Sphinx. I said to myself: *Non raggionam di lor, ma guarda e passa.* It was not altogether easy to look. Sand had half buried the base of all these monuments, and we were there, pert and self-conscious pygmies, incapable of imagining or understanding what they signified, and playing with their ruins like a child with his rocking-horse. There remained only the vain traveller's satisfaction in saying, yes, I have been there, I have seen the Pyramids; and the fact of having seen them, however flightily, certainly leaves in the psyche a material *point d'appui* for anything that we may otherwise learn about them. I have since read two or three books about Egypt, and there have been notorious discoveries, so that nowadays a young girl can't stand still in the street without reproducing the outlines of the ancient Egyptians. This was probably not the immortality for which they cared so much; but I am at a loss to conceive what that immortality could have been. It is not a subject to which anything in me responds. Let the dead, I say, bury their dead; let those who have no sense for eternity try to prolong their existence by desiccating their bodies or disembodying their souls. It is in either case a sham, ghastly or ghostly. Leaving that, I thank the Egyptians for the standard they have set up for mankind in the solidity of their architecture. We may refine all we like; unless we rival or surpass that solidity, that superhuman permanence, those symbols of silent potentiality and eternal peace, we shall always remain secondary, temporary, capricious, and childish. We shall always be doing things that are partial failures, that we must abandon at once for something different, and that even when they are in fashion, disquiet us more than they satisfy.

Palestine the cradle of fanaticism. It was not as a pious pilgrim that I went to Palestine; nothing that I could expect to find there would affect my personal religion or philosophy. I went as a sceptic, to visit the birthplace of religion in others and if possible to understand that religion better. These parched Semitic deserts have been the fountain of inspiration to the whole modern West and to a great part of the East; only pagan antiquity, India, and China have reflected rationally upon the subject, and leaving inspiration to take the forms it likes, have naturalised it in a calm philosophy. Nor was the expression

of religion in art, as in Europe and in Egypt, that which I looked for
here. Here the chief art was religious eloquence, and that can be
studied more quietly by one's own fireside. The rest was barbarous
and secondary. But the primitive condition of the country—then (1905)
still under Turkish rule—the mixture of races, languages, and costumes,
the religious feuds, the medley of ruins and shrines, and the petrified
deathlike aspect of these ravines and river-beds without water, and
these hills without verdure, formed an ominous theme for historical
meditation.

First contact   I was now alone, having parted from Mrs. Beal at
with Asia.   Assouan. She was bound further up the Nile; but with
the first cataract, the great dam, and the half submerged temple of
Phylae my journey had come to its proper end. Nubia lay beyond my
range: sun, sand, and natives were nothing to my purpose. I had made
for the Holy Land in the only way then practicable, by sea to Jaffa.
The little port, which we entered in a row-boat by scooting on the
top of a wave between two rocks, the little town clinging to the face
of the cliffs, and the little railway climbing the mountains to Jerusalem,
were much to my taste: small, indifferent material things, to be disregarded by souls full of great passions. And the country, not unlike
Castile, all rock and moor, also preached frugality, austerity, reserve.
It taught the overfed, overdressed, overworked child of the West how
unnecessary were most of his burdens.

A mechanical   In Jerusalem I was in the hands of a guide assigned
guide to   to me by Cook's Agency, a short middle-aged native
closed doors.   who spoke English and had been converted to Anglicanism from his doubtless Jewish affiliations. He had no sense for the
matters, historical and artistic, that really interested me, and thought
it his duty merely to point out sites and name names, none of which
were worth remembering. I staid three weeks in Jerusalem, waiting
for the rain to stop, for I had planned to go by carriage through
Samaria and Galilee to Damascus. It would have been a memorable
trip; but the roads, people said, would be impossible, and I finally
gave up the idea. So long a stay rather taxed my poor guide's ingenuity
to think of new sights to show me; but some of the last were among
the best. For instance, he took me one day to a Greek monastery
some miles away in the country; the drive was not uninteresting, and
the glimpse of the religious life of the Orthodox, and of their persons,
was just what I was looking for and seldom found. My guide, while
not unknown or turned away, seemed not to be on very good terms

with the natives of any persuasion: doubtless they thought him a renegade for not being converted to their own sect. I seemed to be an object of curiosity to these Greek monks, as much as they were to me. Unfortunately, I couldn't say anything to them directly; but we exchanged courtesies through the interpreter. Meantime I observed their aspect and ways. Nothing religious: a sort of childish animality; no trace of Greek features, except in some the very large, thick-lidded eyes. They were all rather small, and of course long-haired and bearded. One couldn't help thinking of Christ, who no doubt in the pictures has been made to look somewhat like them: but to me the assimilation was distinctly unpleasant. Christ should never be painted to look like a savage or like a woman. There should be the dazzling apparition of a god, breaking through an ascetic figure.

Another afternoon, on foot, we went to a Catholic monastery on the Mount of Olives. Here the trouble with my guide didn't matter. An Italian monk showed us the garden; I at once established friendly relations; and he explained to me that the ancient olive was not the same that had stood there in Christ's time, but was an offshoot of it; they had planted other offshoots near by, against the time when the present hollow contorted old tree should crumble altogether; and he gave me a few leaves of this, which I sent in a letter to Mercedes. I felt at home: my vocation to live in Italy began to show itself.

The Dead Sea. We had of course been to Jericho, the Jordan, and the shores of the Dead Sea. Geographically, this was of the highest interest. What a cleft in the crust of the earth, to prove how rotten it is inside! The view across the Dead Sea from the Mount of Olives, with the mountains of Moab opposite, shows the same cleft in a grander light: the rottenness is not felt, only the sublimity of the depths and the heights, the gamut of nature keyed up to that of the Hebrew prophets.

As to Christian associations, legendary or historical, my own ignorance and the insensibility of my guide completely smothered them. I saw everything, but without even a borrowed illusion or devotion, such as I could have caught easily from a pious Catholic. Turkish soldiers kept guard at the supposed birthplace of Christ, lest Christian sects should come to blows over it; and everywhere ecclesiastical quarrels and modern desecration vulgarised sacred and poetic things.

My dream of romantic Islam. Of the Mussulmans I had a better opinion: they were openly warlike, openly sensual, proud, chivalrous, and capable of friendship. They were exquisite and manly, bold and bravely resigned to the will of God. They didn't overestimate their own importance in the universe; but they despised a servile mind. All this, however, was a mere ideal, a fancy of my own; I had no means of verifying or disproving it. It would have required a youthful and adventurous courage to explore the East like a Doughty or a Charles de Foucault, and in the first place a sportsman's agility and endurance, with a perfect command of Arabic. I was reduced to catching glimpses here and there of men and manners, and filling in the rest with memories of the Arabian Nights. My reading of the Koran had not awakened me to anything new: the lyric parts were inferior to the Psalms, and the legends inferior to those in the Old Testament; whereas to compare with the parables and the maxims of the New Testament there was absolutely nothing. Ritual sublimity the Koran, in the original, may well possess. Eloquence and nobleness belong to speech even in Spain, and they have a quality that is not Roman, but must be Moorish.

The Thousand and One Nights as an introduction to the East.   As to the Arabian Nights, I had feasted on them recently with unexpected pleasure. What I had read of them in boyhood had inspired me with a priggish contempt. I thought the tales (as they are) chaotic and demoralising, although I read them in a drastically expurgated translation. But now Mrs. Berenson, who had charitably received me at Settignano when I was ill with a bad catarrh, had piled the sixteen volumes of the French version of Mardrus upon the table by my bedside; and if they didn't cure me, at least they reconciled me to being laid up. The view of life, like the life reviewed, is still chaotic; and I can understand the dislike expressed by pious Moslems at having them regarded as true pictures of their family life. The pictures belong to the general tradition of the whole East, India and China included: they are satirical, poetical, realistic, exquisite, and entertaining. The exaggeration, Gargantuan or love-sick, has irony in it; the popular story-teller indulges our unrestrained dreams, and at the same time laughs at them. The ribaldry renders all this more piquant and joyous than it otherwise would be; also less narcotic and vainly imaginary, because sensuality after all belongs to real life, and experience can at once justify the interest in it and discount the illusion. I don't find the Arabian Nights, unexpurgated, demoralising, as I did, expurgated, when I was a boy. I see now that they are playful, and how much they adorn and embroider the commonplaces that they play upon. There is indeed no moralising in them, nothing by way of a lesson; wisdom and poetry only in scraps, comedy only in episodes, tragedy hardly at all. Yet we have the daily texture of life spread before us in its crudity and in its magic: the experience and imagination of an unabashed creature that understands nothing, but meets everything with the strength and cunning of a man and the impulses of a child.

Scenes in Damascus.   In Damascus I remembered the judgment that my young friend Duer Irving had passed on Seville. Seville was nothing unless you had a horse and a love-affair, and then it was everything. The horse and the love-affair being out of the question for me at Damascus, the place threatened to mean nothing to me: yet that was not altogether the case. The suk was the best I saw in the East; there was also a most picturesque market or exchange or caravansary, where merchants and travellers gathered, where the merchandise was on view, and where the central fountain, under the open sky, and the surrounding domes and cloisters, produced most wonderful effects of light and shade. Here leisure and business, profit and enchantment, were not divided. The suk was comparatively lofty and wide, like the nave of a church, with much the same effects of light, for it was covered partly by stone arches, partly by wooden roofs, and in places only by awnings, so that patches of sunlight shone out here and there, to dazzle the eye and deepen the grateful shadows of the rest. The ground was earth, to be trodden by beasts of burden, led in familiarly without undue regard for pedestrians; and the booths on either side for the most part had no depth, but displayed all their wares within reach of the hand. One of these booths especially attracted my attention, and as a stubborn client happened one day to be bargaining and making his choice for half an hour, I was able to watch the scene unmolested at a discreet distance. It was a carpet shop. There was a broad counter in front, at one end of which sat the venerable merchant, impassive and apparently indifferent, dressed in black, red, and white, with a long grey beard. Behind him were two rows of rugs rolled up and standing on their edges, like so many barrels. The quality, colours, and pattern of each were sufficiently visible to entice the eye, and provoke a request that the precious thing should be unfolded. Then the youthful assistant would leap up from the other end of the counter, pull the particular carpet down and spread it out, over the counter or if need be on the ground outside. This agile young man was beautifully dressed and fit to represent any of the adolescents in the Arabian Nights. He wore a red fez, a white and green striped tunic reaching down to the ankles, with tight sleeves, but growing full at the bottom and held together at the waist by an ample sash, that served also for pockets, and was made of a yellow brocaded stuff; and he was shod with yellow babouches. After many rugs, some of them lovely, had been spread out and rolled up again, he had to bring down and extend the heaviest of all, a great red one that covered the whole width of the road; but I didn't stay to see whether the bargain was finally struck. A great camel was coming up the path: he couldn't be allowed to tread on that invaluable carpet, so up it had to come again in the twinkling of an eye; and I took advantage of the excitement to slip away. It is an awkward position for the curious not to wish to buy anything: if they look, the tradesman at once thinks he has a likely customer, and begins to exhibit and praise his wares. You feel like an intruder and have to hurry away. For this reason I have never been able to examine precious objects, even books, except in shop windows.

Historical speculations at Baalbek. Of architectural beauties I found little in Damascus; it was at Baalbek, on the way back, that the imagination was stirred, if not with beauty, at least with wonder. The scale and extent of the monuments here rivalled the Egyptian, while the style and the religious inspiration remained Greek. Perhaps of all periods in history the Hellenistic, between Alexander and Caesar, corresponds best to my feeling. In reading Plutarch, who lived later himself, but most of whose heroes lived earlier, I am put out by his doctrinaire morality, as if all men and ages ought to follow the same model; also by the limitations of the older heroes' minds. They were wonderful, they were perfect, but they were slaves to local traditions and special passions. The full grown human soul should respect all traditions and understand all passions; at the same time it should possess and embody a particular culture, without any unmanly re-laxation or mystical neutrality. Justice is one thing, indecision is another, and weak. If you allow all men to live according to their genuine natures, you must assert your own genuine nature and live up to it. Now, with Alexander a great part of the East in fact and the whole world in prospect were introduced into the sphere of the West, into the narrow military life of the ancient city: yet the gods of the city, the gods of the open rational philosophic mind, were retained to preside over a universal empire. Heliopolis, the City of the Sun, seemed to me to represent this ideal fusion. It was immense like the East, but unlike the East it was not miscellaneous. The miscellaneous East very soon overwhelmed it, as the miscellaneous North overwhelmed the Western Empire. Yet ruins give ground for hope; for although nothing can last for ever, now and then good seasons may return.

Glimpses of Greek landscape. On the way from Beirut to Athens, we saw the coasts of Cyprus and Rhodes, and stopped at a small island and then at Samos. In these islands I first trod Hellenic ground, but without emotion: hardly a stone, hardly a head, reminded me of Hellas. Athens itself, for the most part, was uninspiring. I engaged a youngish man, a Cypriot journalist, as a guide and as teacher of Greek; but in both respects, in my two months at Athens, I gathered little new knowledge. The social foreground was too cosmopolitan, and the material foreground too ugly and insignificant. We went on one excursion, intending to reach Delphi; but at Corinth we found that the steamer had been purloined by a private pleasure-party, and I had to be satisfied with a trip to Nauplia, to Tiryns and Mycenae, and to Epidaurus. This last, my most remote point, proved the most inspiring. Whether it was the light and the solitude, the steepness of the pit, the completeness of the theatre (except for the stage) or the sombre wooded hills above, somehow all the poetry of early Greece seemed to flood the place: small, heroic, earthly, open to sea and sky, lyric, and divinely haunted.

Notes on the Acropolis. In the Acropolis I had two or three unexpected intuitions. One regarded the vitality, the dash, the solidity of Greek architecture. The lion's head at the corner of the immensely projecting cornice in the Parthenon seemed to have all the picturesqueness of a gargoyle: and the entablature was not what its name and usual aspect imply, a wooden beam laid across posts: it was a great wall built up over a foundation of columns, like the wall of the Doge's palace in Venice, even if not so high. On the other hand, that bold cornice and those broad pediments lent it an even greater dignity. This effect, of the temple raised over the peristyle, was new to me, and important. It removed the reproach that pursues buildings of one storey, of lacking weight and altitude and being set up on stilts, propped up, rather than built. Here the burden carried seemed sufficient to ennoble the bearers, and to justify their stoutness, their number, and their fidelity to one model, like hoplites in a phalanx. This architecture was not merely utilitarian and economical: it was religious and martial.

Beautiful beyond words seemed to me the door and the Ionic porch at the back of the Erechtheum. Byzantine, Saracenic, and Gothic cannot surpass such a thing in loveliness; their advantage lies only in allowing greater variety, so that in a larger and more complex world they could diffuse disparate beauties, more picturesque and romantic than those of Greek buildings.

I renounce travel except in thought.   I left Greece disappointed, not with Greece but with myself. I should have been young and adventurous, knowing the language well, both ancient and modern, and travelling alone, with indefinite time before me. Then, if the historic Ilyssus proved to be a rubbishy ditch in a dusty waste, I could have found another Ilyssus in some mountain gorge in which to bathe my feet like Socrates and Phaedrus, and pass in dialectical thought from sham rhetoric to rational love. But the foreground was a dreadful impediment, and I was the worst of impediments, with my middle-aged ignorance, my academic ties, and my laziness. Hellas must remain for me an ideal, a thing to recompose, as the Evangelists recomposed their idea of Jesus, so as to individualise and replenish their ideal of Christ. The real Greece is dead, pulverised, irrecoverable. There remain only a few words and a few relics that may serve to suggest to us a rational ideal of human life.

Impressions of St. Sophia.   With this the moral object of my journey was attained, or shown to be unattainable; but there remained one more scene to peruse, and I took ship from the Piraeus for Constantinople. Galata, where the hotels are, was nothing; but I could walk across the bridge, guided the first time, afterwards alone, to St. Sophia, the other mosques, and the stray sights of the old city. No exterior effects at St. Sophia, even from a distance. Remove the picturesque accident of the minarets, and you have a flat dome little more beautiful than that of the Pantheon in Rome; in character almost like the Baths of Diocletian. Was this dome intended to be a marvel externally, like that of the Mosque of Omar? In any case, it is a marvel internally: as if a tent held down by a dozen pegs had been lifted by the wind, and crystallised in mid-air. The eye, as it travels down over the great arches to the arcades of the galleries and aisles, is a little distracted by the oblique lines of the Mohammedan carpets and pulpit, and the hideous yellow discs hung high on the walls; but discounting this, and examining things more closely, wonder returns. What columns, what capitals, what walls! Roman luxury refined by oriental taste, Roman grandeur of scale and mass, spiritualised by mystic aspiration. This vast chamber is a sanctuary, regal in magnificence but open to the sky and air; this unity is infinitely rich in detail, this heaven has its hierarchy of dignities and beauties. A theocratic and imperial Church displays its poetry here, as it displays its pride at St. Peter's.

All roads lead to Rome. After this, at once surfeited and disappointed, I wanted to see nothing more, suppressed my love of new places, and stopped only to rest at Buda-Pesth and Vienna. I meant to leave Vienna, at least, for another occasion, when I might make a long stay, and see the Catholic, gay, and courtly aspects of Germany, so utterly ignored in the view of Germany obtainable from America: but I have never been in Vienna again. In fact, I have never again travelled for the sake of travelling. My orbit has become narrower and narrower, dropping one loop-line after another: somewhat as the ball at the gaming-table runs round in smaller and smaller circles, more and more slowly, hesitates at the edge of this socket and that, and finally flops down and settles comfortably into the predestined resting-place. And the predestined socket in my case was Rome: *omnium urbis et orbis ecclesiarum*, says the inscription at the Lateran, *mater et caput*. Mother and head of my moral world, surely, and central enough even today: balmy also, humanly habitable at all seasons, full of ancient and modern and even of recent beauties, and inhabited by a people that more than any other resembles the civilised ancients. I could not be more at home anywhere, while preserving my essential character of stranger and traveller, with the philosophic freedom that this implies. Thus I renounce travel here, where I may still continually travel in thought to all ages and countries and enjoy the divine privilege of ubiquity without moving from my fated centre of gravity and equilibrium.

XXVIII
On the South Downs

The top of the South Downs. Not far from Petersfield in Hampshire, just above the village of South Harting, a steep road climbs up the side of the Downs. The valley, as you ascend, begins to look more and more like a map, with its variegated patches of green fields, hedgerows and woods, and an occasional house that seems remarkably neat and toylike in the distance. At the top, the back of the Downs becomes rolling and bare, with rough heather and grass and here and there a copse in the hollows. The sweep of the horizon is unbroken all round, the wind blows free and invigorating, and in clear weather the sparkling line of the Channel is visible, and the Isle of Wight. The silence is primeval. Here, sheltered in part by some high hedges that enclosed squares of grass as if for tennis courts or gardens, stood a little white pavilion with a flag-staff; the cottage for the man once in charge of the "semaphore" or signal service from London to Portsmouth. That form of communication was now obsolete, although bonfires were still occasionally lighted on the topmost knoll. I don't know by what chance this spot attracted Russell's attention, but it appealed to his love of space and of unchallenged dominion. There was not a house in sight, and a vast stretch of moor and woodland was available for purchase. He bought it, using it at first as a retreat for week-ends and holidays, but eventually enlarged it, put on another storey, a library in a wing, and even a tower, made roads, and turned it into his chief residence.

The natives for some reason had fallen into the habit of calling the place the telegraph house. Russell was not sensitive to the magic of names. He had consented, I suppose at the Scotts' suggestion, to call his ugly villa at Maidenhead *Amberley Cottage*, Amberley being his second title, by which his father had been known; and now when he had a place of some character and potential beauty he adopted for it that absurd name, *Telegraph House*. Soon, however, in the jolly English way, the absurdity was domesticated, and everybody called the place

T.H. It was comfortable, had no pretensions, and yet a magnificent position, a wild and varied domain, and the charm of solitude and freedom. I visited it repeatedly, during thirty-two years, under its three mistresses, all three of whom I found hospitable and friendly; and of all places it is perhaps the place where I have breathed most freely.

A *fauxménage*. When first Russell took me there, no road existed within the grounds, and the cart that met us at the nearest country station cut deep ruts in the grassy hillside as we wound and tilted, like a boat over the waves, up to the little house. I had expected that we should be alone there, in a sort of bungalow; but at the door we were welcomed by two modest-looking women, evidently mother and daughter, who smiled and spoke not exactly as servants would. Mrs. Turner, for so the mother was called, must be, I thought, a sort of landlady or housekeeper; and then I remembered, on hearing the daughter called Martha, that a Martha Turner had been the secretary at Swinburne & Co., Engineers, where Russell was a partner. When those ladies unhesitatingly sat down at table with us, I began to understand how matters stood. Martha Turner was now his private secretary. He was a married man unable to get a divorce, because Lady Scott, no less proper if more fashionable than Mrs. Turner, chaperoned her daughter everywhere, even to hotels where the young man of the moment occupied the adjoining room. Nevertheless, Russell was engaged to be married to Martha Turner prospectively, in case he should ever be free: and meantime he occupied the room next to hers and her mother's at T.H. To non-plus Mrs. Grundy, his identity was concealed from the servants and from people at the village; Mrs. Turner was the legal tenant, and all letters had to be addressed under cover to her. He was only Martha's young man who came for an occasional visit.

Good Martha Turner. I never disliked Martha Turner. She was a clean honest young woman, reasonable, docile, with a good complexion and a copy-book hand. She was the absolute slave and adorer of her lord and master, and juster to him than his other lady-loves. It must not be supposed that in this case or in that of Emma Billings a promise of marriage was a treacherous means of seduction. There was no need of such a promise. Talk of marriage may have come in, in both cases, as a vague ideal; but Martha Turner was honest enough to know that her love-affair was its own reward. The motive force had not been ambition to be a countess: it had been old, simple, irresistible human nature. She loved him truly and was too faithful to rebel at anything. A separation was inevitable, I don't know on what terms they managed it; but he never wholly deserted her as a friend or perhaps even as a lover. There was nothing in him of the poet or the Don Juan, nothing of the gallant, fanciful, volatile lover. His ideal was the home, or several homes: in a polygamous way he was essentially the faithful husband, like Isaac and Jacob, or like Louis the Fourteenth. Had he been an Eastern potentate or a very rich man he might have managed better, keeping all his wives going at once in separate establishments. But in England that was inadmissible. He wanted each wife to be his legal spouse, as did Henry the Eighth; and they too demanded it. Hence his embarrassments and their tears.

Russell at Harvard again.   This idyl had a romantic setting, worthy of Rousseau; but the conversation at table was like that in a respectable boarding-house; and Russell was discretion personified, explaining nothing, and leaving me to gather my impressions undisturbed. That was in 1891; I saw and heard nothing of T.H. or Martha Turner for the next two years; but in July 1894, when for various reasons I was lying low in America, a new chapter opened in this romance. "I was so glad", Russell wrote, "to get your cable and to know that I shall find you in Cambridge . . . It would be so nice of you if you would get me lodgings in Cambridge or a room in an hotel—anyway so long as I am near where you are." Why he should so unexpectedly come to America was a mystery; but I knew that he liked long slow sea voyages, and was not surprised that he should choose the *Cephalonia*, the most Bostonian of Boston boats, for the trip. When people cable to you, and suddenly express an affectionate desire to be near where you are, though that place be Cambridge, Massachusetts, in August, it is a sure sign of trouble; and I was rather puzzled on my part how to find a suitable place where Russell might lodge. I was living at my mother's in Roxbury, where we couldn't ask him to stay; no hotel existed in Cambridge and no lodgings of the English sort, with a sitting-room and food served separately. I could move, however, to my rooms in the Yard, and put him up at the Colonial Club where the restaurant was in working order, and pleasantly deserted. Except for the extreme heat, this arrangement proved pleasant enough. My room was comparatively cool and comfortable, with an outlook on trees and grass, and not much noise, and I took my meals with him at the Club.

One day, when we were at luncheon, in walked William James, with his usual vivacity. "You remember Lord Russell", I explained, "who visited you here eight years ago." "Ah, yes. You have put on flesh", James observed with a medical smile, as they shook hands. It was very true; and Russell's loose white flannels, with the jacket ridiculously short, did nothing to disguise the fact. Nor was it a comic or jolly fatness. He was already suffering acutely from varicose veins. His air was preoccupied and at the same time a little vacant. He had too many things to think of, and none of them rewarded thought.

Problem of a wife and two fiancées. The mystery of his journey—he was on his way to California—was solved one day when he took two photographs out of his capacious breast pocket and asked me which of those two women I thought he had better marry. As he was legally married already and not likely to be free for years, the question was speculative, and for my speculative mind easy to answer. I replied at once, "Neither." One was Martha Turner, looking like a particularly tidy policeman or soldier, conscious of being photographed. She had no superfluous hair, or anything else superfluous. Russell said she was a brick, and I readily believed it. But why marry a brick? In the other lady, quite unknown to me, everything on the contrary seemed to be superfluous. Veronica (for I never saw her and that is all I know of her name), Veronica didn't look very young; rather battered, theatrical and unhealthy. No doubt she was appealing, being unhappy and perhaps intelligent. Russell explained that she belonged to an Irish but prosperous family in San Francisco, had lived long in Europe, was a Catholic and called herself an artist. All this, in 1894, went very well with being at once fashionable and advanced. It was to her, I could see plainly, that Russell's heart inclined for the moment. He suffered at the thought of giving her up, and he might never have had the strength to do it. It was she who thought better of it, and broke off their relations.

Veronica. That she had been greatly tempted, I can well believe. Imagine a woman of thirty, not particularly beautiful, frail, sensitive, thinking herself highly cultivated and a woman of the world, but idle and homeless: what a divine vocation, to capture a superman, to tame him, to save his soul and to become a British peeress, with a lovely home and a fixed nationality! But she seems to have had a shrewd elder brother who managed her property, and kept an eye on her generally; and I suspect that she also had an experienced confessor. Doubtless they warned her. Anyhow, Russell wrote from San Mateo: "I am thrown back rather than forward . . . and am rather upset again. . . . There will be an issue some day." And some months later from Maidenhead: "Veronica has retired into an inscrutable silence. . . . It was very painful as a blow to one's vanity, that abrupt breaking off: and yet the relief was immense . . . Veronica saved the situation by cutting the knot—what I regret is that fear and pique were the cause of the step. I wish I could attribute it to unselfish consideration of Martha's interests." So I discovered that Veronica had known all about Martha. The lady had been aware that she was being asked to promise to marry a man who not only had a legal wife but had promised to marry somebody else whenever he should be free!

Helplessness of the Superman. When Russell says that being finally jilted by Veronica was a "great relief", but regrets that her action was not due to "unselfish consideration of Martha's interests" he reveals two sides of his character that afterwards reappeared on various occasions. One was a certain passivity or fatalism in his actions and feelings. He doesn't see the absurdity of asking one rival lady-love to sacrifice herself for the sake of another, while never thinking of making the sacrifice himself and cutting the knot in the beginning. That falling in love is often fatal and involuntary may be granted, although it can sometimes be headed off; but then reason and duty come in, in a strong soul, to suppress or sacrifice the passion. But what is reason or duty? Either another passion—the passion for harmony and integrity in the soul—or social conventions, expediencies, and taboos. Against everything of the latter kind a transcendental free spirit rebels; and there I see the secret of tragic strength being often mixed with an extraordinary fatalistic weakness. You are tossed by every wave, and yet something in you observes your plight and fundamentally despises you. Most of the heroes and heroines in Racine suffer from this intellectual elevation in moral helplessness, Phèdre especially;* and if

---

*J'aime. Ne pense pas qu'au moment que je t'aime,
 Innocente à mes yeux, je m'approuve moi-même,
 Ni que du fol amour qui trouble ma raison
 Ma lâche complaisance ait nourri le poison.
 Objet infortuné des vengeances célestes,
 Je m'abhorre encor plus que tu ne me détestes. . . .
 Que dis-je? Cet aveu que je te viens de faire,
 Cet aveu si honteux, le crois-tu volontaire?
 Tremblante pour un fils que je n'osais trahir,
 Je te venais prier de ne le point hair.
 Faibles projets d'un coeur trop plein de ce qu'il aime!
 Hélas! je ne t'ai pu parler que de toi-même.

Phèdre, Acte II.

Titus in *Bérénice* masters his passion, he does it behind the scenes under political pressure and against his will, so that his exercise of freedom seems but another instance of slavery. And it was this complete helplessness that Racine felt to be tragic: he wrote *Bérénice* because he found in Suetonius the phrase: *invitus invitam*. Now in Russell the passion for harmony and integrity was entirely absent: the transcendental spirit, though conscious of itself, had no representative on the stage, nor even a chorus to fill up the interludes; it was silent, and therefore, for the public nonexistent. He explains this himself in an unusually reflective letter written during this visit to America:

San Mateo, Cal. 12 Aug. 1894.

Paris, 19 Oct. 1894.

"You will think I have been remiss in not writing to you before to thank you for the lovely time you gave me at Cambridge. It was very peaceful and very restful: just what I wanted . . . I don't think I ever took in your character before so distinctly as I did this time: we are opposed as entirely as possible. You are all for rest in the perfection of form with the negation of an end as either existent or important: I am all for the emotional strife and struggle, however vague and however formless, as being at least a reaching towards some end unknown, & seen only by faith as existing at all. Is not that so?" This he modifies two months later: "Why do you refer to me as loving strife for its own sake? . . . I desire peace and rest above all things now, & hate to be involved in a personal turmoil wh. invades & makes impossible a philosophic calm. Of course I may have said, and it is true, that strife does me good, braces me, & brings out my best qualities: but I don't welcome it."

The romantic hero survives his errors.

Strife undoubtedly brought out his ability, his cleverness, wit, and gift of satire and invective; they say he was an excellent debater. But that was play-acting: it made him unfair and superficial. He had learned too well from cheap politicians and expensive lawyers to defend his brief and to close his eyes to truth and to justice. Nor does "reaching towards some end unknown & seen only by faith",—an endless end, or the eternal feminine—seem his best side to Platonists like Lionel Johnson and me. His best side in our opinion was his intellectual freedom or transcendental detachment. In the midst of his shabby adventures, which whatever he may have been reaching towards brought him nothing but "expense of spirit in a waste of shame", this heroic spirit remained alive, as in all romantic prodigals; it was proud and brave enough not to be overwhelmed by any folly or any mischance. For this I admired him to the end, as I do Byron, not for what he did or thought, but for what he was.

This time, however, the well-advised Veronica saved him in saving herself, and he made his trip to San Francisco to no purpose. I profited by it in having his company for a week at Cambridge and then receiving various confidential letters and a copy of *Leaves of Grass*, as a memento of his visit. He had been patient in the extreme heat of a Boston August, and had taken pains to be civil; yet he was not at his best in a strange environment. He was not adaptable, and found queer things wrong rather than amusing. In England, where he freely found fault with everything, his satire was intelligent, his misrepresentations witty, and his discomfort feigned. He still felt himself there the cock of the walk, as in his first youth, and that pose became him. At first it was justified enough by his intelligence, his physique, and his title; it was dramatically proper and carried off with great effect, even if destined in the end to become tragic. But now the pose of moral high-mindedness seemed less becoming, as when, for instance he wrote that he "feared" that Veronica acted from pique and not from "unselfish consideration of Martha's interests". This tone is an echo of his Low Church breeding. When he was in prison for bigamy he composed a book of "Lay Sermons", and published it. Russell was not only an engineer, he was also a member of the bar and had practised for years as an attorney. Applied science naturally figures in the budget of the superman and the enlightened despot: it developed Russell's *virtù*; but applied sophistry, used in the service of any prejudice or passion, narrowed and cheapened his mind. In these "Sermons" he preaches against tradition and legal control, with crushing texts from the Gospels quoted maliciously by an unbeliever. It sounds like cant and hypocrisy; yet Russell was blurting out his sincerest convictions, like any poor man ranting in Hyde Park. Indignant dogmatism was another helpless passion that would invade him before he could stop to look and to think: the more tart and feeble his maxims, the prouder he felt in defending them. His brother Bertie had the same satiric gift and the same temperamental fanaticism; but in him perverseness was partly redeemed by historical knowledge and speculative acumen. It seems to me a great pity that their sympathies in politics, as in love, should have been so ill directed, and that both should wear the crown of martyrdom for such cheap delusions.

To speak of martyrdom is hardly a metaphor. The two brothers were not executed, but both were imprisoned, ostracised, ruined, and driven very largely to waste their talents. At the end some official amends were made to each of them, but too late and only when British standards of propriety had broken down, partly perhaps through their influence. Yet had they found no opposition, I doubt that their fate would have been happier.

Enter: That their own independent principles exposed them
Mollie. to singular delusions, quite apart from politics, may be proved in Russell's case by the change of mistress found at T.H. on my next visit there. I first got wind of something new in the realm of Venus when I was asked to "join a house-party" at Amberley Cottage. A house-party in Maidenhead? Who could the woman be? I didn't join the party, because that year, 1895, I was but a short time in England; but I did spend a night or two at Amberley Cottage, and at tea one day the lady turned up: "Mollie" I will call her. She was a fat, florid, coarse Irishwoman of forty, with black curls, friendly manners and emotional opinions: a political agitator and reformer. She took me aside at once and began to lament that Russell should be attached to that dreadful dull stupid girl, Martha Turner. He must be rescued. I smiled intelligently, but found myself in rather an awkward position, treated at once as a confidential friend, when I had no right to betray Russell's confidence and no wish that he should jump from the frying-pan into the fire, such as this red-cheeked lady's heart would surely be. Nor could I as yet say: "Rescuing him is not for me to attempt: perhaps *you* might do it." I didn't think he wished to be rescued; and I knew nothing about her except what she had now revealed, which rather suggested that to be rescued from her would be more urgent than to be rescued by her. So I said nothing but discreet commonplaces, and we parted amiably; and amiably we always got on afterwards, during the many years when she was Russell's comfortable wife, and even later, when they had been divorced.

Mollie was a good soul. I think it was a relief to her to give up her politics and "social work"; she retained only a natural motherly kindness to servants and to village children, and to me also, for which I was grateful. She knew what poverty was, and didn't overdo acting the grand lady; remained simple and active, and ready, as it were, to relapse at any moment into her native paddydom without much minding it. She had been an orphan or a foundling, picked up and adopted by a small Irish official or tradesman, who married her later; and she had a grown-up son who bore his name. The old man had died, and now she had two small boys by a second husband, who had brought her to live in London and introduced her to politics and social reform. In those circles she had caught sight of Russell, and Cupid had done the rest.

The cost of bliss. What could Russell find in this old frump completely to upset him, to make him abandon poor Martha Turner (of whose interests he had been so unselfishly jealous) and to drive him into bigamy, into a grand trial in the House of Lords, into prison, and into long years of placid married life? Was it intellectual or political sympathy? The absence of antipathy — an antipathy which he would have found in almost any lady — may have helped; but Mollie had no positive intelligence, no real concern about reform; she was simply kind and accustomed to move among social reformers. Could it be sexual attraction? I have not the means of knowing Russell's feelings on this point: he was never ribald or indiscreetly frank in such matters; but the affair with Lady Scott may have been more than an initiation; it may have established an inveterate leaning towards mature charms and motherly indulgence. Anyhow, Mollie's determination to extricate Russell, and his headlong propensity to be re-entangled overcame every obstacle. She abandoned her two little boys and her husband, who duly divorced her; and she and Russell moved for six months to Reno, Nevada, where he too was divorced, and the two innocents were duly married. The British authorities would not recognise this divorce and remarriage and he was condemned for bigamy by the House of Lords and sentenced to three months in the first division. But this added nothing to his disgrace: on the contrary, it added a touch of antique dignity to his position. His speech in self-defence — duly censored by his lawyers — was excellent, and the only regrettable consequence of having been in prison was the book of sermons that he wrote there.

Mollie mistress of T. H. What had become of Martha Turner? I was never informed, nor as far as I can remember was I at all curious about it. All those years after 1897 were a somnambulistic period for me, and now seem a blank. But in 1895 she had written me from Newnham, where he had evidently sent her to polish up her education and make her fit to be a Countess: very like the Russells to think College a good preparation for that and for wedded happiness!

This move, however, had at least left the hermitage of T.H. empty, and ready in 1900 to welcome the blooming bride fresh from Reno, Nevada. For the next fifteen years I periodically found her presiding over that place, attached to it more and more, and as happy as an exacting husband and a dwindling income could allow her to be. She mollified the servants, when Russell had exasperated them; she knew how to control him; she toddled about in her loose tea-gowns with her pack of little white lap-dogs tumbling about her feet, and blinded by the hair in their hidden eyes; and she disappeared for long intervals to her hut or to her tower, for a little solitude, a little nap, or a little effort to write some child's story that some publisher would at last consent to print. She had no religion, but was humble, prudent, and resigned. I never heard her sigh as if she regretted her little boys; her troubles seemed to be about the present, about Russell's affairs and expenses. He had become a County Councillor in London, where they had taken a house in Gordon Square, and had card-parties. Bridge and motoring were his most obvious employments and expenses; he took a boyish pleasure in them. He had been the first to apply for a motorist's licence, so that the number of his car was A1.

Motoring.   Sitting by him as he drove was an unmixed pleasure: he did it perfectly, with sureness and ease, and his casual observations, as the road opened up before us and various little scenes appeared, belonged to the original sphere of our friendship. This sphere was play of mind, intellectual light; not philosophy, not theory, but quick intelligence turned upon common things, inquiringly, fearlessly, and universally. Theory and philosophy would have crept in, had we pursued any subject very far; but we never did. I was no more professional at heart than he was, and didn't want to be entrapped by my thoughts. Ours were flying comments, made for the pleasure of making them; a purer pleasure than is to be found in the things on which the comments are made. Speed—never forced speed—and fresh air and the gentle homely charm of the English roads, winding in and out of neat villages and respectfully skirting any hedged and private domain, made the hours pass gaily and without fatigue: and we had enough sense of things great and distant for these little passing things not to seem too important, and to be judged merrily. We never laughed much, but we were always laughing a little.

A waning
friendship
and a
crescent love.
Between 1914 and 1919, having been stranded in England by the war, I was often at T.H. I didn't perceive it at the time, but now I suspect that although it was always Russell that wrote to me, it was perhaps rather his wife, first Mollie and very soon Elizabeth, who really thought of asking me so many times to stay. Their husband was their problem, and they thought I might throw light upon it. Another thing that I then overlooked, and now perceive retrospectively, is that I was no longer young: my presence could not in itself give anybody pleasure; and as to what I might say, or my reputation as a writer, Russell was entirely indifferent. He too was much changed physically for the worse; but in his ways and spirit, at least towards me, he seemed exactly the same; only, being much preoccupied with matters unknown to me, he now had no impulse to unbosom himself as in our younger days. I had lapsed into an old but unimportant acquaintance in his eyes, while in mine he remained the most interesting of mortals. Mollie, being a woman of experience, must have felt this shift in her husband's relations with me, and instinctively made me her confidant, when I was no longer Russell's. The whiskey and water that she drank at meals—and between meals also, I imagine—comforted her a good deal; she wasn't hard to comfort; yet one day she confided to me that she was troubled about Russell. He was in love with somebody else. The truth is I had wondered that this hadn't happened before. More than ten years of contentment with fat old Mollie seemed miraculous. Naturally I couldn't put the matter to Mollie in these terms; but I suggested that Russell was still young, that his temperament was vehement, that he was polygamous without being inconstant, and that it would be wiser to overlook any passing infidelity on his part. They were very happily married and he would return to her.

"No," Mollie said rather gravely, "she wants to be his wife; she wants me to divorce him." Why? Did the silly woman wish to be a countess? No: she wasn't silly, and was a countess already. She was the Countess von Arnim, author of *Elizabeth and Her German Garden*. Russell was very much in love with her.

Elizabeth out
of her German
Garden.
When I returned to Oxford I procured *Elizabeth and Her German Garden*, asked people about the authoress, and read other books of hers. They were charming, light, witty, showing love of flowers and of solitude, and full of delicate and satirical insight into character, without bitterness or false expectations. In *The Caravaners* she was hard on the Germans; fairer, with greater

reason for resentment, in *The Pastor's Wife*. With such horror of domestic tyranny, this extraordinary woman was going to marry Russell! Truly, *la raison n'est pas ce qui règle l'amour*.

My regrets.   I was sorry for Mollie; she had made great sacrifices, almost justified so far by the result. Adaptably she had become attached to T.H. and had helped to render the place more comfortable and homelike. There was a dell of which she was especially fond, just below the house: sloping grassy reaches under great trees, with rabbits sitting alert, or galloping away, their white tails bobbing in the air. Here you unexpectedly found deep shade and a sense of being lost and hidden in a green wilderness; while the prevailing notes of that highland solitude were rather openness, buffetting winds, an invitation to adventure, at least in thought, and the freedom of wandering unattached between earth and heaven. Mollie had also attempted a garden, but the site was too exposed, the soil not very rich, and it proved pleasanter to sit indoors, or to stroll through the wilder parts. What folly, after having found a remote refuge and domestic peace with this good woman, and tested the union for so many years, that he should now drive her away, and not only launch upon a new and dangerous voyage, but destroy his home port! As I had been on Martha Turner's side against Mollie, so I was now on Mollie's side against Elizabeth. Russell knew it; of course my external, cynical, Tory view of human affections could make no difference in his conduct; nor did it make any difference in my attachment to him, which had never rested on being much pleased with his actions or opinions, but entirely on sympathy with his indomitable person and on admiration of his powers. Naturally we both were silent on the subject of his new love-affair, and events went on without my knowledge. Mollie simply dropped out of the picture. I knew she had been bought off: but this had to be concealed, because English law prohibited divorce by collusion. Divorce might be granted to the injured partner as a release, and as punishment for the offender: but not if the offender were going to be made happy by it. Such was the wicked fact in this case, at least for the moment; but by some legal machination the divorce was obtained, and Russell and Elizabeth were married. I had no notice of the fact, nor invitation to the wedding, but found her installed at T.H. as a matter of course on my next visit.

Euthanasia   By chance, however, I did see Mollie again. I had gone
of Mollie.   from Oxford to Brighton for a change of scene and of air; and walking one afternoon along the Front, I perceived a bevy

of little white dogs, like lumps of cotton-wool, moving about the pavement. I looked up, and there was Mollie, richly draped in furs, and rounder than ever. She greeted me amiably, and insisted that I should come up to her lodgings, which she had taken with friends for a week or two. Luckily I never played bridge, or cards of any sort: otherwise I should have found it impossible to avoid taking a hand. There were card-tables, glasses and bottles, and four or five men and women of easy-going manners. I escaped; and to clear my conscience wrote that same evening to Russell, relating briefly but accurately, just what had happened. Nevertheless, it seems he was displeased. I suppose I ought not to have gone to Brighton, or ought not to have seen those little white dogs. He could not have expected me not to recognise Mollie, who had been my very friendly hostess at his house for fifteen years. For my own part, I was rather glad to have come upon her and found her looking so well and so much in her element. Was she perhaps happier? No: her pride had been wounded; yet it was not the first wound, and now she was free, with a fixed income, and could grow old in peace. She could keep warm and comfortable, while mad wars raged in the world, with her lap-dogs, her cronies, her game of cards and her tipple.

First contacts with Elizabeth. When eventually one afternoon I arrived at Petersfield, on my next visit to T.H., and looked about for the car, I could see it nowhere. After waiting a moment, when the traps that had been there were gone, I asked the guard. No: he hadn't seen Lord Russell's car. "Yes," said another man; "that's it over there, with Lady Russell." Then I noticed a small grey motor, with what seemed to be a young girl at the wheel. I was accustomed enough to being a traveller and a foreigner everywhere not to doubt anything because it seemed odd; and as I ran up to the fair stranger, she waved to me. We had never before set eyes on each other. Russell had written as usual, without saying a word about her, yet here she was alone to meet me. Even at close quarters in the open air she seemed very young: a little thing with a little nose, little eyes, and a little innocent mouth. Yet she had three grown-up daughters and a son of fifteen at Eton. I got in, my things were placed somewhere behind, and we started. She explained at once that she wanted to speak to me before I saw Russell; yet I found that she had nothing in particular to tell me. Evidently it was only that she wished to conciliate me, and thought it would be easier in a *tête-à-tête*. And the reason for this manoeuvre, that seemed unnecessary, was a letter I had written to Russell, which he had shown her, when I first learned that he was divorcing Mollie and marrying somebody else. He ought not to have been displeased with that letter, in which I compared him with Henry the Eighth and with Goethe. Like Henry the Eighth he desired to *marry* all his lady-loves; but that only made him wish later to cut their heads off, that each might make room for the next. Goethe, less bigoted morally and calmer, had finally married only one, the humblest, of his women, who had been his mistress and housekeeper for years. Russell then found himself married in the same sensible way as Goethe. Mollie was used to all his ways, and kept his house economically and in good order. What a mistake to send her away and insist on marrying Frau von Stein! That he *loved* Elizabeth, Gräfin von Arnim, I could well believe; also that she loved him: but why *marry?* She was a widow, a novelist, and a freethinker. Surely she might accept him for a lover. But if she put herself in his power legally, there would be trouble. With his fixed habits, it would be difficult for a lady to live with him long.

Her hopes in marrying Russell.   All this was not put so clearly in my letter, but could be read between the lines; and it evidently caused some stir and possibly some alarm in their breasts. Russell protested in a perfunctory way, as a lover and as a Christian, which he thought he was; and I knew only long after that she had seen the letter at all, when she admitted the profound truth of it. At first, however, she wished to demonstrate—and I was a sort of dummy audience to convince in lieu of the world and of her own conscience— that she was the first *decent* woman to take Russell in hand, and that she had character, intellect, charm, beauty, and sufficient youth ,to hold him permanently and make a new man of him; or rather, to make him himself again, because his associations, since he fell into Lady Scott's hands at the age of twenty-three, had smothered and degraded his true nature. Clever and experienced as she was, she felt that this would appeal to me; that I also *believed* in Russell, against all apparent evidence; and that I should retract the horrid immoral suggestions of my letter, and admit that she was the providential Frau von Stein destined to lift her happier Goethe into a great statesman and a man of the world.

The plausible grounds for them.   And in spite of the fatal issue, there were elements of truth in her prognostications. She did hold his affections; he spoke of the "anguish" he suffered when she deserted him; protested that he still "loved and worshipped her", that his life was blighted, and that all had been wanton cruelty on her part, because she was incapable of loving anybody, even her own children. These reproaches were absurd; Elizabeth was a cool but tender person; they merely proved how much he was upset and exasperated by losing her. It was also true that he was worth saving: and a certain side of his real gifts actually came to public notice at the end, not especially under her influence, but in politics. Yet, as he knew and admitted, those external occupations didn't touch his heart; they were parts of Maya, traditional whirlpools in which birth plunges us, such as making money, making war, or making love. They compel us to care intensely, as in a dream, for things of no ultimate consequence: and this not merely because those things are transitory, but because the effects of our efforts are incalculable in the end, and we may be bringing about results that, could we foresee them, would appal us. I think that this conviction, perhaps unconsciously, encouraged Russell to let himself go and to plunge into irrational ventures. In him, however, these courses left their mark and became automatisms, soon impossible to withstand or to correct. Maya might be an illusion, but she held him tight.

The marvel was that so many women, by no means fools, thought they could manage him, and that each in her turn believed herself predestined to redeem him and anchor him in the safe haven of her arms. Martha Turner thought so, Lady Scott thought so, Mollie thought so, and now Elizabeth thought so: the simplest, the most battered, the most intelligent of women were alike in their infatuation and blindness. I suppose their vanity conspired with his persuasiveness to deceive them; and he was persuasive: very different as a lover, Elizabeth said, from what he was as a husband.

The fatal obstacles. That his society was charming, his personality dominant, that there was nobody in whose good graces one would rather be, I knew by my own experience. But in friendship liability is limited; each preserves his privacy and freedom, and there is no occasion for jealousy or tyranny. Towards his women, once they were enveigled into an unlimited partnership, Russell was a tyrant. He imposed on them an infinity of petty habits and rules, with the gravity of a strict moralist, and laid down heavily the most puerile and hackneyed saws of politics and conduct as if self-evident. To me these absurdities were amusing and harmless. I knew them by heart; they were parts of his imperious personality, which I accepted merrily when I was with him. He never dreamt that I should accept them for myself. He left me abundantly alone; I was an *hors-d'oeuvre* in his menu; so much so that he was genuinely puzzled when in the last years I wrote him that he had been very important in my life. Certainly he had had no influence on my career; but my career was not my life. Mine has been a life of reflection, which he couldn't understand; and he had given me much to think of, many pleasures and many lights. But his wives and his cats were his prisoners, condemned to be petted at pleasure. They had only secret hours for being fondled, and were treated in public, and ordinarily in private, with a virtuous austerity. His ways of making love were said to be somewhat capricious and exacting: Elizabeth once called them sadistic. And love-making for him was no laughing matter, no playfulness of a mad moment. It was a loving wife's sworn duty to be obedient; and if she rebelled and fled from her husband, he said she was cruel.

The inevitable break.   Elizabeth in the beginning was simply the amiable hostess: always prettily dressed, witty, full of little amusing anecdotes about her life in Germany. She would walk with me in the dell, and show me her knowledge of flowers and discriminating love of them. It was only gradually that she became confidential. She had money and furniture of her own—not much, as I suppose the war had cut off whatever her first husband may have left her—but enough for her to be somewhat independent; and with her love of solitude, she had found it necessary to set up a bungalow of her own, where no one was allowed to disturb her. It was a spacious apartment, charmingly furnished with books, flowers, and gaily coloured chintz. Here she retired to rest and to work. This was the first symptom of domestic division that came to my notice; but ultimately she began frankly to confess the difficulties she found in living with Russell. What they were in essence she made public afterwards in her novel *Vera*. As she said to me, she began by making the man in it quite unlike Russell; but as the theme was her own domestic tragedy, he became more and more like Russell as the story developed. It is not a good portrait because the fundamental structure is wrong, if it were meant to represent Russell; but many of the details are photographic: and I think it may truly be called cruel to publish them during his life-time. But he had driven her to desperation; and she developed the spite of a hunted animal.

T.H. loses its charm. For me the scene closes on T.H. rather distressingly; as on an interrupted performance. The place was materially much improved, the grounds developed, the hall panelled, the rooms freshened up and adorned; but Russell was preoccupied and silent, Elizabeth hardly visible save at table, and a mysterious emptiness seemed to pervade the place where, in good Mollie's day, I had felt so free and happy. After the rupture, Elizabeth and I remained, or rather became, very good friends. She occasionally came to Italy; finally she took a house on the French Riviera where at last, she said, she had a garden after her own heart. But no garden can be paradise when all within is a desert. She was desolate and bitter in her old age, and pronounced life to be "a very bad joke".

Elizabeth hears of Russell's death. It was there that she heard of Russell's death, which occurred at Marseilles, not very far from her: for he too had come to the Riviera for a little rest. One of his relations one day turned up at her place, and Elizabeth, on recognising the approaching lady, waved a welcome to her, but noticed a strange solemnity in her manner. "Why are you so serious?" she asked. "Frank!" the lady gasped tragically. "What is *he* up to now?" Elizabeth inquired without emotion. "Dead and cremated!" cried the other; and closed the chapter of that love-affair sardonically, in sympathy with its theme. For it had been, for both, a false and hollow revival of youth in old age.

Bertie's school at T.H. vs. my old memories. After Elizabeth deserted it, T.H. passed for me, and I think for Russell also, into a sort of penumbra. I was living abroad, and visited it only once again, in 1923.* At the time of my last trip to England, nine years later, Russell was already dead, and had bequeathed the place to his brother Bertie. Then it underwent a curious transformation. Bertie was temporarily married to his second wife, who had been a teacher at Girton; they had young children and advanced ideas on education. Wasn't T.H. an ideal oasis for an unimpeded experiment in liberty? They would turn the house into a school where children should do exactly as they liked until they found it unpleasant; and they should learn only what they felt like learning. I don't know what were the results; perhaps the experiment was interrupted prematurely; for before long Bertie and his wife were divorced and the school was merged and lost in that universal experiment in education which

---

*Cf. "Farewell to England", towards the end.

nature has always been making just on Bertie and Dora's simple and cruel principles. I have not heard, and hardly wish to hear, what has become of T.H. For me it belongs to the happy past, rescued by being past from being ever changed.

XXIX

Oxford Friends

My first acquaintance with Oxford is recorded in the chapter on Russell; it was memorable, but ended in a blind alley. Russell himself I never saw there, nor had he any affection or respect for that place; and Lionel Johnson and the others who had been his Oxford friends soon vanished into the outer wilderness. My other visits there, except in 1896–7 and after 1911, necessarily fell in the long vacation, since during the working terms I was in America. The colleges were deserted and only married Dons, caged like canaries in suburban villas, could be expected to be in residence. It was my Oxford, therefore, that I first learned to know, not that of the Oxonians.

"Old Higgs". There was, however, Louis Dyer, my old professor of Greek at Harvard, who lived in Banbury Road; and through him I made the most useful and faithful of my Oxford friends. Like Dyer, he was a Balliol man but not a Don, and they sometimes met at dinner on feast days at the High Table. There I first saw him: a monkey-like creature with a pasty round face, fringed on all sides by patches of black hair; for some disease made it difficult for him either to shave properly or to grow a decent beard. He was a little man, unobtrusive yet always watching everything with a critical experienced eye. In summer he wore a short alpaca coat and grey trousers, and a little cloth hat with a limp brim curling up all round. His shirt was starched, with a corresponding evening waistcoat that left it uncovered; and often the one black stud, expected to keep the two halves together, would slip out and let them fly apart, revealing a hairy chest immediately beneath. With this he sported a very low turned-down collar, and a drooping black evening tie. At a distance he could be recognised by his meditative way of walking, with occasional stops at a crossing or at a shop window; for he lived to observe. His hands were habitually clasped behind his back, and trailed a loose umbrella. Everybody called him "Old Higgs".

Higgs was a private tutor in modern history. In his younger days, when asthma didn't keep him at home, he had travelled a great deal, often on foot, especially through the Baltic countries, and had a rich collection of photographs showing the picturesque aspects of the North. I liked his conversation; for without talking shop or showing any political bias or academic jealousies, he was full of curious information and credible gossip about men and events, recent and remote; and like the learned men of other times, he knew the identity of human nature in all ages, and felt no contempt for manners or ideas that had now gone out of fashion. His standards were those not of a pedant or of a reformer, but of a man of taste. His taste and his diction were thoroughly Oxonian, and not more limited or local than anything has to be that is definite; they were pleasant to come upon and to profit by, not as models to be copied elsewhere but as attainments to be prized where they belonged.

A guide to the pedestrian. Yet his great service to me was of another kind. He showed me all the possible walks about Oxford; after going over each of them two or three times under his guidance, I was able when alone to recognise every turning and every stile, where there was a right of way through a field; and he encouraged me to go rather further than I should have ventured alone, to Islip, for instance, or to Abingdon. His antiquarian lore helped to make the way seem shorter and the sights more individual; and when the distance was too great for a comfortable day's walk, I learned the possible ways of shortening it by taking a train or 'bus to some intermediate point. This Higgs wouldn't do, for economy; and tea also sometimes became a difficulty, because he didn't like to pay more than sixpence for it. Afterwards, during the war, when I started out in the morning, this experience, together with an ordnance-survey map, very much lengthened the radius of my excursions, and I could easily go to Radley and Nuneham, or to Stanton Harcourt without fatigue. Tea, in winter, would be at a shop in Oxford on my return; but at any inn in the country I could have bread and cheese, with beer, for luncheon: eggs or cold meat the good people never could supply. Old Higgs's days were then over, yet invisibly he often guided my steps; and I may say that I have never seen so many lovely views as through his eyes, because he would not only point them out to me in the first instance, but would find some just epithet to describe them. These modest landscapes rather require a poet to appreciate them; the tourist and even the painter might think them commonplace; their delicacy is aerial, moral, and fugitive, and a happy phrase arrests them best.

I almost saw poor Higgs die. I have called his trouble asthma, but there was a complication of troubles; and while he looked much as usual—that is, very queer—I was startled one day, when strolling with him in the Cornmarket, to have him suddenly stop and stand still, like Socrates struck by epilepsy or by inspiration. He half recovered after a moment and made at once for his lodgings, which were near by, in the first house to the left in Market Street: pleasant lodgings, sunny with a glimpse of town life from the corner windows, by which he sat and kept the fire going day and night all the year round. I never saw him after that day. A poor devil, no doubt; but I am sure I might easily have led a life like his, had I been less lucky and more studious; and I shouldn't have been unhappy. Unattached academic obscurity is rather a blessed condition, when it doesn't breed pedantry, envy, or ill-nature.

Robert Bridges. Of notabilities (for which in general I have no liking) the most distinguished who was my friend in Oxford was Robert Bridges. Our friendship began late and was entirely his doing. A friend of his, at the turn of the century, had shown him a copy of my *Interpretations of Poetry and Religion*, saying, "Here is somebody whose philosophy seems to be much like yours. Perhaps you might care to look into him." And in fact I received in America a very kind and appreciative letter on the subject. Still, I never looked Bridges up when I was in Oxford. He was Poet Laureate, I hadn't read him, and I prefer to remain free and perfectly unknown in the places where I am happy. Higgs was not a commitment; but a Poet Laureate . . .

However, when I was caught in England by the war and settled down in Oxford, I somewhere came across him, probably at Corpus. He was an imposing person, twenty years older then I, tall, a little too thin and spare for Olympian Zeus, but otherwise of the same noble and leonine aspect. His manners, however, and his conversation were of the most unpretending, easy, and charming kind, those of the simple, affable English gentleman who remains always young. Soon I began to go sometimes to Chilswell for my walk. Mrs. Bridges proved no less friendly than her husband. I suspect that she, too, had read something of mine and, dear lady, had thought it edifying. Fortunately the religion of that household was not controversial, and until the very end I succeeded in giving them no offence. With her, moreover,

I had another point in my favour. When their only son, Edward, came back wounded from the war, I liked him very much, and felt at once, as I told them, as if I had known him all my life. Youth and experience together make a charming combination: the youthfulness secures plasticity, and the experience gives a ground to build upon securely.

A domestic incident.   Yet in some things my lack of discipline betrayed itself: I hadn't been brought up in an English nursery and an English public school, nor served in any war. Once, only once, they asked me to spend the week-end at Chilswell. All went well until Sunday morning, when in order to be ready for breakfast down stairs I had to get up rather early. I opened my door, and there were my boots, but no hot water. No mention had been made of any bathroom, and not knowing what to do, I rang, and waited a moment with the door half open. Then I heard an agitated voice saying: "He has rung!" Feeling guilty, I closed my door again. Presently there was a knock, and I said perfunctorily, "Come in", thinking it was the housemaid, recalled to her neglected duties. But no, no one came in, and I went to open the door myself. There stood Mrs. Bridges, ghost-like, and without her front hair. She gasped: "What is the matter?" "Nothing, nothing. I only rang to ask the maid for some hot water." "Hot water!" cried Mrs. Bridges, as if shocked. "Only a little, just for shaving", I said apologetically, realising that tubs were not in order, at least not lukewarm tubs. "The maids have gone to church", Mrs. Bridges explained more calmly. "I'll see if I can get you a little." I was really very sorry, and ashamed of myself: I ought to have brought my hot water with me in a thermos-bottle, since I was such a Sybarite as to require it; but never before in England had hot water not appeared of itself in the morning, wherever I had lodged, and before dinner also, wherever I was a guest. Abashed, I now accepted a small white china jug of hot water from my hostess's hand, and did the best I could with it, a hard beard, a tender skin, and not too sharp a razor. The blessed days of Gillette and of shaving creams had not dawned, and like Olympian Zeus, I should have let nature take her course and possessed a rich and curly beard. Yet Apollo, Hermes, and even Edward Bridges shaved, and also Mars, who needn't have been so young. It would be hard to go back to nature without going back to savagery. That priests and monks should shave, even their crowns, is no doubt a matter of hygiene and cleanliness in warm countries; perhaps, also, as in the case of nuns' hair, a surrender of personal emphasis and boasts. My own instinct would choose hairlessness, long straight robes, and hands hidden in one's sleeves: such an aspect standardises one's personality in the world, and concentrates and purifies it in oneself. **The sinfulness of hot water.** On quite another occasion Bridges, who was a medical man, inveighed against the use of hot water. So bad for the nails and for the hair! With his magnificent *chevelure* contrasting with my baldness, I was reduced to a bashful silence in regard to hair; and I kept it also in regard to nails, although not without casting a furtive glance at his hands. They were large, thin, strong hands, that had been used for doing miscellaneous things, and were not dirty: but they hadn't the nursery-maid's pink cleanness produced by soap and hot water. The nails were grey and thick, like talons. Admirable, no doubt, for certain purposes; but in ages when hot water is available for the toilet, delving is no longer done with the claws, and even jealous ladies do not attempt to scratch each other's eyes out. This does not prove, I admit, that hot water is not a luxury, and unheroic. Even cold water is abhorrent, for external use, to lions and eagles. I admired Bridges' Spartan ablutions, but prefer in this respect to remain a Sybarite. Different animals and different nations cannot be models for one another.

Happy luncheons at The George. Pleasant as Chilswell was, it was not Bridges at home that showed the grounds of his interest in me. It was Bridges afloat in Oxford. He would often come into the town in the morning; sometimes he was detained, or had business of some kind to do in the afternoon; and, then, knowing my habits, he would come to my lodgings in Beaumont Street at about half past twelve, when I was finishing dressing, and go with me to lunch at *The George*. Conviviality, for me, has been a great discoverer and cementer of affinities, or at least a substitute for them. Luncheon at *The George* was better than, under the stress of rations, it was likely to be at home; and we habitually enlivened it with a bottle of good burgundy. On these occasions Bridges became again a young man and a bachelor. He had been long a bachelor; he had once spent a whole season in Rome, delighted with riding about the Campagna, and no doubt composing verses; whereas when later in life he returned to Rome, everything disgusted him, especially the churches. All that to the free traveller had seemed romantic seemed now to the elderly Anglican false and dead. He could not bear the contrast with the English landscape and with English religious music and sentiment. So, reverting with me, even in familiar Oxford, to the atmosphere of the wandering student and poet, he relaxed his acquired habits of mind. It was for mocking English prejudices, while adoring England, that he valued my writings; and though we seldom or never discussed our respective works, I knew that it was this liberating outlook, partly in the Catholic and partly in the naturalistic direction, that he cared for in me.

Our agreement and divergence in philosophy.   That he was influenced by my philosophy is not admissible. A thinker is seldom influenced by another much younger than himself, and Bridges besides did not *understand* my philosophy. His own position was not clear to me until, with reference to his *Testament of Beauty*, he asked me expressly to criticise it and then replied, in a long letter, to my criticisms. He agreed with me (or rather with Kant) as to the *necessarily original* form of the mind, in sensation no less than in religion; but he clung to the belief that this inevitable originality was inspired, and revealed a sympathetic moral spirit in nature at large. Now, my position excludes this belief; because morality and spirit, in my view, express specific and contrary vital interests, as in politics. To assert that one such political or vital interest, say the Jewish or the Anglosaxon, coincides with the total inspiration of the universe, is egotism *in excelsis*, and a plain illusion of animal vanity and egotism. Banish that illusion: the vital and political interest concerned remains standing, but only as one local and temporary movement of animal life on earth. It is its own excuse for being, but it leaves the speculative spirit free to transcend it and to admit equally, in their places, all the other vital and political interests that may arise. I would relax English prejudices in the Catholic and in the naturalistic direction by a single and consistent insight, not by casual contrary sympathies. Catholicism is paganism spiritualised: it is fundamentally naturalistic; and the transcendental spirit and the wise statesman may accept Catholicism, where it naturally arises, as a good poetic symbol for the forces and the issues of human life in that phase; not, however, as a scientific revelation of reality or a history of literal facts. Religion is valid poetry infused into common life. It is not a revelation truer than perception or than science. Nature, where it breeds life, is undoubtedly animated by a spirit kindred to man's and to human morality; hence the dramatic sympathy in us with all real or imagined vitality in the universe. Yet this sympathy should chasten rather than inflate us, because it reveals to us how accidental are the objects of our love.

Harold Fletcher of Christ Church. At Christ Church, about 1895, there was a young American whose name I have forgotten, but whom I had known slightly at Harvard. He was pale, quiet, very well dressed, evidently rich but also aesthetic. He seemed always to have a bunch of violets in his button-hole. It was not surprising that he should have found his way to Oxford, and in particular to Christ Church. There he had spacious but singularly placed rooms that had been occupied by Lord Rosebery. They were in the cellar, immediately to the left as you come in through Canterbury Gate, with the windows in pits so far below the level of the pavement that they had large iron cages to protect them. On the other side, however, towards the garden and the meadows, the ground was lower, and there was sunshine and even, through the shrubbery, the suggestion of a view. I found myself there at a large luncheon with sporting youths most of whom I never saw again; I suspect they were all members of the Bullingdon Club. At least this was the case with the very blond modest young man who sat next to me and whom I might also have forgotten had he not taken the trouble to follow up our acquaintance. His name was Harold Fletcher. I had spoken of Oxford architecture, especially of the churches, defending the intrusion of the baroque amid the Gothic, as in the lovely porch of St. Mary's. This, although I didn't say anything about religion, was also a defence of Catholic sentiment and practice, and happened to strike in Fletcher a sympathetic cord. This I discovered long afterwards, for he was as silent as he was sensitive; at the moment he only asked me if I should like to drive some morning to Dorchester and see the church there, which was an interesting one.

To Dorchester with a tandem. We started at the appointed time, with the best of weather, in a smart dog-cart, but came to a stop a little beyond Folly Bridge, I wondered why. It was only, Fletcher said, that they were not allowed to drive a tandem through the town, and the groom had to bring the leader down here, to be added on as an afterthought. Unexpectedly for me, the drive now acquired a picturesque interest of its own, apart from the landscape and whatever was to be seen in Dorchester. It became a festive occasion. Fletcher drove as quietly and as modestly as he spoke, and as much to the purpose, for he seemed perfect master of his horses and of himself. I have always liked to put myself in the hands of skilful people, especially when I am absolutely ignorant of their art. That is a part of my confident faith in nature. Nature may be trusted to do her job even in living creatures, when they are clean-cut and docile, like Fletcher and his two beautiful horses. I afterwards learned, however, that driving with Fletcher was not without its risks, as trusting to nature is also. He was extremely near-sighted, and the story went that one day, when the leader in his tandem had turned completely round, he had gone on driving merrily with the wheeler in the opposite direction. But in my time he wore glasses, and never had the least accident.

Other excursions.   When he had left the university and come into his money, being an orphan and much attached to Oxford, he bought the stables in Holywell Street and set up in the coaching business. More than once I had the honour of sitting on the box with him in the coach to Woodstock and Blenheim, and admiring his skill and precision as a whip. Those were public occasions, imposing on him a professional gravity, like that of a captain at sea. Jollier and freer was a trip that his brother and I made with him driving a newly bought four-in-hand, from Leicester to Oxford, fifty miles in one day. It was a lovely trip, taken leisurely, with a long halt for luncheon and rest. We drove into Oxford at a steady slow trot; and at the end, after inspecting the horses minutely, Fletcher came radiant out of the stable. "By Jove," he said, "fifty miles, and never turned a hair!"

So pleasant were these outings that I went with him—though this had to be by train—to the cattle fair at Bicester, and enjoyed the scene greatly, while he did his business. The English air and the English country, apart from mankind, were enough to satisfy me; but here I was entertained also by the country types and the show animals; and there is always a convivial side to such excursions, that brings us back to our chosen friends, to a roast joint and a gooseberry tart and a great mug of ale or of porter.

A religious side.   A simple horsey chap, Harold Fletcher, and ten years younger than I: how much out of my line! Yet everything in this world has an explanation, and there was another side to my friend; something that I should not have required in him, yet without it he would never have been so attentive to me. He was religious: he felt the presence of the invisible. Not that he spoke of such things, for he was sensitive and reserved, but a caricature of his feelings appeared openly in his brother, in many ways his opposite and yet of the same blood. The brother was short and dark, quick and voluble, wished to be an actor, and believed in second sight and in haunted places. He lived in London and knew the personages and gossip of Bohemia. In Harold the taste for the supernatural took the nobler form of an orthodoxy, edifying and well-ordered. This feeling, held in reserve, gave a moral background to his ways and to his tastes, even about horses. Horses were made by God; if we saw them from that point of view, we should understand them. That is just what I felt about young men like Fletcher; they are to be approached from within, by way of their genesis and vital impulses, and not to be judged by their utility to other people. Nothing living is a means: all is automatic, spontaneous, justified by whatever it tends to and loves.

I began to see what Fletcher cared for on that first excursion to Dorchester. After visiting the Roman Camp, about which his knowledge was perfunctory (or at least seemed so to me, with my avidity for the setting of ancient life in all its details) we went to see the church, large and perpendicular. In one place a frescoed wall had been recently uncovered. To me it was not very clearly visible or specially interesting, a pastel imitation of stained glass, confused without being brilliant; but what could be made out of the figures sufficed to show the style and spirit of a religious art: quaintly realistic, naïve, and devout. This was evidently what interested Fletcher. His taste had worked back, behind the Renaissance, to the sentiment of the Middle Ages, to the familiar supernatural, to Catholic piety. There was no pre-Raphaelite affectation in him: he was looking beyond boastful material realism and theatricality to homely truth, to humble devotion, to revelations in solitude and comfort in hardship. He was no collector or picture-dealer; it was not the old clothes of mediaevalism that interested him but the faith that had worn them.

Father Waggett. Fletcher was indeed a devoted friend, perhaps a disciple or penitent, of Father Waggett's. He asked me expressly to meet Father Waggett at tea in his rooms; I found a most engaging clergyman, still young, with no clerical absurdities or insolence, but with the manners of the world and yet a frank expression of his apostolic vocation. I was reminded of my *tío Nicolás*, the canon of Tarragona; only that Waggett was much younger and less indolent. I think he may have seen my *Interpretations of Poetry and Religion*, then recently published; for this was some years after I had made Fletcher's acquaintance, and not the source of it. Waggett talked of religion freely and familiarly, like a Catholic; but it appeared that he was also a naturalist, a zoölogist, and was writing something that Fletcher had already seen and admired—I think concerning the instincts of birds. When I expressed a desire to see it, Waggett said he would be glad to come the next day to Fletcher's again, and read it to me, for it was not yet printed. I was delighted; but when the next day came, I found Fletcher alone. Father Waggett had sent word that he was very sorry, but wasn't able to come. "Do you know", Fletcher observed, "what has probably happened? Waggett, last night, in making his examination of conscience, asked himself why he was coming here to read that paper. Was it in the hope of converting you or making you realise how compatible religion is with science? No: it was in order to hear himself praised. He mustn't come."

Pleasant to see how shrewd the simple Fletcher could be in spiritual matters. He was no fool in anything. Our friendship took root, as if it had been an old family friendship; for instance, he and his brother, who were orphans, took me for a week-end to visit a maiden aunt of theirs, Lady Mary Marsham, the sweetest of perfectly deaf old ladies in the neatest of country houses. I have seldom been happier than with these unexpected friends.

A visit to the monastery of the Cowley Fathers. One Sunday Father Waggett invited Fletcher and me to the mid-day dinner at Cowley. The refectory was imposing: plain high white walls, with only a large crucifix over the Abbot's chair, and a long narrow table, with a white table-cloth, running to right and left of him along three sides of the room. The monks all sat with their backs to the wall, leaving the inside of the square empty, as in the pictures of the Last Supper; only two chairs, like that sometimes assigned to Judas, were placed inside, for Fletcher and me. Waggett, in this setting, was absolutely at his ease, and like himself elsewhere. Had we been at a military mess or at a duchess's table, he would have been the same.

Waggett's transcendental argument for immortality. As I found in a conversation we had afterwards in the garden about immortality, he was an *original*: I mean, that he drew his convictions from his own inspiration, even when they were, in words, perfectly conventional.

Immortality was presumable and according to nature, because spirit, the witness, is essentially independent of any world it may discover, prior to it, and in no way held down to that particular world. Admirable, I thought, if only he had brought in his natural history at this point, to explain the inevitably transcendental character of perception or thought, not because thought is materially independent of animal life, but precisely because animal life, in interaction with its environment, has imposed such thought. Now this *originality* in Waggett's sentiments, rendered him a perfect man of the world, not to be put out or embarrassed by the oddity of his surroundings: he was ready for anything, because what was active in himself, spirit, could survive anything unscathed, even death. This is the transcendental principle of courage and of simplicity. It enabled him to put up, I suppose, with the extreme artificiality, self-consciousness, and affectation of everybody else in that monastery.

The handicap of his environment.   If I described all the poses and movements of those poor monks, especially of the young ones, it would be thought a gross caricature. Even to me now it seems incredible that I actually should have seen the idiotic manners that I saw; may I not have dreamt the whole thing afterwards? Yet there was pathos in those absurdities, because these souls, in need of religion, were groping for expression and for support in an age and in a church that had subordinated religion to national pride and to worldliness. They had to rediscover or to imitate a cultus: but for discovery they had no genius and for imitation no taste and no innocence. They therefore seemed fools or hypocrites, when they were sincerely groping after spiritual re-birth. Not all, perhaps; because in the revival of Catholicism in England, both Anglican and Roman, there was also a silly aesthetic sensual side, all vanity and pose and ritualistic pedantry, as in Frederick Rolfe; and this may have contributed something to the affectations of the Cowley monastery.

Father Waggett some years later went to America and lectured, I believe, at the Episcopal Theological Seminary at Cambridge. I went to hear him preach there one afternoon, but I was disappointed. He wasn't the man who, in the garden at Cowley, had talked about immortality. He was commonplace, cautious, dry. What wonder, when he found himself bound by politic ties to people utterly alien to his insights and offensive to his tastes?

The last time I was in Oxford, in 1923, I saw Fletcher's name, half washed out by the rain, still legible on the gates of the stables in Holywell, which looked closed and abandoned. Very likely his enterprise was not successful; such ventures seldom are, and by that time the motor had dethroned the horse. But Fletcher had also become a local politician and agent for the Conservative Party, and seemed, when I last saw him, very pleasantly settled, with his sister, at Wolvercote. I sent them a large brass knocker for their new house; and saw it later, brightly burnished, decorating the door that led from the road to their walled garden. I was leaving England, and didn't knock; but

I hope that good fortune and happiness have done so, and have found their way in.

Aldous Huxley, Grattan Esmonde and Raymond Mortimer at Balliol. During the war Oxford was not deserted even by the young: there was a remnant of boys under military age with others returning wounded or unfit for service, not to speak of a host of privates become cadets and studying to pass examinations for a commission. Somehow, I don't remember how, I made the acquaintance of two sets of undergraduates, one at Balliol and one at Magdalen. Three of the Balliol men remain in my memory, and one at least has become a celebrity: Aldous Huxley. He was then apparently almost blind, with a great shock of curly black hair, and I had no occasion to talk with him. Later, I saw him again, already a popular novelist, with his wife and child at Cortina; but I think there was a latent antipathy in our natures and affections which prevented any spontaneous intercourse. More interesting at the time was Grattan Esmonde, an Irish Catholic already deep in politics, and also devoted to painting in several incongruous styles at once, Byzantine and French. Affectation and enthusiasm were so combined in him with insularity, and this with scraps of exotic knowledge, that it was impossible for me to make out whether he could be taken seriously in any direction. If you took him seriously, he might have seemed a re-incarnation of Lionel Johnson, this time genuinely Irish and at home in the political world. If you took him for an intellectual ballet-dancer, he would turn into the Lord Basil Kilcoole in my *Last Puritan*; except that Esmonde, when I knew him, was really young and handsome, although his elegance was not borne out by everything in his person, as it should be in a genuine beau. Beau Brummel would have shuddered at the sight of those hands.

More my friend was the third of those youths, and he seemed the youngest and least significant, Raymond Mortimer. He was affectionate and literary, read my books, and took me out in a punt to his favourite sylvan resorts. He was an adopted child, perhaps a foundling, and there was a certain mystery or ambiguity about his whole person. He quoted to me the phrase "affected and disaffected", as describing him; but though disaffected politically, a pacifist, conscientious objector, and universal rebel, he was not affected: at least not more than a young man must be who picks up a great deal that he hadn't imbibed traditionally and without selecting it. Something of the waif or the bastard, a prior grudge against everything, seemed to lurk in him, together with the assumption of universal competence: an attitude with which I have some sympathy, being myself something of a waif and a detached critic; but I see the inversion and folly in it, and its hollowness, because the order of nature is the contrary, and we must be true to ourselves before we can be just to other things, and consistently love our enemies. *The pure spirit* in us may safely cultivate universal sympathies; for it can have no grudge against anything and will be tender also to our accidental natural selves and our home world; but *the man* must remain loyal to himself and his traditions, or he will be morally a eunuch and a secret hater of all mankind.

Civilisation   I saw Mortimer later in Paris; and during a season I
in extremis.   spent at the Hôtel du Palais Royal he would sometimes join me at ten in the evening at the Café de la Régence, where I usually had a *camomille* or a beer before turning in. France was perhaps more congenial to him than his own country: it was more of a universal vanity fair and intellectual market, where the surviving moral and national elements would be more hidden and less obstructive to a foreigner than they were in England. For this reason I too preferred to live in Paris and to read French books: not that, like Mortimer, I detested the old France or the old England, but because the new France afforded a more lucid medium through which to observe the dissolution of Christendom. This dissolution might be regretted; yet it was imperative to understand the forces and know the facts that were bringing it about. Harvard also, if you were morally an outsider, afforded such a medium; but there, as in England, the intellectual grab-bag was offered by a missionary hand and with a single purpose, though perhaps an unconscious one: namely to equip everybody as well as possible in the service of national wealth and industrial dominance. The intellectual result, if you forgot that political purpose, was utter confusion; yet this chaos itself was welcome to the dilettante, the parasite, and the *viveur*. It enabled him to pick sweets out of the grab-bag at will, and to indulge all his impulses for the moment, yet sadly in the end: an intellectual brothel.

At Balliol those stray young men, with Urquhart and perhaps another Don or two, had formed an ephemeral club called the Thuliots, which they asked me to join; and I had begun to scrawl a paper on ultimate things, to be read at the next meeting, when the wind that blew towards *Ultima Thule* seemed to die down. The term ended, and the next meeting never took place.

Like my first acquaintances in Oxford, so the last, were made through the Russells, pronounced anti-Oxonians. One day I received a telegram, signed <u>Russell</u>, asking me to come on a certain day to luncheon at a certain farm-house in Garsington. I replied accepting with pleasure, and un-questioningly addressed the telegram to Earl Russell; for I had no reason to expect such a message from Bertie. The next day a note came explaining that it was Bertie who had wired, and hoping I should come just the same. Of course I went, had to go; although it was a new excursion rather beyond my walking range, and involving a journey by the local line to a way station. I arrived duly; it was a real farm-house; and I found Bertie in a spacious upper chamber, with plank walls, and many books strewn about; but nothing about the landlady or the house seemed to forebode luncheon; and I had a good appetite. Presently Bertie said: "We'll go now to the Manor: I have my meals there." So we crossed the road and came to a renovated ancient stone house, a bit below, which I hadn't noticed on arriving, and which proved to be a rather elaborate establishment, with a great garden. There, without previous explanation, I was introduced to a marvellous creature, very tall, very thin, in blue silk flounces, pearls, and black cross-garters (like Malvolio) over bright yellow stockings. She was Lady Ottoline Morrell, had an aristocratic nose, pale blue eyes, with dark straggling locks, and now appeared to be my hostess. She had a husband who I learned afterwards was a Liberal M.P. and a brother of my friend Mrs. Warren. Lady Ottoline had married the son of a brewer, and not an excessively rich one; but he was nice-looking, and her action, together with his politics, which came out at once in his talk, prepared me to understand how Bertie came to be there. Later I gathered that there was a very close old friendship, or perhaps love-affair, between him and Lady Ottoline, which I know to subsist to this day. He was spending his holiday with the Morrells, but slept and worked at the farm-house for greater quietness and freedom.

I soon gathered that it was this lady, ostrich or tropical bird as she seemed, that had wished to discover me, and had caused Bertie to summon me. He and I have always been on pleasant terms, personally and intellectually; yet just as our philosophies are separate without being opposed, except in technicalities and in politics, so our lives and interests are separate, and we were never friends in the sense of looking each other up simply for pleasure or liking to live together.

Lady Ottoline was an intellectual, and cultivated the society of intellectuals; it was in that capacity that she had heard of me, no doubt through Bertie or perhaps through Bridges, and thought of adding me to her collection.

Strange aspect of Lytton Strachey. If I had been younger and interested in forming acqaintances in England, I might have profited by her hospitality, and met various distinguished people at her house, such as Mr. Asquith, then Prime Minister. As it was, I came upon two notabilities worth mentioning: Lytton Strachey and Siegfried Sassoon. Strachey, who was then youngish, looked like a caricature of Christ; a limp cadaverous creature, moving feebly, with lank long brown hair and the beginnings of a beard much paler in colour, and spasmodic treble murmurs of a voice utterly weary and contemptuous. *Obscene* was the character written all over him; and his expertness in secret history and in satire expressed that character intellectually. That it was not merely intellectual appeared one day, when I found Lady Ottoline out, but expected, the maid said, to return shortly; and being left alone in the drawing-room, I picked up a beautifully bound small book that lay at hand on the table. It was a French tale of the eighteenth century, and as obscene as possible. Naturally I read on in it, for I like obscenity well enough in its place, which is behind the scenes, or bursting out on occasion in a comic, rollicking, enormously hearty mood, as in Aristophanes; and when Lady Ottoline arrived, and found me reading it, she took pains to say it was not her book, but Mr. Strachey's. Certainly it wasn't likely to be her book; but he might have put it in his pocket and not left it lying on the drawing-room table.

Siegfried Sassoon and the spiritual ghetto. Siegfried Sassoon showed at first sight more of Siegfried than of Sassoon: a large blond young man sprawling in a large arm-chair, and saying little, as if he were dreaming of the mountains and the open fields. I saw him only once; but he obligingly drove me back to Oxford that afternoon, and from casual words he dropped and what I have seen of his poems, I daresay that the Sassoon side would soon have cropt out. He seemed to be swimming socially on the crest of every wave and to be universally informed, with moral chaos and bitterness beneath. Jewish millionaires cannot feel really at home in the plutocracies they have conquered. These were not originally plutocracies of financiers, but of landed proprietors or blue-sea merchants, bred in military monarchies or in

free commercial cities. The heyday of these comparatively health
plutocracies was past when the Jews came upon the scene, no longe
as foreign pedlars and money-lenders, but as leading citizens. In vai
might they masquerade for a moment as British noblemen or Germa
magnates or even as American men of commercial enterprise, lik
the old Astors or the recent Rockefellers. They had no roots in th
earth, in the race, in the traditions, or in the religion of their countrie
They were surface phenomena, as are actors, professors, critics, an
journalists. While they remained humble artisans or solitary thinker
like Spinoza, they could live content and blameless in the crevices o
the Christian edifice; but when they grew mighty, they could onl
hasten its ruin, and the ruin of their own power over it. A premonitio
of this fate, a sense of this hopeless discord seems to me to distur
the self-assurance of all the Jews I have known, and to keep the
inconsolably envious in their prosperity and profoundly vindictive i
their humanitarianism. A sign of this is that the better of them pin
for Zion, no matter how dominant their position may be in liber
Europe and America. Zion, if worthy of its ancient prophets, wou
not be liberal at all, but tightly compulsory internally, and destructi
or enslaving to all that remained outside.

**I didn't
belong
in the
Intelligentsia.**
Politically, such an ambition seems mad, but moral
and spiritually it is inevitable. I have no Zion, past o
future, to pine for; and yet I sympathise with the Jew
who will not accept the position of weeds and parasite
clinging to the ruins of other Zions, or hastening that ruin. What divide
them from me is only the worldly and competitive form they give t
their prophetic displeasure. They want a forced political paradise o
earth; whereas I am convinced that all glimpses of such a materi
paradise are illusions. My only Zion lies in the fourth dimension, i
heaven, and is composed of the galaxy of all fugitive joys and sincer
ecstasies: a heaven that hides in the heart of earth. Content, lik
Spinoza, with my small share of that, I dislike all the quarrels an
panaceas of the political moralists, turn my back on the disaffecte
and on the fanatics of every sect, and on that conceited Intelligentsi
which sometimes, under a complete misapprehension, asks me t
come into its parlour.

**Nor in
Oxford.**
Lady Ottoline was most kind to me and I liked he
the better the better I knew her; yet I resisted her in
vitations to stay at Garsington, and was repelled by the idea of nibblin

the edges of her social and political world. It was the antithesis and the scornful enemy of the Oxford I could love. Unfortunately this lovable Oxford was imaginary or extinct or evanescent. It could be recaptured only in odd persons and stray glimpses. My bad scholarship, my Romanism, my connection with America and my friendship with the Russells made me unpalatable to the very people that I might have liked best. The conservatives and the poets had never heard of me, or wished they hadn't. Robert Bridges, Father Waggett, and Professor Stewart were the only exceptions; and I was not young enough to profit much by their friendliness. My path, thank God, had led me through Oxford, but it also, thank God, led me away from it.

XXX

Farewell to England

Proposal that I should take root in England. In the year 1919, when the peace of Versailles was being debated, Robert Bridges made a determined effort to induce me to settle for good in England. He said I had things to say that the English needed to hear. Save for the deference I always showed him, who was the only real friend I ever had much older than myself, I might have replied that it would be more becoming and more efficacious for *him* to say these things, if he thought them worth saying. He was Poet Laureate, official prophet to Royalty, psalmist and vicar of King David. He knew the cords to strike and had the ear of the public; and if the public didn't pay much attention to him, what attention would they ever pay to me, a foreigner and a sceptic? Moreover, it was not my vocation to address the British public or any public, but to record as best I could the inwardness of things for a free spirit.

I loved England only too much. Living there I was in danger of losing my philosophical cruelty and independence. Omens of this contagion in sentiment, if not in doctrine, had already appeared in my little book on *Egotism in German Philosophy*: yet the English, far from being propitiated, only felt the more sharply the radical divergence of my mind from theirs. The reviewers accused me of debasing criticism into propaganda. That is what my position would have been in them, if they had assumed it: a philosophical inconsistency caused by political animus. They didn't understand, though they may have felt instinctively, that the egotism I attacked was far from being exclusively German, but was present in them and in the Americans whenever they turned their national ideal into something cosmic and eschatological, and felt themselves to be the chosen people. That if they did so they were themselves neither good philosophers nor good Christians was one of the things they needed to hear: but they wouldn't listen. Did Bridges himself understand it?

I am sounded about becoming a member of Corpus.

It was the net of Oxford that he spread in order to detain me. I had lived there off and on for five years, but absolutely unattached. The point now was to attach me, because I didn't conceal my intention of running away to Paris, to Spain, and to Italy. Now Bridges was a member of Corpus Christi College, and I had more than once been to luncheon there with him in the Senior Common Room; while F. R. S. Schiller, for many years, had asked me to dinner there in Hall, each time that I turned up at Oxford. Besides, a Boston acquaintance of mine, Edward Warren, was also living at Corpus; but he always invited me to his own rooms, where we might be *tête-à-tête* and freely discuss Boston and other delicate subjects. I was thus not unknown at Corpus; but now Bridges induced the Head of the College to ask me to luncheon, in order to inspect me. Apparently I passed muster. In those days I was thoroughly at home in the Oxford atmosphere of moderately comic anecdote—never roisterous—and sly hits at one another's heresies. A well-established Don, like Conybeare, whose scholarship was impeccable, might cry across the table, if someone asked what is orthodoxy, "Orthodoxy is reticence." But I knew better than to take such liberties. I smiled, and remembered the advice of Job to hold my peace, that peradventure I might be thought a wise man. At any rate a few days later Warren approached me with a confidential communication. He had been commissioned to sound me on the subject of residence in Oxford. Should I like to become, for life, a member of the High Table and Common Room at Corpus? For the moment, and during the war, they could let me have rooms in College, but in normal times all their rooms would be needed for undergraduates, and I should have to live in lodgings. When I politely shook my head, and gave merely civil reasons for declining, Warren asked—so little did he or the others understand me,—whether I should prefer to teach. Oh, no: I had never wished to teach. I had nothing to *teach*. I wished only to learn, to be always the student, never the professor. And with being eternally a student went the idea of being free to move, to pass from one town and one country to another, at least while enough youth and energy remained for me to love exploration and to profit by it.

Material pros and cons.

That was all true enough, but I had other far more decisive reasons for not accepting this invitation. Certainly it had its tempting side. I was happy in Oxford, and I needed a centre in which to keep my books and papers, and in which to hibernate and feel at home. The centre I had in Paris, and was about to return to, possessed certain advantages: it was cheap—as I was largely Strong's guest there—and it was convenient for Spain and Italy; yet rooms in an Oxford College, with the privileges of a Don, would have been far more comfortable and dignified. Had I had more money, I might have been seriously tempted to accept: but not at Corpus. Especially not ushered in there, as it were, by Warren, a Bostonian, and with Schiller every day at dinner, as my only other old friend. They were both individuals that a novelist might like to study, interesting cases; but to be sandwiched between them as if intellectually I were such another tramp (as externally indeed I was) would have been a perpetual mortification. Warren was unfortunate, yet I objected to him less than to Schiller, because I pitied him, and our connection with Boston was a true link; but Schiller, with the airs of a professed and shameless sophist, was an English Churchman, for that reason tolerated at Oxford where otherwise he would have been taboo. Perhaps it was his German blood that prevented him, in his simplicity, from seeing himself as others saw him. He earnestly presented himself as a candidate for *the professorship of logic in Oxford*, and asked *me* to write a testimonial recommending him for that position!

The question of moral allegiance. Bridges, who understood me better, must have suspected that my refusal was based on reasons that I hadn't mentioned. Perhaps I didn't like Corpus, and should prefer another college. Now Bridges belonged also to New College, just the college to attract me: beautiful chapel, beautiful music, beautiful garden, old monastic cloisters, old city walls, classical traditions, High Church atmosphere, an undemolished statue of the Virgin still over the College Gate! It happens, that except Lionel Johnson and Bridges himself, I had never had a New College friend, while I have had so many at Balliol, Christ Church, and Magdalen. But that would not have been an objection, if the present residents, masters and pupils, had proved sympathetic, as some of them surely would have done. Bridges on several occasions tried to introduce me to the Warden of New College; but I smelt a rat; perhaps I was afraid that I might be inveigled into some rash commitment. In any case I eluded all contacts in that direction, and so markedly that I am afraid Bridges was a bit offended.

He said that my abandonment of England was "deplorable". Yet nothing was further from my thoughts than to "abandon" England. I hoped to return often, and I had never lived there except as a stranger and a guest. I was simply avoiding a misunderstanding, a false position. I could never abandon *my* England, because that was a part of myself, just as *my* America and *my* Spain are parts of myself: but these are not to be confused with the real, public, ever-changing England, Spain or America of geography and politics. My England was only the illusion with which the real England had inspired me. This illusion contained some truth; but it sprang from a few contacts, many of them indirect, and supplied by other poetic fictions. Shakespeare and Dickens were important sources, and especially Shakespeare's comedies and comic scenes in the histories and tragedies; for the histories officially depict mediaeval passions that are not English now, nor elements in my England. They are noisy. But in the songs, and in Shakespeare's wit and wistfulness everywhere, I find the spirit of my England purer than in any later poet. He was not puritan, he smacked of the country air and of young blood. I am well aware that the real England has many a virtue appreciable from points of view other than mine, virtues that are their own reward; but that is not my affair. It would have been treason to myself and a false profession of faith to have *wedded* the real England or the real America. They are variable material complexes; I could draw from them the pleasures and lessons of travel, but they are not ideal objects to which I could pledge my troth.

Mrs. Berenson once observed with feminine insight that my reasons for not living in England were not those which I gave out, such as my health, or the advantages of living with Strong in Paris or at Fiesole. My real reason, she said, was that England was too much like America. Not yet, perhaps, in 1920; but I felt in my bones, and divined everywhere, the tyrant flood of democracy in England and of commercial imperialism in America, visibly undermining my England in England, and swallowing up my America in America. I was protecting, by fleeing from both, the memory of them in myself.

The veiled offer of a home comes also from Queen's Acre. In those same months a suggestion that might have enticed me twenty-five years earlier came to me from a different quarter: it was that I should go to live as a paying guest with Howard Sturgis and the Babe. But twenty-five years earlier, Howard was rich and would not have dreamt of making me such a proposal, while I was poor, and could not have accepted it. Now the tables, in some measure, were turned. He was old, desolate, ill, and hard up; and I was a friend of long standing, free, with a comfortable income, and beginning to be esteemed as a writer. Moreover, I had always been on pleasant terms with the Babe, liked him, and didn't despise him for not being intellectual or for letting Howard adopt him and support him. If anything it was the Babe that was making the greater sacrifice; which indeed Howard would not have demanded if his affection had been more heroic and his character less feminine. He could perfectly well have helped the Babe to find some comfortable post and to marry, and not have allowed him to grow old in an ambiguous dependence, and incidently to waste Howard's fortune, not in riotous living, but in foolish speculation. The Babe was certainly a minor personage, and feeble; but he kept his head and his spirits up in a difficult position, and was really the victim of the devotion that Howard insisted on showing him.

It was the Babe, on my last visit to them, who dropped a hint, evidently in consequence of confabulations that they had had together. Why didn't I settle down in England? Didn't I have a thousand pounds a year? No? Not so much? Anyhow, I could contribute a tidy sum, if I lived with friends who already had an establishment, but were suffering from the hard times. It would be so much more comfortable for me than living always in temporary quarters, in foreign countries, entirely alone.

Folly of chasing a gay past into a sad future.   How came Howard, with his knowledge of the world and of all his friends' weaknesses, to entertain such a project? He was living in the past. He saw himself, Queen's Acre, and me as we had been twenty-five years before. He knew how enchanting he and his circle had seemed to me then: a little Russian ballet in real life, great airs, extreme elegance in a diminutive setting, wide margins left on every side for glimpses of high life, of Royalty, of politics, of poetry, of grotesque philosophy and grotesque morals; he himself a figurine, a voluntary caricature, sitting with his golden hair beautifully brushed, his small feet daintily crossed, in the middle of a square carpet on the emerald lawn, with his work-basket and menagerie of little dogs about him. His sparkling talk, while he embroidered some large design in gold thread, was alternately tender and merciless, mimicking and ridiculing everyone not present; yet he trembled, like a universal mother, at the mention of any illness, any death, any public disaster. And through all this a drift of charming relatives, guests, and casual visitors, all perfectly at home there, yet all in a holiday mood, acting their various parts appropriately in the comedy, and saying delicate things with a dancing mind.

Reason at home in comedy, not in tragedy. The happy presence of reason in human life is therefore better exemplified in comedy than in tragedy. In comedy we see no terrible sub-human or super-human fatality to render reason vain. Reason therefore can make its little runs and show its comic contradictions and clever solutions without disturbing the sound vegetative substance and free flowerings of human society. We laugh at our foolish errors, correct them with a word, and know no reason why we shouldn't be happy ever after.

Sparks of this free spirit of comedy flew constantly from Howard in his youth; but soon each spark threatened to be extinguished by a little suppressed gasp of compunction. Ridicule and pity seemed to chase each other in his mind. When pity had the start, ridicule dropped out in despair; but when ridicule came first, as it usually did, pity was sure to overtake and smother it before the finish. Sentimental plays with comic relief do not make good comedy; and that was the trouble with Howard's life. He lacked genuine British stamina to keep him jolly in old age, and religion or genius would have been requisite to stiffen the sentimental side.

Gradual fading of his brilliance. A change at Howard's had to come. Long before the war, during my summer visits, I had seen it approach. In 1890, when I first saw him at home, it seemed a bower of roses. Life there was a pantomime in which he played by turns the fairy prince and the disconsolate Pierrot, now full of almost tearful affection, now sitting dressed in sky-blue silk at the head of his sparkling table, surrounded by young dandies and distinguished elderly dames; or when he drove his waggonette and high-stepping pair skilfully and festively, holding high the reins in his white-gloved hands, as if he were dancing a minuet.

Gradually all that gaiety and joyfulness had faded from the scene. First his fancy clothes were discarded: they had lost their freshness and perhaps they had got too tight, for he was no longer very slender. Anyhow masquerades at home were ridiculous and unsuitable. Then he gave up mimicking people, except involuntarily in little touches when he repeated what anyone had said. His imitations had been works of art, taking off not only voice and manner to perfection, but supplying diction and sentiments to suit, and only slightly exaggerated. But mockery, his aging conscience warned him, was unkind; and if he gave up being kind, what would remain of him? The irony of fate would have it that now when he disciplined himself in kindness he was really far less kind than he had been when merry and ready to make fun of everybody; for just as he had loved lame little mongrel dogs for being lame and mongrel, so he had really loved us all in his youth for being absurd and full of little weaknesses; whereas now the merry sentimentalist had become a melancholy one, and sadly censorious. And while the freedom and light faded from his spirit, the sunshine seemed also to fade from his garden and the joyousness from his house.

Anticipations had not been realised. The house had been enlarged, but seemed smaller, the furniture old-fashioned and worn, the once flowering garden grey and bald like our respective heads. The ribaldry had been expunged from conversation, but also the wit, the frankness, the variety. Political intolerance had set in, and a thick mist of sadness. Any straggling guest like myself caused evident disturbance. I knew that some white wine had been ordered expressly on my arrival, so that it might not seem that there was nothing to drink. If I came to live with them I should be an expense, as well as a help: nor could it be an act of kindness on my part in other ways, because our views now clashed not in merriment any longer but in displeasure. People do not grow better when they grow old; they remain the same, but later circumstances cause them to exhibit their character sometimes in a minor key with the soft pedal, so that they seem to us grown sweeter, and sometimes more harshly and disagreeably, when we think them soured or depraved. No: we are no longer charmed by their virtues or interested in their vices.

My selfishness. With the lapse of years Howard and I had begun to see each other in this less favourable light. He thought I was abominably selfish. Certainly, I am profoundly selfish in the sense that I resist human contagion, except provisionally, on the surface, and in matters indifferent to me. For pleasure and convivially, I like to share the life about me, and have often done it: but never so as, at heart, to surrender my independence. On the other hand, I am not selfish in a competitive way. I don't want to snatch money or position or pleasures from other people, nor do I attempt to dominate them, as an unselfish man would say, for their own good. I sincerely wish them joy in their native ways of living, as if they were wild animals; but I decidedly refuse to hunt with them unless the probable result recommends itself to me independently.

To heartlessness of this kind I am ready to plead guilty, and see clearly that it is inhuman. Sympathy with nature, however, is the source of it, and not any aggressive selfishness. Every need or passion evokes dramatic sympathy; but the contrariety among the passions gives that sympathy pause and evokes reason. Now reason, confronted with the chaos and hell of all these conflicting passions and needs, often takes a Mephistophelian turn. Reason can never be malignant, because it is a complex of sympathies, but it may sometimes be cynical, when it shows how many needs are needless and how many passions artificial. I confess that I often like the sayings of Mephistopheles and Iago as much as I dislike the conduct of Othello and Faust. In those sayings there is light; but in the action of these heroes there is no light, only the blind will of protoplasm to stir and to move on, or the blind errors of a bull fighting a shadow. As to the action of Mephistopheles or Iago, there is properly none. There is no human motive for it, only the traditions of a puppet-show, with devils popping up to do the mischief. And this explains the inhumanity of these stage villains. They develop reasoning in the modern drama without acquiring the generic animal needs and passions requisite to evoke reason in the human mind. The rational man cannot cease to be an animal, with the bias of his race and its passions. Reason can serve to control and harmonise these human interests; it cannot take their place.

Howard's distress at the war. I happened to be at Queen's Acre in 1914 shortly after the outbreak of war, when Howard was suffering from a cruel sense of the folly of mankind. What could be more senseless than destruction, destruction, destruction? Yet in his intense liberalism he had applauded the destruction of ancient institutions and ways of life, because destruction there had made room for liberty. The destruction of modern works, on the contrary, would make for poverty; and like a true child of the Great Merchants, Howard was convinced that riches exalted worthy people and made them beneficent. Destruction is indeed cruel and odious when it is carried on for its own sake, malignantly or covetously, like the destruction of the monasteries during the Reformation and the Revolution; but if we take a broad cosmic view, destruction is only the shady side of progress. Like natural death it is inevitable; and though we regret it when premature or needlessly painful, there would be as much sentimental folly in disallowing it as in mourning the coming on of night or of autumn. So the war of 1914–18 was intended by the Germans to be, for them and for the future of the world, a step in industrial and political progress; and so too the next war, wickedly destructive and arrogant on both sides, was conceived, first again by the Germans, and then by all the combatants. The Great Merchants' wealth and the whole economic system of which they were the flower, proved in fact less beneficent and much less durable than the *ancien régime*. Howard himself was a pathetic victim of this system; he was generosity and refinement personified; but he couldn't help envying the dying aristocracy that he imitated and denounced; and the necessary soil to sustain his wealth, refinement, and generosity slipped visibly from under his feet.

During that first climacteric war, I heard that Howard had taken lodgings in London in order to do "War Work" by reading, censoring and readdressing German prisoners' correspondence. This was a marked sacrifice of his comfort and leisure; but solitary comfort with moral irritation and loneliness is not happiness; and the change of scene, the dutiful occupation, and the sense of helping to console mothers, sweethearts, and wives, in spite of possible bombs, was surely some compensation. But there was a tragic background to this charitable act. Howard was beginning to suffer from a mortal illness, cancer in the bowels; and though he had been reprieved by one dangerous operation, another was destined to be necessary. Fortune proved faithless to him with a vengeance; but he showed a remarkable fortitude, not stoical but tender. The fountains of pleasure and gaiety, so sparkling in his youth, had run dry. It was not difficult to surrender them, when the affections remained which need never be surrendered.

This whole story passes into the region of Once upon a Time.   When months later, in Italy, I saw in *The Times* that Howard was dead, and on writing to the Babe received assurances that Howard had died peacefully, without pain, and nobly resigned, then the whole long and curious chapter of my friendship with him came up before me, much as I have recorded it here; and I was glad that the end, which had to be sad, at least had not been harrowing. If I had jumped at the chance of going to live at Queen's Acre, thinking I had found a home at last, my illusion would have been short-lived, and our brief life in common would not have been happy. Still, when I returned to England in 1923, I went to see the Babe where he was living with his father near Bath; but it was an unsatisfactory postscript. What a ghastly pleasure this is, to pull the dead out of their graves! My morning tea was served me in a beautiful china cup, one of a familiar set in the old days at Howard's, now apparently the last survivor, glued and rivetted together in many places, like a mutilated veteran of the Guard. Was I sorry that Howard was dead? No: but I was glad that he had lived. And here I repeated the experience of my uncle Santiago on the death of his daughter. "I had already lost her", he said, "when she was married." I had already, gradually and insensibly, lost Howard when he began to shed his rare self, with its inimitable honest mixture of effeminacy and courage, sensibility and wit, mockery and devoted love.

Decline and immortality of friendships. Meantime a curiously similar cloud had obscured my other chief friendship, my other Mecca, in England. Russell too had become estranged and resentful; and here also, while there was no open breach, there could be no pleasure or simplicity in keeping up the old intimacy. I have described already the circumstances and the issue of this misunderstanding: if now I compare what happened there with what had happened to me with Howard Sturgis, I see a fundamental difference. With Howard the chief trouble was that we had both grown old, that the natural period of our intimacy was past, and could not be prolonged honestly. Howard complained of this, because he was motherly, tender, affectionate, and jealous. He would have wished the Babe to be always a babe, and me to be always the delighted young traveller. I made no such claims, and felt only the melancholy that pervades a world where everything is transitory. By that time I was inured to the cyclical character of all my friendships, that set a period to the best of them, sometimes a very brief one. For me this involved no estrangement, no disillusion; on the contrary, the limits of each friendship perfected that friendship, insured it against disaster, enshrined it in the eternal. Spirit can immortalise events without being able to prolong them; it can virtually survey all seasons at every season. That is what I am doing now to my love of England and of my English friends. My farewell to them, in so far as it was my doing, was only temporal; they belonged to my past; materially we had to separate; it was better and wiser to do so in time. In that way nothing need grow stale, nothing need lapse, or contradict itself or confuse the affections.

Russell also estranged a little. With Russell the bond had little to do with externals, whether in our persons or in our circumstances. Conventionally, without the quickness and simplicity of youth, we should never have become friends; and many people always wondered how it could have happened. The affinity between us lay beneath the surface, and I, at least, felt it at once very strongly: and in two directions. There was physical or vital affinity, or rather attraction by contrast: I admired his fearlessness, agility, and skill in doing things entirely beyond my powers; and he found me sympathetic and calm. Then, intellectually, in independent and disinterested judgment, we coincided; but since this was only a transcendental identity, it could pass unobserved, and could seem to be destroyed by our contrary prejudices in concrete matters. Nevertheless this double affinity could hardly be affected by the lapse of time: and I think that if Russell had finished his career in the world as early as I did, before the age of fifty, we might have been ideal old cronies in our declining years, grumbling of course at each other, yet perfectly happy together. But before he was rid of his matrimonial embarrassments, he had plunged into the troubled waters of unsuccessful business and unsuccessful politics; and he succumbed, exhausted, in the heat of the day, without ever feeling the cool of the twilight. I on the contrary have been enjoying peace for thirty years, in the midst of prodigious wars.

In regard to Russell, I had really been guilty of an indiscretion in questioning the wisdom of his change of wives, when his mind was probably made up. But my motive had been sympathy with his new love, not disapproval; and I feared that legal commitments towards both wives at once would lead to a catastrophe. Had he and Elizabeth retained their freedom, the episode might have ended in comparative peace. Undoubtedly, on the day when Elizabeth had come for me at the station, to win me for her cause, Russell could reasonably have said: "Allow that you were a fool. You didn't know Elizabeth, and you couldn't conceive how happy she would be with me." But soon *she was not happy*; and her unhappiness led her to confide in me, and deepen the sympathy naturally inspired by her delicate mind and person. Russell perceived this, and disliked it; his displeasure even became a kind of jealousy. Not that he imagined for a moment that Elizabeth and I were making love; that would have been absurd; but we seemed to be more confidential and sympathetic about him than with him. This was unfortunately the case, entirely against our will and expectation. We were both interested only in him, and troubled about what threatened to cloud our relations with him or in her case to make them impossible. I couldn't help recognising her difficulties, and the qualities in him that caused them; to me they were an old story, and I had, as he knew, foreseen them and warned him of what would happen. That this now should irritate him, was only human; but here a confusion seems to have arisen in his mind. He thought that I too had become *hostile* to him; that I was *abandoning* him and becoming her ally. He was angry because I saw her once or twice in London after she had left him. He seemed to demand that I should break with her, and because I refused to do so, he said I was "disloyal".

Dominance of the present in Russell's mind. There was a marked peculiarity in Russell's mind that helps to explain this misunderstanding. Perspectives for him were sharply limited: he saw only what, for the moment, touched the matter in hand. All the rest of the truth lapsed altogether. He used to say in the early years that he cared nothing for what his friends might do when he wasn't present. I noticed, for instance, even when he seemed glad to have me as a companion, that he never remembered that any such things existed as my family, my prospects, my opinions, or my books. I was nothing but what I was *for him*. Far from resenting this, I had liked it. It helped me also to shed my past and my future, and to live for a moment in another's life. I was being treated justly and generously in my capacity of friend available for that occasion; I was not meddled with, judged, or misrepresented in my other capacities.

Limited claims and liabilities in friendship. It is characteristic of spontaneous friendship to take on trust, without inquiry and almost at first sight, the unseen doings and unspoken sentiments of our friends: the part known gives us evidence enough that the unknown parts cannot be much amiss. Nor does this imply that the unknown parts must be intelligible to us or after our own taste; on the contrary, it is almost better that they should extend into the inimitable. Friendship may then be touched at the edges with admiration and love. Russell knew that I was a being apart, dependent on him for nothing except the pleasure of his society; he was well aware that in politics my views were different from his: not contradictory but at another level. I never aired them; and I heartily enjoyed the satirical expositions he would make of English law, custom, and prejudice. I learned a lot from him, and was silently confirmed in my affections and philosophy. We never argued. If by chance our divergences came to the surface, he grunted and I laughed. I knew that English opinions had to grow like that, with that scent and that promise of fruit: they were instrumental or edifying opinions, and it would have been unprofitable for them to bother to be true. I on my side was allowed to remain ineffectual and negligible in my wise fools' paradise.

Blind spots in memory. Russell's indifference to everything not involved in his present surroundings or sentiments produced odd lapses in his memory. I have mentioned his forgetting altogether that I had pulled him into the water at Richmond, something that at the time had infuriated him. This might conceivably have been suppressed by Freud's "Censor"; there were other cases of forgetfulness regarding inconvenient or regrettable facts that, in early days, he himself had told me of; and here the pressure of a later *parti pris* evidently had first ignored and then erased the contrary memory. Yet in general it was more what Bergson describes: urgent practical business absorbing attention and driving irrelevant ideas from consciousness. Russell's worries fatigued, distracted and narrowed his mind. A curious sign of this, in his last years, was that he repeatedly called me Sargeaunt. Sargeaunt was a Latin master at Westminster, the translator of Terence in *Loeb's Classics*, who no doubt had been a friend of Russell's at school or in Oxford, and who sometimes came for a week-end to T.H. They had nothing now in common save that old sense of familiarity. This was identically what, from his present point of view, Russell saw in me. Both Sargeaunt and I were obviously inoffensive unimportant elderly persons shuffling about abstractedly: both teachers and old bachelors and old acquaintances, who knew his ways and were not nuisances, and whose names began with an S and had A's and NT's in them. Sargeaunt or Santayana, what difference did it make?

The truth behind the illusion. No doubt this was only a slip of the tongue, in moments of abstraction. A Freudian treatment would have elicited that I had been the only one of his old friends, besides his brother, to stick to him openly through thick and thin for thirty years; that I had been the witness or confidant of many of his love-affairs (though not of all) and had given testimony for him in the most scandalous of his lawsuits, without a thought of the possible risk to my own reputation and livelihood. But all this lay in the past, hidden by the fog of the present, and to be brought to light only at the Last Judgment. To see now only what counted now was a sign of being a man of action and a good politician. And in his life now I counted for very little; perhaps at last I had even become a nuisance.

Yet at the very time when he was confusing me with Sargeaunt, he was complaining that I was "disloyal", and this reproach presupposes allegiance. It asserts regal claims that only long years of fidelity could justify; so that the past remained virtually present *in him*, though banished from his conscious memory. Precisely because he knew that I was loyal, he was hurt to find that I understood Elizabeth's grievances and rebellion. *I* had no grievances, *I* was not deserting him; and in his last letter to me, dictated a week before his death, he crossed out the secretary's word "sincerely" at the end and wrote as usual, "Yours ever".

Last visit to T.H.   When I returned to England in 1923 I had written to him announcing my presence and asked if he wished me to go and see him. He had replied, "Do as you like." I went for a short week-end. He was alone, and spent his day, as he had always done, exactly as if I hadn't been there. I found him busy over the wires of his new radio—it was then a novelty—and in the evening, without dressing, we went to dine at a retired Admiral's in a neighbouring village, where Russell, with his radio, was to give a talk to the villagers at the church vestry or schoolhouse. The radio didn't work very well; it refused to connect with Paris, as Russell had planned; but a fragment of a fragment of a music hall performance in London was heard with satisfaction and wonder. On Sunday we went for a long motor drive; I was not forewarned, but I found that we were bound to a particular cottage where an interesting widow was expecting us for tea. She and Russell afterwards strolled aside in earnest and somewhat troubled conversation. Evidently the course of true love here didn't run smooth. Five years had passed since the flight of Elizabeth, and I ought to have expected to find a lady in the picture. No doubt he had a secretary or other companion in London; but that wasn't enough. He was haunted by the need of a happy home.

The next morning he took me back to town in his motor; and here there was a significant change. It was a closed motor, that is to say, it had a glass front and a roof, but Russell drove and I sat beside him as usual on the front seat. However, there was a chauffeur, something not known formerly; and Russell said that now he sometimes let him drive while he himself dozed on the back seat. He was tired. For thirty years he had lived a distracted life under high pressure and a forced draught, a life absorbed not in doing what he was fit to do but in getting rid of obstacles and wasting his energies on trifles and his affections on impossible women. He needed relaxation, yet couldn't relax. He never drank: a glass of wine would upset him. Continual discomfort had crept into his system; it could be soothed or forgotten only by the greater strain of fast motoring or playing cards, with stakes rather higher than he could afford. For he had become poor; lawsuits and losses in business had nearly ruined him; he was kept going precariously by being director of various precarious companies. He had forgotten his youthful cultivated tastes; he had lost his old friends; he had repudiated his wives or been abandoned by them.

Politics casts a subdued sunset glow over Russell's end. Luckily politics, his hereditary calling, came after a fashion to the rescue. He was elected to the London County Council, and afterwards played a useful if not distinguished part in the House of Lords and in the Government. But for me this was small comfort. I knew what a sham it all was, how unhappy it left him, how it buried the truly masterful side of him under a load of ridiculous servitudes. He thought life had to be like that; that it was a rough fast game you must play; after which your ashes should be scattered to the winds. Peace would come soon enough in death. He could not conceive peace to be something positive, like laughter or intelligence, that lived in the midst of life and was the true triumph over it. Yet he had possessed that peace in his first youth most emphatically; and we had enjoyed it together.

Two final flying visits to England. Such, on the sentimental side and in regard to my friends, was my farewell to England. I yet expected to return often to England, and to revisit my old haunts there, and find other pleasant places. I might see them in an autumnal colouring; that would be a new beauty; it might almost be worth the old. I should stop in London only in transit, but revisit Oxford, Cambridge, Windsor, and perhaps even T.H. for the old solitary walks over fields and downs, or by quiet rivers. All this was not to be, and I am glad of it. Materially, however, I did return to England twice, and for a tell-tale reason. I was invited to give lectures. The author, the professor, went; the spirit did not accompany him. The first time was in 1923, when they asked me to give the Herbert Spencer lecture at Oxford. I was glad to accept; this was my first and last official connection with that University. The question might be what to say about Spencer, whom I had not read or thought of since my undergraduate days, when William James lectured about him. To have re-read Spencer would have been too severe a penance; I chose *The Unknowable* for a subject, as admitting no investigation. I chose also the earliest possible date in October for my lecture, so as to get back to Italy before the winter set in. However, with my romantic notion of revisiting old haunts, and composing elegies about *La Chute des*

Feuilles, I went, as I have already related, to see Russell; and Howard being dead I went to see the Babe, and then retired to lodgings in Cambridge in order to finish writing my lecture. There the always amiable Lapsley put me up at the High Table at Trinity, where I had pleasant conversations with MacTaggart and with Housman. But I was not well, persecuted by my bronchial catarrh, and without heart to attempt to re-evoke any Oxford ghosts.

Oxford and I hopeless survivals.   There, I went to the Clarendon Hotel, walked one day to Iffley, and saw nobody except young Randolph Chetwynd, who was charming, but busy trying to argue I don't know what socialists back to liberalism. He lived in an old stable or coach-house in New College Lane which had been turned into chambers: the sloping roof was open to the eye, plastered, and made picturesque by beams painted black and by iron brackets and lanterns. He dined with me at my hotel and after dinner left me alone to sit by his fire, with a glass of port, and a book said to be interesting; but no, I couldn't feel at home. Nor was my age the only cause. Oxford also was not itself. I couldn't walk through New College Lane or Merton Lane without being startled, as by a cavalry charge, by troops of young women on bicycles, wearing caps and gowns. Was it worth while for Randolph to stem the tide of Socialism? Better let the flood come, I thought, and perhaps something genuine after its kind might emerge after the deluge.

I lecture in the Natural History Museum.   As to my lecture, it was kindly received, but by the oddest of audiences in the oddest of places. I never felt less in Oxford at Oxford than on that occasion. I had been put in communication with a scientific Don, doubtless of the committee for the Spencer Lectureship; and when I called at his house by appointment an hour before the time for the lecture, his wife said he was so sorry but he had been called away to receive 4,000 butterflies that had just arrived from South America. He turned up later, however, and took me to the Natural History Museum, not to see the butterflies, but to read my lecture in a hall like an operating-theatre, with a deep pit, and great black-boards and maps on the walls. He wore no gown and instead of introducing me said simply, "Oh, you might as well begin." The audience, sprinkled about the steep semicircle of seats, comprised a good many Indians and Japanese, and a few ladies. I recognised only old Professor Stewart, always most kind to me, and F. R. S. Schiller. This audience, however, soon became sympathetic, perceived that they were expected to laugh, and applauded heartily at the end. Several dusky youths brought me books to be autographed. Did they feel that I was one of them at heart? We might have been in Singapore.

And read a chapter of *The Realm of Essence* to an uncomprehending Philosophical Society. This occasion had been graceless externally, but morally it left a pleasant impression. I felt that my labour had not been wasted. Not so the evening before, when I had been invited to dine at Wadham and to read a paper before a philosophical club. I had nothing with me except the first chapter of *The Realm of Essence*, so I read that. There was no sympathy in the air, and I read without warmth. When it came to the discussion everybody seemed at sea, and caught at phrases or trifles that struck them as odd. Nobody had heard of *Scepticism and Animal Faith*, published not long before. Samuel of New College, Robert Bridges' son-in-law, but white-bearded like a Hebrew prophet, observed sarcastically that "there seemed to be a thing called substance." Only one little chap, perhaps an Irishman or a Catholic, said something that showed comprehension. How glad I was not to be at New College with the Prophet Samuel and the Prophet Joachim! Wasn't I at heart more English than these "Englishmen" and more Oxonian than these Oxonians? How much at home I should have felt in fleeing from them to Harold Fletcher and Father Waggett, to old Higgs and Robert Bridges!

A thousand silent isolated wits, if I could have got at them, would not only have understood my philosophy but would have fortified my love of England and of mankind. But my lot was cast among the heretics and the radicals, and I seemed insignificant to the professional ideologues who had never had the courage to face the cruel truth about anything, much less to utter it.

There was then a through train from Oxford direct to Dover, passing through the pleasant hilly country south of the Thames and avoiding London. I took it the next morning and found it most comfortable and almost empty. Apparently it was not yet the season for continental travel from Liverpool and the North; but it was lovely autumnal weather, pleasant to the eyes and suitable for a timely but still affectionate farewell to England.

Professional last trip to London only. Nevertheless I returned nine years later for another visit. I had agreed to go in September, to the Spinoza tercentennial meeting at The Hague, and had already finished my address for that occasion when I received an invitation from the Royal Society of Literature in Bloomsbury Square to speak there about Locke, born, like Spinoza, in 1632. Holland is not far from England geographically or morally, and after my heavy work on Spinoza it would be entertaining to write something lighter about the English worthy. The meetings at the Domus Spinozana had pleased me: I had paid my homage to the *numen* of the place, I had learned something about my hero, namely, how *theological* his youth had been (just like mine), and I had breathed gladly again the air of the Netherlands, their vast horizons and their homely ways. I would risk crossing the North Sea, and would ask Cory, who was in London, to engage rooms for me somewhere in Saint James's, where I should feel at home. I didn't mean to leave town or to revive any sentimental associations. Oxford was vulgarised, Cambridge was stale, Russell was "dead and cremated". I would devote the mornings to finishing my lecture, and get some book—it happened to be Aldous Huxley's latest—to while away the evenings; Cory would come to lunch with me every day at Hatchett's, and then I would go for a solitary walk in Hyde Park, and a comfortable tea before turning in. I carried out this programme to the letter. My rooms in Saint James's Place were not like lodgings in Jermyn Street of old: bad service, gas fires (at which I had to finish toasting my toast in the morning, holding it with a fork) and a dismal outlook over mews and chimney-pots. Besides, I was suffering from my bronchial catarrh, not severely, but enough to mar the pleasure of mere existence. However, I should have ended my visit in a neutral state of somnambulism, but for the disgusting experience of the day of my lecture.

Failure of contact. This lecture was a *jeu d'esprit*, it was gay, it was addressed to the free and unprejudiced mind. It also presupposed a certain familiarity with the quality of modern ideologies, seen satirically. I had counted on an audience like the blessed one at the British Academy in 1918 who laughed merrily when they heard that, for a pragmatist, the real past was the idea of the past that he would have in the future. But I found a Bloomsbury audience that didn't consent to smile. Nor was it intellectual opacity alone that enveloped me. All the lights in the room were in my eyes and none on the reading-desk. I had purposely brought my own manuscript, written large and clear on alternate lines, but I couldn't see to read it. What was I to do? Finally, by having the lights at the rear of the room put out, I found that I could manage, though with great difficulty and uncertainty. Sir Rennell Rodd (not yet a peer) who had been ambassador at Rome, pompous and vacuous, introduced me in a vague little speech, saying nothing about Locke and repeatedly calling me a-a-a thinker and a-a-a writer, fortunately not a-a-a professor. It was evident that he knew nothing about me. Disgusted as I was about the lights, and chilled by the chairman and the audience, I couldn't fall into the spirit of my paper, or assume the facile and confidential tone that it demanded. However, I pulled through somehow, and at the end I was surprised that they applauded with some persistence, as if to say: "Your lecture was a bit queer, and disconcerting in places, and we haven't quite caught the drift of it; but we realise that it was a superior lecture, as lectures go." Even Sir Rennell Rodd, in his speech of thanks, had a happy thought. He observed, between two little pauses, that perhaps there was subtlety in what I had said. Yes, Sir Rennell; there were insinuations.

Characteristic comments.   When we broke up, an Indian came to ask me some leading questions about Locke. He wished to be confirmed in thinking Locke superficial. When I explained that Locke was a pioneer, more important in his influence than in his insight, my dusky friend showed his white teeth. Yes, he said, Locke wasn't *profound*. A lady also came up who said that she was Mrs. Inge and that her husband had been sorry not to be able to come and hear me. When I spoke of my sympathy with the Dean's views on the history of religion, and my debt to his *Plotinus*, she shifted the subject at once, repeating how much he liked what I had written about *the English character*. Was it entirely as poetry, as description, as analysis that those words of mine in the *Soliloquies* were so often noticed? Are they juster than what I said of other things? I am afraid they were valued a little as testimonials. The English now had begun to relish praise even from an obscure foreigner! I am confirmed in this suspicion by the fact that Bertrand Russell, who retained the old British pride in Baconian England, its science, philosophy, and politics, actually resented my sentimentality about the *boyish* Englishman, and complained that I cared for nothing except undergraduates and the families they come from. Quite so: there I found human virtue pure and not distorted by any fanaticism, intellectual or moral, or by any shams.

In the midst of change all is immortal.   After this unpleasant last visit, my farewell to England seemed almost an escape. It was a relief to feel that this chapter, rich as it had been, was closed for ever. It was like burying a wife long ago divorced: there was peace in the finality of it. No more attempts to patch things up, no more fresh disappointments to cloud the memory of old embraces. For I had once embraced England with a deep and quiet pleasure. She had seemed perfect in her simplicity, in her distinction, in the comfort of her ways. How decent, how wise, how gentle these ways had been, how beautiful her eyes and voice, how healthful her affections! And although I was avowedly a wayfarer, not fit to be her acknowledged lover or husband, yet she had sometimes seemed to love me a little. She had understood that I was to be trusted, that I saw things as they were, and was not shocked at the truth. She had felt that I loved her as a poet should love, without claims, without flattery, and with an incurable pang in his unfeigned rapture.

XXXI

Old Age in Italy

My belated *Wanderjahre.*   When at the threshold of old age I found myself free and looked about for a place of retirement and finally found it in Italy and particularly in Rome, I was not at all in search of an ideal society or even of a congenial one. I was looking only for suitable lodgings, where the climate, the scene, and the human ways of my neighbours might not impede but if possible inspire me in my projected work and where I might bring my life to a peaceful end. As to society, I was quite content with that which naturally surrounded me; for I still had my family and my friends in America, in England and in Spain: while in Italy later the Anglo-American residents, with their fringe of distinguished Italian acquaintances, would have been accessible to me, if I had cared to cultivate them more assiduously. But essentially I desired solitude and independence: not in the English form of quiet home-life in the country, but rather after the fashion of ancient philosophers, often in exile, but always in sight of the market-place and the theatre.

Nor was I at first entirely adrift. Even my relations with Harvard were not suddenly severed. President Lowell had resisted my wish to resign and we had come to an agreement that, after eighteen months' leave, I should return for the first half of each year. I meant to carry out this plan so long as my mother lived; but she died soon after my departure, and my sister Josefina returned to live in Spain. I had henceforth no home in America. At the same time my income was somewhat increased, and I resigned my professorship by letter. The question of an official residence thus presented itself immediately, and remained more or less open during the next ten years.

Headquarters in Paris.   My nominal headquarters, as well as my books, remained for some time at Strong's in the Avenue de l'Observatoire, and my passport was periodically renewed by the Spanish Consulate in Paris. But Strong and I were never there in winter, and he usually went in summer to see his parents. Sometimes I spent a season there alone, in a silence most favourable for concentration of mind. Then, in the evening, I could remember that all Paris lay at my feet, behind that screen of green trees, and I would go to the Boulevards or to the Champs Elysées for a stroll and for dinner.

There was evidently no finality, no sense of home, in such a *pied-à-terre*. Nor was Paris a place where, even if I had been younger and richer, I should have cared to live. It did very well for an occasional season of cosmopolitan pleasures, but even its intellectual and artistic movements, though they greatly attracted and rewarded attention, were episodes, fashions, and extravagances with which no one would wish to be identified. Even distinguished and philosophical persons that I came across never inspired any confidence in my mind. Three of these might be mentioned: Bergson, Boutroux, and Dr. Cazalis, who wrote under the name of Jean Lahore. None of these three were Catholics, so that in them all there was a certain strain or self-consciousness, as of outsiders who always felt a little aggrieved and a little insecure in the French atmosphere. I have never had a French friend. In the most charming of them I felt something false, as if an evil spell bound them to some secret and sinister cause, and they were feigning all their amiability for an ulterior reason. They could never be disinterested, never detached. They had in their hearts a sort of covert intensity and stubborn nearsightedness that I could not endure. On the other hand I have fed with perpetual delight on the French way of putting things: everything was perceived by them, everything tolerated, nothing overdone, nothing insisted upon. The French mind is an exquisite medium for conveying such things as can be communicated in words. It is the unspoken things of which one feels the absence or mistrusts the quality.

My unsatisfactory *milieu* in Madrid. During my first free years I instinctively turned to Spain, and besides long visits in Avila, I lived awhile with Mercedes in Madrid, in a circle composed of twenty-seven women and not one man. For partial relief, I then went with her and Josefina to Seville. After a while they were bored there, and left me to enjoy the air in the gardens, the Cathedral, the little plays at 10.30 at the *Teatro del Duque*, the bull-fights, and the processions of Holy Week. I even went sometimes to the music hall *Novedades* to see the local dancing and hear the local songs. It was well enough for once, or for the young natives who can enjoy it all gracefully, and escape to higher things. But for me, with my tastes and at my age, it was only a flimsy spectacle, a surface without volume or depth and with nothing to hold me. During another winter, being cold and bored in Madrid with Mercedes and her intimates, I made a trip to Valencia, Alicante, and Murcia. I saw some lovely spots along the coast, where a Spanish *Riviera* might exist; but the towns and the life were distinctly second-rate, and even the language, as far as Murcia, not Castilian. Avila, I perceived, was the only place in Spain where I might live happily. I kept that in reserve; for the moment I would look about elsewhere. Before long, however, war had broken out, and by chance had caught me in Cambridge at the *Red Lion*; and in England I remained for five years.

Anglophobia in Avila.   When I returned to Avila after the war I felt a distinct change in the moral climate. My long residence in England and the fact that my sympathies during the struggle had been strong on the English side, produced a chill towards me in my sister's family. Their sentiments had been, and continued always to be inspired by clerical and nationalist Spanish opinion, which anticipated what it is now, during the second general war. At that time I didn't altogether appreciate the grounds of such violent Anglophobia. It was not founded on knowledge of England gained in England, as my feelings were. It arose indirectly, through traditional fear and hatred of English influence in other European countries; and to this was added the detestation of French influence in Spain, both in politics and in religion. These good people did not suspect (although the Pope did) that modern Germany was more anti-Catholic than England or even than republican France, in that it preached an enthusiastic return to heathenism; whereas England and France were merely Erastian, worldly, greedy and money-loving, as the Catholic soul of Castile certainly was not. Yet they did not preach a racial war on the Jewish foundations of Christianity, nor propose to saddle a Nietzschean morality on peaceful lands like Austria, Bavaria, and the Rhineland that were traditionally Catholic.

My amphibious neutrality.   Not that my own philosophy was partisan or afraid of Nietzsche. Neither tribal nor commercial morality inspired me with particular horror. I knew that the first was brutal and the second vulgar; but they both were intelligible phases in human civilisation, just as Catholicism was; and it was an accident of temperament or circumstances how far my sympathies were enlisted with one or the other. Essentially I could sympathise with them all, but could identify myself with none. That I was a philosopher, that I could identify myself willingly only with intelligence and with the truth, offended my friends in Avila, as it now seems to offend some of my friends in other places.

Unsuccessful experiment of living in the *Riviera*.   The idea of eventually living in Avila, with one of my sisters or with both, remained with me; but the moment had not arrived. Meantime I would make trial of the Riviera, the common refuge of the lazy in exile; and I took rooms, with only first breakfast served, first at Monte Carlo and then in Nice, going to Italian restaurants for my other meals. I should have liked the old town of Monaco, with its gardens overhanging the sea, but there was no hotel there, and no likely lodgings. In Nice I had a bad attack of my chronic catarrh, and moved to a clinic, where lying comfortably in bed by a wide open window, I had a pleasant convalescence spent reading Spengler's *Untergang des Abendlandes*, all but the mathematical part, which I couldn't understand and distrusted *a priori*; for it is a marvel that mathematics should apply so well to the material world, and to apply it to history or ideas is pure madness.

Most people seen to better advantage at home than abroad.   The atmosphere of the Riviera, physical and moral, didn't agree with me very well. And the same may be said of Florence, in spite of the presence there of some old friends, Strong, Loeser, and Berenson. They, Strong especially, with his new villa, caused me often to stop there, as I never did again at the Riviera; yet even in Fiesole I was never happy. All nationalities are better at home, where they are less conspicuous as special nationalities, and may pass for common humanity. When you transplant the species, it suffers constraint and becomes sickly or intrusive, or both at once. I like to be a stranger myself, it was my destiny; but I wish to be the only stranger. For this reason I have been happiest among people of all nationalities who were not of my own age, class, or family circle; for then I was a single exceptional personage in their world, and they a complete harmonious milieu for me to drop into and live with for a season. Where there were other foreigners among whom I was classed, and with whom I was expected to be more at home than with the natives, I was ill at ease in both camps, and disliked each for not knowing how to live with the other. For this reason in America I avoided all foreigners, especially all Spanish people; and in England or Spain or even Italy, I suffered when I was with Americans. Only in Paris, a cosmopolitan caravansary in itself, did Americans and other foreigners fall nicely into the picture and spoil nothing in the charm of the place. This would probably not have been the case even there, if I had known the best French people; but I saw only persons already cultivating foreigners and making up to them for interested reasons; and it was not among such that I cared to move.

Rome, Venice, and Cortina become my yearly orbit. It might seem that I turned to Italy and especially to Rome as a last resort, but that was not the case. Italy and Rome were my first choice, my ideal point of vantage in thought, the one anthropological centre where nature and art were most beautiful, and mankind least distorted from their complete character. But I had wished to look about first to see if my own country, or places more allied to my later associations, like England, would not be, for me, more desirable retreats: for it was a retreat I was looking for, not a field of action. No: upon trial I was sure that none of them would be better. Therefore I began to spend my winters in Rome in 1920, as I have done ever since. For the summer I still went to Paris, to Avila, sometimes to Glion over the lake of Geneva, a short walk to the clinic where Strong often took refuge. But I remembered the terms in which my poetic friend Stickney had eulogised Cortina, an ideal Tyrolese village in an emerald green valley amid the mountains of the moon; and now, after the war, Cortina was in Italy. I tried it, going to the Hotel Cristallo high on a hillside, and found it cool, free from insects, and rich in walks short or long at pleasure, and always exhilarating. It was here, in a bare little bedroom on the top floor, that I wrote at one stretch, *Platonism and the Spiritual Life*. In that year (1926) the valley of Ampezzo was still green and rustic, with only a few roofs clustering about the church, with its noble spire. The peasants were ideal peasants and the strangers few, and true lovers of nature.

My love of Venice. Cortina had extraneous advantages for me as well; it could be easily reached, yet not so easily as by a night express direct from Rome. It was almost inevitable to stop in Venice; and I fell into the habit of stopping there for some weeks in each year, especially in September and October. The fashion in Venice had moved to the Lido, where I didn't follow it; and the sea front, the Piazza and the Piazzetta preserved an Italian rather than a cosmopolitan character. I found a book by an old-fashioned English resident on *Walks in Venice* with accurate little maps indicating the turns to take at each point in the labyrinth of lanes; and with this guide I walked all over Venice, without ever taking a gondola, except on my arrival and departure, when I had luggage. The eye was feasted in Venice as nowhere else on light and colour. The sea, most inhuman of elements, met in perfect friendship here with the soft and pleasure-loving side of man; and the mixed architecture of a by-gone plutocracy reconciled me to the experiments of today.

Causes of Venetian effects.   Here too the desire to be splendid is in evidence, rather than vital greatness betrayed by a splendour that was unintended. How different these palaces, so rich and ornamental outside, so evidently striving to outshine one another, from the severe grandeur of the palaces in Rome, each turned inwards, walled and barred like a castle or a monastery against the outer world, plain like a fortress or a prison, yet imposing by the scale of the monumental doors and spaced windows, the cliff-like walls and the defiant cornices! In Venice, originally on the human scale, all was pleasant loggias and balconies, where the gay inmates might crowd to see and to be seen. Business was not hidden; it might be transacted in the great Piazza or on the frequented Rialto; but Pleasure soon drove it in doors, into the secret cabinets of rich men, while the young and gallant paraded the squares or the Grand Canal, to display their finery and plot their amours. Venice would have been vulgar but for two blessed accidents, that made it inimitably beautiful. One was the magic of that lagoon on which it seems to float, and that mesh of canals vivifying it as the veins vivify the body, and everywhere mirroring a sky itself softened and dyed by the denser tints that earth and water have reflected back upon it. The other happy accident was the age in which Venice flourished and from which it borrowed its arts. The model at first was Byzantium, also a commercial city, although an oriental and hieratic one; so that everything, even nautical things, came to the Venetians already mellowed and refined by the traditions of many ages and many empires. These Venetians were *nouveaux riches*; they could never so have developed their arts from within; but they had many contacts, such as other Christian nations generally lacked, and they could adopt and combine many fashions, not without a festive originality in combining them. So later, when it became the fashion in Italy to be classical, the Venetians again had models nobler than their own genius; yet those models gained a new charm and elegance when reproduced, on a smaller scale, in the incomparable stage-setting of Venice.

Daily round in Venice. I lodged habitually at Danieli's, going out to Martini's by the *Teatro Fenice* for luncheon, because it was quiet and pleasant there at that hour, sitting under an awning in the well-paved square, with interesting façades before one, and not too much food, as happened then in good hotels. For dinner I usually went to the Olympia, where a table at the back was reserved for me; and when the band began to play at nine o'clock, I was ready to go and stand in the Piazza, or walk about in the upper end of it, where few people gathered. The public seems to think that to hear music is to see the musicians fiddle and blow. I preferred not to see them. Here, and in the Pincio in Rome, I had my only taste of instrumental music: shocking confession, no doubt, for a person supposed to relish the fine arts. But music bores me if I am sitting penned in among a crowd in a hot place, with bright artificial lights, and a general pretense at intelligent interest, whether such interest exists or not. It is too much like sitting through a service in a Protestant church. At the opera I can forget this discomfort because the impression, visual as well as auditory, is violent enough to hold my attention; but for pure music I desire the open air, solitude if possible, and liberty to move about, and to go away. There is a wonderful sense of freedom in standing on one's two legs. It adds, in my feeling, to the sincere enjoyment of both nature and art. Music and landscape then come as a gift, not as a thing procured for a ticket that constitutes a promise and imposes a sort of pledge. I prefer that the beautiful should come upon me unannounced, and that it should leave me at liberty.*

My lodgings there. At Danieli's my favourite room was a little one in the entresol, No. 8, close over the entrance, where I could sit during my writing hours in the morning and during my reading hours in the early afternoon, by my low-silled window, open but discreetly curtained, little above the level of the Riva degli Schiavoni. Here I was conscious of the life of the place but not disturbed by it and refreshed, whenever I looked up, by the lovely picture of San Giorgio Maggiore across the Bacino di San Marco. If I stretched my neck a little, I could also see the Dogana and the domes and belfry of La Salute; but this, although more ornate, seemed to me less beautiful

---

* . . . veniam subito, nec quisquam nuntiet ante,
sed videar caelo missus adesse tibi. . . .

Tibullus, III, *ad finem.*

than San Giorgio, less naturally perfect and individual; because the brick and marble harmonies of San Giorgio, with the green roof of the tower, were a happy gift of fortune. Doubtless the plutocratic rebuilders of the old convent and hospital would have liked to face everything with white marble; but the rich, on their lavish scale, are no less or even more hampered than the poor; and in this case they had the exquisite taste of Palladio to redeem and to glorify their comparative poverty. The new west front should be shining white, to be gilded and mellowed by the setting sun; while the walls, the dome, and the outlying low buildings should preserve their weathered pink, with only touches of white and grey in the lintels and cornices. And fortune smiled again when the campanile was added, a slenderer and more graceful copy of that of Saint Mark's, *matre pulchra filia pulchrior*: for it completes the harmony of its church, as the great campanile does not, lends it height and unity, rhymes the same russet with the same white, and caps the whole, in the hood of the spire, with a touch of aerial green. So nature has blessed and adopted this work of art, as if it had descended like a vision from the clouds and remained suspended between the sparkling sea and the depths of air.

Once, in 1939–40, when the Hotel Bristol in Rome was closed and about to be rebuilt, I spent a whole winter in Venice, not a thing to be recommended; yet a pleasant walk had just been opened along the sea front uninterruptedly to the Public Gardens. There were nine little bridges, I counted some 400 steps, to go up and down on the way; but from each bridge there was a new vista, and the varied shipping carried the mind from ancient wars to the one then beginning, and from those placid lagoons to the Southern Seas.

The Rev. Luciano Zampa.   In Rome fortune at first lent me a living guide in the person of the Rev. Luciano Zampa of Gubbio, a modernist priest who had translated my *Egotism in German Philosophy*. It was with him that I first ventured into Italian conversation. He helped me without discouraging me by too many corrections; and I could always put in an English or Spanish or French or even Latin word if my Italian failed me. Besides, he could often guess what I wished to say before I quite said it; my later friend Michele Petrone used to do the same; and with these two I could even become eloquent in Italian, in spite of my insecure hold on the language. But the great service that Zampa did me was to show me the less obvious sights of Rome. Being a provincial priest—at first dressed as a layman, having been unfrocked for his modernism, but afterwards restored to his clerical privileges—he had a traditional admiration for all that was ecclesiastically important. Great ancient columns and rich marbles inspired him with respect, apart from their beauty: and this proprietary human esteem for the arts was a good corrective to the priggish aestheticism of my English-speaking artistic friends. Later some of these artistic friends—Geoffrey Scott, for instance, in Florence—abetted this ecclesiastical view in so far as they renounced pre-Raphaelism and learned to love the baroque; but that was an aesthetic fashion also, and corrupt, Aubrey Beardsley substituted for Burne-Jones; whereas my honest Zampa was simply impressed by the positive qualities of great size, rarity, cost, or splendour.

Walks in   In spite of these lessons, however, I soon retreated
Rome.   into my aesthetic, or rather my poetic, shell, and limited my diet of visual impressions to a few chosen sights. The central streets came in inevitably for a person who lives in them and frequents cafés; but my usual walk was to Trinità de' Monti, the Pincio and the Villa Borghese. On some days I would go instead to the Tiber, St. Peter's, and (when it was made) the admirable garden at Castel Sant'Angelo; or else to the Janiculum, San Pietro in Montorio and, above all, the Aqua Paola, where I always read the monumental inscription over the fountain, until finally I knew it by heart. And if any friend turned up, not familiar with Rome, I would explain my aversion to museums and picture galleries, but would offer to take them, after luncheon, to see three things, the Pantheon, Michaelangelo's Moses, and the Forum from the top of the Capitoline, which included admiring the two pavilions of Michaelangelo and the statue of Marcus Aurelius. Of these things I never tired: but of seeing more things or other things I had had enough. Fresher thoughts came and I could transmit more pleasure in reconsidering these old objects than in staring at new ones.

Yet when not compelled to talk or to avoid useless explorations, I took many other casual turns in the labyrinth of the old streets: sometimes purposely making little circuits in search of odd variations on the theme of doors and windows, not to speak of church fronts and of fountains. Sometimes lovely things turned up in this way: for instance the German burying ground by the sacristy of St. Peter's, and the court of the hospital adjoining the church in the Borgo Santo Spirito, not far distant. Monte Cavallo, at the tip of the Quirinal, where also a band played, was another spot to loiter in at sunset, when the level light gilded the whole length of the Alta Semita, as far as the Porta Pia, a caprice of Michaelangelo's. Many things depended on the time of day and the weather for their full effect, as landscape necessarily does; and great weathered works of architecture become parts of the landscape and move the mind to poetry, not to pedantic criticism.

Meditation in St. John Lateran. This for me, with my imperfect eyesight wrapping everything in a second often merciful atmosphere, applies even to interiors. With Spanish preconceptions of what a church should be—sombre, devotional, and rich in shrines—Italian interiors are apt to strike me as empty and cold; and even the great basilicas in Rome seem to lack a focus and to be too much like artists' models and too little like places of worship. But this may be due to personal prejudice, which a new personal experience may correct. Now (1942) that I live not far from the Lateran, I often cross San Giovanni, as I used to do the Cathedral of Avila, in order to avoid the hot sun or the rough pavement; and being old and fond of sitting upon public benches, I rest for a moment on one of the wooden seats that are found there (but not, alas, at St. Peter's); and in those calm moments my eye has learned to frame wonderful vistas in that great church, forward to the restored apse with its golden mosaics and its papal throne, or across aisles and aisles, into vast side chapels, each a church in itself. And then the whole place seems to lose its rigidity and its dead pomp, and to become a marvellous labyrinth, as if it were a work of nature or of fancy rather than of human art. The gigantic violent Apostles in the nave cease to seem monstrous, as great rocks or great trees are not monstrous; they become baroque works of nature, as if water by chance had molded the sides of a cliff into the likeness of Titans. And what might have disappointed in the mother of cathedrals, the moderate height, becomes only the condition of unlimited breadth; and you cannot complain that in the centre you have a ceiling instead of a vault or a soaring dome, when you see beyond, quite subordinate to this rectangular space, soaring domes and vaults, enclosing other spaces and shedding variously coloured lights on other elaborate altars. Thus familiarity discloses the richness of what seemed bare at first glance, and you find amplitude, time, and silence intensely present in what you had passed by as insignificant.

Constancy in an inconstant world. It might seem that with age places gained upon persons in interest to my mind; and that my pleasure grew in intercourse with things rather than with ideas. Yet what held me in things was only their aspects, the picturesque or moral suggestions in them; for to things as material weights or forces I have never become attached. The old animal passion for fetiches, for hugging and hoarding particular objects because of their material identity, seems to have been entirely extinct in me; and it was precisely this indifference to physical identities that made me episodical in friendship and Platonising in love. I was far from inconstant or variable in affection towards the *true* objects of my choice; but these were not the material things or persons that chance put in my way, in their necessarily mixed and changing compositon. I saw only the gifts and virtues of which, perhaps for the first time, they gave me a clear idea. They became to that extent my local shrines or the saints for that day in my calendar; but never did the places or the persons turn into idols for my irrational worship. It was only the *numen* in them that I loved, who, as I passed by abstracted, whispered some immortal word in my ear.

It is true that persons, however changed in aspect, at least keep their memories. They may hark back to the scenes and the interests that may have bound them once to their old friends; and beneath memory there is also a soul, an innate disposition and character that may be recognised at moments in spite of all the incrustations of age, servitude, and vice. And besides that, there are lessons of experience; acquirements and renunciations brought about by fortune, that some-times transform the most commonplace persons, or the least pre-possessing originally, into noble minds; and then the Holy Ghost, that is no respecter of persons, speaks to us through those softened and pathetic masks. I would not nurse my animal aversions any more than my animal favouritisms. Without disowning in any way the bonds of blood or of comradeship or of social utility, I gladly recognise the good and the beautiful in unexpected quarters; and I am not in the least daunted in my cult of those divine essences when I find that they have disappeared from a place or a person that had once seemed to possess them.

Old age in renouncing all things may possess them all ideally. Never have I enjoyed youth so thoroughly as I have in my old age. In writing *Dialogues in Limbo*, *The Last Puritan*, and now all these descriptions of the friends of my youth and the young friends of my middle age, I have drunk the pleasure of life more pure, more joyful, than it ever was when mingled with all the hidden anx-ieties and little annoyances of actual living. Nothing is inherently and invincibly young except spirit. And spirit can enter a human being perhaps better in the quiet of old age and dwell there more undisturbed than in the turmoil of adventure. But it must be in solitude. I do not need or desire to hob-nob artificially with other old men in order to revisit them in their salad days, and to renew my own. In Rome, in the eternal city, I feel nearer to my own past, and to the whole past and future of the world, than I should in any cemetery or in any museum of relics. Old places and old persons in their turn, when spirit dwells in them, have an intrinsic vitality of which youth is incapable; precisely the balance and wisdom that come from long perspectives and broad foundations. Everything shines then for the spirit by its own light in its own place and time; but not as it shone in its own restless eyes. For in its own eyes each person and each place was the centre of a universe full of threatening and tempting things; but old age, having less intensity at the centre has more clearness at the circumference, and knows that just because spirit, at each point, is a private centre for all things, no one point, no one phase of spirit, is materially a public centre for all the rest. Thus recognition and honour flow out to all things, from the mind that conceives them justly and without egotism; and thus mind is reconciled to its own momentary existence and limited vision by the sense of the infinite supplements that embosom it on every side.

XXXII

Epilogue on My Host,
The World

Private poetical character of these reminiscences. · Persons and places people the world; they individuate its parts; and I have devoted this book to recording some of them that remain alive in my memory. Mine are insignificant recollections: for even when the themes happen to have some importance as persons and places in the great world, it is not at all in that capacity that I prize and describe them. I keep only some old miniature or some little perspective that caught my eye in passing, when the persons perhaps were young and the places empty and not dressed up to receive visitors, as are museums, libraries, ball-rooms and dinner-tables. Those were free glimpses of the world that I could love and could carry away. They were my consolations.

Yet I loved land and sea in their inhumanity. ˙ Yet the very contrast between these glimpses, all picturesque and aerial, and the vast obscure inexorable world from which they came, forced me gradually to form some notion of that material world also. We were a blue-sea family; our world was that of colonial officials and great merchants. From the beginning I learned to think of the earth as a globe with its surface chiefly salt water, a barren treacherous and intractable waste for mankind, yet tempting and beautiful and swarming with primitive animals not possible to tame or humanise but sometimes good to eat. In fine, I opened my eyes on the world with the conviction that it was inhuman: not meant for man, but habitable by him, and possible to exploit, with prudence, in innumerable ways: a conviction that everything ever since has confirmed.

One peculiarity was common to all these possible satisfactions: they brought something perfect, consummate, final. The sea, after no matter what storms, returned to its equilibrium and placidity; its gamut was definite. Voyages all led to some port. The vastness and violence of

538   Persons and Places

nature, in challenging and often decimating mankind, by no means tend to dehumanise it. The quality of attainable goods may change, and also the conditions for attaining them; but the way is always open, at the right time, for the right sort of animal and for the right sort of mind. Dogs have their day; arts have their dates; and the great question is not what age you live in or what art you pursue, but what perfection you can achieve in that art under those circumstances.

The great master of sympathy with nature, in my education, was Lucretius. Romantic poets and philosophers, when they talk of nature, mean only landscape or other impressions due to aerial perspectives, sensuous harmonies of colour or form, or vital intoxications, such as those of riding, sea-faring, or mountain-climbing. Nature is loved for heightening self-consciousness and prized for ministering to human comfort and luxury, but is otherwise ignored as contemptible, dead, or non-existent. Or when people's temper is hardy and pugnacious, they may require nature as a buffer on which to rain their mighty blows and carve their important initials. Where human strength comes from or what ends human existence might serve, they neither know nor care.

My own person an annoying part of my world. The spirit in me felt itself cast upon this social and political world somewhat like Robinson Crusoe upon his island. We were both creatures of the same Great Nature; but my world, in its geography and astronomy, like Robinson Crusoe's island, had much more massive and ancient foundations than the small utterly insecure waif that had been wrecked upon it. In its social and political structure, however, my world was more like Crusoe's energetic person; for my island was densely inhabited; an ugly town, a stinted family, a common school; and the most troublesome and inescapable of its denizens was the particular body in which my spirit found itself rooted; so rooted that it became doubtful whether that body with its feelings and actions was not my true self, rather than this invisible spirit which they oppressed. I seemed to be both; and yet this compulsive and self-tormenting creature called "Me" was more odious and cruel to the "I" within than were the sea and sky, the woods and mountains or the very cities and crowds of people that this animal "Me" moved among: for the spirit in me was happy and free ranging through that world, but troubled and captive in its close biological integument.

Yet spirit must be incarnate.   This is the double conflict, the social opposition and the moral agony, that spirit suffers by being incarnate; and yet if it were not incarnate it could not be individual, with a station in space and time, a language and special perspectives over nature and history: indeed, if not incarnate, spirit could not *exist* at all or be the inner light and perpetual witness of a *life* in its dramatic vicissitudes.

My accidental foreignness favoured my spiritual freedom.   If it be the fate of all spirit to live in a special body and a special age, and yet, for its vocation and proper life, to be addressed from that centre to all life and to all being, I can understand why I have been more sensible to this plight and to this mission than were most of my contemporaries. For by chance I was a foreigner where I was educated; and although the new language and customs interested me and gave me no serious trouble, yet speculatively and emotionally, especially in regard to religion, the world around me was utterly undigestible. The times also were moving, rapidly and exultingly, towards what for me was chaos and universal triviality. At first these discords sounded like distant thunder. Externally they were not yet violent; the world smiled in my eyes as I came to manhood, and the beauties and dignity of the past made the present unimportant. And as the feeling of being a stranger and an exile by nature as well as by accident grew upon me in time, it came to be almost a point of pride; some people may have thought it an affectation. It was not that; I have always admired the normal child of his age and country. My case was humanly unfortunate, and involved many defects; yet it opened to me another vocation, not better (I admit no absolute standards) but more speculative, freer, juster, and for me happier.

Landlord and guest.   I had always dreamt of travel, and it was oftenest in the voluntary, interested, appreciative rôle of the traveller that I felt myself most honest in my dealings with my environment. The world was My Host; I was a temporary guest in his busy and animated establishment. We met as strangers; yet each had generic and well-grounded ideas of what could be expected of the other. First impressions made these expectations more precise; the inn was habitable; the guest was presumably solvent. We might prove mutually useful. My Host and I could become friends diplomatically; but we were not akin in either our interests or our powers. The normal economy of an innkeeper, though incidentally and in a measure it supplies the wants of his guests, knows nothing of their private moral

economy. Their tastes in wines, in service, or in music may entirely
outrun or contradict his long-established practice, which he will impose
on his guests with all the authority of a landlord; and there may not
be another inn in the place, or only worse ones. The guest has no
right to demand what is not provided. He must be thankful for any
little concessions that may be made to his personal tastes, if he is
tactful and moderate in his requirements, pays his bills promptly and
gives decent tips.

Virtues of a commercial age and country.   Such at least was the case in the nineteenth century
when the world made itself pleasant to the traveller; and
not to rich travellers only but to the most modest, and
even to the very poor in their little purchases and popular
feasts. Personal freedom produced a certain dignity and good humour
even in bargaining; for to buy and sell, to patronise a shop or a
boarding-house, was an act of kindness; and bills, at least in civilly
commercial England, were always receipted "with thanks". Having
lived a peaceful independent life, free from hardship or misfortune,
I have found it easy to conform externally with the mechanism of
society. Matter has been kind to me, and I am a lover of matter. Not
only aesthetically but dynamically, as felt by Lucretius, nature to me
is a welcome presence; and modern progress in mechanical invention
and industrial luxury has excited joyously my materialistic imagination,
as it did prophetically that of Bacon. Moreover, I inherited from my
father a bond with matter which Bacon and Lucretius probably did
not feel: the love of employing leisure in small mechanical occupations.
I should never have read and written so much if the physical side of
these employments had not been congenial to me and rich with a
quiet happiness. Any common surroundings and any commonplace
people pleased me well enough; it was only when sugary rapture was
demanded about them or by them, as happened almost everywhere
in my youth, that my stomach rose in radical protest. Then I discovered
how much the human world of my time had become the enemy of
spirit and therefore of its own light and peace.

Radical disease of Western civilisation.   How had this happened? Not at all as lovers of antiquity
or of the middle ages seem to think, because of me-
chanical inventions or natural sciences or loss of Christian
faith. These transformations might all have occurred in
the normal growth of society. Variety in cultures is not due to ab-
errations any more than is the variety of animal species. But there

may be aberration in any species or any culture when it becomes *vicious*; that is, when it forms habits destructive of its health and of its ability to prosper in its environment. Now modern sciences and inventions are not vicious in this sense; on the contrary, they bring notable additions to human *virtù*. And I think that the Renaissance, with the historical learning and humanism which it fostered, was also a great gain for human happiness and self-knowledge. Of this the surface of the modern world during my youth gave continual evidence, in spite of an undercurrent of unrest and disaffection sometimes heard rumbling below. "My Host's" establishment made a brave appearance; and I was particularly conscious of many new facilities of travel, breadth of information, and cosmopolitan convenience and luxury. Though there was no longer any dignity in manners, or much distinction in costume, fashion had not lost all its charm. In literature and the fine arts talent could give pleasure by its expertness, if not by its taste or savour. I have described how in Boston and in England I sometimes sipped the rim of the plutocratic cup; and this was a real pleasure, because beneath the delicacy of the material feast there was a lot of shrewd experience in that society, and of placid kindness.

I displease other intellectuals.   There was another cosmopolitan circle, less select and less worldly, but no less entertaining and no less subject to fashion and to ironical gossip, the Intellectuals, into whose company I was sometimes drawn. I was officially one of them, yet they felt in their bones that I might be secretly a traitor. "Ah, yes," cried a distinguished Jesuit recently when I was casually mentioned, "he is the *poetical* atheist." And an Italian professor, also a Catholic but tinged with German idealism, remarked of me: "The trouble with him is that he has never succeeded in outgrowing materialism." Finally a faithful diehard of British psychologism, asked why I was overlooked among contemporary philosophers, replied: "Because he has no originality. Everything in him is drawn from Plato and Leibniz." This critical band is democratic in that it recognises no official authority and lets a fluid public opinion carry the day; yet it is, on principle, in each man, private and independent in judgment. Few, however, have much time to read originals or to study facts. Leaders and busybodies must obey their momentum. A personal reaction on what other people say is socially sufficient; it will do for the press; and it will corroborate the critic's opinion in his own eyes.

Fatuity militant. I cannot overcome a settled distrust of merely intellectual accomplishment, militant in the void. I prefer common virtues and current beliefs, even if intellectually prejudiced and simple, when the great generative order of nature has bred them, and lent them its weight and honesty. For I do not rebel in the least at political and moral mutations when this same generative order brings them about spontaneously; for it is then on the side of change that clear intelligence discerns the lesser danger and the wider interests. I should have loved the Gracchi; but not the belated Cato or the belated Brutus. All four were martyrs; but the first two spoke for the poor, for the suffering half of the people, oppressed by a shortsighted power that neglected its responsibilities; while the last two were conceited ideologues, jealous of their traditional rights, and utterly blind to destiny. If I were not too old and could venture to write in French, I should compose a short history of *Les Faux Pas de la Philosophie*; by which title I should not refer to *innocent* errors, with which all human speculation must be infected, nor to the symbolic or mythological form of the wisest wisdom, but only to militant heresies and self-contradictions due to wilful conceit, individual or tribal, verbal or moral; and there is little in European philosophy that is not infected with these *unnecessary* errors. Let the reader compose his own catalogue of these blind alleys explored by the ancients and by the moderns; since this is a biographical book, I will limit myself to the first and principal *Faux Pas* that the world has seemed to me to have taken in my time.

Two chief demands of rational morals. The contemporary world has turned its back on the attempt and even on the desire to live reasonably. The two great wars (so far) of the twentieth century were adventures in enthusiastic unreason. They were inspired by unnecessary and impracticable ambitions; and the "League" and the "United Nations" feebly set up by the victors, were so irrationally conceived that they at once reduced their victory to a stalemate. What is requisite for living rationally? I think the conditions may be reduced to two: First, self-knowledge, the Socratic key to wisdom; and second, sufficient knowledge of the world to perceive what alternatives are open to you and which of them are favourable to your true interests.

The modern world has plenty of mechanical science, but no self-knowledge.

Now the contemporary world has plenty of knowledge of nature for its purposes, but its purposes show a positively insane abandonment of its true interests. You may say that the proletariat knows its interests perfectly; they are to work less and to earn more. Those are indeed its interests so long as it remains a proletariat: but to be a proletariat is an inhuman condition. Proletarians are human beings, and their first interest is to have a home, a family, a chosen trade, and freedom in practising it. And more particularly a man's true interest may exceptionally be not to have those things, but to wander alone like the rhinoceros; or perhaps to have a very special kind of home, family, and occupation. There must be freedom of movement and vocation. There must be *Lebensraum* for the spirit.

Simpler societies know better their place in nature.

There have always been beggars and paupers in the world, because there is bound to be a margin of the unfit—too bad or too good to keep in step with any well organised society: but that the great body of mankind should sink into a proletariat has been an unhappy effect of the monstrous growth of cities, made possible by the concentration of trade and the multiplication of industries, mechanised, and swelling into monopolies.

The natural state of mankind, before foreign conquerors dominate it or native ideologues reform it, is full of incidental evils; prophets have ample cause for special denunciations and warnings; yet there is, as in all animal economy, a certain nucleus of self-preserving instincts and habits, a normal constitution of society. Nature with its gods is their landlord of whose fields and woods they are local and temporary tenants; and with this invincible power they make prudent and far-seeing covenants. They know what is for their good, and by what arts it might be secured. They live by agriculture, the hunting and breeding of animals, and such domestic arts as their climate and taste lead them to cultivate; and when a quarrel arises among them, or with strangers, they battle to preserve or to restore their free life, without more ambitious intentions. They are materially and morally rooted in the earth, bred in one land and one city. They are *civilised*. Wandering nations, with nothing of their own and working havoc wherever they go, are *barbarians*. Such "barbarians" were the proletariat of antiquity. When they occupied some civilised region without exterminating the natives, and established in the old strongholds a permanent foreign domination, they became half-civilised themselves, without shedding altogether the predatory and adventurous practices of their ancestors. This is the compound origin and nature of modern Western governments.

Barbarism in the romantic mind coexists with civilisation in mechanical arts.   Varied, picturesque, and romantic mixtures of civilisation beneath and barbarism above have filled the history of Christendom, and produced beautiful transient arts, in which there was too little wisdom and too much fancy and fashion: think of Gothic architecture, or of manners, dress, poetry, and philosophy from the middle ages to our day. Civilisation had become more enterprising, plastic, and irresponsible, while barbarism seemed to retreat into sports, and into legal extravagances in thought and action. Intellectual chaos and political folly could thus come to coexist strangely with an irresistible dominance of mechanical industry. The science that served this industrial progress by no means brought moral enlightenment. It merely enlarged acquaintance with phenomena and enabled clever inventors to construct all sorts of useful or superfluous machines. At first perhaps it was expected that science would make all mankind both rich and free from material cares (two contradictory hopes) and would at the same time enlighten them at last about the nature of things, including their own nature, so that adequate practical wisdom would be secured together with fabulous material well-being.

Deluded optimism of the Great Merchants.   This is the dream of the moderns, on which I found My Host boastfully running his establishment. He expected his guests also to act accordingly and to befuddle and jollify one another, so that all should convince themselves that they were perfectly happy and should advertise their Host's business wherever they went. Such forced enterprise, forced confidence, and forced satisfaction would never have sprung from domestic arts or common knowledge spontaneously extended. It was all artificial and strained, marking the inhuman domination of some militant class or sect. This society lacked altogether that essential trait of rational living, to have a clear, sanctioned, ultimate aim. The cry was for vacant freedom and indeterminate progress: *Vorwärts! Avanti! Onward! Full speed ahead!* without asking whether directly before you was not a bottomless pit.

This has been the peculiar malady of my own times. I saw the outbreak of it in my boyhood, and I have lived to see what seem clear symptoms of its end. The Great Merchants of my parents' youth had known nothing of it on their blue-sea voyages round Cape Horn or the Cape of Good Hope. Their good hope had been to amass a great fortune in fifteen or twenty years, and return home to bring up a blooming family in splendour and peace. They foresaw an orderly diffused well-being spreading out from them over all mankind. The fountains of happiness were ready to flow in every heart and mind if only people were suffered to have their own way materially and socially. That the masses would crowd out, exclude, indoctrinate, enslave, and destroy one another could not cross their genial and innocent minds, as they skimmed those immense oceans in their tight, strictly disciplined, white-sailed little craft.

Perverse militancy in politics. Alas! The healthy growth of science and commerce had been crossed, long before the rise of the Great Merchants, by an insidious moral and political revolution. From the earliest times there have been militant spirits not content with inevitable changes and with occasional wars between neighbouring states, not usually wars of conquest or eternal hatred, but collisions in readjusting the political equilibrium between nations when their actual relations were no longer the same. Indeed, the tragic causes of conflict and ruin in civilisations are fundamentally internal to each society. A whole city or state may sometimes be destroyed, like Carthage; but history, then, comes to an end for that particular society, and the others continue their course as if their vanished rival had never existed. This course may be cut short, however, by internal disruption and suicidal revolutions. Every generation is born as ignorant and wilful as the first man; and when tradition has lost its obvious fitness or numinous authority, eager minds will revert without knowing it to every false hope and blind alley that had tempted their predecessors long since buried under layer upon layer of ruins. And these eager minds may easily become leaders; for society is never perfect; grievances and misfortunes perpetually breed rebellion in the oppressed heart; and the eloquent imagination of youth and of indignation will find the right words to blow the discontent, always smouldering, into sudden flame. Often things as they are become intolerable; there must be insurrection at any cost, as when the established order is not only casually oppressive, but ideally perverse and due to some previous epidemic of militant madness become constitutional. Against that domination, established in wilful indifference to the true good of man and to his possibilities, any political nostrum, proposed with the same rashness, will be accepted with the same faith. Thus the blind in extirpating the mad may plant a new madness.

Present free fight of egotistical follies.   That this is the present state of the world everyone can see by looking about him, or reading the newspapers; but I think that the elements in this crisis have been working in the body-politic for ages; ever since the Reformation, not to say since the age of the Greek Sophists and of Socrates. For the virulent cause of this long fever is subjectivism, egotism, conceit of mind. Not that culture of the conscience and even the logical refinements of dialectic are anything but good for the mind itself and for moral self-knowledge, which is one of the two conditions that I have assigned to political sanity; but the same logical arts are fatal if they are used to construct, by way of a moral fable, an anthropomorphic picture of the universe given out for scientific truth and imposed on mankind by propaganda, by threats, and by persecution. And this militant method of reforming mankind by misrepresenting their capacities and their place in the universe is no merely ancient or mediaeval delusion. It is the official and intolerant method of our most zealous contemporary prophets and reformers. Barbarism has adopted the weapons of flattery and prophecy. Merciless irrational ambition has borrowed the language of brotherly love.

But earthquakes do not destroy the earth.   The very fact, however, that these evils have deep roots, and have long existed without destroying Western civilisation, but on the contrary, have stimulated its contrary virtues and confused arts,—this very fact seems to me to counsel calmness in contemplating the future. Those who look for a panacea will not find it. Those who advise resignation to a life of industrial slavery (because spiritual virtues may be cultivated by a slave, like Epictetus, more easily perhaps than by rich men) are surrendering the political future to an artificial militant regime that cannot last unaltered for a decade anywhere, and could hardly last a day, if by military force it were ever made universal. The fanaticism of all parties must be allowed to burn down to ashes, like a fire out of control. If it survives, it will be only because it will have humanised itself, reduced its dogmas to harmless metaphors, and sunk down a tap-root, to feed it, into the dark damp depths of mother earth. The economy of nature includes all particular movements, combines and transforms them all, but never diverts its wider processes, to render them obedient to the prescriptions of human rhetoric. Things have their day, and their beauties in that day. It would be preposterous to expect any one civilisation to last for ever.

Had it happened in my time (as by chance it did happen) that my landlord should give me notice that he was about to pull down his roof over my head, I might have been a little troubled for a moment; but presently I should have begun to look for other lodgings not without a certain curious pleasure, and probably should have found some (as I did, and better ones) in which to end my days. So, I am confident, will the travelling Spirit do,—this ever-renewed witness, victim, and judge of existence, divine yet born of woman. Obediently it will learn other affections in other places, unite other friends, and divide other peoples; and the failure of over-exact hopes and over-weening ambitions will not prevent Spirit from continually turning the passing virtues and sorrows of nature into glimpses of eternal truth.

EDITORIAL
APPENDIX

LIST OF ABBREVIATIONS AND EDITORIAL SYMBOLS

The following abbreviations are used to designate the sources of readings:

A American Edition (Scribner's, 1944, 1945, 1953)

At The Atlantic Monthly (1943, 1948, 1949)

CE The present Critical Edition

E English Edition (Constable, 1944, 1947; Cresset, 1953)

F1 Humanities Research Center typescript of "Farewell to England", p. 14, with George Santayana's revisions

F2 Humanities Research Center typescript of "Farewell to England", p. 14, corrected

F3 Humanities Research Center typescript of "Farewell to England", p. 18

F4 Humanities Research Center typescript of "Farewell to England", p. 18, corrected

MS1 Holograph manuscript of part one of *Persons and Places*

MS2 Holograph manuscript of part two of *Persons and Places*

MS3 Holograph manuscript of part three of *Persons and Places*

P Proof (Scribner's, 1944)

T Atoms of Thought [:] *An Anthology of Thoughts from GEORGE SANTAYANA* (1950)

W1 Columbia University typescript of "We Were Not Virtuous"

W2 Humanities Research Center typescript of "We Were Not Virtuous"

The following editorial symbols are used in the *Editorial Appendix*:

The Lemma Bracket]
    Critical Edition readings and their sources are listed to the left of the lemma bracket in the *List of Emendations*; rejected copy-text readings are listed to the right of the lemma bracket. Copy-text readings are listed to the left of the lemma bracket in the *List of Substantive Variants*; the variant readings are listed to the right of the lemma bracket. In the *Notes to the Text* and the *Discussions of Adopted Readings* the Critical Edition reading is to the left of the lemma bracket and editorial notes and discussions are to the right.

The Wavy Dash or Tilde ~
    The wavy dash or tilde stands for the word or words cited to the left of the lemma bracket in the *List of Emendations* and in the *List of Substantive Variants*.

The Caret ∧
    The caret indicates the absence of a punctuation mark.

The Ellipsis . . .
    The ellipsis indicates material omitted from the citation to the left of the lemma bracket in the *List of Emendations* and the *List of Substantive Variants*.

The Asterisk *
    The asterisk precedes emendations which are discussed in the *Discussions of Adopted Readings*.

The Slash or Virgule /
   The slash or virgule is used to indicate separate lines of verse or lines of a title.

Similar
   Similar begins a parenthetical listing of additional lines where the forms of emendation are identical.

The Paragraph Symbol ¶
   The paragraph symbol indicates the beginning of a new paragraph.

Superscript Number [1]
   In the *List of Emendations* and the *List of Substantive Variants* the position of a word which occurs more than once on a line is indicated by a superscript number.

Marginal Heading MH
   The marginal headings are those phrases or sentences in bold print which appear on the left-hand side of the page in the Critical Edition text.

NOTES TO THE TEXT

3.8 Santayana] Don Agustín Ruiz de Santayana (1814–1893), Santayana's father.

3.9 Zamora] principal city of modern Province of Zamora.

3.9 Borrás] Josefina Borrás y Carbonell de Santayana (1826–1912), Santayana's mother.

3.10 Nicolás] Don Nicolás Ruiz de Santayana, Santayana's paternal grandfather.

3.10 Badumès] Possibly Badames, a town in the Province of Santander.

3.11 Reboiro] Doña María Antonia Reboiro Ruiz de Santayana, Santayana's paternal grandmother.

3.12 Don José] Don José Borrás y Bufurull (1835–?), Santayana's maternal grandfather.

3.13 Reus] A city in the Province of Tarragona.

3.13 Carbonell] Doña Teresa Carbonell Borrás, Santayana's maternal grandmother.

3.15 Santayana] Don Nicolás Ruiz de Santayana (1819–?), Santayana's godfather and paternal uncle, a major in the Spanish army.

3.15 Sturgis] Susana Sturgis y Borrás [later Señora de Sastre; American legal name in marriage: Susan Parkman Sturgis de Sastre] (1851–1928), Santayana's godmother and half sister. She was the first daughter of Santayana's mother's first marriage.

5.22 *mayorazgo*] The Spanish inheritance law of primogeniture.

6.13 Ferdinand VII] Ferdinand VII (1784–1833), King of Spain (1808–1833).

6.25 Mahon] Principal city of Minorca, Balearic Islands, which were under British control (1713–1802).

7.12 Jackson] Andrew Jackson (1767–1845), seventh president of the United States (1829–1837).

10.2 first marriage] Santayana's mother had married George Sturgis (1817–1857) in 1849.

10.24 School] The Boston Latin School, a public high school, was founded in 1635.

11.12 village] Santillana del Mar, a village in the Province of Santander.

11.13 Espinosa] Espinosa de los Monteros, a village in the Province of Burgos.

11.14 Montesa] Antonio Marichalar y Rodriguez, Marqués de Montesa (1893–?), Spanish historian.

11.17 Spinoza] [Baruch] Benedict de Spinoza (1632–1677), Dutch-Jewish philosopher.

12.38 Blas] Santayana's allusion is to Gil Blas de Santillana, the picaresque hero of the novel by Alain-René Lesage (1668–1747).

13.17 Zorilla] José Zorilla y Moral (1817–1883), Spanish poet and author of *Don Juan Tenorio*. The lines which Santayana prints are a misquotation of *Don Juan Tenorio*, Part One, IV, iii, 2169–73: *Ah! No es cierto, ángel de amor, / que en esta apartada orilla / mas pura la luna brilla / y se respira mejor?*

15.15 Seneca] Lucius Annaeus Seneca (*c.*3B.C.–65A.D.), Roman Stoic philosopher and statesman, born in Spain.

15.25 Johnson] Lionel Pigot Johnson (1867–1902), British poet and critic.

15.27 Bridges] Robert Bridges (1844–1930), English poet and editor; Poet Laureate from 1913.

15.27 Waggett] Rev. Philip Napier Waggett (1862–1939), an Anglican clergyman prominent in the late period of the Catholic revival in the Church of England. Perhaps the most noted of his several books was *The Scientific Temper in Religion* (1905). He served as Select Preacher at Oxford, 1902–1903, and at Cambridge, 1906–1913, and subsequently gained fame as a preacher, missioner, and conductor of retreats.

15.30 Newman] John Henry Newman (1801–1890), English churchman, author, and leader of the Oxford Movement in theology; later a convert from Anglicanism to Roman Catholicism; made cardinal (1879).

15.37 Augustine] Saint Augustine (354–430), bishop and theologian; author of autobiographical *Confessions* (*c.*397–400).

16.4–5 Leonardo] Leonardo da Vinci (1452–1519), Florentine sculptor, painter, architect, and engineer.

16.7 *El Pasmo de Sicilia*] Raphael's painting *Lo Spasimo di Sicilia* ("The Bearing of the Cross"), now in the Prado, was commissioned by the Olivetan Monks of the monastery of Santa Maria dello Spasimo as an altarpiece for their church, which has given the painting its second name.

16.11 Goyas] Francisco José de Goya y Lucientes (1746–1828), Spanish painter.

16.14 Watteau] Jean Antoine Watteau (1684–1712), French painter.

17.23 Epicurus] Epicurus (340–270 B.C.), Greek philosopher and founder of the Epicurean school of philosophy.

17.35 Quintilian] Marcus Fabius Quintilian (*c.*35–95), Roman rhetorician and teacher of oratory, born in Spain.

17.36–37 *Ad cognoscendum . . . domus:*] In a letter of November 25, 1944, following Scribner's publication of *Persons and Places*[:] *The Background of My Life*, Santayana wrote to his editor at Scribner's concerning this "alleged quotation from Quintilian": "I have lately been rereading Latin poets . . . and have come upon a passage in Juvenal that says in verse what I quoted in prose; and I am afraid my father, or more likely I myself, must have confused the memory of this with the name of Quintilian."

Decimus Junius Juvenalis (60?–140?) was a Roman poet and satirist. His Satire XIII (lines 159–160) contains the passage recalled by Santayana's father: *Humani generis mores tibi nosse volenti / Sufficit una domus.*

18.40 Manet] Edouard Manet (1832–1883), French painter.

19.2 Ribera] Jusepe de Ribera [called *"Lo Spagnoletto"*] (1588?–1656?), Spanish painter.

19.3 Rembrandt] Rembrandt Van Rijn (1606–1669), Dutch painter.

19.24 Pavía] Manuel Pavía y Lacy, Marqués de Novaliches (1814–1896), Spanish general and Governor General of the Philippines (1853–1854).

19.27 Prim] Juan Prim y Prats (1814–1870), Spanish general and statesman.

19.27 Serrano] Francisco Serrano y Dominguez, Conde de San Antonio y Duque de la Torre (1810–1895), Spanish general and political figure.

19.27 battle] The battle of Alcolea took place on September 27, 1868.

22.10 Robert] Robert Shaw Sturgis (1854–1921), Santayana's half brother.

22.36 Locke] John Locke (1632–1704), English philosopher.

22.36 Rousseau] Jean Jacques Rousseau (1712–1778), Swiss-born French philosopher.

22.36–37 *Nathan der Weise*] A play (1779) by Gotthold Ephraim Lessing (1729–1781).

23.28 Lucretius] Titus Lucretius Carus (96?–55 B.C.), Roman poet and philosopher. The line quoted by Santayana appears in *De Rerum Natura.*

25.35 Raphael's frescoes] Raffaello Sanzio (1483–1520), Italian painter. The frescoes to which Santayana refers are in the Vatican.

31.24 Brutuses] Marcus Junius Brutus (85?–42 B.C.), Roman politician.

31.24 Catos] The reference may be to either Marcus Porcius Cato [called "the Elder" and "the Censor"] (234–149 B.C.), Roman statesman; or Marcus Porcius Cato [called "the Younger"] (95–46 B.C.), Roman Stoic philosopher.

32.9 Diogenes] Diogenes (c.412–323 B.C.), Greek cynic philosopher.

33.2 *Essay on Man*] An Essay on Man (1733), a poem in heroic couplets by Alexander Pope (1688–1744), expressing Deistic optimism in reason.

34.18 Batang] Apparently Batan Island, of which there are two, widely separated but bearing the same name, among the Philippine Islands.

36.28 Hegel] Georg Wilhelm Friedrich Hegel (1770–1831), German philosopher.

39.10 young man] George Sturgis (1817–1857), American-born first husband of Santayana's mother.

40.35 Victor] James Victor Sturgis (1856–1858), fifth and last child of Santayana's mother by her first marriage.

41.7 boy] Joseph Borrás Sturgis [José Borrás Sturgis; called "Pepín" and "Pepe"] (1850–1852), first son of Santayana's mother's first marriage.

41.11 sister] [See Note at 1.15]

41.30 Josefina] Josephine Borrás Sturgis [called Josefina] (1853–1930), Santayana's half sister, the third child of his mother's first marriage.

46.5 Norton] Charles Eliot Norton (1827–1908), American author and educator; Dante scholar and professor of art history at Harvard (1873–1898).

46.6 Lowell] James Russell Lowell (1819–1891), American literary critic, poet, and humorist; professor of French and Spanish at Harvard (1855–1886); minister to Spain (1877–1880) and to England (1880–1885).

46.6 Longfellow] Henry Wadsworth Longfellow (1807–1882), American poet and professor of French and Spanish at Harvard (1836–1854).

46.7 Holmes] Oliver Wendell Holmes (1809–1894), American essayist and lecturer; professor of anatomy and physiology at Harvard (1847–1882); father of Supreme Court Justice Oliver Wendell Holmes, Jr.

46.8 Emerson] Ralph Waldo Emerson (1803–1882), American essayist and poet.

46.40 Nathaniel] Nathaniel Russell Sturgis (1779–1856), father of Santayana's mother's first husband.

47.17 Robert] Robert ("Uncle Robert") Shaw Sturgis (1824–1876), youngest son of Nathaniel Russell Sturgis and brother of Santayana's mother's first husband.

48.15–16 brother-in-law] Russell ("Uncle Russell") Sturgis (1805–1887) was the eldest son of Nathaniel Russell Sturgis. He was not, as Santayana states, twice married, but actually had *three* wives: Lucy Lyman Paine (married April 3, 1828; died August 23, 1828); Mary Greene Hubbard (married September 28, 1829; died September 17, 1837); and Julia Overing Boit (married June 4, 1846; died May 31, 1888), mother of Howard Overing Sturgis (1855–1920), the novelist. (Sturgis family genealogy.) He, like his brother Henry, made a fortune as a young man in the Far East trade. After their early years in China and the Philippines both brothers settled in London.

51.11 Parkman] Susan Parkman married Nathaniel Russell Sturgis in 1804. As a young woman, she was Sturgis's next-door neighbor on Tremont Row in Boston, the daughter of Samuel Parkman.

51.14 Shaw] Sarah Blake Sturgis (1815–1902) married Francis George Shaw in 1835.

51.14 Shaw] Robert Gould Shaw (1837–1863), as an army colonel was in command of the first black regiment in the field in the Civil War, the 54th Massachusetts. He was slain in July 1863, at Morris Island, South Carolina and is memorialized in the Saint-Gaudens statue on Boston Common.

52.8 twice married] [See Note at 48.15–16.]

52.38 Henry Sturgis] Henry Parkman Sturgis (1847–1894), son of Russell Sturgis (1805–1887) by his third wife, was naturalized in England and became a Member of the House of Commons during Gladstone's last ministry. He was first married to Mary Cecilia Brand, daughter of the Speaker of the House, and subsequently to Mary Eveleen Meredith, daughter of George Meredith.

53.23 Henry Sturgis] Henry Parkman Sturgis (1806–1869), brother of Santayana's mother's first husband.

53.31–32 Fred and Nena Sturgis] Frederic Russell Sturgis (1844–1919) and Mary Trinidad Howard ("Nena") Sturgis (1845–1890) were the last two of the eight children of Henry Parkman Sturgis (1806–1869).

53.40 Her] Mary Georgiana Howard married Henry Parkman Sturgis in 1835. She died in 1850, after bearing eight children.

54.14 Middlemore] Samuel George Chetwynd Middlemore married Mary Trinidad Howard ("Nena") Sturgis in 1881. Both died in 1890.

54.35 step-mother] Elizabeth ("Aunt Lizzie") Orne Paine was the second wife of Henry Parkman Sturgis, marrying him in 1851. She was a widow during the last 42 years of her life, and died in 1911. The marriage was childless.

57.9–10 Samuel] Samuel ("Uncle Samuel") Parkman Sturgis (1808–1877), son of Nathaniel Russell Sturgis and brother of Santayana's mother's first husband. He was never married.

66.13 White] Amy White (1848–?) was one of two children of William Abijah White and Harriet Tilden (Sturgis) White (1820–1850).

67.1 Norton] Grace Norton (1834–1926), a writer and sister of Professor Charles Eliot Norton.

67.8 James] James ("Uncle James") Sturgis (1822–1888).

67.21 John] John Hubbard Sturgis (1834–1888).

67.24 Clipston] Richard Clipston Sturgis (1860–1951).

67.27 Groton School] Private boys' school in Groton, Massachusetts, founded in 1884 by Endicott Peabody.

67.29 one] Henry Parkman Sturgis (1847–1894).

67.30 other two] Julian Russell Sturgis (1848–1904) and Howard Overing Sturgis (1855–1920).

68.7 wife] Mary Catharine Townsend married James Sturgis in 1845.

70.23 great fire in Boston] The fire broke out on Saturday evening, November 9, 1872. It consumed 65 acres of the business district, and 776 buildings were gutted.

72.16 Charley and Frank] Charles Wilkins Sturgis (1849–1913) and Francis Shaw Sturgis (1853–1922).

73.3 Susie] Susan Sturgis (1846–1923), first child of James Sturgis, was married to Henry Horton McBurney in 1867 and to Henry Bigelow Williams in 1876.

75.30 Maisie] Mary Howard ("Maisie") Sturgis (1872–1944). She married Edgar Thomson Scott in 1898.

78.17 La Granja] The Palacio Real de la Granja, the royal palace and grounds at San Ildefonso, in the Province of Segovia.

78.17 Escurial] San Lorenzo del Escorial, the royal palace and monastery in the Province of Madrid.

78.18 Isabella] Queen Isabella II succeeded her father, Ferdinand VII, as Spanish monarch in 1833. She was dethroned in 1868 and renounced the throne in favor of her son, Alfonso XII, in 1870. [See Note at 326.34.]

79.29 Isabel] Isabel (1851–1931), the Infanta of Spain. She was the daughter of Isabella II and sister of Alfonso XII.

82.5 Lowell] Sara Putnam Lowell (1843–?), daughter of John Amory Lowell, married George Baty Blake in 1876.

83.2 the Homers] Mrs. Homer was the daughter of Horatio and Victorine (Flechelle) Sprague. Horatio Sprague, a native Bostonian, established a mercantile business at Gibraltar in 1812, and served as U.S. consul there from 1832 until his death in 1848. He was succeeded in that office by his son, Horatio Jones Sprague (1823–1901).

83.3 the Iasigis] Joseph Iasigi, an affluent Meditteranean merchant and Turkish consul, established his family in the 1840's at No.3 Louisburg Square. Joseph and his wife, Eulalie Loir Iasigi, were the parents of Octavie Iasigi, the fourth of their daughters and the only one who "came later within my [Santayana's] range." The "young Bostonian" whom Octavie married (in 1876) was William Apthorp, a teacher and music critic for various Boston newspapers.

83.17 *The Last Puritan*] *The Last Puritan*[:] *A Memoir in the Form of a Novel* was Santayana's only novel, first published in 1935.

85.29 Gardner] Isabella Stewart (Mrs. "Jack") Gardner (1840–1924), Boston hostess, art collector, and patroness.

85.30 Sembrich] Marcella Sembrich [originally Praxede Marcelline Kochanska] (1858–1934), Galician-born operatic soprano; American debut in 1893.

85.31 Eames] Emma Eames (1865–1952), operatic soprano. Born in China of American parents, she sang with the Metropolitan Opera (1891–1909).

85.31 Paderewska] Madame Paderewska, née Rosen (?–1934), wife of Jan Paderewski, Polish pianist, composer, and statesman.

88.23 the widow] Susan Brimmer Inches (?–1900) married Robert Shaw Sturgis in 1858. They had seven children.

89.20 Teresa] Saint Teresa of Avila (1515–1582), Spanish Carmelite nun and mystical writer.

89.24 Fulton] Rev. Robert Fulton, S.J. (1826–1895), president of Boston College (1870–1880 and 1888–1891).

89.38 Royce] Josiah Royce (1855–1916), American philosopher and member of the Harvard philosophy faculty (1882–1916). He supervised Santayana's dissertation on Lotze.

92.25 Sastre] Celedonio Sastre (c.1840–1930), husband of Santayana's half sister, Susan Parkman Sturgis, whom he married in 1892.

101.18 Alain] "Alain" was the *nom de plume* of the philosopher Émile-Auguste Chartier (1868–1951).

105.28 Rafael] Rafael Sastre Gonzalez, the third son of Celedonio Sastre's first marriage.

129.25 Portugalete] Spanish port on the Bay of Biscay, near Bilbao.

134.28 Russell] John Francis Stanley, the second Earl Russell (1865–1931), was the eldest son of John Russell (Viscount Amberley) and Katharine Louisa (Stanley) Russell. A barrister and politician, he served for nine years as an alderman in the London County Council, and later acted in the Labour government as the secretary of the Ministry of Transport, 1929, and under secretary of state for India (1929–1931). He was prominent in England through his efforts to alter the divorce law, and was also known as a Fabian socialist, engineer, and "motorist."

137.15 Davis] Charles P. Davis. Following the death of Santayana's sister, Susana, he maintained for several years (1932–1938) a correspondence with Santayana.

138.19 Ruskin] John Ruskin (1819–1900), art critic and social-reforming essayist. He praised Gothic architecture in *The Stones of Venice* (1851–1853) and attacked the "pestilent art of the Renaissance."

138.19 Richardson's] Henry Hobson Richardson (1836–1888), American architect.

142.5 *Arabian Nights*] In 1840, E. W. Lane published a new scholarly English translation (three volumes).

142.8 Optic's] Oliver Optic was the pseudonym of William Taylor Adams (1822–1897), a prolific author of stories for boys and girls.

142.9 *Lives*] The brothers John S. C. Abbott (1805–1877) and Jacob Abbott (1803–1879) were the joint authors of "Abbotts' Illustrated Biographical Histories," thirty-two in all, ranging from Genghis Khan to Peter the Great.

142.10–11 Motley's and Prescott's pseudo-Spanish histories] John Lothrop Motley (1814–1877), American historian famous for his histories of the Netherlands under Spanish rule. William Hickling Prescott (1796–1859), American historian of Spanish New World colonialism.

142.14 *Lives*] Plutarch (c.46–120 A.D.), Greek historian and author of *Parallel Lives*.

142.15 Gibbon] Edward Gibbon (1737–1794), British historian, author of *The Decline and Fall of the Roman Empire* (1777–1788).

142.23 *Un Servilón y un Liberalito*] "Fernán Caballero" was the *nom de plume* of Cecilia Boehl von Faber (1796–1877), whose *Un Servilón y un Liberalito, o tres almas de Dios* appeared in 1857.

142.31 *Don Juan*] Poem (1819–1824) of nearly 16,000 lines left incomplete by George Noel Gordon, Lord Byron (1788–1824).

142.36 Napoleon the Third] Napoleon III (1808–1873) nephew of Napoleon I and Emperor of the French (1852–1870).

142.36 Eugénie] Empress Eugénie (1826–1920), Eugénie Marie de Montijo de Guzmán, Empress of France (1853–1871), wife of Napoleon III.

143.20 *History of Architecture*] Santayana apparently refers to James Ferguson's *A History of Architecture in All Countries from the Earliest Times to the Present Day*, the several editions of which derive from Ferguson's *Handbook of Architecture*, which was first published in 1855.

146.6 *Fiction and Truth* or *Poetry and Truth*] Santayana's translation of Johann Wolfgang von Goethe's (1749–1832) *Dichtung und Warheit* (1811–1814).

148.32 Gardner] Francis Gardner (1812–1876), headmaster of the Boston Latin School (1851–1876).

149.22 Capen] Charles James Capen (1823–1910), member of the Latin School faculty (1852–1910).

150.1 Schoolhouse] The Latin School was located in Bedford Street (1844–1881). See Santayana's poem "Lines on leaving the Bedford Str. School House," *The Complete Poems of George Santayana*, pp. 363–66.

151.31 Fiske] Arthur Irving Fiske (1848–1910), member of the Latin School faculty (1873–1910), and headmaster (1902–1910).

151.32 Groce] Byron Groce, member of the Latin School faculty (1878–1915).

157.3 Merrill] Moses Merrill (1833–1902), headmaster of the Latin School.

157.26 Chadwick] Joseph Webber Chadwick (?–1917), member of the Latin School faculty (1866–1906).

157.32 Smith] Robert Dickson Smith, Jr. [later Robert Dickson Weston-Smith and later still Robert Dickson Weston] (1864–1956). Robert Dickson Smith is reported in the *Latin School Register* as Battalion Major during the fall term of his senior year. He graduated in Santayana's Harvard class of 1886 and subsequently became a Boston lawyer.

158.14 Eliot] Charles William Eliot (1834–1926), chemist and president of Harvard (1869–1909).

162.4 O'Connor] Rev. Jeremiah O'Connor, S.J. (1841–1891), president of Boston College (1880–1884).

163.32 *Assumption*] Titian (*c*.1488/90–1576) painted the *Assumption* for the Santa Maria Gloria del Frari altarpiece (1518) and the Verona cathedral (1530's).

164.7 Murillo] Bartolomé Esteban Murillo (1617–1682), Spanish painter.

168.32 *At the Church Door*] Santayana, who here as so often quotes from memory, mistakenly writes "thrift" for "love" in the seventh quoted line of "At the Church Door". See *The Complete Poems of George Santayana*, p. 419.

173.32 Hubbard] Gorham Hubbard (1864–1921), later a Boston real estate and insurance broker.

174.17 Warren] Bentley Wirt Warren (1864–1947), later a lawyer.

174.35 father] William Wirt Warren (1834–1880), a lawyer and congressman from Massachusetts' 44th Congressional district (1875–1877).

174.40 Warren] Mary Adams Warren, wife of William Wirt Warren.

175.2-3 Harry and Jim Garfield] Harry Augustus Garfield (1863–1942), later professor of politics at Princeton and president of Williams College (1908–1934). James Rudolph Garfield (1865–1950), a lawyer and, during 1907 to 1909, United States Secretary of the Interior in the cabinet of President Roosevelt.

175.3 President] James Abram Garfield (1831–1881), president of the United States (1881).

175.14 Thoron] Ward Thoron (1867–1938), son of Joseph and Ann Barker (Ward) Thoron, graduated with Santayana in the class of 1886. A business executive for nearly fifty years, he retired in 1932 and turned to literary work, including the editing of *The Letters of Mrs. Henry Adams*.

175.17 Burden] Probably Chester Griswold ("Ja") Burden, whose early home was Lenox, Massachusetts. Burden was a student at Harvard (1907–1910), and later practiced architecture in New York City.

175.40 Bayley] Edward Bancroft Bayley (1864–1936), after his graduation in 1882 from English High School, became a Boston merchant.

176.40 Potter] Warwick Potter (1870–1893), a student of Santayana's at Harvard, graduated in the Harvard class of 1893.

177.11 Peabody] Endicott Peabody (1857–1944), founder of the Groton School in 1884.

178.17 *Nature*] Ralph Waldo Emerson's first book (1836).

179.14 Hollis] Hollis Hall, Harvard residence hall dedicated in 1764.

179.32-33 *La Revue des Deux Mondes*] Paris literary journal published since 1829.

180.23 the Institute] The Institute of 1770 was a Harvard undergraduate club which held fortnightly meetings devoted to lectures and debates. In 1926, it combined with the Hasty Pudding Club.

180.23 the Pudding] The Hasty Pudding Club, founded in 1795.

180.24 the O.K.] The O.K. (The Orthoepy Klub) was a Harvard literary society founded in 1858.

181.25 Thayer] Thayer Hall, a Harvard residence hall constructed in 1870–1872.

181.27 Fletcher] Jefferson Butler Fletcher (1865–1946), instructor in English at Harvard (1890–1902), and assistant professor of comparative literature there (1902–1904); thereafter professor of comparative literature at Columbia.

182.10 Stoughton] Stoughton Hall, a Harvard residence hall completed in 1805.

182.19 Cushing] Howard Gardiner Cushing (1869–1916), graduated in the Harvard class of 1891. He spent the subsequent five years as a student of painting at the Académie Julien in Paris, returning to Boston to become a professional painter. In 1904 he moved to New York, where he maintained a studio until his death.

185.1 Holden Chapel] Holden Chapel, later a lecture hall, was completed in 1744.

185.21 Holworthy] Holworthy Hall, a Harvard residence hall, was completed in 1812.

185.23 Little's Block] Harvard Square building at the corner of Massachusetts Avenue and Dunster Street since removed for construction of Holyoke Center building.

185.24 Beck] Beck Hall was a Harvard dormitory built in 1876.

187.11 Felton] Cornelius Conway Felton (c.1864–1890), after graduating from Harvard in 1886, took a law degree from the University of Pennsylvania in 1888. He died two years later of pneumonia.

187.11 Sanborn] Thomas Parker Sanborn (1865–1889) was, for two years following his graduation from Harvard in 1886, a literary and drama editor of *The Springfield Republican* (Massachusetts).

187.13 Baldwin] William Woodward Baldwin (1862–1954), one of the founders, with Santayana, of the *Harvard Monthly*; later a lawyer and, during the Cleveland administration, third assistant secretary of state (1893–1897).

187.27 Shaler] Nathaniel Southgate Shaler (1841–1906) was Harvard professor of paleontology (1869–1888), and professor of geology (1888–1906), serving as dean of Harvard's Lawrence School of Science (1891–1906).

189.12 Thayer] Ernest Lawrence Thayer (1863–1940), graduated from Harvard a year before Santayana. At the invitation of his classmate, William Randolph Hearst, he joined the staff of the San Francisco *Examiner* for two years. Following his resignation, he wrote "Casey at the Bat," engaged "half-heartedly" in the woolen business for eight years, and in 1902 began to spend a good deal of his time abroad.

189.24 Hearst] William Randolph Hearst (1863–1951), American newspaper publisher.

190.3 Maupassant] Guy de Maupassant (1850–1893), French novelist and short-story writer, author of *La Maison Tellier* (1881).

190.3 Gautier] Théophile Gautier (1811–1872), French poet and novelist, author of *Mademoiselle de Maupin* (1835); exponent of "art for art's sake."

190.19 Institute Theatricals of 1884] Amateur entertainments staged by the Institute of 1770.

190.31 Whitman] Crosby Church Whitman (1863–1916), later a medical doctor, having received his M.D. from the University of Paris in 1894. He practiced in Paris from 1901 until his death.

190.34 Anderson] Mary Anderson (1859–1940), American actress known for her great beauty.

191.3 *Harvard Monthly*] The *Harvard Monthly* was founded in the fall of 1885 "primarily to preserve . . . the best literary work that is produced in college by undergraduates." Its first editor-in-chief was A. B. Houghton, its business manager William Woodward Baldwin, and its board of editors was comprised of Santayana, George Rice Carpenter, William Morton Fullerton, and Thomas P. Sanborn. Both as an undergraduate and later, as a young faculty member, Santayana contributed numerous poems and essays to the *Monthly*.

191.20 Houghton] Alanson Bigelow Houghton (1863–1941), later the executive president of Corning Glass (1909–1918), congressman from New York's 37th District (1918–1922), ambassador to Germany (1922–1925), and ambassador to England (1925–1929).

192.32 Lowell] Abbott Lawrence Lowell (1856–1943), political scientist and president of Harvard (1909–1931).

200.38 *New Atlantis*] Published in 1624, by Francis Bacon (1561–1626), English philosopher and statesman.

201.39 Castillo] Antonio Cánovas del Castillo (1823–1897), Spanish politician and historian.

202.4 Sagasta] Praxedes Mateo Sagasta (1827–1903), Spanish political leader and prime minister.

203.31 Spengler] Oswald Spengler (1880–1936), German philosopher of history; author of *Der Untergang des Abendlandes* ["The Decline of the West"] (1918–1922).

203.37 *La Lonja*] The Saragossa merchants' hall.

206.15 Manuel] Manuel Ruiz de Santayana, Santayana's father's youngest brother.

206.17 "niece"] Hermenegilda Zabalgoitia de Santayana, illegitimate daughter of Nicolás Zabalgoitia and Mariquita Santayana.

206.24 Manuela] Manuela Ruiz de Santayana y Zabalgoitia (*c.* 1868–1936), Santayana's maiden cousin.

207.35 Tarraco] The ancient Roman name for Tarragona.

211.30 Bernhardt] Sarah Bernhardt [originally Rosine Bernard] (1844–1923), French actress whose many American tours began in 1880.

212.10 Sardou] Vincent Sardou (1831–1908), French dramatist who wrote several of Bernhardt's most successful plays.

215.16 Loeser] Charles Alexander Loeser (1864–1928), an art connoisseur and collector, long resident in Florence.

216.13 Berenson] Bernard Berenson (1865–1959), Lithuanian-born art critic and connoisseur of Italian Renaissance art; like Santayana, a graduate of both the Boston Latin School and Harvard College.

216.23 Salvini] Tommaso Salvini (1829–1916), Italian actor who specialized in tragic roles, especially those of Shakespeare.

216.23 Ristori] Adelaide Ristori (1822–1906), Italian tragedienne who played a variety of classical roles on American tours following her 1866 New York debut.

218.3 wife] Olga Lebert married Charles Loeser in 1912.

218.23 Thorold] Algar Labouchere Thorold (1866–1936) was the son of Anthony Wilson Thorold (1825–1895), Bishop of Rochester (1874–1890), and of Winchester (1890–1895). The younger Thorold was a journalist, editor, and philosophical writer. He married Teresa Mary Mansel in 1894.

218.28 wife] Teresa Mary Mansel married Algar Labouchere Thorold in 1894.

221.36 Mr. and Mrs. "Sam" Ward] Samuel Gray Ward (1817–?) was a Boston and (later) a New York banker for Baring Brothers of London. Like his wife, Anna Barker, Ward was a young friend of Emerson and Margaret Fuller. He contributed poems and articles to the transcendentalist journal, *The Dial*, and was a sometime member of Boston's Saturday Club. He resettled his family in New York in 1862, and retired to Washington in 1887.

224.6 Adams] Henry Brooks Adams (1838–1918), American man of letters and assistant professor of history at Harvard (1870–1877).

224.8 Norton] [See Note at 46.5.]

224.36 Lyman] Herbert Lyman (1864–1941), later a Boston businessman.

224.37 Bullard] Francis Bullard (1862–1913). After graduation, Bullard continued to be, through travel and the taking of additional courses at Harvard, a student of philosophy and art. Later he became an art collector, and made significant contributions to the collections of the Boston Museum of Fine Arts.

224.37 Beal] Boylston Adams Beal (1865–1944). A Boston lawyer, he served as an officer in the American Embassies at Berlin and London (1922–1929), under Ambassador A. B. Houghton. Beal and Santayana maintained an intermittent correspondence throughout most of their lives.

225.15 Cortina] Cortina d'Ampezzo, a resort in the northern Italian Tyrol.

225.25 Turner] Joseph Mallord William Turner (1775–1851), English Romantic painter.

231.3 Dyer] Louis Dyer (1851–1908), graduated from Harvard in 1874, and took a B.A. at Oxford in 1878. After serving as tutor in Greek at Harvard (1878–1881), and as assistant professor of Greek and Latin (1881–1887), he settled in England in 1890. A translator, editor, and writer in classical and Renaissance literature, he was appointed lecturer in German and French at Balliol College, Oxford (1893–1895). In subsequent years he continued to serve on various committees and as an examiner at Oxford, and as a friend to American students there was known as "the Consul."

231.3-4 Miss Macmillan] Margaret Anne Macmillan, the eldest daughter of the publisher, married Louis Dyer in 1889.

232.13 James] William James (1842–1910), American psychologist and philosopher; son of the theologian Henry James, Sr., and brother of the novelist, Henry James, Jr.; Harvard instructor and subsequently assistant professor in physiology (1872–1880); assistant professor of philosophy (1880–1885); professor of philosophy (1885–1907).

232.13 De l'Intelligence] Hippolyte Taine (1828–1893), French philosopher and literary critic. Santayana's reference is to his two-volume De l'Intelligence, first published in 1870.

232.24 Spencer] Herbert Spencer (1820–1903), English philosopher and social theorist.

234.4 Pollock's sympathetic book] Sir Frederick Pollock (1845–1937), English legal philosopher, professor of jurisprudence at Oxford (1883–1903); Santayana's reference is to Pollock's Spinoza: His Life and Philosophy (1880).

234.32 Thales] Thales (c.634–546 B.C.), Greek philosopher, mathematician, and astronomer.

234.33 Democritus] Democritus (c.460–357 B.C.), Greek philosopher.

236.8 Bowen] Francis ("Fanny") Bowen (1811–1890), Alford Professor of Natural Religion, Moral Philosophy and Civil Polity at Harvard (1853–1889).

236.33 Palmer] George Herbert Palmer (1842–1933), member of the philosophy faculty at Harvard (1872–1913); he succeeded Francis Bowen as Alford Professor in 1889.

237.11 Hobbes and Mandeville] Thomas Hobbes (1588–1679), English philosopher. Bernard Mandeville (1670–1733), Dutch-born English philosopher.

237.12 Shaftesbury] Anthony Ashley Cooper, third Earl of Shaftesbury (1671–1713), English philosopher.

237.14 Mill] John Stuart Mill (1806–1873), English philosopher.

237.19 Bangs] Francis Reginald ("Swelly") Bangs (1869–1939), later a prominent Boston lawyer and civic leader.

238.5 Russell] Bertrand ("Bertie") Arthur William Russell, third Earl Russell, (1872–1970), English philosopher and mathematician.

239.38 Strong] Charles Augustus Strong (1862–1940), American philosopher and psychologist; instructor at Cornell (1887–1888); assistant professor of psychology, University of Chicago (1892–1895); lecturer, Columbia (1896–1900); professor of psychology, Columbia (1903–1910).

253.15 boarding house] Santayana's Göttingen address was 16D Obere Karspule.

254.14 Wagner] Richard Wagner (1813–1883), German composer.

254.14 Gudehus] Heinrich Gudehus (1845–1909), German tenor.

254.14 Malten] Therese Malten [originally Müller] (1855–1930), German soprano.

255.5 Lymans] Herbert Lyman was the son of Arthur Theodore and Ellen Bancroft (Lowell) Lyman. The father was a Harvard overseer (1892–1899).

255.28 Apthorp] William ("Billy") Foster Apthorp (c.1848–1913), Boston music critic and professor of music composition, history, and criticism at Boston University (1876–1887).

258.4 Paulsen] Friedrich Paulsen (1846–1908), member of the philosophy department at Berlin from 1871 and professor from 1893.

258.4 Ebbinghaus] Hermann Ebbinghaus (1850–1909), Privatdozent at Berlin (1880–1894), and subsequently professor at Freiburg and Halle.

258.13 Bergson] Henri Bergson (1859–1941), French philosopher.

258.23 Gezycki's] Santayana, apparently writing from memory, misspells the name of Georg von Gizycki (1851–1895), professor of philosophy at Berlin and a founder of the German Society for Ethical Culture.

258.32 Salter] William MacKintire Salter (1853–1931), had been a graduate student at Göttingen before being active with the Ethical Culture Society in Chicago and Philadelphia (1883–1908), and professor of philosophy at the University of Chicago (1909–1913). Gizycki translated his writings into German.

259.3 Herodotus] Herodotus (484–432 B.C.), Greek historian.

259.3 Solon] Solon (?–c.560 B.C.), lawgiver of ancient Athens.

259.4 Croesus] Croesus (?–546 B.C.), wealthy king of Lydia.

260.10 Wagner] Adolph Wagner (1835–1917), after holding professorships at Dorpat and Freiburg, he became professor of philosophy at Berlin beginning in 1870.

260.11 Lasson] Adolf Lasson (1832–1917), a member of the Berlin Philosophy Department after his habilitation there in 1877 and later holder of professorships in the University's philosophy, theology, and law faculties.

260.11 Fichte] Johann Gottlieb Fichte (1762–1814), German philosopher.

260.11 Deussen] Paul Deussen (1845–1919), passed his Berlin habilitation in 188. and became professor in 1887 before going to Kiel in 1889.

260.12 Simmel] Georg Simmel (1858–1918), German philosopher, known for essays on the methodology of sociology.

261.7 *Three Philosophical Poets*] First published by the Harvard University Press in 1910.

261.25 Loisy] Alfred Loisy (1857–1940), French scriptural scholar.

268.33 Bank] The Bank of England in Threadneedle Street in the city of London.

268.37 Dickens] Charles Dickens (1812–1870), English novelist.

268.37 Cruikshank] George Cruikshank (1792–1878), English illustrator (of Dickens' *Sketches by Boz* and *Oliver Twist*) and caricaturist.

268.38 Thackeray] William Makepeace Thackeray (1811–1863), English novelist.

268.40 St. Paul's] St. Paul's Cathedral, London, was rebuilt after the Great Fire of 1666 on the design of Sir Christopher Wren; completed 1701.

269.5 Wren's] Sir Christopher Wren (1632–1723), English architect of churches and public buildings.

269.16 Swinburne] Algernon Charles Swinburne (1837–1909), English poet associated with the Pre-Raphaelite Brotherhood.

269.17 Arnold] Matthew Arnold (1822–1888), English poet and critic.

273.23 Aristophanes] Aristophanes (c.450–380 B.C.), the greatest of Greek comic dramatists.

273.37 Woolwich] Site of the Royal Military Academy, Royal Arsenal and other institutions; since 1965 part of the London Boroughs of Greenwich and Newham.

273.37–38 Kensington Palace] Royal residence located in the London Borough of Kensington.

273.38 Hampton Court] Palace built in 1515 by Cardinal Wolsey and subsequently (until George II) a royal residence.

273.38 Windsor Castle] Chief residence of English monarchs since William the Conqueror, located in Berkshire.

281.15 Guardsman] A cancellation on the holograph manuscript identifies the guardsman as "Geoffrey Stewart."

281.30MH *Decorum est pro patria mori*] An abridgement of Horace, *Odes*, Book Three, line 13: *dulce et decorum est pro patria mori.*: "It is agreeable and honorable to die for your country."

283.21 Dent] John Malaby Dent (1849–1926), English publisher.

283.21 Scribner] Charles Scribner (1854–1930), head of the publishing house which printed, in the United States, most of Santayana's books.

283.24 wife] Eugenie Sellars Strong (1860–1943), classical archaeologist, Assistant Director and Librarian of the British School of Archaeology in Rome (1909–1925).

283.26 Strong] Sandford Arthur Strong (1863–1904), English orientalist and historian of art, appointed Librarian at the House of Lords in 1897.

283.27 the Prince of Wales] Later Edward VII (1841–1910), eldest son of Queen Victoria and King of England (1901–1910).

285.19 member] Logan Pearsall Smith (1865–1946), Anglo-American essayist. Later, Smith would edit a book of *Little Essays: Drawn from the Writings of George Santayana* (1920).

285.26 sisters] Alys Pearsall Smith (1867–1951), first wife of Bertrand Russell (1894–1921).

285.26 the other] Mary Whitall Smith (1865–1945) lived with Bernard Berenson for some ten years prior to their marriage in 1900. Her first marriage, to Benjamin Francis Conn Costelloe in 1885, eventuated in a legal separation in 1893. Costelloe died in 1899.

285.30 Smith] Robert Pearsall Smith (1827–1898), Quaker evangelist and father of Logan Pearsall Smith.

285.35 Mrs. Smith] Hannah Tatum (Whitall) Smith (1832–1911), evangelist, religious writer, feminist, and temperance reformer. Like her husband, Robert Pearsall Smith, she was descended from a long line of colonial American Quakers.

286.1 *Prue and I*] Published in 1857.

286.2 "Aunt Sarah's"] [See Note at 51.14.]

286.2 Curtis] George William Curtis (1824–1892), novelist, editor, university chancellor, and reformer; married Anna Shaw in 1856.

286.15 brother] John Francis ("Frank") Russell, second Earl Russell (1865–1931), elder brother of Bertrand Russell, later a barrister.

286.30–31 "Michael Field"] Joint pen name of Katherine Harris Bradley (1846–1914) and Edith Emma Cooper (1862–1913).

287.10 first wife] [See Note at 285.26.]

287.15 James] Henry James (1843–1916), American novelist; son of the theologian-author Henry James, Sr. (1811–1882) and brother of the psychologist-philosopher William James (1842–1910).

287.23 Mérimée] Prosper Mérimée (1803–1870), French novelist.

288.18 Madame de Fontenay] Probably the Viscountess de Fontenay, née Renée Pichon. The Viscount (Joseph-Étienne) de Fontenay (1864–1946) served variously as French ambassador to Spain, minister to Denmark, and ambassador to the Vatican. Well known for their hospitality, the de Fontenays had many American friends.

288.22–23 son-in-law and granddaughter] Charles Augustus Strong had married Elizabeth ("Bessie") Rockefeller (1866–1906). Their daughter Margaret married

George de Cuevas, later the Marquis de Piedrablanca de Guana, in 1927. By a second marriage she became the Marquesa Margaret Rockefeller de Lorrain. John D. Rockefeller (1837-1939), was the American oil billionaire and philanthropist.

289.6 Lady Russell] Lady Frances Anna Maria Elliot (?-1898), daughter of the second Earl of Minto, was the second wife of Lord John Russell, the first Earl Russell (1792-1878). They had four children: John (Viscount Amberley, father of John Francis Stanley and Bertrand Russell), George Gilbert William, Francis Albert Rollo, and Mary Agatha.

289.11 *The Bible in Spain*] George Henry Borrow (1803-1881), author of *The Bible in Spain* which was first published in 1842.

289.14 Agatha] Mary Agatha Russell (1853-1933) was the fourth and youngest child of Lord John Russell (first Earl Russell) and Lady (Frances Anna Maria Elliot) Russell. She did not marry, and lived with her mother until the latter's death in 1898.

289.17 Gladstone] William Ewart Gladstone (1809-1894), British statesman and prime minister (1868-1874, 1880-1885, 1886, 1892-1894).

289.23 Stanley] Henrietta Maria Stanley, Lady Stanley of Alderley (1807-1895). Widely known in social and governmental circles for her uncompromising frankness, she was called *"notre chef-d'état major"* by Lord Palmerston, in whose government her husband, Edward John Stanley, held several important posts. She was a leading figure in the movement to open education to women.

290.7 Stanley] Hon. Maude [*sic*] Alethea Stanley (1833-1915), daughter of the second Baron Stanley of Alderley, noted for her social work.

290.8 Ogilvie] Griselda Johanna Helen Drummond (1865-1934), daughter of David Graham Drummond, fifth Earl of Airlie (1826-1881) and the Hon. Henrietta Blanche (Stanley) Drummond (?-1921). Her mother was the second daughter of Edward John Stanley, second Baron Stanley of Alderley.

291.5 Jarvis field] Principal Harvard sports facility from 1869 until Soldiers Field was presented to the University in 1890.

292.8 *Atalanta in Calydon*] Poetic drama in classical Greek form by Swinburne, first published in 1865.

292.22 *The Bookbills of Narcissus*] Richard Le Gallienne (1866-1947), English man of letters. His *Bookbills of Narcissus* first appeared in a private printing of 1891 and was subsequently reprinted for public sale.

298.14 Lady Scott] Maria Selina Burney (*c.*1846-1909) married Sir Claude Scott in 1861.

299.5 Jepson] Edgar Alfred Jepson was later a prolific English novelist, author of half-a-hundred novels published between 1895 and 1931.

299.34 Billings Girls] These are pseudonyms devised by Santayana to protect the identity of two young women, Nelly and Kate Williams.

301.15 *To a Spanish Friend*] Johnson's "To a Spanish Friend," written in 1894, appears on pp. 86–87 of *The Complete Poems of Lionel Johnson*, ed. Iain Fletcher (London: The Unicorn Press, 1953).

303.27 Paul] Charles Kegan Paul (1828–1902), English author and publisher.

305.2 *Thy heart with splendid passion, a great fire of dreams*,] Santayana frequently errs in writing from memory. The text of this poem in *The Complete Poems of Lionel Johnson* (p. 100) has "soul" for "heart."

305.5 Wilde] Oscar Fingal O'Flahertie Wills Wilde (1859–1900), Irish writer and famous wit.

305.19–23 *Because of thee . . . of cares.*] Lionel Johnson, "The Dark Angel."

305.28–29 *Lonely, unto the Lone . . . to the Divinity.*] Lionel Johnson, "The Dark Angel."

306.3–9 *We will not wander . . . and loveliness.*] Lionel Johnson, "Gwynedd," lines 116–20.

306.15–18 *Because of thee . . . of useless tears.*] Lionel Johnson, "The Dark Angel."

307.28 Jowett] Benjamin Jowett (1817–1893), Oxford Greek scholar. He was named Regius Professor in 1855 and Master of Balliol College in 1870, and served as University Vice-Chancellor (1882–1886).

307.30 Elizabeth] Russell's reference is to his third wife, Mary Annette Beauchamp (1866–1941). [See Note at 479.5.]

310.8 Winchester] Winchester College, one of the great public schools of England, in the city of Winchester, county of Southampton. It was founded in 1387 by William of Wykeham. Russell was a student there (1879–1883).

310.27–28 Richardson, whose amiable wife] Rev. G. Richardson and Sarah ("Mrs. Dick") Richardson. Richardson held the office of Second Master at Winchester and, by tradition of that office, was also House Master of "College," the original foundation comprised of seventy scholars.

313.7 Curzon] George Nathaniel Curzon, first Marquess Curzon of Kedleston (1859–1925), British statesman.

313.12 Clemenceau] Georges Clemenceau (1841–1929), French statesman.

316.28 Scott] Sir Claude Edward Scott (1840–1880).

316.34 Mabel Edith] Mabel Edith Scott (?–1908) was the third daughter of Sir Claude Edward Scott and Lady (Maria Selina) Scott. Russell's first wife, she married him in 1890 and obtained a divorce in 1901 after several ugly law suits.

324.10 Habana] Spanish spelling for "Havana" (Cuba).

326.34 Isabel] The Infanta Isabel (1830–1904), daughter of Ferdinand VII; later Queen Isabella II of Spain (1833–68). [See Note at 78.18.]

326.34 Cristina] Queen María Cristina (1858-1929), wife of Alfonso XII. Widowed on November 25, 1885, she bore the future Alfonso XIII on May 17, 1886, and served as regent until his accession in 1902.

326.35 Eugénie] Queen Victoria Eugénie Julia Ena (1887-?), wife of Alfonso XIII.

335.1 brother] Robert Sturgis (1854-1921), Santayana's half brother.

341.11 Barlow] Ellen ("Nelly") Shaw, daughter of Sarah Blake (Sturgis) and Francis George Shaw, married General Francis Channing Barlow in 1867. She was his second wife.

341.12 Barlow] Francis Channing Barlow (1834-1896), a much-decorated Union officer in the Civil War, practiced law in New York. He was a founder of the Bar Association and held many New York state offices, including secretary of state, U. S. marshal, and attorney general.

341.13 Bob] Robert Shaw Barlow (1869-?), was a member of the Harvard class of 1891. Later he practiced law in New York, serving as assistant corporation counsel of the City of New York (1891-1898). After returning to Boston in 1898, he continued to practice law with a number of different partners including, from 1898 to 1907, his old Harvard classmate, Francis ("Swelly") Bangs.

343.4 *The Spee*] The Harvard chapter of Zeta Psi, the national fraternity, had been founded in 1852.

343.36 "*Le Monde où l'on s'ennuie*"] A comedy by Édouard Jules Henri Pailleron (1834-1899), in 1881.

344.16 *Cape Cod*] "Cape Cod" appears in *The Complete Poems of George Santayana*, pp. 160-61.

344.16 Moody] William Vaughn Moody [formerly William Vaughn Story Moody] (1869-1910), American poet and dramatist.

344.24 Julian] Julian Codman (1870-1932), was the son of Lucy Lyman Paine Sturgis and Charles Russell Codman. He was a student of Santayana's and a member of the Harvard class of 1892. He was later a corporate and real estate lawyer, and was a leader in efforts to repeal Prohibition.

344.25 "cousin Lucy"] Lucy ("Cousin Lucy") Lyman Paine Sturgis married Charles Russell Codman in 1856. "Cousin Lucy" was the daughter of "the great Russell Sturgis of London" (1805-1887) by his second wife—not, as Santayana states, by his first.

344.27 a Bostonian] Charles Russell Codman (1829-1918) married "Cousin Lucy" Sturgis. A lawyer, he served two terms in the Massachusetts Senate and three in the Massachusetts House of Representatives, and was Harvard overseer (1878-1890 and 1891-1897).

344.31 Brooks] Phillips Brooks (1835-1893), Episcopalian bishop (1870-1882) and Harvard overseer (1883-1889).

345.18 Stickney] Joseph Trumbull Stickney (1874–1904), after his graduation from Harvard in 1895, studied for seven years at the Sorbonne, and was the first American to receive its degree of *Docteur ès lettres*. He was appointed instructor in Greek at Harvard (1903–1904). A poet, he is best known for his *Dramatic Verses* (1902).

345.30 Aiken] Conrad Potter Aiken (1889–1973), a member of the Harvard class of 1912, went on to gain fame as a poet, fiction writer, and critic.

346.16 Forbes] William Cameron Forbes (1870–1959) graduated from Harvard in 1892. He was appointed Harvard's head football coach (1897–1899). Later a financier and member of the board of directors of several American corporations, he was appointed Governor-General of the Phillipines (1909–1913), ambassador to Japan (1930–1932), and Harvard overseer (1914–1920). His poem "On Life and Death" was published anonymously in 1914 in *The Atlantic Monthly*.

346.18 Forbes] John Murray Forbes (1813–1898), railroad builder active in public affairs.

346.31 grandson] Cameron Forbes' father married Edith Emerson, second daughter of Ralph Waldo Emerson, in 1865.

347.39 Forbes] William Hathaway Forbes (1840–1897), called "Colonel Forbes" after his service in the Civil War, was founder and president of the Bell Telephone Company (1878–1887), a director of several other companies, and a horse breeder.

349.33 wooden house] Samuel Eliot Morison, *Three Centuries of Harvard, 1636–1936* (Cambridge, Mass., 1936), pp. 425–26, tells of the club's evolution but fixes the house's location as having been on Brattle Street.

350.5 Woodworth] William McMichael Woodworth (c. 1866–1912), later an instructor in microscopical anatomy at Harvard (1891–1897).

350.11 Bob] Robert Burnside Potter (1869–1934), received the B.A. from Harvard in 1891 and the A.D.G.F. from the École des Beaux Arts in 1900. Later an architect in New York, he gradually retired from practice after 1911 and devoted much of his time to astronomy.

350.22 Scott's] Edgar Thomson Scott (c. 1870–1918), a wealthy Philadelphian and owner of the steam yacht *Sagamore*. He attended Harvard in the early 1890's but did not graduate. He later (1898) married Mary Howard ("Maisie") Sturgis.

354.26 Sturgis, Jr.] Russell Sturgis, Jr. (1831–1899), eldest son of Mary Greene Hubbard and Russell Sturgis (1805–1887). "Cousin Russell" was the father (by two wives) of eight children.

354.38*fn* Sturgis, 3rd] Russell Sturgis, 3rd (1856–1899), eldest son of Susan Codman Welles (?–1862) and Russell Sturgis (1831–1899).

355.8 Gray] Horace Gray (1828–1902), a learned jurist, chief justice of the Massachusetts Supreme Court (1873–1882); later appointed justice of the U.S. Supreme Court (1882–1902).

357.21 two elder sons] Russell Sturgis Codman (1861–?) and John Sturgis Codman (1868–?).

357.31 Sturgis] Howard Overing Sturgis (1855–1920), London-born novelist; a close friend of Henry James and Edith Wharton.

358.4 mother] Julia Overing (Boit) Sturgis (?–1888), third wife of Russell Sturgis (1805–1887). [Also see Note at 48.15–16.]

360.9 Ainger] Arthur Campbell Ainger (1841–1919), teacher of Latin and Assistant Master at Eton (1864–1901). "Carmen Etonense" was one of the songs published in his collection of *Eton Songs*.

360.38 Smith] Willie Haines Smith (*c.* 1870–?), distant cousin of Howard Sturgis.

361.3 two daughters] Anne Macmaster Codman (1864–?) married Henry Bromfield Cabot in 1892. Susan Welles Codman (1866–?) married Redington Fiske in 1896.

364.1 Whitman] Sarah Wyman (*c.* 1845–?) was the wife of Henry Whitman, a Boston wool merchant and banker. She was well known in Boston for her church work and as an interior decorator.

368.8 Holmes] Oliver Wendell Holmes, Jr. (1841–1935), professor of law at Harvard (1882–1883), justice and later chief justice of the supreme judicial court of Massachusetts, (1883–1902), justice of the United States Supreme Court (1902–1932).

368.10 Mrs. Gray's] Amy Heard, married Russell Gray.

368.33 *The Nation*] Periodical published from 1865.

368.37 Wolcott] Roger Wolcott (1847–1900) was governor of Massachusetts (1896–1900).

372.14 Bessie] [See Note at 288.22–23.]

372.24 Strong] Augustus Hopkins Strong (1836–1921), Baptist clergyman, president of the Baptist Theological Seminary in Rochester, New York (1872–1912).

375.19 Margaret] [See Note at 288.22–23.]

379.20 Fish] Nicholas Fish (1846–1902), diplomat; minister resident to Belgium (1882–1886).

380.1 Potter] Elizabeth Stephens Clare Fish married Robert ("Bob") Potter in 1894.

381.12 Butler] Lawrence Smith Butler (1875–1954) graduated in the Harvard class of 1898. After three years as a special student in architecture at MIT (1898–1901), he enrolled at the École des Beaux Arts in Paris.

381.25 mother] Cornelia Stewart Butler.

381.26 wife] Bessie Smith married Stanford White.

382.7 Reszke] Jean de Reszke [originally Jan Kieczyslaw] (1850–1925), Polish operatic tenor.

383.13 friends] Conrad Hensler Slade (1871–?), son of Mina Louise Hensler and Daniel Denison Slade, graduated from Harvard in 1893. An expatriate, he spent most of his life painting in Paris and the south of France, but returned to the United States (Los Angeles) in 1941. He was married to a niece of Renoir.

383.18 Slade] Daniel Denison Slade practiced privately in Boston (1852–1863), and subsequently was appointed professor of applied zoology at Harvard (1870–1882). He was a frequent contributor to scientific and medical journals.

384.19MH Esser . . . fato.] Translation of marginal heading in Italian: *Esser beato nega ai mortali il fato.* (Fate denies mortals happiness.)

384.24 boy] Conrad Slade's child, John Louis Slade (1920–?), was subsequently cured, as Santayana learned from Slade after the war.

384.33 Green] Andrew Hugh Green (1869–1939) received his B.A. degree from Harvard in 1892 and a Bachelor of Science in Civil Engineering from MIT in 1896. An inventor, designer, and engineer, Green went in 1902 to live in Dominica, British West Indies, where his thousand-acre plantation produced lime juice, vanilla beans, rum, and kapok.

387.14 Hubert] Henri Hubert (1872–1927), archaeologist of early Europe, especially of the Celts.

387.35–36 *Les Sentences dans la Poésie Grècque*] *Les Sentences dans la poésie grecque d'Homère à Euripide* (Paris: Société Nouvelle de Librairie Et D'Édition, Librairie Georges Bellais, 1903) was Stickney's University of Paris degree thesis.

387.39 *Die Samkyaphilosophie*] Santayana's reference is to Richard Garbe, *Die Sâmkhya-philosophie: Eine Darstellung des indischen Rationalismus nach den Quellen* ["Sâmkhya-Philosophy: A Representation of Indian Rationalism According to the Sources"] (Leipzig, 1894).

389.9 Lotze] Rudolph Hermann Lotze (1817–1881), German philosopher who, conceding that the physical world is governed by mechanical laws, explained relation and development in the universe as functions of a world mind.

389.9 *Microcosmos*] Rudolph Hermann Lotze, *Mikrokosmus* (Leipzig, 1856–1864). English translation *Microcosmus*, by E. Hamilton and E. E. C. Jones (New York: Scribner and Welford, 1885).

389.21 *Principles of Psychology*] William James's *The Principles of Psychology* was first published in 1890.

390.20 "Angels and ministers of grace defend me."] An adaptation of "Angels and ministers of grace defend us!", *Hamlet* (I, iv, 39).

393.19 Wendell] Barrett Wendell (1855–1921), Harvard instructor in English (1880–1888); assistant professor (1888–1898); professor of English (1898–1917).

394.15 Dickinson] Goldsworthy Lowes Dickinson (1862–1932), fellow of King's College, Cambridge (1887–1920), and lecturer in political science (1896–1920). An agnostic interested in mysticism, his first love was Plato and the Greeks, the subjects of many of his books. His book, *The Greek View of Life*, was first published in 1896. Dickinson made two lecture tours in the United States, in 1901 and 1909.

394.16 Wedd] Nathaniel Wedd (1864–1940), fellow of King's College, Cambridge (1888–1940). A tutor and lecturer in classics, he translated Euripides' *Orestes* in a new English edition of 1895.

394.29 Colonial Club] A Cambridge social and dining club, founded in 1890, which boasted that its elected members were "the leading men of the University and of the town." The club, at 20 Quincy Street, maintained a restaurant, several rooms for overnight visitors, bowling alleys, and a billiards room.

395.23 Browning] Robert Browning (1812–1889), English poet and husband of Elizabeth Barrett Browning.

397.15 Cutting] William Bayard Cutting, Jr., (1878–1910) was granted the Harvard B.A. degree in 1900, one year after he had taken up an appointment as secretary to Ambassador Joseph H. Choate in the American Embassy in London. Subsequently he was appointed vice-consul in the American Consulate in Milan (1908–1909), and secretary of the American Legation, Tangier, Morocco (1909). He was forced to resign from the latter post because of ill health, and died at Assouan, Egypt, at the age of 31.

397.20 Cuffe] Lady Sybil Marjorie Cuffe (1879–1943) married Bayard Cutting, Jr., in 1901. She was later married to Geoffrey Scott (Bernard Berenson's secretary) and to Percy Lubbock.

397.22 Iris] Iris Margaret Cutting (later Marchesa Iris Origo) (1902–?), biographer, historian, and literary critic. Santayana wrote the foreword to her *Leopardi: A Biography* (1935) reissued as *Leopardi: A Study in Solitude*.

398.3 Toy] Crawford Howell Toy (1836–1919), professor of Hebrew and Oriental languages at Harvard (1880–1909).

398.3 wife] Nancy Saunders Toy. She was a correspondent of Santayana's in his later years.

398.9 Coolidge] Archibald Cary Coolidge (1866–1928), member of the history department at Harvard (1893–1928), and director of the Harvard University Library (1910–1928).

399.34 Everett] Charles Carroll Everett (*c.* 1828–1900), Bussey Professor of Theology at Harvard (1869–1900) and dean of the Divinity School (1878–1900).

400.5 Cruthers] Rev. Samuel McChord Crothers (?–1927) was made pastor of the old First Church in Cambridge in 1894, and became one of greater Boston's most popular preachers. Santayana misspells his name.

400.17 Tavern Club] A Boston male dining and social club, founded in 1884. Its members, primarily Boston and Cambridge business and professional men, artists, and professors, were (and are) elected. Santayana was elected in 1894, together with Justice Holmes and fourteen others. The club often hosted visiting dignitaries.

400.24 Fiske] John Fisk [formerly Edmund Fisk Green] (c.1841-1901), American historian and philosophical writer.

401.1 Kipling] Rudyard Kipling (1865-1936), English poet and fiction writer.

402.18 Palmer] [See Note at 236.33.]

403.21 McKinley] William McKinley (1843-1901), president of the United States (1897-1901).

407.5 Copeland] Charles Townsend Copeland (1860-1952), member of the English department at Harvard (1892-1928). He was well known for his platform readings.

407.28 la Rose] Pierre de Chaignon la Rose (1873-1941), instructor in the English department at Harvard (1895-1902), later a literary critic and decorative and heraldic designer.

408.15 Phelps] William Lyon Phelps (1865-1943), professor of English at Yale (1896-1933).

408.18 Child] Francis James Child (c.1824-1896), member of the Harvard English faculty from his graduation in 1846; Boylston Professor of Rhetoric and Oratory (1851-1876), and professor of English (1876-1896).

408.18 Kittredge] George Lyman Kittredge (1860-1941), professor of English at Harvard (1888-1936).

409.19 Palmer] Alice Freeman (1855-1902). Prior to her marriage to Professor George Herbert Palmer in 1887, she was professor of history (1879-1881), and president (1881-1887), of Wellesley College. Subsequently she was dean of the women's department at the University of Chicago (1892-1895).

410.7 wife] Annabel Hubbard (?-1939) married William Lyon Phelps in 1892.

411.35 Hyde] The "rich and isolated student" was James Hazen Hyde (1876-1959), a member of the Harvard class of 1898. As liberal in his benefactions to Harvard as he was in his entertainments, he was known at the turn of the century as "Wonderful Jimmy, the Golden Boy of New York."

420.21-22 *Ich . . . Welt*] Goethe, *Vanitas! Vanitatum Vanitas!*, lines 1, 3.

420.28-29 *Nun . . . Welt,*] Goethe, *Vanitas! Vanitatum Vanitas!*, lines 43, 45.

427.28-31 *This . . . resigning.*] Emerson, "Threnody," lines 162-65. Santayana, apparently quoting from memory, has supplied "true and sure declining" for Emerson's "slow but sure reclining" in line 164.

428.15 La Vallière] Françoise Louise de La Baume Le Blanc, Duchesse de la Vallière (1644-1710), mistress of Louis XIV and mother of four of his children. She withdrew to a convent in 1674.

428.25 *A perfect love is founded on despair*] Santayana here misquotes the first line of Sonnet XXXIII of the second sonnet sequence: "A perfect love is nourished by despair." See *The Complete Poems of George Santayana*, pp. 111, 582.

428.36–37 *De l'Amour*] The reference is to Stendhal's treatise on the psychology of love, published in 1822.

431.20 Lapsley] Gaillard Thomas Lapsley (1871–1949), took his undergraduate and graduate degrees at Harvard, receiving his Ph.D. in 1897. From 1904 to 1929 he was fellow, lecturer, and assistant tutor at Trinity College, Cambridge, and subsequently Cambridge University reader in constitutional history prior to his return to the United States in 1939.

431.31 Wharton] Edith Wharton (1862–1937), American novelist.

434.25 about them] Santayana apparently refers to his poem, "King's College Chapel." See pp. 169–73 of *The Complete Poems of George Santayana.*

435.32 Browning] Oscar Browning (1837–1923) was Master at Eton (1860–1875), and subsequently held various appointments at Cambridge University (1876–1909). He was a prolific writer of history and biography.

435.37*fn* Trevelyan] Robert Calverley Trevelyan (1872–1951), English poet and playwright. He was educated at Harrow and Trinity College, Cambridge.

435.38*fn* Keynes] John Maynard Keynes (1883–1946), English economist, pioneer of the theory of full employment. He was born at Cambridge and educated at Eton and King's College. In 1909 he was elected fellow of King's College.

435.38*fn* Bury] John B. Bury (1861–1927), Irish-born classicist and historian; Regius Professor of Modern History at Cambridge (1902–1927).

439.3 Jackson] Henry Jackson (1839–1921) in 1906 became Regius Professor of Greek at Cambridge.

439.4 Moore] George Edward Moore (1873–1958), English philosopher. He was made a fellow of Trinity College, Cambridge, in 1898, was appointed University Lecturer in moral science (1911–1925), and professor of philosophy (1925–1939).

439.4 MacTaggart] John M'Taggart Ellis M'Taggart [also spelled "MacTaggart"] (1866–1925), English philosopher. MacTaggart was made a fellow of Trinity College, Cambridge, in 1891 and was appointed lecturer in moral science (1897–1923). Three of his five books were on Hegel.

439.34 Lord Acton] Sir John Emerich Edward Dalberg-Acton (1834–1902), Regius Professor of Modern History at Cambridge (1895–1902).

440.33 *Principia Mathematica*] The English philosophers Bertrand Russell and Alfred North Whitehead (1861–1947), both of Cambridge, first published their *Principia Mathematica* in 1910–1913.

444.29 *Encyclopaedie der Wissenschaften*] Hegel's *Enzyklopadie der philosophischen Wissenschaften im Grundrisse* was first published in Heidelberg in 1817.

445.8 *Truth*] Line 14 of Sonnet V in Santayana's second sonnet sequence. See pp. 93 and 568 of *The Complete Poems of George Santayana.*

450.10 Sargent] John Singer Sargent (1856–1925), American painter.

451.6 *The Life of Reason*] In five volumes, was published in 1905–1906.

456.22–33 *Renowned . . . of the air*] The first two lines of a sonnet which Santayana never finished.

456.26 Beal] Louise Adams Beal, wife of James H. Beal and mother of Santayana's friend, Boylston Adams Beal.

456.34 Evans] Sir Arthur John Evans (1851–1941), English archaeologist famous for his excavations of Cretan antiquities.

457.3 Racine] Jean Baptiste Racine (1639–1699), French dramatist.

457.9–12 *Pourquoi . . . retraite*] Racine, *Phèdre*, II, v, 67–70.

462.5 Doughty] Charles Montagu Doughty (1843–1926), English poet, scientist, and explorer; author of *Travels in Arabia Deserta* (1888).

462.6 Foucault] Santayana here misspells the name of Charles Eugène, Viscomte de Foucauld (1858–1916), French explorer.

462.23 Settignano] The location of Berenson's Villa I Tatti near Florence.

463.9 Irving] Alexander Duer Irving (1873–1941), a Harvard student, graduated in 1895 and was later an insurance broker.

470.25 Grundy] Proverbial person of conventional propriety and morality, named after character in Thomas Morton's 1798 comedy, *Speed the Plough*.

473.30–41fn J'aime! . . . toi-même.] *Phèdre*, II, v, 93–97, 112–17.

474.1 *Bérénice*] Tragedy (1670) by Racine.

475.4 Byron] George Noel Gordon, Lord Byron (1788–1824), English Romantic poet.

476.18 "Mollie"] Marion ("Mollie") Cooke (*c.*1855–?), the second Countess Russell, married Russell in Reno, Nevada, in 1900. The marriage was not recognized under English law and Russell was charged with bigamy, inasmuch as he had been unable previoulsy to obtain an English divorce from his first wife, Mabel Edith Scott. Mabel Edith's petition in the following year to have her marriage dissolved was granted, however, and Russell and Mollie were legally wed in England in October of 1901. Mollie's petition for divorce from Russell was granted in 1916.

479.5 Elizabeth] "Elizabeth," the pen name of Mary Annette ("May") Beauchamp (1866–1941), was the author during her lifetime of more than a dozen books of fiction and autobiographical reflections. Born in Australia, the daughter of a prosperous merchant, she moved with her family to London at an early age. She was married in 1891 to the German Count (Henning August) von Arnim-Schlagenthin (1851–1910). At the time of her first meeting with Russell she had been a widow for three years. "Elizabeth" became the third Countess Russell in 1916; she left him in 1919, subsequently refusing him a divorce on the grounds that no woman should be permitted to marry him again.

479.33 *Elizabeth and Her German Garden*] First published *c.*1898.

479.40 *The Caravaners*] First published in 1909.

480.1 *The Pastor's Wife*] First published in 1914.

484.30 *Vera*] First published in 1921.

485.30 second wife] Dora Winifred Black, second wife of Bertrand Russell; formerly, she had been a fellow of Girton College, Cambridge.

485.33 school] Beacon Hill School was begun in 1927.

487.32 "Old Higgs."] Arthur Hibble Higgs (1850–1915), Oxford private tutor.

489.21 *Interpretations of Poetry and Religion*] First published in 1900.

489.36 Bridges] Monica Waterhouse, eldest daughter of the architect Alfred Waterhouse, married Robert Bridges in 1884.

490.1 Edward] Edward Bridges (1892–1959), son of Robert Bridges, later chancellor of Reading University.

492.10 *Testament of Beauty*] First published in 1929.

493.8 Lord Rosebery] Archibald Philip Primrose, fifth Earl of Rosebery (1847–1929), British statesman, educated at Eton and Christ Church, Oxford, which he left without a degree. Foreign secretary under Gladstone in 1892, Lord Rosebery succeeded Gladstone as prime minister (1894–1895).

493.16 Bullingdon Club] Oxford sporting club.

493.19 Fletcher] Harold John Fletcher (*c*.1876–?), Christ Church commoner (1894–1898).

497.21 Rolfe] Frederick Rolfe (1860–1913), English schoolmaster, painter, and writer.

498.11 Huxley] Aldous Leonard Huxley (1894–1963), English novelist, essayist, and critic.

498.16 Esmonde] Sir Osmond Thomas Grattan Esmonde (1896–1936), later Member of Dail Eireann for County Wexford.

498.30 Mortimer] Charles Raymond Bell Mortimer (1895–1980), English journalist and author.

499.34 Urquhart] Francis Fortescue Urquhart (1868–1934), tutor in modern history and senior dean of Balliol.

500.22 Morrell] Lady Ottoline Violet Anne Morrell (1873–1938), wife of Philip Edward Morrell (1870–1943); as hostess she entertained at Garsington Manor, her home near Oxford.

501.8 Asquith] Herbert Henry Asquith (1852–1928), English statesman and prime minister (1908–1916).

501.9 Strachey] Giles Lytton Strachey (1880–1932), English biographer and essayist.

501.9–10 Sassoon] Siegfried Sassoon (1886–1967), English poet.

503.9 Stewart] John Alexander Stewart (1846–1933), White's Professor of Moral Philosophy at Oxford (1897–1927), and professorial fellow of Corpus Christi College. Stewart is best known for his *Notes on the Nicomachean Ethics of Aristotle* (1892) and *The Myths of Plato* (1905).

505.20 *Egotism in German Philosophy*] First published in 1915.

506.8 Schiller] Ferdinand Canning Scott Schiller (1864–1937), English pragmatic philosopher. He was educated at Balliol College, Oxford, taught philosophy at Cornell University in 1893, was a fellow of Corpus Christi College, Oxford (1897–1926), and professor of philosophy at the University of Southern California (1929–1936). (Santayana misidentifies him as F. R. S. Schiller rather than F. C. S. Schiller.)

506.10 Warren] Edward Perry Warren (1860–1928) took the Harvard B.A. in 1883, an Oxford B.A. in 1888, and the M.A. in 1911. Although he established his permanent home in Sussex, he was frequently in residence at Oxford after 1916, when he was made an honorary fellow of Corpus Christi College. Warren was a classical archaeologist and art collector, and made significant contributions to the collections of the Boston Museum of Fine Arts.

506.17 Conybeare] Frederick Cornwallis Conybeare (1856–1924), fellow and praelector in philosophy at University College, Oxford (1880–1887). A philologist and translator, he published several studies and translations of classical and Christian texts. His candor and skepticism (and his defense of Dreyfus) made him a controversial figure.

517.15 Sargeaunt] John Sergeaunt (1857–1922), Latin teacher at Westminster School.

519.35–36 *The Unknowable*] Santayana delivered his Herbert Spencer Lecture on "The Unknowable" at Oxford, October 24, 1923; it was published the following year.

520.5 Housman] Alfred Edward Housman (1859–1936), English classical scholar and poet.

520.10 Chetwynd] Wentworth Randolph Chetwynd (*c.*1904–?), student at New College.

521.10 *The Realm of Essence*] *The Realm of Essence*[:] *Book First of Realms of Being* was first published in 1927.

521.14 *Scepticism and Animal Faith*] First published in 1923.

521.15 Samuel of New College] Walter Horace Samuel (1882–?).

521.20 Joachim] Harold Henry Joachim (*c.*1870–1938), Wykeham Professor of Logic at Oxford and Sub-Warden of New College.

522.40 Rodd] James Rennell Rodd (1858–1941), English diplomat, historian, and classical scholar.

523.20 Inge] Mary Catharine Spooner married William Inge in 1905.

523.22 the Dean's] Dean William Ralph Inge (1860–1954), Anglican prelate and dean of St. Paul's, London; author of numerous philosophical, religious, and historical books.

523.23 *Plotinus*] The 1929 British Academy Lecture, published in the same year.

523.26 *Soliloquies*] *Soliloquies in England and Later Soliloquies,* published in 1922.

526.13 Boutroux] Émile Boutroux (1845–1921), French philosopher.

526.13 Cazalis] Henri Cazalis [pen name Jean Lahore] (1840–1909), French medical doctor and poet.

528.13 *Untergang des Abendlandes*] [See Note at 203.31.]

529.24–25 *Platonism and the Spiritual Life*] First published in 1927.

531.36–37*fn* . . . *veniam* . . . *tibi* . . .] Santayana here quotes from Tibullus, *Carmina,* I, iii, 89–90.

533.6 Geoffrey Scott] Geoffrey Scott (1884–1929), an English art historian, biographer, and editor. In 1907 he became librarian and secretary to Bernard Berenson in Florence, Italy, and designed (with Cecil Pinsent) the library and gardens of Berenson's Villa I Tatti. In 1918 he married Lady Sybil Cuffe, widow of Santayana's Harvard friend and student, Bayard Cutting.

535.33 *Dialogues in Limbo*] First published in 1925.

TEXTUAL COMMENTARY

I. Summary Statement of Textual Principles and Procedures

A. *The Works of George Santayana* and Editorial Scholarship

The volumes of *The Works of George Santayana* are unmodernized, critical editions of Santayana's published and unpublished writings. An "unmodernized" edition retains out-dated and idiosyncratic punctuation, spelling, capitalization, and word-division in order to capture the full intent of the author as well as the original texture of the work; a "critical" edition allows the exercise of editorial judgment in making corrections, changes, and choices among authoritative readings. The goal of the editors is to produce texts that accurately represent Santayana's final intentions regarding his works, and to record all evidence on which editorial decisions have been based.

Editorial judgments are based on an assessment of all available evidence manifest in Santayana's works, letters, annotations, and other authorial material. The editors determine the authority of all documents containing the text in question, establish the critical text on the most authoritative documents, record all textual data for appropriate documents, and account for any divergence, whether substantive or accidental, from the copy-text. When completed, this procedure enables scholars, using the information presented in the editorial apparatus, to recover readings of the documents used in preparing the text and to evaluate the editorial judgments made in establishing the critical text.

B. The Theory of Copy-Text

The central editorial decision for unmodernized, critical editions is the choice of copy-text, the document on which a critical text is based. The texts for *The Works of George Santayana* are constructed according to the theory of copy-text formulated by Sir Walter Greg.[1] Greg distinguishes between substantives (the words themselves)

---

[1] Sir Walter Greg, "The Rationale of Copy-Text," *Studies in Bibliography*, 3 (1950–51): 19–36, reprinted in *The Collected Papers of Sir Walter W. Greg*, ed. J. C. Maxwell (Oxford: Clarendon Press, 1966), 374-391. Guidelines for the application of this method were taken from Fredson Bowers,"Textual Criticism," in *The Aims and Methods of Scholarship in Modern Languages and Literatures*, ed. James Thorpe (New York: Modern Language Association of America, 2d ed., 1970), pp. 29–54, and the *Statement of Editorial Principles: A Working Manual for Editing Nineteenth*

and accidentals (punctuation, spelling, capitalization, word-division, paragraphing, and devices of emphasis). This is a pragmatic distinction used to choose a copy-text, not a theoretical distinction used to determine meaningful from non-meaningful elements in the text. Simply stated, Greg maintains the copy-text should be the most authoritative source of accidentals (not substantives), and, unless clear and certain evidence indicates otherwise, that source will be the document closest to the author's hand, i.e., the fair-copy manuscript, or, when a manuscript does not exist, the typed or printed document that is closest to it.

Basing the choice of copy-text on the most authoritative source of accidentals provides the strongest evidence to make the most difficult decisions on variant readings. Greg's reasoning in this matter is predicated on the known behavior of authors and of intermediaries involved in publishing a work. In practice, authors tend to regard accidentals as less important than substantives. In proofreading, they concentrate on the fidelity of the words and more freely permit or overlook changes in formal matters made by typists, copy-editors, and compositors. As a result, evidence of the author's preferred accidentals is ordinarily less clear than evidence for deciding the author's preferred substantives. The author's intention for changes in substantives can usually be determined by thorough and disciplined research; but the behavior of authors in general—and of Santayana in particular—results in a paucity of evidence concerning preferred accidentals. Greg maintains that the copy-text should be a foundational authoritative document that provides a clear base for the critical edition and sets specific parameters for editorial decisions. To publish a text with accidentals closest to the author's own form, he concludes that it is best to choose the document that the fewest intermediaries have had a chance to alter, i.e., the fair-copy manuscript if it exists or the form closest to it.

Santayana always produced a hand-written manuscript, usually after earlier drafts (pre-copy-text forms). The holograph manuscripts of some of his later writings were given to a typist[2] and the typescript corrected by Santayana. Because a typescript may contain errors in accidentals that Santayana overlooked, the fair-copy manuscript best represents Santayana's preferred use of accidentals, even when a corrected typescript is extant. Hence, in *The Works of George Santayana* the fair-copy manuscript, when extant, is the copy-text. When a manuscript is not extant, the form closest to it is chosen as the copy-text. This may be the typescript, or the first printing of the first edition, or, if Santayana is known to have read proof for the edition, the marked proof.

Century American Texts, rev. ed., prepared by the Center for Editions of American Authors (New York: Modern Language Association of America, 1972). Two exceptional essays on the art of modern scholarly editing that have been very helpful to the editors of this Critical Edition of Santayana's autobiography are by G. Thomas Tanselle: "Greg's Theory of Copy-Text and the Editing of American Literature," *Studies in Bibliography*, 28 (1975): 167-229, and "Some Principles for Editorial Apparatus," *Studies in Bibliography*, 25 (1972): 41-88.

[2] Miss Evelyn Tindall, an Englishwoman employed at the British Legation to the Holy See in Rome, began typing Santayana's handwritten manuscripts late in 1933, beginning with his novel, *The Last Puritan* (1935), and made typescripts of all of Santayana's subsequent work through *Dominations and Powers* (1950).

C. Divided Authority in Critical Editions

Critical editions are eclectic in that readings may be drawn from several different authorial sources or from corrections by the editors. The authority for accidentals is the copy-text; however, the authority for substantive variants may shift to later editions known to be revised by Santayana. Such editions may contain the author's substantive corrections and additions, so that questionable readings of substantives may be decided in favor of the later editions rather than the copy-text. This practice is based on the existence of evidence of authorial revision in later editions. But even when such evidence exists, some substantives may have been altered by other persons and overlooked by Santayana; in such cases the editors rely on the authority of the copy-text to reject the later change.[3]

Establishing critical texts thus requires the utmost scholarly rigor. The relative authority of each textual document and the relationships among these documents are determined by establishing a genealogy of each text. This process involves locating all relevant forms of the texts and collating them to prepare tables of variants that can be used to delineate the development of and the relationships among the texts.

D. Locating Material, Collating Texts, Determining the Relationships of the Texts

All material bearing on the history of the text must be examined. This includes items related to the publication of the work (letters, publishers' files, printers' ledgers), sources quoted in the text, and every text that has *prima facie* authority (pre-copy-text forms, fair-copy manuscripts, all impressions of all editions of the work prior to the death of the author).

To determine the authority of all documents containing the text for previously published works of George Santayana, all true editions up to Santayana's death are collected, collated, and their variants are recorded.[4] Each variant is studied to determine whether it is an authorial revision or the result of other factors such as house styling or type damage. If there is evidence that Santayana revised an edition, the editors must distinguish between his revisions and nonauthorial ones such as those introduced by copy-editors or compositors. As each printing or impression of a single edition may also have been revised by Santayana, the editors collect and collate the first and last impressions of each edition to locate possible authorial variants. When variants are found, the intermediate impressions (if any) are studied to determine when the variants were introduced and whether they are authorial.

---

[3] G. Thomas Tanselle, "Textual Scholarship," *Introduction to Scholarship in Modern Languages and Literatures*, ed. Joseph Gibaldi (New York: Modern Language Association of America, 1981), 40.

[4] All true editions of Santayana's works up to his death are listed in *George Santayana: A Bibliographical Checklist, 1880-1980*, eds. Herman J. Saatkamp, Jr. and John Jones (Bowling Green, Ohio: Philosophy Documentation Center, 1982).

The order and relationship of editions and impressions are determined by internal as well as external evidence. Printing records or publisher's markings in the printed volume may indicate separate impressions, and correspondence sometimes provides clues to the existence of new printings of an edition. Lacking such external evidence, the editors may distinguish between otherwise apparently identical impressions by internal evidence, such as wear and deterioration of the plates. Variants between impressions may be discovered by extensive collation of copies of the edition collected from disparate regions in which the work was marketed.

E. Selection and Emendation of the Copy-Text

When the genealogy of the text has been established and the relationships of all textual documents determined, the editors choose the document that will serve as copy-text. Greg's theory of copy-text, described above, is the basis for this choice. The text of the critical edition adheres to the copy-text except where there is compelling evidence to justify emendation. Substantives are emended when a corresponding reading in another version of the text reflects Santayana's clear intention, or, in those instances where the copy-text is a published form (book or article), when the editors judge that Santayana's usual practice has been altered in the printing and publishing of the work.

For *The Works of George Santayana*, the apparatus for each volume records editorial decisions in three sections: (1) *Discussions of Adopted Readings*, (2) *List of Emendations*, and (3) *Report of Line-End Hyphenation*. A fourth section, the *List of Substantive Variants*, permits the reader to compare the critical text with all substantive variant readings in every other possibly authoritative text. By recording all editorial decisions and providing a historical record of substantive variant readings in all authoritative forms of the text, the editorial apparatus enables the reader to reconstruct the copy-text and to evaluate judgments made by the editors in establishing the text of the critical edition.

F. Use of Computer Files in Transcribing, Editing, and Typesetting

Computer files are used in transcribing, editing, and typesetting *The Works of George Santayana*. The initial transcription of a copy-text includes typesetting codes for all the text elements (chapter headings, sub-headings, marginal headings, standard paragraphs, extracts, poetry lines, footnotes, etc.). The codes are for the Penta Front-End System (a front-end phototypesetting system) used by MIT Press, and they are usually mnemonic. They consist of two or more characters and are based on the character set of the American Standard Code of Information Interchange (ASCII) and, as a result, do not employ print-control codes unique to any one particular word-processing program. If the copy-text is a holograph manuscript, its transcription also includes codes indicating authorial alterations of the text (deletions, insertions, and other corrections). When there is a need for a transcription without the typesetting codes, they are deleted from a duplicate file containing the transcription. Each transcription receives at least two independent sight collations against the copy-text to assure its accuracy. These collations are made using transcriptions with or without the typesetting codes, depending on whether the codes interfere with the clarity of the text. Independently, the typesetting codes are proofed at least twice.

A duplicate computer file of the corrected copy-text transcription serves as the basis for the critical edition, and all emendations are entered in it with appropriate typesetting codes. This is a straightforward process when the copy-text is a first edition of a work, but when the copy-text is a holograph manuscript, intermediate steps are necessary before the file is ready for emendations. First, computer files of holograph transcriptions are converted from word-processing files to ASCII files. Second, programs written in Basic strip the ASCII files of material that will not appear in the clear-text of the critical edition. For example, they are stripped of text that Santayana deleted while inscribing the holograph and of symbols indicating inserted material. (The original transcription of the holograph is coded in a manner that enables the Basic programs to strip this unwanted matter.) The editors then have the beginnings of a clear-text for the critical edition that has already received at least two independent sight collations against the copy-text.

All material associated with the critical edition is placed in computer files: the textual commentary, variants list (substantive and accidental), list of emendations, record of line-end hyphenations, notes to the text, manuscript alterations lists, index. This material is transcribed with typesetting codes (though, as in the case of accidental variants, not all of it will be published). Various software programs aid the editors in locating, counting, and compiling copy-text material needed in making editorial decisions. This software, in conjunction with the computer file containing a transcription of the copy-text, is used to identify all alterations in the manuscript, patterns of punctuation and spelling, and all line-end hyphens in the copy-text. A "Word Book" indicating Santayana's usage and spelling of problematic words is placed in a computer file for future use. Software programs also aid the editors in locating and identifying index entries.

The transition from computer files to phototypesetting is accomplished in three stages: the text of the critical edition, of the apparatus, and of the index are typeset separately. Each of these stages produces galleys and then page proofs. To typeset the critical text, the word-processing files containing the established text are converted to ASCII files, and these files are structured for use by the Penta Front-End System in conjunction with an Autologic Aps Micro 5 (a digital typesetter). These ASCII files are sent on floppy discs to MIT Press where they are transferred to magnetic tape, and galleys of the text are produced for the editors. The galleys receive two independent sight collations against the copy-text and are checked against the emendations list. If any corrections are required, the galleys are marked and returned to MIT Press which then produces page proofs. The page proofs are carefully examined (particularly the page breaks) but no formal collation process is normally required at this point. Typesetting the apparatus and other material of the Editorial Appendix occurs after the page proofs of the text have been received and checked by the editors. All page references in the files containing the apparatus and index are then changed to the new critical edition pages (previously they referred to the pages of the copy-text). This material, coded for typesetting when first placed in the file, is sent on floppy discs to MIT Press where, as before, it is transferred to magnetic tape and galleys are produced. The galleys for the apparatus are proofed twice by independent readings and returned to the Press. Page proofs are sent to the editors for a final review, though a formal collation is normally not necessary at this point. In the final stage, the index is completed by including references to page numbers from the critical edition text and apparatus. The index file is sent to MIT Press, and the process of galleys to page proofs, as in the preceding sections of the volume, is repeated.

The technology of "desk-top typesetting" employed in *The Works of George Santayana* greatly facilitates the editing and publication process. It is significant that once the copy-text is transcribed in a computer file, the integrity of that text is maintained throughout the editing process. Except for the added emendations, the final critical edition text is identical to the original copy-text transcription. When the galley proofs of the critical edition text are collated against the copy-text and checked against the emendations list, this is actually the fourth independent collation the text has received: two independent collations when transcribed from the copy-text plus the final two collations of the galley proofs. Hence, not only do the editors of *The Works of George Santayana* have direct control over the printing process, but also the integrity of the critical edition text is better safeguarded by this modern technology than by standard typesetting procedures.

II. Description and Development of the Text of
Persons and Places

A. Manuscript

There are three stages in the development of the manuscript: (1) pre-copy-text forms, (2) the fair-copy manuscript, and (3) the typescript.[5]

1. Pre-Copy-Text Forms

Pre-copy-text documents consist of four notebooks and several essays that were evidently composed as possible chapters of the autobiography. The four pre-copy-text *Autobiography Notebooks* are written mainly in pencil in ruled composition books. Their contents are as follows:

Notebook I:[6] rough drafts of the following topics:

---

[5] The first two of these stages—the three autobiographical essays and the "*Autobiography Notebooks*", together with the fair-copy holograph manuscript of *Persons and Places*[:] *Fragments of Autobiography*— are in the George Santayana Papers, Rare Book and Manuscript Library, Columbia University. The third stage—the corrected and revised typescript made from the fair-copy holograph— has not been located.

[6] The numbering of these "*Autobiography Notebooks*" has evidently been done by the librarians of the Rare Book and Manuscript Library, Columbia University, for the purposes of cataloguing and bears no relation to the probable dates of inscription of the individual notebooks. The numbering of the notebooks is, in fact, directly contrary to the order in which they relate to the later fair-copy stage of the autobiography.

"Farewell to England" (becomes Chapter 6 of part three of the fair-copy holograph manuscript); Robert Bridges, Harold Fletcher and Father Waggett, Howard Sturgis in his later years, Santayana's Locke and Spinoza lectures (become Chapter 5, "Oxford Friends" and Chapter 6, "Farewell to England" of part three of the fair-copy holograph manuscript); and "Younger Harvard Friends" (becomes Chapter XXI of part two of the fair-copy holograph manuscript); "Notes on the Ethics of the Old Testament" and "Alexander in Olympus" (rough drafts of unpublished essays); and the young Howard Sturgis (included in Chapter XXII of part two of the fair-copy holograph manuscript).

Notebook II: contains rough drafts of materials later included in the second part of the fair-copy holograph manuscript: "Germany I" (Chapter XVII: "Germany"); "First Visit to England" (Chapter XVIII:"London"); "Germany continued" (Chapter XVII: "Germany"); and "Official Career at Harvard" (Chapter XXIV).

Notebook III: contains rough drafts of materials later found in the first part of the fair-copy holograph manuscript: "My Father's Family continued" (Chapter VII: "Early Memories" and Chapter XIV: "First Return to Spain"); "Buggies" (Chapter VIII: "I Am Transported to America"); material relating to the story of his cousin Elvira (Chapter IV: "Changes in Avila"); and a draft of a piece entitled "The Duke of Parcent" not included in the later stage of the *Persons and Places* holograph manuscript and which remains unpublished.

Notebook IV: written mainly in ink, with pencil corrections and insertions, this notebook is entitled "Parts of Autobiography[:] Russell[,] Lionel Johnson[,] Jepson[,] Burke". (The names "Jepson" and "Burke" being added later in pencil.) A section beginning on page 27 of the notebook is entitled "III How to keep a friend from becoming a nuisance". It is an incomplete but fairly polished draft of Chapter XIX of the second part of the fair-copy holograph manuscript entitled "Russell".

Besides the notebooks, several autobiographical essays are handwritten on the cross-hatched ruled stationery that Santayana favored for writing letters and composing essays during his last years. Typed versions of some of these essays are extant, and these typescripts will be described in relation to their corresponding holographs. One of the essays entitled *"Towers or Magdalen Tower"* consists of ten pages written in pencil and describes the charm of the celebrated tower of Magdalen College, Oxford University. That this essay was originally intended to be part of the autobiography is indicated by the title *"Persons & Places"* written in the upper left-hand corner of the first leaf.

There are also two pages of handwritten matter and a five-page typewritten piece entitled *"Elvira."* The two handwritten pages refer to what Santayana considered eugenic abnormalities in the children of his mother and her first husband, George Sturgis (which Santayana discusses in Chapter III of *Persons and Places*). There are also comments on the character and personality of Santayana's half brother, Robert Sturgis. The first of these two handwritten pages carries an inscription at the top, upper left-hand side: "Reserve this for a separate chapter later." Some of the material on these two pages was incorporated into *Persons and Places* as indicated above. But the discussion in these pages of Robert's nature and his thoughts and feelings regarding religion is nowhere completely represented in the finished holograph manuscript or the published versions of *Persons and Places*. The typewritten piece entitled "Elvira", a portrait of Santayana's cousin, finds its way, with some refinements, into "Changes in Avila", Chapter XX of the second part.[7]

The last of these essays consists of two separate and rejected drafts of the Epilogue to the autobiography. The first rejected draft consists of three pages written in pencil on cross-hatched ruled stationery and is entitled *"Epilogue[:] The World in my Time."* These three holograph pages appear to be a rough and incomplete draft of the fair-copy version of the Epilogue that was published in the third volume of the Scribner's and Cresset editions. The second rejected draft of the Epilogue consists of twenty-five holograph pages on cross-hatched ruled stationery and is entitled "XXXII *Epilogue on the Idler and his Works."* (There is also a cover sheet bearing the title in Daniel Cory's hand.) Written above the title in ink are the words: *"Rejected first draft of Epilogue to Persons and Places."* This rejected epilogue became the title piece in *The Idler and His Works and Other Essays*, edited and with a preface by Daniel Cory (New York: George Braziller, 1957). It also appeared earlier in *The Saturday Review*, 37 (May 15, 1954): 7–9.

2. Fair-Copy Manuscript: Three Parts, One Volume

The second stage of the manuscript is the fair-copy holograph. It was written in three distinct parts, all of which are at present in the collection of the Rare Book and Manuscript Library of Columbia University.[8] It is clear from Santayana's letters and the original consecutive roman numeral numbering of chapters throughout the three parts that Santayana intended them to constitute a single work. The numbering of chapters was later modified on the holograph for publication in three separate volumes. The holograph manuscript is inscribed in black ink on cross-hatched ruled stationery. The first part consists of sixteen chapters, totalling seven hundred and seventy-eight leaves; the second and third parts consist of eight chapters each, and the total number of leaves is three hundred and forty-five for the second part and two hundred and sixty-six for the third. Santayana has numbered the leaves in the upper right-hand corner, but the numbering, due no doubt to revisions, is not perfectly consecutive in every chapter. In part one, chapter numbering of the holograph manuscript is one through sixteen in roman numerals; in part two, seventeen through twenty-four in roman numerals; in part three the original roman numeral chapter numbers have been erased and arabic numbers, one through eight substituted.[9]

Included with the holograph of part one is an essay entitled "We Were Not Virtuous." It is located between Chapters XII and XIII as a distinct unit with its

---

[7] For a description of the "Elvira" materials and an analysis of their development and incorporation into Chapter XX, see *Discussions of Adopted Readings*, 322.20–324.38.

[8] Following Santayana, the editors use the term "part" when referring to the three sections of the holograph manuscript or, more generally, when simply referring to the three sections of the autobiography. This Critical Edition is divided into the three parts of the holograph manuscript. Each of these three parts was published as a separate book in both the American and English editions, and the editors use "book" or "volume" when referring to these specific publications.

[9] In referring to the manuscript chapter numbers we follow Santayana's pattern by using roman numerals for parts one and two (Chapters I through XXIV) and arabic numbers for part three (Chapters 1 through 8).

own heading. However, it is not numbered as a separate chapter nor is it a part of Chapters XII or XIII. It is written in ink, and though undoubtedly conceived as a chapter of *Persons and Places*, it was omitted from publication. At the top of the first page of Chapter XII of the fair-copy holograph manuscript (*MS1*, page 42), which is headed "XII First Friends", Santayana has written in pencil "or *We Were Not Virtuous*", indicating the possibility that he originally planned to include the essay at this place in the autobiography. Two typewritten versions of this piece followed the holograph manuscript. One of these typescripts is currently in the Rare Book and Manuscript Library of Columbia University; the other is in the Harry Ransom Humanities Research Center of The University of Texas at Austin. Study of the typescripts in relation to the holograph manuscript reveals that the Texas typescript is the later of the two and represents Santayana's latest intentions regarding this essay. The essay is a discussion of Santayana's mother's dissatisfaction with both of her husbands and with her four surviving children. Apparently, this is material about Santayana's American family that he did not want published before his death, and he perhaps hoped to assure its future publication by including it with the fair-copy manuscript of part one, though without fully incorporating it into a specific chapter.[10]

The holograph manuscript for all three parts of *Persons and Places*, written in Santayana's fine, clear hand, is in a good state of preservation. The handwriting on the third part, completed in 1947, is shakier than that on the two earlier parts and is also more heavily revised. After inscribing each of the three parts in black ink, Santayana evidently went over them and made corrections and revisions. Many of these revisions are erasures, with the corrected or revised version written over the erasure. Other corrections and revisions were made by pasting strips of paper containing the revision directly over erased, crossed out, or otherwise cancelled words, phrases, or sentences. The vast majority of revisions are in ink, but there are some clear revisions in black pencil. There is also a set of apparent revisions in red pencil that are very faint and some appear to have been erased. None of these red-pencil revisions, unless reentered in ink, appears in the printed forms of the autobiography; this also indicates that they were not included in the typescript sent to the publisher. Apparently Santayana made some tentative revisions in red pencil and later indicated his final intentions with ink.[11]

Santayana's original conception of his autobiography was that it be published as one volume posthumously. As a concession to externally imposed conditions, he wrote his memoirs in three separate parts and allowed both his American and English publishers to produce the work as three distinct books. This concession was due primarily to his desire to provide financial assistance for his friend and literary secretary Daniel Cory. Cory was, at the start of the Second World War, living in New York City; he was married, unemployed, and had very little money. To insure that immediate publication of the work would provide Cory financial relief, Santayana designated him recipient of the rights and royalties to the manuscript. The Scribner's

---

[10] See Section III.E. (pp.610–11) of the Textual Commentary for a discussion of the placement of this essay in the Critical Edition.

[11] These tentative red-pencil revisions are not included in the Critical Edition unless they were reentered in ink by Santayana.

edition of *Persons and Places*[:] *The Background of My Life*, the first volume of the published autobiography, was a Book-of-the-Month Club selection and earned a considerable amount of money. Another reason why Santayana agreed to a three-volume publication of his autobiography was that his Scribner's editor, John Hall Wheelock, was very anxious to publish the work at once. Finally, the correspondence suggests that Santayana himself became reconciled to publication of the parts of his autobiography in three separate volumes when he realized that the three sections would stand individually. Perhaps he was also concerned that the war might otherwise prevent publication of the work through loss or destruction of the manuscripts. In any case, he sent the typescripts of parts one and two of *Persons and Places* to Scribner's (in 1941 and 1944, respectively) with permission to publish immediately. It was only with the final section that he insisted publication occur after his death. Though accommodating the exigencies of immediate publication for parts one and two, Santayana never relinquished hope that his autobiography would one day appear in a corrected and more complete one-volume edition.

3. Typescripts

The typescripts for all three parts of Santayana's original handwritten manuscript of *Persons and Places* have disappeared. Miss Evelyn Tindall, an Englishwoman employed at the British Legation to the Holy See in Rome, made the typescript, which Santayana read and revised. It was the thin-paper carbon copy of this typescript, not the handwritten manuscript, which was sent to New York and used as printer's copy for the American (Scribner's) edition. This in turn served as the basis for the English edition (parts one and two published by Constable Publishers and part three published by Cresset Press).

B. Part I: Transmission and Publication

By September 13, 1941, Santayana had completed work on the first part of *Persons and Places*.[12] By October 12, 1941, he had posted the typescript to Scribner's in New York, with instructions that it be delivered to Daniel Cory.[13] But shortly afterward the parcel was returned to Santayana by the Italian postal authorities, who, because of wartime regulations, refused to forward it. However, in mid-July 1942, the typescript was successfully transported by diplomatic pouch to Scribner's in New York through a remarkable set of international channels. In a letter dated October 28, 1942, John Hall Wheelock expresses his gratitude to Padraic Colum for his influence in "effecting the transmittal of this manuscript from Rome to the Scribner offices."[14] Scribner's had hoped to promote the autobiography by advertising the international intrigue

[12] George Santayana to Evelyn Tindall, 13 September 1941, Harry Ransom Humanities Research Center, The University of Texas at Austin.
[13] George Santayana to George Sturgis, 12 October 1941, Collection of Robert S. Sturgis (Santayana's grandnephew, the son of George Sturgis), Cambridge, Massachusetts.
[14] Wheelock to Colum, 28 October 1942, Archives of Charles Scribner's Sons, Princeton University Library, Princeton University.

necessary for them to receive the typescript. But Hugh S. Cumming, Jr., Assistant Chief of the United States Division of European Affairs, asked that the information not be released because the United States was at war and the transmission of the typescript involved two neutral governments, Spain and the Vatican City.[15] The following is the release proposed by Scribner's but never published.

> After an intriguing journey which involved numerous diplomats, the manuscript of George Santayana's autobiography, "Persons and Places," to be published by Charles Scribner's Sons early in 1943, has reached this country. Mr. Santayana, now in his eightieth year, is staying at a nursing-home in Rome. He was unable to leave Italy before war was declared, since the only two immediate avenues of escape were both closed to him. Switzerland would accept him, as any other foreigner, for only two weeks. To reach Spain it was necessary to fly, and this his doctor forbade. There was no choice but to remain in Rome. Mr. Santayana, however, at once took steps to get his manuscript, upon which he has been working for some years, out of the country. Since we were by that time at war, the Italian Government was unwilling to permit this. It became necessary, therefore, to enlist the aid of the Department of State in Washington, and especially of Sumner Welles. The further cooperation of the Papal Secretary of State, Cardinal Maglione, together with that of the Papal Nuncio in Madrid, of Carlton J. H. Hayes, the American Ambassador to Spain, and the Spanish Ambassador, Senor Cardenas, finally made possible the transmission of the manuscript by Diplomatic Pouch to the United States. Santayana is known to a large section of the general reading-public for his novel, "The Last Puritan." His most important philosophical work has been collected into the single volume, "Realms of Being," which appeared in the spring of 1942.[16]

Santayana's title for the entire autobiography appears on the first page of the fair-copy holograph: *"Persons & Places: Fragments of Autobiography"*. This is the only title for the entire autobiography originated by Santayana himself. The subtitles to volumes one and two of the Scribner's and Constable editions, *"The Background of My Life"*, and *"The Middle Span"*, were originated by Daniel Cory. The subtitle to volume three, *"My Host the World"*, was developed by John Hall Wheelock from the title of the final chapter: *"Epilogue on My Host The World"*.

In his letters of this time Santayana acknowledges the advisability of cutting the romantic story of the love and marriage of Jessie Grew and Jack Morgan from the manuscript version of Chapter IV.[17] Omitted were ten pages of the typescript (sixteen and a half pages of the holograph manuscript) from the Scribner's and Constable

---

[15] Cumming to Scribner's, 7 December 1942, Archives of Charles Scribner's Sons, Princeton University Library.

[16] Release, 20 November 1942, Archives of Charles Scribner's Sons, Princeton University Library.

[17] Santayana to Boylston Adams Beal, 4 September 1941, Houghton Library, Harvard University; also Santayana to Evelyn Tindall, 13 September 1941, Humanities Research Center, The University of Texas.

editions of *Persons and Places*[:] *The Background of My Life* (1944). Santayana regretted the omission of this material from publication of the first part of his autobiography, saying in a letter to his friend Boylston Beal, whom he had consulted on the question of the advisability of the cuts and who had encouraged him to make them, that "frankness and realism are the soul of these memoirs. . . ."[18] He writes to Cory that "perhaps the omissions can be restored in a few years", and to Beal, that this material can be published later, "in twenty years. . . ."[19]

The first publication of *Persons and Places* was in *The Atlantic Monthly*. John Hall Wheelock suggested serial publication of excerpts from the autobiography in a magazine. Santayana seconded the suggestion in a letter to Cory of October 12, 1941. The purpose of the magazine publication was to bring some immediate relief to Cory's financial distress. The carbon copy of the typescript was evidently used by Daniel Cory, in collaboration with the editor of *The Atlantic Monthly*, to prepare copy for publication in the magazine. In 1943, three separate issues of the magazine carried excerpts from the autobiography. "Persons and Places[:] Time, Place, and Parents" appeared in the March issue, consisting of excerpts from the first three chapters ("Time, Place and Ancestry", "My Father", and "My Mother"). "Persons and Places[:] Early Memories and Schooling" appeared in the April issue, consisting of excerpts from Chapters VII ("Early Memories"), VIII ("I am Transported to America"), IX ("No. 302 Beacon Street"), and X ("The Latin School"); and "Persons and Places[:] First Friends and Harvard College" appeared in the May issue, consisting of excerpts from Chapters XII ("First Friends"), XIII ("The Harvard Yard"), and XIV ("First Return to Spain").

The Scribner's edition of the work was published on January 1, 1944. The Constable edition also appeared that same year, having been set from copy sent to London by Scribner's. Correspondence between Italy and the United States had, however, been cut off in October 1941. Santayana had no opportunity to receive or read proof of either the Scribner's or Constable volume. He first saw a copy of the published version late in June 1944, when a visiting war correspondent or photographer with the American occupation forces in Rome brought him a copy of the Scribner's edition. Thus Santayana learned that the manuscript picked up by the Vatican messenger two years earlier had, in fact, reached New York.

Santayana was not wholly displeased with the form and substance of the Scribner's volume, but he noticed certain changes and omissions and was dissatisfied with the American spellings that Scribner's had substituted for his own habitual British forms. When writing to Otto Kyllmann, editor at Constable Publishers of London, on June 9, 1945, Santayana assumes that Kyllmann will have "corrected" the spelling to proper British forms and will also have corrected the obvious printer's errors in the Scribner's volume.[20] In a letter to Cory of April 8, 1945, Santayana says that Wheelock of Scribner's has promised him "English spelling" in volume two and that "ultimately

[18] Santayana to Beal, 4 September 1941, Houghton Library, Harvard University.
[19] Santayana to Cory, 17 October 1941, Rare Book and Manuscript Library, Columbia University; Santayana to Beal, 4 September 1941, Houghton Library, Harvard University. This deleted material is included in the Critical Edition (pp. 58.23–65.3).
[20] Santayana to Kyllmann, 9 June 1945, Rare Book and Manuscript Collection, Temple University Libraries, Temple University.

all three volumes will be bound in one." But that, he says, "is not at all my dream of the final illustrated and completed edition! . . . You must manage to have, some day, an *édition de luxe*, to appease my Shade." The Constable edition of the first part of Santayana's autobiography does in large measure use traditional British spellings; however, by the middle of the twentieth century many of the older British spellings had converted to the modern American forms. Although the Constable edition was set up specially, it does depend upon the Scribner's edition for its text; thus many of the corruptions (editorial revisions and compositorial errors of the Scribner's edition) are simply perpetuated in the Constable edition. The Scribner's edition has a single illustration: Santayana's graduation portrait from the Harvard College Class of 1886 is the frontispiece. The English edition contains no illustrations in any of the three volumes.

C. Part II: Transmission and Publication

As with the first part of his autobiography, Santayana eventually acceded to requests for publication of the second part. By June 23, 1944, he had completed the fair-copy holograph manuscript of the second part.[21] He regretted having to cut sections that he believed impossible to publish at that time. In his June 23, 1944 letter to Cory, Santayana writes that he hated to "mutilate my memories for the sake of giving the public what they might like only, or what is good for them to hear." But he adds that if he had some assurance that eventually "a complete version of both volumes shall appear, I might bring myself to omit, for the present, a great part of what I have written."

Evelyn Tindall, by July 3, 1944, was typing up the second part of Santayana's autobiography, and by early November the typescript was completed and ready to be sent to Cory and Scribner's in New York. Again Santayana was faced with the problem of a means of conveyance, as the post between Rome and New York had not yet been reestablished. The U. S. Army censors would not permit transportation of the manuscript through the mails because it contained a chapter (XVII) entitled "Germany". This time, however, transportation of the manuscript of the second part of the autobiography was facilitated by Master Sergeant Harry A. Freidenberg of the American Army. He arranged for the typescript to be carried to New York by his commanding officer, Colonel Lee Miller, who was flying there on official business.[22] The typescript was received by Scribner's in New York during November or December 1944. In gratitude for this assistance, Santayana made Sergeant Freidenberg a present of the handwritten manuscript.

[21] Santayana to Daniel Cory, 23 June 1944, Rare Book and Manuscript Library, Columbia University.
[22] Freidenberg to William G. Holzberger, 27 September 1982, Collection of William G. Holzberger. (This is the man whom Santayana referred to as "the invaluable Sergeant Freidenberg": the soldier who befriended Santayana during the American occupation of Rome in 1944, brought him presents of food, coffee, and tea from the Army mess, and drove him to the pharmacy in his jeep.)

Discussion of the plans for publication of the second part of Santayana's auto-biography occurs in his correspondence, particularly in the letters to Cory, Wheelock, George Sturgis (Santayana's nephew), Andrew Onderdonk (a friend), and Otto Kyllmann. This correspondence makes clear Santayana's original intention to withhold publication of the second part of his autobiography until after his death and then his change of mind in order to come to the financial assistance of his friend Cory. In a letter to Otto Kyllmann of August 23, 1947, Santayana says, "I wrote these memoirs intending them to be posthumous; when circumstances led me to publishing them, I made some excisions . . . "; and in a letter to Rosamond Sturgis (wife of his nephew, George Sturgis) of October 3, 1947, he writes: ". . . I counted on dying, so that my indiscretions would all have acquired the impersonal authority of historical documents. I rely on Scribner to issue an edition [deluxe] eventually, if they think they can make money out of it. My idea had been, on the contrary, to help finance an edition that would have been a work of art."[23]

The letters that Santayana wrote to John Hall Wheelock are textually significant. In a letter to Wheelock of January 21, 1945, Santayana asks that galley proofs of the second part of the autobiography be shown to Daniel Cory: "Perhaps he might soften some of my words. This book was meant to tell the naked truth, but I see it is imprudent and not worthwhile."[24] In two letters to Wheelock written in February 1945, Santayana discusses the question of the title to be assigned to the second volume of his memoirs.[25] " 'On both sides of the Atlantic' occurs to me" he writes. To the title possibilities suggested by Wheelock—"The Middle Years" or "The Middle Span" (the latter being the eventual title of the volume, and originated by Daniel Cory)—Santayana responds that these titles do not describe the real character of the book: "the true subject is *the impressions left in me* by the various persons and places I came across, and I don't hesitate to skip about chronologically, and say on each occasion all that I have to say on that theme. I also return in some cases, or anticipate." And he adds: "I assume that the final standard edition in one volume, with some of the suppressed passages restored, will retain *Persons & Places* for its title."[26] To Daniel Cory he writes, on March 14, 1945, "I regard this edition of *Persons and Places* [implying both volumes one and two and perhaps three by anticipation] as a mutilated victim of war, and dream of a standard edition, which probably I shall never see, in which the original words, the omitted passages, and the marginal comments (not headings, as in the Triton Edition) shall be restored, and the portraits and other illustrations shall be well reproduced."[27]

The Scribner's edition of part two of Santayana's autobiography, entitled *The Middle Span*[:] *Vol. II Persons and Places*, was published in New York in March 1945.

[23] Santayana to Kyllmann, 23 August 1947, Temple University Libraries; Santayana to Rosamond Sturgis, 3 October 1947, Collection of Robert S. Sturgis.
[24] Santayana to Wheelock, 21 January 1945, Archives of Charles Scribner's Sons, Princeton University Library.
[25] Santayana to Wheelock, 17, 23 February 1945, Archives of Charles Scribner's Sons, Princeton University Library.
[26] Santayana to Wheelock, 17 February 1945, Archives of Charles Scribner's Sons, Princeton University Library.
[27] Santayana to Cory, 14 March 1945, Rare Book and Manuscript Library, Columbia University.

The volume contains a single illustration: a frontispiece portrait of Santayana in his middle years. The marginal headings (or "marginal comments" as Santayana calls them) which appear in the fair-copy holograph manuscript are missing. Santayana regarded these marginal headings as important elements in his autobiography, yet they appear in no published version of the work. In a letter to his friend Andrew Onderdonk of June 8, 1945, Santayana writes that the book was entitled *The Middle Span* "without my knowledge or consent for commercial reasons: but it is an integral part of the whole book and will ultimately, I hope, appear, with volume third, in an edition with illustrations, marginal comments (omitted, I suppose, for economy) and the suppressed passages: but I shall not see that edition, so that I can indulge in the illusion that it will be magnificent."[28]

Among the passages suppressed for the original publication is Santayana's description of the so-called "Oxford scandal" involving his friend, the young Earl Russell (elder brother of Bertrand Russell). Under mysterious circumstances, the Earl was "sent down" from Oxford in May 1885 by Benjamin Jowett, Master of Balliol College. This passage (and all other originally suppressed passages in all three parts of *Persons and Places*) has been restored in the text of the Critical Edition (308.26–309.27). Santayana's account of the incident constitutes the first authoritative explanation of a critical event in the young life of the English nobleman who, during his notorious courtroom battles with his first wife and her mother, was dubbed by journalists "the Wicked Earl".[29]

The English edition of the second part of Santayana's autobiography was set from printed copy sent to London by Scribner's. Despite the fact that Santayana had expressed his objections to the title of the Scribner's edition in a letter to Kyllmann,[30] the Constable edition is titled "*The Middle Span*[:] *By the Author of 'Persons and Places'* ". This English edition was published during the autumn of 1947, and only after much correspondence between Santayana and editor Otto Kyllmann. The London publisher was worried about the possibility of libel suits developing from Santayana's descriptions of and comments about persons in the book, and particularly British persons, who might still be alive or whose descendants might bring suit. Kyllmann was especially concerned about Santayana's comments about John Francis Stanley, the second Earl Russell, and he pressed Santayana to revise a passage referring to the "Billings sisters" and their relations with the young earl. Santayana was annoyed by what he considered unwarranted fears on the part of the English publisher, but he obliged by thoroughly rewriting the passage. He eventually came to prefer the rewritten version to the original and requested Cory to assure that the rewritten version be included in any future edition of the work (see *Discussions of Adopted*

---

[28] Santayana to Onderdonk, 8 June 1945, Rare Book and Manuscript Library, Columbia University. In 1963, Scribner's issued a single-volume version of the autobiography, with an introduction by Daniel Cory. This was not, however, a new edition; it merely combined the three previously published Scribner's volumes (*Persons and Places*[:] *The Background of My Life* [1944], *The Middle Span* [1945], and *My Host the World* [1953]) into a single volume.

[29] Lord Russell's own account of the incident, in his autobiography, *My Life and Adventures* (London, New York, Toronto, Melbourne: Cassell & Co., Ltd., 1923), is vague, incomplete, and evasive.

[30] Santayana to Kyllmann, 9 June 1945, Temple University Libraries.

Readings, 314.15–38).[31] Kyllmann and his editors carefully went through the text revising and softening statements as they deemed fit. The result of this editorial bowdlerization is particularly evident when comparing the wording of the English edition to that of the holograph manuscript or to the Scribner's edition in the passages dealing with Earl Russell (Chapter XIX, "Russell"). Although both the English and American editions of the second part of the autobiography contain essentially British spelling forms, both editions vary considerably from Santayana's characteristic punctuation, and when compared the two editions differ at many points. Neither the English nor the American edition is a complete or fully accurate realization of Santayana's intentions as they are revealed in the holograph manuscript or in his letters.

D. Part III: Transmission and Publication

Santayana completed the fair-copy holograph of the third part of *Persons and Places* by June 9, 1945,[32] but he told Cory that he did not want it published during his lifetime. The work, he said, "will certainly remain over, to be published by you eventually."[33] He did, however, permit Cory to publish excerpts in *The Atlantic Monthly*. "A Change of Heart" (excerpted from Chapter 1: "A Change of Heart") appeared in the December 1948 issue; and "Epilogue On My Host The World" (except for some changes in words and phrases, the complete text of Chapter 8: "Epilogue on My Host, The World") appeared in the issue of January 1949. Santayana gave Cory the holograph and typescript while Cory was in Rome in the autumn of 1947. Cory took the manuscript and typescript with him back to London, where he and his wife were then living. On February 26, 1952, Cory wrote Wheelock that he was sending the manuscript (the typescript) for "safekeeping."[34] Wheelock, in a letter to Santayana of February 29, 1952, expressed his pleasure at the prospect of receiving the manuscript of the third part of Santayana's memoirs. On April 8, 1952, Wheelock wrote Cory acknowledging the arrival of the typescript; and on April 11 Wheelock wrote to Santayana asking permission to read the typescript before sealing it away.[35] Santayana willingly granted this permission in a letter to Wheelock of April 17, 1952. Wheelock then read through the text before sealing away the typescript for publication after the author's death. Santayana was quite definite about his unwillingness to publish the third part of *Persons and Places* during his lifetime.

The author himself supplied a subtitle to the third and final part of his autobiography: "In the Old World" appears on the holograph. But on February 26, 1952, Cory wrote Wheelock saying that Santayana had changed his mind and wished

---

[31] Santayana to Cory, 21 May 1948, Rare Book and Manuscript Library, Columbia University.
[32] Santayana to Kyllmann, 9 June 1945, Temple University Libraries.
[33] Santayana to Cory, 4 November 1944, Rare Book and Manuscript Library, Colombia University.
[34] Cory to Wheelock, 26 February 1952, Archives of Charles Scribner's Sons, Princeton University Library.
[35] Wheelock to Cory, 8 April 1952, Archives of Charles Scribner's Sons, Princeton University Library; Wheelock to Santayana, 11 April 1952, Archives of Charles Scribner's Sons, Princeton University Library.

the third volume to be subtitled "Seeking Places for a Chosen Life". Wheelock, however, did not like this title and wrote Cory asking his agreement to "My Host the World" as a title for the third volume, to which Cory assented. Wheelock agreed to preserve Santayana's British spelling forms for the third volume but expressed his intention to "standardize" punctuation. Thus, though the spelling of the Scribner's edition of the third part of Santayana's autobiography is mainly British, the punctuation is American. Cory also wrote to Wheelock that although Santayana had given a subtitle to the third part of his autobiography, his intention clearly was that all subtitles for the individual books or volumes be dropped whenever the work was published as a unit.[36] Then the book should be entitled simply *Persons and Places*[:] *Fragments of Autobiography.*

Scribner's edition of the third part of the autobiography was published in New York in 1953, the year following Santayana's death in Rome on September 26, 1952. Entitled *My Host The World*[:] *VOL. III • Persons and Places*, it includes a single illustration: a pencil drawing of Santayana in old age done from life by Lino S. Lipinsky in 1950. The English edition appeared in the same year (1953) in London, published by The Cresset Press, Ltd., and is entitled simply *My Host The World*, with no subtitle and no illustrations. The English edition was set up separately from copy supplied by Scribner's. It varies mainly from the American edition in its British punctuation and, as in the case of the second part, in softening and bowdlerizing descriptions of persons and events. The British publishers remained more fearful than their American counterpart of causing offense and incurring libel suits.

III. Establishment of the Critical Text for *Persons and Places*

A. Authority of the Texts

1. Choice of Copy-Text

Based on Greg's theory of copy-text (discussed above in Section I), the fair-copy manuscript for all three parts of the autobiography serves as copy-text for *Persons and Places*. Theoretical alternatives to this choice were the typescripts, which are missing, and the first edition of each part of the autobiography. However, if the copy-text is to be the most authoritative source of accidentals, as Greg's theory proposes, there is no question but that the holograph of the autobiography is that source. Even if the missing typescripts were available, they might well contain alterations in accidentals that Santayana overlooked (and indeed, the extant typescripts of essays not included in the published autobiography do reveal such variants in accidentals from their corresponding handwritten manuscripts). Furthermore the

---

[36] Cory to Wheelock, 13 October 1952, Archives of Charles Scribner's Sons, Princeton University Library.

standard house-styling of Scribner's (about which Santayana complained) makes their edition of the autobiography suspect regarding Santayana's use of accidentals. Hence, the clear choice for copy-text was the handwritten manuscript.

When the editing of the present Critical Edition began, the manuscript for the second part of the autobiography was missing, and locating it constituted something of an editorial adventure. The holographs of the first and third parts were given by Santayana as gifts to Daniel Cory, who later sold them to the Rare Book and Manuscript Library of Columbia University. The whereabouts of the holograph of the second part of the autobiography was a total mystery until recently when the correspondence between Santayana and John Hall Wheelock for the years 1946 through 1952 was deposited by the firm of Charles Scribner's Sons in the Scribner's Archives in Princeton University Library. In a letter from Santayana to George Sturgis of December 4, 1944,[37] Santayana describes a member of the American occupation army in Rome, Sergeant Freidenberg, who had called upon him in the Blue Sisters' nursing home on the Via Santo Stefano Rotondo, where Santayana spent the last eleven years of his life. Sergeant Freidenberg had been very kind to him, bringing him little presents of food, and had been invaluable in assisting in the transportation of the typescript of the second part of *Persons and Places* to New York. Santayana observes in this letter that Sergeant Freidenberg, a mature and evidently well-to-do man, had offered to purchase one of his manuscripts. Also among the recently deposited letters at Princeton is a letter from Mr. Harry A. Freidenberg to Wheelock, dated November 16, 1952, in which he writes that he has the "original copy" of *The Middle Span*. Though virtually inconceivable for Santayana to *sell* one of his manuscripts, it was characteristic of him to give one away, or that is generally what he did with his manuscripts after publication. To whom would he be more likely to give the manuscript of the second part of his autobiography than to the man who had made possible its publication by arranging for its transportation to New York? With the assistance of the Department of the Army in Washington, D.C., the editors of the Critical Edition were able in 1982 to contact Mr. Freidenberg at his home in Los Angeles. The holograph manuscript of the second part, the whereabouts of which had been for forty years a mystery, had indeed been given to him by Santayana as a present. Freidenberg had it bound in half and kept it by him all those years.

After giving the manuscript to Freidenberg, Santayana later wrote to him: "I should like a good illustrated and unexpurgated edition of the whole three parts to be issued . . . and as you have the MS of part Second in full, Scribner's might then be much obliged to you if you could let them (or Cory) see it."[38] Mr. Freidenberg kindly lent the holograph to the General Editor to use in preparing the present Critical Edition. This holograph was then used in preparing the transcription of part two and for collating that transcription against the holograph. It was also photocopied for later reference. Through the generosity of Dr. Corliss Lamont, the Rare Book and Manuscript Library of Columbia University was able to obtain the Freidenberg

[37] Santayana to Sturgis, 4 December 1944, Collection of Robert S. Sturgis.
[38] Quoted in letter from Freidenberg to Wheelock, 16 October 1952, Archives of Charles Scribner's Sons, Princeton University Library.

manuscript. It is housed at Columbia together with the holographs of the first and third parts of Santayana's autobiography.

With the holograph manuscript serving as copy-text for all three parts of the Critical Edition, the editors were able to restore significant passages that had been omitted from all prior publications. These include sections on Spinoza, John Stanley Russell, Lionel Johnson, and members of Santayana's American family, as well as 644 marginal headings. All this material is part of Santayana's holograph and was omitted from the American and English editions for a variety of reasons, including: Santayana's wish that portions be published only after his death, publishers' sensitivity about potential lawsuits, printing and production convenience, and a general desire to "soften" some of Santayana's remarks. Restoring these passages provides the first version of Santayana's autobiography that embodies his full and final intentions regarding this work.

2. Typescripts and Published Editions

The authority of the typescripts and of all published editions is problematic. Presumably, the first edition would be closer to the missing typescript and would incorporate the revisions that Santayana had made on the typescript. However, a study of Santayana's correspondence (most of which is as yet unpublished) dealing with the publication of *Persons and Places*, revealed that sections of the handwritten manuscript were omitted by Santayana from the typescript (sections which, for the time at least, he did not wish printed), and collations of the handwritten manuscript against the American (Scribner's) and English (Constable, Cresset) editions revealed numerous instances where editors of the Scribner's edition (including Daniel Cory) had revised or "improved" Santayana's writing both in substantives and in accidentals. In Santayana's unpublished letter to Cory of March 14, 1945, he gently chides: "I see by your letter of Jan. 29th, that you have been officially debasing my pure and legitimate English to conform with the vernacular . . ." and goes on to decry the general habit of substituting "on" for "in", insisting that one goes down to the sea "in" ships, lives "in" an island, and walks "in" a street.[39] We know from unpublished correspondence between Cory and Wheelock that Cory had been licensed by Scribner's to make deletions and revisions in the typescript.[40] And, indeed, Santayana had asked Wheelock to let Cory see the galleys of the second part of the autobiography and perhaps "soften" passages.

The English edition (parts one and two by Constable and part three by the Cresset Press) was even less trustworthy. Not only had it been set from copy sent by Scribner's, but—particularly in the second book, arbitrarily entitled "*The Middle Span*" without either Santayana's knowledge or consent—numerous revisions and deletions had been made by the British publishers out of fear that the original wording might invite libel actions from persons or their heirs described and discussed in the book.

Santayana had no opportunity to read proof for any of the three published volumes of *Persons and Places* in either the American or English editions. The Second

---

[39] Santayana to Cory, 14 March 1945, Rare Book and Manuscript Library, Columbia University
[40] Wheelock to Cory, 23 November 1942, and 7 April 1943, Archives of Charles Scribner's Sons, Princeton University Library.

World War prevented Santayana, who was living in Rome, from receiving proofs of either the first or second volumes of the Scribner's edition (published in 1944 and 1945 respectively). The third volume, entitled "My Host the World", was not published until 1953, the year following his death. There was only one edition each of the American and English versions of the text. For the American edition there were three impressions of the first volume and two impressions of the second. The English edition had only one printing for each volume. Except for certain later corrections and substitutions requested by Santayana, the only variants from the handwritten manuscript that could be considered authorial would be those in the missing typescript made from the handwritten manuscript and corrected and revised by Santayana.[41] These authorial revisions would presumably appear in the Scribner's edition. The problem for the editors of the present Critical Edition was to decide—based on evidence and on their knowledge of Santayana's style and habitual usage of substantives and accidentals—which variants from the handwritten manuscript were likely to be by Santayana himself and which variants were not. Variants determined or judged to be authorial were therefore emended into the critical text; those determined or judged to be nonauthorial were rejected.

B. Historical Collation

In order to determine the variants both in substantives and in accidentals between the handwritten manuscript of *Persons and Places* and the printed forms, all authorized editions and publications of the autobiography have had at least two independent collations. Transcriptions of the holograph manuscript were first proofread against Xerox copies of the holographs. Then the corrected transcriptions were sight collated by the editors against the original manuscript.[42] Sight collations were done comparing the transcript of the holograph against the Scribner's first edition and also comparing the American against the English first edition. At least two independent sight collations were always completed, one by a team of readers including the General Editor, and the other by the Textual Editor alone. This balance of team and individual sight collations was approved by the Chairman of the Committee on Scholarly Editions.[43]

---

[41] An interesting example of a revision made unwillingly by Santayana for the second volume of the English edition is the section regarding the relations of the young Earl Russell with the 'Billings Girls" (see *Discussions of Adopted Readings*, 314.15–38).

[42] The term "sight collation" refers to the process of comparing two versions of a text "by eye"; that is, in collating (comparing) a handwritten version against a typewritten version, or comparing two different editions (necessarily involving two different settings of type), the task cannot be done on a collating machine. "Machine collations" can be done only between impressions (printings) of a given edition. In the machine collations done for the present Critical Edition the Lindstrand Comparator was used. The various editorial terms used in this edition, including *edition, impression (printing), issue, state*, etc., are used according to the definitions found in Fredson Bowers, *Principles of Bibliographical Description* (Princeton: Princeton University Press, 1949), 379–426.

[43] David J. Nordloh to William G. Holzberger, 5 February 1980, Collection of William G. Holzberger.

It proved a valuable safeguard against oversights characteristic of collations confined to a single method. Whenever more than two sight collations were made, the additional collations were done by an independent team of readers.

The precise pattern of sight collations is as follows:

1. Typewritten literal transcriptions of the photocopied manuscripts of parts one, two, and three against the original holograph manuscripts (parts one and three at the Rare Book and Manuscript Library, Columbia University, and part two at the University of Tampa).

Two independent sight collations.

2. The checked and corrected literal transcriptions of the holograph manuscripts of parts one, two, and three against the first impression of the American (Scribner's) edition.

Three independent sight collations for parts one and three; two independent sight collations for part two.

3. First impression of the American edition (Scribner's) against the first impression of the English edition (Constable, volumes one and two; Cresset, volume three).

Two independent sight collations.

4. First impression of the American (Scribner's) edition against sections of the autobiography published in *The Atlantic Monthly* ("Time, Place and Parents," 171, no. 3 [March 1943]: 45–54; "Early Memories and Schooling," 171, no. 4 [April 1943]: 49–56; "First Friends and Harvard College," 171, no. 5 [May 1943]: 80–86; "A Change of Heart," 182, no. 6 [December 1948]: 52–56; and "Epilogue On My Host The World," 183, no. 1 [January 1949]: 26–30).

Two independent sight collations.

5. First impression of the American (Scribner's) edition against uncorrected and unrevised Proof (extant for Chapters I through VII of volume one only) of the Scribner's edition.

Two independent sight collations.

6. First impression of the American (Scribner's) edition against selections from the autobiography included in *Atoms of Thought*[:] *An Anthology of Thoughts from George Santayana* (1950).

Two independent sight collations.

Machine collations were used for comparing different copies of the same published volume and for identifying different impressions (printings). Editorial personnel trained on the Lindstrand Comparator made these collations. Publishers records did not indicate the number of impressions for any of the three volumes of either the American or English editions. The first impressions for the three volumes of the Scribner's edition were identifiable by the symbol "A" appearing on the title verso. Constable Publishers lent the General Editor their file copies of the first impressions of their two volumes. There were no external markings indicating different impressions in the third part of the English edition published by Cresset Press. The identifiable first impressions were chosen as the master-copies (the text against which other copies are machine collated). For the third part of the English edition, a master-copy had to be designated arbitrarily, and since this particular text had not been marketed widely or extensively, this procedure proved satisfactory.

Because the exact number of printings for each work was not known, the editors collected published versions of each part of the autobiography from disparate regions in which the volumes had been marketed. These published versions were either purchased by the editors or were borrowed from libraries and publishers. This effort to identify impressions for the six published books (three volumes each in the American and English editions) resulted in a large number of machine collations. The pattern consisted of two independent machine collations comparing each published version against the master-copy. At a minimum, three books were collated against the master-copy of each volume. In some cases, additional single machine collations were made to explore the possibility of identifying a later impression, even though the likelihood of doing so was small. The number of collations made for each volume depended, in part, on the extent to which the book was marketed, i.e., more collations were conducted on volumes that were extensively marketed than on those whose market was small. Since we had no identifiable first impression for part three of the English edition, six copies of the book were machine collated against the designated master-copy. These collations identified: (1) three impressions of Scribner's first volume; (2) two impressions of Scribner's second volume; (3) a single impression of Scribner's third volume; and (4) a single impression of each volume of the Constable/Cresset edition.

The precise pattern of machine collations is as follows:

1. Master-copy of the first volume of the American (Scribner's) edition against seven copies of the first volume of the American edition.

Two independent machine collations of each copy.

2. Master-copy of the second volume of the American (Scribner's) edition against seven copies of the second volume of the American edition.

Two independent machine collations of four copies and three single machine collations of three copies.

3. Master-copy of the third volume of the American (Scribner's) edition against six copies of the third volume of the American edition.

Two independent machine collations of four copies and two single machine collations of two copies.

4. Master-copy of the first volume of the English (Constable) edition against three copies of the first volume of the English (Constable) edition.

Two independent machine collations of each copy.

5. Master-copy of the second volume of the English (Constable) edition against four copies of the second volume of the English (Constable) edition.

Two independent machine collations of each copy.

6. Master-copy of the third volume of the English (Cresset) edition against six copies of the third volume of the English (Cresset) edition.[44]

Two independent machine collations of each copy.

---

[44] The printed copies used for these collations are here recorded. Identification numbers are given for books in the personal collections of the editors of the present edition; library name and call numbers are given for books obtained from libraries. Sight collation for volume I: (1.) Scribner's vol. I (H-100) *vs.* photocopy of Constable vol. I, Constable Public Library. (2.) Scribner's vol. I (S-001) *vs.* Constable vol. 1, Constable Public Library. (3.) Scribner's vol. I (S-001) *vs. Atlantic Monthly*, vol. 171, nos. 3, 4, and 5; vol. 182, no. 6; and vol. 183, no. 1. (4.) Scribner's vol. I (S-001) *vs. Atoms of Thought* (PL-001). Machine collation for vol. I: (5.) Scribner's vol. I (S-001) *vs.* (S-002), (S-003), (S-004), (S-005), (S-006), (S-007), and (S-008); Constable vol. I, Constable Public Library, *vs.* (C-002), (C-003), and (C-004). Sight collations for vol. II: (6.) Scribner's

The formal process of historical collation is further supported by the routine procedures of compiling, checking, and proofreading associated with preparing the material of this edition for publication. All work has been conducted with the utmost care and attention to detail.

Analysis of the variant readings discovered by these collations has resulted in the adoption of 775 emendations in the copy-text; 569 more emendations not taken from the authorized texts have been made by the editors of the present Critical Edition. Of the total number of emendations made in the copy-text, 155 are in substantives and 1189 are in accidentals.

C. Treatment of Substantives

The single greatest problem for the editors in establishing the text of this Critical Edition was created by the disappearance of the typescript for all three parts of the handwritten manuscript. It served as printer's copy for the Scribner's edition and for the excerpts published in *The Atlantic Monthly*. We know from Santayana's letters that the typescript for each part of the autobiography was made in Rome by Evelyn Tindall, and that it was read, corrected, and revised by Santayana before being sent to New York for publication. The typescript, therefore, represented a further revision and refinement of the holograph manuscript. However, this typescript of *Persons and Places* was not complete because sections had been deleted. These deleted sections contained material that Santayana did not want published before his death.

Since the American (Scribner's) edition was based on the revised typescript, one might assume that it incorporated the revisions made by Santayana on the typescript, and thereby the substantive variants of the first edition would have authority over

---

vol. II (S-121) *vs.* photocopy of Constable vol. II, Constable Public Library. (7.) Scribner's vol. II (S-121) *vs. Atoms of Thought* (PL-001). Machine collation for vol. II: (8.) Scribner's (S-121) *vs.* (S-122), University of Wisconsin (B945.S24), University of Central Arkansas (B945.S24 A3), State University College of Brockport, New York (B945.S24 A3 V2), Arizona State University (B945.S24 A3), Felician College Library (B945.S24 A3), Pasadena Public Library (92 Santayana V2). (9.) Constable (C-111) *vs.* (C-112), (C-113), (C-114), and (C-115). Sight collations for vol. III: (10.) Scribner's vol. III, (H-300A) *vs.* photocopy of Cresset (C-301). (11.) Scribner's vol. III, Scribner's Public Library *vs.* Cresset vol. III (C-301). (12.) Scribner's vol. III, Chapter 8, Scribner's Public Library *vs. Atlantic Monthly*, vol. 182, no. 6 (Dec. 1948): 52-56, and vol. 183, no. 1 (Jan. 1949): 26-30. (13.) *Atlantic Monthly*, vol. 182, no. 6 (Dec. 1948): 52-56, and vol. 183, no. 1 (Jan. 1949): 26-30 *vs. Atoms of Thought* (PL-001). Machine collation for vol. III: (14.) Scribner's vol. III, Scribner's Public Library *vs.* University of Wisconsin (B945.S24 A3), State University College of Brockport, New York (B945.S24 A3 V3), Arizona State University (B945.S24 A3), Pomona Public Library (92 S233s), Florida State University (B.Santayana), University of Central Arkansas (B945.S24 A3). (15.) Cresset vol. III (C-301) *vs.* State University of New York at Buffalo (PS2773 A4), Boston State College (B945.S24 A3), Riverside Public Library (923 S233-San), University of South Carolina (B945.S2M8), University of Southern California (191.S233m), Yale University Library (K81 Sa59m9).

The process of collation inevitably involves making judgments about the text of an impression on the basis of inductive reasoning from the copies actually examined. Collation, therefore, cannot guarantee identical readings in all of the copies of a given impression. The existence of states within the impression for which copies are not available to the editors for collation remains a possibility.

the holograph manuscript. However, correspondence between Santayana and Daniel Cory (Santayana's friend and literary secretary), between Santayana and John Hall Wheelock (Scribner's editor), and between Cory and Wheelock makes it clear that Cory, Wheelock, and perhaps other editorial personnel at Scribner's altered words and phrases in the text without Santayana's consent or final approval. To some extent this was done with the author's implicit acquiescence, as suggested in the letter to Wheelock in which Santayana requests that the typescript of his autobiography be given to Cory to read and perhaps "soften" some of the things that Santayana had written.[45] However, as noted above, Santayana objected when Cory and Scribner's editors actually made changes affecting the tone and substance of his writing: he resented their "softenings" and "improvements". We also know from his letters that it was with a sense of resignation rather than approbation that Santayana accepted the "softenings" and bowdlerizations of his text and that he repeatedly expressed his hope for an "unexpurgated edition". These facts made it impossible simply to accept the Scribner's edition as representative of Santayana's final wishes or intentions regarding the wording of his autobiography. As far as the English (Constable/Cresset) edition is concerned, we know from the correspondence between Santayana and his British publishers that he was required to submit to many changes in the text that they considered necessary to avoid suits for libel. Some of these changes Santayana made himself, one of which (as noted above) he actually came to prefer over the original;[46] others were simply made by the English publishers at their own discretion.

These manipulations of the text without Santayana's knowledge or consent, made it impossible to rely upon the published editions as fully accurate representations of Santayana's intentions for his published work. No doubt some of the substantive variants in the published texts do indeed represent Santayana's own revisions of his manuscript, but in the absence of the revised typescripts there is no way of knowing with perfect accuracy whether a particular variant from the holograph manuscript is by Santayana or by someone else. The present editors, therefore, have had to weigh each variant and decide to the best of their knowledge whether to accept or reject the change. In accordance with the Greg theory, we have acted conservatively, following the handwritten manuscript unless convinced by clear evidence or the great likelihood that a variant reading represented Santayana's own revision. Therefore, although we have been as careful and consistent as possible in applying the Greg theory to the establishment of the text of this Critical Edition of *Persons and Places* and believe that we have, consequently, established a text as close as possible to the one that Santayana desired, we recognize that there is no way in which any editors or editorial theory can insure a perfectly reliable product. Modern scholarly editing is a careful and accurate but not perfect science.

The present Critical Edition is a dramatic example of the application of the principles of the Greg theory. It conforms to no single version of the text of the autobiography, but rather, starting with Santayana's handwritten fair-copy manuscript as a basis, it incorporates all those variants in both substantives and accidentals

---

[45] Santayana to Wheelock, 21 January 1945, Archives of Charles Scribner's Sons, Princeton University Library (regarding part two of the autobiography).

[46] Regarding Russell and the "Billings Girls" (see footnote 41).

found in the printed versions that could be determined as likely to be by Santayana himself and is an eclectic text based on the authoritative versions of *Persons and Places*. It also includes all corrections and revisions requested by Santayana in his letters and noted by him in his copies of volumes one and two of the American edition.

Decisions to emend the copy-text are based on different arguments, depending on the nature of the variant. We have seen that the published forms of Santayana's autobiography can have no independent authority apart from the possibility of including revisions that Santayana made on the typescript, or requested in a letter or other document that would represent a further development of his intentions beyond the holograph. When a reading, therefore, is adopted from any source other than the copy-text, it is justified only by the certainty or great likelihood that it represents a revision by Santayana. Such emendations of the copy-text are made when the variant reading in a published version of the text is clearly an expression (a word or phrase) that, based upon the editors' long familiarity with Santayana's works and style, may be deemed authorial. Similarly, in those instances where the present editors supply a reading not found in any of the other sources, they do so only on their judgment that it reflects Santayana's intention. In no case is such emendation based upon the preference or notions of the editors as to what is better or worse form, but rather exclusively upon their judgment of what was intended by the author. Where judgment on these grounds is indeterminable, the copy-text reading has been preserved.

The editors of the Critical Edition have emended the copy-text in substantives in the following circumstances:

1. To correct obvious slips of the pen by Santayana; and to correct obvious errors of misquotation of titles or contents of books, novels, plays, or other works. The *List of Emendations* reveals correction of the following slips of the pen: "outlasted" for "outlusted"; "haunted souls" for "hunted souls"; "an" for "on"; and "is" for "in" (in Chapter V, 89.7; Chapter XII, 176.26–27; Chapter XVIII, 273.8; and Chapter XXVI, 434.4, respectively). Misquotation is not uncommon in Santayana's autobiography because, having relatively few books at hand in the Blue Sisters' nursing home, he generally quoted from memory, and though his memory was very good, it was not perfect. Furthermore, he often requested that his quotations be corrected since he did not have the quoted source at hand. Misquotations corrected by emendation include: "*Un Servilón y un Liberalito*" (the title of a novel by "Fernán Caballero") for Santayana's "*El Servilón y el Liberalito*"; "*Fiction and Truth* or *Poetry and Truth*" (English translation of Goethe's *Dichtung und Wahrheit*) for Santayana's "*Truth and Fiction* or *Truth and Poetry*" (Chapter IX, 142.23, and Chapter X, 146.6, respectively); and the French word "Faibles" for "Vains" in his quotation from Racine's *Phèdre* (Chapter XXVIII, 473.40).

2. To reflect authorial revisions evidently made by Santayana on the typescript of his holograph manuscript. Examples include "exotic" for the less precise "foreign" and two footnotes not found in the holograph: "*I . . . circumcised." and "*Cf. Saint Bernard . . . Par. xxxii, 109–111." (Chapter V, 84.39, and Chapter XI, 165.38 and 166.34, respectively).

3. To make corrections and revisions based on external evidence, particularly Santayana's correspondence with his publishers and Daniel Cory. An example of a

substantive emendation based on external evidence is Santayana's revision of his comment about the Chicago Fire of 1871 when he learned that it had preceded the Boston Fire by a year: "Chicago had had an even bigger fire" was substituted for "Chicago soon had a fire that beat it" (Chapter IV, 71.3–4); this revision is requested by Santayana in an unpublished letter to Wheelock, dated March 17, 1945. Another example of emendation based on external evidence is the revision of the title of Chapter XXV, originally entitled "Metanoia". It was revised by Santayana to the English equivalent "A Change of Heart" when Daniel Cory suggested that the Greek word sounded pedantic (reflected in Santayana's unpublished letter to Cory of August 27, 1948). These are the only conditions under which substantive emendations have been made in the copy-text.

D. Treatment of Accidentals

Thanks to the fortunate survival of all three parts of the holograph manuscript, we have been able to preserve Santayana's characteristic spelling and punctuation. The published versions of the text are often confused and confusing regarding these accidentals. Santayana generally preferred British forms of spelling and placement of punctuation. When he was learning to read and write English during the 1870's, these British forms were often the standard American forms. But even then, usage was moving toward what we think of today as typically American. However, Santayana was never perfectly consistent in his usage, particularly regarding punctuation.

The various printed versions of the text of *Persons and Places* make a remarkable hodge-podge in terms of spelling and punctuation. The first volume of the American (Scribner's) edition changes Santayana's British spellings on the holograph to American forms: "civilise" becomes "civilize" and "savour" becomes "savor"; and the placement of punctuation is standardized to American forms. Because Santayana was dissatisfied with the Americanization of his spellings and punctuation (after all, he was *not* American either by birth or naturalization, but kept his Spanish passport current to the end of his life), John Hall Wheelock agreed to retain Santayana's British spellings for volumes two and three of the American edition.[47] However, the American punctuation was retained in these later volumes. The English edition generally preserves most of Santayana's British spellings, but it is inconsistent in this regard. For instance, in volume two, we have an ironic situation: the American (Scribner's) edition adopts the British spellings, and the English (Constable) edition has mainly American spellings. The two other published forms of the text of *Persons and Places*, the excerpts in *The Atlantic Monthly* and in *Atoms of Thought*[:] *An Anthology of Thoughts from George Santayana*, Selected and Edited by Ira D. Cardiff (New York: Philosophical Library, 1950), regularly standardize Santayana's spelling and punctuation to American forms. Thus, the present Critical Edition is the first publication of Santayana's autobiography that not only presents the complete text, but also preserves Santayana's characteristic spellings and punctuation.

[47] Wheelock to Santayana, 5 March 1945, Archives of Charles Scribner's Sons, Princeton University Library.

We have observed that although Santayana preferred British spelling and placement of punctuation, he was not perfectly consistent in his usage. The editors of the Critical Edition, therefore, decided to regularize certain instances of spelling and punctuation according to Santayana's usual practice. Santayana almost invariably uses British "-our" spellings in his holograph manuscripts: "colour", "flavour", "savour", etc.[48] The "-ise"/"-ize" spellings create a problem for Santayana editors that is resolved by normalization, because the medial "s" and "z" in Santayana's hand are, apart from a few exceptional instances, utterly indistinguishable. For all words, therefore, in either nineteenth or twentieth-century spelling, that can be spelled with either "s" or "z" we have adopted the more traditionally British "s" spelling which Santayana favored.[49]

Santayana's customary old-fashioned forms such as "sempstress" have been pre-served in the Critical Edition text, but normalization of spelling occurs in the following instances: titles of books, long works of literature (such as novels, plays, or lengthy poems), and names of newspapers and ships are italicized, according to conventional publishing practice; superscripts are reduced to the line; digraph spellings are changed to spellings with two letters, according to modern typographical usage; ampersands are changed to "and" (except where the ampersand is preserved for special effect, as in the case of "Bangs & Barlow", Santayana's inseparable young Harvard friends whose names together, always iterated in the same sequence, suggested a Dickensian law firm); and numbers in digits on the holograph are generally spelled out in the Critical Edition text.

A regularization based on Santayana's normal pattern of usage concerns the initial capital and lowercase letters in the titles of relatives. For example, as is customary in English, he usually, but not always, capitalizes "Aunt" or "Uncle" when referring to his American Sturgis relations (or more precisely those of his half brother and two half sisters, whose father, Santayana's mother's first husband, was George Sturgis "of Manila"). The opposite is true when Santayana refers on the holograph of his autobiography to his Spanish relations: here the title is usually in lower-case, as is customary in Spanish (*tía* or *tío*), but again he is not perfectly consistent although his pattern is clear. We have, therefore, normalized the forms to initial capitals for American relations and to lower-case for Spanish relatives, thus providing a consistency which we believe Santayana would not only approve, but which, except for occasional lapses, he evidently intended.

Santayana's punctuation, always a problem for his editors, has likewise required certain normalization and regularization in the Critical Edition text of the auto-biography. Two major punctuation problems requiring regularization are the use of quotation marks with on-line punctuation, and distinguishing between Santayana's handwritten colon and semicolon. Santayana generally preferred the traditional British system of placing on-line punctuation before or after the quotation marks

---

[48] A few exceptions may be found in handwritten drafts of some of his early poems, written during the 1880's.

[49] This spelling is present in the Triton Edition of Santayana's works—a limited, collector's edition published by Scribner's in fifteen volumes between 1936–1940. The Triton Edition does not, of course, include the autobiography, but it effectively demonstrates the significance that Santayana attached to his British spelling.

depending on whether the punctuation is a part of the quoted material, but he is not perfectly consistent in his practice. Frequently, the on-line punctuation mark falls directly beneath the quotation mark and its exact placement inside or outside the quotation mark is not clear. Because Santayana's general preference and practice in punctuation, as in spelling, is for British forms, we have followed Bowers in his recommendations for dealing with the problem by normalizing according to the following principles: both modern British and American practice, in every instance, place colons and semicolons outside the quotation marks; British practice places commas, periods, question marks, and exclamation marks "inside or outside quotation marks . . . according as they form part of the actual quoted matter or else as they belong, instead, with the syntactical pointing of the sentence."[50]

Deciding whether to read a colon or semicolon in Santayana's holograph manuscripts is itself a problem. Not only are the two marks frequently indistinguishable in his hand, but he sometimes used the colon in unconventional ways, and he also used it rather more frequently than most authors.[51] It might be assumed that since Daniel Cory read and edited the typescript printer's copy of the autobiography that the Scribner's edition could be taken as authoritative in the matter of Santayana's colons and semicolons, but this is not the case. Not only did Cory himself have difficulty with Santayana's colons and semicolons,[52] but Scribner's imposed house styling on Santayana's punctuation in all three volumes of their edition. The editors of the Critical Edition, in determining how to read these marks on the holograph of *Persons and Places*, decided on the following policy: when both parts of the mark are above the line it is read as a colon, unless an instance clearly calling for the semicolon; similarly, when the lower part of the mark falls below the line, it is read as a semicolon, unless clearly a place where Santayana characteristically (and sometimes unconventionally) uses the colon. This is the chosen procedure for dealing with an otherwise insoluble problem, and consequently, the Critical Edition differs from the Scribner's edition—and therefore also from the Constable/Cresset edition—in many places regarding Santayana's use of the colon or semicolon.

Another instance of regularization of Santayana's punctuation is in the period following each marginal heading in the holograph manuscript of his autobiography. Although Santayana usually supplies a period at the end of a marginal heading, he does not always do so. The marginal headings in the Critical Edition (they occur in no other published version of the text) are all concluded by a period; for some of these the period has been supplied by the present editors.[53] Conversely, the occasional period included by Santayana at the end of a chapter heading has been deleted by the present editors.

---

[50] Fredson Bowers, "Transcription of Manuscripts: The Record of Variants," *Studies in Bibliography*, 29 (1976): 212–64.

[51] Santayana once told Daniel Cory that his frequent use of the colon derived from his habit of "thinking in opposition." (Cory to William G. Holzberger, 14 March 1972, Collection of William G. Holzberger.)

[52] Cory to William G. Holzberger, cited in footnote 51.

[53] This practice is supported by the extant typescripts of "Elvira", "Farewell to England", and "We Were Not Virtuous", which contain seventeen marginal headings concluded by a period and one without a period.

The editors have also regularized the placement of Santayana's marginal headings. Santayana normally inserts one marginal heading three lines down from the beginning of a paragraph, but he is not perfectly consistent in this and there are eight paragraphs that have two marginal headings. Santayana's only stated preference regarding his marginal headings is that they not be like those found in the Triton Edition: centered on the page as if section headings for chapters. Using computer files for typesetting limited the positioning of marginal headings that are set within the text. The MIT Penta Front-End System cannot vary the placement of the marginal headings, nor can it place them anywhere but at the beginning of the paragraph. Therefore, in the Critical Edition, each begins at the first line of the paragraph beside which Santayana wrote it. In the case of paragraphs having two marginal headings, the first is separated from the second by a bullet [•].

In addition to the normalization and regularization described above, the editors of the Critical Edition have made certain emendations in accidentals into the present text that are also duly recorded in the *List of Emendations*. Emendations in spelling are to correct errors that are either slips of the pen in inscribing the manuscript or words that Santayana habitually misspelled. Examples of the latter are "parliament" and "profited" which were habitually misspelled by Santayana as "parliament" and "profitted". His spelling of "Pre-Raphaelite" and "Pre-Raphaelitism" as "preraphaelite" and "preraphaelitism" is corrected by emendation to the standard English form, and the various spellings on the holograph of the name of the great Italian artist, Michelangelo (including "Michael Angelo", and "Michaelangelo") are also emended to "Michaelangelo", Santayana's predominate usage.

A group of words requiring correction in spelling by emendation are those Spanish words on the holograph manuscript that require accent marks. Spanish custom is generally to dispense with accent marks when writing by hand; thus, the handwritten manuscript of *Persons and Places* (like Santayana's handwritten correspondence in Spanish) is generally devoid of the diacritical marks which, as a matter of course, are usually supplied in printed forms. The editors of the Critical Edition, therefore, have supplied the necessary diacritical marks in the present text of the autobiography. Examples are the acute accent in the Spanish words *tía* and *tío* which Santayana almost never accented when he wrote them. As a Spaniard, however, Santayana, who, though modest about the matter, knew his native language well, would have expected these accents to appear in published versions of his writing, as they generally do not appear in the Scribner's and Constable/Cresset editions of his autobiography.

Emendations in punctuation have also been made to provide for inadvertent authorial omissions, such as a period at the end of a sentence or a possessive apostrophe. They supply punctuation or correct to proper punctuation where Santayana has made revisions on the holograph but where he has overlooked necessary deletion, insertion, or change in the original punctuation.

E. *Addendum* to Part I of the Critical Edition of *Persons and Places*

The location of the unpublished essay, "We Were Not Virtuous" (described above in Section II), between Chapters XII and XIII of the holograph manuscript presented a problem for its placement in the Critical Edition. Evidently, Santayana composed the essay as a chapter of the autobiography, but then omitted it from the original publication of *Persons and Places* because of its unattractive portrayal of his half-brother, Robert Sturgis, whose children and grandchildren Santayana did not wish to offend. The piece is of finished quality, having gone through three separate stages of development, but it was not made a cohesive part of any existing chapter in the holograph, nor did Santayana give it a separate chapter number. That Santayana included this essay in part one of the holograph when he gave it to Daniel Cory indicates his intention that it eventually be published. There is, however, no authorial basis for incorporating the material into an existing chapter or for creating an additional chapter number for it. The compromise adopted by the editors has been to include the essay as an *Addendum* to part one of the Critical Edition (the part with which it has the greatest affinity in chronology and content). This placement assures its inclusion in future editions of the autobiography based on the Critical Edition.

IV. Editorial Appendix

Textual information constituting the evidence upon which the text of the Critical Edition is based is presented in four lists following this *Textual Commentary*. The first three of these lists concern editorial decisions; the fourth is a historical record. A fifth list (*Notes to the Text*) provides information of general interest but is not part of the evidence for the Critical Edition text.

Discussions of Adopted Readings: editorial decisions to emend or not to emend, requiring, in the opinion of the editors of the Critical Edition, more information than that reported in the *List of Emendations*, are commented on in these *Discussions*. The reading of the Critical Edition is given first, to the left of the lemma bracket ( ]).

List of Emendations: contains all emendations (changes), both in substantives and in accidentals, made in the copy-text (Santayana's holograph manuscript) for the present Critical Edition. The Critical Edition reading is given to the left of the lemma bracket, the rejected copy-text reading to the right. The symbols following the emended readings indicate the source of the emendations. Readings followed by the symbol CE have been supplied by the present editors.

Report of Line-End Hyphenation: since some possible compound words (not customarily hyphenated) are hyphenated at the ends of lines in the copy-text (holograph manuscript), the intended forms of these words (i.e., with or without hyphen) must be determined by editorial decision. When a word hyphenated at line-end appears elsewhere in the copy-text in only one form, that form is followed; however, when the spelling of the word is not consistent (and the inconsistency is acceptable as a form of the word), the form appearing more frequently in the copy-text is adopted for the Critical Edition text. If the word does not occur elsewhere in the copy-text, the form of the word is then determined by comparing it to Santayana's preferred form for similar words in the copy-text or, if necessary, in other Santayana manuscripts.

The first list in the *Report of Line-End Hyphenation*, called the *Copy-Text List*, records editorial decisions by noting the Critical Edition forms of possible compounds which are hyphenated at the ends of lines in the copy-text. This list shows the editorially established form of each of these words, with or without hyphens, when appearing within the line. The *Copy-Text List* records information necessary to the reader in evaluating editorial decisions or in reconstructing the copy-text. The second list, called the *Critical-Text List*, records the copy-text forms of possible compounds which are hyphenated at the ends of lines in the Critical Edition text. The second list is for the purpose of recording only those line-end hyphens that are to be retained in quoting from or otherwise transcribing the Critical Edition text. The *Critical-Text List* does not, of course, involve editorial decisions, but rather provides information necessary for reproducing or quoting from the Critical Edition text.

List of Substantive Variants: variant substantive readings in all versions of the text of Santayana's autobiography published during his lifetime are recorded in this list, constituting a historical record. (These variant readings are discovered in the process of collation, that is, comparing the various texts. Therefore, this section is often referred to as the "Historical Collation.") Readings to the left of the lemma bracket are those of the copy-text. Listed to the right of the lemma bracket are those readings that are at variance with the readings of the copy-text. When a Critical Edition reading differs from the copy-text reading and also from that of any published form of the text, it appears to the left of the copy-text reading, followed by the symbol *CE*, in order to provide a reference to the text. Symbols for publications reported in the *List of Substantive Variants* are the same as those used in the *List of Emendations*.

Symbols employed in the editorial apparatus are explained in the *List of Abbreviations and Editorial Symbols*. The wavy dash or tilde (~) stands for the word or words cited to the left of the lemma bracket in the *List of Emendations* and in the *List of Substantive Variants*. The caret ($_\wedge$) indicates the absence of a punctuation mark. The ellipsis (. . .) indicates material omitted from the citation to the left of the lemma bracket in the *List of Emendations* and the *List of Substantive Variants*. (The ellipsis is used to make the citation of manageable size for presentation in the lists.) The beginning and end of the material cited is keyed to the page and line numbers of the Critical Edition text for ready reference.

Notes to the Text: identify persons, places, books, and quotations referred to in the text. They provide translations of foreign terms and quotations, and generally supply information useful to a fuller understanding of Santayana's autobiography. Organization is by order of appearance of the item in the text. These notes do not pretend to be complete, since information was often unavailable (as, for instance, for many of Santayana's Spanish relations).

In addition to the material published in the *Editorial Appendix*, the editors have assembled a *List of Alterations in the Manuscript* containing all discernible changes made by Santayana on the holograph manuscript of his autobiography. This extensive list is not included in the *Editorial Appendix* to the Critical Edition, but it has been deposited, together with the transcription of the holograph, in the George Santayana Papers, Rare Book and Manuscript Library, Columbia University.

DISCUSSIONS OF ADOPTED READINGS

7.19*fn* No ye] Following page 8 of the first chapter of the holograph manuscript is a leaf bearing the typewritten text of the footnote containing the appointment by President Andrew Jackson, in 1835, of Santayana's grandfather, José Borrás, to the position of American Consul at Barcelona. At the foot of page 8 of the holograph, Santayana wrote: "Copy of appointment as consul here, in a note". At the top left of the typewritten leaf, a note in Santayana's handwriting reads: "Preserve this priceless spelling, please!" His request was observed by the editors of *A* and *E* as well as by those of the present Critical Edition.

17.37 *domus:**] See 17.38–40*fn*.

17.38–40*fn* *Probably a confused memory, mine or my father's, of Juvenal, *Satire XIII . . . domus.*] This footnote does not appear in the holograph manuscript, in the first printing of the Scribner's edition of *Persons and Places*, or in the Constable edition. It does appear in later impressions of the Scribner's edition.

The Scribner's edition of *Persons and Places*[:] *The Background of My Life* was published in New York on January 1, 1944; however, Santayana did not see a copy of the book until mid-June of that year, when one of the war correspondents or photographers who had called upon him at the Blue Sisters' nursing home in Rome, left his copy of the book with Santayana (related by Santayana in an unpublished letter to Cory of June 23, 1944, Rare Book and Manuscript Library, Columbia University). As Santayana read through this copy of the first volume of his autobiography, he made pencil notations in the margins, indicating typographical errors and other changes and additions that he wished to have included in future printings. (This copy of the Scribner's book, now in the library of the University of Waterloo, in Ontario, Canada, has provided the source and authority for several emendations found in the text of the present Critical Edition.)

Santayana's first version of this footnote, inscribed in pencil at the bottom of page 17 of his copy of the Scribner's edition, reads: "*Probably a reminiscence of Juvenal, Satire XIII 159-60: Humani generis mores tibi nosse volenti / sufficit una domus." The rationale of the need for an explanatory footnote appears in an unpublished letter by Santayana to Scribner's editor John Hall Wheelock, dated Rome, November 25, 1944. In the first paragraph of this letter, Santayana writes: "On page 17 is an alleged quotation from Quintilian: I am sure that my father sometimes quoted Quintilian; but I have lately been rereading Latin poets . . . and have come upon a passage in Juvenal that says in verse what I, quoted in prose; and I am afraid my father, or more likely I myself, must have confused the memory of this with the name of Quintilian. It is a matter of no importance, but curious, and might be noticed (in a note) in the future complete edition." (Letter currently in the Princeton University Library.) In an *"Errata"* list included with this letter to Wheelock, Santayana requests the following: "Page 17: Add a note to the Latin quotation as follows: Probably a confused memory, mine or my father's, of Juvenal, *Satire XIII*, 159–60:" [the Latin quotation from Juvenal follows this request and is identical to that pencilled at the foot of page 17 of Santayana's copy of the book, with the single exception that in the "*Errata*" list the word "*Sufficit*" is capitalized].

The version of this footnote addition in the "*Errata*" list accompanying the letter to Wheelock of November 25, 1944, is clearly an elucidation of Santayana's original pencilled version at the foot of page 17 of his Scribner's edition copy and is therefore the form of the footnote included in the present Critical Edition.

19.35 Sonsolès] The grave accent on the "e" is an orthographic symbol commonly used in manuscripts and publications in Spanish from the advent of mechanical printing through the end of the nineteenth century. Since Santayana usually put the accent on "Sonsolés", the use of the grave accent on "Sonsolès" has been regularized by the editors. "Badumès" at 3.10 is another example of Santayana's archaistic orthography, which seems limited to these types of names.

21.20 fifteen] The holograph manuscript reading is retained over the reading "twelve" in all printed forms. Santayana and his father left Spain for America in June 1872. Fifteen years later, in the spring of 1887 (a date which Santayana writes twice in this paragraph, inserting it first into line 9 of the manuscript and then moving it to line 10), Santayana, who was then twenty-three and who had been studying in Germany, made his third return to Spain. On September 2, 1887, he sailed from Malaga to Gibraltar where he met his sister Susana for a few weeks' tour of southern Spain before he would return to Germany. The references here to Gibraltar and to his knowledge of the German language establish the correct date as 1887.

22.8–9 especially a few years later when] The reading of all printed forms is accepted over the *MS1* reading "especially when", as is also the case in 22.12 "my father or my sisters or me" over "my father or me" as probably reflecting Santayana's revision on the typescript made from the holograph manuscript. The visit to Spain here being described occurred in 1887, but Robert Sturgis was not married until April 9, 1890.

22.12 my father or my sisters or me] See 22.8–9.

23.25 requirements] This reading, which appears in both the proof of the Scribner's edition and in the edition itself and also in the Constable edition, is a revision of the holograph manuscript reading "requisites". That the revision is by Santayana is indicated by a pencil note in his hand in the left-hand margin of the original (and later revised and rewritten) page 30 of the holograph manuscript of *MS1*, Chapter III, which reads: "change requisites to requirements". (The original pages 30 and 31 of *MS1*, Chapter III, were not included in the holograph manuscript of *Persons and Places*; rather, they were placed together with the holograph of the previously unpublished chapter entitled "We Were Not Virtuous." Rare Book and Manuscript Library, Columbia University.)

27.39 sacrament] In Santayana's hand the initial lowercase and capital s's are sometimes indistinguishable. Scribner's editors read a capital here, and the capital appears in *P*, *A*, and *E*. The *At* reading is lowercase as is ours. Customary usage has the lowercase letter when referring generally to the sacraments of the Catholic Church, reserving the capital for the Blessed Sacrament (Eucharist) and this is clearly Santayana's usage in 28.8.

28.8 sacrament] See 27.39.

36.24 in] The *MS1* reading "in a tropical island" stands over the "on" in *P*, *A*, and *E*. For Santayana, one was definitely *in* an island, street, or ship, and not *on* them. (An unpublished letter to Daniel Cory [in the Rare Book and Manuscript Library of Columbia University] dated Rome, March 14, 1945, makes this point wittily and unequivocally.)

45.37 certainly the aura] The *MS1* reading is retained over "the enlightened center" in *At*, *P*, *A* (~ centre *E*). The significant omissions and changes made in the published versions of the paragraph immediately preceding the sentence in which this phrase occurs result in the loss of much of the satire of Santayana's treatment here of mid-nineteenth century Boston culture. The substitution in line 37 of "and" in all published versions for "but" in *MS1*, together with the variant phrase in line 37, lose sight of Santayana's satiric, tongue-in-cheek intent. These variants, therefore, appear to result from a "softening" of the typescript text by Cory or by Scribner's editors.

50.28 *daemonic*] The reading of all printed forms is accepted over the reading "*external*" in *MS1* because the substitution seems an unlikely one to be made by anyone but the author. The final sentence of the chapter might be seen as an objection to this emendation, but a *daemonic* force, after all, may be an obscure, irrational, and not readily identifiable one.

51.7 five] The reading of all printed forms is accepted over the *MS1* reading "several" since the refinement is one likely to have been made by Santayana himself when correcting the typescript made from his holograph manuscript.

65.36 was] An interesting characteristic of Santayana's style and usage—generally so traditional—is his preference for the imperfect or simple past tense of the verb "to be" where the subjunctive would ordinarily be called for. The presence of the subjunctive "were" in *P*, *A*, and *E* is evidently a "correction" made either by Cory or Scribner's editors. Another instance of this substitution occurs at 111.17. In both cases we have preserved Santayana's characteristic usage.

69.16 1868] Santayana's mother left him and his father behind in Spain and took her three Sturgis children to America when Santayana was five years old. Thus, she first went to live in Boston in 1868, the date in *MS1*. The reading 1858 in *P*, *A*, and *E* is incorrect.

71.2–4 People wouldn't speak of the London fire any more; they would say the Boston fire. Unluckily for Boston, Chicago had had an even bigger fire] Santayana confused the dates of the three great city fires, mistakenly thinking that the Boston Fire (November 9, 1872) preceded the Great Chicago Fire (October 8, 1871). (The Great Fire of London had occurred on September 2, 1666.) The original *MS1* reading was: "People wouldn't speak of the London fire any more; they would say the Boston fire. Unluckily for Boston, Chicago soon had a fire that beat it". Recognizing the chronological confusion, Scribner's editors revised the passage to: "People wouldn't speak of the Chicago fire any more; they would say the Boston fire. Unluckily for Chicago, Boston had had a more recent fire". In an unpublished letter to Scribner's editor John Hall Wheelock, dated Rome, March 17, 1945 (Archives of Charles Scribner's Sons, Princeton University Library), Santayana, having seen a copy of the Scribner's edition of *Persons and Places* (1944), refers to the error and, expressing his dissatisfaction with the revision of his words on page 72 of the Scribner's volume, requests another revision: "But of course the false memory that the Chicago fire followed the Boston one ought not to have passed uncorrected, because it would have spoilt the fun I was making for those who knew the facts. Still, I am not reconciled to the omission of London, which makes the reference to Wren uncalled for: and I think I see a simple way of putting things right without violating the moral duty of telling the truth. Why not read: *People wouldn't speak of the London fire any more; they would say the Boston fire. Unluckily for Boston, Chicago had had an even bigger fire; etc?*" (This revision supplants—and is slightly different from—the original revision of the passage requested by Santayana in an unpublished letter to Wheelock of November 25, 1944.)

92.6–7 the house in Boylston Place and India Building] The reading of all printed forms ("The houses in Boylston Place and India Building") is clearly inferior to that of *MS1*. At this time, 1887, Santayana's sisters and brother were living with their mother in her house at 26 Millmont Street, Roxbury, Massachusetts. There had been only one house in Boylston Place owned by Santayana's mother, No. 17; that house had been mortgaged in order to purchase the one at 302 Beacon Street. His mother had also been part owner of the India Building in Boston.

97.24MH *Aussichtsthurm*] We have retained Santayana's archaic spelling of this German word (as we have with "Thiergarten" at 257.3). The letter "h" following the "t" (or "T") in these words is characteristic of German spelling until about the beginning of the present century.

97.32fn *Abŭla*] In the footnote explaining the correct pronunciation of the Spanish town of Avila, Santayana cites the Latin origin of the name, using the diacritical mark over the "u" merely as a guide to pronunciation, indicating the shortness of the vowel: ['abələ]. The diacritical mark, not actually part of the spelling, is appropriately omitted when the Latin word recurs at 99.15. (These are the forms of the word in *MS1*, *P*, *A*, and *E*.)

101.18 Alain] The roman type reading of *A* and *E* is selected over the italicization of the name in *MS1* and *P*. The French author's name (pen name of Émile-Auguste Chartier [1868–1951]) occurs again in this chapter in *MS1* at 9.5, but without underlining. In the earlier instance, Santayana, thinking of the name as a foreign term, may have included the underline accidentally, since he usually underlined foreign words or phrases.

106.6–7 church and state] In Santayana's hand, it is sometimes difficult to determine whether, at the beginning of a word, the letter "c" or "s" is capital or lowercase.

His lowercase "c" is often oversized and his lowercase "s" (especially when followed by a tall letter like "t") tends to be tallish and top-looped. (Santayana's usual capital "S" is open and unlooped.) In the present instance, there is no doubt that the intial letter of "church" is lowercase: it is much smaller than the three initial capital "C's" on the same page of the holograph (*MS1*, chapter 6, page 19) in the words "Celedonio", "Chapel", and "Church" (*CE* page 106, lines 1, 19, and 23). The initial letter of "state" is more ambiguous, but it is somewhat smaller and less open than the initial letter in "Sundays" and in "Sonsolès", both of which appear on this page of the holograph ("Sonsolès" apearing twice). The same general institutional usage of the two words occurs at 142.18 (*MS1*, chapter 9, page 11) and at 247.14–15 (from the previously unpublished "We Were Not Virtuous" essay [holograph manuscript page 7D, line 26]), in the former instance the intial "c" of "church" is distinctly lowercase and the intial "s" of "state" somewhat ambiguous, as in the instance under discussion. However, in the example from "We Were Not Virtuous", both the initial "c" of "church" and "s" of "state" are unmistakably lowercase. Based on these characteristics of Santayana's handwriting, and the evidence of initial lowercase letters in the two analogous examples cited, we have followed the holograph reading in spelling "church" and "state" with initial lowercase letters in all three instances. Our reading is in contrast to that of *P*, *A*, and *E* at 106.6–7, all of which use initial capitals ("Church" and "State"), and of *A* and *E* at 142.18. It is highly unlikely that Santayana, after using lowercase letters on the holograph, would afterward capitalize them in all three instances on the missing typescript. It is possible, however, that Evelyn Tindall, in transcribing the holograph, read and typed some of these letters as capitals, and that her capitalization, perhaps overlooked by Santayana, influenced Cory and Wheelock to capitalize both words in all three instances.

110.6 a myriad lovely settings] The reading of *A* and *E* inserting the preposition "of" ("a myriad of lovely settings") is rejected in favor of the reading of the holograph manuscript. *The Oxford English Dictionary*, vol. I, page 810, cites an example of this usage, from W. W. Story's *Fiametta* (189) 1886: "The crickets were trilling a myriad infinitessimal bells in the grasses." Also, the first line of Sonnet XXI (the first poem in Santayana's Second Sonnet Series) is: "Among the myriad voices of the Spring". The appropriateness of this form, and the fact that Santayana uses it in his sonnet, suggests that the more usual "myriad of" found in *A* and *E* was not on the missing typescript but was probably supplied by Cory or Wheelock.

111.17 was] See 65.36.

113.5–6 two charming pulpits] The two hammered-iron pulpits of Avila Cathedral are not identical; therefore the reading "charming twin pulpits" of *P*, *A*, and *E* is rejected in favor of the more precise reading on the holograph manuscript.

119.5–6 as if I had not been there before] The reading "as I had not been there before" in *P*, *A*, and *E* is evidently either a compositorial error or a mistaken "correction" by Cory. Here Santayana is describing the superfluous solicitude of his aunt María Josefa's brother in taking him to visit the University at Granada: "as if I had not been there before, or had no guidebook"—the sarcasm is unmistakable. Moreover, this visit to Granada was in 1893, but Santayana had been in southern Spain before. Early in September 1887, he had met Susana on Gibraltar and together they had made a few weeks' tour of the region. Among the principal cities visited, Granada was likely to have been included.

120.13 Antonia] See 120.15.

120.15 Antonia] The reading "Antoñita" of *A* and *E* suggests that Cory, or perhaps a Scribner's editor, did not realize that it is the diminutive of "Antonia", Santayana's cousin's given name. That "Antonia" appears at these places both in the Scribner's proof as well as in the holograph manuscript suggests that this form of the name also appeared at these places on the missing typescript used as printer's copy and that use of both forms was intended by Santayana.

122.7 like those] The reading "just like" appearing in both the holograph manuscript and the Scribner's proof indicates that this was also the reading of the missing typescript revised by Santayana. However, Santayana clearly intends the red damask coverlet as well as the lace flounces of the sheets (both mentioned earlier) to be similar to or the same as those he had seen on Raphael's mother's bed. Therefore, in order better to realize Santayana's intentions, the manuscript is emended to the wording of *A* and *E*.

138.11 four storeys] The reading "five stories" of *A* and *E* is rejected in favor of the manuscript reading. The American spelling of "stories" indicates that at least part of the revision is not by Santayana, and there is no evidence that Santayana revised "four" to "five". Santayana is most likely using "storey" here in the British sense, in which the first storey is one flight up from street level. Thus, the British "fourth storey" is the American "fifth story". The change in *A* and *E* to "five stories" may well derive from the intention of Cory and Scribner's editors to make Santayana's description of these Boston buildings accurate in the American sense.

138.36 advantages] The reading of *At*, *A*, and *E* is accepted over the "attractions" of the holograph manuscript. The occurrence of "attractive" at 138.38 and of "attraction" at 139.8 suggests a probable authorial revision on the missing typescript in order to avoid this repetition.

142.4 eighth] The holograph manuscript reading "ninth edition of the Encyclopaedia Britannica" is emended to the reading in all three printed versions (*At*, *A*, and *E*). The eighth edition of the *Britannica* was published during the years 1853–1860. Santayana is here describing the presence of the encyclopedia in the sitting-room beside the front door of his mother's house at 302 Beacon Street, the house purchased when she first came to Boston to live, in 1868. The family dwelt in that house until 1881. The ninth edition of the *Britannica*, however, was not published until 1875–1889. Assuming that Santayana is referring to the complete set of volumes, he must be referring to the eighth edition.

142.23 *Un Servilón y un Liberalito*] Santayana mistakenly supplied the definite rather than the indefinite article in two places in the title of this Spanish novel. His incorrect "*El Servilón y el Liberalito*" was perpetuated in *A* and *E*, but it was given correctly in *At*. The English equivalent of the title of this novel by "Fernán Caballero" is *A Loyalist and a Liberal*.

146.6 *Fiction and Truth* or *Poetry and Truth*] The holograph manuscript reads "*Truth and Fiction* or *Truth and Poetry*", but Santayana includes a note to Scribner's editors in the left-hand margin of the manuscript: "Is it Dichtung and Wahrheit or Wahrheit and Dichtung? I have no books!" The title of Goethe's autobiographical essay is *Dichtung und Wahrheit* ("*Poetry and Truth*"). Scribner's editors corrected the order of Santayana's first translated version of the title to "*Fiction and Truth*" but neglected to do so for his second version, keeping the incorrect word order of "*Truth and Poetry*". The error is perpetuated in the Constable edition.

163.4 Carcassonne] Although misspelled "Carcassone" on the holograph manuscript (and also in *A* and *E*), Santayana does correctly spell the name of the ancient town in southern France on his handwritten "*Persons & Places Errata*" list.

166.7 performance.*] See 166.34–38*fn*.

166.34–38*fn* *Cf*. Saint Bernard in Dante: . . . "*Baldezza e leggiadria / quant' esser puote in angelo e in alma, / tutta è in lui; e sì volem che sia . . .*" *Par*. xxxii, 109–111.] The quotation from the *Paradiso* does not appear on the holograph manuscript but must have been inserted by Santayana into the missing typescript. In the "*Errata*" list, Santayana requests deletion of three accent marks incorrectly added by Scribner's editors (*èsser*, *può*, and *volém*) which occur in the published versions. The form of the Italian quotation included in the present Critical Edition differs slightly from that in the Scribner's and Constable editions and evidently from that supplied by Santayana; it is taken from the text of the Mandelbaum edition (*The Divine Comedy of Dante Alighieri*, A Verse Translation with Introduction and Commentary by Allen Mandelbaum [Berkeley, Los Angeles, London: University of California Press, 1982], Vol. 3, 287). Mandelbaum's English rendering of these lines is: . . . "All of the gallantry / and confidence that there can be in angel / or blessed soul are found in him, and we / would have it so. . . ."

169.1 thrift] Santayana misquotes this line of "At the Church Door", substituting the word "thrift" for "love". Since Santayana is here quoting his own work, we have kept the misquotation.

175.17 "Ja" Burden] Although this young friend's name appears in *MS1* as "Jay" (without quotation marks), there is evidence to indicate that the form "Ja" in *A* and *E* reflects a correction or change made by Santayana in the missing typescript. The name "Ja Burden" (without quotation marks) appears in line 75 of an untitled verse fragment first published in *The Complete Poems of George Santayana* (1979), page 542.

176.26 haunted] The change from "hunted" to "haunted" in *A* and *E* avoids the awkwardness of "hunted souls, hunting they know not what."—the reading of *MS1*. Santayana probably intended to write "haunted" souls, but with the word "hunting" in mind, as the soon to be expressed futile activity of these souls, wrote "hunted" by mistake. This may well have been the reasoning of Scribner's editors in making the emendation, or the correction may have been made by Santayana himself on the now missing typescript.

177.22 dreamt] The substitution of "dreamt" (in *A* and *E*) for "thought" in *MS1* seems, because of the more forceful and poetic quality of "dreamt", to be the sort of substitution that Santayana himself would make.

178.24 with warm blood] The reading of *At*, *A*, and *E* is accepted over the "who could pray" of *MS1*. Elsewhere, Santayana criticizes Emerson for "coldbloodedness", and this revision appears to be Santayana's.

189.11MH Ernest] See 189.12.

189.12 Ernest] The reading "Eugene" Thayer of *MS1* and *At* is emended to "Ernest" Thayer in *A* and *E*. The emendation corrects an evident slip by Santayana. Ernest Lawrence Thayer was a member of the Harvard Class of 1885 and appears to be the Thayer associated with the Harvard *Lampoon*.

203.26 love] The reading of *MS1* is preserved. The form "loves" would perhaps be more grammatical, but the occurrence of "love" in *A* and *E* indicates that that was the reading in the now missing typescript from which those editions were set. In correcting the typescript, Santayana had the opportunity to change this reading, but apparently did not do so.

204.3 itself.*] See 204.35–38*fn*.

204.35–38*fn* *Voir ... Hernani] These lines from the Victor Hugo drama, *Hernani* (Act 3, scene 2), were added by Santayana in a footnote written in his copy of *Persons and Places* (Scribner's, 1944), page 213, now in the collection of the library of the University of Waterloo. Quoting from memory, Santayana somewhat misrepresented the passage. Based upon his expressed desire that his misquotations be corrected, we have made the following emendations in accord with the Hugo text: "Notre-Dame" for Santayana's "la Sainte Vierge"; "corridor," for "~."; "châsse" for "chasse"; "chape d'or," for "chappe d'or."; and "Victor Hugo, *Hernani*" for "*Victor Hugo, Ernani*" (here Santayana confused the Italian spelling of Verdi's opera with the silent "h" of the French title of Hugo's play). Hugo's lines may be translated: "To see Our Lady, at the end of the somber corridor, / Gleaming in her silver shrine with her cope of gold, / And then return whence I came."

207.3 turn] Describing the onset of smallpox, Santayana writes on the holograph that his "head began to turn". The word "turn" in Santayana's handwriting could easily be misread as "swim", the word that appears in *A* and *E*, and it is possible that Miss Tindall in transcribing the holograph typed "swim", and that Santayana missed the substitution in reading the typescript or accepted it as unimportant. But it is also possible that the missing typescript, like the holograph, read "turn" and that Scribner's editors changed the word to "swim" because more idiomatic. However, "turn" in this usage is idiomatic in other languages, which in fact may have influenced Santayana's choice of the term. In any case, the word on the holograph is undoubtedly "turn" (it appears twice on this page of the holograph [page 25 of Chapter XIV], first in line 8, and in the reading in question in line 31).

209.9 piety;*] See 209.36–38fn.

209.36–38fn *Cf. Psalm . . . timentibus eum.] These two verses, 9 and 10 from Psalm
33, were added by Santayana in a footnote written in his copy of *Persons and
Places* (Scribner's, 1944), page 219, currently at the University of Waterloo. We
have made a single emendation to correct Santayana's slip of the pen in writing
the fourth word of the ninth verse where he wrote "quan" (an impossible form)
for "quam". The Latin of the Vulgate differs from Santayana's version both in
substantives and accidentals: "Gustate, et videte quoniam suavis est Dominus;
beatus vir qui sperat in eo. / Timete Dominum, omnes sancti ejus, quoniam non
est inopia timentibus eum." (*Biblia sacra juxta Vulgatae exemplaria et correctoria Romana
. . . denuo edidit . . . or navit Aloisius Claudius Fillion, ed. 10* [Paris: Librairie Letouzey
et Ané, 1887], 569.)

Because Santayana's version of the verses is distinctive, we have chosen to
include it in the Critical Edition, rather than correct it according to the Vulgate.
The English translation of these verses in *The Revised Standard Version* of the Bible
(where they are verses 8 and 9 of Psalm 34) is as follows: "O taste and see that
the Lord is good! Happy is the man who takes refuge in him! / O fear the Lord,
you his saints, for those who fear him have no want!"

215.26 squirm and fawn] John Hall Wheelock of Scribner's, in a note to Santayana
of October 4, 1944, objected to this description of "most" modern Jews. Santayana
replied in an unpublished letter to Wheelock, dated November 12, 1944, proposing
the words be changed to "court the world". Santayana's letter, however, indicates
the proposed change to be a concession to Wheelock's wishes. Therefore, the
original *MS1* reading (which appears in both the Scribner's and Constable editions)
stands.

219.35–37 "But my servant Antonio," he had added, "doesn't approve of her. I
asked him if he was shocked. 'Chè,' said Antonio, 'she is too thin.'"] The reading
of *MS1* is preferred to that of *A* and *E* (which do not italicize *Chè*, insert double
quotes following the word "shocked", include double quotes around Antonio's
observations, and substitute an exclamation mark for Santayana's period following
the word "thin"). Santayana's form of the quotation within a quotation is made
consistent with conventional practice simply by emending his double quotes around
"*Chè*" (in *MS1*) to single quotes.

220.13 Verna] See 220.15.

220.15 Verna] The correction of "La Vernia" to "La Verna" is included in the
"*Errata*" list accompanying Santayana's unpublished letter to Wheelock of November 25, 1944.

226.15–16 Counsellor] The reading of *A* and *E* is accepted over the reading "Chancellor" of *MS1*. The Harvard University Archives record that Boylston Adams
Beal was "Honorary Counsellor" to the American Embassy in London, 1916–1928.
(He had also been "Special Assistant" to the American Embassy at Berlin, 1914.)
It is possible that Santayana himself made the correction on the missing typescript,
or perhaps the change was made by Cory or Wheelock. In any case, it is the sort
of correction that Santayana would approve.

226.21-23 I did have it, in an obscure modest way that perhaps ran deeper, if less sparklingly, than official or fashionable society] The reading of *MS1* is preferred to that of *A* and *E* because the sense of the original statement is different from and more accurate than that of *A* and *E* ("I did taste such happiness in obscure modest places where perhaps it ran deeper, if less sparklingly, than in official or fashionable society"). The subject here is the *happiness* that Beal and Santayana experienced among refined and distinguished persons. The *places* where they experienced this happiness were either the same or were at least of equal significance (London, Boston, Rome, Paris, etc.); the emphasis here is on the *way* (i.e., the conditions and scale) in which this happiness was experienced, rather than where it was experienced. The *A* and *E* reading distorts or changes this meaning and is therefore rejected as probably unauthorial. Similarly, the reading of "to him" and "to me" in *A* and *E* are rejected in favor of the manuscript readings "for him" (at 226.18-19) and "mine" (at 226.20). These changes are part of what appears to be an editorial effort to "improve" the style of Santayana's description in this passage.

230.34 reality] The substitution of the term "substance" here in *A* and *E* probably reflects a change introduced into the missing typescript by Cory, who perhaps feared that Santayana appeared to be attributing "reality" to the gods. For Santayana, however, as for Lucretius, matter is the essential reality of which the gods are poetic representations. Hence, the word "reality" here in *MS1* seems neither inaccurate nor misleading and is retained.

231.14 gods] The manuscript reading is retained over the reading "god" in *A* and *E*. "Dionysiac inspiration" derives not from Dionysus alone, but rather from the numerous irrational promptings of nature, represented metaphorically by several deities.

231.28 one] The reading "ones" of *MS1*, *A*, and *E* is emended to the singular. Sonnet III, Santayana states, was his first sonnet, and Sonnets I and II were composed afterwards "to frame in" Sonnet III. (In fact, there is manuscript evidence that three of Santayana's sonnets were composed a year or two earlier than Sonnet III. For discussion see Introduction, footnote 16, page 28 of *The Complete Poems of George Santayana* [1979].)

233.3-4 Spencer in his "principles" was an "objective idealist"] The reading in *A* and *E* is: "Such 'principles' might serve an 'objective idealist' . . . " The manuscript reading, however, directly describing Herbert Spencer as an "objective idealist" is retained in the absence of any evidence of authorial revision, and also because the last sentence of the paragraph serves to explain Santayana's referring to Spencer as an "objective idealist" by asserting that Spencer's doctrine inadvertently subverted his intended naturalism, turning him into an "idealistic metaphysician".

233.26-28 Nature thereby has changed, but not evolved; change is called evolution when sense and language are thereby enabled to distinguish its form better.] The reading in *A* and *E* is: "Nature thereby has changed, but only intelligence has advanced; change is called evolution when sense and language are thereby enabled to distinguish their objects." The style of the revision is smoother, but the meaning may be somewhat changed. The absence of any evidence that the revision is by Santayana himself (rather than by Cory or Scribner's editors), and the risk of distorting Santayana's meaning, argues for retention of the reading in the holograph manuscript.

237.1 "rhythmic"] Santayana corrects the misspelling "rhymic" of the holograph manuscript (perpetuated in *A* and *E*) to "rhythmic" in the margin of page 246 of his copy of *Persons and Places* (Scribner's, 1944), currently at the University of Waterloo.

245.31 Portoricans] We retain the archaic spelling of the holograph manuscript. The modern spelling of "Puerto Rico" was changed officially in 1932 from "Porto Rico".

254.22 Zwinger] Santayana's misspelling "Zwingler" on the holograph manuscript (*MS2*) of the name of the palace in Dresden which houses one of the great art collections of the world, was probably a mere slip of the pen. The misspelling was perpetuated in both *A* and *E* but is corrected in the Critical Edition.

257.3 Thiergarten] See 97.24MH.

288.39 Jenkins] The *A* and *E* reading "Watkins" is evidently a compositorial error. Sir Lawrence Hugh Jenkins (1858–1928) was chief justice of the High Court of Bengal during 1909–1915.

290.8–9 charming in the latest fashion and smiling with an easy grace] The holograph manuscript reading "charming and smiling in the latest fashion with an easy grace" is rejected in favor of the reading of *A* and *E* because probably representative of Santayana's revision on the missing printer's copy typescript. Inversion of the phrases "and smiling" and "in the latest fashion" implies that "fashion" be interpreted as "costume" thus reducing the likelihood of attaching a pejorative connotation to the description of Lady Griselda's manner, which Santayana seems not to intend.

291.5 Jarvis] The name of "the college playground" was "Jarvis" Field, the spelling on the holograph manuscript (not "Jervis", the form in *A* and *E*). In 1874, Jarvis Field was the site of the first intercollegiate rugby game played in the United States. (Harvard University Archives)

302.38 three] Lionel Johnson was at Oxford during the period 1886–1890; therefore, the holograph manuscript reading "three years at Oxford" is retained over the "two years of Oxford" of *A* and *E*.

303.2–3 Heddon's Mouth, Barnstable] In the margin of his copy of the Constable edition of *The Middle Span* (volume II of *Persons and Places*), Santayana corrects the spelling of the word "Hedder's" to "Heddon's" in the date-line of Russell's letter to him. He does not, however, correct "Barnstable" to "Barnstaple", an evident misspelling since the place in England is spelled "Barnstaple", whereas "Barnstable" is in Massachusetts. Russell's letter has not been located; thus, we do not know whether the misspelling is by Russell or by Santayana and have therefore allowed it to stand. (Santayana's copy of the Constable edition of *The Middle Span* is currently at the University of Waterloo.)

304.11 Don Juan] Here Santayana is comparing the young Earl Russell to the title character of Byron's poem rather than to the poem itself. The italicized version of *A* and *E* is therefore rejected in favor of the form on the holograph manuscript.

311.22-24 Pyrennees . . . on route] Although the original of Russell's note has not been located, the form of Santayana's quotations from it suggests that Santayana probably had the note by him when writing this passage. It seems desirable, therefore, to preserve what appear to be Russell's idiosyncrasies of spelling and usage. (By contrast, *A* reads "Pyrenees" [the conventional English spelling] and *E* reads "Pyrennes". [The French spelling is *Pyrénées*.] Both *A* and *E* read "en route".)

314.15-38 Broom . . . was,] This passage was composed by Santayana at the insistence of Otto Kyllmann, Constable's editor, who feared the possibility of libel actions resulting from the original passage describing the second Earl Russell's relations with the "Billings" sisters, "Jennie" and "Emma", who in reality were Nelly and Kate Williams. Santayana considers the matter in an unpublished letter to Kyllmann of October 4, 1947, in which he expresses reluctance to revise the passage. On the following day, he again writes to Kyllmann, enclosing the revised passage, but adding that he hopes that "it may not be necessary to make these changes." On May 21, 1948, however, Santayana wrote to Daniel Cory. He had by then seen a copy of the Constable edition of the second volume of his autobiography and was not only reconciled to the change of passage but actually preferred the revision: " . . . I think the passage on pp. 77-8 [actually pp. 76-77], instead of that about the "Billings Girls" is an improvement in tone and just feeling. I hope you will have this correction retained if there ever is a standard complete edition." This leaves no doubt that Santayana genuinely preferred the substitution and it is therefore included in the present Critical Edition. The original passage, which, with slight variation, appeared in the Scribner's edition, is included in the *List of Substantive Variants*, 314.15-38. (The two unpublished letters to Otto Kyllmann are in the Temple University Libraries and the unpublished letter to Daniel Cory is in the Rare Book and Manuscript Library, Columbia University.)

320.9 private] The reading of the holograph manuscript is preferred to the reading "primitive" of *A* and *E*. In this discussion, "private passions or whims" are contrasted with convention (i.e., public morality); the word "primitive" does not so effectively point up this contrast and is therefore likely to be either a compositor's error or an error on the typescript.

320.27 desperate] The reading of *A* and *E* is adopted over the reading "unhappy" of the holograph manuscript. This intensification is unlikely to be by anyone other than the author himself and probably reflects a revision made by Santayana on the missing typescript.

322.20-324.38 The . . . sufficient] In addition to the holograph manuscript (*MS2*), two typewritten versions of this description of Santayana's cousin Elvira exist. One of these is currently in the Rare Book and Manuscript Library at Columbia University; the other is at the Humanities Research Center at The University of Texas. These two typescripts (done on different machines) are identical; however, the Texas typescript contains some handwritten revisions and may therefore be the later of the two. It is possible that Santayana wrote this sketch of Elvira and had it typed up before composing Chapter XX of *Persons and Places*, because a pencil notation in Santayana's hand at the top of the Texas typescript reads: "Introduce in Avila in 1883-8". The version of this "Elvira" material in the holograph manuscript, which occurs on the second page of Chapter XX, entitled "Changes in Avila", is, however, more accurate in details and more polished in form than either typescript and is evidently the latest version. Also, the *MS2* version is almost identical with the readings of the Scribner's and Constable editions and would therefore have been closest to the unlocated typescript used as printer's copy.

As pre-copy-text forms, the variant readings of these two "Elvira" typescripts do not appear in the *List of Substantive Variants*. However, a very interesting statement occurs in all three manuscript versions of this section of the text (at page 149/4 *bis* of the holograph, lines 18-21 and page 3, lines 6-8 of each typescript), which is cancelled only on the holograph manuscript and does not appear in any published form. It follows the sentence (at 323.9-10) "But we got on very well together." and reads, "She [Elvira] soon perceived that if I was unenterprising, it was not because I was innocent. . . ." Given the context, which is undoubtedly sexual, this cancellation is of considerable biographical interest.

363.39 I hardly ever saw her husband] The reading of *A* and *E* is accepted over the reading of *MS2* ("I never saw her husband") since it is most unlikely that anyone but Santayana would make this change, which probably appeared on the missing typescript made from *MS2*.

377.24 Marquise de l'Enfernat] See 379.4.

377.32 Madame de l'Enfernat] See 379.4.

378.13 Madame de l'Enfernat] See 379.4.

379.4 Madame de l'Enfernat] This Parisian is referred to in *A* and *E* only by the pseudonym of "the Marquise de Blanc-Blanc" and "Madame de Blanc-Blanc"; however, she is identified by name in *MS2*. Whether the decision to conceal the real name of the scheming Marquise was made by Santayana or by Cory and Wheelock is now relatively unimportant and there seems to be no reason for not now using the actual name.

379.27 *distingué*] It seems unlikely that anyone but Santayana, in his description of Bob Potter, would substitute "*distingué*" (the form in *A* and *E*) for "distinguished" in *MS2*. Bob Potter's artistic talent (he was to become an architect) and other virtues, combined with the linguistic accomplishments of his wife-to-be (Lily Fish), probably combined to make Santayana prefer the French term (which perhaps carries more the connotation of general personal refinement than does the English word), and resulted in a revision by Santayana on the missing typescript.

380.28 organic, moral and physical, energies] The positioning of commas on the holograph manuscript indicates that the phrase "moral and physical" modifies "organic energies" and that the terms "moral" and "physical" are not merely parts of a series of three words modifying "energies", as they appear in *A* and *E* where the comma after "physical" is deleted and a comma following "moral" is inserted (giving a somewhat changed reading: "organic, moral, and physical energies").

384.39–385.1 he could see his friend Richmon Fearing every day, whereas otherwise they would never come across each other. This was because Fearing was a swell and Green an outsider.] On the holograph manuscript, this reading contains four red pencil "revisions": "a" is written above "his"; "Richmon Fearing" is deleted; "om" is written above "whereas" (suggesting revision to "whom"); and "the friend" appears very faintly above the repeated surname "Fearing", which is lightly drawn through in red pencil. The reading in *A* and *E* substitutes "a particular friend of his" (for "his friend Richmon Fearing"); "the friend" (for "Fearing" [following the word "because"]); and "leader in the College world" (for "swell").

Given the obviously tentative character of these red pencil revisions on the holograph manuscript and the substitution of the rather verbose and imprecise "leader in the College world" for the more terse and characteristically Santayanan "swell", we have retained the holograph manuscript reading over that of *A* and *E*.

389.9 *Microcosmos*] Santayana's spelling on the holograph manuscript of the title of Lotze's treatise is retained over the original German *Mikrokosmus*. The form of the title in *Persons and Places* is the same used by Santayana in his doctoral dissertation, "Lotze's System of Philosophy" (Harvard, 1889). There was an English translation *Microcosmus: An Essay Concerning Man and His Relation to the World*, by Elizabeth Hamilton and E. E. Constance Jones (New York: Scribner and Welford, 1885) at that time and *"Microcosmos"* represents perhaps Santayana's English translation of the title.

390.19 Hamlet's Ghost] The reading of *A* and *E* is *"Hamlet's"*, the italicization being intended to eliminate the ambiguity of the reading and make clear that the Ghost is that of the play (i.e., that of the murdered King) and not that of the Prince himself. However, the unitalicized possessive of *MS2* is quite appropriate here. The Ghost *is*, in a manner of speaking, "Hamlet's Ghost": it is the Ghost with which he converses; and, in the following sentence, Santayana, identifying himself with the Prince, quotes (imprecisely) Hamlet's words upon encountering the Ghost.

393.20 Scribner] See 393.24.

393.21 Scribner] See 393.24.

393.24 Scribner] Santayana's habit (frequently encountered in his letters) was to refer to his publishers by the name of the founder or head of the firm: "Scribner" or "Constable" or "Dent". Therefore, the holograph reading is retained over the "Scribner's" of *A* and *E*, a change undoubtedly introduced by Scribner's as more consistent with the official name of the firm, Charles Scribner's Sons.

413.17 lectures] Santayana's slip of the pen "lecture's" is corrected to "lecture" in *A* and *E*, doubtless in consequence of his earlier reference to the Rector of the University of Lille, who, when Santayana said he was prepared to give "one or two lectures in English", insisted that he give only one (see page 412.23). It is, however, clear that Santayana had prepared more than one lecture for his tour of the French universities, so the plural "lectures" appears to be what he intended on the holograph and to be correct.

[Contents Page] Epilogue on My Host, the World] The absence of double quotation marks surrounding the words "My Host", on the holograph first page of the final chapter of the autobiography, and the absence of the quotation marks from the contents page of both the Scribner's and Constable editions of *My Host the World*, vol. III of *Persons and Places*, as well as from the first page of the final chapter of these editions, suggests that Santayana probably deleted the quotation marks from the contents page in the missing typescript. We have not, however, felt justified in adopting the form of A and E ("*Epilogue*[:] *My Host the World*"—not italicized in *E*) over that of the copy-text, *MS3*, because of the actual chapter title to *MS3*, 8.

417.2 *A Change of Heart*] The title of this chapter on the holograph manuscript is "*Metanoia*". The English title, which appears in all published versions, results from Santayana's rendering the Greek word into its English equivalent at a hint from Daniel Cory, to whom Santayana writes from Rome, on August 27, 1948: " . . . I myself have felt that 'Metanoia' was a trifle pedantic. It can be readily translated into '*A Change of Heart*'. Wouldn't that be attractive to the general (feminine) reader? '*At the Crossroads*' would be another equivalent, but I think not so good."

427.28 . . . this] See 427.30.

427.29 down-lying;] See 427.30.

427.30 . . . this . . . reclining,] In this quotation from memory of lines 163–166 of Emerson's poem *Threnody* (a lamentation for Emerson's first child, Waldo, who died of scarlet fever in 1842, at the age of five), Santayana slightly misrepresents the lines. His inexact version ("This losing is true dying, / This is lordly man's down-lying, / This his true and sure declining, / Star by star his world resigning.") perpetuated in A and E, was caught and corrected by the editors of *The Atlantic Monthly* (whose version is identified with the established forms of the original, except that *At* retains Santayana's comma following "down-lying", whereas the established form has a semicolon, the form of punctuation included in the present Critical Edition). The Critical Edition editors, observing Santayana's wishes that his misquotations be corrected, follow *At* in substituting an ellipses for the word "For" (the first word of the first line of the quoted verses) and in correcting "true and sure declining" in the third line to "slow but sure reclining".

428.25 founded on] The first line of the thirty-third sonnet of Santayana's Second Sonnet Series is "A perfect love is nourished by despair." His misquotation here is retained because of its interest and significance in this context.

428.38 *l'amour-physique, l'amour de vanité, l'amour-goût*] See 429.11.

428.39 *l'amour-passion*] See 429.11.

429.3 *amour passion*] See 429.11.

429.9 *amour-goût*] See 429.11.

429.11 *amour de vanité*] Santayana's misspellings on the holograph manuscript of
Persons and Places of Stendhal's *"quatre amours différents"* are perpetuated in *A* and
E, where the hyphen is omitted from *"l'amour-goût"* and *"l'amour-physique"* and
the *"de"* from *"l'amour de vanité"*. Santayana also incorrectly refers to Stendhal's
"l'amour-passion" as *"la grande passion"*. The terms are correctly spelled in *At*, whose
editors evidently checked the French original.

432.19 Quad] See 432.24.

432.24 Quad] The view from the East front of Gibbs, or the Fellows' Building of
King's College, is toward the great Chapel on the left and what is usually called
the "Entrance Court", with a stone screen, and beyond to the street called King's
Parade. The English edition corrects Santayana's term to "Court", but we follow
Scribner's in retaining the holograph manuscript reading.

434.5 us] The reading "us" of *A* and *E* suggests the likelihood of Santayana's having
changed the reading to this form on the missing typescript, because the holograph
manuscript reading "it" makes the sentence illogical. ("Halfway down the nave
there is a screen, with an elaborate organ above, separating it from the choir.")
The problem derives from Santayana's conception of the nave of King's College
Chapel as running the full length of the vault, and regarding the choir—located
on the opposite side of the screen—as the "other half" of the nave. Thus, the
word "it" in the holograph reading refers to the nave and illogically represents
it as separated from itself by the screen. (Descriptions of this great Chapel usually
refer to the sections west and east of the oak screen as the "nave" and the "choir",
respectively.) Substituting "us" for "it" allows for Santayana's conception of the
nave as divided by the screen, with the area on the opposite "east" side of the
screen constituting the choir. The rest of the paragraph describes the interior of
the Chapel as viewed from the perspective of the nave or area west of the screen
that divides "us" from the chancel consisting of the choir (occupied by the fellows
of the College and the choristers) and the sanctuary and altar.

435.6 garden] Santayana's view through the west windows of Nathaniel Wedd's
room in Gibbs, the Fellows' Building of King's College, was toward the "Backs",
with the South front of Clare College on the right. This side of Clare faces directly
the great lawn described by Santayana, with only a pathway (and no garden)
between the building and the lawn. Thus, the reading of *E*, "South front", referring
to the side of Clare that Santayana saw from Wedd's windows, is more accurate
than the "garden front" of *MS3* and *A*. However, in the absence of any evidence
that Santayana authorized the reading of *E*, the reading "garden front" is retained.
The third volume of the autobiography was published in 1953, the year following
Santayana's death, and the English edition (by the Cresset Press) was set from
copy sent by Scribner's. The correction to "South front" is evidently an effort by
the Cresset editors to render Santayana's description more accurate.

439.29 the Cloisters] The reading of the holograph manuscript and the Scribner's
edition is retained over the reading "Nevile's Court" in the Cresset Press edition.
The English publisher evidently "corrected" the reading to the more specific term;
however, Nevile's Court of Trinity College is also referred to as "the Cloister
Court", so that Santayana's term on the holograph is natural and not inaccurate.

440.29 "logical realists"] The reading of *MS3* and *A* is retained over the "logical positivists" of *E*. There is no evidence that Santayana authorized such a change in the posthumously published third volume of the English edition of his autobiography. The early philosophical position of Bertrand Russell is appropriately described as "logical realism", a term that Santayana again associates with Russell at 443.33 (and which again, without authorization, is changed in *E* to "logical positivism").

443.33 "logical realism"] See 440.29.

462.9 Arabian Nights] See 462.37.

462.17 Arabian Nights] See 462.37.

462.37 Arabian Nights] We have kept the capitalized but not italicized form of the holograph manuscript (as have both *A* and *E*). In thus referring to the "Arabian Nights", Santayana distinguishes between the tales themselves and the book containing them—*The Thousand and One Nights*—which he refers to on the same page (*MS3*, page 439/35) in the marginal heading, underlining the title of the book.

465.16 to Tiryns] The reading "for Tiryns" in *A* and *E* is unidiomatic and obviously an error. On the holograph manuscript the word "for" has been cancelled and the word "to" inserted, but the change was done in such a way that a misreading was quite possible. The error was probably made by Evelyn Tindall when making the typewritten copy from Santayana's manuscript. The error was evidently missed by Santayana when reading and revising the typescript, which served as printer's copy for the Scribner's edition, which in turn served as printer's copy for the Cresset Press edition.

Santayana's plans to visit Delphi had to be cancelled because in order to reach Delphi a ship was needed to cross the Gulf of Corinth. Instead, he merely travelled by land to nearby Nauplia, Tiryns, Mycenae, and Epidaurus, all of which lie in the Peloponnesus or southern part of Greece, south of the Gulf of Corinth.

478.2 ready in 1900] There seems to be no reason to adopt the reading of "ready after 1898" of *A* and *E*. Russell and "Mollie" returned to England from America in May 1900.

481.13 for fifteen years] The reading of *A* and *E*, "for so many years", is rejected in favor of the reading on the holograph. Russell and "Mollie" were married for fifteen years (1901–1916).

490.17 But no, no one came in] This phrase occurs on the last line of page 494/7 and the first line of page 495/8 in Chapter 5 of the third part of the holograph manuscript (*MS3*). The word "no" is the final word on page 494/7 and is repeated as the first word on page 495/8 of the holograph, with no punctuation in between. It is possible that this merely represents an unintentional repetition of a word used at the end of one page and at the beginning of the next (something that Santayana occasionally does elsewhere on the holograph). However, the reading "no, no one" in *A* and *E* suggests that the repetition was on the missing typescript and that either the comma was automatically inserted by Evelyn Tindall in transcribing the holograph, or it was deliberately inserted by Santayana in reading and revising the typescript. It is also possible that Santayana overlooked an unintentional repetition of "no" on the typescript and that the comma was inserted later. If, however, the punctuation were inserted by Cory or Wheelock, it would more likely be a semicolon, the standard form of punctuation for this construction. While both forms of the reading are possible ("But no, no one came in" or "But no one came in"), the context makes the repetition of the word "no" appropriate, and the appearance of the repetition on the holograph as well as in *A* and *E* makes it likely that this form was on the missing typescript. The intended repetition of the word "no" in this instance is further supported by the fact that Santayana uses the locution "But no" at three other places in *Persons and Places* (pp. 65.39, 237.14, 520.17).

496.36 materially] The holograph reading is retained over "existentially" of *A* and *E*. Santayana's view is that the organizing material substance of animal life (i.e., the psyche) generates consciousness (or spirit) as an epiphenomenon of the psyche's interaction with its physical environment. Thus, while transcending matter, the existence of consciousness is dependent upon matter for its inception, content, and continuation. Retaining the holograph reading preserves Santayana's original intent, though "existentially" could have been an authorial emendation to the missing typescript.

515.19–27 to Russell . . . said] Two typewritten revisions of this section of the holograph manuscript are in the Harry Ransom Humanities Research Center of The University of Texas at Austin. They are evidently early versions of page 14 of the missing typescript which was used as printer's copy. The holograph *MS3* reads: "In regard to Elizabeth, he could have said: 'Allow that you were a fool. You didn't know Elizabeth, and you couldn't conceive how happy she would be with me.' But *she was not happy.* . . ." The earlier of the two typescript revisions reads: "At first, in regard to Elizabeth, on that day when she had come to meet me at the station, Russell could have said: 'Allow that you were a fool. You didn't know Elizabeth, and you couldn't conceive how happy she would be with me.' But soon *she was not happy.* . . ." The text of the second typewritten version of this revised passage is identical with the first; however, on the second typescript the handwritten revision on the first typescript is now typewritten. The considerably fuller version of this passage found in the Scribner's edition represents a still further revision undoubtedly by Santayana and was most likely included in the now missing typescript. (The Constable text is identical here with that of the Scribner's edition, except the Constable editors refined "the station" to "Petersfield station".) The Scribner's reading of this passage has therefore been incorporated into the text of the present Critical Edition as an emendation of the holograph manuscript.

518.4 him; and] Twenty-five words and a semicolon included in the holograph manuscript copy-text are cancelled by emendation. The cancelled material ("I was only recognising the existence of a conflict that I had foreseen to be inevitable. He knew this perfectly in his heart of hearts;") does not appear in the Scribner's or Constable editions and is cancelled by hand in ink on a typewritten revision of this section of the text in the Humanities Research Center of The University of Texas. This typewritten page is designated at the top, in Santayana's hand: "[Farewell to England; p. 18, revised.]". Another typewritten revision of this same section of text, also at Texas, a refinement of the earlier typewritten page, omits the cancelled material altogether. The typewritten pages at Texas represent a later stage of this material than the holograph manuscript copy-text and evidently reflect the reading of the missing typescript which served as printer's copy for the Scribner's edition. The holograph copy-text has therefore been emended in accord with these later revisions reflected in the texts of *A* and *E*.

518.9 asked] The two typewritten revision pages at Texas cited above also represent further revision of this part of the holograph text. Both typewritten revision pages substitute "asked" for the "asking" of the holograph manuscript. The reading of *A* and *E* is also "asked", indicating that this revision was evidently present also in the missing printer's copy typescript.

518.12 there. I] The two typewritten revision pages at Texas cited above (518.4 and 518.9) also include a revision deleting the phrase "On the Saturday afternoon" (which, on the holograph manuscript, follows "there.") The phrase is also absent from the texts of *A* and *E* and was evidently omitted from the missing printer's copy typescript.

531.25 liberty.*] See 531.36–38*fn*.

531.36–38*fn* * . . . veniam . . . *finem*.] This quotation from Tibullus (*c*.54–19 B.C.), Roman elegaic poet, was undoubtedly inserted into the missing typewritten version of *MS3* by Santayana himself. He was reading Tibullus during the 1940's and translated twenty-two lines of Part III of Book One of *Albii Tibulli Carmina*, lines 1–10 and 83–94. (See *The Complete Poems of George Santayana*, pp. 281–82 and 678–80.) The lines quoted are 89–90; however, Santayana here omits the first word of line 89, "*Tunc*". This omission is not indicated in *A* or *E*, but is expressed in the Critical Edition text by means of the ellipsis.

LIST OF EMENDATIONS

This is a list of changes made in the copy-text by the present editors. The following abbreviations are used to designate the sources of readings:

A American Edition (Scribner's, 1944, 1945, 1953)
At The Atlantic Monthly (1943, 1948, 1949)
CE The present Critical Edition
E English Edition (Constable, 1944, 1947; Cresset, 1953)
F1 Humanities Research Center typescript of "Farewell to England", p. 14, with George Santayana's revisions.
F2 Humanities Research Center typescript of "Farewell to England", p. 14, corrected.
F3 Humanities Research Center typescript of "Farewell to England", p. 18.
F4 Humanities Research Center typescript of "Farewell to England", p. 18, corrected.
P Proof (Scribner's, 1944)
T Atoms of Thought [:] *An Anthology of Thoughts from GEORGE SANTAYANA* (1950)
W1 Columbia University typescript of "WE WERE NOT VIRTUOUS"
W2 Humanities Research Center typescript of "WE WERE NOT VIRTUOUS"

For discussion of emendations marked with an asterisk (*), see the Discussions of Adopted Readings, pp. 613–631. The wavy dash (~) stands for the word or words cited to the left of the lemma bracket and indicates that a punctuation mark is emended. The caret (˄) indicates the absence of a punctuation mark. *Similar* begins a parenthetical listing of additional lines where the forms of emendation are identical. When a word occurs more than once on a line, a superscript number indicates its position on the line.

1 I *CE*] *George Santayana / Persons & Places: / Fragments of / Autobiography*
3.3 Place, Time, *CE*] ~ ˄ ~ ˄
3.8 Agustín *At,P,A,E*] Agustin
3.10 Nicolás *At,P,A,E*] Nicolas
3.11 María *CE*] Maria
3.15 Nicolás *At,P,A,E*] Nicolas
3.16 Joaquín *At,P,A,E*] Joaquin
4.10 Nicolás *P,A,E*] Nicolas
4.17 separately, *At,A,E*] ~ ˄
4.21 were in fact secretly *At,P,A,E*] were secretly
5.32 grandfather's *At,P,A,E*] grandfathers
7.9 testimonial *At,P,A,E*] testemonial
8.10 everyone *P,A,E*] every one
8.23 her official *P,A,E*] this

8.39*fn* John Forsyth, *A,E*] (Unintelligible Signature)
11.3 name *P,A,E*] surname
11.4 from that of a *P,A,E*] from a
11.4MH Santayana. *CE*] ~ ˄ (*Similar* 11.8MH; 12.14MH; 13.29MH; 14.12MH; 15.39MH; 16.37MH; 17.33MH; 20.4MH; 20.28MH; 21.18MH; 22.33MH; 23.10MH; 26.3MH; 26.26MH; 31.7MH; 31.18MH; 31.37MH; 35.36MH; 37.27MH; 38.27MH; 40.31MH; 42.27MH; 43.38MH; 44.12MH; 46.39MH; 47.14MH; 50.3MH; 65.6MH; 66.10MH; 67.9MH; 68.12MH; 68.15MH; 69.4MH; 70.1MH; 70.23MH; 73.3MH; 73.31MH; 77.4MH; 77.24MH; 78.12MH; 80.26MH; 82.5MH; 83.3MH; 83.38MH;

84.39MH; 85.37MH; 87.4MH; 88.25MH;
89.15MH; 90.8MH; 90.31MH; 91.36MH;
92.17MH; 94.3MH; 94.26MH; 97.4MH;
98.12MH; 98.30MH; 99.17MH; 100.6MH;
101.2MH; 101.38MH; 102.32MH;
104.16MH; 105.18MH; 106.20MH;
107.24MH; 108.17MH; 109.26MH;
115.12MH; 116.11MH; 118.21MH;
119.21MH; 120.27MH; 121.20MH;
123.15MH; 125.22MH; 127.4MH;
127.26MH; 130.13MH; 130.33MH;
131.16MH; 131.34MH; 132.34MH;
133.33MH; 134.14MH; 138.24MH;
139.37MH; 141.28MH; 141.31MH;
146.16MH; 146.33MH; 147.39MH;
148.16MH; 148.34MH; 150.34MH;
151.28MH; 153.25MH; 154.35MH;
156.28MH; 157.19MH; 159.6MH;
159.27MH; 162.22MH; 165.7MH;
165.28MH; 167.13MH; 168.13MH;
170.18MH; 179.4MH; 180.3MH;
180.31MH; 182.25MH; 183.4MH;
183.17MH; 183.38MH; 184.23MH;
185.3MH; 186.21MH; 187.11MH;
187.21MH; 188.22MH; 189.22MH;
190.11MH; 190.30MH; 191.3MH;
191.23MH; 192.30MH; 195.10MH;
196.3MH; 196.26MH; 198.20MH;
199.14MH; 201.25MH; 202.12MH;
202.21MH; 204.21MH; 206.34MH;
207.20MH; 208.5MH; 209.16MH;
210.2MH; 215.4MH; 215.15MH;
217.31MH; 218.18MH; 221.14MH;
221.36MH; 222.27MH; 223.7MH;
224.35MH; 225.22MH; 225.37MH;
226.7MH; 229.4MH; 230.4MH;
231.25MH; 232.16MH; 232.38MH;
233.34MH; 238.31MH; 239.18MH;
239.38MH; 240.22MH; 241.14MH;
242.10MH; 243.32MH; 245.5MH;
246.32MH; 247.31MH; 248.6MH;
248.24MH; 253.6MH; 253.12MH;
254.2MH; 254.20MH; 254.30MH;
255.28MH; 256.8MH; 256.23MH;
257.7MH; 257.35MH; 258.5MH;
258.26MH; 259.20MH; 260.33MH;
263.32MH; 269.12MH; 270.8MH;
270.38MH; 271.30MH; 271.39MH;
274.15MH; 276.3MH; 276.16MH;
276.37MH; 277.18MH; 279.13MH;
280.17MH; 284.8MH; 286.15MH;

286.30MH; 287.10MH; 288.5MH;
288.34MH; 289.6MH; 291.3MH;
291.15MH; 292.33MH; 294.10MH;
295.1MH; 295.25MH; 296.6MH;
298.6MH; 298.35MH; 299.22MH;
300.1MH; 300.22MH; 302.38MH;
304.15MH; 306.27MH; 307.3MH;
309.28MH; 310.6MH; 310.27MH;
312.37MH; 314.15MH; 317.24MH;
318.20MH; 319.8MH; 321.3MH;
321.22MH; 322.5MH; 323.18MH;
324.14MH; 324.23MH; 326.6MH;
327.16MH; 329.6MH; 329.17MH;
332.3MH; 332.20MH; 333.24MH;
334.2MH; 335.3MH; 335.33MH;
336.21MH; 337.3MH; 342.12MH;
343.3MH; 344.38MH; 346.15MH;
347.13MH; 349.19MH; 350.10MH;
350.38MH; 351.15MH; 354.13MH;
355.25MH; 356.25MH; 359.22MH;
360.28MH; 361.1MH; 361.36MH;
364.6MH; 365.1MH; 365.26MH;
365.32MH; 368.26MH; 373.8MH;
374.7MH; 375.38MH; 379.15MH;
380.23MH; 381.3MH; 381.11MH;
381.32MH; 382.38MH; 383.13MH;
384.20MH; 385.21MH; 386.5MH;
386.29MH; 387.3MH; 387.30MH;
388.7MH; 391.9MH; 391.38MH;
393.29MH; 394.25MH; 395.36MH;
397.9MH; 398.4MH; 399.1MH;
400.19MH; 401.2MH; 403.16MH;
405.8MH; 407.1MH; 407.27MH;
408.14MH; 408.36MH; 411.11MH;
412.19MH; 417.5MH; 420.11MH;
422.16MH; 423.38MH; 431.21MH;
432.28MH; 433.8MH; 434.21MH;
434.34MH; 435.16MH; 437.8MH;
438.4MH; 439.1MH; 439.29MH;
440.19MH; 440.35MH; 441.24MH;
442.14MH; 442.30MH; 443.2MH;
444.1MH; 447.4MH; 448.8MH;
449.1MH; 450.3MH; 451.2MH;
452.4MH; 452.17MH; 454.9MH;
454.30MH; 455.23MH; 456.33MH;
457.18MH; 458.26MH; 461.23MH;
461.39MH; 465.6MH; 465.23MH;
466.20MH; 467.4MH; 469.4MH;
470.6MH; 472.9MH; 472.30MH;
479.3MH; 479.36MH; 480.4MH;
480.38MH; 483.30MH; 484.16MH;

485.1MH; 487.13MH; 489.17MH;
490.6MH; 491.21MH; 493.29MH;
494.8MH; 495.26MH; 496.18MH;
498.7MH; 499.11MH; 501.6MH;
502.23MH; 502.37MH; 505.5MH;
507.21MH; 509.24MH; 510.5MH;
511.28MH; 514.37MH; 527.11MH;
528.5MH; 529.8MH; 529.29MH;
530.7MH; 531.26MH; 532.29MH;
533.12MH; 535.36MH; 537.18MH;
538.22MH; 540.36MH; 541.21MH;
543.17MH; 544.25MH; 546.24MH)

11.7 *J* *A,E*] J
11.8 *i* *A,E*] i
11.8 *y¹* *A,E*] y
11.8 *y²* *A,E*] y
11.9 *ll* *A,E*] ll
11.10 *gl* *A,E*] gl
11.13 south east *CE*] South east
11.15 etymology), *A,E*] ∼)ᴧ
11.28 unmistakably *P,A,E*] unmistably
12.18 than on love of political
    independence *At,P,A,E]* *than of political*
    dependence
13.20 ángel *P,A,E*] angel
14.26 *ad libitum* *At,A,E*] ad libitum
16.12–13 sensuality of the eighteenth-
    century notion *P,A,E*] eighteenthᴧcentury
    sensuality of the notion
16.23 everything *At,P,A,E*] everthing
17.15 insistence *At,P,A,E*] insistance
*17.37 *domus:** *CE*] ∼:ᴧ
*17.38–40*fn* *Probably . . . domus. CE*] [not
    present]
18.2 4,000 *CE*] 4000
18.3 boulders *P,A,E*] bowlders
18.19 boulders *P,A,E*] bowlders
19.25 general, then in Spain again, *At,P,A,E*]
    ∼ᴧ now in Spain againᴧ
*19.35 Sonsolès *E*] Sonsoles
20.11–12 the fact escapes them that light
    and shade or outlines in themselves are
    something *At,P,A,E*] light and shade or
    outlines in themselves meaning nothing
    escape them
21.25 a *At,P,A,E*] of
*22.8–9 especially a few years later when
    At,P,A,E] especially when
*22.12 father or my sisters or me *At,P,A,E*]
    father or me
*23.25 requirements *P,A,E*] requisites

25.34 aqueduct *P,A,E*] acqueduct
26.11 donkey, *CE*] ∼ᴧ
26.39 dining-room *E*] ∼ᴧ∼
27.11 sea voyages *At*] sea-voyages
27.23 alien, *At,P,A,E*] ∼ᴧ
29.27 presently *P,A,E*] immediately
30.16 daughter, *At,A,E*] ∼ᴧ
31.27 mother's *P,A,E*] mothers
32.30 her² *P,A,E*] he
34.8 Despatches *P,A,E*] Despaches
34.29 devote *P,A,E*] devout
36.1 friendly. *At,P,A,E*] ∼,
40.2 extreme *P,A,E*] ex-extreme
42.1 pronounced *At,P,A,E*] propounced
44.2 roundabout *P,A,E*] round about
44.29 said, *A,E*] ∼.
45.18 Church *At,E*] church
45.34 pirouette *CE*] piroutte
47.19 one-eleventh *A,E*] ∼ᴧ∼
48.4 sonnets *P,A,E*] Sonnets
48.12 *Fearless A,E*] Fearless
48.32 Civil War *A,E*] civil war
48.36–37 locutions . . . I *CE*] locutions I
49.28 Toribio, *P,A,E*] ∼ᴧ
50.5 Doña *At,P,A,E*] doña
*50.28 *daemonic At,P,A,E*] *external*
*51.7 five *P,A,E*] several
51.13 eighth *P,A,E*] eightth
52.25 Rothschilds *P,A,E*] Rothchilds
52.35 offered *P,A,E*] offerred
53.4 distinguished *P,A,E*] brilliant
53.6–7 no longer possessed those abilities.
    He *P,A,E*] had lost those abilities. He,
53.15 lieu *P,A,E*] place
54.12 Pyrenees *P,A*] Pyrennees
54.25 drawing-room *E*] drawingroom
54.26 forty-three *A,E*] 43
54.26 twenty-three *A,E*] 23
54.28 *despreocupada A,E*] ∼,
55.2 break *P,A,E*] brake
55.4 boarding-houses *E*] boardingᴧhouses
55.11 Uncle *P,A,E*] uncle
55.20 Aunt *P,A,E*] aunt
56.21 Aunt *P,A,E*] aunt
56.38 Aunt *P,A,E*] aunt
57.1 staple *P,A,E*] stable
57.7 Chinese *P,A,E*] chinese
57.17 mild *P,A,E*] ∼,
57.37 Brummel *P,A,E*] Brum-
57.39*fn* Danvers. *P,A,E*] ∼ᴧ
58.27 instance, *CE*] ∼ᴧ

58.32 daughter, *CE*] ∼ ͺ

59.26 thought *CE*] thoughts

59.27 thirty-four *CE*] ∼ ͺ ∼

62.2 ambassador *CE*] embassador

62.23 Jennie" *CE*] ∼ ͺ

62.40 ineradicable *CE*] inerradicable

65.12 godmother *P,A,E*] god-mother

65.26-27 *¿Reconoces los compañeros de tu infancia? P,A,E*] ¿Reconoces los compañeros de tu infancia?

66.15 course *A,E*] ∼,

66.20 faces *P,A,E*] eyes

66.23 *Scarlet P,A,E*] Red

66.25 her. *P,A,E*] ∼,.

67.18 temporarily *P,A,E*] temporarilly

67.21 sons *P,A,E*] son's

67.27 but all this *P,A,E*] but this

67.29 Parliament *P,A,E*] Parlaiment

67.30 unmistakable *P*] unmistable

68.5 Micawber *P,A,E*] Miccawber

68.15 caprice *P,A,E*] egotism

68.28 Michaelangelo's *CE*] Michael Angelo's

68.30 beard like Saint Peter's is *P,A,E,T*] beard is

69.29 $10,000— *P,A,E*] ∼ ͺ

69.39 married *P,A,E*] ∼,

70.23 1872 *A,E*] 1873

*71.3-4 Chicago had had an even bigger fire *CE*] Chicago soon had a fire that beat it

71.5-6 the era of an abominable architectural *CE*] the abominable era of an abominable architectural

71.8 1872 *A,E*] 1873

72.6 James's *CE*] James

72.18 sixty-four *A,E*] 64

72.18 sixty-nine *A,E*] 69

72.21 mother's *P,A,E*] mothers

74.14 for him; *CE*] for;

74.30 Robert's *CE*] Roberts

75.3 however. *CE*] ∼,

75.29 had, *CE*] ∼,,

75.38 tour. *CE*] ∼,

76.9 bureaucracy *CE*] burocracy

77.1 V *E*] ∼.

77.2 *My Sister Susana CE*] My Sister Susana.

77.31 that in Boston, local *P,A,E*] that local

78.24-25 cry: *P,A,E*] cry ͺ

78.26 inquired: *P,A,E*] ∼ ͺ

78.27 me?" *P,A*] ∼."

80.36 principal *P,A,E*] principle

81.10 impressions *P,A,E*] impression

82.20 practised *P,A,E*] practiced

82.37 and never *P,A,E*] but not

83.30 impoverished *CE*] empoverished

84.39 exotic *P,A,E*] foreign

85.31 Paderewska *A,E,T*] Paderewski

85.38 Iasigis *A,E*] Iasigi's

86.15 carriages, *P,A,E*] ∼ ͺ

87.31 Fiji *P,A,E*] Figi

88.5 Fiji *P,A,E*] Figi

88.11 connoisseurs *P,A,E,T*] connaisseurs

88.29 *Robinson Crusoe E*] Robinson Crusoe

88.34 aunt *E*] Aunt

89.5 scalloped *P,A,E*] scollaped

89.7 outlasted *P,A,E*] outlusted

90.1 *a priori A,E*] a priori

90.18 thirty-four *P,A,E*] ∼ ͺ ∼

91.16 months *P,A,E*] month's

92.10 Spain, *P,A,E*] ∼ ͺ

93.4 exigencies *P,A,E*] exigences

94.18 himself. *P,A,E*] ∼..

94.28 mother's *P,A,E*] mothers

95.24 Dominican *P,A,E*] Domican

95.25 Tomás *P,A,E*] Tomas

98.30 *oppidum, A,E*] ∼ ͺ

101.9 Aristophanic *P,A,E*] Aristaphanic

*101.18 Alain *A,E*] *Alain*

101.21 solstice *P,A,E*] soltice

101.23 tapestries *P,A,E*] taprestries

101.24 coverlet *P,A,E*] covelet

101.31 mystic *P,A,E*] mysic

102.22 rose-leaves *P,A,E*] ∼ ͺ ∼

104.2 obeisances *P,A,E*] obeissances

104.4 obeisance *P,A,E*] obeissance

104.26 imperturbably *A,E*] imperturbedly

105.9 Tomás *A,E*] Tomas

105.12 amongst *CE*] amongs

105.30-31MH brother-in-law's *CE*] ∼ - ∼ ͺ ∼

106.11 dining-room *E*] ∼ ͺ ∼

106.23 Chapel *P,A,E*] chapel

106.24 Our *P,A,E*] our

106.28 Our¹ *P,A,E*] our¹

106.28 Our² *A,E*] our²

106.28-29 would have been *P,A,E*] would been

107.14 Sonsolès *P,A,E*] Sonsoles

107.21 Sonsolès *P,A,E*] Sonsoles

108.20 mediaeval *P,A,E*] medieval

108.22 6,000 *P,A,E*] 6000

108.23 30,000 *P,A,E*] 30000

108.26 nondescript *P,A,E*] nondiscript
108.29 wrought-iron *A,E*] ~ ∧ ~
110.29 soared *P,A,E*] sored
110.32 churches, *CE*] ~ ∧
111.20 Chapter *P,A,E*] chapter
111.30 sacrificed *P,A,E*] sacrified
113.4 examining *P,A,E*] examing
113.4 nondescript *A,E*] non-descript
113.11 circumstance, *P,A,E*] ~ ∧
113.11 itself, *P,A,E*] ~ ∧
116.34 with a *At,P,A,E*] with, with a
117.4 parents' *At,P,A,E*] parent's
117.28 War *At*] war
118.7 María *CE*] Maria
118.21 María *CE*] Maria
118.21MH María *CE*] Maria
118.25 Jaén *At*] Jaen
119.1 María *CE*] Maria
119.18 Jaén *CE*] Jaen
119.20 *tía María CE*] tia Maria
119.21MH love-affairs *CE*] ~ ∧ ~
119.28 María *CE*] Maria
119.29 María *CE*] Maria
120.38 coverlet *P,A,E*] covelet
121.24 as² *P,A,E*] a
*122.7 like those *A,E*] just like
122.17 Vegases *CE*] Vegas
124.7 profited *P,A,E*] profitted
124.17 María *CE*] Maria
125.15 María *CE*] Maria
125.39 essence, *A,E*] ~ ∧
126.1 however, *A,E*] ~ ∧
126.3 everything *P,A,E*] every thing
127.22 cockleshell *A,E*] cockelshell
128.31 3,000 *CE*] 3000
128.38 seasick *A,E*] sea-sick
132.5 frustrated *A,E*] frustated
132.10 arts *A,E*] art
133.8 twenty-one *At,A,E*] ~ ∧ ~
133.14 mantelpiece *At,A,E*] mantel piece
133.17 examining *At,A,E*] examing
134.28 grandmother's *A,E*] grand-mother's
137.2 No. 302, Beacon Street *CE*] № *302,*
　　Beacon Street.
137.27 time *A,E*] ~,,
138.21 *Venice. A,E*] ~;
*138.36 advantages *At,A,E*] attractions
139.14 occasional *A,E*] occasion
139.33 upstairs *At,A,E*] up stairs
139.34 bedrooms *At,A,E*] bed-rooms
140.36 love-affairs *CE*] ~ ∧ ~

141.15 backyard *E*] back-yard
141.16 façade *A,E*] facade
*142.4 eighth *At,A,E*] ninth
142.5 *Encyclopaedia Britannica E*]
　　Encyclopaedia Britannica
142.8 Optic's *At,A,E*] Optick's
142.14 *Lives E*] lives
*142.23 *Un Servilón y un At*] El Servilón y el
142.23 Fernán *At*] Fernan
143.18 *Encyclopaedia CE*] Encyclopaedia
143.33 have never *A,E*] have have never
143.37 never *A,E*] ~;
143.39 place, *E*] ~;
145.9 everything *A,E*] every thing
145.20 are not *A,E*] are are not
145.25 preoccupy *A,E*] pre-occupy
146.3 vision, *A,E*] ~ ∧
*146.6 *Fiction and Truth A,E*] Truth and Fiction
*146.6 *Poetry and Truth CE*] Truth and Poetry
147.11 fisticuffs, *A,E*] ~ ∧
147.30 profited *At,A,E*] profitted
148.13 Somnambulistic *A,E*] Somnabulistic
148.14 two-thirds *A,E,T*] ~ ∧ ~
148.26 asinine *A,E*] assinine
149.5 *bonne*", *CE*] ~ ∧,
149.31 profiting *At,A,E*] profitting
149.38MH Schoolhouse *E*] schoolhouse
150.29 thundering, *A,E*] ~ down,
152.37 χαράδρα *CE*] χάραδρα
156.6 involuntary. *A,E*] ~,
157.37 School *A,E*] school
158.8 Battalion *A,E*] battalion
160.20 announcements *A,E*] announcement
161.11 belfry. *A,E*] ~:.
*163.4 Carcassonne *CE*] Carcassone
163.8MH Baroque *CE*] Barocque
163.30 vault, *A,E*] ~ ∧
164.8 sun *A,E*] ~,
164.8 Apocalypse), *A,E*] ~) ∧
164.18 gowns (except *A,E*] ~ ∧ ~
164.18 bare), one *A,E*] ~ ∧ ∧ ~
165.14 *a priori.* *A,E*] ~. ∧
165.35 no less *A,E*] as
165.38-39fn *"I . . . circumcised. A,E*] [not
　　present]
166.7 performance. *A*] ~. ∧
*166.34-38fn *Cf. . . . 109-111. CE*] [not
　　present]
169.8 1880's), *A,E*] ~) ∧
170.26 *a priori A,E*] a priori
173.8 *amourette At,A,E*] amourette

173.12 actresses: *At*] ~;
173.14 cotillion *At,A,E*] cotillon
174.3 judgment *A,E*] judgement
174.6 moral. *A,E*] ~:
174.8 a *A,E*] ~,
174.9 charm: *CE*] ~ ∧
174.10 risks. *A,E*] ~,
174.33 made an exile *A,E*] made exile
175.4 second class *At,A,E*] ~-~
175.7 Headmaster *A,E*] head master
175.15 Lenox *A,E*] Lennox
175.16 Lenox *A,E*] Lennox
*175.17 "Ja" *A,E*] Jay
175.18 twenty-five *At,A,E*] ~ ∧ ~
175.18 Harry *A,E*] James
175.25–29 When . . . friendship. *At,A*] [not present]
175.29 Room *A,E*] room
175.40 appeared, Edward Bayley. I *At,A,E*] appeared. I
*176.26 haunted *A,E*] hunted
177.9 pontiff *A,E*] pontif
*177.22 dreamt *A,E*] thought
177.27 absence *A,E*] absense
177.32 civilised. *CE*] ~ ∧
177.33 Bayley *A,E*] Bayle
177.34 education *A,E*] edcation
177.40 he *A,E*] the
178.2 blamelessness), *A,E*] ~) ∧
*178.24 with warm blood *At,A,E*] who could pray
178.33 he *At,A,E*] ne
179.14 north-east *E*] ~ ∧ ~
179.15 forty-four *A,E*] 44
179.18 have been thought *A,E*] have thought
182.14 biscuits *At,A,E*] buiscuits
183.20 earthen *At,A,E*] earthern
184.35 side-windows *CE*] ~ ∧ ~
186.8 hard-coal *At,A,E*] ~ ∧ ~
186.21MH *Lampoon CE*] Lampoon
186.32 Mérimée *A,E*] Mérimé
187.1 *Lampoon A,E*] Lampoon
187.5 Board *A,E*] *Board*
187.8 of *A,E*] a
187.9 Board *At,A,E*] *Board*
187.25 Freshmen *A,E*] Freshman
187.37 than *A,E*] that
188.4 *Springfield A,E*] *Springfied*
188.6 College *A,E*] college
188.22 *Lampoon A,E*] Lampoon

188.24 crotchets *A,E*] crochets
188.30 *Lampoon At,A,E*] Lampoon
188.34 *Lampoon At,A,E,T*] Lampoon
189.3 *Lampoon At,A,E*] Lampoon
189.11 *Lampoon At,A,E*] Lampoon
*189.11MH Ernest *CE*] Eugene
*189.12 Ernest *A,E*] Eugene
189.21 *Lampoon At,A,E*] Lampoon
189.29 *Lampoon At,A,E*] Lampoon
190.13 Athletics *At,A,E*] Athelics
191.2 O.K. *At,A,E*] O.K ∧
191.3 *Harvard Monthly At,A,E*] Harvard Monthly
191.5 *Lampoon At,A,E*] Lampoon
191.5 O.K., *At,A,E*] O.K. ∧
191.7 athletic *At,A,E*] althletic
191.20 *Harvard Monthly At,A,E*] Harvard Monthly
191.20MH *Harvard Monthly CE*] Harvard Monthly
191.22 contrast *At,A,E*] constrast
191.22MH Bigelow *CE*] Biglow
192.12 cigar, *At,A,E*] ~,,
196.7 5,000 *A,E*] 5000
197.39 provided myself with *CE*] provided with
198.7 fifteen *A,E*] 15
198.8 thirty-six *At,A,E*] 36
198.20 fifteen *A,E*] 15
198.21 Irún *At*] Irun
198.36 dishevelled *CE*] disshevelled
199.2 María *CE*] Maria
199.26 events *A,E*] event
200.19 asceticism *A,E,T*] ascetism
201.19 side of Anglosaxon *A,E*] side Anglosaxon
202.19 parliamentary *A,E*] parliamentary
203.34 eschatological *A,E*] eschatoligal
204.3 itself. *CE*] ~. ∧
204.20 calls *A,E*] call's
204.21 tío *CE*] tio
204.20–21MH tío *CE*] tio
204.23 godfather *A,E*] god-father
204.30 tío *CE*] tio
204.32 tío *CE*] tio
204.34 Nicolás *A,E*] Nicolas
*204.35–38fn *Voir . . . Hernani CE*] [not present]
205.35 tío *CE*] tio
206.7 ones *A,E*] one's
206.16 Nicolás *A,E*] Nicolas

206.25 *tío* *CE*] *tio*
206.34MH ill *CE*] in
206.37 *tío* *CE*] *tio*
206.39 insignificant *A,E*] insignicant
207.15 precisely *A,E*] preciously
208.1 *tío* *CE*] *tio*
208.1 *Nicolás* *A,E*] *Nicolas*
208.10 *tío* *CE*] *tio*
208.16 *tío* *CE*] *tio*
208.39 *tío* *CE*] *tio*
208.39 *Nicolás* *A,E*] *Nicolas*
209.2 canon *A,E*] Canon
209.9 piety; *CE*] ~;_∧
209.15 *tío* *CE*] tio
209.15 *Nicolás* *A,E*] Nicolas
209.28 *tío* *CE*] *tio*
209.28 *Nicolás* *A,E*] *Nicolas*
*209.36–38*fn* *Cf.* . . . eum. *CE*] [not present]
210.13 *tío* *CE*] *tio*
210.33 forty *A,E*] 40
210.33 eight *A,E*] 8
211.4 Intelligentsia *A,E*] Intelligensia
211.12 *Tío* *CE*] *Tio*
211.12 *Nicolás* *A,E*] *Nicolas*
211.27 Rhône *CE*] Rhone
212.2 contrary, *A,E*] ~ _∧
212.14 8th. *A,E*] 8th_∧
212.15 9th *A,E*] 9th_∧
212.22 [*lo ha maliciado*] *A,E*] (~)
212.36 her *A,E*] he
216.32 Maecenas *A,E*] Mecaenas
216.40 responsibility *A,E*] responsability
217.6 twenty *A,E*] 20
218.36 Michaelangelo's *CE*] Michelangelo's
218.38 Michaelangelos *CE*] Michelangelo's
*219.36 'Chè,' *CE*] "Chè,"
220.9 Apennines *A,E*] Appenines
*220.13 Verna *CE*] Vernia
*220.15 Verna *CE*] Vernia
221.17 Mario *A,E*] *Mario*
222.19 grandparents *A,E*] grand-parents
223.14 *War and Peace* *A,E*] *Peace & War*
224.12 Adams' *A,E*] Adams_∧
224.29–30 adaptability *A,E*] adaptivity
225.2 had been thoroughly sound *A,E*] had thorough sound
225.14 seventy-seven *A,E*] 77
225.16 fifty-five *A,E*] 55
*226.15–16 Counsellor *A,E*] Chancellor
230.38 ninety per cent *A,E*] 90%
231.5 *Gods of Greece* *A,E*] "Gods of Greece"

*231.28 one *CE*] ones
233.36*fn* essences", *CE*] ~".
234.7 The *E*] the
234.13 Dog-Star *A,E*] dog-star
234.23 heavy, *A,E*] ~ _∧
235.31 they *CE*] the
236.34 headmaster *A,E*] head-master
*237.1 rhythmic *CE*] rhymic
237.11 Mandeville *A,E*] Manderville
237.17–18 of utilitarianism *A,E*] or Utilitarianism
240.8 candidates *A,E*] canditates
240.30–31 good-looking *A,E*] good looking
241.22 whoever *A,E*] who ever
241.38 whoever *A,E*] who ever
242.6 rather *A,E*] ~,
242.25 $2,500 *A,E*] $2500
242.29 headquarters *A,E*] headquarter
242.39 to a point *A,E*] to point
243.9 hand *A,E*] had
243.13 was less *A,E*] was a less
243.20 psychologically *A,E*] psycholically
244.10–11 Angoulême *A,E*] Angouleme
244.11 Bordeaux *A,E*] Bordeau
245.10 Church *W1,W2*] church
245.14 *hijo.*" *W1,W2*] ~ ",
247.7 or curiosity *W1,W2*] or in curiosity
247.14 church, *CE*] ~ _∧
247.23–24 busy with science *W1,W2*] business, science,
248.21 kept *W2*] taken
249.1 tentacles *CE*] tenticles
251 II *CE*] *Persons and Places* / *The Background of my Life* / by / *George Santayana* / *Volume Second*
253.12 recommendation *A,E*] recommentation
253.13 autumn *A,E*] autunn
253.29 *nichts* *A,E*] *Nichts*
254.10 *Julius Caesar* *CE*] Julius Caesar
254.12 *Hamlet* or *Othello* *A,E*] Hamlet ~ Othello
*254.22 Zwinger *CE*] Zwingler
254.22 Katholische *A,E*] Catholische
255.38 November. *A,E*] ~,
256.18 *Gemütlichkeit* *A,E*] *Gemüthlichkeit*
256.18 hearty, *A,E*] ~ _∧
256.23 modernness, *A,E*] ~ _∧
256.31 compote *A,E*] compôte
256.32 dessert *A,E*] desert
256.37 Louisenplatz *A,E*] Louisen platz

260.12–13 "Ten Different Interpretations of the Essence of Kant's *Critique of Pure Reason*" *CE*] Ten Different Interpretations of the Essence of Kant's Critique of Pure Reason
261.13 me than between *A,E*] me between
261.19 correspondence *A,E*] correspondance
262.10 No. *A,E*] Nº
262.23 invalid *A,E*] invalide
262.31 seasickness *A,E*] sea-sickness
263.26 requisitioned *A,E*] requisioned
265.23 King, *A,E*] ∼ ₐ
267.5 enamoured. *A,E*] ∼ ₐ
267.33 first-class *A,E*] ∼ ₐ ∼
268.3 deferential *A,E*] deferencial
268.8 to suspect *A,E*] to to suspect
268.32 traffic *A,E*] trafic
269.11–12MH boarding-house *CE*] ∼ ₐ ∼
269.18 horrid *A,E*] hoerid
270.8 family friends *A,E*] ∼-∼
270.15 Tussaud's *A,E*] Toussaud's
270.18 Jermyn Street *A,E*] ∼-∼
270.27 linen. *A,E*] ∼,
271.5 Jermyn Street *A,E*] ∼-∼
272.24 Parks— *A,E*] ∼,—
272.29 summer *A,E*] Summer
273.8 an *A,E*] on
273.10 pre-Raphaelite *CE*] preraphaelite
273.12 passed *A,E*] past
273.12 London, *A,E*] ∼ ₐ
273.35 imperceptibly *A,E*] inperceptibly
276.22 smoking-room *A,E*] ∼ ₐ ∼
276.22 smoking-room *A,E*] ∼ˑ ₐ ∼
277.25 Guards' *E*] Guard's
278.22 said, *CE*] ∼ ₐ
278.37 walnut *A,E*] wallnut
278.39 walnut *A,E*] wallnut
280.5 War *CE*] war
280.19 better"— *A,E*] ∼,"—
281.4 cynical, *E*] ∼ ₐ
281.14 looked *A,E*] look
281.21 second-class *A,E*] ∼ ₐ ∼
281.25 home, *A,E*] ∼ ₐ
283.39–40 pre-Raphaelite *CE*] preraphaelite
284.6 Berensons' *A,E*] ∼ ₐ
285.11 resilience *CE*] resalience
285.40 old-fashioned *A,E*] ∼ ₐ ∼
287.3 Unfortunately *A,E*] Unfortunely
287.14 Berensons *A*] Berenson's
289.9 old-fashioned *A,E*] ∼ ₐ ∼
289.11 *The Bible in Spain A,E*] "The Bible in Spain"

289.34 silhouetted *A,E*] silhoutted
290.7 middle-aged *A,E*] ∼ ₐ ∼
*290.8–9 charming in the latest fashion and smiling *A,E*] charming and smiling in the latest fashion
291.1 XIX *CE*] *Chapter XIX*
292.36 days' *A,E*] ∼ ₐ
292.37 accommodation *A,E*] accomodation
293.38 triumphantly, *A,E*] ∼ ₐ
293.39 is." *A,E*] ∼.".
294.5 defiance. *A,E*] ∼..
295.2 *Royal A,E*] "Royal"
295.2MH *Royal CE*] "Royal"
295.23 *Royal A,E*] "Royal"
296.40 boat-hook *E*] boathook
297.5 Rosencrantz *CE*] Rosencranz
297.5 Guildenstern *A,E*] Guildernstern
297.17 heels *A,E*] heals
298.8 you", *A,E*] ∼" ₐ
299.22 One *A,E*] 1
300.8 *veneris A,E*] *Veneris*
301.21 reflection *E*] reflexion
302.1 Rimbaud *A,E*] Ribaud
*303.2 Heddon's *CE*] Hedder's
303.18 many a *A,E*] a many
304.1 aestheticism, *A,E*] ∼;
304.2 pre-Raphaelitism *CE*] preraphaelitism
305.17 absorption *A,E*] absorbsion
306.3 [Wales] *A*] (∼)
306.29 Baudelairean *A,E*] Baudelarian
308.17 death-bed *E*] deathbed
309.9 summoned *CE*] summonsed
310.19 restrained *A,E*] retrained
310.22 Boer War *A,E*] ∼ war
310.33 perjure *A,E*] purjure
311.12 ferrule *A,E*] ferule
311.27 *Royal A,E*] "Royal"
311.35 *Royal A,E*] "Royal"
312.1 Civitavecchia *A*] Cività Vecchia
312.6 'Royal' *A,E*] "∼"
312.12 profiting *A,E*] profitting
312.13MH *Royal A,E*] "Royal"
312.17 Rhône *A,E*] Rhone
313.5 middle-class *A,E*] ∼ ₐ ∼
313.12 Clemenceau *A,E*] Clèmenceau
314.5 top, *A,E*] ∼ ₐ
314.5 also *A,E*] ∼,
314.11 *Royal A,E*] "Royal"
*314.15–38 Broom . . . was, *E*] In the afternoon we were to go out in the launch; I was a bit surprised that Jennie,

the housemaid, seemed to be coming with us; but I knew she was one of the Billings children. Their mother had been Russell's nurse, and they had played together in their early days. That might be an explanation; but not for the presence of a second young woman, silent and dejected, with all her hair loose, already sitting in the stern of the launch, next to the wheel, where Russell would certainly sit. "That is my sister Emma", said Jennie, observing my surprise. I asked if she was drying her hair. No, Lord Russell (Jennie didn't call him "His Lordship") liked her to have it like that. *Zo!* I said to myself (having been lately in Germany) and I discreetly went to sit with Jennie in the bow, leaving Russell with his dishevelled and rather mad-looking sweetheart in the stern. But how could he be carrying on such an intrigue in public? I thought of Steerforth and Little Emily. And what could be Jennie's position in the matter? An accomplice, a jealous rival, or perhaps a second mistress? For Jennie's eyes were very bright, and she moved about with the freedom of a member of the family, and with some coquetry as well. Accustomed though I was to the wild oats and the love-affairs of my friends, these complications at Broom Hall troubled me a little. It might not prove such a peaceful and dignified retreat as I had fancied.

315.15 anyone *A,E*] any one
315.15 about? . . . *A,E*] ~? . . . .
315.35 this. *A,E*] ~ ₍
316.18 desk, *A,E*] ~ ₍
316.18-19 mantelpiece *A,E*] mantlepiece
317.18 other's *A,E*] others
317.19-20 than the housemaids and the lady-secretaries that *A*] than the lady secretaries that
318.15 mantelpiece *A,E*] mantel-piece
318.16 Billings, *CE*] ~;
318.20 Billings, *A*] ~ ₍
319.5 cues *A,E*] queus
319.35 love-affairs *CE*] ~ ₍ ~
*320.27 desperate *A,E*] unhappy
321.1 XX *CE*] Chapter XX

321.8 María *CE*] Maria
321.21 Nicolás *CE*] Nicolas
321.21-22 godfather *A,E*] god-father
323.28 practitioner *A,E*] practioner
325.5 Spain *A,E*] ~,
325.31 irritants: *CE*] ~;
326.34 María *CE*] Maria
328.16 house, *A,E*] ~ ₍
328.16 continuity, *A,E*] ~ ₍
328.16 union, *A,E*] ~ ₍
328.17 Madorells' *A,E*] Madorell's
328.30 years' *A,E*] ~ ₍
330.6 Celedonio *A,E*] Celodonio
330.22 boys' *A,E*] boy's
331.27 Upstairs *A,E*] Up stairs
332.16 night air *A,E*] night of air
332.29 pencil *A,E*] paper
332.31 Avila, *A,E*] ~ ₍
333.3 muleteers *A,E*] muletiers
333.5 dam *A,E*] damm
333.25 years' *A,E*] ~ ₍
334.16 pastimes *A,E*] pasttimes
334.28 doubtfully *A,E*] doubfully
335.38 taking *A,E*] taken
336.29 committed *A,E*] comitted
338.2 sons *A,E*] son's
338.3 sons' *A,E*] son's'
338.23-24 and of having won *A,E*] and won
341.1 XXI *CE*] Chapter XXI
342.15 squad *A,E*] squard
342.30 Norfolk *E*] norfolk
343.13 company, *A,E*] ~ ₍
343.24 scalloped *A,E*] scollaped
343.36 *s'ennuie A,E*] *s'ennui*
344.5 Easter *A,E*] easter
344.17 that[1] *A,E*] than
345.14 attainments, *A,E*] ~ ₍
345.18 or, as he *A,E*] or he
345.28 end . . . Julian's *A,E*] end. Julian's
346.19 War *A,E*] war
346.36 Emerson, *CE*] ~ ₍
346.36 him, *A,E*] ~ ₍
347.3 brothers' *A,E*] brother's
348.27 off *A,E*] out
349.5 fluently *A,E*] ~,
349.6 Louisiana), *A,E*] ~) ₍
349.16 seemed *A,E*] seem
349.27 assessments *A,E*] assesments
350.16 Beaux-Arts *A,E*] ~ ₍ ~
350.16 Julien's. *A,E*] ~,.
350.27 before, *A,E*] ~ ₍

350.33 new, *CE*] ∼ ‸
351.34MH Evanescence *CE*] Evanessence
353.1 XXII *CE*] Chapter XXII
354.28 children: *A,E*] ∼;
354.29*fn* *This *CE*] ‸ ∼
354.38*fn* Russell *A,E*] ∼,
355.35 strange, *A,E*] ∼ ‸
355.35 everyone *A,E*] every one
356.15 murmured *A,E*] murmurred
356.16 Prayer *A,E*] prayer
356.32 although, *E*] ∼ ‸
356.35 plutocracy, *A,E*] ∼,,
357.9 region *A,E*] ∼,
358.13 imitative, *A,E*] ∼ ‸
360.17 *belles-lettres CE*] ∼ ‸ ∼
360.17 do. *A,E*] ∼,
360.22 old-fashioned *A,E*] ∼ ‸ ∼
360.22 pre-Raphaelite *CE*] preraphaelite
361.6 good-looking *CE*] ∼ ‸ ∼
362.16 out of a *A,E*] out a
363.28 were, *A,E*] ∼ ‸
*363.39 hardly ever *A,E*] never
364.15 perseverance *A,E*] ∼,
364.15 that, *A,E*] ∼ ‸
368.9 blond *A,E*] blonde
368.17 *Winds of Doctrine A,E*] "Winds of Doctrine"
371.24–25 Englishmen, *A,E*] ∼ ‸
372.8 spring *A,E*] Spring
372.22 settle *A,E*] settled
373.26 thanksgiving *A,E*] Thanksgiving
373.27 Piccadilly *A,E*] Picadilly
375.36MH Phantom *CE*] Phatom
376.18 psychology? *A,E*] ∼.
376.38 *Closerie A,E*] *Cloiserie*
377.7 reddish-grey *E*] ∼ ‸ ∼
378.12 husband." *A,E*] ∼. ‸
378.24 indecision." *A,E*] ∼. ‸
378.39 Everyone *A*] Every one
*379.27 *distingué A,E*] distinguished
379.36 parents' *CE*] parent's
379.40 friend, *A,E*] ∼ ‸
381.4 Beaux-Arts *A,E*] ∼ ‸ ∼
381.11 Rue *A,E*] rue
381.13 Beaux-Arts *A,E*] ∼ ‸ ∼
382.7 Reszke *A,E*] Retsky
382.19 Reszke *CE*] Retsky
382.27 freethinker *CE*] free thinker
383.5 South *A,E*] south
384.1 southern *A,E*] Southern
387.36 *Grecque E*] *Grècque*

389.1 XXIV *CE*] Chapter XXIV
390.15 $1,000 *CE*] $1000
390.29 answer?" *A,E*] ∼".
391.30 that various *A,E*] that that various
392.7 conscientiously *CE*] conscienciously
392.19 invalids' *A,E*] invalid's
393.19 Barrett *A,E*] Barret
394.29 fifty *A,E*] 50
394.30 were *A,E*] we
395.2 $2,000 *CE*] $2000
395.5 $4,000 *CE*] $4000
395.6 years, *A,E*] ∼ ‸
395.6 1904–1906, *A,E*] ∼ ‸
395.11 imperceptibly *A,E*] inperceptibly
396.11 forty-in-hand *A,E*] ∼ ‸ ∼ ‸ ∼
396.26 parliamentary *A,E*] parliamentary
396.31 of the whole *A,E*] of whole
396.35 parliamentary *A,E*] parliamentary
397.20 Cuffe *A,E*] Guff
397.31 old-fashioned *A,E*] ∼ ‸ ∼
399.10 Burne-Jones *A,E*] ∼ ‸ ∼
399.22 rhythmical *A,E*] rhymical
401.14 James, *A,E*] ∼ ‸
401.39 profited *A,E*] profitted
402.2 presence. *A,E*] ∼ ‸
402.23 library *A,E*] ∼,
402.24 Street), *A,E*] ∼) ‸
402.36 switch *A,E*] swish
403.21 McKinley *A,E*] Mackinley
403.26 McKinley *A,E*] Mackinley
403.31 Irún *CE*] Irun
404.20 it *A,E*] they
404.36 expression *A,E*] expressions
405.15 *Lampoon A,E*] Lampoon
405.35 Dr. *A,E*] D.ͬ ‸
406.14 old-fashioned *A,E*] ∼ ‸ ∼
407.17 proletariat *A,E*] prolitariat
408.10 President *A,E*] President's
409.19 husband), *A,E*] ∼) ‸
409.35 baba-au-rhum *A,E*] baba-au-rum
410.31–32 all together *A,E*] altogether
411.17 views, *A,E*] ∼.,
411.27 Address, *A,E*] ∼ ‸
412.2 years' *A,E*] ∼ ‸
412.25 Paris, *A,E*] ∼ ‸
413.7 universities *A,E*] ∼'
*413.17 lectures *CE*] lecture's
414.18 sincere. We all move together when we pursue the truth. [¶] The *A,E*] sincere. [¶] The
414.19 posthumous *A,E*] pothumous

414.30–31 with the universe *A,E*] with universe

415 III *CE*] "In The Old World" / (Original Title Vol. III) / of / *Persons & Places*

417.1 XXV *CE*] 1

*417.2 A Change of Heart *At,A,E*] *Metanoia*

417.7 inexhaustibly *At,A,E*] inexhaustably

418.5 but his spirit *A,E*] but it

420.30 in *At,A,E*] is²

424.26 forty-one *At,A,E*] ~ ∧ ~

424.38*fn Purgatorio CE*] Purgatorio

*427.28 . . . this *At*] This

*427.29 down-lying; *CE*] ~,

*427.30 slow but sure reclining *At*] true and sure declining

428.36 Stendhal *At,A,E*] Stendahl

*428.38 *l'amour-physique CE*] ~ ∧ ~

*428.38 *l'amour de vanité At*] *l'amour vanité*

*428.38 *l'amour-goût CE*] ~ ∧ ~

*428.39 *l'amour-passion CE*] *la grande passion*

429.1 craving, *At,A,E*] ~ ∧

*429.3 *amour-passion CE*] *grande passion*

*429.9 *amour-goût CE*] ~ ∧ ~

*429.11 *amour de vanité At*] *amour vanité*

431.1 XXVI *CE*] 2

431.16 open. *A,E*] ~,

432.19 east *A,E*] East

432.26 College, *A,E*] ~ ∧

432.38 shouldn't *A,E*] shouldnt

432.39 smile, *A,E*] ~,,

434.4 is *A,E*] in

*434.5 us *A,E*] it

435.10 granite-like *A,E*] ~ ∧ ~

435.25 cage.* *A,E* [has¹]] ~. ∧

435.36–39*fn* *The . . . him. *A,E*] [not present]

436.19 O.B., *A,E*] O.B. ∧

436.34 ferreting *A,E*] furretting

437.12 Oxford . . . for *A,E*] Oxford; for

437.14 Cambridge . . . but *A,E*] Cambridge, but

438.8 *Greek View of Life A,E*] "Greek View of Life"

440.3 Civil War *A,E*] civil war

442.2 many-sided, *A,E*] many-sided ∧

442.25 Liberal *A,E*] liberal

443.7 practise *A,E*] practice

444.29 *Wissenschaften A,E*] *Wissensschaften*

445.7 sonnets: *A,E*] ~,:

445.8 *true A,E*] ~.

445.28 all-comprehensive *A,E*] ~ ∧ ~

447.1 XXVII *CE*] *3*

448.2 fascinate *A,E*] fascinates

448.10 picturesque *A,E*] pisturesque

450.13 reexamine *A,E*] reexamined

450.20 cross-legged *A,E*] cross-ledged

450.36 tedious, *A,E*] ~ ∧

451.24 exigencies *A,E*] exigences

451.32 Pompeii *A,E*] Pompei

452.21 middle-aged *A,E*] ~ ∧ ~

453.12 vague, *A,E*] ~ ∧

453.18 not, *A,E*] ~ ∧

453.18 philosophers, *A,E*] ~ ∧

454.22 connoisseur *A,E*] connaisseur

454.28 Moreover *A,E*] Moreoer

455.12 than it *A,E*] than than ~

455.25 day, *A,E*] ~ ∧

456.9 town. *A,E*] ~,

456.16 Agrigentum *A,E*] Agrigentium

456.34 archeologist, *A,E*] ~ ∧

457.5 *Laws E*] Laws

457.11 *Crète, CE*] ~ ∧

458.26 Denderah *A,E*] Dendarah

458.29 Denderah *A,E*] Dendarah

458.29 late *A,E*] ~,

458.30 perhaps), *A,E*] ~) ∧

458.33 mannerisms *A,E*] manerisms

459.5 Arab *A,E*] arab

459.25 architecture. *A,E*] ~.,

460.4–5 then (1905) still *A,E*] then still

460.22 West *A,E*] west

461.25 cleft *A,E*] clelft

461.36 ecclesiastical *A,E*] ecclesiastial

464.10 tread *A,E*] tred

465.5 Beirut *A,E*] Bairut

465.27 gargoyle *A,E*] gargoile

465.37 model, *A,E*] ~ ∧

466.20MH Impressions *CE*] Impresions

466.31 had been *A,E*] had had been

466.39 chamber *A,E*] chambre

469.1 XXVIII *CE*] 4

470.1 yet *A,E*] yet,

470.16 Co. *A*] C͞o

470.33 lady-loves *A*] ~ ∧ ~

470.36–37 in, in *A*] ~ ∧ ~

470.37 cases, *CE*] ~ ∧

470.38 love-affair *A*] ~ ∧ ~

471.14 boarding-house *A,E*] ~ ∧ ~

472.17 believed *A,E*] believe

472.20 name), *A*] ~) ∧

472.31 thirty, *A,E*] ~ ∧

473.30*fn* J'aime. *CE*] ~!

473.30*fn* qu'au moment *CE*] qu'en disant
473.31*fn* moi-même *E*] moimême
473.33*fn* Ma *CE*] Une
473.34*fn* des vengeances célestes *CE*] d'une vengeance céleste
473.35*fn* détestes *CE*] déteste
473.39*fn* hair. *CE*] ~:
473.40*fn* Faibles *CE*] Vains
473.41*fn* toi-même *E*] toimême
475.7 profited *A,E*] profitted
476.33 afterwards, *A,E*] ~;
477.20 established *A*] ~,
479.29 her. *A,E*] ~ ˄
479.33 *Elizabeth and Her German Garden.* *A,E*] "Elizabeth and her German Garden."
479.35-36 *Elizabeth and Her German Garden* *A,E*] "Elizabeth and her German Garden"
479.40 *Caravaners* *A,E*] *Caravanners*
480.28 love-affair *A,E*] ~ ˄ ~
481.34 grown-up *A,E*] ~ ˄ ~
481.39 *tête-à-tête* *A,E*] ~ ˄ ~ ˄ ~
482.7 bigoted *A,E*] bigotted
482.14 freethinker *A,E*] free thinker
483.7 end, *A,E*] ~ ˄
484.25 her. It *A,E*] ~, ~
485.4 preoccupied *A,E*] pre-occupied
485.20 now? *A,E*] ~,
485.21 love-affair *CE*] ~ ˄ ~
485.39*fn* *Cf.*"Farewell to England" *CE*] Cf. *Farewell to England*
485.39*fn* end. *CE*] ~ ˄
487.1 XXIX *CE*] 5
487.22 alpaca *A,E*] alpacca
487.26 together, *A,E*] ~,,
488.27 sixpence *A,E*] six pence
489.9 Market Street *E*] ~-~
*490.17 no, no *A,E*] ~ ˄ ~
490.25 hot water *A,E*] ~-~
490.26 Sybarite *CE*] sybarite
490.39 nuns' *CE*] nun's
491.33 Campagna *E*] Campania
493.13 shrubbery *A,E*] shubbery
493.21 Gothic *CE*] gothic
494.22 Bicester *E*] Bicister
495.19 Middle Ages *A,E*] middle ages
495.20 pre-Raphaelite *A,E*] preraphaelite
495.31 *tío CE*] tio
496.3 "Do *A,E* [has single instead of double quotation marks]] '''~
496.4 Waggett, *A,E*] ~ ˄

496.37 life,[1] *A,E*] ~ ˄
497.5 artificiality, *A,E*] ~ ˄
497.19 Catholicism *A,E*] Catholiscism
497.36 Wolvercote *E*] Wolvercott
498.17-18 incongruous *A,E*] incongrouous
499.34 Urquhart *A*] Urckhart
500.23 eyes, *A,E*] ~ ˄
501.11 cadaverous *A,E*] little
501.18 drawing-room *E*] ~ ˄ ~
501.34 daresay *A,E*] dare say
501.39 blue-sea *CE*] ~ ˄ ~
503.11 also, *A,E*] ~;
505.1 XXX *CE*] 6
505.10 Poet Laureate *E*] poet laureate
506.8 Room *A,E*] room
506.11 *tête-à-tête E*] tête-à-tête
506.13 College *A,E*] ~,
506.17 well-established *A,E*] ~ ˄ ~
506.39 side. *A,E*] ~ ˄
507.3 there *A,E*] ~,
507.30 Magdalen *E*] Magdalene
507.35 inveigled *A,E*] enveigled
508.12 Shakespeare's *A,E*] Shakespear's
509.16 settle *A,E*] settled
509.36 mother, *A,E*] ~ ˄
509.37 death, *A,E*] ~ ˄
512.29 works, *A,E*] ~ ˄
*515.19-27 to . . . said *A,E*] to Elizabeth, he could have said
515.28 But soon *she A,E*] But *she*
517.17 *Classics A,E*] *Clasics*
517.17 school *A,E*] School
518.1 *in him A,E*] to him
518.4 him; and *F3, F4,A,E*] him; I was only recognising the existence of a conflict that I had foreseen to be inevitable. He knew this perfectly in his heart of hearts; and
518.9 asked *A,E*] asking
518.10 replied, *CE*] ~ ˄
*518.12 there. I *A,E*] there. On the Saturday afternoon I
519.39 *Chute A,E*] *Chûte*
520.1 went, *A,E*] ~ ˄
520.1 related, *A,E*] ~ ˄
520.18 couldn't *A,E*] couldnt
520.31 4,000 *CE*] 4000
520.36 Oh *A,E*] oh
521.14 *Scepticism . . . Faith A,E*] "~"
521.26-27 the heretics *A,E*] the the heretics
521.39 The *CE*] the

523.9 "Your *A,E*] ˄ ~
523.35 moral, *A,E*] ~ ˄
525.1 XXXI *CE*] 7
525.11 America, *A,E*] ~ ˄
525.13 acquaintances, *A,E*] ~,,
525.21 months' *A,E*] ~ ˄
526.24 everything was perceived by them,
   everything *A,E*] everything perceived,
   everything
527.9 me *A,E*] ~,
528.15 *a priori A,E*] a priori
531.25 unannounced *A,E*] un unanounced
531.25 liberty. *A*] ~. ˄
*531.36–38*fn* * . . . veniam . . . *finem*. *CE*]
   [not present]
531.27 No. *A,E*] no.
532.13 *pulchra A,E*] *pulchrâ*
532.33 Spanish or French or even Latin *A,E*]
   Spanish or even Latin
533.22 museums *A,E*] Museums
533.26 pavilions *A,E*] pavillions
533.26 Michaelangelo *CE*] Michael Angelo
533.40 Michaelangelo's *CE*] Michael
   Angelo's
535.12 loved, *A,E*] ~ ˄
535.29 essences *A,E*] essenes
537.1 XXXII *CE*] 8
537.10 them. *At,A,E*] ~ ˄
537.17 aerial *At,A,E*] aereal
537.19–20 blue-sea *At,E*] ~ ˄ ~
537.28 everything *At,A,E*] every thing
538.29 particular *At,A,E*] particularly
539.5 incarnate, *At,A,E*] ~ ˄
539.27 vocation, *At,A,E*] ~ ˄
540.37 These *At,A,E*] There
540.38 Variety *At,A,E*] Variaty
542.17 mythological *At,A,E*] mytholigal
543.9 practising *A,E*] practicing
543.16 good to *A,E*] good—to
545.1 Cape *At,A,E*] cape
546.7 Greek *At,A,E*] Greeks
547.14 glimpses *At,A,E*] glimpes

Report of Line-End Hyphenation

I. Copy-Text List

The following are the editorially established forms of possible compounds which were hyphenated at the ends of lines in the copy-text (i.e., the holograph manuscript).

3.12 grandparents		49.15 self-defence	
5.9 cockle-shell		53.11 family-picture	
6.11 Free-mason		57.7 dovetailing	
6.24 grandfather		58.12 brother-in-law	
7.5 well-rooted		64.5 lady-gossips	
8.28 self-reliant		65.2 banking-house	
13.37 field-marshal		69.8 money-matters	
16.15 workmanlike		69.30 water-side	
19.19 supernatural		71.38 thirty-four	
20.15 unconscious		74.10 side-whiskers	
23.10MH Anglomaniac		82.30 step-mother	
23.15 quarter-deck		86.36 overcome	
24.23 mankind		89.7 outlasted	
24.31 well-dressed		91.7 commonplace	
25.34 semicircular		97.11 ne'er-do-wells	
26.21 love-making		98.26 grab-bag	
27.7 old-fashioned		100.6MH Market-days	
27.25 semi-blindness		100.35 threshing-ground	
29.20 singing-lessons		100.37 market-towns	
29.21 half-understand		101.30 snowflakes	
30.2 pruning-hook		102.18 overshadowed	
30.20 half-naked		104.36 table-land	
31.6MH old-fashioned		105.4 brother-in-law's	
32.40 commonplace		105.25 mid-summer	
33.4 self-evident		105.30MH brother-in-law's	
35.7 grandfather		105.37 brother-in-law's	
35.24 grandfather		106.9 multi-form	
35.38 sailing-vessel		106.16 hiding-place	
37.32 shoulder-blades		106.17 well-known	
38.37 love-making		118.3MH stage-setting	
40.23 bridegroom		119.6 guide-book	
40.31 background		123.12MH mankind	
40.33 thirty-second		124.2 outright	
41.3MH first-born		133.13 dining-room	
41.20 womankind		138.12 apartment-houses	
46.14 out-of-focus		139.34 bath-room	
47.17 brother-in-law		140.20MH non-Freudian	

141.30 sitting-room
143.1 churchyard
149.37MH Schoolhouse
150.15 ill-lighted
150.17 overshadowed
150.28 nailed-hoofed
150.33MH school-teacher's
151.32 headmaster
153.1 down-flowings
157.33 Headmaster
163.40 super-abundant
167.3 poverty-stricken
168.30 prize-poem
174.36 congressman
175.4 second class
175.40 Lieutenant-Colonel
179.17 bedroom
179.23 undergraduate's
180.16 pocket-money
180.17 money-present
182.32 bathroom
183.23 hip-bath
183.33 working-people's
184.24 window-seats
185.3MH outlook
186.13 willy-nilly
186.23 stable-yard
186.29 commonplace
187.34 over-intellectualized
188.36 lady-like
191.2MH after-dinner
196.22 nightmares
198.31 Englishman's
199.24 nutshell
205.6 grandmother
205.39 overlooked
206.27 ill-furnished
207.11MH small-pox
207.25 overshadowing
207.37 northeastern
212.39 seasickness
216.23 everything
218.36 Michaelangelo's
219.25 landlady
222.26MH everything
224.23 mother-in-law's
225.28 pre-Raphaelite
226.34 flower-pots
239.36MH life-long
248.23MH non-affectionate
253.27 land-lady

256.13 sky-blue
256.39 twenty-four
260.18 all-embracing
262.5 half-mental
262.12 starting-point
263.12 overcoming
264.5 thirty-third
269.21 well-set-up
269.28 semicircle
269.36 fairyland
272.25 by-gone
277.22 well-known
278.35 commonplace
285.2 Englishmen
288.18 handwriting.
288.34MH Midshipman
295.6 semicircle
299.33 commonplace
302.38MH twenty-one
304.5 all-mocking
310.26 overpoweringly
312.15MH inland
322.15 well-turned
324.36 well-being
325.33 strawberries
326.8 horse-back
327.37 ill-natured
331.34 dining-room
332.3MH Tête-à-têtes
336.20 seventy-seven
337.13 dressing-room
341.3MH grandson
343.5 dining-room
344.21MH grandson
346.9 undergraduate
346.12 background
346.15MH grandson
354.36 dining-room
354.40 flat-bottomed
355.6 note-paper
355.23MH Small-Boys'
356.40 well-built
361.36MH Match-making
362.15MH uprooted
363.7 uprooted
363.32 errand-boy
367.14 half-bottle
373.11 commonplaces
374.28MH self-made
375.4MH extraordinary
375.7 eyelashes

376.29 Steamship
379.16 love-affair
380.1 good-fellowship
384.35 football
385.5 self-reliance
385.20MH Mammon-worship
391.2 undergraduates.
391.12 rethink
391.19 undergraduates
394.20 revisit
394.29 undergraduates
395.1MH Assistant-Professor
396.25 object-lesson
402.8 quicksands
407.38 undergraduates
410.35 Whoop-her-up!
421.19 ill-bred
424.30 step-mother
424.37 step-mother
435.35 club-footed
436.28 breeding-holes
437.7MH northeastern
438.11 super-sensitive
441.35 outdoor
442.3 best-educated
442.26 anti-military
442.26 anti-clerical
444.6 clear-headed
448.8 picture-books
451.6 middle-aged
451.22MH curtain-raiser
452.32 self-satisfaction

455.5 country-like
455.12 short-lived
459.25 mankind
461.19 offshoots
465.12 foreground
466.12 foreground
467.11 loop-line
469.7 hedgerows
470.11 modest-looking
480.16 indoors
484.2 *hors-d'oeuvre*
490.18 ghost-like
490.26 thermos-bottle
496.25 elsewhere
510.28 high-stepping
512.16 puppet-show
518.16 schoolhouse
519.33 undergraduate
523.32 Englishman
525.3MH *Wanderjahre*
525.29MH Headquarters
526.22 nearsightedness
527.11MH Anglophobia
533.7 pre-Raphaelism
539.29MH Landlord
539.34 well-grounded
540.28 commonplace
541.7 self-knowledge
543.4MH self-knowledge
544.5MH coexists
546.15 mankind
546.22MH earthquakes

II. Critical Edition List

In quotations from the present critical edition, no line-end hyphens are to be retained except the following.

8.1 home-coming
8.28 self-reliant
17.6 self-assertion
26.21 love-making
41.7 blue-eyed
45.20 window-panes
46.11 water-colourish
48.15 brother-in-law
55.26 one-windowed
57.7 tea-tables

65.38 pet-name
72.35 well-bred
74.25 well-meaning
80.33 billiard-room
83.22 well-off
85.27 concert-halls
86.2 self-banished
86.16 well-informed
91.20 boarding-house
100.9 checker-board

100.19 clod-coloured
105.4 brother-in-law's
105.30MH brother-in-law's
106.17 well-known
107.36 bull-ring
116.15 baby-brother
118.3MH stage-setting
121.22 cow-bells
122.4 well-filled
129.37 sailor-hat
130.17 dining-room
132.30 fifty-five
137.31 cross-street
139.34 bath-room
141.37 study-hour
150.33MH school-teacher's
150.35 shabby-genteel
167.9 willy-nilly
182.31 week-end
184.26 chimney-stack
184.33 "bed-sitting-room"
202.11 brother-in-law
202.32 near-sighted
210.35 non-commissioned
225.39 "bird-witted"
237.9 stepping-stones
238.23 Mammon-worshippers
240.30 good-looking
245.28 servant-girl
248.23MH non-affectionate
256.12 many-coloured
268.2 well-spoken
269.4 Law-courts
269.11MH boarding-house
270.23 well-varnished
283.39 pre-Raphaelite
287.9 better-known
288.29 motor-busses
291.16 steel-blue
302.27 death-beds
302.38MH twenty-one
303.24 self-satisfied
315.18 ash-heaps
323.32 shop-keeper
324.17 banking-house
326.1 thirty-six
326.22 step-daughter
329.36 step-daughter
330.27MH brother-in-law's
335.6 twenty-seven
337.28 living-room

348.36 well-bred
349.14 golden-red
356.13 right-about-face
359.23 living-room
365.37 dinner-table
366.14 working-girl's
366.17 palm-trees
375.31 well-chosen
376.7 lecture-room
382.23 hunting-songs
384.23 step-motherly
385.20MH Mammon-worship
395.1MH Assistant-Professor
401.27 self-interrupted
406.7 pigeon-hole
420.11MH self-knowledge
425.4 self-esteem
432.30 statue-columns
435.8 amber-like
439.36 ultra-empirical
450.30 story-teller
451.26 mid-winter
455.13 poet-philosopher
456.11 sea-walls
466.13 middle-aged
495.23 picture-dealer
500.26 nice-looking
517.30 love-affairs
519.34 re-read
520.33 operating-theatre
526.5 pied-à-terre
526.31 twenty-seven
527.26 money-loving
531.3 well-paved
537.19 blue-sea
542.18 self-contradictions
543.4MH self-knowledge
543.28 far-seeing

LIST OF SUBSTANTIVE VARIANTS

This list is a historical record of the substantive variants in the authorized forms of Santayana's autobiography, including the fair-copy holograph manuscript and all printed forms published during Santayana's lifetime. Copy-text readings are listed to the left of the lemma bracket; variant readings are listed to the right. (In the few instances where a Critical Edition reading [constituting emendation of the copy-text] differs from both the copy-text reading and that of any published form, the Critical Edition reading is situated to the left of the lemma bracket, preceding the copy-text reading, in order to provide a reference to the text. In some instances the works cited to the left of the lemma bracket have identical substantive readings but differ in accidentals. This is indicated by the bracketed remark "[. . . substantive reading same as . . .]".

1 I *CE; George Santayana / Persons & Places: / Fragments of / Autobiography MS1*] PERSONS AND PLACES / *MEMORIES OF / CHILDHOOD AND YOUTH* / BY / GEORGE SANTAYANA *P;* PERSONS / and / PLACES / *The Background of My Life* / BY / GEORGE SANTAYANA *A;* PERSONS AND PLACES / *The Background of My Life* / By / GEORGE SANTAYANA *E*

3.1–3 Fragments of Autobiography / I / My Place, Time, and Ancestry *CE; Fragments / of / Autobiography / I / My Place Time & Ancestry MS1*] PERSONS AND PLACES / *Time, Place, and Parents* / *by* GEORGE SANTAYANA *At;* CHAPTER I / TIME, PLACE AND ANCESTRY *P,A;* I TIME, PLACE AND ANCESTRY *E*

3.15 Santayana and Doña *MS1,P,A,E*] Santayana, and his half-sister, Doña *At*

3.16 Carrasco *MS1*] Cabrasco *At,P,A,E*

3.18 duties".① *MS1*] ~." [superscript numeral omitted] *At,P,A,E*

3.19–35, 4.28–31*fn* Don . . . (rubricado) *MS1*] [omitted] *At,P,A,E*

4.2–14 Where . . . society. *MS1* [*P, A* and *E* substantive reading same as *MS1.*]] [omitted] *At*

4.21 Glasgow. They were *MS1*] Glasgow, were *At,P,A,E*

4.21 were secretly *MS1*] were in fact secretly *At,P,A,E*

4.25–5.9 Not . . . precipice. *MS1* [*P, A,* and *E* substantive reading same as *MS1.*]] [omitted] *At*

5.9 Now *MS1,P,A,E*] For *At*

5.15 My grandfather *MS1,P,A,E*] My maternal grandfather *At*

5.16 Reus, of *MS1,P,A,E*] Reus, in Catalonia, of *At*

5.17–21 In . . . London." *MS1* [*P, A,* and *E* substantive readings same as *MS1.*]] [omitted] *At*

5.25 *Lebensraum MS1*] territory *At,P,A,E*

5.34–6.9 The . . . that *MS1,P,A,E*] [omitted] *At*

6.10 monk . . . became *MS1* [*P, A,* and *E* substantive readings same as *MS1.*]] monk, became *At*

6.19–23 In . . . solving. *MS1,P,A,E*] [omitted] *At*

6.24 One . . . my *MS1,P,A,E*] I do not know why my *At*

6.25 and *MS1,P,A,E*] or *At*

6.25–36 Mahon . . . climate. *MS1* [*P, A,* and *E* readings same as *MS1,* except for variants listed below.]] [omitted] *At*

6.28 these *MS1*] those *P,A,E*

6.35 government and art may *MS1*] government may *P,A,E*

6.35 and his heart *MS1*] and heart *P,A,E*

7.1–7 virtue. With slavery? Perhaps . . .
freedom. Be that as it may, José *MS1* [*P*,
A, and *E* substantive readings same as
MS1.]] virtue. ¶ José *At*

7.9 as florid *MS1*] as a florid *At,P,A,E*

7.17–40*fn*, 8.35–39*fn* The . . . State. *MS1* [*P*,
A and *E* readings same as *MS1*, except
for variants listed below.]] [omitted] *At*

8.39 (Unintelligable Signature) Secretary of
State *MS1*] (Unintelligible Signature)
Secretary of State P; John Forsyth, *Secretary
of State A,E*

8.39 X Seal. *MS1*] (SEAL) *P,A,E*

8.1–30.2 An . . . pruning-hook. *MS1* [*P*, *A*,
and *E* readings same as *MS1*, except for
variants listed below.]] [omitted] *At*

8.23 this *MS1*] her official *P,A,E*

11.1 II / *My Father MS1*] 4 [section number]
At; CHAPTER II / MY FATHER *P*;
CHAPTER II / *MY FATHER A*; II MY
FATHER *E*

11.3–12.12 The . . . *sento. MS1* [*P*, *A*, and *E*
readings same as *MS1*, except for variants
listed below.]] [omitted] *At*

11.3 surname *MS1*] name *P,A,E*

11.3MH Origin . . . Santayana [marginal
heading] *MS1*] [omitted] *P,A,E* (*Similar*
11.6MH; 12.13MH; 12.36MH; 13.28MH;
14.12MH; 14.38MH; 15.38MH; 16.36MH;
17.33MH; 18.32MH; 19.9MH; 20.1MH;
20.28MH; 21.16MH; 22.31MH; 23.9MH;
23.26MH; 24.12MH; 24.34MH; 26.3MH;
26.17MH; 26.26MH; 27.7MH; 29.3MH;
30.3MH; 31.6MH; 31.17MH; 31.37MH;
32.30MH; 33.9MH; 34.3MH; 34.24MH;
35.35MH; 36.20MH; 36.34MH; 37.27MH;
38.27MH; 39.27MH; 40.30MH; 41.3MH;
42.8MH; 42.27MH; 43.36MH; 44.8MH;
45.13MH; 46.15MH; 46.38MH; 47.14MH;
48.6MH; 49.21MH; 50.1MH; 65.4MH;
66.9MH; 67.8MH; 67.11MH; 68.12MH;
68.14MH; 69.4MH; 70.1MH; 70.23MH;
71.8MH; 72.10MH; 73.3MH; 73.30MH;
74.16MH; 75.9MH; 77.3MH; 77.24MH;
78.9MH; 79.9MH; 80.8MH; 80.26MH;
81.18MH; 82.4MH; 83.1MH; 83.37MH;
84.19MH; 84.39MH; 85.37MH; 86.8MH;
86.27MH; 87.3MH; 87.30MH; 88.22MH;
89.15MH; 90.6MH; 90.30MH; 91.24MH;
91.36MH; 92.14MH; 92.31MH; 93.16MH;
94.1MH; 94.26MH; 95.27MH; 97.3MH;
97.24MH; 98.11MH; 98.30MH; 99.15MH;
100.6MH; 101.1MH; 101.37MH;
102.32MH; 103.27MH; 104.15MH;
105.17MH; 105.30MH; 106.19MH;
107.23MH; 108.17MH; 109.26MH;
110.20MH; 111.15MH; 112.1MH;
115.12MH; 116.10MH; 117.1MH;
118.1MH; 118.21MH; 119.20MH;
120.27MH; 121.20MH; 122.13MH;
123.12MH; 124.12MH; 125.9MH;
125.21MH; 127.3MH; 127.25MH;
128.16MH; 129.20MH; 130.13MH;
130.32MH; 131.15MH; 131.33MH;
132.34MH; 133.32MH; 134.13MH;
137.3MH; 137.27MH; 138.22MH;
139.36MH; 140.20MH; 141.10MH;
141.28MH; 141.30MH; 142.33MH;
143.18MH; 145.3MH; 146.15MH;
146.31MH; 147.23MH; 147.38MH;
148.16MH; 148.31MH; 149.21MH;
149.36MH; 150.33MH; 151.26MH;
152.19MH; 153.3MH; 153.23MH;
154.16MH; 154.35MH; 155.14MH;
156.9MH; 156.28MH; 157.17MH;
158.1MH; 159.3MH; 159.25MH;
161.1MH; 161.30MH; 162.21MH;
163.8MH; 163.24MH; 165.7MH;
165.28MH; 166.18MH; 167.12MH;
168.12MH; 169.17MH; 170.1MH;
170.18MH; 170.31MH; 179.3MH;
180.3MH; 180.29MH; 181.18MH;
182.9MH; 182.24MH; 183.1MH;
183.3MH; 183.17MH; 183.37MH;
184.23MH; 185.3MH; 185.21MH;
186.19MH; 187.10MH; 187.20MH;
188.22MH; 189.11MH; 189.21MH;
190.11MH; 190.30MH; 191.1MH;
191.20MH; 192.9MH; 192.29MH;
195.9MH; 196.1MH; 196.26MH;
197.26MH; 197.36MH; 198.20MH;
199.14MH; 199.29MH; 200.11MH;
200.34MH; 201.25MH; 202.10MH;
202.20MH; 203.14MH; 204.17MH;
204.32MH; 206.1MH; 206.34MH;
207.10MH; 207.20MH; 208.3MH;
209.15MH; 210.1MH; 211.8MH;
211.22MH; 212.12MH; 215.3MH;
215.15MH; 216.10MH; 217.10MH;
217.31MH; 218.17MH; 219.15MH;
220.8MH; 221.13MH; 221.36MH;
222.26MH; 223.6MH; 223.17MH;

224.17MH; 224.35MH; 225.20MH;
225.37MH; 226.7MH; 226.28MH;
229.3MH; 229.23MH; 230.4MH;
231.1MH; 231.23MH; 231.35MH;
232.13MH; 232.36MH; 233.34MH;
234.30MH; 236.3MH; 236.30MH;
238.3MH; 238.30MH; 239.16MH;
239.35MH; 240.20MH; 241.11MH;
242.8MH; 242.36MH; 243.30MH;
245.5MH; 246.28MH; 247.31MH;
248.6MH; 248.23MH; 253.3MH;
253.12MH; 254.1MH; 254.20MH;
254.29MH; 255.25MH; 256.8MH;
256.22MH; 257.7MH; 257.34MH;
258.4MH; 258.22MH; 258.26MH;
259.1MH; 259.18MH; 260.31MH;
261.1MH; 261.11MH; 262.10MH;
262.27MH; 263.1MH; 263.31MH;
264.1MH; 265.6MH; 267.3MH;
267.29MH; 268.23MH; 269.9MH;
270.5MH; 270.37MH; 271.28MH;
271.38MH; 272.35MH; 273.25MH;
274.13MH; 275.20MH; 276.3MH;
276.16MH; 276.36MH; 277.17MH;
278.8MH; 279.13MH; 280.17MH;
281.5MH; 281.30MH; 282.6MH;
282.29MH; 283.19MH; 283.32MH;
284.8MH; 284.31MH; 285.19MH;
286.15MH; 286.30MH; 287.9MH;
288.4MH; 288.34MH; 289.5MH;
291.3MH; 291.15MH; 292.17MH;
292.31MH; 293.22MH; 294.10MH;
295.1MH; 295.24MH; 296.5MH;
296.20MH; 297.30MH; 298.6MH;
298.35MH; 299.22MH; 300.1MH;
300.22MH; 300.30MH; 301.13MH;
302.3MH; 302.20MH; 302.38MH;
304.15MH; 304.32MH; 306.25MH;
307.1MH; 308.1MH; 308.26MH;
309.28MH; 310.6MH; 310.27MH;
310.38MH; 311.20MH; 312.12MH;
312.36MH; 313.19MH; 314.1MH;
314.15MH; 315.3MH; 316.1MH;
316.25MH; 317.22MH; 318.19MH;
318.32MH; 319.8MH; 319.38MH;
321.3MH; 321.20MH; 322.5MH;
322.37MH; 323.16MH; 323.30MH;
324.13MH; 324.23MH; 325.1MH;
325.19MH; 326.3MH; 326.21MH;
327.16MH; 328.19MH; 329.6MH;
329.17MH; 330.13MH; 330.26MH;

331.8MH; 332.3MH; 332.20MH;
333.23MH; 334.1MH; 335.1MH;
335.21MH; 335.33MH; 336.20MH;
337.1MH; 338.1MH; 341.3MH;
342.12MH; 343.3MH; 344.3MH;
344.21MH; 344.38MH; 345.25MH;
345.34MH; 346.15MH; 347.11MH;
347.33MH; 348.16MH; 348.35MH;
349.19MH; 350.10MH; 350.37MH;
351.14MH; 351.34MH; 353.3MH;
354.12MH; 355.1MH; 355.23MH;
356.22MH; 357.6MH; 357.30MH;
358.1MH; 358.32MH; 359.8MH;
359.21MH; 360.27MH; 361.1MH;
361.36MH; 362.15MH; 363.11MH;
363.25MH; 364.6MH; 364.25MH;
365.1MH; 365.26MH; 365.32MH;
366.9MH; 366.27MH; 367.34MH;
367.37MH; 368.26MH; 371.3MH;
371.30MH; 373.5MH; 373.23MH;
374.6MH; 374.28MH; 375.4MH;
375.13MH; 375.36MH; 376.33MH;
377.20MH; 378.25MH; 379.14MH;
379.37MH; 380.21MH; 381.3MH;
381.11MH; 381.30MH; 382.37MH;
383.13MH; 383.32MH; 384.19MH;
384.29MH; 385.19MH; 386.3MH;
386.29MH; 387.1MH; 387.28MH;
388.7MH; 389.3MH; 390.3MH;
391.8MH; 391.26MH; 391.37MH;
392.26MH; 393.10MH; 393.26MH;
394.7MH; 394.24MH; 395.1MH;
395.14MH; 395.34MH; 396.25MH;
397.7MH; 397.27MH; 398.1MH;
399.1MH; 399.34MH; 400.17MH;
401.1MH; 401.14MH; 402.8MH;
402.35MH; 403.16MH; 403.34MH;
404.32MH; 405.8MH; 405.34MH;
406.24MH; 407.1MH; 407.27MH;
408.14MH; 408.36MH; 409.27MH;
410.9MH; 411.10MH; 411.33MH;
412.16MH; 412.33MH; 413.29MH;
414.19MH; 417.3MH; 417.8MH;
417.29MH; 418.9MH; 418.34MH;
419.23MH; 420.10MH; 420.13MH;
421.5MH; 422.5MH; 422.14MH;
423.1MH; 423.20MH; 423.38MH;
424.18MH; 425.22MH; 426.3MH;
427.1MH; 427.15MH; 428.7MH;
428.26MH; 431.3MH; 431.20MH;
432.9MH; 432.28MH; 433.8MH;

434.3MH; 434.21MH; 434.34MH;
435.15MH; 435.26MH; 436.23MH;
437.6MH; 438.4MH; 439.1MH;
439.29MH; 440.19MH; 440.35MH;
441.24MH; 442.12MH; 442.30MH;
443.1MH; 444.1MH; 444.18MH;
445.20MH; 447.3MH; 448.6MH;
449.1MH; 449.24MH; 450.1MH;
451.1MH; 451.20MH; 452.3MH;
452.17MH; 452.34MH; 453.30MH;
454.8MH; 454.30MH; 455.23MH;
456.32MH; 457.17MH; 457.35MH;
458.25MH; 459.1MH; 459.32MH;
460.10MH; 460.24MH; 461.23MH;
461.38MH; 462.17MH; 463.8MH;
464.18MH; 465.5MH; 465.23MH;
466.5MH; 466.20MH; 467.3MH;
469.3MH; 470.6MH; 470.30MH;
471.12MH; 472.8MH; 472.30MH;
473.11MH; 474.11MH; 474.14MH;
474.27MH; 476.10MH; 477.8MH;
477.34MH; 478.20MH; 479.1MH;
479.35MH; 480.4MH; 480.38MH;
481.21MH; 482.18MH; 482.37MH;
483.30MH; 484.16MH; 485.1MH;
485.13MH; 485.24MH; 487.13MH;
488.16MH; 489.17MH; 490.6MH;
491.3MH; 491.20MH; 492.6MH;
493.1MH; 493.28MH; 494.8MH;
494.29MH; 495.26MH; 496.16MH;
496.27MH; 497.7MH; 498.3MH;
499.11MH; 500.1MH; 501.5MH;
501.28MH; 502.21MH; 502.37MH;
505.3MH; 506.1MH; 506.37MH;
507.21MH; 508.31MH; 509.22MH;
510.3MH; 510.21MH; 511.28MH;
512.23MH; 513.26MH; 514.10MH;
514.36MH; 516.7MH; 516.21MH;
517.3MH; 517.26MH; 518.8MH;
519.6MH; 519.19MH; 520.8MH;
520.24MH; 521.5MH; 521.37MH;
522.27MH; 523.15MH; 523.36MH;
525.3MH; 525.27MH; 526.29MH;
527.11MH; 527.31MH; 528.3MH;
528.17MH; 529.5MH; 529.29MH;
530.6MH; 531.1MH; 531.26MH;
532.28MH; 533.12MH; 534.4MH;
534.35MH; 535.32MH; 537.4MH;
537.16MH; 538.20MH; 539.1MH;
539.8MH; 539.29MH; 540.9MH;
540.34MH; 541.20MH; 542.1MH;

542.26MH; 543.1MH; 543.14MH;
544.4MH; 544.23MH; 545.12MH;
546.3MH; 546.22MH)

11.4 from a *MS1*] from that of a *P,A,E*
11.10 variously *MS1*] obviously *P,A,E*
11.11 Iliana *MS1*] Lliana *P,A,E*
11.31–12.12 Through . . . *sento. MS1*]
[omitted] *P,A,E*
12.18 than of political dependence *MS1*]
than on love of political independence
At,P,A,E
12.18–19 author . . . My *MS1,P,A,E*] author
was a man of affairs, not an ecclesiastic.
My *At*
12.36–14.11 If . . . it. *MS1* [*P, A,* and *E*
readings same as *MS1*, except for variants
listed below.]] [omitted] *At*
13.20 No *MS1*] Nos *P,A,E*
13.29–31 Oriental, utterly contrary to the
venemous hatred and envy, lined with
ambition, of the democratic demagogue.
MS1] Oriental. *P,A,E*
13.36 (which . . . be) *MS1*] [omitted] *P,A,E,T*
13.37–38 them . . . me. *MS1*] them. *P,A,E,T*
14.1–2 equally . . . dew; *MS1*] sprinkled
over it like dew: *P,A,E,T*
14.12 This *MS1*] The *At,P,A,E*
14.15 not in the *MS1*] not the *At,P,A,E*
14.31–15.11 That . . . first. *MS1* [*P, A,* and *E*
readings same as *MS1*, except for variants
listed below.]] [omitted] *At*
14.31 not only *MS1*] [omitted] *P,A,E*
15.6 the *MS1*] a *P,A,E*
15.12–13 know first under what
schoolmaster *MS1,P,A,E*] know under
what schoolmaster first *At*
15.15 all *MS1*] [omitted] *At,P,A,E*
15.19–15.37 His . . . Seneca? *MS1* [*P, A,* and
E readings same as *MS1*, except for
variants listed below.]] [omitted] *At*
15.24 and the gifted *MS1*] and gifted *P,A,E*
16.5–14 In . . . Watteau. *MS1* [*P, A,* and *E*
readings same as *MS1*, except for variants
listed below.]] [omitted] *At*
16.12–13 eighteenth century sensuality of
the notion *MS1*] sensuality of the
eighteenth-century notion *P,A,E*
16.15 no *MS1*] not *At,P,A,E*
16.22 And I doubt *MS1,P,A,E*] I rather
doubt *At*
17.3–13 But . . . ideal. Not *MS1* [*P, A,* and *E*
readings same as *MS1*, except for variants
listed below.]] [omitted] ¶ Not *At*

17.13 disclosed *MS1*] discovered *P,A,E*
17.20-26 make . . . nature. He *MS1* [*P, A,* and *E* readings same as *MS1*, except for variants listed below.]] make. He *At*
17.25 so many *MS1*] many *P,A,E*
17.29 the *MS1*] an *At,P,A,E*
17.33-19.8 In . . . begun. *MS1* [*P, A,* and *E* readings same as *MS1*, except for variants listed below.]] [omitted] *At*
18.24 *molde* in black and white." *MS1*] *molde.*" *P,A,E*
18.34 his *MS1*] this *P,A,E*
19.10-13 His success as an official *MS1*] [omitted] *At,P,A,E*
19.18-21 Modesty . . . behaved. My *MS1,P,A,E*] [omitted] ¶ My *At*
19.25 general now in Spain again *MS1*] general, then in Spain again *At,P,A,E*
19.27-28 he . . . defeated. *MS1,P,A,E*] he was easily defeated and wounded. *At*
19.28 Now in *MS1*] In *At,P,A,E*
20.11-12 light . . . them *MS1*] the fact escapes them that light and shade or outlines in themselves are something *At,P,A,E*
20.28-21.15 My . . . waves. *MS1* [*P, A,* and *E* readings same as *MS1*, except for variants listed below.]] [omitted] *At*
20.28 have particularly *MS1*] particularly have *P,A,E*
21.1-15 anything . . . waves. *MS1*] anything. *P,A,E*
21.20 fifteen *MS1*] twelve *At,P,A,E*
21.22 (1887) *MS1*] 1883 *At,P,A,E*
21.25 of *MS1*] a *At,P,A,E*
21.28 my German *MS1*] my elementary German *At,P,A,E*
22.3-5 cut . . . have *MS1*] [omitted] *At,P,A,E*
22.8-9 especially when *MS1*] especially a few years later when *At,P,A,E*
22.9 it then would *MS1,P,A,E*] it would *At*
22.12 father or me *MS1*] father or my sisters or me *At,P,A,E*
22.21 No date *MS1,P,A,E*] *No date At*; [omitted] *T*
22.38-24.11 My . . . Remus. *MS1* [*P, A,* and *E* readings same as *MS1*, except for variants listed below.]] [omitted] *At*
23.3 He had lived *MS1,P,A,E*] We lived *T*
23.24 hands. "*¡Cuantos MS1*] hands, and asked the waitress for some soap. *¡Cuantos P,A,E*

23.25 exclaimed, how many requisites! *MS1*] exclaimed. How many requirements! *P,A*; (How many requirements!) *E*
24.1-2 conflicts rather than provoke them, but *MS1*] conflicts, but *P,A,E*
24.16 in the *MS1,At*] of the *P,A,E*
24.17-18 he had been when *MS1*] when he had been *At,P,A,E*
24.23 more *MS1*] else *At,P,A,E*
24.36-25.20 was . . . Station, *MS1* [*P, A,* and *E* readings same as *MS1*, except for variants listed below.]] [omitted] *At*
25.5 to Spain from Boston; anyhow *MS1*] from Boston to Spain. Anyhow *P,A*; from Boston to Spain. Anyhow, *E*
25.20 the Church and convent of *MS1,P,A*] the Church and Convent of *E*; the Convent of *At*
25.24 aunt, for *MS1*] aunt, and for *P,A,E*
25.29-26.2 This . . . composition. *MS1* [*P, A,* and *E* substantive readings same as *MS1*.]] [omitted] *At*
26.17-27.6 Going . . . Elvira. *MS1* [*P, A,* and *E* substantive readings same as *MS1*.]] [omitted] *At*
27.31 experience. Yet intelligence *MS1*] experience. Intelligence *P,A,E*; experience. ¶ Intelligence *At*
29.1-2 III / *My Mother MS1*] CHAPTER III / *MY MOTHER P,A*; III / MY MOTHER *E*
29.27 immediately *MS1*] presently *P,A,E*
30.3-4 appointment as consul in Barcelona lapsed *MS1*] appointment lapsed *At,P,A,E*
30.10 further *MS1,P,A,E*] farther *At*
30.16 daughter who *MS1,P*] daughter, who *A,E*; daughter,— my mother,—who *At*
30.20-23 The . . . now. *MS1,P,A,E*] [omitted] *At*
30.24-39 They . . . go. *MS1* [*P, A,* and *E* substantive readings same as *MS1*.]] [omitted] *At*
31.11-13 My mother . . . learned *MS1* [*P, A,* and *E* substantive readings same as *MS1*.]] My mother learned *At*
31.17-34.6 And . . . test. *MS1* [*P, A,* and *E* substantive readings same as *MS1*, except for variants listed below.]] [omitted] *At*
31.28-29 time . . . Had *MS1*] time. Had *P,A,E*
32.30 he *MS1*] her *P,A,E*
34.6 even going round *MS1,P,A,E*] even round *At*

34.9 departure, had reached *MS1,P,A,E*]
    departure, reached *At*

34.13-14 enjoyed some of the *MS1,P,A,E*]
    enjoyed the *At*

34.24-35.17 I . . . natives. *MS1* [*P*, *A*, and *E*
    substantive readings same as *MS1*, except
    for variants listed below.]] [omitted] *At*

34.29 devout *MS1*] devote *P,A,E*

34.34 nature, for *MS1,P,A,E*] nature (natives
    of Batang) for *T*

35.21-27 It . . . average. *MS1,P,A,E*]
    [omitted] *At*

35.29 of life *MS1*] of his life *At,P,A,E*

36.9 even from *MS1*] from even *At,P,A,E*

36.11-15 Although . . . it. *MS1,P,A,E*]
    [omitted] *At*

36.17 accident that I *MS1,P,A,E*] accident I
    At

36.18-19 Yet . . . quoted. *MS1,P,A,E*]
    [omitted] *At*

36.23 sent from *MS1*] sent out from *P,A,E*

36.24 in *MS1*] on *P,A,E*

36.35-37 Manila . . . was *MS1,P,A,E*]
    Manila, by the name of *At*

36.38-38.37 and . . . arranged. *MS1* [*P*, *A*,
    and *E* substantive readings same as *MS1*,
    except for variants listed below.]]
    [omitted] *At*

37.5 without distinction *MS1,A,E*] with
    distinction *P*

37.15 Scotch *MS1,P,A*] Scots *E*

38.7 that *MS1*] who *P,A,E*

38.10 night, in case of need, as an extra
    coverlet. *MS1*] night in case of need.
    P,A,E

38.19-20 novena, to confession and
    communion, punctually *MS1*] novena,
    punctually *P,A,E*

38.32 hats, the *MS1*] hats and the *P,A,E*

38.33 *Maria*, and the horses made water.
    MS1] *Maria*. *P,A,E*

38.40 and Juliet *MS1*] and a Juliet *At,P,A,E*

39.4 Iparraguirres. Victorina any *MS1,P,A,E*]
    Iparraguirres. Her special friend,
    Victorina Iparraguirre, any *At*

39.11 blue-eyed like herself, an *MS1*] blue-
    eyed, an *At,P,A,E*

39.35 Everybody, including the Archbishop
    MS1,P,A,E] ¶ Even the Archbishop *At*

40.1 principle *MS1*] principles *P,A,E*

40.4-13 I . . . children. *MS1* [*P*, *A*, and *E*
    substantive readings same as *MS1*.]]
    [omitted] *At*

40.13 simpler *MS1,P,A,E*] simple *At*

40.20 truly apostolic *MS1*] true Apostolic
    At,P,A,E

40.23 House *MS1,P,A,E*] firm *At*

40.26 ensign, borne to the frigate *MS1*]
    ensign, to the frigate *At,P,A,E*

40.28 jovial . . . there *MS1,P,A,E*] jovial,
    there *At*

40.32-33 for being the *MS1,P,A,E*] because
    it was the *At*

40.34 is *MS1,P,A,E*] was *At*

40.36 be some day *MS1,P*] some day be
    At,A,E

40.39 apt *MS1,P,A,E*] likely *At*

41.6 no longer could *MS1*] could no longer
    At,P,A,E

41.6 or could wound *MS1*] or wound
    At,P,A,E

41.8-9 hair . . . and *MS1,P,A,E*] hair; and *At*

41.11 calling their *MS1*] calling away their
    At,P,A,E

41.14 the two babies *MS1,P,A,E*] the babies
    At

41.17 as I have said, *MS1,P,A,E*] [omitted] *At*

41.20 womankind *MS1*] womenkind *At,P,A,E*

41.21-38 So . . . lead. *MS1* [*P*, *A*, and *E*
    substantive readings same as *MS1*.]]
    [omitted] *At*

42.4-26 There . . . death. *MS1* [*P*, *A*, and *E*
    substantive readings same as *MS1*, except
    for variants listed below.]] [omitted] *At*

42.6 worn *MS1,A,E*] worm *P*

42.39 home, expressing *MS1,P,A,E*] home to
    Boston, expressing *At*

42.40 in *MS1*] of *At,P,A,E*

42.40-43.1 She . . . children *MS1,P,A,E*] She
    bore children *At*

43.15-23 She . . . positivism. *MS1,P,A,E*]
    [omitted] *At*

43.39-40 their three little children *MS1*]
    their little children *At,P,A,E*

44.1-45.12 leave . . . Sunday. *MS1* [*P*, *A*,
    and *E* substantive readings same as *MS1*,
    except for variants listed below.]]
    [omitted] *At*

44.3-4 and even Niagara *MS1*] and Niagara
    P,A,E

44.10 very[2] *MS1*] same *P,A,E*

45.17 It *MS1,P,A,E*] Victor *At*

45.17 hotel that stood in Tremont
    MS1,P,A,E] hotel on Tremont *At*

45.31-36 Here . . . religion!" *MS1*] [omitted] *At,P,A,E*

45.37 certainly the aura *MS1*] the enlightened center *At,P,A*; the enlightened centre *E*

45.37 but *MS1*] and *At,P,A,E*

45.40 variously *MS1*] various *At,P,A,E*

46.7-14 saw . . . useless. *MS1*] saw. *At,P,A,E*

46.21-37 The . . . things. *MS1* [*P*, *A*, and *E* substantive readings same as *MS1*.]] [omitted] *At*

47.5 But my mother *MS1*] My mother, however, *At,P,A,E*

47.14-49.39 Yet . . . potatoe! *MS1* [*P*, *A*, and *E* substantive readings same as *MS1*, except for variants listed below.]] [omitted] *At*

47.14 this *MS1*] such a crisis *P,A,E*

47.22-23 usual civilities and the usual charities *MS1*] usual charities *P,A,E*

47.27 case *MS1,A,E*] cases *P*

47.34-35 of the Old Adam, of all earthly *MS1*] of all earthly *P,A,E*

47.37 the same *MS1*] a similar *P,A,E*

48.14 and *MS1*] or *P,A,E*

48.26 in her *MS1*] on her *P,A,E*

48.36-37 locutions I *MS1*] locutions, such as "make haste" instead of "hurry up," I *P,A,E*

49.13 Perhaps in Boston she *MS1*] Perhaps she *P,A,E*

49.19 elsewhere *MS1*] in some other place *P,A,E,T*

49.34 in *MS1*] on *P,A,E*

50.1 Madrid there *MS1,P,A,E*] Madrid, to which my mother returned four years later, there *At*

50.3 and who liked *MS1,At*] and also liked *P,A,E*

50.5 officials, at that moment, was *MS1,P,A,E*] officials was *At*

50.5 father. Don *MS1,P,A,E*] father. My mother's friends from Manilla, Don *At*

50.6 Victorina . . . knew *MS1,P,A,E*] Victorina, knew *At*

50.6-7 him . . . liked *MS1,P,A,E*] him. They liked *At*

50.7 liked for his *P,A,E*] liked his *At*

50.7 and for his *P,A,E*] and his *At*

50.17 illusion *MS1,At,P,A*] illusions *E*

50.20-28 I . . . love. *MS1* [*P*, *A*, and *E* substantive readings same as *MS1*.]] [omitted] *At*

50.28 external *MS1*] daemonic *At,P,A,E*

50.28-29 circumstances *MS1,P,A*] circumstance *E*

50.32-37 My . . . project. *MS1* [*P*, *A*, and *E* substantive readings same as *MS1*.]] [omitted] *At*

51.1-2 IV / *The Sturgises MS1*] CHAPTER IV / THE STURGISES *P*; CHAPTER IV / *THE STURGISES A*; IV THE STURGISES *E*

51.6 some *MS1*] two *P,A,E*

51.7 several *MS1*] five *P,A,E*

53.4 brilliant *MS1*] distinguished *P,A,E*

53.6-7 had lost those abilities. He *MS1*] no longer possessed those abilities. He *P,A,E*

53.9 nor *MS1*] or *P,A,E*

53.15 place *MS1*] lieu *P,A,E*

53.25 died in time scarcely to witness *MS1,P*] barely lived to experience *A,E*

54.12-13 certainly was *MS1*] was certainly *P,A,E*

54.26 I was 23 *MS1,P*] I twenty-three *A,E*

54.27 or else very *MS1,P*] or very *A,E*

54.40-55.1 had had a law-suit *MS1*] had a lawsuit *P,A,E*

55.6 a safe self-restrained *MS1*] a self-restrained *P,A,E*

55.25 always provided *MS1*] provided *P,A,E*

55.31 unintendedly *MS1*] unintentionally *P,A,E*

56.6 understand *MS1*] understood *P,A,E*

56.40 and of one's *MS1*] and one's *P,A,E*

57.25 them *MS1*] the Sturgises *P,A,E*

57.26 been *MS1*] become *P,A,E*

58.23-65.3 Decay . . . part. *MS1*] [omitted] *P,A,E*

65.7 branch, which *MS1*] branch. This *P,A,E*

65.19-21 me . . . disappointed *MS1*] me, perhaps in order not to count on too much and then be disappointed, seems to have been that I should be a simpleton too *P,A,E*

65.24-25 walk . . . he *MS1*] walk, he *P,A,E*

65.36 was *MS1*] were *P,A,E*

66.20 eyes *MS1*] faces *P,A,E*

66.23 with *The Red MS1*] to *The Scarlet P,A,E*

66.28-29 wooers . . . There *MS1*] wooers. There *P,A,E*

67.6-7 her . . . went *MS1*] her, at least in the mind of other people *P,A,E*

67.22 Ruskin and perpetrated *MS1*] Ruskin; it was he would built *P*; Ruskin; it was he who built *A,E*

67.27 but this *MS1*] but all this *P,A,E*

67.30 unmistable *MS1*] unmistakable *P*; unmistakably *A,E*

68.15 egotism *MS1*] caprice *P,A,E*

68.20 this *MS1*] thus *P,A,E*

68.30 beard is vulgar *MS1*] beard like Saint Peter's is vulgar *P,A,E,T*

69.16 1868 *MS1*] 1858 *P,A,E*

69.18 '60's *MS1*] '50's *P,A,E*

69.25 boarding and other houses *MS1*] boarding‸houses *P,A*; boarding-houses *E*

70.1-2 "Uncle . . . Grew *MS1*] some wiser friend *P,A,E*

70.23 1873 *MS1,P*] 1872 *A,E*

70.33-34 bed . . . and *MS1*] bed and *P,A,E*

70.38 was *MS1*] were *P,A,E*

71.2 London *MS1,P*] Chicago *A,E*

71.3-4 Boston, Chicago had had an even bigger fire *CE*; Boston, Chicago soon had a fire that beat it *MS1,P*] Chicago, Boston had had a more recent fire *A,E*

71.5-6 the era of an abominable architectural *CE*; the abominable era of an abominable architectural *MS1*] the era of an architectural *P,A,E*

71.7 artists: the scourge of Ruskinism. *MS1*] artists. *P,A,E*

71.8 1873 *MS1,P*] 1872 *A,E*

71.16 amount . . . to *MS1*] amount to *P,A,E*

71.21 all out of *MS1,A,E*] all of *P*

71.29-40 For . . . dollars. *MS1*] [omitted] *P,A,E*

71.40 That *MS1*] This *P,A,E*

72.1-2 came nominally to *MS1*] came to *P,A,E*

72.2-3 as . . . place. *MS1*] as a regular allowance. *P,A,E*

72.4-9 To . . . canvasses. *MS1*] [omitted] *P,A,E*

72.17 they both remained *MS1,P*] they remained *A,E*

72.18 64 and 69 respectively. *MS1*] 64 and 69, respectively. *P*; sixty-four and sixty-nine. *A,E*

72.23 and *MS1*] or *P,A,E*

73.2 on *MS1*] of *P,A,E*

73.14-16 religion . . . absurd. *MS1*] religion. *P,A,E,T*

73.20 and unreliable *MS1*] and considered unreliable *P,A,E*

73.30-76.10 I . . . intelligentzia. *MS1*] [omitted] *P,A,E*

77.1-2 V / My Sister Susana *CE*; V / My Sister Susana. *MS1*] CHAPTER V / MY SISTER SUSANA *P*; CHAPTER V / *MY SISTER SUSANA A*; V MY SISTER SUSANA *E*

77.18 be only fragmentary *MS1*] be fragmentary *P,A,E*

77.22 then tell *MS1*] tell then *P,A,E*

77.31 that local *MS1*] that in Boston, local *P,A,E*

80.3 towards Susana from the first. Susana *MS1*] towards Susana. Susana *P,A,E*

80.6 clutches *MS1*] snares *P,A,E*

80.14 comedy or even of mockery. *MS1*] comedy. *P,A,E*

80.34 stage to it. *MS1*] stage. *P,A,E*

81.10 impression *MS1*] impressions *P,A,E*

81.17 in *MS1*] at *P,A,E*

81.29 or of their *MS1,P*] or their *A,E*

81.40 and to protect *MS1*] and protect *P,A,E*

82.14 passing always conscientious *MS1*] passing conscientious *P,A,E*

82.24 this *MS1*] their *P,A,E*

82.29 by *MS1*] through *P,A,E*

82.37 but not the *MS1*] and never *P,A,E*

83.28-84.38 The . . . world. *MS1*] [omitted] *P,A,E*

84.39 foreign *MS1*] exotic *P,A,E*

85.3 [not present] *MS1*] I was not at home among them. *P,A,E*

85.3-85.17 There . . . hearts. *MS1*] [omitted] *P,A,E*

85.18-19 ladies . . . part *MS1*] ladies for the most part *P,A,E*

85.21-22 whose . . . dipping *MS1*] who had dipped *P,A,E*

85.23 learning *MS1*] learned *P,A,E*

85.24 studying *MS1*] studied *P,A,E*

85.24 then *MS1*] well *P,A,E*

85.34 meant *MS1,P,A,E*] means *T*

86.38 only loved *MS1*] loved only *P,A,E*

86.38 certainly was *MS1*] was certainly *P,A,E*

87.4 our own household *MS1*] our household *P,A,E*

87.6 any *MS1*] a *P,A,E*

87.8 and naturally *MS1,P*] and I naturally *A,E*

87.24 on my part *MS1*] in my case, *P,A,E*

87.32 those ways were *MS1*] those were *P,A,E*

88.12 will be only *MS1*] will only be *P,A,E*

88.26 sympathetic; for while *MS1*]
   sympathetic. While *P,A,E*
88.29 Susie" seemed *MS1*] Susie," his wife,
   seemed *P,A,E*
89.22 her family *MS1*] the family *P,A,E*
90.6-7 I . . . Roxbury. *MS1*] [omitted] *P,A,E*
90.13 by *MS1,P*] of *A,E*
90.15 injunction *MS1*] injunctions *P,A,E*
90.22-23 strange . . . she *MS1*] strange; she
   P,A,E
90.24-25 hostility . . . about. *MS1*] hostility.
   P,A,E
90.33 of Novices *MS1*] of the Novices *P,A,E*
90.35 nuns' *MS1*] nun's *P,A,E*
90.39 allowance *MS1*] allowances *P,A,E*
91.20-21 boarding-house in *MS1*] boarding-
   house at *P,E*; boarding͵house at *A*
91.31 trust my *MS1*] Trust that my *P*; trust
   that my *A,E*
92.6 house *MS1*] houses *P,A,E*
92.34 It *MS1*] This *P,A,E*
93.7 a totalitarian moral *MS1*] a moral *P,A,E*
93.20-21 she turned *MS1,A,E]* she had
   turned *P*
93.22 and was worried *MS1*] and worried
   P,A,E
93.28 sweet *MS1*] beneficent *P,A,E,T*
94.10 called the psyche *MS1,P,A,E*] called
   psyche *T*
94.12 accidental *MS1,P,A,E*] accident *T*
94.30-31 fibre; and yet in *MS1*] fiber; and
   yet even in *P,A*; fibre; and yet even in *E*
95.16 dumpy *MS1,A,E*] dummy *P*
95.36 are all always *MS1*] are always *P,A,E*
95.39 *Lebensraum MS1*] breathing space
   P,A,E
96.2 body or the words or the works
   MS1,A,E] body or the works *P*
97.1-2 VI / *Avila* MS1*] CHAPTER VI /
   AVILA* *P*; CHAPTER VI / *AVILA* A*; VI
   AVILA¹ *E*
97.22 and to die *MS1*] and die *P,A,E*
100.10 and the straggling *MS1*] and
   straggling *P,A,E*
101.24 these *MS1*] they *P,A,E*
101.35 into *MS1*] in *P,A,E*
102.1-2 What . . . recognise *MS1*] What a
   pagan satirist might recognize *P,A,E*
102.3 indeed not go beyond *MS1*] be only
   P,A,E
102.4 not without *MS1*] with *P,A,E*

102.30 the *MS1,P,E*] he *A*
102.35-36 woman . . . not *MS1*] woman.
   Santa Teresa is not *P,A,E*
103.33 right the *MS1*] right and the *P,A,E*
104.3 delighted *MS1,P,A*] delightful *E*
104.25 of battlements *MS1*] of the
   battlements *P,A,E*
104.31 stony *MS1*] stone *P,A,E*
105.8 church *MS1*] churches *P,A,E*
105.8 belfry *MS1*] belfries *P,A,E*
105.12 amongst *CE*; amongs *MS1*] among
   P,A,E
106.28-29 would been *MS1*] would have
   been *P,A,E*
107.38 coarse *MS1,A,E*] course *P*
108.3 beside *MS1*] besides *P,A,E*
108.23 day; for almost *MS1*] day. Almost
   P,A,E
108.23-24 area . . . that *MS1*] area that
   P,A,E
108.26 rubbish, and a *MS1*] rubbish, a *P,A,E*
108.27 stone *MS1*] some *P,A,E*
108.30 attesting *MS1*] attested *P,A,E*
109.35 is *MS1*] was *P,A,E*
109.36 unintended *MS1,P,A*] untended *E*
109.38 mean *MS1*] speak *P,A,E*
110.6 myriad lovely *MS1*] myriad of lovely
   P,A,E
110.8 to *MS1*] for *P,A,E*
110.20 The *MS1*] This *P,A,E*
110.34 allows *MS1*] allow *P,A,E*
111.10-11 American . . . for *MS1*] American
   for *P,A,E*
111.17 was *MS1*] were *P,A,E*
112.9-11 living . . . The *MS1*] living. The
   P,A,E
113.3-4 eye, examing *MS1*] eye, and
   examining *P,A,E*
113.5 obscure *MS1,A,E*] obscene *P*
113.5-6 two charming pulpits *MS1*]
   charming twin pulpits *P,A,E*
115.1-2 VII / *Early Memories MS1*] PERSONS
   AND PLACES / *Early Memories and
   Schooling* / *by* GEORGE SANTAYANA *At*;
   CHAPTER VII / EARLY MEMORIES *P*;
   CHAPTER VII / *EARLY MEMORIES A*;
   VII EARLY MEMORIES *E*
115.7-11 For . . . variations. *MS1,P,A,E*]
   [omitted] *At*
115.16 that *MS1,At,P*] who *A,E*
115.21 *siete MS1,At,P*] *seis A,E*

115.30–116.9 Yet . . . me. *MS1,P,A,E*]
[omitted] *At*
116.9 about me. *MS1,P,A,E*] about me.
Age 3. *T*
116.11 brother *MS1,P,A,E*] half-brother *At*
116.29 and the shapely *MS1*] and shapely
At,P,A,E
116.34 with, with a *MS1*] with a *At,P,A,E*
116.38–40 The . . . it. *MS1,P,A,E*] [omitted]
At
117.9 Boston; my father *MS1,P,A,E*] Boston
to her property and to the family of her
first husband. My father *At*
117.19 to *MS1*] for *At,P,A,E*
117.34 She *MS1,P,A,E*] My half-sister *At*
118.8–21 live . . . benefit. ¶ My *MS1,P,A,E*]
live with us. ¶ My *At*
118.32–119.19 For . . . letters. *MS1,P,A,E*]
[omitted] *At*
119.5 as if I *MS1*] as I *P,A,E*
119.25–27 Besides . . . sympathetically.
MS1,P,A,E] [omitted] *At*
119.29 deserved *MS1,At*] observed *P,A,E*
119.30–125.20 Moreover . . . years.
MS1,P,A,E] [omitted] *At*
120.13 Antonia *MS1,P*] Antoñita *A,E*
120.15 Antonia *MS1,P*] Antoñita *A,E*
121.24 dark a possible *MS1*] dark as
possible *P,A,E*
122.3 breakfast *MS1,A,E*] breakfasts *P*
122.7 just like *MS1,P*] like those *A,E*
123.12 that *MS1,A,E*] her *P*
123.40 needs *MS1,E*] need *P,A*
125.27 teacher—I think *MS1,P,A,E*]
teacher—who was, I think *At*
125.30–126.17 I . . . things. *MS1,P,A,E*]
[omitted] *At*
127.1–2 VIII / *I am Transported to America
MS1*] 6 [section number] *At*; CHAPTER
VIII / *I AM TRANSPORTED TO AMERICA
A*; VIII I AM TRANSPORTED TO
AMERICA *E*
127.9 believe *MS1*] believed *At,A,E*
127.9 Biscay in such a craft confirmed
MS1,A,E] Biscay confirmed *At*
127.10 was *MS1,A,E*] were *At*
127.11–24 A . . . them. *MS1,A,E*] [omitted]
At
127.24 and to obey *MS1*] and obey *A,E*
127.25 were in *MS1,A,E*] were then in *At*
127.32–128.15 For . . . England. *MS1,A,E*]
[omitted] *At*

128.31 vessel was *MS1*] was vessel *A,E*; was
a vessel *At*
128.37–129.19 I . . . so. *MS1,A,E*] [omitted]
At
129.31 there *MS1*] along *At,A,E*
129.32 a . . . youth *MS1*] a youth *At,A,E*
129.37–38 sailor-hat *MS1*] hat *A,E*
129.38–131.14 Of . . . afresh. *MS1,A,E*]
[omitted] *At*
129.39–130.1 royal blue *MS1*] royal blues
A,E
130.1 passages *MS1*] crossings *A,E*
130.3 hat-maker's *MS1*] hat-makers *A,E*
131.13 it . . . and *MS1*] it, and *A,E*
131.20–132.33 The . . . us. *MS1,A,E*]
[omitted] *At*
131.31 ethics *MS1,A*] ethic *E*
132.6–10 prosper . . . When *MS1*] prosper.
When *A,E*
132.10 art *MS1*] arts² *A,E*
132.21 seas *MS1*] sea *A,E*
132.22 interests. But Faith *MS1*] ~. Faith
A,E
132.40 that *MS1*] the *At,A,E*
133.22 Sturgises . . . As *MS1,A,E*] Sturgises.
As *At*
133.37–134.12 The . . . freedom. *MS1,A,E*]
[omitted] *At*
134.2 being *MS1*] creature *A,E*
134.3–4 or to do *MS1*] or do *A,E*
134.13 As to my pronunciation, it improved
MS1,A,E] My pronunciation improved *At*
134.18–24 For . . . pure. *MS1,A,E*] [omitted]
At
134.26 finer *MS1*] fine *At,A,E*
134.28–30 In 1887 . . . Lady *MS1,A,E*] In
1887, I met Lady *At*
134.37–39fn The . . . Bertie". *MS1* [*A* and *E*
substantive readings same as *MS1*.]]
[omitted] *At*
137.1–2 IX / No. 302, Beacon Street *CE*;
IX / *№ 302, Beacon Street MS1*] 7 [section
number] *At*; CHAPTER IX / *NO. 302*₍
BEACON STREET A; IX NO. 302 ₍
BEACON STREET *E*
137.3–25 The . . . dissensions. *MS1,A,E*]
[omitted] *At*
137.3 though *MS1*] although *A,E*
137.25–26 It . . . claims. *MS1*] [omitted]
At,A,E
137.32–138.22 houses . . . theatrical. ¶ Ours
MS1,A,E] houses. ¶ Ours *At*

138.6 in *MS1*] by *A,E*
138.11 four storeys *MS1*] five stories *A,E*
138.17 watch *MS1*] see *A,E*
138.36 attractions *MS1*] advantages *At,A,E*
138.38–139.25 which . . . government.
MS1,A,E] [omitted] *At*
139.6–7 and seasons the *MS1*] the seasons
and *A,E*
139.14 occasion *MS1*] occasional *A,E*
139.26 Our . . . offered *MS1,A,E*] It offered
At
139.37–140.1 Entertaining . . . rooms.
MS1,A,E] [omitted] *At*
140.1–2 She therefore *MS1,A,E*] My mother
therefore *At*
140.17 instincts *MS1*] instinct *At,A,E*
140.18 adjoining little room *MS1,A,E*] little
room adjoining *At*
140.20–141.9 The . . . sympathies. *MS1*]
[omitted] *At,A,E*
141.10–27 The . . . dozen. *MS1,A,E*]
[omitted] *At*
141.35–142.3 It . . . scholarship. *MS1,A,E*]
[omitted] *At*
142.3 that little sitting-room *MS1*] our
family sitting room *At,A*; our family
sitting-room *E*
142.4 ninth *MS1*] eighth *At,A,E*
142.12–20 The . . . wits. *MS1,A,E*] [omitted]
At
142.15 out of *MS1*] from *A,E*
142.22–23 Don Quixote . . . and *MS1,A,E*]
Don Quixote and *At*
142.23 *El Servilón y el MS1,A,E*] *Un Servilón y
un At*
142.38*fn* Facetious . . . *moles. MS1* [*A* and *E*
substantive readings same as *MS1*, except
for variants listed below.]] [omitted] *At*
142.38*fn* Tales interspersed *MS1*]
interspersed Tales *A,E*
143.11 *healthy and wealthy MS1,A,E] healthy,
wealthy At*
143.18–146.14 The . . . mankind. *MS1,A,E*]
[omitted] *At*
145.1–2 X / *The Latin School MS1*] Chapter
X / THE LATIN SCHOOL *A*; X THE
LATIN SCHOOL *E*
145.22 remembered *MS1*] remember *A,E*
146.6 *Truth and Fiction MS1*] *Fiction and Truth
A,E*
146.21 helpless it is without *MS1*] helpless
without *A,E*

146.23–24 children . . . and *MS1,A,E*]
children; and that *At*
146.29 awaking *MS1*] awakening *At,A,E*
147.11–22 Only . . . failure. *MS1,A,E*]
[omitted] *At*
147.25–26 to . . . recent *MS1*] until my day,
at least *At*; until my day ‸ at least *A,E*
147.32 School old boy *MS1*] School boy
At,A,E
147.34–37 Both . . . schoolhouses. *MS1,A,E*]
[omitted] *At*
147.37 to all those *MS1*] to those *A,E*
148.2 oases *MS1,At,A,E*] cases *T*
148.6 later . . . often *MS1,A,E,T*] later
often *At*
148.13 name . . . such *MS1,A,E,T] name.
Such At*
148.16–30 Certain . . . them. *MS1,A,E*]
[omitted] *At*
148.31 remember also my *MS1,A,E*]
remember my *At*
148.36–39 Was . . . out? *MS1,A,E*] [omitted]
At
149.6 like *MS1*] as *At,A,E*
149.16–17 was sure *MS1,A,E*] was as sure *At*
149.24 acquiring *MS1,A,E*] imparting *At*
149.24 accent without needing to *MS1,A,E*]
accent—there was no need to *At*
149.38–39 places . . . But *MS1,A,E*] places.
But *At*
150.4–10 usage . . . it *MS1,A,E*] usage. ¶ It
At
150.11–17 last . . . No *MS1,A,E*] last long.
No *At*
150.23 hours! In *MS1,A,E,T*] ~! Even in *At*
150.25–33 mischief . . . And *MS1,A,E*]
mischief. And *At*
150.28 nailed-hoofed *MS1*] nail-hoofed *A,E*
150.29 thundering down, *MS1*] thundering,
A,E
150.31 than hold *MS1*] than to hold *A,E*
150.32 trampled *MS1*] tramped *A,E*
150.37–38 me . . . school *MS1,A,E*] me the
school *At*
150.40 knew of no *MS1*] knew no *At,A,E*
151.3–26 them . . . Those *MS1,A,E*] them.
Those *At*
151.33–36 education . . . I *MS1,A,E*]
education. ¶ I *At*
151.39 and my *MS1*] and to my *At,A,E*
152.1 interests *MS1*] interest *At,A,E*

152.5-24 they . . . inflections. *MS1,A,E*]
[omitted] *At*

152.21 *Tyrannos MS1*] Tyrannus *A,E*

152.25 remember *MS1*] remembered *At,A,E*

152.26-153.3 studying . . . Very *MS1,A,E*]
studying. Very *At*

152.31 looking *MS1*] reaching *A,E*

152.37 χαράδρα *CE*; χἀραδρα *MS1*]
χἄρᾰδρα *A,E*

152.39 καταρρέω *MS1*] κατἀρρέω *A,E*

153.22-156.28 prize . . . My *MS1,A,E*] prize.
My *At*

153.39-154.34 Criticism . . . slight. *MS1*]
[omitted] *A,E*

154.37-155.11 part . . . event. Very *MS1* [*A*
and *E* substantive readings same as *MS1*.]]
part. . . . [editorial ellipsis] Very *T*

156.7 laughter; that *MS1*] laughter. Laughter
A,E

156.17-18 of the good *MS1*] of good *A,E*

156.18 and as evanescent *MS1*] and
evanescent *A,E*

156.39 above *MS1,A,E*] here *At*

157.9 Farewell public *MS1*] public Farewell
At; Farewell Public *A,E*

157.17-27 It . . . blow. *MS1,A,E*] [omitted] *At*

157.29-30 This . . . term. *MS1,A,E*] [omitted]
At

158.1-30 These . . . sincerity. *MS1,A,E*]
[omitted] *At*

158.3 being at the *MS1*] being the *A,E*

158.16 School; but *MS1*] School. Now *A,E*

158.18 as performer *MS1*] as a performer
A,E

159.1-2 XI / *The Church of the Immaculate
Conception MS1*] CHAPTER XI / *THE
CHURCH OF THE IMMACULATE
CONCEPTION A*; XI THE CHURCH OF
THE IMMACULATE CONCEPTION *E*

159.32 round *MS1*] around *A,E*

160.20 announcement *MS1*] announcements
A,E

161.9 bosky *MS1*] shady *A,E*

161.10 or temple *MS1*] or a temple *A,E*

161.17 the whole *MS1*] this interior *A,E*

161.36 Jesuit *MS1*] Jesuit's *A,E*

162.25-26 one . . . other *MS1*] one of them
two or three yards above the other *A,E*

163.8 models *MS1*] model *A,E*

163.22-23 heaven . . . philosophy *MS1*]
oneself than are dreamt of in our too
economical philosophy *A,E*

163.30 that *MS1*] the[1] *A,E*

164.20 home, yearned *MS1*] home, all
yearned *A,E*

165.35 as *MS1*] no less *A,E*

165.37 of the faith *MS1*] of faith *A,E*

165.38-39 [not present] *MS1*] *I refer to
Catholic theology. In the *Jewish Book of the
Jubilees*, assigned to about 100 B.C., we
are informed that the angels in heaven
are circumcised. *A* [*E* substantive reading
same as *A*.]

166.18 or[1] *MS1*] of *A,E*

166.18 of *MS1*] in *A,E*

166.34-38fn *Cf.* . . . 109-111. *CE*; [not
present] *MS1*] *Cf.* Saint Bernard in Dante:
*Baldezza e leggiadria, / Quanta èsser può in
angelo ed in alma, / Tutta è in lui: e sì volém
che sia. / Par. XXXII, 109-111. A* [Reading
is the same in *E*, except for form of
canto number and punctuation: xxxii.
109-111.]

167.38 upset facts; and *MS1*] upset the facts.
Thus *A,E*

167.38-168.9 facts . . . dreaming. You *MS1*
[*A* and *E* substantive readings same as
MS1.]] facts. . . . You [editorial ellipsis] *T*

168.26 easily the *MS1*] easily in the *A,E,T*

168.26-27 than that *MS1*] than in that *A,E,T*

169.22 philosophy *MS1*] opinions *A,E*

169.30 excellent *MS1*] excellently *A,E*

169.36fn breasts . . . I[1] *MS1*] breasts. I *A,E*

170.26-27 no even empirical *MS1*] even no
empirical *A,E*

170.29 or perpetuity *MS1*] of perpetuity *A,E*

170.31-38 intuition . . . this *MS1*] intuition:
yet this *A,E*

171.2 unrealised: to *MS1*] unrealized: the
A,E

171.10-11 call animal faith; *MS1*] call faith:
A,E

173.1-2 XII / *First Friends MS1*] PERSONS
AND PLACES / *First Friends and Harvard
College / by* GEORGE SANTAYANA *At*;
CHAPTER XII / *FIRST FRIENDS A*; XII
FIRST FRIENDS *E*

173.3 It was also at the *MS1,A,E*] At the *At*

173.3 sixteen that I *MS1,A,E*] sixteen I *At*

173.15 afterwards *MS1*] since then *At,A,E*

173.25-30 order . . . Let *MS1,A,E*] order.
Let *At*

173.32-174.16 He . . . world. *MS1,A,E*]
[omitted] *At*

174.2 have *MS1*] had *A,E*
174.4 author *MS1*] guide *A,E*
174.5 and sureness *MS1*] and a sureness *A,E*
174.8-9 them . . . charm *MS1*] them a chivalrous and aristocratic charm *A,E*
174.9 namely, independence, indifference *MS1*] namely, indifference *A,E*
174.11 sort: but the *MS1*] sort. The *A,E*
174.19-34 Warren . . . mine. *MS1,A,E*] [omitted] *At*
174.29 among the children *MS1*] among children *A,E*
174.30 in me *MS1*] me in *A,E*
174.31 luxurious American *MS1*] luxurious of American *A,E*
174.33 made exile *MS1*] made an exile *A,E*
174.34 at all a temperament *MS1*] a temperament at all *A,E*
174.40 apt *MS1,A,E*] likely *At*
174.40 on holidays to tea *MS1,At*] to tea on holidays *A,E*
175.7 tiff which his *MS1*] tiff his *A,E*
175.9-10 would have been desolate, but for a mere chance. Not that *MS1*] might have been desolate. ¶ Not that *At,A,E*
175.14-15 Ward . . . visits. I *MS1,A,E*] [omitted] ¶ I *At*
175.15-18 I² . . . James *MS1* [*A* and *E* substantive readings same as *MS1*, except for variants listed below.]] ¶ I went to Williams again twenty or twenty-five years later, to read a lecture on Shelley. Harry *At*
175.17 Jay *MS1*] "Ja" *A,E*
175.18 James *MS1*] Harry *A,E*
175.25-29 When . . . friendship. *CE* [not present] *MS1*] When I mentioned Bentley Warren, Garfield said: "Oh, yes. He is one of the Trustees of our College." From this I gathered two things: that Warren had been "successful" and was now rich; and that for Garfield this fact was what counted in Warren rather than their early friendship. *At,A* [*E* substantive reading same as *At* and *A*.]
175.29-38 I . . . pictures. *MS1,A,E*] [omitted] *At*
175.40 appeared. I *MS1*] appeared, Edward Bayley. I *At,A,E*
176.3 On *MS1*] In *At,A,E*
176.10 together . . . that *MS1* [*A* and *E* readings same as *MS1*, except for variants listed below.]] together. That *At*

176.10 months *MS1*] weeks *A,E*
176.22-33 There . . . eternal. *MS1* [*A* and *E* readings same as *MS1*, except for variants listed below.]] [omitted] *At*
176.26 hunted *MS1*] haunted *A,E*
176.28 love, rest *MS1*] love and rest *A,E*
176.36-177.35 I . . . things? *MS1* [*A* and *E* substantive readings same as *MS1*, except for variants listed below.]] [omitted] *At*
177.22 thought *MS1*] dreamt *A,E*
177.26 As *MS1*] And *A,E*
177.40 the *MS1*] he *A,E*
178.2-19 He . . . himself. *MS1* [*A* and *E* substantive readings same as *MS1*, except for variants listed below.]] [omitted] *At*
178.18-19 mediocrity . . . I *MS1*] mediocrity. I *A,E*
178.22 more that those great men *MS1,A,E*] his spiritual forebears *At*
178.22-23 I . . . renunciation *MS1*] I mean humility and renunciation *At,A,E*
178.24 who could pray *MS1*] with warm blood *At,A,E*
178.30-31 silence for *MS1*] silence, at least on my side, for *At,A,E*
179.1-2 XIII / *The Harvard Yard MS1*] CHAPTER XIII / *THE HARVARD YARD A*; XIII THE HARVARD YARD *E*
179.3 has *MS1,At*] had *A,E*
179.5 to places *MS1,A,E*] to the places *At*
179.10 as instructor *MS1*] as an instructor *At,A,E*
179.16 in *MS1*] on *At,A,E*
179.16 rooms desired *MS1*] desired rooms *At*; rooms *A,E*
179.18 have thought *MS1*] have been thought *A,E*
179.20 or affect *MS1,A,E*] or to affect *At*
179.22 in *MS1*] at *At,A,E*
179.29-180.2 I . . . judgments. *MS1* [*A* and *E* substantive readings same as *MS1*.]] [omitted] *At*
180.5 to air *MS1*] to be aired *At,A,E*
180.16-22 Sometimes . . . help. *MS1,A,E*] [omitted] *At*
181.3 shooting or dancing. What *MS1,A,E*] shooting. ¶ What *At*
181.10-15 gentleman² . . . valet. To *MS1,A,E*] gentleman. To *At*
181.26-182.8 The . . . could. *MS1,A,E*] [omitted] *At*

182.17 grocer's *MS1*] grocers *At,A,E*

182.32-39 In . . . health. *MS1* [*A* and *E* substantive readings same as *MS1*.]] [omitted] *At*

183.20 earthern *MS1*] earthen *At,A,E*

183.21 fetch *MS1*] carry *At,A,E*

183.23-36 Yet . . . aired. *MS1,A,E*] [omitted] *At*

183.24 unknown even in *MS1*] unknown in *A,E*

183.31 there on *MS1*] across *A,E*

183.32 Complexions certainly were *MS1*] Complexions were *A,E*

184.4-7 decoration . . . On *MS1* [*A* and *E* readings same as *MS1*, except for variants listed below.]] decoration. ¶ On *At*

184.7 end *MS1*] ends *A,E*

184.16 did know *MS1,A,E*] knew *At*

184.18 in *MS1*] of *A,E*

184.23-185.20 In . . . places *MS1* [*A* and *E* substantive readings same as *MS1*, except for variants listed below.]] [omitted] *At*

185.16 fishermen's *MS1*] fisherman's *A,E*

185.21 Holworthy in *MS1,A,E*] Holworthy Hall in *At*

185.21-27 day . . . baths *MS1* [*A* and *E* substantive readings same as *MS1*.]] day had no baths *At*

186.10 fuel *MS1*] fire *At,A,E*

186.19-187.9 The . . . Board. *CE* [*MS1*, *A*, and *E* substantive readings same as *CE*, except for variants listed below.]] [omitted] *At*

186.28 and to talk *MS1*] and talk *A,E*

186.35 that *MS1*] the *A,E*

187.8 a *MS1*] of *A,E*

187.10 This . . . in *MS1,A,E*] My election to the *Lampoon* Board—because of some drawings I submitted—was a decisive event in *At*

187.14 so that I *MS1*] so I *A,E*

187.15 and seeing them *MS1*] that congregated *At,A,E*

187.16 from any personal *MS1,A,E*] from personal *At*

187.17 myself *MS1,A,E*] me *At*

187.22-23 were therefore likely *MS1,At*] were likely *A,E*

187.25 Freshman *MS1*] Freshmen *A,E*

187.26 remember especially in *MS1,At*] remember in *A,E*

187.29-30 overlook one another's *MS1,A,E*] look at each other's *At*

187.33-188.29 Sanborn . . . *forty-year."* *MS1* [*A* and *E* substantive readings same as *MS1*, except for variants listed below.]] [omitted] *At*

187.37 that *MS1*] than *A,E*

188.5-6 the company of loose women *MS1*] rather undesirable company *A,E*

188.7 disgracefully *MS1*] ungracefully *A,E*

188.29 Their room, No. 1 *MS1,A,E*] ¶ The room where Felton and Baldwin lived, No. 1 *At*

189.5-10 In . . . pleasure. *MS1,A,E*] [omitted] *At*

189.11 Ernest [marginal heading] *CE*; Eugene [marginal heading] *MS1*] [omitted] *At,A,E*

189.12 Eugene *MS1,At*] Ernest *A,E*

189.19 of any sort *MS1,A,E*] [omitted] *At*

189.19-20 rounded all *MS1*] rounded out all *At,A,E*

189.22 everywhere known *MS1*] known everywhere *At,A,E*

189.35-190.10 Yet . . . room. *MS1* [*A* and *E* substantive readings same as *MS1*.]] [omitted] *At*

190.23-40 moment . . . world *MS1* [*A* and *E* substantive readings same as *MS1*, except for variants listed below.]] [omitted] *At*

190.27 so that I *MS1*] so I *A,E*

191.4 these two *MS1*] the two *At,A,E*

191.11-19 I . . . convention. *MS1* [*A* and *E* substantive readings same as *MS1*, except for variants listed below.]] [omitted] *At*

191.17 by *MS1*] in *A,E,T*

191.23 was also *MS1,A,E*] were also *At*

191.31-192.8 In . . . distinction. *MS1* [*A* and *E* substantive readings same as *MS1*, except for variants listed below.]] [omitted] *At*

192.7 marked *MS1*] indicated *A,E,T*

192.13 try to *MS1,At*] try and *A,E*

192.18-30 speed . . . I *MS1* [*A* and *E* substantive readings same as *MS1*, except for variants listed below.]] speed. ¶ I *At*

192.26 and the *MS1*] and in the *A,E*

192.26 being *MS1*] as *A,E*

192.30 add *MS1,A,E*] say *At*

192.30 that place *MS1,A,E*] the Harvard Yard *At*

192.38 become . . . important *MS1,A,E*]
become too important *At*

195.1-2 XIV / *First Return to Spain MS1*] 12
[section number] *At*; CHAPTER XIV /
FIRST RETURN TO SPAIN A; XIV FIRST
RETURN TO SPAIN *E*

195.14 a certain sense *MS1,A,E*] her view *At*

195.17 could *MS1*] would *At,A,E*

195.17 or to go *MS1*] or go *At,A,E*

195.27 knew *MS1,At,A*] know *E*

196.2-3 New York . . . for *MS1*] New York
for *At,A,E*

196.19-25 The . . . purpose. *MS1,A,E*]
[omitted] *At*

196.36-197.28 Now . . . movements. *MS1* [*A*
and *E* substantive readings same as *MS1*,
except for variants listed below.]]
[omitted] *At*

196.39 there *MS1*] that *A,E*

197.1 that of course *MS1*] of course that *A,E*

197.28 I had *MS1,A,E*] At Antwerp I had *At*

197.38-39 I . . . with *CE*; I had provided
with *MS1*] I was provided with *At,A,E*

198.9 day . . . I *MS1,At*] day; I *A,E*

198.11-19 During . . . independent.
MS1,A,E] [omitted] *At*

198.20 were only just *MS1,At*] were just *A,E*

199.26 event *MS1*] events *A,E*

199.28 became *MS1*] become *A,E*

200.19 mysticism, Platonism, and *MS1,A,E*]
mysticism, and *T*

200.32 or sympathies *MS1*] or in sympathies
A,E

201.19 side Anglosaxon *MS1*] side of Anglo-
Saxon *A,E*

201.26-33 His . . . advocated. *MS1* [*A* and *E*
readings same as *MS1*, except for
marginal heading in *MS1*.]] [omitted] *T*

201.36-205.29 Don . . . up, *MS1* [*A* and *E*
substantive readings same as *MS1*, except
for variants listed below.]] [omitted] *T*

202.9 greatness is a *MS1,A,E*] greatness a *T*

202.30 and *MS1*] had *A,E*

204.28 and two *MS1*] and their two *A,E*

205.2 except a *MS1*] except for a *A,E*

206.16 find his *MS1*] find that his *A,E*

206.17 had[2] *MS1*] thus *A,E*

206.34 ill [marginal heading] *CE*; in
[marginal heading] *MS1*] [omitted] *A,E*

207.3 turn *MS1*] swim *A,E*

207.15 preciously *MS1*] precisely *A,E*

207.34 an *MS1*] the[1] *A,E*

209.7 Lord . . . that *MS1*] Lord, that *A,E*

210.22 and all so-called *MS1*] and so-called
A,E

210.31 and the famous *MS1*] and famous
A,E

210.34 married an honest member *MS1*]
married a member *A,E*

210.35-36 soldier or non-commissioned
MS1] private or a non-commissioned *A,E*

211.11 succeeded in marrying her *MS1*]
contrived the marriage of her *A,E*

211.18 nothing; at this *MS1*] nothing wrong;
at their *A,E*

211.26 that *MS1*] the *A,E*

212.9-10 liberates you from *MS1*] liberates
from *A,E*

212.33 the . . . X *MS1*] the Reginald X *A,E*

212.33 Cincinnati. *MS1*] Cincinnati, Ohio.
A,E

215.1-2 XV / *College Friends MS1*] CHAPTER
XV / *COLLEGE FRIENDS A*; XV
COLLEGE FRIENDS *E*

215.3 deeper *MS1*] DEEPEST *A,E*

215.11 other *MS1*] chosen *A,E*

216.12 seen . . . and *MS1*] seen everything,
and *A,E*

217.4-5 plans . . . were *MS1*] plans that
were *A,E*

217.34 America . . . isolated *MS1*] America.
I was not isolated *A,E*

217.39 prowl *MS1*] prowled *A,E*

219.7 streets *MS1*] street *A,E*

219.8 hobby *MS1*] theory *A,E*

219.24 the top *MS1*] the very top *A,E*

219.24 in *MS1*] on *A,E*

219.28 in[2] *MS1*] on *A,E*

220.2 This *MS1*] That *A,E*

220.28 were little *MS1*] were but little *A,E*

220.29 but *MS1*] yet *A,E*

221.19 man *MS1*] men *A,E*

221.27 and of a *MS1*] and a *A,E*

222.11 I ever had *MS1*] I had *A,E*

223.4 is well *MS1*] is as well *A,E,T*

223.14 *Peace & War MS1*] *War and Peace A,E*

223.17-40 I . . . it. *MS1*] [omitted] *A,E*

224.1 The impression *MS1*] A feeling *A,E*

224.1-2 was confirmed *MS1*] came over me
A,E

224.8 tone that we *MS1*] tone we *A,E*

224.21 no *MS1*] not *A,E*

224.21 mere accident *MS1*] indifferent *A,E*
224.22 private *MS1*] personal *A,E*
224.23 public *MS1*] social *A,E*
224.24 desire *MS1*] admire *A,E*
224.25 changes *MS1*] transforms *A,E*
224.31 and me *MS1*] or to me *A,E*
224.37 three *MS1*] these *A,E*
224.38–39 that Boston "culture" had at *MS1*] of Boston "culture" at *A,E*
225.2 had thorough sound *MS1*] had been thoroughly sound *A,E*
225.11 to music entirely *MS1*] entirely to music *A,E*
225.16 days, 55 *MS1*] days that, fifty-five *A,E*
226.15–16 Chancellor *MS1*] Counsellor *A,E*
226.18–19 for *MS1*] to¹ *A,E*
226.20 mine *MS1*] to me *A,E*
226.21–22 I . . . deeper *MS1*] I did taste such happiness in obscure modest places where perhaps it ran deeper *A,E*
226.22 than official *MS1*] than in official *A,E*
226.29 tradition *MS1*] traditions *A,E*
226.38 faithful *MS1*] tender *A,E*
227.8 wishes *MS1*] desires *A,E,T*
229.1–2 XVI / *College Studies MS1*] CHAPTER XVI / *COLLEGE STUDIES A*; XVI COLLEGE STUDIES *E*
229.32 wouldn't *MS1*] couldn't *A,E*
230.5 we *MS1*] I *A,E*
230.9 horse-car *MS1*] horse ₍ₐ₎cars *A,E*
230.11 theories seemed *MS1,A,E*] theories (of Lucretius) seemed *T*
230.12 finalities, as if *MS1*] finalities, if *A,E,T*
230.13 could be *MS1*] is *A,E,T*
230.34 is *MS1*] sets *A,E,T*
230.34 reality *MS1*] substance *A,E*
231.14 gods *MS1*] god *A,E*
231.32 the *MS1*] that *A,E*
231.38–39 if . . . but *MS1*] in the assumptions made inevitably in daily life; yet *A,E*
232.7 say to a *MS1*] say a *A,E*
232.10 worldly *MS1*] sensuous *A,E*
232.15 aspect *MS1*] aspects *A,E*
233.3 Spencer . . . was *MS1*] Such "principles" might serve *A,E*
233.27 not evolved *MS1*] only intelligence has advanced *A,E*
233.28 to . . . better *MS1*] better to distinguish their objects *A,E*

234.16 cosmic "mind" *MS1*] "universal thought" *A,E*
234.35 him *MS1*] Spinoza *A,E*
235.4 this . . . is *MS1*] there is a fixed good *A,E*
235.11–236.2 Now . . . stars. *MS1*] [omitted] *A,E*
236.34 orator or head-master *MS1*] parson or headmaster *A,E*
237.11 Manderville *MS1*] Mandeville *A,E*
237.17–18 Or Utilitarianism *MS1*] of utilitarianism *A,E*
237.38 don't do) *MS1*] don't) *A,E*
238.18 or ground *MS1*] and occasion *A,E*
238.19 spirit *MS1*] result *A,E*
238.19–29 What . . . mastered. *MS1*] [omitted] *A,E*
238.39 place *MS1*] places *A,E*
239.11 poetic *MS1*] poetical *A,E*
239.34 Fable *MS1*] Experience *A,E*
240.35 Now how *MS1*] How *A,E*
241.13 and *MS1*] or *A,E*
241.18 things Strong *MS1*] things that Strong *A,E*
242.39 to point *MS1*] to a point *A,E*
243.8 enforcing *MS1*] forcing *A,E*
243.13 was a less *MS1*] was less *A,E*
243.14 politically *MS1*] financially *A,E*
243.23–24 friendliness . . . the *MS1*] friendly partnership originally formed by us in dividing the *A,E*
243.26 at *MS1*] of *A,E*
243.34 lie *MS1*] be *A,E*
243.37 of my mediocre *MS1*] of mediocre *A,E*
245.2–249.22 *We . . . virtuous. MS1 [W1 and W2 same as MS1, except for variants listed below.]]* [omitted] *At,A,E*
247.7 or in curiosity *MS1*] or curiosity *W1,W2*
247.23–24 business, science *MS1*] busy with science *W1,W2*
247.31 seemed *MS1*] been *W1,W2*
248.21 taken *MS1,W1*] kept *W2*
251 II *CE; Persons and Places / The Background of my Life* / by / *George Santayana / Volume Second MS2*] The / MIDDLE / SPAN / VOL. II / *Persons and Places* / BY / GEORGE SANTAYANA *A*; GEORGE SANTAYANA / THE MIDDLE SPAN / *By the Author of* / *"Persons and Places" E*

[Contents Page] [not present] *MS2*]
CONTENTS / CHAPTER / I. Germany /
II. London / III. Russell / IV. Changes in
Avila / V. Younger Harvard Friends / VI.
Boston Society / VII. Americans in
Europe / VIII. Official Career at
Harvard / Index *A,E*
253.1-2 XVII / *Germany MS2*] CHAPTER I /
GERMANY A; I GERMANY *E*
254.7 for performances *MS2*] for the
performances *A,E*
254.10-11 I have never seen done *MS2*]
that is not often done *A,E*
255.12 exciting, a slightly *MS2*] exciting,
slightly *A,E*
256.32 desert *MS2*] dessert *A,E*
256.32 with a half-bottle *MS2,E*] with half-
bottle *A*
256.34 for coffee *MS2*] for the coffee *A,E*
257.3 could *MS2*] would *A,E*
257.8 not very important in himself *MS2*]
not in himself *A,E*
257.22 what more *MS2*] what is more *A,E*
258.25 had emotional *MS2*] evoked
emotional *A,E*
259.20 staid in *MS2*] stayed at *A,E*
259.28 is *MS2*] was *A,E*
261.13 & me between me & *MS2*] and me
than between me and *A,E*
261.27 He always *MS2,A,E*] ¶ He
(Westenholz) always *T*
261.40 Burghermaster *MS2*] burgomaster
A,E
263.15 regarded *MS2*] was with *A,E*
264.29 Burghermaster *MS2*] Burgomaster
A,E
265.8 mark *MS2*] make *A,E*
265.28 conquests, but fragmentary, poor
MS2] conquests; yet their instincts were
crude *A,E*
265.32 intellectuals *MS2*] enthusiasts *A,E*
265.35 officialism *MS2*] officialdom *A,E*
267.1-2 XVIII / *London MS2*] CHAPTER II /
LONDON A; II LONDON *E*
267.14 then *MS2*] yet *A,E*
267.31 Meantime *MS2*] Meanwhile *A,E*
268.8 to to suspect *MS2*] to suspect *A,E*
268.29 tops *MS2*] top *A,E*
268.29-30 often (since we started at the
start) on the front seat, only *MS2*] often
sitting (since we started at the start), only

A; often sitting (since we started at the
start)_∧_ only *E*
268.40 at the corners *MS2*] at corners *A,E*
269.33 walked the *MS2*] walked in the *A,E*
270.13 strait *MS2*] straight *A,E*
272.9 and means *MS2*] and a means *A,E*
272.9-10 being much *MS2*] being very
much *A,E*
272.17 had *MS2*] has *A,E*
273.8 on *MS2*] an *A,E*
273.12 past *MS2*] passed *A,E*
274.9 he shows *MS2,A,E*] he (the
Englishman) shows *T*
274.15 secret *MS2*] sacred *A,E*
274.20 make *MS2*] makes *A,E*
274.35-36 thrifty labour, *MS2*] thrift, labor;
A; thrift, labour *E*
275.32 in *MS2*] at *A,E*
275.36 when *MS2*] where *A,E*
275.37 when *MS2*] where *A,E*
276.7 Englishmen, tall, well dressed *MS2*]
Englishmen, well dressed *A,E*
276.28 chairs or benches where *MS2*] chairs
where *A,E*
276.32 incidentally that they *MS2*]
incidentally they *A,E*
277.23 some of the other *MS2*] some other
A,E
277.25 Guard's *MS2,A*] Guards' *E*
278.19 eight in *MS2*] eight o'clock in *A,E*
278.28 that *MS2*] the *A,E*
278.34 when *MS2*] where *A,E*
279.7 day of pacing *MS2*] day pacing *A,E*
279.11 authority and weight *MS2*] weight
and authority *A,E*
279.18-19 leave . . . we had *MS2*] leave. We
had *A,E*
279.19-20 philosophical *MS2*] philosophic
A,E
280.2-17 slaughter . . . Our *MS2*] slaughter.
Our *A,E*
281.14 look *MS2*] looked *A,E*
281.20 But *MS2*] Yet *A,E*
281.22 in great-coat *MS2*] in a great-coat *A*;
in a greatcoat *E*
282.10 or go *MS2*] or to go *A,E*
283.1 Decent *MS2*] Direct *A,E*
283.11 been dismal and monotonous *MS2*]
been monotonous *A,E*
283.27-28 for . . . He *MS2*] for the speeches
of the Prince of Wales, later King Edward
VII. He *A,E*

283.29-32 be connected somehow . . . large *MS2*] be somehow connected. Mrs. Strong was a large *A,E*

283.39 forward *MS2*] forwards *A,E*

283.39 upward *MS2*] upwards *A,E*

284.4 in *MS2*] on *A,E*

284.10 literature, and his *MS2*] literature. His *A,E*

284.23-24 *things* . . . that *MS2*] *things*: that *A,E*

284.30-285.19 result . . . There *MS2*] result. There *A,E*

285.20 whom later I *MS2*] whom I *A,E*

285.20-21 this subject *MS2*] high subjects *A,E*

285.20-23 subject . . . Of *MS2*] subject. Of *A,E*

285.27 to his wife's family *MS2*] to the Smith family *A,E*

286.17 girls speak of the latter *MS2*] young women speak of the elder brother *A,E*

286.30 Haslemere . . . they *MS2*] Haslemere, they *A,E*

287.23 us *MS2*] me *A,E*

288.5 time . . . is *MS2*] time is *A,E*

288.11 I lived *MS2*] I had lived *A,E*

288.39 Jenkins *MS2*] Watkins *A,E*

289.36 lavender *MS2*] discreet *A,E*

290.8 other side her *MS2*] other her *A,E*

290.8-9 charming and smiling in the latest fashion *MS2*] charming in the latest fashion and smiling *A,E*

291.1-2 *Chapter XIX / Russell MS2*] CHAPTER III / RUSSELL *A*; III RUSSELL *E*

291.5 Jarvis Field *MS2*] Jervis field *A,E*

294.4 a *MS2*] the² *A,E*

294.15 —tea *MS2*] —the tea *A,E*

294.29 Russell, not *MS2*] Russell, and not *A,E*

294.30-31 querulous . . . It *MS2*] querulous. It *A,E*

295.21-22 saw, even during *MS2*] saw during *A,E*

295.22 weeks that I *MS2*] weeks I *A,E*

295.22-23 in the "Royal" *MS2*] on board the *Royal A,E*

296.7 stones *MS2,E*] steps *A*

296.14 sweet *MS2*] gentle *A,E*

297.5 Guildernstern *MS2*] Guildenstern *A,E*

297.18 Sunday *MS2*] sundry *A,E*

297.23 great *MS2*] good *A,E*

297.32 believe he *MS2*] believe that he *A,E*

298.31 lasted for so *MS2*] lasted so *A,E*

299.37-300.1 acquaintance . . . I *MS2*] acquaintance. I *A,E*

300.11-22 interest me . . . Number *MS2*] interest me. Number *A,E*

300.35 was of the *MS2*] was the *A,E*

302.1 Ribaud *MS2*] Rimbaud *A,E*

302.28 life¹ . . . the¹ *MS2*] life: the *A,E*

302.38 three years at *MS2*] two years of *A,E*

303.18 for a many *MS2*] for many a *A,E*

304.11 Don Juan *MS2*] *Don Juan A,E*

306.22 as . . . where *MS2*] as, in the line about Wales, where *A,E*

307.23-24 say I minimise *MS2*] say that I minimise *A*; say that I minimize *E*

308.6-7 would be *MS2*] would have been *A,E*

308.21 spirit lyrically and *MS2,A*] spirit and *E*

308.25-310.6 Earl." . . . But *MS2*] Earl." But *A,E*

310.19 retrained *MS2*] restrained *A,E*

310.29 She instantly perceived *MS2*] She perceived *A,E*

310.30 and became *MS2*] and instantly became *A,E*

311.10 admirable the setting here *MS2*] admirable here the setting *A,E*

311.23 too much pleased *MS2*] too pleased *A,E*

311.24 on *MS2*] en *A,E*

313.14-15 intonation . . . I *MS2*] intonation. I *A,E*

313.18 waking *MS2*] rational *A,E*

314.15-38 In the afternoon we were to go out in the launch; I was a bit surprised that Jennie, the housemaid, seemed to be coming with us; but I knew she was one of the Billings children. Their mother had been Russell's nurse, and they had played together in their early days. That might be an explanation; but not for the presence of a second young woman, silent and dejected, with all her hair loose, already sitting in the stern of the launch, next to the wheel, where Russell would certainly sit. "That is my sister Emma", said Jennie, observing my surprise. I asked if she was drying her hair. No, Lord Russell (Jennie didn't call him "His Lordship") liked her to have it like that. *Zo!* I said to myself (having been lately in Germany) and I discreetly went to sit with Jennie in the bow, leaving Russell with his dishevelled and rather mad-looking sweetheart in the stern. But how could he be carrying on such an intrigue in public? I thought of Steerforth and Little Emily. And what could be Jennie's position in the matter? An accomplice, a jealous rival, or perhaps a second mistress? For Jennie's eyes were very bright, and she moved about with the freedom of a member of the family, and with some coquetry as well. Accustomed though I was to the wild oats and the love-affairs of my friends, these complications at Broom Hall troubled me a little. It might not prove such a peaceful and dignified retreat as I had fancied. *MS2* [Substantive reading of *A* same as *MS2*, except for absence of comma after "dejected", position of comma inside quotation marks following "Emma", and word "Zo" in roman type.]] Broom Hall has acquired in my mind an ominous aspect, like that of a smiling landscape about to be overshadowed by lowering clouds. Here were treasures piously gathered, as if Russell meant to pick up the threads of his family traditions and of his own chosen interests. Here were his father's books, many of them uniformly and richly bound, lining the upper shelves; not probably to be much read, for they were too intentionally edifying in their virtuous adherence to a pure old-fashioned liberalism. Yet they seemed, by their mere presence, to shed, as if they had been ikons, the simple and ardent spirit of the young Lord Amberley, for whom his son retained a profound affection. Lower down were ranged school classics and the latest scientific and engineering manuals, to keep his yachting and mechanical tastes enlightened and allied to public and intellectual interests. Yet all this, compared with his masterful person,

seemed rather a false background, put there according to plan and intention, but disregarded in the talk of the day. Sometimes, indeed, a paragraph from some address at the Royal Society would be read aloud for my benefit or some ponderous platitude, maliciously, from *The Times.* Something else, however, would blow in, something less definite but more alive, a breeze from the climes of Venus, a call from the open that made those walls and those relics seem strangely sombre and frigid. I saw only a casual intrigue; but something more serious and fateful lay hidden behind which later was revealed to me. ¶ As it was, *E*

316.10 lawn . . . stately *MS2*] lawn and the stately *A,E*

317.16 Scott had persuaded *MS2*] Scott persuaded *A,E*

317.19-20 than the lady secretaries that *MS2*] than the housemaids and the lady-secretaries that *A*; than others who *E*

317.29 attractive and important *MS2*] important and attractive *A,E*

318.3 and her borrowed *MS2*] and borrowed *A,E*

318.10 in life *MS2*] of life *A,E*

318.16 Emma Billings *MS2* [*A* substantive reading same as *MS2*]] a young person *E*

318.16 for breach of promise *MS2,A*] claiming a promise *E*

318.19-23 I . . . , yet *MS2,A*] Russell never wished to abandon his old loves, but could not help being charmed by his new ones. In a society that excludes polygamy, he had to seem fickle against his will. So now, when captured by Lady Scott, he settled his first compromising affair out of court; yet some points in it were mysterious and pathetic, and *E*

318.37 wrote, "accompanied *MS2*] wrote to me, "accompanied *A,E*

319.8-37 him . . . Thus *MS2*] him. Thus *A,E*

320.9 private *MS2*] primitive *A,E*

320.15-16 Yet a young *MS2,A,E*] ¶ A young *T*

320.27 unhappy *MS2*] desperate *A,E*

321.1-2 XX / Changes in Avila *CE*; Chapter XX / *Changes in Avila MS2*] CHAPTER

IV / *CHANGES IN AVILA A*; IV CHANGES
IN AVILA *E*
321.23 same who *MS2*] same man who *A,E*
323.2-3 came back to *MS2*] came to *A,E*
323.28 Don Cándido *MS2,A*] Cándido *E*
324.21 he provide *MS2*] be provided *A,E*
325.3 a quiet month *MS2*] a month *A,E*
325.25 unnecessary *MS2*] insignificant *A,E*
325.31 disproportionally *MS2*]
   disproportionately *A,E*
327.20 rake . . . Elvira *MS2*] rake. Elvira *A,E*
327.32 therefore had *MS2*] had therefore
   A,E
328.33 gesticulations *MS2*] gesticulation *A,E*
329.1 Susana . . . perhaps *MS2*] Susana
   liked him better, perhaps *A,E*
329.32 would *MS2*] could *A,E*
329.34 thereby *MS2*] therefore *A,E*
331.21 down as in *MS2*] down in *A,E*
331.23 land here turned *MS2*] land turned
   A,E
331.24 deep . . . and *MS2*] deep room, and
   A,E
331.28 on *MS2*] of[1] *A,E*
332.5 reminiscence *MS2*] reminiscences *A,E*
332.11 nominally *MS2*] normally *A,E*
332.16 night of air *MS2*] night air *A,E*
332.29 paper *MS2*] pencil *A,E*
332.38 ups . . . and *MS2*] ups were all steep
   and *A,E*
332.39 are *MS2*] were *A,E*
333.34 in *MS2*] during *A,E*
335.23 and of all *MS2*] and all *A,E*
335.38 taken *MS2*] taking *A,E*
336.15 ships *MS2*] bridges *A,E*
336.36-37 *De sa main MS2*] *De ses mains A,E*
337.1 and had *MS2*] and who had *A,E*
337.9 were *MS2*] was *A,E*
337.17 would *MS2*] could *A,E*
338.23-24 and won *MS2*] and of having
   won *A,E*
338.29 such as *MS2*] like *A,E*
341.1-2 XXI / Younger Harvard Friends
   CE; Chapter XXI / *Younger Harvard
   Friends MS2*] CHAPTER V / YOUNGER
   HARVARD FRIENDS *A*; V YOUNGER
   HARVARD FRIENDS *E*
341.13 This *MS2*] The *A,E*
341.16 in *MS2*] at *A,E*
341.22 at *MS2*] in *A,E*
342.8 demanding any *MS2*] demanding
   from him any *A,E*

342.35 were *MS2*] was *A,E*
342.35 pupils *MS2*] pupil *A,E*
343.32 with younger *MS2*] with the younger
   A,E
344.17 than[1] *MS2*] that *A,E*
344.21 Cotuit . . . lived *MS2*] Cotuit, lived
   A,E
345.18 or he *MS2*] or, as he *A,E*
345.28 end. Julian's *MS2*] end, except *The
   Cenci.* Julian's *A,E*
346.8-10 company . . . Our *MS2*] company.
   Our *A,E*
346.12-13 age . . . or *MS2*] age, or *A,E*
347.34 by me for *MS2,A*] for me by *E*
348.21 another marked *MS2*] another sense
   they marked *A,E*
348.27 out of *MS2*] off *A,E*
349.8 *look* . . . of *MS2*] *look* of *A,E*
349.16 seem *MS2*] seemed *A,E*
350.19 in our *MS2*] during our *A,E*
350.19 in[2] *MS2*] on *A,E*
350.31 presently *MS2*] later *A,E*
350.32 whole *MS2*] public *A,E*
350.33 new, a more *CE*; new a more *MS2*]
   new and more *A,E*
351.18 is *MS2*] was *A,E*
351.27 merry *MS2*] alert *A,E*
351.33 complete life *MS2*] complete view of
   life *A,E*
351.33 strength *MS2*] light *A,E*
351.37 diversities *MS2*] divergences *A,E*
352.22 And in each *MS2,A,E*] ¶ In each *T*
353.1-2 XXII / Boston Society *CE*; Chapter
   XXII / *Boston Society MS2*] CHAPTER VI /
   BOSTON SOCIETY *A*; VI BOSTON
   SOCIETY *E*
353.11 occurred *MS2*] took place *A,E*
353.23 in *MS2*] within *A,E*
354.20 world . . . and *MS2*] world, and *A,E*
354.22 circle *MS2*] circles *A,E*
354.24 in *MS2*] at[2] *A,E*
354.28 once his *MS2*] once, many years ago,
   his *A,E*
355.10 seemed *MS2*] appeared *A,E*
355.35 standing *MS2*] standing up *A,E*
356.14 chair *MS2*] chairs *A,E*
356.36 moved *MS2*] lived *A,E*
357.8 in *MS2*] on *A,E*
358.7 and beyond *MS2*] and surrounded
   beyond *A,E*
358.22 earlier *MS2*] early *A,E*

359.27 case, and an *MS2*] case. He had an *A,E*

360.1 him *MS2*] the lad *A,E*

361.5–6 designate . . . whom *MS2*] designate the one in whom *A,E*

361.6–36 interested . . . ¶ This delicate *MS2*] interested. I liked them both; but to choose a wife was the last thing that I was thinking of; my friends knew it, and this delicate *A,E*

362.5 to tell *MS2*] to go and tell *A,E*

362.16 out a *MS2*] out of a *A,E*

363.2 traditions *MS2*] tradition *A,E*

363.10 onto *MS2,A*] on to *E*

363.23 no thought *MS2*] not thought *A,E*

363.39 never *MS2*] hardly ever *A,E*

364.37 surrounding *MS2*] surrounded *A,E*

365.36 or *MS2*] nor *A,E*

365.36 symbolical *MS2*] symbolic *A,E*

366.10 with not learning *MS2*] without learning *A,E*

366.13–14 colours . . . something *MS2*] colours, something *A,E*

366.31 in *MS2*] of *A,E*

369.5 flourish *MS2*] flourished *A,E*

371.1–2 XXIII / *Americans in Europe MS2*] CHAPTER VII / *AMERICANS IN EUROPE A*; VII AMERICANS IN EUROPE *E*

371.10 and thought *MS2*] and of thought *A,E*

372.13 family, that *MS2*] family, and that *A,E*

372.22 settled *MS2*] settle *A,E*

372.27 all Baptist *MS2*] all the Baptist *A,E*

373.38 record[1] *MS2*] score *A,E*

373.38 record[2] *MS2*] score *A,E*

375.20 this hobby *MS2*] This habit *A,E*

375.38 in *MS2*] on *A,E*

376.30 in *MS2*] on *A,E*

377.9–10 by its three *MS2*] by three *A,E*

377.24 l'Enfernat *MS2*] Blanc-Blanc *A,E*

377.32 l'Enfernat *MS2*] Blanc-Blanc *A,E*

378.2 only could *MS2*] could only *A,E*

378.5–6 It is taking the wrong path whenever *MS2*] It is the right to do wrong whenever *A,E*

378.13 l'Enfernat *MS2*] Blanc-Blanc *A,E*

378.21 woman *MS2*] women *A,E*

379.4 l'Enfernat *MS2*] Blanc-Blanc *A,E*

379.12 was as well *MS2*] was well *A,E*

379.27 distinguished *MS2*] *distingué A,E*

379.34–37 future . . . During *MS2*] future. During *A,E*

379.37 following *MS2*] next few *A,E*

379.37–38 only rarely *MS2*] but rarely *A,E*

380.22–23 limited . . . it *MS2*] limited. It *A,E*

380.31 its *MS2*] in its *A,E*

381.6–7 the cost of their common table *MS2*] the common cost of their table *A,E*

381.25–26 and his *MS2*] and to his *A,E*

381.33 helpless fashionable herd-instinct *MS2*] helpless herd-instinct *A,E*

382.9–36 heartily . . . petered out. *MS2*] heartily. But like my luckless hero— Oliver Alden, to whom he contributed this trait—he could sing only what he felt. *A,E*

382.37 Petering out *MS2*] Falling short *A,E*

383.9 pedantic *MS2*] titanic *A,E*

383.32 At Harvard, for some *MS2*] For some *A,E*

384.23 had had *MS2*] had *A,E*

384.35 rowing *MS2*] running *A,E*

384.39 his friend Richmon Fearing *MS2*] a particular friend of his *A,E*

385.1 Fearing was a swell *MS2*] the friend was a leader in the College world *A,E*

385.21 away . . . lead *MS2*] away and hide and lead *A,E*

385.21 a useless *MS2*] an empty *A,E*

385.29 make *MS2*] earn *A,E*

386.5–6 mind . . . He *MS2*] mind. He *A,E*

386.11 or *MS2*] of *A,E*

386.16–22 States . . . All *MS2*] States. All *A,E*

386.27 fruit *MS2*] fruits *A,E*

387.9 something . . . warmer *MS2*] something more troubled and warmer *A,E*

387.32 were *MS2*] was *A,E*

387.33 lovely little edition *MS2*] lovely edition *A,E*

388.31 severely. Perhaps *MS2*] severely. But perhaps *A,E*

389.1–2 XXIV / Official Career at Harvard *CE*; Chapter XXIV / *Official Career at Harvard MS2*] CHAPTER VIII / OFFICIAL CAREER AT HARVARD *A*; VIII OFFICIAL CAREER AT HARVARD *E*

389.18 in *MS2*] at[2] *A,E*

390.6 their *MS2*] the *A,E*

390.19 Hamlet's *MS2*] *Hamlet's A,E*

391.30 that that various *MS2*] that various *A,E*

392.7 anxiously, conscientiously, with *CE*; anxiously, conscienciously, with *MS2*] anxiously, with *A,E*

392.13 would willingly go *MS2*] would be willing to go *A,E*

392.19 invalid's *MS2*] invalids' *A,E*

392.23 categories *MS2*] allegories *A,E*

393.20 Scribner *MS2*] Scribner's *A,E*

393.21 Scribner *MS2*] Scribner's *A,E*

393.24 Scribner *MS2*] Scribner's *A,E*

394.13 polite society *MS2,A*] polite social *E*

394.26 in¹ *MS2*] at² *A,E*

394.28 expenses *MS2*] expense *A,E*

394.30 we *MS2*] were *A,E*

395.3-4 it actually *MS2*] actually it *A,E*

396.31 of whole *MS2*] of the whole *A,E*

396.36 seemed *MS2*] seem *A,E*

397.20 Guff *MS2*] Cuffe *A,E*

398.1 hardly had *MS2*] had hardly *A,E*

398.18 asked why *MS2*] asked him why *A,E*

398.27 and try *MS2*] and to try *A,E*

398.35 or . . . never *MS2*] or of having a purely documentary mind, he never *A,E*

399.26 and fresh *MS2*] and a fresh *A,E*

400.27 as is usual *MS2*] as usual *A,E*

401.39 was really addressing *MS2*] was addressing *A,E*

402.8 on the quicksands *MS2*] on quicksands *A,E*

402.22 upon *MS2*] on *A,E*

402.24 felt that he *MS2*] felt he *A,E*

403.5 to a tragic *MS2*] to tragic *A,E*

403.10 was *MS2*] had been *A,E*

403.37 motives *MS2*] ideals *A,E*

404.2 serve *MS2*] engage *A,E*

404.20 they *MS2*] it *A,E*

404.22 gave the *MS2*] gave to the *A,E*

404.22-23 declaration of their independence timeliness *MS2*] Declaration of Independence its timeliness *A,E*

404.36 expressions *MS2*] expression *A,E*

405.9 in the official *MS2*] in official *A,E*

405.25 proprieties *MS2,A*] properties *E*

406.2-3 carried . . . he *MS2*] carried; he *A,E*

406.14 wouldn't *MS2*] couldn't *A,E*

406.31 prevalent *MS2*] present *A,E*

406.40-407.1 unorganized private initiative. *MS2*] incorporated private interests. *A,E*

407.13 boy's *MS2*] boys' *A,E*

407.22 impersonal *MS2*] personal *A,E*

407.27 in *MS2*] on *A,E*

407.37 upon *MS2*] on *A,E*

408.21 become *MS2*] became *A,E*

409.15 harmonious *MS2*] harmonising *A*; harmonizing *E*

409.25 Rousseau *MS2,A*] Rosseau *E*

410.8 and the better *MS2*] and better *A,E*

410.31-32 altogether *MS2*] all together *A,E*

410.35-36 was . . . my *MS2*] was, my *A,E*

411.21 and in other *MS2*] and other *A,E*

413.17 lectures *CE*; lecture's *MS2*] lecture *A,E*

414.7-12 feelings . . . Having *MS2*] feelings. Having *A,E*

414.18-19 sincere. ¶ The last *MS2*] sincere. We all move together when we pursue the truth. ¶ The last *A,E*

414.27 and in the *MS2*] and the *A,E*

414.30-31 with universe *MS2*] with the universe *A,E*

415 III *CE*; *Persons and Places / Vol. III / In the Old World MS3*] MY HOST / THE / WORLD / GEORGE / SANTAYANA / VOL. III * *Persons and Places A*; GEORGE SANTAYANA / *My Host* / *The World E*

[Contents Page] [not present] *MS3*] CONTENTS *A,E*

[Contents Page] Chapter 1. Metanoia *MS3*] CHAPTER / I. A Change of Heart *A* [*E* substantive reading same as *MS3*.]

[Contents Page] 8. Epilogue on "My Host," the World. *MS3*] VIII. Epilogue: My Host the World *A*; VIII ᴧ *Epilogue: My Host the World E*; [Titles of other chapters same in *MS3*, *A*, and *E*, except for use of roman numerals in *A* and *E* and italics in *E*.]

[Contents Page] [not present] *MS3*] Index *A* [*E* substantive variant reading same as *A*.]

417.1-2 XXV / A Change of Heart *CE*; 1 / *Metanoia MS3*] A CHANGE OF HEART / *by* GEORGE SANTAYANA *At*; CHAPTER I / *A CHANGE OF HEART A*; CHAPTER ONE / A CHANGE OF HEART *E*

418.1 repent . . . he *MS3*] repent; he *At,A,E*

418.5 but it *MS3,At*] but his spirit *A,E*

419.8 ideas that the *MS3,At,A,E*] ideas the *T*

419.12 life . . . in² *MS3*] life in *At,A,E*

419.16 invincible . . . youthful *MS3,A,E*] invincible. My youthful *At*

420.30 is *MS3*] in² *At,A,E*

420.35 depths *MS3*] depth *At,A,E*
421.7 to drown *MS3,A,E*] that we drown *At*
421.21 agreed *MS3,A,E*] agree *At*
422.34–35 or . . . clinic *MS3,A,E*] or as now in the clinic *At*
423.3 idea and *MS3*] idea of it and *At,A,E*
423.14 could *MS3*] would *At,A,E*
423.20–426.2 This . . . other-worldliness. *MS3,A,E*] [omitted] *At*
424.37 and a step-mother *MS3*] and stepmother *At,A,E*
425.5 old little *MS3*] little old *At,A,E*
425.10 then *MS3*] later *At,A,E*
425.22 disillusion *MS3*] disillusionment *At,A,E*
425.24 disillusion *MS3*] disillusionment *At,A,E*
426.3 Here . . . four *MS3,A,E*] Eventually four *At*
426.3 merging *MS3,A,E*] merged *At*
426.4 carrying *MS3,A,E*] carried *At*
426.18 in *MS3,A,E*] on *At*
426.24 no . . . up. *MS3,A,E*] no less ready to give them up than to enjoy them. *At*
427.30 *true and sure declining,* *MS3,A,E*] slow but sure reclining, *At*
428.38 *l'amour vanité MS3,A,E*] *l'amour de vanité At*
428.39 *l'amour-passion CE; la grande passion MS3,A,E*] *l'amour passion At*
429.10 thought *MS3,A,E*] thoughts *At*
429.11 *amour vanité MS3,A,E*] *amour de vanité At*
431.1–2 XXVI / King's College, Cambridge *CE;* 2 / *King's College, Cambridge MS3*] CHAPTER II / *KING'S COLLEGE, CAMBRIDGE A;* CHAPTER TWO / KING'S COLLEGE, CAMBRIDGE *E*
431.3 in 1895, only for the day *MS3*] on a flying visit *A,E*
431.4 by Russell *MS3,A*] by Lord Russell *E*
431.8–10 Oxford . . . Bertie *MS3*] Oxford. Bertie *A,E*
431.14–15 gone . . . in *MS3*] gone in *A,E*
432.19 Quad *MS3,A*] Court *E*
432.22 proud, sensitive *MS3*] respectable *A,E*
432.24 Quad *MS3,A*] Court *E*
433.3 thick one at *MS3*] thick at *A,E*
433.18 our special tombs *MS3*] our tombs *A,E*
434.4 in *MS3*] is *A,E*

434.5 it *MS3*] us *A,E*
434.18 of *MS3*] at *A,E*
435.6 garden *MS3,A*] South *E*
435.26 these *MS3*] the *A,E*
435.29 antiquarian James—later I believe provost *MS3*] antiquarian James—later, I believe Provost *A;* antiquarian M. R. James—later, Provost *E*
435.33 paederasty *MS3*] promiscuity *A,E*
435.36–39fn [not present] *MS3*] *The year 1896-7 seems to have been an unlucky one for finding genius at King's. Several literary lights, including Trevelyan, the poet, had just disappeared and several public celebrities, including Keynes, had not yet come up. I believe Bury, the historian, was in residence but I never came across him. *A* [Same reading in *E,* except use of raised one instead of asterisk and "R. C. Trevelyan" instead of "Trevelyan".]
436.11 that had introduced *MS3*] that introduced *A,E*
436.23 Personal friends at King's I had two, Wedd *MS3*] At King's I had two personal friends, Wedd *A,E*
437.9 at *MS3*] with *A,E*
437.12 Oxford; for *MS3*] Oxford where I had spent the previous summer; for *A,E*
437.14 Cambridge, but *MS3*] Cambridge out of term, but *A,E*
437.20 seems *MS3*] seemed *A,E*
437.25 needs *MS3*] needed *A,E*
437.29 splendours *MS3*] splendour *A,E*
439.4 Russell, and G. E. Moore *MS3*] Russell, G. E. Moore *A,E*
439.5 person, might *MS3*] person, he might *A,E*
439.11–12 and . . . get *MS3*] and, as I needed a translation to help me in my reading, he recommended me to get *A,E*
439.25–26 facts . . . Facts *MS3*] facts. Facts *A,E*
439.29 the Cloisters *MS3,A*] Nevile's Court *E*
440.29 "logical realists." *MS3,A*] 'logical positivists'. *E*
440.30–31 whole, relatively to his capacities, he was a failure. He petered out. He squandered his time *MS3*] whole, relative to his capacities, he was a failure. He petered out. He squandered his time *A;*

whole, it seemed to me that his achievements were less than his capacities. He was capable of squandering his time *E*

440.32 He . . . the *MS3,A*] Yet he has left one monument—the *E*

441.13 war *MS3,A*] first World War *E*

441.15 Rockefeller *MS3*] capitalism *A,E*

441.18 and ruined *MS3,A*] and for a time ruined *E*

441.20 Holloway *MS3,A*] prison *E*

441.22 his judgment *MS3,A*] his political judgment *E*

442.30-31 way . . . would *MS3,A*] way would *E*

442.37 Newton *MS3,A*] Newton's *E*

443.23 in *MS3*] into *A,E*

443.33 "logical realism", *MS3*] "logical realism," *A*; 'logical positivism' *E*

444.1-17 When . . . persecuted. *MS3*] [omitted] *A,E*

444.20 person, sidled *MS3*] ~, who sidled *A,E*

445.32 existentially *MS3*] essentially *A,E*

447.1-2 XXVII / Travels *CE; 3 / Travels MS3*] CHAPTER III / *TRAVELS A;* CHAPTER THREE / TRAVELS *E*

447.19 this *MS3*] my *A,E*

448.2 fascinates *MS3*] fascinate *A,E*

448.38 and to die *MS3*] and die *A,E*

449.18 got *MS3*] gone *A,E*

450.13 reexamined *MS3*] reexamine *A,E*

450.20 cross-ledged *MS3*] cross-legged *A,E*

451.17 indispensable *MS3*] indisputable *A,E*

452.31 hand *MS3*] hands *A,E*

452.31 *braccia MS3,A*] *braccie E*

454.11 served a *MS3*] served with a *A,E*

455.4 the long days *MS3*] the days *A,E*

455.5-6 country-like . . . the *MS3*] country-like in the *A,E*

455.10 perfect *MS3*] final *A,E*

455.12 than than it *MS3*] than it *A,E*

455.14 the model *MS3*] the literary model *A,E*

455.17 in other words *MS3*] that is to say *A,E*

456.33-34 heard Evans *MS3,A*] heard Arthur Evans *E*

457.15 that *MS3*] who *A,E*

457.39 bank *MS3*] banks *A,E*

459.14 anything that we *MS3*] anything we *A,E*

460.4-5 then still *MS3*] then (1905) still *A,E*

460.22 overdressed, overworked child *MS3*] overdressed child *A,E*

460.33 impossible *MS3*] impassable *A,E*

461.10 has *MS3*] had *A,E*

461.17 olive was *MS3*] olive tree was *A,E*

461.20 tree *MS3*] stem *A,E*

461.23 Jericho, the Jordan, and *MS3*] Jericho, and *A,E*

461.33 or *MS3*] of *A,E*

461.40 exquisite *MS3*] poetical *A,E*

462.30 poetical *MS3*] summary *A,E*

463.4 and imagination *MS3*] and the imagination *A,E*

463.26 no depth *MS3*] no great depth *A,E*

463.36 a *MS3*] at *A,E*

464.37-38 city, the gods of the open rational philosophic mind, were *MS3*] city were not abandoned; but exalted into gods of the open rational philosophic mind, they were *A,E*

465.10 as teacher *MS3*] as a teacher *A,E*

465.16 to³ *MS3*] for *A,E*

465.21 earthly *MS3*] silvan *A,E*

465.30 even *MS3*] firmer *A,E*

465.34 altitude *MS3*] height *A,E*

466.8 indefinite *MS3*] infinite *A,E*

466.31 had had been *MS3*] had been *A,E*

467.7 aspects *MS3*] elements *A,E*

467.13-14 of this socket and that, and finally *MS3*] of each socket and then finally *A,E*

467.24 divine *MS3,A*] diving *E*

469.1-2 XXVIII / On the South Downs *CE; 4 / On the South Downs MS3*] CHAPTER IV / *ON THE SOUTH DOWNS A;* CHAPTER FOUR / ON THE SOUTH DOWNS *E*

469.11 free *MS3*] fresh *A,E*

469.19 Russell's attention *MS3,A*] the attention of Stanley, Bertrand Russell's elder brother *E*

469.27 Russell *MS3,A*] Lord Russell *E*

469.28 Scotts' suggestion *MS3,A*] suggestion of his wife's parents *E*

470.2-3 solitude and freedom. *MS3*] solitude. *A,E*

470.12-29 daughter . . . visit. *MS3* [*A* substantive reading same as *MS3*, except for variants listed below.]] daughter. The daughter was now his private secretary and Russell hoped to marry her in the event of his marriage being dissolved, meantime her mother was there to chaperone her. *E*

470.20 if *MS3*] and *A,E*

470.30 Martha Turner *MS3,A*] the daughter *E*

470.33 lady loves *MS3*] lady-loves *A*; ladyfriends *E*

470.34–471.3 It . . . lover. *MS3* [*A* substantive reading same as *MS3*]] She had no ambition to be a countess. She loved him truly and was too faithful to rebel at anything. *E*

471.3 him *MS3,A*] Russell *E*

471.8 all his *MS3,A*] several *E*

471.10 his *MS3,A*] a *E*

471.16–17 T.H. or Martha Turner *MS3,A*] Russell *E*

471.20–21 nice of you if you *MS3*] nice if you *A,E*

471.31 lodgings *MS3*] lodging *A,E*

471.33 Yard *MS3,A*] Harvard Yard *E*

471.33 him up at *MS3*] him at *A,E*

472.3 with the jacket *MS3*] with jacket *A,E*

472.11 which of those two women I thought *MS3,A*] which of the women portrayed I thought *E*

472.11–13 As . . . question *MS3,A*] As he was married already, the question *E*

472.14 Martha Turner *MS3,A*] the young woman I had met at T.H. *E*

472.17 believe *MS3*] believed *A,E*

472.19–20 Veronica . . . name) *MS3,A*] [omitted] *E*

472.20 Veronica *MS3,A*] She *E*

473.1 Veronica *MS3,A*] She *E*

473.2 as *MS3*] and *A,E*

473.3 Veronica *MS3,A*] She *E*

473.5–7 step . . . The *MS3,A*] step.' The *E*

473.7 lady had *MS3,A*] lady, after all, had *E*

473.11 Veronica *MS3,A*] her *E*

473.12–13 relief," . . . he *MS3,A*] relief', he *E*

473.16 lady-love *MS3,A*] lady *E*

474.21 later: "Why *MS3*] later, writing from Paris, October 19th, 1894: "Why *A,E*

474.23 & *MS3*] I *A,E*

474.32 does *MS3,A*] did *E*

475.6 Veronica *MS3*] young woman *A,E*

475.20–23 becoming . . . breeding. *MS3* [*A* substantive reading same as *MS3*]]

becoming, and a reflection of his Low Church breeding. *E*

475.35 and to think *MS3*] and think *A,E*

475.37–38 was partly redeemed *MS3,A*] was redeemed *E*

476.1 ill directed *MS3* [*A* substantive reading same as *MS3*]] misdirected. *E*

476.1–2 and . . . delusions. *MS3,A*] [omitted] *E*

476.3 To . . . metaphor. *MS3,A*] [omitted] *E*

476.3–5 The two brothers were not executed, but both were imprisoned, ostracised, ruined, and driven *MS3,A*] Both brothers were imprisoned, ostracised, and for a time driven *E*

476.10 them *MS3,A*] the two brothers *E*

476.12 Russell's *MS3,A*] the elder's *E*

476.12 change of mistress *MS3,A*] changed situation *E*

476.13–14 new . . . when *MS3,A*] new when *E*

476.20 and reformer *MS3*] and a reformer *A,E*

476.22 that dreadful dull stupid girl, *MS3*] "~," *A;* '~', *E*

476.22 Martha Turner *MS3,A*] his secretary *E*

476.25 Russell's *MS3,A*] my host's *E*

476.40 relapse *MS3*] lapse *A,E*

477.9 poor Martha Turner *MS3,A*] his poor secretary *E*

477.18–21 matters . . . Anyhow *MS3,A*] matters. Anyhow *E*

477.34 Martha Turner *MS3,A*] the secretary *E*

477.35 as *MS3*] so *A,E*

477.40 for . . . wedded *MS3*] for wedded *A,E*

478.2 in 1900 *MS3*] after 1898 *A,E*

478.11 write *MS3*] rewrite *A,E*

478.17 employments *MS3*] enjoyments *A,E*

478.33 neat *MS3*] clean *A,E*

479.4 perhaps rather *MS3*] always *A,E*

479.9 could not in itself *MS3*] in itself could not *A,E*

480.21 Martha Turner's *MS3,A*] the young secretary *E*

480.21 I was now *MS3*] now I was *A,E*

480.25 being much pleased *MS3*] being pleased *A,E*

480.32 as punishment *MS3*] as a punishment *A,E*

480.39–40 and of air *MS3*] and air *A,E*
481.12 to recognise *MS3*] to have recognised *A,E*
481.13 fifteen *MS3*] so many *A,E*
481.21–22 Petersfield, on *MS3,A*] Petersfield station on *E*
481.24 the guard *MS3,A*] a porter *E*
482.29 associations, since *MS3*] associations, ever since *A,E*
482.29–30 Lady Scott's *MS3,A*] an older woman's *E*
483.24–25 Martha . . . so[2] *MS3,A*] They had all thought so *E*
484.27 and to work *MS3*] and work *A,E*
484.35–36 and . . . cruel *MS3,A*] and it was, perhaps, cruel *E*
485.30 was temporarily married *MS3,A*] was married *E*
485.34–35 and they should *MS3*] and should *A,E*
485.39*fn* Cf. "Farewell to England", towards the end. *CE;* Cf. *Farewell to England,* towards the end *MS3*] Cf. *Farewell to England,* towards the end of this book. *A,E*
487.1–2 XXIX / Oxford Friends *CE;* 5 / *Oxford Friends MS3*] CHAPTER V / *OXFORD FRIENDS A;* CHAPTER FIVE / OXFORD FRIENDS *E*
487.3–4 Oxford is recorded in the chapter on Russell; it was *MS3*] Oxford is recorded in the early chapter on Russell; it was *A;* Oxford was *E*
487.14 in Banbury *MS3,A*] in the Banbury *E*
487.19 disease *MS3,A*] skin affection *E*
487.25 uncovered *MS3,A*] exposed *E*
487.31 clasped *MS3*] crossed *A,E*
488.10 had *MS3*] have *A,E*
488.28 the war *MS3,A*] the first World War *E*
489.3–4 I have called his trouble asthma, but there *MS3,A*] I knew that his trouble was asthma, but, in fact, there *E*
490.17 no no one *MS3*] no, no one *A,E*
490.39 of nuns' hair *CE;* of nun's hair *MS3*] of a nun's hair *A,E*
490.39 of[2] *MS3*] to *A,E*
491.6 to a bashful *MS3*] to bashful *A,E*
491.10 cleanness *MS3*] cleanliness *A,E*
491.31 man and a bachelor. *MS3*] man. *A,E*
491.34 later in *MS3*] in later *A,E*

493.9 come in through *MS3*] come through *A,E*
494.21–22 this had to be by *MS3,A*] we had to go by *E*
496.1 when the next *MS3*] when next *A,E*
496.36 materially *MS3*] existentially *A,E*
498.3 the war *MS3,A*] the first World War *E*
498.25 my *Last MS3*] my *The Last A,E*
498.29 those *MS3*] these *A,E*
498.32–33 He was an adopted child, perhaps a foundling, and there was *MS3* [*A* substantive reading same as *MS3*]] There was *E*
498.35–36 pacifist, conscientious objector, and *MS3*] pacifist, and *A,E*
498.38–39 waif or the bastard, a *MS3*] waif, a *A,E*
499.34 Urckhart *MS3*] Urquhart *A;* 'Sligger' Urquhart *E*
500.1 Like my first acquaintances in Oxford, so the last, were *MS3* [*A* reading same as *MS3,* except *A* has 'at Oxford']] My last acquaintances at Oxford, like the first were *E*
500.5 in *MS3*] at *A,E*
500.11 way *MS3,A*] wayside *E*
500.16–17 renovated ancient stone *MS3*] renovated stone *A,E*
500.25 Mrs. Warren *MS3,A*] Mrs. Edward Warren *E*
500.25–27 the . . . together *MS3,A*] the son of a well-known Oxford solicitor; he was good-looking, and her distinction, together *E*
500.30 perhaps love-affair *MS3*] perhaps a love-affair *A;* perhaps a romance *E*
500.30–31 Ottoline . . . He *MS3,A*] Ottoline. He *E*
500.35 that *MS3,A*] who *E*
501.8 Mr. Asquith *MS3,A*] Herbert Asquith *E*
501.11 little *MS3*] cadaverous *A,E*
501.24–25 but Mr. Strachey's *MS3,A*] but Strachey's *E*
501.36–502.36 Jewish . . . parlour. *MS3*] [omitted] *A,E*
505.1–2 XXX / Farewell to England *CE;* 6 / *Farewell to England MS3*] CHAPTER VI / *FAREWELL TO ENGLAND A;* CHAPTER SIX / FAREWELL TO ENGLAND *E*
506.17–18 Don, like Conybeare, whose scholarship was impeccable, might cry

MS3] Don, whose scholarship was
impeccable, might like Conybeare cry A;
don, whose scholarship was impeccable,
might like Conybeare cry E
506.18-19 someone asked MS3] someone
had asked A,E
506.39 its MS3] a A,E
507.3 Strong's MS3,A] Charles Strong's E
507.15 Churchman, for MS3] Churchman,
probably for A,E
507.16 would MS3] might A,E
507.33 occasions MS3,A] occasion E
508.21 could MS3] would A,E
508.25 reason MS3,A] reasons E
508.31 those MS3] these A,E
509.16 settled MS3] settle A,E
509.26 seemed MS3] been A,E
510.3 therefore MS3] perhaps A,E
510.9 society. We MS3] society. In comedy
we A,E
510.12 soon MS3] even then A,E
510.14 When MS3] Where A,E
510.21 A change at Howard's had to come.
MS3] At Howard's the transformation
had been gradual. A,E
510.24 roses. . . . he MS3] roses. He A,E
510.31 gaiety and joyfulness MS3] joyfulness
and gaiety A,E
511.15-16 variety . . . Any MS3] variety.
Any A,E
511.22 old MS3] older A,E
512.12 these MS3] those A,E
512.14 errors MS3] error A,E
512.18 acquiring MS3] possessing A,E
512.19-21 in the human mind. The . . .
Reason MS3] in any creature. Reason A,E
512.22 these human MS3] such natural A,E
512.34 Revolution; but MS3] revolutions still
to-day malignant; but A,E
512.35 view, destruction is MS3] view of
destruction it is A,E
513.17-18 wives, in spite of possible bombs,
was surely some compensation MS3]
wives was surely some compensation, in
spite of possible bombs A,E
513.20 though MS3] although A,E
513.24 them MS3] the world A,E
513.25 which need MS3] which alone need
A,E
513.38 What a ghastly MS3] What ghastly
A,E

514.30 am MS3,A] was E
515.18-19 wars. ¶ In regard MS3; wars. ¶
At first, in regard F1,F2] wars. In regard
A,E
515.19-27 to Elizabeth, he could have said:
MS3; to Elizabeth on that day when she
had come to meet me at the station,
Russell could have said: F1,F2] to Russell,
I had really been guilty of an indiscretion
in questioning the wisdom of his change
of wives, when his mind was probably
made up. But my motive had been
sympathy with his new love, not
disapproval; and I feared that legal
commitments towards both wives at once
would lead to a catastrophe. Had he and
Elizabeth retained their freedom, the
episode might have ended in comparative
peace. Undoubtedly, on the day when
Elizabeth had come for me at the station,
to win me for her cause, Russell could
reasonably have said ₍ A [E reading same
as A, except E text has "Petersfield
station" instead of "the station" and a
colon after "said".]
515.28-29 But she was not happy MS3; But
soon she was not happy F1] But soon she
was not happy F2,A,E
515.39 that caused them MS3] that could
cause them A,E
516.1 now should MS3] should now A,E
516.4 once MS3,A] one E
516.9 sharply MS3] strictly A,E
516.17 a MS3] the A,E
516.34-35 my affections MS3] my silent
affections A,E
516.37 that scent and that promise MS3] the
scent and the promise A,E
517.1 fools' MS3] fool's A,E
517.5 I have mentioned his MS3,A] I recall
his E
517.5-6 had pulled MS3,A] had once
pulled E
517.14 narrowed MS3] harrowed A,E
517.20 identically MS3] incidentally A,E
517.31 not of all) MS3] not all of them) A,E
518.1 to him MS3,F3,F4] in him A,E
518.4 him; I was only recognising the
existence of a conflict that I had foreseen
to be inevitable. He knew this perfectly
in his heart of hearts; and MS3] him; and
F3,F4,A,E

518.9 asking *MS3*] asked *F3,F4,A,E*

518.10 He had replied *MS3,F3,F4*] He replied *A,E*

518.12 On the Saturday afternoon I found *MS3*] I found *F3,F4,A,E*

518.39 could *MS3*] would *A,E*

519.20 England. I *MS3*] England. I recognised that that chapter was closed. I *A,E*

520.5 Housman. *MS3,A*] A. E. Housman. *E*

520.6-7 heart to attempt to re-evoke *MS3*] heart to re-evoke *A,E*

521.27 the the heretics *MS3*] the heretics *A,E*

521.30 train from Oxford direct to *MS3*] train direct from Oxford to *A,E*

522.2 there *MS3*] to them *A,E*

522.11 in Saint *MS3*] at St. *A;* in St. *E*

522.33 a Bloomsbury audience *MS3,A*] an audience *E*

523.34 come *MS3*] came *A,E*

525.1-2 XXXI / Old Age in Italy *CE;* 7 / *Old Age in Italy MS3*] CHAPTER VII / OLD AGE IN ITALY *A;* CHAPTER SEVEN / OLD AGE IN ITALY *E*

526.14-15 of . . . Catholics *MS3*] of these were Catholics *A;* of them was a Catholic *E*

526.15 or *MS3*] of¹ *A,E*

526.17 insecure *MS3*] insincere *A,E*

526.29 free *MS3*] three *A,E*

527.16-17 it is now *MS3*] it became *A,E*

527.17 general war *MS3*] World War *A,E*

527.19 England . . . as *MS3*] England, as *A,E*

527.27 Yet they did *MS3*] The Latin peoples did *A,E*

527.28 war on *MS3*] war based like the Teutonic claims on *A,E*

527.37 with one or the other. *MS3*] on one or the other side. *A,E*

528.1-2 it now seems to offend some *MS3,A*] it seems to have offended some *E*

528.22 at *MS3,A*] on *E*

529.22-23 hillside . . . It *MS3*] hillside. It *A,E*

529.27 strangers few *MS3*] strangers very few *A,E*

530.10 in *MS3*] of² *A,E*

530.22 seems *MS3*] seemed *A,E*

530.31 never so have *MS3*] never have *A,E*

530.36 those *MS3*] these *A,E*

531.8 in² *MS3,A*] at *E*

531.36-38*fn* * . . . veniam . . . *finem. CE;* [not present] *MS3*] *Veniam subito, nec quisquam nuntiet ante, / sed videar caelo missus adesse tibi. / Tibullus, III, *ad finem. A* [*E* reading same as *A*, except *E* text has raised 1 instead of asterisk and "Sed" instead of "sed".]

532.12 slenderer *MS3*] slender *A,E*

532.33 Spanish or *MS3*] Spanish or French or *A,E*

533.21 friend *MS3*] friends *A,E*

533.22 up, not familiar with Rome, I *MS3*] up, I *A,E*

533.28 thoughts *MS3*] thought *A,E*

533.29 reconsidering *MS3*] recognising *A,E*

534.2 parts *MS3*] part *A,E*

534.6 With Spanish *MS3,A*] With my Spanish *E*

534.9 artists' *MS3*] artist's *A,E*

534.12 Now (1942) that I live *MS3,A*] Later (1942) when I lived *E*

534.12 cross *MS3,A*] crossed *E*

534.14 or *MS3*] on *A,E*

534.15 I rest *MS3,A*] I would rest *E*

534.17 eye has learned *MS3,A*] eye learned *E*

534.23-24 monstrous . . . they *MS3*] monstrous; they *A,E*

535.5 inconstant *MS3*] inconsistent *A,E*

535.10 became *MS3*] become *A,E*

535.21 renunciations *MS3*] remunerations *A,E*

535.24 those softened *MS3*] those so softened *A,E*

535.34 now all these *MS3,A*] now these *E*

536.9 come *MS3*] comes *A,E*

537.1-3 XXXII / Epilogue on My Host, / The World *CE;* 8 / *Epilogue on My Host, The World MS3*] EPILOGUE ON MY HOST THE WORLD / *by* GEORGE SANTAYANA *At;* CHAPTER VIII / EPILOGUE: MY HOST THE WORLD *A;* CHAPTER EIGHT / EPILOGUE: MY HOST THE WORLD *E*

537.5 devoted . . . recording *MS3,A,E*] devoted my leisure hours to recording *At*

537.19 We were *MS3,At*] Mine was *A,E*

537.26 was common to all these possible satisfactions *MS3*] was common to all possible satisfactions *At;* seemed common to all satisfactions *A,E*

538.2 goods *MS3,A,E*] good *At*

538.2-3 change, and also the *MS3,At*]
change with the *A,E*

538.3 them *MS3,A,E*] it *At*

538.5 mind. . . . arts *MS3*] mind. Arts *At,A,E*

538.15 people's *MS3,A,E*] their *At*

538.16 they *MS3,A,E*] people *At*

538.23 but *MS3*] and *At,A,E*

538.29 particularly *MS3*] particular *At,A,E*

539.4 station *MS3,At*] situation *A,E*

539.4 perspectives *MS3,At*] perspective *A,E*

539.6 of a *life MS3*] of *life At,A,E*

540.27-28 with *MS3,A,E*] in *At*

540.37 There *MS3*] These *At,A,E*

541.17 sipped the *MS3,At*] sipped at the *A,E*

541.20 was another *MS3,A,E*] was also
another *At*

541.20 circle, less *MS3,At*] circle, however,
less *A,E*

541.25 recently *MS3,At,A*] once *E*

541.33 lets a fluid *MS3*] lets fluid *At,A,E*

542.22-23 moderns . . . I *MS3,A,E*]
moderns; I *At*

542.28 wars (so far) of *MS3,A,E*] wars of *At*

542.33 requisite *MS3*] required *At,A,E*

543.27 their *MS3*] the *At,A,E*

543.30 and *MS3,At*] or *A,E*

543.35 and *MS3,At*] or *A,E*

544.7 was *MS3,A,E*] were *At*

544.37 my own times *MS3,At*] my times *A,E*

545.28 that had tempted *MS3,A,E*] that
tempted *At*

546.7 Greeks *MS3*] Greek *At,A,E*

546.24 but on the contrary, have *MS3* [*A*
and *E* substantive variant reading same
as *MS3*]] and even have *At*

Genealogy of the members of the Santayana family
who appear in **Persons and Places**

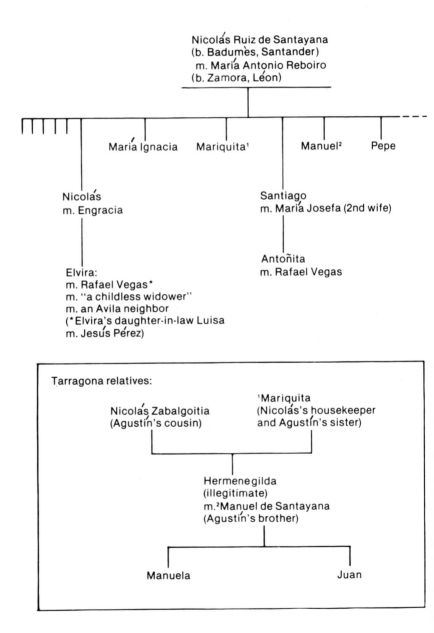

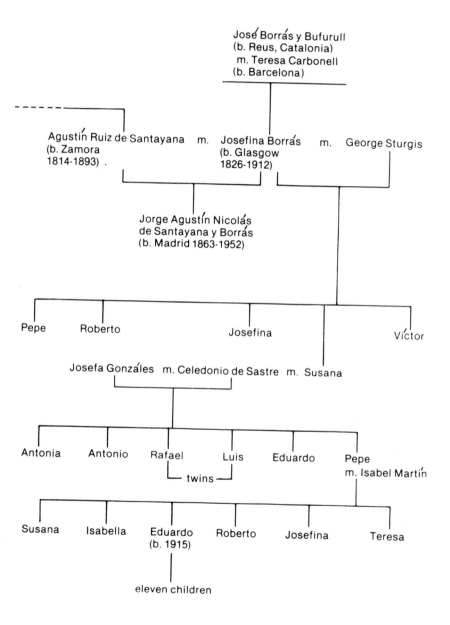

José Borrás y Bufurull
(b. Reus, Catalonia)
m. Teresa Carbonell
(b. Barcelona)

Agustín Ruiz de Santayana   m.   Josefina Borrás   m.   George Sturgis
(b. Zamora   (b. Glasgow
1814-1893) .   1826-1912)

Jorge Agustín Nicolás
de Santayana y Borrás
(b. Madrid 1863-1952)

Pepe   Roberto   Josefina   Víctor

Josefa Gonzáles   m. Celedonio de Sastre   m. Susana

Antonia   Antonio   Rafael   Luis   Eduardo   Pepe
                    └── twins ──┘   m. Isabel Martín

Susana   Isabella   Eduardo   Roberto   Josefina   Teresa
                        (b. 1915)

eleven children

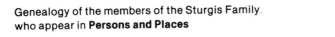

Genealogy of the members of the Sturgis Family.
who appear in **Persons and Places**

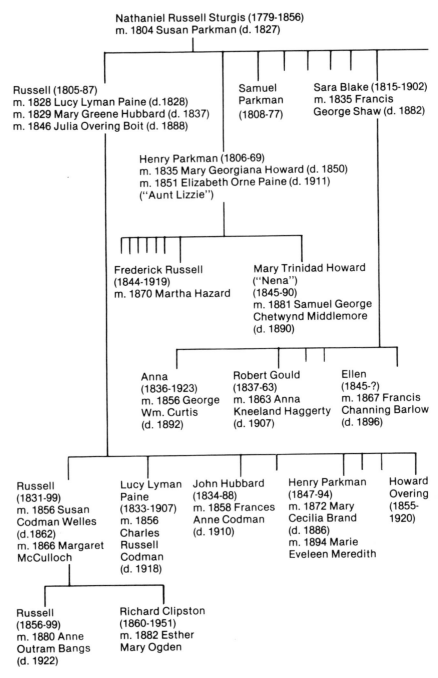

Nathaniel Russell Sturgis (1779-1856)
m. 1804 Susan Parkman (d. 1827)

Russell (1805-87)
m. 1828 Lucy Lyman Paine (d.1828)
m. 1829 Mary Greene Hubbard (d. 1837)
m. 1846 Julia Overing Boit (d. 1888)

Samuel
Parkman
(1808-77)

Sara Blake (1815-1902)
m. 1835 Francis
George Shaw (d. 1882)

Henry Parkman (1806-69)
m. 1835 Mary Georgiana Howard (d. 1850)
m. 1851 Elizabeth Orne Paine (d. 1911)
("Aunt Lizzie")

Frederick Russell
(1844-1919)
m. 1870 Martha Hazard

Mary Trinidad Howard
("Nena")
(1845-90)
m. 1881 Samuel George
Chetwynd Middlemore
(d. 1890)

Anna
(1836-1923)
m. 1856 George
Wm. Curtis
(d. 1892)

Robert Gould
(1837-63)
m. 1863 Anna
Kneeland Haggerty
(d. 1907)

Ellen
(1845-?)
m. 1867 Francis
Channing Barlow
(d. 1896)

Russell
(1831-99)
m. 1856 Susan
Codman Welles
(d.1862)
m. 1866 Margaret
McCulloch

Lucy Lyman
Paine
(1833-1907)
m. 1856
Charles
Russell
Codman
(d. 1918)

John Hubbard
(1834-88)
m. 1858 Frances
Anne Codman
(d. 1910)

Henry Parkman
(1847-94)
m. 1872 Mary
Cecilia Brand
(d. 1886)
m. 1894 Marie
Eveleen Meredith

Howard
Overing
(1855-
1920)

Russell
(1856-99)
m. 1880 Anne
Outram Bangs
(d. 1922)

Richard Clipston
(1860-1951)
m. 1882 Esther
Mary Ogden

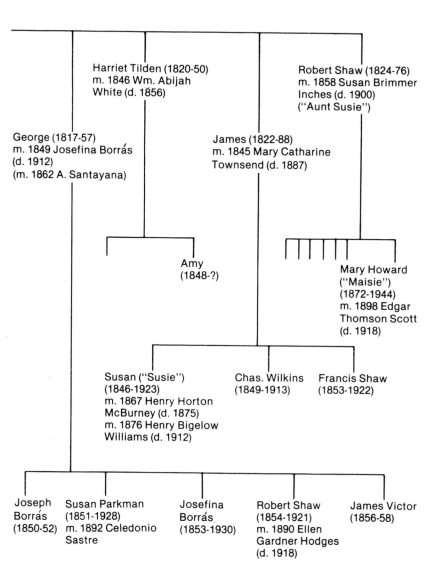

Harriet Tilden (1820-50)
m. 1846 Wm. Abijah
White (d. 1856)

Robert Shaw (1824-76)
m. 1858 Susan Brimmer
Inches (d. 1900)
("Aunt Susie")

George (1817-57)
m. 1849 Josefina Borrás
(d. 1912)
(m. 1862 A. Santayana)

James (1822-88)
m. 1845 Mary Catharine
Townsend (d. 1887)

Amy
(1848-?)

Mary Howard
("Maisie")
(1872-1944)
m. 1898 Edgar
Thomson Scott
(d. 1918)

Susan ("Susie")
(1846-1923)
m. 1867 Henry Horton
McBurney (d. 1875)
m. 1876 Henry Bigelow
Williams (d. 1912)

Chas. Wilkins
(1849-1913)

Francis Shaw
(1853-1922)

Joseph
Borrás
(1850-52)

Susan Parkman
(1851-1928)
m. 1892 Celedonio
Sastre

Josefina
Borrás
(1853-1930)

Robert Shaw
(1854-1921)
m. 1890 Ellen
Gardner Hodges
(d. 1918)

James Victor
(1856-58)

INDEX

696   Persons and Places

Cooper, Edith Emma. *See* Field, Michael
Copeland, Charles Townsend
  identified, 576
  and Harvard College, 407
  and Norton, 407
  and Palmer, 407
  reading, 407
  and Wendell, 407
Copley Square (Boston), 67, 138
Copy-text, 582–587
  editorial decisions determining choice
    of, 598–600
  emendation of, 604, 606–607
  establishment of, 582–587
  Greg's theory of, 582, 598, 605
Cordova (Spain), 457
Corinth, 465
  Gulf of, 629
Cornell University, 375, 566
Cornmarket (Oxford), 489
Corpus Christi, the feast of, 101–102
Corpus Christi College
  Santayana offered membership in, 506
  mentioned, 489, 580
Cortina d'Ampezzo (Italy)
  identified, 564
  Santayana at, 529
  mentioned, xxxi, 178, 225, 498, 529
Cory, Daniel
  comments concerning spelling and
    punctuation forms, 607
  correction of manuscript by, 617
  letter from Santayana to, 594
  and placement of Addendum, 611
  his possession of the holographs for
    the first and third parts of the
    autobiography, 599
  possible changes made by, 621, 624
  his problems with Santayana's
    punctuation, 608
  and publication of the third part of the
    autobiography, 597
  questions of proper grammatical terms,
    615
  and Santayana, 522
  suggests change in title in third part of
    autobiography, 607
  mentioned, xxxii, 589, 590, 591, 592,
    593, 595, 600, 605, 609*fn*, 613, 625
Cosmic Evolution (Fiske), 400

Cosmology, Christian *Weltanschauung* as,
  419
Costelloe, Benjamin Francis Conn, 568
Cotuit (Cape Cod), 344, 357, 361
Country(ies)
  French hatred of foreign, 414
  and history of the world, 404
  and ideals, 404
  James and loss of his, 403, 404
  Mohammedan, 449
  mother, 403
  mentioned, 460
Courage
  of Dorians, 453
  to explore the East, 462
  and Goethe's drinking-song, 427
  Bertrand Russell's, 440
  Susana's, 425
Cowley Fathers, monastery of, 496–497
Cresset Edition
  publication of the, 598
  typescripts of, 600–601
  use in collation process, 602–604
  use in emendation process, 605
  mentioned, 589, 591
Crete, 456–457
Critic(s)
  of *The Sense of Beauty*, 393
  traveller as, 449
Critical Edition
  Addendum to the, 610–611
  establishment of text, 605–606
  marginal headings, placement of,
    609*fn*, 610
  restoration of omitted passages, 600
  spelling and punctuation forms, 607–
    610, 614
  mentioned, 582, 584, 587, 604
Criticism
  affection and, 424–425
  literary, 411, 422
  and Bertrand Russell, 443
Critique of Practical Reason (Kant), 258
Critique of Pure Reason (Kant), 260
Croesus, 259
  identified, 566
Crucifix, and screen of King's College
  Chapel, 434
Crucifixion, depicted in central window
  of King's College Chapel, 434

Ghost(s)
  President Eliot as Hamlet's, 390
  and James, 402
Gibbon, Edward, 142
  identified, 560
Gibbs (King's College), his rooms in,
    432, 434, 435, 628
Gibraltar
  impressions at, 450
  mentioned, 21, 91, 119, 198, 207, 259,
    614, 618
Girton College, 579
Gladstone, William Ewart, 289, 557
  identified, 569
Glasgow, 3, 4, 6, 8
Glion (Switzerland)
  Santayana at, 529
  mentioned, 375
God(s)
  and Celedonio, 105–106
  and Christian Doctrine, 125–126
  Emerson on, 411
  Empedocles as, 455
  and history, 402
  idea of, 453
  and the Jews, 220–221, 419
  laughing at the world, 448, 453
  Johnson and, 302
  Lucretius as, 455
  and Moslems, 203
  of pantheism, 433
  and salvation, 161
  Santayana and, 122, 128, 146, 168,
    200, 208, 284, 419, 453
  Susana and, 93, 332, 338, 419
  view of the world, 455
  will of, 462
  mentioned, 62, 68, 124, 263, 374, 378,
    495, 503
Godparents, his, 3
Gods of Greece (Dyer), 231
Goethe, Johann Wolfgang von
  compared to Russell, 482
  drinking-song by, 420, 427
  motto from, 420, 426
  Santayana reading, 420
  soldier in drinking-song, 420, 421, 427
  in Three Philosophical Poets, xxxiv
  mentioned, 146, 178, 261, 619

Good, the
  Warwick Potter, Bayley, and, 350–351
  his loss of, 423
  honest loves as, 427
  and possession, 428
Goodness
  and The Last Puritan, 410
  of Phelps, 410
  mentioned, 351
Gordon Square (London), Russell's
    house in, 478
Gospel(s)
  Russell quoting, 475
  mentioned, 230
Gothic
  architecture, 109–110, 431, 433, 465,
    493
  charm, 434
Göttingen, 253
Gounod, Charles, 161
Government(s)
  American, 402
  American aristocracy and, 405
  Cuban, 402
  French, 412–413
  guiding a, 404
  of Harvard, 396
  illusion of self-, 396
  individuals and, 403
  and liberty, 442
  minimum of, 442
  monarchy, 396
  popular, 406
  power of, 442
  Bertrand Russell and, 442
  Russell and the British, 308, 320
  sectarian, 412–413
  students, 413
  United States', 441
  Western, 543–544
  mentioned, 6
Goya y Lucientes, Francisco José de
  paintings of, 16
  identified, 554
Gracchi, the, and Santayana, 542
Granada, 118
  University of, 617
Grand Canal, 530
Grantham (England), 25

White, Bessie (Smith), 381
identified, 573
White, Harriet Tilden (Sturgis) (sister-
in-law of Santayana's mother), 66
identified, 557
White, Stanford, 381, 573
White, William Abijah, 557
Whitehead, Alfred North
in America, 444
and *Principia Mathematica*, 440
quoted, 444
and Bertrand Russell, 440, 444
Whitman, Crosby Church, 190
identified, 563
Whitman, Henry, 573
Whitman, Sarah (Wyman), 363–367
identified, 573
at William James's supper, 366–367
Whitman, Walt, 72
Wigglesworth, Jane. *See* Grew, Jane
"Cousin Jennie" (Wigglesworth)
Wigglesworth, Michael, 62
Wilde, Oscar, 305, 319
identified, 570
Wilhelm Meister (Goethe), 253
Will
concept expressed in *Bérénice*, 473–474
of God, 461–462
good, 444
ideals relative to the, 447
James as, 404
renunciation of world as, 426
mentioned, 239
Williams College, 175, 561
Williams, Henry Bigelow (second
husband of Susan Sturgis), 73, 558
Williams, Kate and Nelly. *See* Billings
sisters
Williams, Susan "Susie" (Sturgis)
MacBurney (daughter of "Uncle
James"), 72, 73
identified, 558
Williamstown, 175
William the Conqueror, 567
Wilson, Edmond, xv
Winchester, Bishop of, 218
Winchester College
identified, 570
Johnson at, 306
Russell at, 293

his visit to, 310
mentioned, 302
Winchester (Virginia), 7, 8
Winds of Doctrine, 368
Windsor Castle
first glimpse of, 296
identified, 567
mentioned, 273
Windsor (England)
his first visit to, 296
mentioned, 288, 357, 519
Winslow, Mrs. Frederick, his letter to,
xxx–xxxi
Wisconsin, Santayana in, 411
Wisdom
in Arabian Nights, 463
Epicurean, 426
human, 454
of the traveller, 449
Wiseman, Cardinal, 301
Wise Men of the East, 49
Wit
and life, 426
Norton's, 400
Russell's, 474
Wedd's, 436
Wendell as, 405
Wolcott, Roger
attacks *The Nation*, 368–369
identified, 573
a stalwart, 369
Wolvercote (England), Santayana and
Fletcher at, 497
Women
colleges for, 411
mentioned, 421
Woodstock (Oxfordshire), 494
Woodworth, William "Billy" McMichael
at the Gashouse, 350
identified, 572
Woolwich (London), 273
identified, 567
Worcester (Massachusetts), 55
Wordsworth, William, 187
Work
American attempts to drown
unhappiness in, 421
of man, 452–453
Mollie and social, 477
Bertrand Russell's, 441, 442, 443

Colophon

This book was designed and set in Baskerville
by The MIT Press Computergraphics Department.
It was printed on 60-pound Moistrite Opaque/Mead paper
and bound with Roxite B 51545, vellum finish,
by Halliday Lithograph.